P9-DWA-112

Dictionary *of* **Natural Resource Management**

Julian and Katherine Dunster

Dictionary *of* **Natural Resource Management**

UBCPress / Vancouver

Printed in Canada on acid-free paper ∞

ISBN 0-7748-0503-X

Canadian Cataloguing in Publication Data

Dunster, Julian A. (Julian Andrew), 1954-
Dictionary of natural resource management

ISBN 0-7748-0503-X

1. Natural resources – Management – Dictionaries. I. Dunster, Katherine Jane, 1955- II. Title.

S922.D86 1995 333.7'03 C95-910798-3

UBC Press gratefully acknowledges the ongoing support to its publishing program from the Canada Council, the Province of British Columbia Cultural Services Branch, and the Department of Communications of the Government of Canada.

Set in Minion and Frutiger by George Vaitkunas
Printed and bound in Canada by Friesens
Designer: George Vaitkunas
Selected illustrations: Irma Rodriguez

UBC Press
University of British Columbia
6344 Memorial Rd
Vancouver, BC V6T 1Z2
(604) 822-3259
Fax: 1-800-668-0821
E-mail: orders@ubcpress.ubc.ca

This book is dedicated to the wonderful memories of our association with the late Robert S. Dorney, one of Canada's foremost natural resource planners: a supervisor, friend, and mentor beyond compare. He showed us how to turn dreams into realities.

Si monumentum requiris, circumspice.

And to Flora, our hope for the future.

Contents

Acknowledgments

Researching and compiling a book of this nature has involved the cooperation of many people and organizations around the world as sponsors of the work, as reviewers of the data entered, as sources of critical (but mostly helpful) advice, or as suppliers of additional materials. Without this assistance the project would have failed, and we are indebted to the many people who have helped us.

The research work was cooperatively funded by government and non-government agencies: British Columbia Conservation Foundation; Department of Fisheries and Oceans (Habitat Management); Natural Resources Canada; British Columbia Ministry of Forests (FRDA II); British Columbia Ministry of Environment, Lands and Parks, Integrated Resource Management; Environment Canada, Inland Waters; Environment Canada: Fraser River Action Plan, Forest Ecosystem/Biodiversity, Fraser Pollution Abatement Office. To all of them we extend our thanks for their assistance and faith in the project.

Wherever possible we have tried to provide definitions that do not infringe on the copyright of individual authors or publishers. However, in some cases, terms were so well defined that it was difficult to improve the text without making the entry clumsy. In other cases, we have merged several definitions to provide more comprehensive entries or to ensure that we have captured the many meanings being attached to any one term. The following people graciously permitted us to utilize materials from their books and articles:

- Paul Aird, 'Conservation for the Sustainable Development of Forests Worldwide: A Compendium of Concepts and Terms,' *Forestry Chronicle* (70) 6:666-74
- American Fisheries Society, for permission to use terms from their publication *Aquatic Habitat Inventory – Glossary and Standards Methods* (Bethesda, MD: American Fisheries Society 1985)
- Joan Baxter, ed., *Agroforestry Today*, International Centre for Research in Agroforestry, Nairobi, Kenya, for comments and suggestions regarding agroforestry terminology
- Benjamin-Cummings Publishing Company, for permission to reproduce the term 'Ideal Population' from C.M. Schonewald-Cox, S.M. Chambers, B. MacBryde, and W.L. Thomas, eds., *Genetics and Conservation* (Menlo Park, CA: Benjamin-Cummings 1983)
- Dr. Charles Blem, ed., *Wilson Bulletin*, for permission to use terms in the article by R. Koford et al., 'A Glossary for Avian Conservation Biology,' *Wilson Bulletin* 106, no. 1 (1994):121-37
- Dr. Peter Bobrowsky and Dr. June Ryder, British Columbia Resources Inventory Committee, for help with geomorphology and terrain-mapping terminology, and for permission to use many of the terms in their forthcoming *Guidelines and Standards to Terrain Mapping in British Columbia* (Victoria: Resources Inventory Committee 1995)
- Gerry Cormick, for selected terms from *A Glossary of Dispute Resolution Terms* (Mill Creek, WA: Mediation Institute 1990)
- Cornell University Press, for permission to use terms from Wayne A. Sinclair, Howard H. Lyon, and Warren T. Johnson, *Diseases of Trees and Shrubs* (Ithaca: Cornell University Press 1987), and from Warren T. Johnson and Howard H. Lyon, *Insects That Feed on Trees and Shrubs* (Ithaca: Cornell University Press 1991)
- Dr. Bill Crepet, L.H. Bailey Hortorium, Cornell University, for permission to use some terms from *Hortus Third: A Concise Dictionary of Plants Cultivated in the United States and Canada* (Cornell University: L.H. Bailey Hortorium 1976)
- Alan Drengson, University of Victoria, BC, for selected environmental philosophy terms
- Fulcrum Publishing, for permission to use terms from J.C. Hendee, G.H. Stankey, and R.C. Lucas, *Wilderness Management* (Golden, CO: North American Press 1990)
- Herb Hammond, for selected terms developed as a practitioner in alternative forestry
- International Society of Arboriculture and Hortscience, for permission to use terms from N.P. Matheny and J.R. Clark, *A Photographic Guide to the Evaluation of Hazard Trees in Urban Areas,* 2nd edition (Savoy: International Society of Arboriculture 1994)
- Lone Pine Publishing, for permission to use and adapt terms from D.H. Vitt, J.E. Marsh, and R.B. Bovey, *Mosses, Lichens, and Ferns of Northwest North America* (Edmonton: Lone Pine Press 1988), and from J. Pojar and A. MacKinnon, *Plants of Coastal British Columbia* (Edmonton: Lone Pine Press 1994)
- Dr. Joe Lowe, Natural Resources Canada, Petawawa, for assistance with inventory terminology and for permission to use terms in B.D. Haddon, ed.,

Forest Inventory Terms in Canada, 3rd edition, Canadian Forest Inventory Committee (Ottawa: Forestry Canada 1989)

- Queen's Printer, British Columbia, for permission to use terms from the publication *Pesterms: A One-word Term to Designate a Glossary of Forest Pest Management Terms, Pest Management Report No 3* (Victoria: BC Ministry of Forests 1986)
- Society of American Foresters, for their permission to use terms from F.C. Ford-Robertson, ed., *Terminology of Forest Science Technology Practice and Products,* 2nd printing (Bethesda, MD: Society of American Foresters 1983), and G.R. McPherson, D.D. Wade, and from C.B. Phillips, *Glossary of Wildland Fire Management Terms Used in the United States* (Washington, DC: Society of American Foresters 1990) (reprinted from the Society of American Foresters and not for further reproduction)
- Soil Science Society of America, for permission to use terms from their publication, *Glossary of Soil Science Terms* (Madison, WI: Soil Science Society of America 1987)
- Bryce Stokes, for permission to use terms from B.J. Stokes, C. Ashmore, C.L. Rawlins, and D.L. Sirois, *Glossary of Terms Used in Timber Harvesting and Forest Engineering,* General Technical Report SO-73 (New Orleans: USDA, Forest Service, Southern Experiment Station 1989)
- Storey Communications, Pownal, Vermont, for permission to use terms from Henry W. Art, ed., *The Dictionary of Ecology and Environmental Science* (New York: Henry Holt 1993)
- World Conservation Union, Gland, Switzerland, for permission to use the internationally defined Protected Areas designations
- World Resources Institute, for permission to use terms from the publication by Walter V. Reid and Kenton R. Miller, *Keeping Options Alive* (Washington, DC: World Resources Institute 1987)

Many of the technical terms included are extremely esoteric, yet have quite different meanings within several very narrow areas of science. In order to try to ensure the widest possible review of the terms and definitions, the entries have been scrutinized by practitioners and academics across North America and other parts of the world. We are particularly indebted to these reviewers for their comments, criticisms, and corrections, as well as for suggesting additional terms that needed inclusion. They are: Hamish Kimmins and Hal Salwasser (ecology); Joe Lowe (inventory); Bruce Dancik, James Beck, Ellen McDonald, and William Hyde (comprehensive review of the first draft); Gordon Weetman and John Worrall (silviculture); Tim Ballard (soils); June Ryder (geomorphology); James Clark (arboriculture); Alex Downie (botany); Michael Dunn (wildlife); Vince Poulin and John Payne (fisheries and water); John Muir (disease); Herb Hammond (emerging terms in new forestry); Joan Baxter (agroforestry); and Alan Drengson (environmental philosophy).

During two years of research and writing, many other people have offered encouragement, provided suggestions and comments, and directed us toward additional sources of material. To all of you, our thanks.

UBC Press has provided constant encouragement and support throughout the research and editing phases. Special thanks are due to Peter Milroy and Jean Wilson for their expertise and faith in the project, and to many very helpful staff who so willingly helped us to mould the manuscript into its final form. Their patience in waiting for us to deliver the manuscript and revisions is much appreciated.

Finally, as is so often the case, thanks to our families and friends, and particularly to Flora, for putting up with seemingly endless excuses and a lack of time to do much more interesting things.

Introduction

I know you think you understand what I said, but do you realize that what you think you heard me say, is not what I meant?

Words are the essence of language; their use determines how we communicate thoughts and ideas to each other. Yet the way in which we use words can also be a very powerful means of manipulation and a source of serious misunderstanding. Nowhere is this more apparent than in the area of natural resource management, where common or obscure words are bantered around, often without a good understanding of what the words mean or might imply. All words have one, and sometimes more than one, specific meaning.

As an interdisciplinary approach to resource management becomes more common, specific words from one technical area are increasingly being applied to another. Often, these words are intended to have very narrow meanings but, in the absence of clear definition, misunderstanding multiplies. Consequently, it is common to see technical words that we thought we understood being applied in a context that we do not recognize. Hence the reason for this dictionary, which has two primary goals.

The first goal is to assemble a comprehensive collection of words that are used in one or more aspects of natural resource management. The definitions are not intended to be absolutes, although many do in fact have only one very specific meaning; rather, they are intended to serve as a starting point for understanding so that if someone else proposes a different definition, its context and meaning can be more clearly understood. We hope the questions raised by reading one definition will be answered by examination of other terms in the book, thus leading to some degree of enlightenment.

The second goal is to bring these definitions together in a single source document so that most of the terms are in one place, rather than in many different glossaries or specialized dictionaries. Undoubtedly, we have missed words and terms of importance to some resource managers and included others of no immediate interest. However, we see the aim of the dictionary to be more than just a source of terminology. We hope that it will also serve as an education, a place where one can browse and learn more without the need for mountains of additional books or reports. (They come later.) And, of course, we hope it will be fun to use; if nothing else, it provides the avid Scrabble player with new horizons!

The selection of words for inclusion in this book posed an interesting challenge. The scope of the dictionary was broadly limited to terms related to the theory, practice, or discussion of natural resource management, generally at the field or policy level, so the technical aspects of manufacturing or processing of natural resources are not included in great detail. For reasons of accessibility, much of the data has been drawn from North American or European sources. However, not all of the terms are specific to any one part of the world, nor are they all globally applicable; some regional variation has been included.

We have tried to select those words that are now, or are in the process of becoming, commonly used in the lexicon of natural resource management in its broadest sense, although we admit to having forests and the management of forested landscapes as our starting focus. Thus, terms peculiar to conservation biology, landscape ecology, and geographic information systems are included because these aspects are assuming much greater significance world-wide in the management of natural resources.

A conservative estimate suggests that there are probably at least double, and maybe triple, the number of words we have selected, in usage somewhere in resource management. Many of these are regional, even colloquial, in nature. Rather than include everything, the definitions selected are based on extensive review of contemporary literature, glossaries, our own professional knowledge, discussions with people around the world, and the comments of our many reviewers. Even so, we recognize that there will be continuing debate about some of the definitions. This is to be welcomed since it heralds active discussion and vocal testing of the definitions.

We have been fortunate to have most of the terms and definitions reviewed and critiqued by many very knowledgeable people in different parts of North America. The definitions included provide (we hope) the most commonly accepted meaning of the terms listed. Nonetheless, the entries given do not necessarily provide an absolute definition in the legal sense. They do provide the best available definition at the time of publication but, in some cases, there may be other equally valid interpretations of the definitions or terms that we have not included.

Despite this rigorous review process, we are keenly aware that within narrowly defined specialities, some very arcane meanings exist for certain terms. This raises the interesting challenge of providing the 'right' definition. In fact, several terms had similar but distinct definitions; for example, 'Association.' This seems to reflect an evolution in the underpinning ecological theory of the terms and a shift in contemporary usage. Other terms examined were clearly defined incorrectly. For example, we found one definition of 'dispersion' that included the ideas of movement of propagules and their *establishment* at a new location. But, dispersion is not necessarily correlated with establishment; many propagules may be dispersed, but of these, only a few may actually survive and get established at the new location.

In order to include as many of these subtleties as possible, we sought several sources of definition for each term to ensure we have comprehensive coverage and to be sure we had some consensus on the meaning of the term. In some cases, one term has many very specific meanings, such as 'drift' (seven distinct applications), or 'index' (five distinct applications). This process was further helped by the many reviewers who pointed us in the right (in their opinion) direction.

A further problem is that some people use one of several synonyms. Thus 'Ballochore' is a form of 'Autochore,' and 'Choripetalous' is defined under the term 'Polypetalous.' We have included the many synonyms found and these are cross-referenced throughout. In some cases, we have placed classes of terms under one heading, with the associated terms cross-referenced to the main root term. Thus 'alpha diversity' is defined under the heading 'diversity.' Adopting this approach allowed us to provide the reader with a more complete sense of the main term and its associated derivatives without the need to be constantly moving around in the text. Several terms have different spellings for the same term, such as 'aeolian' or 'eolian.' Again, we have tried to systematically include these subtleties as they arose.

While the authors and the University of British Columbia Press accept no responsibility or liability for the way in which the reader chooses to use or interpret the words contained in this book, we are interested in hearing how we might improve the coverage and contents. Suggestions for change and additional terms are welcomed and we hope that readers will send these to us for inclusion in the next edition. Our address is P.O. Box 109, Bowen Island, BC, Canada V0N 1G0 (e-mail: jdunster@mindlink.bc.ca).

Finally, we acknowledge our historical debt to Samuel Johnson, the first lexicographer to assemble a comprehensive dictionary of the English language. Throughout this work we have tried to assemble the best definitions available, but have been forced to recognize that some disagreement still exists. Should there be any major mistakes, we offer, with due deference, the riposte given by Dr. Johnson, when a lady asked him why he had defined 'pastern' as 'a horse's knee.' He replied, 'Ignorance, madame, pure ignorance.'

Dictionary *of* **Natural Resource Management**

A

ABANDONED ROADS Roads that have served their purpose and are no longer required for any form of vehicular access.
ABATEMENT **1** The reduction of a nuisance or harmful effect, such as pollution. **2** In arboriculture, the reduction of hazard potential by treatment or removal of the hazardous tree, or by removal of the target.
ABAXIAL **1** Describes the surface of a lateral organ located away from, or on the opposite side of, the main axis of the structure or entire organism; dorsal. **2** In describing plants, the side of a leaf that is turned away from the main axis during development, typically the underside. *See also* Adaxial.
ABC PLANNING A comprehensive planning tool that broadly classifies component parts into Abiotic (A), Biotic (B), or Cultural (C) and uses an interdisciplinary approach to ensure a sound technical basis for decision-making.
ABDOMEN **1** In vertebrate animals, that part of the body containing the kidneys, liver, stomach, and intestines, collectively termed the viscera. The diaphragm separates the abdomen from the thorax. **2** In arthropods, that part of the body, which may or may not be segmented, located directly behind the thorax, that bears no functional legs. *See also* Butterfly (for illustration); Thorax.
ABERRANT Unusual, atypical; not the 'normal' form.
ABIOTIC The nonliving components of the planet, not currently part of living organisms, such as soils, rocks, water, air, light, and nutrients.
ABIOTIC DISEASE *See* Disorder.
ABIOTIC PATHOGEN A nonliving cause or inducer of disease, such as an air pollutant, a toxic metal ion in the soil, or a nutrient imbalance caused by nutrient shortages or excesses in the soil, or inadequate development of mycorrhizae, extremes of temperature, or extremes of water availability.
ABLATION The loss of ice and snow on glaciers by melting, evaporation, and calving of icebergs.
ABLATION MORAINE A moraine resulting from ablation; typically hummocks of ablation till formed by the melting of stagnant ice.
ABLATION TILL The material accumulated on top of a melting glacier; it is coarser in texture and less consolidated than basal till. Commonly seen where glacier recession is dominated by downwasting of stagnant ice.
ABNEY LEVEL A hand-held clinometer used to measure slopes in percentage.
ABORT **1** To drop an unused load of water or fire retardant from an aircraft; synonymous with jettison. **2** The spontaneous or induced expulsion of a fetus from the womb or uterus before it has the capability for survival. **3** Botanically, ovules that fail to develop into seeds.
ABORT AREA A designated area where unused quantities of water or fire retardant may be dropped, usually to permit an airtanker to land with less than a full load.
ABORTIVE Botanically, a plant organ or feature that is undeveloped or imperfectly developed and therefore barren.
ABRASION The wearing down or rubbing away of materials as a result of frictional processes.
ABSCISSA The horizontal axis (x) on a graph. *See also* Axes; Ordinate.
ABSCISSION The process by which plants shed fully developed fruits, leaves, or leaf stems, by developing a specialized layer of cells (the abscission layer) at the base of the part to be shed, thus protecting the remaining twig from decay.
ABSENTEE OWNERSHIP The holding of property by one or more persons who do not live or work on the premises and who are not regularly present to oversee its use or maintenance.
ABSOLUTE DOMINANCE In point-centred quarter forest sampling, the mean basal area of the trees in a species times the number of individual trees in a species.
ABSOLUTE HUMIDITY The total amount of water vapour in a given volume of air. *See also* Relative Humidity.
ABSORPTION The process where one substance is taken up by another. Solids or liquids can take up gases; solids can take up liquids; matter can take up light (e.g., a sponge absorbs water). *See also* Adsorption.
ABSTRACT **1** The first part of a report, which gives an overview of the main text. An abstract contains three main parts: (1) the description of the problem studied and the goals and objectives of the study undertaken; (2) an outline of the methods employed to fulfil the goals and objectives; and (3) an outline of results, their implications, the conclusions, and the recommendations. **2** A method of considering problems in which the possible solutions are considered in the mind without quantitative translation to paper. *See also* Conceptual Model.

ABUNDANCE The total number of individuals or amount of resources present in a specific area. Typically used in a qualitative, relative, or subjective manner rather than an absolute number or amount. *See also* Diversity; Relative Abundance.

ABUTMENT The structure supporting the ends of a bridge and retaining the fill material that terminates at each side of the approach road. *See also* Bridge (for illustration).

ACARICIDE A pesticide used to control or kill mites or ticks.

ACAULESCENT Stemless or apparently so. A stem is usually present, but subterranean or very short. It is a descriptive rather than morphological term.

ACCELERANT Any substance applied to fuel to expedite the burning process.

ACCELERATED EROSION Erosion occurring more rapidly than normal, typically as a result of disturbances by animals (often humans). *See also* Erosion for other associated terms.

ACCEPTABLE BURN *See* Allowable Burned Area.

ACCEPTABLE DAMAGE Damage that does not impair the flow of benefits from wildlands beyond a level previously judged acceptable by some external criterion.

ACCEPTABLE FIRE RISK The potential fire loss a community is willing to accept rather than provide the resources to reduce such losses.

ACCESSIBILITY **1** The degree to which an area of forested land is accessible, usually in the context of a road, but could be by foot, air, or water. Accessibility is a reflection of the topography (slopes, soils, and distances to next nearest access connection point). It is also influenced by the money available to create access corridors, and the potential value of goods (such as timber values) and services (such as recreation opportunities) that may result from the creation of better access. **2** In wood chemistry, the degree to which the wood fibres are penetrated by treatment with preservative chemicals.

ACCESSORY FRUIT A fruit or assemblage of fruits in which the conspicuous fleshy parts are not derived from the pistil. For example, the true fruits of a strawberry (*Fragaria* spp.), are the achenes that are embedded in the accessory fruit, which consists of the soft, red, edible flesh.

ACCLIMATION An adaptation, by means of a physiological change in an organism, in response to a change in one specific environmental attribute, such as air temperature or daylight length. *See also* Acclimatization.

ACCLIMATIZATION **1** In a general sense, adapting to a change in climate. **2** More technically, the gradual physiological and behavioural adaptations of an organism, usually lasting a few days or weeks, in response to a change in several environmental attributes. *See also* Acclimation.

ACCRETION **1** In general, the increase in size of inorganic materials due to the addition (accretion) of particles. **2** In stream assessments, the accumulation of silt, sand, or pebbles from flowing waters. **3** In describing channel flows, the gradual increase in stream flow due to seepage inputs. **4** In timber management, the increment of growth, usually applied to the more rapid growth in diameter or volume, of trees given more growing space during the latter part of the rotation.

ACCULTURATION The processes and results of contact between two or more different cultures. Acculturation induces diffusion of cultural traits in one or more directions, the development of new intercultural roles, the growth of new customs not found in either culture, and the disintegration of older cultural traditions.

ACCUMBENT Lying against another organ (e.g., accumbent cotyledons lie face to face). *See also* Conduplicate; Incumbent.

ACCUMULATING SHEAR A shearhead on a feller-buncher that is capable of accumulating and holding two or more stems. *See also* Harvest Machine Classification.

ACCURACY The size of the deviation of a sample estimate from the true population mean. The degree by which measurements differ from their true value. Measurements can be very accurate but imprecise, or inaccurate but very precise. Ideally, they should be both accurate and precise. The mean square error (MSE) is a measure of accuracy and shows the relationship between precision and bias:

$$MSE = (\text{precision})^2 + (\text{bias})^2$$

See also Bias; Precision.

ACERVULUS Plural acervuli. A fruiting structure found in some microfungi. It consists of a layer of conidiophore-bearing hyphae arising subcuticularly, subepidermally, or deeper in plant tissue; colourless to dark, visible with a hand lens and sometimes with the unaided eye, and often appearing like a tiny blister that opens at the plant surface.

ACHENE A small, dry, indehiscent, one-seeded fruit. *See also* Fruit (for illustration).

ACICULAR An object, such as a crystal, sedimentary particle, or certain leaf shapes, that is slender and pointed, or needle-shaped. *See also* Leaf Shape (for illustration).

ACID DEPOSITION The process by which acids are deposited, either as **wet deposition** in the form of rain, snow, sleet, hail, or fog; or as **dry deposition** in the form of particulates such as fly ash, sulphates, nitrates, or as gases like sulphur dioxide and nitric oxide. Dry particles and gases, deposited onto or adsorbed into surfaces, can be converted into acids after deposition or adsorption when they contact water.

ACIDIC ROCK **1** A broad descriptive term for felsic igneous rocks rich in silicate minerals, which is typically more light coloured, such as granite and rhyolite. **2** The ability of certain rock types to generate acidic waters. It is a major concern in mining operations when surface water is percolating through freshly exposed rocks, often in the form of tailings piles or flooded underground workings. It can be a major source of downstream pollution.

ACIDITY The degree to which a substance has a high concentration of hydrogen ions; having a pH value lower than 7.0. *See also* Alkalinity.

ACID PRECIPITATION Rain, snow, sleet, hail, or fog, typically with a pH less than 5.6. The acidity results from chemical reactions occurring when water, sulphur dioxide, and nitrogen oxides, generally released by industrial processes, are chemically transformed into sulphuric and nitric acids. The process typically occurs during atmospheric transport and the products are subsequently deposited downwind. The term acid precipitation is broad. The terms acid deposition and acid rain have more specific meanings. *See also* Acid Deposition; Acid Rain.

ACID RAIN Rain having a pH less than 5.6. Not to be confused with the broader term acid deposition.

ACRE-FOOT A unit of measurement describing water or sediment volumes; equal to a volume that would cover an area of one acre to a depth of one foot. A volume of 43,560 cubic feet or 1,233 cubic metres.

ACROCARPOUS Describes bryophytes where the sporophyte is borne at the tip of the main stem or branch. The apical cell of the branch or stem is involved in the production of archegonia. *See also* Archegonium.

ACROCENTRIC In genetics, a chromosome having the centromere close to one end of the chromosome, such that the chromosome has one short arm and one long arm. *See also* Metacentric; Telocentric.

ACROGENOUS Located at the tip; apical.

ACROPETAL Arising, developing, or opening sequentially from a lower position toward a more apical one. *See also* Basipetal.

ACROPLEUROGENOUS Located at the tip and sides.

ACTINOMORPHIC Describes some flowers and some animals, such as starfish and sea urchins, that have radial symmetry and are capable of division into two or more planes in order to yield identical sections (see illustration). *See also* Bilateral Symmetry; Symmetrical; Zygomorphic.

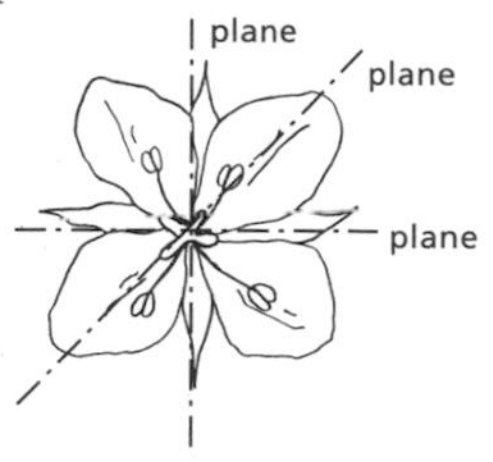

ACTINOMYCETES Soil microbes in the order Actinomycetales that superficially resemble fungi but are in fact non-motile bacteria. They play an important role in the decomposition of organic matter.

ACTIONABLE FIRE Any fire requiring suppression, especially a fire started or allowed to spread in violation of law, ordinance, or regulation.

ACTIVE CROWN FIRE *See* Forest Fire.

ACTIVE FIRE *See* Going Fire.

ACTIVE INGREDIENT **1** The component of a pesticide formulation to which the pesticidal effect is attributed. The rate of pesticide application is determined by the amount of active ingredient. **2** The legal definition of active ingredient, including synergists, under the applicable pest control legislation in the country of application. *See also* Carrier.

ACTIVE LOGGING ROADS Roads that are in current use for logging or other forest management activities.

ACTIVE REPAIR TIME *See* Machine Time (mechanical delay time; scheduled operating time).

ACTIVE SLOPE A mountain or hill slope that is responding to valley incision and has detritus accumulated behind obstructions, indicating contemporary transport of slope colluvium; slope gradient typically exceeds 45 per cent. *See also* Slope.

ACTIVITY FUELS In forest fire management,

fuels resulting from, or altered by, forestry practices such as timber harvest or thinning, as opposed to naturally created fuels. *See also* Natural Fuels.

ACTUAL PRODUCTIVE TIME *See* Machine Time (productive time).

ACULEATE **1** Covered with spines or prickles. **2** Having a spiny margin with long, prickly teeth. *See also* Leaf Margin.

ACUMINATE Tapering at the end; long; pointed. *See also* Leaf Shape.

ACUTE **1** Pointed, tapering with mainly straight sides to a point. *See also* Leaf Shape. **2** An angle less than ninety degrees. *See also* Obtuse.

ACYCLIC Plant parts arranged spirally, not in whorls or pairs.

ADAPTATION **1** Evolutionary changes in structure, morphology, or physiology of populations that enhance their ability to survive and reproduce in the prevailing environmental conditions. These changes are genetic modifications that occur over long periods of time. **2** Shorter term behavioural modifications in response to changed or changing conditions.

ADAPTER A device for connecting hoses of the same size with non-matching hose threads, or connecting a threaded coupling to a quick-connect coupling.

ADAPTIVE MANAGEMENT A dynamic planning or modelling process that recognizes the future cannot be predicted perfectly. In response to these imperfect predictions, planning and management strategies are modified frequently as better information becomes available. It applies scientific principles and methods to improve management activities incrementally, as decision-makers learn from experience and new scientific findings, and adapt to changing social expectations and demands. Adaptive management is based on the adage 'expect the unexpected.' It is a continuous process requiring constant monitoring and analysis of the results of past actions, which are then fed back into current decisions.

ADAPTIVE PLANNING A planning strategy in which planning efforts are directed toward meeting temporary crises that arise in response to changing conditions. The planner responds to external forces influencing the area, identifies potential and current crises, takes advantage of externally developed resources, and attempts to forestall or resolve the crises by creating the proper responses to the pressures generated by those forces.

ADAPTIVE VALUE The degree to which a characteristic confers a selective advantage to an organism by promoting survival, reproduction, and greater overall fitness within the environment.

ADAXIAL Describes the surface of a lateral organ facing toward the main axis; ventral. In describing plants, the upper side of a leaf is typically adaxial because it develops facing the stem. *See also* Abaxial.

ADDITIVE **1** In pesticide formulations, any substance that contributes to the formulation (e.g., stabilizer or adjuvant). **2** In wood panel manufacture, any substance added to impart or improve the endproduct properties, such as preservatives, water-repellents, and fire retardants, but excluding the binders that hold the substrate particles together.

ADDITIVE GENES Different genes interacting only by enhancement of a trait, showing no dominance or recessiveness. If the genes are nonallelic, they show no epistasis.

ADDITIVE WEIGHTING A decisionmaking method in which a number of different resource values that are not easily compared by conversion to an equivalent dollar value are assigned numerical values on the basis of some more or less objective, common-sense notion of their relative importance. The simple summation of the weightings of alternative resource yield mixes is used as the basis for making choices.

Maximization of the net social yield of resource use is either: (1) the mix that maximizes the sum of the additive weights, if numerically larger weights are assigned to more important values; or (2) the mix that minimizes the sum, if relative importance values are assigned on the basis of rankings, with 1 being the most important type of yield and successively less important yields being assigned higher numbers. *See also* Measurement; Optimization.

ADELPHOUS Staminate male flowers with filaments that are fused together. *See also* Diadelphous; Monadelphous; Syncarp.

ADHERENT Botanically, united, sometimes clinging together but not actually fused. It sometimes refers to the joining of dissimilar parts or organs. *See also* Coherent.

ADHESION **1** The force of attraction between different molecules. When combined with surface tension, adhesion is responsible for capillary action. **2** The force of attraction between soil particles.

ADIABATIC PROCESS The thermodynamic change of state in which no heat is added or subtracted from a system. Compression always results in warming, and expansion always results in cooling.

ADJACENCY REQUIREMENTS Management restrictions to regulate the creation of harvest openings. An opening created by harvest must 'close' through a new forest or other vegetation growing to a certain height before another harvest unit can be placed next to it. This requirement has led to the 'staggered setting' approach to timber harvest in which clearcut units, usually over twenty to sixty acres, are scattered over the landscape. *See also* Staggered Setting.

ADJUSTED DUFF MOISTURE CODE *See* Canadian Forest Fire Weather Index System (Buildup Index).

ADJUSTMENT A process in which observations are corrected in an effort to reduce or remove errors or internal consistencies in the results. The term can refer to mathematical procedures or to corrections made to the instruments used in taking the observations.

ADJUSTMENT PERIOD **1** A period following disturbance with increased rates of species colonization, extinction, and changes in population size. **2** The time period required to modify a forest from one growing stock level to another (more desirable) growing stock level.

ADJUVANT A substance (solid or liquid) added to improve the physical or chemical properties of another substance (e.g., to make a fluid flow better, stick to surfaces more effectively, or to enhance the performance of an antigen).

ADMIRALTY SHACKLE A heavy shackle at the tail tree that connects the skyline to the stub line (guyline extension).

ADNATE Completely or nearly fused. It refers to the union in early development of dissimilar parts or organs (e.g., a filament adnate to the corolla). *See also* Connate.

ADNEXED In fungi, describes gills notched next to the stipe.

ADOLESCENT **1** Generally, a transitional stage of development between immaturity and maturity. **2** In silviculture, a tree in a size class immediately preceding the merchantable size class.

ADPRESSED *See* Appressed.

ADSORPTION The process in which a layer of ions, atoms, or molecules are bonded chemically or physically to solid surfaces (e.g., the adsorption of cations by negatively charged minerals such as clay particles). *See also* Absorption.

ADULT The fully grown, usually sexually mature, individual. *See also* Imago; Instar.

ADULT PHASE In phenology, the period of life in a tree during which flowering occurs.

AD VALOREM An assessment or tax that is proportional to the value of the item being taxed. This value does not necessarily reflect the true market value of the item being taxed.

ADVANCED DECAY A stage of wood decay in which the wood has become definitely changed in appearance, character, and composition, with loss of structural strength. *See also* Decay; Intermediate Decay.

ADVANCE REGENERATION The young (or extremely suppressed) trees growing under an existing stand before it is logged. If the advance regeneration survives the logging operation it may form the initial part of a new stand. In some silvicultural systems, the advance growth is the dominant form of regeneration utilized. *See also* Regeneration.

ADVANCING A LINE Moving a hose line toward a specified area from the point where the hose-carrying apparatus has stopped.

ADVANCING FRONT CONVECTIVE STAGE *See* Convective-Lift Fire Phase.

ADVECTION The transfer of atmospheric properties by the movement of air, usually in reference to the transfer of warmer or cooler air, but may also refer to moisture. *See also* Convection.

ADVENTITIOUS Tissue that develops from newly organized meristems. Typically, buds or roots that develop in places and at times outside those considered normal or characteristic (e.g., an adventitious bud arises from any part of a stem, leaf, or root but lacks vascular connection with the pith). They may be a result of defoliation by insect pests or pruning. An adventitious root arises from parts of the plant other than a pre-existing root, such as a stem or leaf; often associated with the placement of excess fill over the existing root mat or with stem decay. Adventitious roots will often develop around areas of root damage and give the tree some continuity of water supply, but seldom function in a structural capacity. Roots growing from a stem cutting are adventitious.

ADVENTIVE **1** An organism introduced or appearing from another region or country and not yet naturalized. **2** Buds developing along a stem instead of at leaf axils; plantlets developing from stem or leaf axils (e.g., viviparous plants) or roots.

ADVERSARIAL PROCEDURES The system or set of legally defined procedures for conducting civil trials under strict rules of evidence with the right of cross-examination and argument accorded to both sides. The plaintiff is the person or organization launching a lawsuit. The defendant is the person or organization defending the suit. Both sides may bring in expert witnesses to prove their version of the 'facts.' The procedure has long been advocated as the best way of resolving (in or out of court) resource management disputes and, in recent decades, there have been thousands of court cases argued along these lines.

The theoretical strength of the approach lies in its strong presentation and contrasting of both pro and con interpretations of what the real facts are for the judge(s). Its weaknesses lie in the distortions of the relative merits of the opposing cases that may result from: (1) the ability or inability to finance presentations and defences; (2) unequal access to information and the financial resources required to secure expert opinion; (3) the theatrical and intellectual capabilities in making presentations and cross-examinations; and (4) the limits on the ability of the judging parties to be truly objective. An additional difficulty results from the extremely complex nature of contemporary resource management issues. In many cases, there is no one right or wrong answer, but merely several interpretations being offered by different experts.

ADVERSE GRADE Describes a highway grade that is an uphill haul that requires trucks to use lower gears. Generally, a gradient that slopes uphill in the direction of log haul. *See also* Grade.

ADVOCACY PLANNING **1** The practice of professional planners voluntarily helping underprivileged sections of society to give expression to their hopes for a better standard of living and improved environmental conditions. **2** Planners working directly with socioeconomically defined special interest groups to translate their aspirations for a livable environment into formal planning goals and a set of procedures for attaining those goals. The manner in which conflicting desires are resolved depends on the context of the issues and the manner in which the authorities having jurisdiction react to the proposed plans. *See also* Alternative Dispute Resolution; Plan; Planner.

ADZE HOE A fire-trenching or digging tool with a sharp, tempered blade; useful for heavy grubbing, trenching, and cutting.

AECIAL The spore state in which aecia are formed in the aecium. It is also termed aecidial.

AECIOSPORE Coming from rust fungi, the aeciospore is a nonrepeating, asexual spore, often yellow to orange in mass, borne in chains in an aecium and incapable of infecting the host on which it is produced.

AECIUM Plural aecia. A fruiting structure that produces aeciospores of a rust fungus. The aecia form after the spermagonium and before the uredinium in the life cycle. They are often cup-shaped or in some cases blisterlike or tubular, often with colourless or white walls.

AEOLIAN *See* Eolian.

AERATION The process in which soil gases are exchanged with atmospheric gases. Aeration may be limited by the number, size, continuity, and drainage patterns of the soil pores. Poor aeration results in anaerobic (anoxic) conditions. The zone of aeration occurs above the water table. *See also* Illuviation (for illustration).

AERENCHYMA A form of parenchymatous tissue; composed of thin-walled cells and large intercellular air-filled cavities. It is found in roots and stems of some aquatic plants and enables effective gaseous exchange above or below water, as well as providing some buoyancy.

AERIAL APPLICATION The application of a pesticide from the air using spray equipment mounted on a helicopter or an airplane.

AERIAL ATTACK *See* Air Attack.

AERIAL DETECTION A system for discovering, locating, and reporting fires from an aircraft. This may be planned or unplanned. **Planned aerial detection (organized)** is in effect when an agency deploys detection aircraft for the specific purpose of detecting and reporting wildfires. **Unplanned aerial detection (random)** occurs when discovery and reporting of wildfires are from aircraft not specifically hired or deployed for detection purposes (includes private aircraft reports).

AERIAL FUELS Standing or supported living and dead vegetation not in direct contact with the ground and consisting mainly of shrub and tree crowns, and draped fuels. It is also termed crown fuels. *See also* Ladder Fuels; Surface Fuels.

AERIAL IGNITION Ignition of fuels by dropping incendiary devices or materials from an aircraft.

AERIAL IGNITION DEVICE (AID) An incendiary apparatus designed to ignite wildland fuels from an aircraft. *See also* Aerial Torch; Ping-Pong Ball System.

AERIAL LOGGING Any yarding system employing aerial lift of logs, such as by balloons or helicopters.

AERIAL OBSERVER A person specifically assigned to discover, locate, and report wildfires from an aircraft and to observe and describe conditions at the fire scene.

AERIAL PHOTOGRAPH Any photographic image taken from the air. It is usually taken as close as possible to vertical over the site being photographed, but sometimes taken at an oblique angle to see a different perspective.

AERIAL PHOTOGRAPH INTERPRETER A person skilled in identifying natural and cultural features or patterns on aerial photographs.

AERIAL PHOTOGRAPH MOSAIC A photographic reproduction of a series of aerial photographs assembled in such a manner that features such as roads and streams match from one photograph to the next and there is no overlap or repetition. **Controlled mosaics** are made by locating some points precisely, as on a map, and using prints that have to some extent been corrected for tilt and topographic distortion. **Uncontrolled mosaics**, which are less expensive, are made by matching edges from one photograph to the next as well as possible; images are distorted and cannot be used for reliable measurements.

AERIAL RECONNAISSANCE **1** In general, the collection of information by visual, electronic, or photographic means from the air. **2** In fire suppression, the use of aircraft for observing fire behaviour, values-at-risk, suppression activity, and other critical factors to facilitate command decisions on the tactics needed for fire suppression.

AERIAL SEEDING The broadcast sowing of seeds from an aircraft.

AERIAL SHOOT The stemlike portion of a dwarf mistletoe plant outside the host plant. Its primary function is reproduction. A collection of aerial shoots is sometimes referred to collectively as an aerial plant.

AERIAL TORCH An aerial ignition device slung from, or mounted on, a helicopter, that dispenses ignited globs of gelled gasoline. It is also termed a flying drip torch or helitorch. *See also* Aerial Ignition Device; Drip Torch.

AERIAL VOLUME TABLE In timber management, a volume table based on measurements such as stand density, visible tree height, and visible crown diameter made from aerial photographs and correlated with a sampling of ground volume measurements. An aerial volume table can be constructed for individual tree volumes or stand volumes.

AEROBIC **1** Environmental conditions in which oxygen is present. **2** Organisms requiring atmospheric oxygen as a gas or dissolved in water in order to survive. *See also* Anaerobic.

AEROSOL Dispersion of fluids in a suspension of very fine particles of liquid or gas.

AESTHETICS Generally, the study, science, or philosophy concerning judgments made about beauty. An evaluation or consideration concerning the sensory quality of resources (sight, sound, smell, taste, touch, and movement) evoked by phenomena, individual elements, or configurations of elements in the landscape surrounding humans, especially with respect to judgments about their pleasurable qualities.

AESTIVATION **1** A period of torpor (resting, sleeping, and generally inactive) in the summer months. Insects may be in aestivation for one or two months. *See also* Diapause; Dormancy; Hibernation. **2** The folding pattern of plant structures prior to opening. It is also spelled estivation.

AETIOLOGY The scientific study of the cause of disease, including the causal factor. It is also spelled etiology.

AFFERENT Leading, or conducting toward an organ or location (e.g., blood vessels conducting fluids toward a specific organ). *See also* Efferent.

AFFIRMS In the United States, the Administrative and Forest Fire Information Retrieval and Management System. A user-oriented interactive computer program that permits entry of fire weather observations and fire weather forecasts, and permits the computation of danger indices.

AFFIXED LOGS *See* Large Organic Debris.

AFFORESTATION The establishment of a forest or stand of trees by sowing, planting, or natural regeneration on an area not previously forested, or in areas where forests were cleared long ago and other land-use patterns have dominated the landscape for many generations (e.g., the moorlands of Great Britain).

A-FRAME Two wood or metal poles mounted in the shape of the letter 'A' with a block and tackle hung in the apex where the poles join. It is used as a loading or unloading device for logs on trucks.

AFTER-HATCHING-YEAR (AHY) BIRD A bird in at least its second calendar year of life.

AFTER-SECOND-YEAR (ASY) BIRD A bird in at least its third calendar year of life.

AFTER-THIRD-YEAR (ATY) BIRD A bird in at least its fourth calendar year of life.

AGAMOSPERMY Asexual seed formation.

AGARIC A mushroom having gills.

AGE In forest management, age is normally counted in years. **1** The age of a tree can usually be determined by counting the number of annual rings across the tree trunk and then adding on a factor to account for the time needed to grow up to the point of measurement. Not all trees produce clearly defined annual rings; some produce extra, or false rings, within any one annual growth period, while others, especially in the tropics, may not produce a clearly defined ring at all since the annual seasonal variation in climate is not large enough to trigger variation in growth patterns. **2** The age of a forest is based either on the year of planting or on the age of dominant and codominant trees. **3** In nursery work, the age of young trees is based on the time elapsed since germination. **4** In fish and wildlife studies, age is measured in years since birth, but may be months since birth for the earlier stages of development.

AGE CLASS The classification of stands in a forest, or trees in a stand, into a series of ages (e.g., 1 to 20 might be Age Class 1, 21 to 40 might be Age Class 2, and so on). Certain age classes would equate to certain points in the average stage of tree, stand, or forest development (e.g., Age Class 1 might be the seedling/sapling stage, Age Class 2 might be the pole stage, and so on). Similar schemes can be devised for any population of organisms.

AGE-CLASS DISTRIBUTION The distribution of different age classes within the population being examined. *See also* Life Table.

AGE-CLASS PERIOD The interval, usually measured in years, within the limits of each age class.

AGENT OF DISEASE Any organism or abiotic factor that causes disease.

AGGLOMERATE A fused mass of large angular fragments of rock mixed with finer material. Often found in the cone or neck of a volcano and resulting from explosive volcanic forces. *See also* Breccia; Conglomerate.

AGGRADATION The geologic process of accumulating deposits of unconsolidated materials that have been eroded elsewhere and are then deposited at a new location. It is the opposite of degradation. *See also* Degradation.

AGGRADING **1** Describes a geomorphic feature being built up by aggradation. **2** In landscape ecology, the steady increase of structure and/or biomass in a system. *See also* Degrading.

AGGREGATE **1** Part of the soil structure, formed by natural processes, containing fine inorganic materials less than two millimetres in diameter that are held together by interaction with each other (e.g., clay flocculation) and/or are bonded together by organic matter or cementing agents. **2** Granular material of mineral composition such as sand, gravel, crushed rock, slag, or similar inert material, used with a cementing medium to form mortar, concrete, and asphalt, or alone as in railroad ballast. Aggregate is described as gravel or coarse aggregate if it is retained on a 4.76-millimetre square (no. 4 sieve screen) and as sand or fine aggregate if it passes this mesh size. **3** A verb describing the process of aggregation, meaning to bring together in one place. Its opposite is disaggregate, or to take apart pieces from the whole. It is also used to describe component parts of an assessment that has integrated many different pieces of data and information.

AGGREGATE FRUIT A 'fruit' comprising the several separate ripened ovaries of a single flower (e.g., blackberry, strawberry). *See also* Fruit (for illustration).

AGGREGATION **1** The clumping of individuals in a biotic community. **2** The massing of male and female adult bark beetles or other insects on a tree under attack.

AGGREGATION PHEROMONE A pheromone either synthetically released or naturally excreted by male or female insects, or by plants (or both plants and insects) to attract other male or female insects to a given location (e.g., bark beetles massing on a tree under attack). *See also* Pheromone.

AGGRESSIVENESS **1** A plant pathogen that has the ability to colonize and cause damage to plants. *See also* Virulence. **2** Animals displaying aggressive behaviour, often as a part of territorial defence during the mating season.

AGGRESSIVE STRAIN A fungus genotype having an enhanced pathogenic capacity.

AGOMOSPERMY A form of asexual reproduction in plants where seeds form without meiosis or fertilization.

AGONIC LINE *See* Isogonic Charts.

AGONISTIC BEHAVIOUR A threat, offensive movement (aggression), or retreat (appeasement) directed at another member of the same species. Agonistic behaviour is associated with territorial behaviour and defence of marked territories.

AGRICULTURAL LAND Land used primarily for the production of plant or animal crops, including arable agriculture, dairying, pasturage, apiaries, horticulture, floriculture, viticulture, animal (including poultry) husbandry, and the necessary lands and structures needed for packing, processing, treating, or storing the produce. Agricultural land may be employed in an unimproved state with few, if any, management inputs (extensive rangeland), or in an intensively managed state with annual inputs of fertilizer, pest-control treatments, and tillage (plant crop production or pasturage).

AGROFORESTRY A distinct form of land use involving the integrated production of trees, other forest plants, agricultural crops, and animals in a manner compatible with the cultural patterns of the local population. Typical of developing countries, agroforestry schemes use the trees to provide fuelwood, lumber, and animal fodder, while at the same time providing shade and soil stability to the agricultural crops that are interplanted with the trees. In its ideal form, agroforestry would be both a stable and a sustainable land use, though this may not always be feasible. The three basic components of trees, agricultural crops, and animals are combined into several main agroforestry systems. **Agrosilvicultural** is the integration of crops and trees, shrubs, and/or vines. **Silvopastoral** is the integration of trees, pasture, and/or animals. **Agrosilvopastoral** is the integration of crops, trees, pasture, and/or animals. **Silvoaquaculture** is the integration of trees, crops, pasture, and fish farming.

AGROSTOLOGY **1** Strictly, the study of grasses. **2** The study of grasses and legumes for animal nutrition.

AIR ATTACK A fire-suppression operation involving the use of aircraft to deliver fire-fighting forces, suppressants, or retardants to or on a fire. It is synonymous with aerial attack. *See also* Helitack.

AIR ATTACK BASE A permanent facility at which aircraft are stationed for use in air-attack operations.

AIR BASE **1** The distance between two camera stations. **2** The ground distance between centres of overlapping photographs. *See also* Base-Height Ratio; Camera Station.

AIR COORDINATOR (AIRCO) In the United States, a light, fixed-wing aircraft with an experienced fire officer on board who serves as the coordinator of air attack on a fire incident. *See also* Birddog Aircraft.

AIRCRAFT NETWORK (AIR NET) A network of radio frequencies primarily used for air operations.

AIR-DRIED LUMBER Lumber or other wood products that have been dried either by exposure to natural atmospheric conditions outdoors, or in an unheated shed; or dried to equilibrium with the surrounding atmosphere. Moisture content of air-dried wood fibre depends on the relative humidity, temperature, and the length of the drying period. It is also termed air-seasoned lumber. *See also* Equilibrium Moisture Content; Kiln-Dried Wood.

AIR-DRY DENSITY The density of wood that has been dried in, and is in equilibrium with, the prevailing atmospheric conditions. *See also* Equilibrium Moisture Content; Kiln-Dried Wood.

AIR-GROUND DETECTION Any fire detection system combining fixed-point coverage of key areas by ground detectors with aerial detection that is varied according to needs.

AIR LAYERING In propagating plants, the induction of root development on an aerial portion of the plant that is still attached, by slightly wounding the portion, treating it with a rooting hormone, and wrapping it in moist material in a waterproof covering. The portion thus treated will develop roots and can then be separated and will grow independently from the original plant.

AIR MASS A meteorological term describing an extensive body of air having similar properties of temperature and moisture in a horizontal plane.

AIR POLLUTION A general term describing the undesirable addition of substances (gases, liquids, or solid particles) to the atmosphere that are foreign to the natural atmosphere, or are present in quantities exceeding natural concentrations.

AIR SHED Conceptually similar to a watershed, but involving a geographically defined air mass, usually regional in scale.

AIR SPEED The speed of aircraft travel, along its longitudinal axis, relative to the surrounding atmosphere. *See also* Ground Speed.

AIRTANKER A fixed-wing aircraft fitted with tanks and equipment for releasing water or fire retardant on fires. It is also termed fire or water bomber. *See also* Helitanker.

AIRTANKER BASE An operational base at which airtankers are held in readiness for action on fires. The base generally includes dispatch facilities, crew day quarters, limited equipment storage, and administrative facilities. It may also be equipped to provide fire retardant, in which case it may be called a retardant base.

ALAR CELLS Specialized cells, located at the basal angles of a leaf, that attach the leaf to the stem.

ALATE **1** Winged. *See also* Alulate. **2** Referring to stems, petioles, and fruit, where the main axis is connected to the stem, fruit, or petiole by a membranaceous tissue. *See also* Samara.

ALBEDO The ratio of shortwave radiation energy reflected back by a surface relative to the amount falling on it. Albedo, expressed as a percentage, is thus:

$$\frac{S_o}{S_i} \times 100$$

where

S_o = reflected radiation

S_i = radiation coming in.

The albedo is affected by surface roughness, water content, and daily and seasonal sun angles. Typically, darker, rougher materials have a lower albedo than lighter, smoother materials (e.g., forest, 5-10 per cent; grass, 25 per cent; snow, 55-80 per cent). *See also* Boreal Forest.

ALBUMEN In plants, the starchy or other nutritive materials in the seed. If the albumen is stored inside the embryo sac, it is called the endosperm; if stored in the surrounding nucellar cells, it is called the perisperm. *See also* Nucellar Embryo.

ALEVIN A stage of embryonic development of salmon or related fish. Refers to fish recently hatched from the egg and before absorption of the yolk sac and emergence from the spawning gravel.

ALGAL BLOOM A readily visible, high concentration of algae or aggregation of algae in or on the surface layer of a water body. *See also* Eutrophication.

ALGORITHM A set of mathematical instructions or problem-solving procedures designed to provide answers to complex problems. Algorithms are used in modelling applications to portray the interrelationships between different sets of data; for example, timber supply, yield tables, wildlife habitat, individual tree growth, fire spread, or insect and disease spread. *See also* Digital Classification; Pixel.

ALIDADE An instrument used in surveying, consisting of a straight-edge rule with two vertical sights whose alignment is parallel with the edge. A modified form is used in locating fires. *See also* Fire Finder.

ALIEN SPECIES *See* Exotic Species.

ALIGNMENT **1** Generally the lining up of two parts so that they join, match, or overlap correctly. **2** The centre line of a road, drain, or track reflecting its actual position on the ground and its corresponding position on a plan or map. It is made up of straight lines, tangent sections, and curves.

ALKALINITY A measure of the degree to which a substance can neutralize hydrogen ions (H^+), usually expressed as pH. Alkaline materials have a value higher than the neutral pH value of 7.0. It is the opposite of acidic. *See also* Acidity.

ALKALOID A group of complex nitrogenous organic compounds that are alkaline, produced in many plants, some of which are highly poisonous, while others have commercial value. Trees containing alkaloids may have toxic effects, even after manufacture into lumber or other wood products. Alkaloids, such as nicotine, quinine, caffeine, strychnine, cocaine, morphine, atropine, etc., produce distinct physiological effects.

ALL-AGED A crop or forest containing examples of all the age classes from young to mature. *See also* Even-Aged.

ALLANTOID Sausage-shaped, slightly curved with round ends.

ALLEE EFFECT A depression in the potential chance of encountering a breeding partner, resulting from low population densities. The probability of finding a mate drops below that required to maintain the reproductive rates necessary to support the population. The result is eventual extinction of the species locally and, if the phenomenon is widespread, would lead to global extinction of the species.

ALLELE A form of gene, typically seen in pairs, one on each homologous chromosome within a diploid cell nucleus. An individual organism having identical alleles is said to be a homozygote; if different alleles are present, it is a heterozygote. Pairs or series of alleles may represent several forms of a gene situated in the same relative position on homologous chromosomes. Different alleles determine alternative characteristics of inheritance.

ALLELOCHEMIC A chemical substance given off by one organism that influences the behaviour or physiology of other organisms. *See also* Allelopathy; Allomone; Kairomone; Pheromone; Synomone.

ALLELOPATHY A competitive strategy of plants in which there is the production of chemical compounds (allelochemicals) by such plants that interfere with the germination, growth, or development of another plant. Allelopathy occurs in three ways: (1) by exudates from roots (e.g., the genera *Typha, Juglans, Solidago, Hieracium*, and *Helianthus*); (2) with rainfall, causing leachates from stems and leaves; (3) as toxins produced upon decomposition of plant parts, including roots, stems, leaves, rhizomes, stolons, and tubers. Allelochemicals may also operate via the effects of mycorrhizal symbionts, or decomposer organisms. The classic North American example is Black Walnut (*Juglans nigra*), which produces the chemical juglone. Juglone is exuded during the decomposition of plant parts, such as leaves and petioles, inhibiting growth in neighbouring plant species. It is sometimes termed antibiosis. *See also* Autoallelopath.

ALLERGENIC A nasal and/or bronchial allergic reaction in mammals caused by inhaling an allergen, usually in the form of fine dust or as an aerosol. It can also be manifested as a skin reaction when contact is made with allergenic substances.

ALLIANCE **1** In ecology, a series of climax ecosystems having identical structural characteristics, dominants that are related species, and an understorey typified by the same or related species. *See also* Association. **2** In the Braun-Blanquet plant community classification system, the unit of next higher rank than the association.

ALLITIC Soils having a clay fraction in which aluminum and iron compounds predominate, with the silica sesquioxide ratio being less than 50 per cent. *See also* Ferrallitic; Ferruginous; Fersiallitic; Laterite; Siallitic.

ALLOCATION **1** The process of deciding where, when, and how management resources are used or management activities are to be directed. The process of deciding which parts of the forest landscape will be managed and for what purposes (e.g., harvesting or other, often mutually exclusive, uses). **2** Within a tree, the physical direction of resources to assist in discrete biological activities, such as photosynthesis, wound compartmentalization, or refoliation following insect attacks.

ALLOCHTHONOUS **1** A substance located away from its original source (e.g., rocks). **2** In freshwater biology, the nutrient inputs (leaves and small twigs) to a stream originating from streamside vegetation, which undergo decomposition and provide an important source of food for the benthic invertebrates. *See also* Autochthonous; Benthic Invertebrates.

ALLOGAMY Cross-fertilization between flowers, including geitonogamy and xenogamy. *See also* Autogamy.

ALLOGENIC The species changes within an ecosystem that result from external influences such as fire, long-term drought, and wind. *See also* Autogenic.

ALLOMETRY The growth of one part of the organism relative to the entire organism.

ALLOMONE A chemical substance given off by an individual of one species which, when contacted by an individual of a second species, induces a behavioural or physiological response favourable to the first species. *See also* Allelochemic; Kairomone; Pheromone; Synomone.

ALLOPATRIC Geographically separated populations of the same species where the isolation is sufficient to prevent the exchange of genetic material. *See also* Parapatric; Sympatric.

ALLOPOLYPLOID An organism with more than two sets of chromosomes in its vegetative cells, derived by cross-breeding two or more species. It is also termed amphiploidy and alloploidy.

ALLOWABLE BURNED AREA A standard or objective of protection effort set for an area of managed forest or other land. It is the maximum average area burned by wildfire over a specified period of years that can be tolerated and sustained for a given area without disrupting overall forest management and other land-use objectives.

ALLOWABLE CUT EFFECT The allocation of anticipated future forest timber yields to the present allowable cut. The effect is typically based on several assumptions about the yields that may develop as a result of activities and decisions taken in the present. Consequently, the allowable cut effect can be a double-edged sword.

The problem can be shown in general terms by reference to Hanzlik's formula (or others), which calculates

$$\text{Annual cut} = \frac{Vm}{R} + I$$

where

Vm = volume of merchantable timber beyond rotation age
R = rotation adopted for future stands, in years
I = annual increment of wood volume.

Shortening the rotation period, raising the increment, or both, increases the annual cut. If the anticipated yields materialize, then past cut levels will have been at about the right level.

However, if the anticipated yields fail to materialize, the allowable cut will have been consistently overestimated, leaving a larger shortfall of wood than was expected, with the consequent need to drastically reduce actual cuts at that time.

ALLOWABLE SALE QUANTITY In the United States, the gross amount of timber volume, including salvage, that may be sold annually from within a specified area or over a stated period, in accordance with management plans of the US Forest Service or the Bureau of Land Management. It was formerly termed allowable cut.

ALLOZYMES In genetics research, isozymes that have different electrical charges and are thus detectable by electrophoresis. One of several forms of an enzyme encoded by different alleles at the same locus. *See also* Isozyme.

ALLUVIAL *See* Fluvial.

ALLUVIAL CONE The material washed down mountain and hill slopes by ephemeral streams and deposited at the mouth of gorges in the form of a moderately steep conical mass descending equally in all directions from the point of issue.

ALLUVIAL FAN A type of floodplain, typically located at the mouth of a tributary valley, created when alluvium is deposited. Usually results from decreased water velocity, increased sediment content, or changing channel shape, with the resulting landform resembling a cone or fan shape. Alluvial fans are sensitive to climatic and tectonic activity and are therefore environmentally significant. Studying them can yield useful information about past climatic and tectonic changes.

ALLUVIAL FLAT A nearly level, graded, alluvial surface.

ALLUVIAL PLAIN **1** *See* Floodplain. **2** A plain underlain by fluvial deposits, including alluvial (fluvial) fans, and lacustrine deposits (stream-transported materials that have accumulated in lakes).

ALLUVIAL SOIL Soil formed in alluvial deposits.

ALLUVIAL STREAM Named after the silts, sands, and gravels of river origin that compose their beds, banks, and floodplains, alluvial streams are characterized by a distinctive S-shaped channel pattern that is free to shift slowly (meander) in the valley. Repeated bank cavings do not widen the channel as they do in erodible bed streams. Alluvial streams have their bed materials conveyed from upstream and they tend to be large.

ALLUVIAL TERRACE *See* River Terrace.

ALLUVIUM Unconsolidated deposits (fluvial materials) of recent origin, especially silts and silty clays, resulting from the direct, or indirect, water transport of sediment. It includes sediments laid down in streams, riverbeds, floodplains, and alluvial fans, but excludes subaqueous sediments in seas and lakes. *See also* Colluvium.

ALPHA DIVERSITY *See* Diversity.

ALPHA SPECIES A species requiring specialized habitats, typically restricted to one particular vegetation type and having a small home range, small size, and high rate of reproduction.

ALPINE **1** The area of land lying above the current altitudinal limits of tree growth, implying a cold climate. **2** A geomorphic structure and its associated environmental conditions resembling the European Alps or similar high mountains.

ALTERNATE Botanically, arranged singly at different heights and on different sides of the axis or stem (e.g., alternate leaves, as illustrated, or branches). *See also* Opposite; Whorl.

alternate leaf
Myrica gale
(Sweet gale)

ALTERNATE HOST One of two or more unlike hosts required by a heteroecious insect (e.g., gall aphid), fungus (e.g., rust), or other organism to complete its life cycle. *See also* Alternative Host; Host.

ALTERNATING GENERATIONS **1** In some plants and animals, the regular alternation of life-forms or reproductive methods in consecutive generations. It may include an alternating switch from sexual to asexual propagation, or between being in the diploid and haploid stages. **2** In some insects and fungi, an obligatory change of host species in consecutive generations. *See also* Generation.

ALTERNATION The successive occurrence of a fungal parasite on two alternate hosts during its life cycle.

ALTERNATIVE The different means (alternatives) by which objectives or goals might be achieved. Alternatives need not be obvious substitutes for one another, or perform the same specific functions. *See also* Environmental Impact Assessment.

ALTERNATIVE DISPUTE RESOLUTION Conflict resolution techniques that do not utilize the normal adversarial approaches typical of court settings. There are a range of techniques available, including arbitration, bargaining, conciliation, consensus seeking, consultation, group processes, mediation, negotiation, and policy dialogues. Each one has distinct characteristics. *See also* Advocacy Planning; Balanced Objectivism.

ALTERNATIVE HOST One of several plant, insect, or other host species suitable for a given parasite, no one of which is essential for completion of the latter's life history. *See also* Alternate Host; Host.

ALTERNE One of two or more plant communities that alternate with each other in space.

ALTIMETER An instrument indicating the vertical distance above a known datum point. Most altimeters consist of an aneroid barometer calibrated to reflect relative changes in atmospheric pressure. Laser and radar altimeters use a laser or microwave beam to determine height above ground by measuring the speed at which the beam travels and the time taken to be reflected back to the point of origin.

ALTIMETER SETTING The pressure value to which an aircraft altimeter scale is set so that it will indicate the altitude above mean sea level of the aircraft on the ground at the location for which the value was determined.

ALTITUDE The vertical distance of an object or point in space above the Earth's surface, relative to a known datum point, usually mean sea level.

ALTRICIAL Any animal that is born blind, in an immature state (without feathers if a bird), and is dependent on its parents. Altricial birds are unable to leave the nest until they mature. *See also* Precocial.

ALULATE Botanically, with a very narrow or small wing. *See also* Alate.

ALVEOLUS In mammals, a tooth socket.

AMBIENT The quality of physical parameters in the surrounding, external, or unconfined conditions (e.g., air temperature or air pollution). The term has no positive or negative connotation.

AMBROSIA BEETLES Small, usually cylindrical, beetles in the family Platypodidae and some genera of the Scolytidae and Lymexylidae. The adults bore into moist wood, typically living; unhealthy, dying, or damaged trees; or green timber, inoculating it with an ambrosia fungus on which they and their larvae feed. The tunnels, the walls of which are often darkly stained, tend to run across the grain of the wood, and the exit holes and their characteristic boring dust give the wood a shothole or pinhole appearance. A cause of significant economic damage to logs in storage.

AMENITY (AMENITY VALUE) **1** An object, feature, quality, or experience that gives the beholder or user sensory pleasure, or makes life more agreeable. **2** Amenity values are non-consumptive and they usually describe features of the landscape that have recognizable resource values that often have no obvious means of quantification in the normal marketplace, and are therefore intangible in an economic assessment. *See also* Intangible Values; Intrinsic Values.

AMENT *See* Catkin.

AMORTIZATION **1** An accounting procedure in which the value of an asset is written-off over a number of years, usually assumed to be equivalent to the expected working life of that asset. **2** The process of repaying a debt, typically a combination of the principal sum and the interest being charged on the unpaid balance still owing on that sum, over a predetermined period of time and at a predetermined rate of interest.

AMPHIBIAN A cold-blooded vertebrate animal in the class Amphibia, which has the following characteristics: (1) glandular skin lacking hair, scales, or feathers; (2) land dwelling as an adult but returns to fresh water when breeding; (3) external fertilization, eggs usually laid in water or moist places; (4) eggs lack a shell and surrounding embryonic membrane; (5) eggs hatch into an aquatic larval stage and transform into adults by metamorphosis (some species may develop directly from egg to young that resemble the adult form); (6) they lack an internal diaphragm for breathing with lungs, and may not have lungs at all; (7) can use the skin and mouth lining for oxygen exchange underwater.

There are three orders of Amphibia: (1) **Anura**, which are frogs and toads; (2) **Caudata**, which are salamanders and newts; and (3) **Apoda**, which are burrowing caecilians found in the circum-tropical regions. *See also* Bird; Mammal; Metamorphosis; Reptile.

AMPHIBIOUS **1** An organism (an amphibian) in the class Amphibia capable of growing equally well on land or in water. **2** A vehicle capable of travelling equally well on land or water.

AMPHIDIPLOID An organism that has a complete chromosome set from each of two different diploid parental strains.

AMPHIGENOUS Growing all around or on both sides.

AMPHIMIXIS Sexual reproduction. *See also* Apomixis.

AMPHISPORE A specially developed urediniospore, with a thicker and occasionally more coloured wall, which acts as a resting or overwintering spore.

AMPHITROPOUS Describes an ovule that is curved back along its supporting stalk (funiculus) so that its base and its micropyle are brought near to each other. *See also* Anatropous.

AMPLEXICAUL Botanically, clasping the stem, with the base partially surrounding it (e.g., leaf base, dilated petiole, or stipule).

AMPLEXUS In amphibians, the mating embrace by the male on the female.

AMPULLA A flasklike or bladderlike organ on plants.

AMPULLIFORM Flask-shaped.

AMUCRONATE In mycology, lacking a mucro. *See also* Mucro.

ANABATIC WINDS An uphill air flow created when air passes over a slope warmed by the sun. The warmer air rises and is replaced with cooler, denser air. It typically occurs in the earlier part of the day. *See also* Katabatic Winds.

ANABIONT A perennial plant that fruits many times.

ANADROMOUS FISH Fish that are born and reared in freshwater, move to the ocean to grow and mature, and return to freshwater to reproduce (e.g., salmon, steelhead, and shad). *See also* Catadromous Fish.

ANADROMOUS POTENTIAL It is also called sportfish potential. Refers to the productive capability of a stream reach to support anadromous or resident sportfish, whether or not fish are or have been present. The presence of fish is determined by the suitability of the stream characteristics (e.g., gradient, water flow, depth, temperature, and quality of spawning gravel). Absence of fish may be attributed to natural barriers or those erected by humans, absence of a specific feature required during one phase of the fish's life history, or a previous catastrophic disturbance in the stream.

ANAEROBIC **1** Environments in which oxygen is absent or present in very low concentrations. **2** Organisms able to survive in the absence of oxygen. *See also* Aerobic.

ANALOGOUS A substance, organism, or form of similar function but different evolutionary descent or origin. *See also* Homologous.

ANALOGUE **1** A synthetic chemical similar in structure to a naturally occurring chemical and capable of mimicking all or some of its effects. **2** In analogue computers, a continuous but variable physical and measurable quantity, such as voltage or electrical resistance, that can be calibrated to represent a series of varying numerical values.

ANAL SHIELD A hard plate on the terminal segment of a caterpillar and certain other immature insects.

ANALYSIS **1** In general, a detailed examination of a body of data, a series of decisions, or the implications of one or more policies, and a determination of what this examination reveals about the nature, function, and/or relationships in effect. Typically, a reductionist approach in which the whole is broken down into smaller component parts for analysis. There may be analytical problems in such an approach when the analyses of the component parts are re-aggregated into a whole. **2** In GIS work, the derivation of new information by bringing together and processing the basic data such as polygons, lines, points, labels, etc. *See also* Manipulation.

ANALYSIS OF COVARIANCE (ANCOVA) In statistics, a process that makes use of ANOVA and regression. The purpose of ANCOVA is to describe the relationship between a continuous dependent variable and one or more nominal independent variables, while controlling for the effect of one or more continuous independent variables. *See also* Analysis of Variance (ANOVA); Nominal Variable.

ANALYSIS OF VARIANCE (ANOVA) An arithmetic process for partitioning a total sum of squares into components associated with recognized sources of variance. The purpose of ANOVA is to describe the relationship between a continuous dependent variable and one or more nominal independent variables. *See also* Analysis of Covariance (ANCOVA); Nominal Variable.

ANAMORPH The imperfect state of a fungus; the asexual, mitotic, diasporic expression of a fungus.

ANAPHASE The third stage of meiosis or mitosis in which the chromosomes migrate to opposite poles of the cell.

ANASTOMOSING Running together irregularly, interlacing, to give a veinlike network.

ANASTOMOSING CHANNEL Describes stream channels that diverge and converge around many islands, where an island is a landform supporting mature vegetation with its surfaces relatively high above mean maximum discharge levels.

ANASTOMOSIS In mycology, the fusion of

hyphal filaments and mixing of cellular contents in one hypha.

ANATROPOUS In botany, describes an ovule that is reversed, with its opening (micropyle) close to the point of attachment of its supporting stalk (funiculus). *See also* Amphitropous, Raphe.

ANCHORAGE The interaction of the soil and root structures of a plant that permit it to stand upright without falling down. Wet or loose soils have weaker anchorage properties.

ANCHOR CABLE In timber extraction work, it is the line used to tie down a yarder to prevent tipping on a heavy pull. *See also* Yarding.

ANCHOR LOG A wooden, concrete, or metal bar buried in the ground to act as an anchor for a guy or anchor line. Also known as deadman.

ANCHOR POINT An advantageous location, generally a fire barrier, from which to start constructing a fire line. It is used to minimize the chance of being outflanked by the fire while the line is being constructed.

ANCIENT FOREST In North America, the late successional, or climax stage of forest development. It could be synonymous with old-growth forest in some definitions. In Great Britain, remnant woodlands are known to have existed before AD 1700.

ANDROECIUM The male element of a flower, referred to as the stamen, being one or many. Each stamen is comprised of an anther and a filament (see illustration). The tissue between the two locules of an anther is known as the connective. An anther attached by its base to the filament is basifixed. An anther attached at the back to the apex of the filament is dorsifixed. The anther is pendulous when the locules are positioned away from the connective. *See also* Flower; Gynoecium; Stamen.

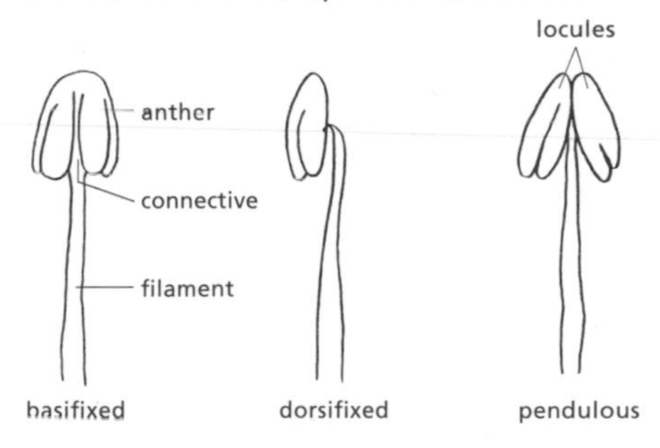

ANDROGYNOPHORE An axis or stalk above the point of perianth attachment, bearing both stamens and pistil.

ANDROGYNOUS Botanically, having both staminate and pistillate flowers in the same inflorescence.

ANDROMONOECIOUS Plants that have separate male and bisexual flowers on the same plant.

ANDROPHORE A stalk bearing the androecium.

ANEMOCHORE A propagule dispersed by wind. Characteristics of anemochory include minute plumose seeds, winged fruits (Samaras), and tumbleweeds. *See also* Autochore; Barochore; Dispersal; Hydrochore; Propagule; Samara; Zoochore.

ANEMOGRAPH An anemometer capable of recording wind speeds graphically (the anemogram).

ANEMOMETER An instrument designed to measure wind speeds.

ANEMOPHILOUS Wind-pollinated. *See also* Entomophilous.

ANEROID BAROMETER An instrument used to determine changes in atmospheric pressure on a flexible diaphragm on an evacuated chamber. Changes in pressure cause the diaphragm to move a needle, which is calibrated to a scale for weather forecasting. Aneroid means without fluid, thus an aneroid barometer is unlike a column of mercury, although the results should be the same. Aneroid barometers are commonly used as altimeters, calibrating the relationship between atmospheric pressure and altitude to provide a direct reading of elevational differences.

ANESTRUS The non-breeding period in animals. It is also spelled anoestrus.

ANEUPLOID A cell having a chromosome number that is not an exact multiple of the base haploid number (i.e., it is missing one or more entire chromosomes, or it has too many). It is a condition called aneuploidy. *See also* Euploid.

ANGIOSPERM Any member of the phylum Anthophyta, also termed in some classification schemes, the Angiospermophyta (the flowering plants), which includes grasses and trees. *See also* Anthophyta; Gymnosperm; Appendix 1: Classification of Organisms.

ANGLE COUNT METHOD *See* Point Sampling.

ANGLEDOZER A heavy steel blade mounted across the front of a crawler tractor. The blade can be raised and lowered, and each end can be advanced and retracted to place the blade at various angles, making it possible to push dirt to either side.

ANGLED STRIP IGNITION *See* Ignition Pattern.

ANGLE GAUGE A class of instrument used in point sampling; it includes the prism and the relascope. It is typically used to project a fixed (critical) angle horizontally from a point.

ANGLE OF REPOSE The maximum slope or angle at which a material, such as soil or loose rock, will remain stable without sliding or slumping. The illustration shows the angle of repose in degrees for different slope materials.

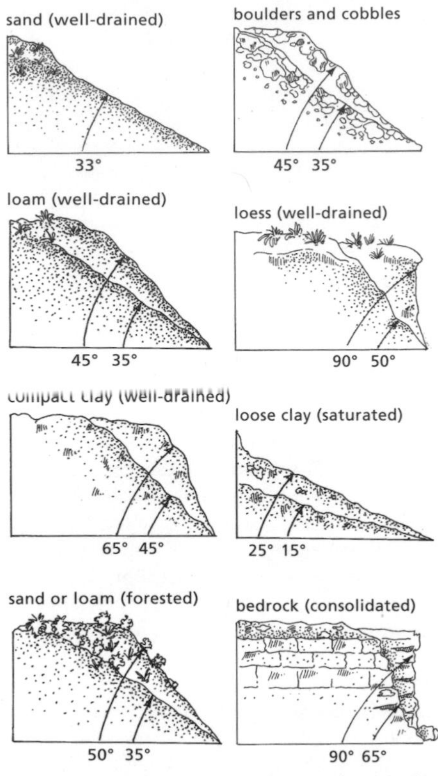

ANGULAR FRAGMENTS Broken rock with sharp edges.

ANIMAL DAMAGE Physical damage to vegetation (forest, tree, seed, saplings, and tree stems) by foraging, browsing, cutting, rubbing, or trampling by mammals and birds.

ANIMAL RIGHTS Refers to a value theory and commitment that extends basic human protection in law and practice to animals. The **Animal Rights Movement** goes beyond the humane treatment movement of earlier times. Animal rights advocates work for humane reforms, but they also advocate vegetarianism and in some cases veganism (eating no animal parts or products). Animal rights activists aim to end human exploitation and mistreatment of animals and see animals as having a certain level of sentience and with inherent rights that should be protected by laws.

ANIMAL UNIT The weight of one cow and calf (1,000 pounds or 455 kilograms). The measure (1 animal unit) is used to assess grazing pressure for different species (e.g., 1 AU = 7.7 white tailed deer or 5.8 mule deer). *See also* Animal Unit Month.

ANIMAL UNIT CONVERSION FACTOR A numerical figure that permits conversion from one category of animal to another (e.g., so many cows of a certain type are equivalent to so many ewes in terms of animal units). The factor supplies a reasonable comparison for the amount of forage required to sustain the animal, but offers no guidance as to the stocking suitable for various types of range.

ANIMAL UNIT MONTH The amount of forage that one animal unit (e.g., a cow with calf) would consume in one month. *See also* Animal Unit.

ANION A negatively charged ion. *See also* Cation.

ANNUAL An organism that completes its life cycle from birth or germination through to death within one year.

ANNUAL ALLOWABLE CUT (AAC) The volume of wood that can be harvested in one year from any area of forest under a sustained yield management regime. The choice of AAC is based on knowledge of the potential fertility of the growing site, the state and potential of the stands currently growing in the forest, and assumptions about how existing or anticipated future stands will continue to grow, the risks of loss, and constraints on operability.

The term allowable cut is generic and represents a class of models applied when substantial inventories of mature timber exist and the management focus is on harvest volumes rather than net revenues. The allowable cut model is predicated on a fixed land base, part of which is actively managed or 'regulated' and part of which contains standing, unmanaged, mature timber or 'old growth.' The primary objective of allowable cut models is to develop a fully regulated forest by maximizing annual harvests from the regulated lands and, converting the unmanaged old-growth forests (over a number of years known as the conversion period) into additional regulated lands by a process of harvesting and replanting. Two basic models apply: the even-aged regime and the uneven-aged regime.

In the even-aged model, the annual allowable volume is calculated as Y_i^1 for each year, and the conversion period T_c is derived by: (1) maximizing annual harvests on the area already under regulation (A_m) where the cumulative timberstand volume Q is normally characterized as a logistic function of time T; and (2) harvesting the area of old-growth forest (A_g) in equal annual segments throughout the period. Successful reforestation is assumed to occur after each area is harvested. Thus the allowable cut is calculated as:

Y_i^1 = max $A_m[Q(T)/T] + A_g[G/T_c]$ for each year$_i$ in the period T

where

Y_i = harvest volume in year$_i$

A_m = number of hectares in the initially regulated (managed) forest

A_g = number of initially unregulated or old-growth hectares

$Q(T)$ = cumulative biological growth per hectare in units of volume

G = stock of old-growth timber per hectare in units of volume

T = time in years of the production period, or rotation age

T_c = conversion period in years ($= T_c \geq T^*$)

T^* = optimal volume maximizing rotation age (culmination of mean annual increment).

The two main decision variables are the production period or rotation age for the regulated lands, and the length of the conversion period T_c for the unregulated lands. This equation is known as the Hanzlik formula and is sometimes simplified to:

$$\text{Annual cut} = \frac{Vm}{R} + I$$

where

Vm = volume of merchantable timber beyond rotation age

R = rotation adopted for future stands, in years

I = annual increment of wood volume.

Hanzlik's formula can be applied in two basic forms, termed *area control* and *volume control.* Area control focuses on the land from which the annual harvests originate. Volume control focuses on the annual harvest level regardless of the area of origin. Area control implies equal annual areas of harvest with variable annual harvest volumes, while volume control equates to uniform annual harvest volumes coming from varying areas of land.

Hanzlik's formula, originally intended for even-aged stands of Douglas-fir, can be adapted for uneven-aged and selectively managed forests. *See also* Allowable Cut Effect; Sustained Yield; Regulation.

ANNUAL CANKER *See* Canker.

ANNUAL RING A distinctive (not always by the naked eye) layer of wood (xylem tissue) formed once a year, starting at the beginning of the growing season and continuing through to the dormant period. The make up of an annual ring is highly variable between species and within any one tree, and depends on the climate and other growth-dependent factors. A count of the annual rings provides the age of the tree at the point of counting. An additional allowance must be made for the time taken to grow to the point of counting.

In periods of severe stress, the annual rings may be small or nonexistent, and may lead to false rings that are only partly complete around the circumference. Detection of false rings is only achieved with a complete cross-section of the stem. In many parts of the world, tree growth cannot be measured so easily, since rings of growth are not produced on a regular annual basis. For a few species, the number of branch whorls can be used as an approximate indication of age, bearing in mind that the branch whorl develops in the year after it is formed, and no whorls may be formed in the early stages. In the absence of annual rings or branch whorls, site history, or external characteristics such as shape or bark texture, may be a useful guide in determining age. *See also* Xylem.

ANNULAR Organs or parts in a circular arrangement, or in the form of a ring.

ANNULATA/ANNELIDA Ringed, or segmented, worms. This phylum contains over 8,800 species.

ANNULATED Having, or composed of, rings.

ANNULES The grooves around the body of a nematode.

ANNULUS It means, literally, a ring. **1** The ring of tissue left on the stalk of a mushroom when the partial veil breaks. *See also* Fungus (for illustration); Volva. **2** In certain plants, a fleshy ring or rim of the corolla. **3** A ring of specialized, thin- or thick-walled cells around the rim of the capsule in mosses, involved in dehiscence of the operculum. **4** A ring, sometimes just a group of specialized cells, on the sporangium of a fern.

ANOMALOUS Describes an object or process that deviates from the general rule; irregular or atypical.

ANOXIC Devoid of oxygen.

ANTAGONISM **1** A relationship between different organisms in which one partly or completely inhibits the growth of the other or kills it, often due to the effects of toxic chemicals (e.g., antibiotics) released into the substrate or to the creation of unfavourable living conditions, such as the depletion or exhaustion of food supplies. **2** The opposing action of two or more chemicals, or activities, such that the action of one is impaired by the other, or the total effect is less than that of one component acting separately. *See also* Synergism.

ANTEMARGINAL Within or not extending quite as far as the margin.

ANTENNA Plural antennae. A jointed appendage, usually found in pairs, on the head of many arthropods. The antennae are used for touching, swimming, and other sensory purposes. Butterflies have clublike antennae, while moths tend to have featherlike antennae. *See also* Butterfly (for illustration).

ANTERIOR **1** In plants, on the front side, furthest away from the axis, abaxial to the subtending bract. Also, the lower or furthest, as in the tip of an organ. **2** In animals, the forward part of the animal or toward the head. *See also* Posterior.

ANTHER The pollen-bearing portion of a stamen. *See also* Androecium or Flower (for illustrations).

ANTHERIDIUM The male organs in cryptogams, producing male gametes (sperms) and corresponding to the anther in flowering plants. In bryophytes, the antheridium is typically a globose or short cylindrical sac one cell layer thick.

ANTHESIS **1** The expansion, or the period of expansion or opening, of a flower, associated with the anthers and stigmas becoming functional, thus permitting fertilization to occur. **2** The process of a flower bud opening, thus the exposure of stamens and stigmas to pollinating agents.

ANTHOPHYTA In the plant kingdom, the phylum containing all flowering plants. The ovules of these plants are enclosed in a carpel and seeds are borne within fruit. It is the most successful group in the plant kingdom, with plants exhibiting very diverse vegetative forms, but always characterized by a flower and the process of pollination. The phylum is divided into two classes, the Magnoliopsida (also termed the Dicotyledonae), and the Liliopsida (also termed the Monocotyledonae). Details of the plant kingdom are given in Appendix 1: Classification of Organisms.

ANTHRACNOSE A plant disease characterized by necrosis around the leaf and shoot veins and the development of acervuli.

ANTHROPOCENTRIC An attitude that sees humanity at the centre of the universe (i.e., more important than any other biotic form). *See also* Anthropomorphism.

ANTHROPOGENIC MATERIALS Earth materials modified by human activities to the extent that their initial physical properties (e.g., structure, cohesion, consolidation) have been drastically altered. It includes spoil heaps and fill.

ANTHROPOGENIC SITE Sites modified by human activity, such as cultural sites, archaeological sites, historic sites.

ANTHROPOLOGY The scientific study of the origin and of the physical, social, and cultural development and behaviour of human beings.

ANTHROPOMORPHISM Refers to the attribution of human characteristics to nonhuman entities or beings. Anthropomorphism need not be based on the bias of anthropocentrism. *See also* Anthropocentric.

ANTIBIOSIS *See* Allelopathy.

ANTIBIOTIC A chemical produced synthetically or by a microorganism that is able to inhibit the growth of or kill another microorganism.

ANTICAL The upper surface or margin of a liverwort leaf.

ANTICLINE An upward fold in sedimentary strata, resembling an arch. *See also* Fold (for illustration); Monocline; Syncline.

ANTIDESICCANT A chemical compound applied to the foliage of plants to greatly reduce water losses due to transpiration. It is typically used during transplanting as a means of reducing transplant shock and subsequent stress.

ANTRORSE Directed upward or forward. *See also* Extrose; Introse; Retrorse.

ANVIL The fixed steel blocks that provide support and resistance for the cutting blade of a single-action tree shear. The hydraulically operated cutting blade slices through the tree toward the anvil. Also termed a bed plate. The same principle applies in the design of pruning shears or secateurs, where the blade moves toward the anvil. *See also* Bed Plate.

APETALOUS Without petals.

APEX Plural apices. The tip, or end furthest from the base or point of attachment; the distal end. *See also* Leaf Shape (for illustration).

APHID A small, pear-shaped, soft-bodied insect in the order Homoptera, usually Aphididae, Eriosomatidae, or Adelgidae (Chermidae). Some aphid forms have delicate, transparent wings. Aphids infest the tender growing portions of plants, sucking their juices and, in some cases, inducing galls and other forms of leaf deformity. They excrete the processed sap as honeydew, which frequently attracts ants.

APHOTOSYNTHETIC SURFACE The surface meristematic tissues of stems, branches, and roots that lack chloroplasts and are not capable of photosynthesis. These areas of tissue development depend upon there being an excess of carbohydrate left over after the plant's respiration needs are met. *See also* Photosynthetic Surface.

APHYLLOUS Without leaves. *See also* Gamophyllous.

APICAL Occurring at the apex.

APICAL CONTROL/APICAL DOMINANCE The manner in which tree forms develop is determined by the way in which the active meristematic tissue develops at different points in the tree crown within any one growing season. Trees that have the lateral growth of branches inhibited by the terminal bud (within any one growing season or flush) are said to have strong apical dominance. Weak apical dominance occurs when lateral shoots do develop in the current growing season or flush.

Apical control refers to the relationship between the central leader and lateral branches of the crown. It operates throughout the lifespan of the tree. Trees with strong apical control have leaders that outgrow all the lateral buds. The resulting tree form is said to be **excurrent**. Where apical control is weak, the central leader cannot maintain its superior position. It may abort or be outgrown by an adjacent lateral shoot, which may itself then be outgrown in later years. Over time, no one single shoot maintains a superior or controlling position and a **decurrent** (sometimes termed deliquescent) form results.

There is no direct relationship between apical dominance and apical control. Trees with strong apical control may have either weak or strong apical dominance. Trees with weak apical control generally have strong apical dominance. Trees with both weak apical dominance and weak apical control are shrubs.

Typically, strong apical dominance of current growth creates weak apical control of the subsequent growth, and vice versa, although many plants may initially exhibit an excurrent growth pattern initially but change to a decurrent pattern in later life. Species like oak, elm, and maple have strong apical dominance when the shoots are first developing. In subsequent years, lateral shoots release and may outgrow the original terminal shoot, thus yielding the classic rounded forms of these species. At that point, the species would exhibit weak apical control. In other species, such as sweetgum, tulip poplar, cedars, and cypresses (random branching conifers), weak apical dominance but strong apical control is typical, leading to the typical conical form. The conifers such as fir, pine, and spruce (whorl-branching conifers) have both strong apical dominance and strong apical control, leading to an excurrent form.

Plant vigour directly influences apical dominance and control, which is why there may be large morphological differences within the same species. For example, within a species, vigorous shoots usually have less apical dominance than weaker, less vigorous shoots. The lateral buds associated with vigorous shoots may therefore be released from apical dominance sooner, leading to a more excurrent habit. By contrast, plants developing under stress tend to exhibit stronger apical dominance, a loss of apical control, and the formation of rounder plant form. *See also* Plant Form.

APICAL MERISTEM In plants, the region of primary tissue initiation. A group of meristematic cells at the tip of a shoot or root that, by division, produce the cells that initiate the primary tissues of root or shoot; may be vegetative or reproductive, initiating vegetative or reproductive tissues and organs. Strictly speaking, roots do not have an apical meristem, because the root cap is at the apex, so the meristem is subterminal. *See also* Intercalary Meristem; Meristematic Tissue; Root (for illustration).

APICULAR Possessing an apicule.

APICULATE Describes an organ terminated by an abrupt, short, flexible point, the apiculus. In spores, a short projection at one end.

APICULE A short, sharp, flexible point. It is also called an apiculus.

APOCARPOUS Having separate carpels, not united. It commonly describes the gynoecium of separate simple pistils. *See also* Syncarpous.

APOMICTIC Reproduced or reproducing asexually, often through viable seeds but without fertilization.

APOMIXIS Reproduction, of many types, in which a nonsexual process has replaced the sexual process and no fusion of male and female gametes is involved. In many plants, seeds regularly develop from unfertilized egg cells or from specialized generative tissue other than egg cells. The resultant plants, termed apomicts, are genetically identical with the mother plant. *See also* Amphimixis; Automixis; Parthenogenesis.

APOPHYSIS The exposed portion of the cone scale of a conifer.

APOSEPALOUS Having the sepals free and distinct from one another, the calyx being composed of separate elements. It is also termed polysepalous. *See also* Gamosepalous.

A POSTERIORI A conclusion derived solely from the observed facts. *See also A Priori.*

APOTHECIUM Plural apothecia. The fruiting body of certain Ascomycotina, which are commonly called Discomycetes or cup fungi, in which the fertile layer of asci is exposed by a wide opening. Apothecia vary from linear and embedded in the substrate to sessile or stalked structures that may be shaped like a cup, saucer, or wine glass. They vary in size from nearly microscopic to several centimetres in diameter and height. *See also* Perithecium.

APPLANATE Having a flattened shape.

APPRAISAL **1** In economics, the economic appraisal of the monetary value of a resource in its raw or manufactured form. **2** A valuation or estimate of quality.

APPRAISED PRICE The price of a particular timber sale based on an estimate of the timber's actual market value. The minimum acceptable price on a sale.

APPRESSED **1** A plant part (indumentum, leaves, etc.) that lies flat and is pressed close to the surface (e.g., against the bark of a tree), or flattened up against but not attached to another (usually larger) plant part (e.g., a bud next to a stem). It is sometimes called adpressed.

APPRESSORIUM Occurring in fungi and some parasitic seeds, the appressorium is a swollen or flattened portion of a germ tube (in fungi) or radicle (in seeds). It provides a point of attachment to the host, from which the parasite will often penetrate the host.

APPROPRIATE TECHNOLOGY Technology designed and used as if humans and nature matter. It is technology that is based on ecocentric values, is of low impact, thermodynamically sound, ecologically balanced, locally controlled, knowledge-rich, and labour-intensive, in contrast to the megatechnology systems currently in use in the dominant culture. Originating in the third world, the concept was defined and popularized by E.G. Schumacher in his 'small is beautiful' approach to technology.

A PRIORI A conclusion derived before the facts have been observed. *See also A Posteriori.*

APRON A protective structure placed below a stream bed to prevent erosion around the foundations of bridge abutments, retaining walls, or dam walls.

AQUATIC Of or concerning water. An organism whose primary habitat for growth, reproduction, and survival is on, in, or partially submerged in water. *See also* Terrestrial.

AQUATIC SYSTEM Any body of water, such as a stream, lake, or estuary, and all organisms and nonliving components within it, functioning as a natural system.

AQUICLUDE An impermeable bed or stratum of material hindering or preventing the movement of groundwater.

AQUIFER A stratum of gravel, sand, or porous, fractured, or cavernous and vesicular rock capable of holding and/or conducting water. When fully charged, an aquifer is saturated with water.

ARBITRATION In conflict resolution, arbitration is an adjudicary process with an arbitrator (or, in some cases, panel of arbitrators) acting in the capacity of a judge. Disputing interests present their arguments and evidence and the arbitrator rules, making a decision on behalf of the parties. The parties will be bound by legislative mandate or contractual agreement to accept and adopt the decision of the arbitrator. Bases for appeal to administrative or judicial bodies are very limited.

Reference is sometimes made to nonbinding or advisory arbitration where the parties are not bound to accept and implement the decision of the arbitrator. This approach to resolving a conflict is more accurately referred to as fact-finding.

Rights and interest arbitration are different; in the former the arbitrator is making a decision within the context of a contract, treaty, or other formally binding agreement between the parties. In the latter, the arbitrator is establishing an agreement or contract between the parties based on equity, other comparative relationships, or such other bases as may be deemed appropriate; for example, where the arbitrator is called upon to establish wage and benefits for employees.

ARBOREAL An adjective describing the habitat defined by species living in the canopies of trees.

ARBORESCENT Having a treelike growth habit.

ARBORICIDE A herbicide used to kill or inhibit

the growth of unwanted trees or, in some cases, a pesticide used to kill the bark beetles known to be under the bark of a trap tree. The herbicide is inclusive and covers all phytocides (plant killers), including arboricides and silvicides. *See also* Trap Tree.

ARBORICULTURE The science and art of growing, tending, and managing trees and shrubs as individuals or in groups, typically for their value as ornaments and aesthetics, their ability to provide visual and noise screening, and climatic moderation, typically in an urban setting. Practitioners are termed arborists.

ARBUSCULE Refers to vesicular-arbuscular mycorrhizae; a much-branched, microscopic haustorial structure of the fungal symbiont that forms within living cortical cells of the root. The interface of the arbuscule with the plant protoplast is a site of exchange of nutrients and growth-regulating chemicals. *See also* Haustorium; Mycorrhizae.

ARCH A supporting device towed behind or mounted on a skidding vehicle. It used to lift one end of a log or logs clear of the ground, and thus reduce the sliding resistance and/or transfer the weight of the load to the skidding vehicle.

ARCHAEOLOGICAL SITE A geographic locale that contains the material evidence and/or remains of human activity.

ARCHEGONIUM In higher cryptogams and gymnosperms, the usually flask-shaped female organ producing the female gamete (egg).

ARCHING Skidding logs or trees using a mounted or trailing arch.

ARCUATE Curved or bowed downwards.

AREA GRID IGNITION *See* Ignition Pattern.

AREA IGNITION *See* Ignition Pattern.

AREA OF CRITICAL ENVIRONMENTAL CONCERN Refers to the US Bureau of Land Management designation of lands where special management attention is needed to protect and prevent irreparable damage to important historic, cultural, or scenic values, fish, and wildlife resources or other natural systems or processes, or to protect life and provide safety from natural hazards. *See also* Environmentally Sensitive Area (ESA).

AREA OF INFLUENCE A delineated area surrounding a base that can be reached first by the ground or air attack units assigned to the base. It is synonymous with influence area or zone of influence.

AREA REGULATION *See* Annual Allowable Cut.

AREA-SENSITIVE SPECIES Any species that responds negatively to shrinkage in the size of its habitat patches.

AREA-SPECIES CURVE *See* Species-Area Curve.

ARENACEOUS **1** In pedology, a soil containing an abundance of sand. **2** Geologically, a clastic sedimentary rock with particle sizes ranging from 0.5 to 2.0 millimetres (e.g., sandstone). *See also* Argillaceous.

AREOLATE Describes a surface that is broken up into small, angular, and irregular patches (areoles), typically with a tile-like appearance.

AREOLE **1** A small area, especially the open space between anastomosing veins. **2** A spine-bearing sunken or raised spot on the stem of cacti. **3** Occurring in an island formed by cracks in the surrounding surface.

ARÊTE A narrow, jagged, mountain crest, often above the snowline, sculptured by alpine glaciers and formed by backward erosion of adjoining cirque walls.

ARGILLACEOUS Rocks or sediments containing more than 50 per cent of clay and silt-sized particles. *See also* Arenaceous.

ARIL A fleshy outgrowth surrounding the seed; commonly brightly coloured. For example, the American bittersweet (*Celastrus scandens*) produces bright orange-red fruit in a terminal cluster that opens to expose a red aril when ripe.

ARISTATE **1** Having a stiff, bristlelike awn or seta. *See also* Leaf Shape (for illustration). **2** Tapered to a narrow, very elongated apex.

ARMATURE Botanically, any covering or occurrence of spines, barbs, hooks, or prickles on any part of a plant.

ARMED **1** A term used in airtanker parlance to indicate that the dropping mechanism is set to allow a programmed release of part or all of the load of fire retardant. **2** Plants bearing thorns, spines, or prickles.

ARRIS The sharp edge formed by the junction of two planar surfaces, such as timber, bricks, crystals.

ARRIS KNOT A knot that is exposed on two adjacent surfaces. *See also* Knot.

ARROYO A flat-bottomed, steep-walled channel that has been cut into sedimentary deposits by a small watercourse, often ephemeral. It is typical of arid regions.

ARSON FIRE *See* Fire Cause Class (incendiary).

ARTHROPODS The animal phylum Arthropoda, which encompasses crustaceans, spiders, mites, centipedes, insects, and related life-forms having articulated bodies and limbs. The largest phylum in the animal kingdom, containing more than three times the number of all the other phyla combined. The role of arthropods in forest management is often poorly understood, but is seen to be of increasing importance, especially within soils.

ARTHROSPORE In fungi, a spore created by the division of a hypha into separate cells.

ARTICULATED **1** Having obvious joints, nodes, or segments, or locations where separation may naturally occur. **2** Describes a vehicle that is hinged at the centre to facilitate turning (e.g., a skidder).

ARTIFACT An object or product of cultural significance that has been modified by human activity or use and differs from a similar object produced without human input. Typically considered to be portable items, they could also be boulders or rock faces. The bones of animals eaten or otherwise used by people are sometimes called ecofacts.

ARTIFICIAL INTELLIGENCE In computer science, the use of computers and design of programs in such a way that they perform operations analogous to the human abilities of learning and decisionmaking (e.g., artificial intelligence is used in the development of expert systems).

ARTIFICIAL REGENERATION The creation of a new stand by direct seeding or by planting seedlings or cuttings. *See also* Natural Regeneration.

ARTIFICIAL SELECTION *See* Selection.

ARUNDINACEOUS Reedlike, or resembling a cane.

ASCENDING **1** Rising upwards through a medium such as air or water. **2** A shape or form that rises or curves upwards somewhat obliquely or indirectly from a horizontal or oblique position.

ASCENDING TYPOLOGY A study that starts by examining attributes of an individual and aggregates upwards to yield broader categories.

ASCOCARP A sexual or perfect fruiting body of the Ascomycete that produces its spores within an ascus.

ASCOMYCETE Any organism belonging to the Ascomycota phylum of fungi (sac fungi), characterized by the production of usually eight sexual spores contained in a saclike structure called an ascus. It includes leaf-infecting and canker-producing fungi, many of which are destructive to trees, as well as cellulose-decomposing fungi, mycorrhizal fungi, and economically important fungi such as yeasts, morels, truffles, and the fungi used in genetic research.

ASCOSPORES A spore produced in an ascus.

ASCOSTROMA Plural ascostromata. In the Ascomycotina, a mass of hyphae within or on which asci form. They are often microscopic, dark in colour, and partially to wholly embedded in dead plant tissue.

ASCUS Plural asci. A membranous sac containing eight, or another multiple of four, sexually formed Ascopores of an Ascomycete fungus. A fungus having asci is said to be ascigerous.

ASEXUAL REPRODUCTION Reproduction without fertilization, no union of gametes occurs, and no exchange of genetic material takes place.

ASEXUAL STAGE or SPORE Either a vegetative stage or a reproductive stage in the life cycle of a fungus in which nuclear fusion is absent and in which reproductive spores are produced by mitosis or simple nuclear division. It is synonymous with imperfect stage. *See also* Sexual Stage.

ASH **1** Fine pyroclastic material, smaller than four millimetres in diameter, emanating from volcanoes. **2** The remnant traces of materials consumed by fire.

ASPECT **1** The compass direction of a slope or surface relative to the sun (e.g., a slope on the south side of a hill has a southerly aspect). **2** The seasonal appearance of vegetation. **3** Loosely synonymous with feature, or factor, as in a problem having many complex aspects to consider.

ASSEMBLAGE A collection of organisms whose patterns of organization, with respect to competition, predation, mutualism, etc., are unknown. *See also* Community.

ASSETS The goods, resources, and services that have monetary value and are attached to a company or organization. They may be **fixed assets,** such as buildings, machinery, and other equipment; **liquid assets,** such as cash in the bank; **intangible assets,** such as a company's good reputation; and **current assets,** such as unsold goods in stock, cash, and unpaid invoices.

ASSIMILATION **1** The process by which plants or animals use metabolic processes to transform nutrient substances into tissue for growth or reproduction. **2** The flow of energy between trophic levels.

ASSOCIATED SPECIES A species found to be numerically more abundant in a particular forest successional stage or type compared to other areas.

ASSOCIATION A group of species living in the same place at the same time.

ASSOCIATION ANALYSIS A monothetic, divisive statistical technique that classifies sites based on species associations. Species associations are determined by computing a chi square value for all possible 2 × 2 tables based on presence/absence data for each species. The species with the highest sum of significant chi squares is considered to be the divisor species. The collection of heterogeneous stands is then statistically divided into two based on the presence or absence of the divisor species. A new set of chi squares is constructed for the two new groups and if neither has significant associations, then each group is considered to be homogeneous. If significant species associations remain, then the process is repeated until homogeneity is achieved in all groups. The final result is that each formed group has greater homogeneity within, rather than between, the groups. *See also* Classification.

ASSORTATIVE MATING The selection of mates based on one or more traits. This is positive when individuals with the same form of a trait mate more frequently than would be expected by chance, but is negative when they mate less frequently.

ASSUMPTION **1** Something taken for granted and accepted as a truth. **2** A judgmental decision made by a planner or decisionmaker that supplies missing values, relationships, or societal preferences for some informational component necessary for making a decision. The true nature of such missing information is either unknown or cannot be readily ascertained within the time and/or budgetary constraints affecting the need to make a decision.

ASSURGENT Ascending, rising.

ASTRINGENT A fruit, juice, or other substance that when tasted has a sharp taste, causing the mouth to 'pucker.' It is sometimes used as a crude qualitative indicator in plant identification.

ASYMMETRICAL Off-centre, eccentric, not symmetrical. For example, an asymmetrical flower has some parts different in form, size, or degree of connation from others of the same whorl, such that it is not possible to divide the flower into two equal halves.

ATAVISTIC Reverting to a form characteristic of remote ancestors.

ATLAS In conservation biology, the results of a comprehensive survey of a large geographical area designed to map the occurrence and, possibly, relative abundance of species in subunits of the larger area. An atlas is typically based on a grid of fixed intervals of distance or degrees of latitude and longitude. For birds and animals, the survey may be restricted to a particular season of the year, usually the breeding season.

ATMOSPHERE **1** The gaseous medium surrounding Earth. The main components of Earth's atmosphere are nitrogen (79 per cent), oxygen (20 per cent), carbon dioxide (0.3 to 0.5 per cent and increasing), and other minor components (0.5 per cent). **2** A mental, moral, or emotional condition surrounding one or more beings.

ATMOSPHERIC PRESSURE The gravitational force exerted by the weight of a column of air extending from the point of concern to the outer limits of the atmosphere. The recommended SI unit is the kilopascal (kPa), although millibar (mb) has been the most common unit of measurement. It is synonymous with barometric pressure. *See also* Bar; Pressure Altitude.

ATMOSPHERIC STABILITY A meteorological term describing the degree to which the atmosphere resists turbulence and vertical (upward) motion. With reference to fire management activities, the atmosphere is usually described as neutral, stable, or unstable with respect to the Dry Adiabatic Lapse Rate (DALR). **Neutral atmosphere** means the temperature decrease with altitude is equal to the DALR (i.e., the atmosphere neither hinders nor aids large-scale vertical motion). **Stable atmosphere** means the temperature decrease with altitude is less than the DALR (i.e., the atmosphere tends to suppress large-scale vertical motion). **Unstable atmosphere** means the temperature decrease with altitude is greater than the DALR (i.e., the atmosphere tends to support large-scale vertical motion).

AT-RISK FISH STOCKS Fish stocks that have been identified by professional societies, fish management agencies, and in the scientific literature as being in need of special management consideration because of low or declining populations.

ATROPHIC An organ of abnormally small size due to pathological reduction in growth (underdevelopment) of its tissues.

ATTACK INTENSITY RATINGS The qualitative evaluation of a pest attack into degrees of severity: heavy, moderate, or light. The degree to which a stand is infested with or damaged by a pest. It is used as a preliminary assessment tool in sketching the extent and severity of pests.

ATTACK LINE A line of hose, preconnected to the pump of a fire apparatus and ready for immediate use in attacking a fire.

ATTACK TIME The elapsed time from the end of report time to the first organized attack, including getaway time and travel time. It is also termed response time. *See also* Speed of Attack.

ATTACK UNIT A single vehicle or aircraft and its associated personnel and material provided for the purpose of responding to and abating a fire or other emergency. It is synonymous with crew.

ATTACK UNIT RESPONSE The response of one attack unit to a fire or other emergency, without regard for the number of return trips to that same fire or emergency.

ATTENUATE A form or shape having a long tapering point, often set off rather abruptly from the main body (e.g., a leaf blade). *See also* Leaf Shape (for illustration).

ATTITUDE **1** The angular orientation of a camera, or of the photograph taken with that camera, with respect to some external reference system. **2** A learned predisposition manifesting itself in a general state of readiness either to evaluate or to react toward an object or class of objects in either a favourable or unfavourable manner in a more or less consistent and characteristic way. Attitudes are relatively stable and have three components: (1) a cognitive or belief component; (2) an affective or feeling component; and (3) a conative or action-disposition component. Behaviour may be a function of attitude, but attitude is not a reliable predictor of behaviour; that is, changes in attitude do not always reflect changes in behaviour. *See also* Belief; Opinion.

ATTRACTANT A substance or odour that affects behaviour by attracting an insect or other animal to a particular area. They are used in population surveys or control. *See also* Primary Attraction; Secondary Attraction.

ATTRIBUTE **1** A characteristic required for describing or specifying some entity (e.g., forest cover type, preferred habitat, or ecosystem function) relative to the requirements of any one organism. **2** A readily definable and inherent characteristic of a plant, animal, habitat, or abiotic feature.

ATTRIBUTE DATA Non-graphic information associated with a point, line, or area element (e.g., descriptive names, colours).

ATTRIBUTE FILE Computer file containing attribute data.

AURICLE An ear-shaped projection or appendage, such as are found at the base of some leaves or petals. *See also* Grass (for illustration).

AURICULATE Having two projecting auricles. *See also* Leaf Shape (for illustration).

AUSTRAL A derivation from the latin word meaning 'south' or 'of the south.' *See also* Boreal.

AUTECOLOGY The study of relationships of individual organisms or species to environmental conditions. *See also* Synecology.

AUTOALLELOPATH Some plant species produce chemical compounds that inhibit their own growth. This activity is thought to be a behavioural adaptation. For example, clonal populations of *Helianthus* become doughnut-shaped because the central part of the clone is inhibited by a chemical compound produced by the decomposing plant. *See also* Allelopathy.

AUTOCHORE A propagule that is self-dispersing. Autochory is characterized by explosive dispersal mechanisms found in plants such as *Impatiens* spp. and by the stoloniferous habits of plants such as the Walking Fern (*Camptosorus rhizophyllus*). It is also termed ballochory. *See also* Anemochore.

AUTOCHTHONOUS **1** A substance originating at its location in the landscape (e.g., rocks, plants). **2** In freshwater biology, the primary biological production within streams (algae production), utilizing chemicals, nutrients, and sunlight, and a very important source of food for the benthic invertebrates. **3** In conservation biology, a species or other taxon of regional origin. *See also* Allochthonous; Benthic Invertebrates.

AUTOECIOUS Describes a parasite, particularly a rust fungus, that completes its life cycle on one host. It is the opposite of heteroecious. *See also* Dioecious; Heteroecious; Monoecious.

AUTOGAMY Self-fertilization; pollination within one bisexual flower. The term includes geitonogamy and xenogamy. *See also* Allogamy.

AUTOGENIC The species changes within an ecosystem that result from internal influences created by the interactions of plants and animals. *See also* Allogenic.

AUTOICOUS In mosses, a plant bearing both archegonia and antheridia, but in separate sheaths of leaves. *See also* Dioicous.

AUTOLYSIS Literally, self-dissolving. A process whereby plants or animals use their own enzymes to break down dead tissues within themselves.

AUTOMATED MAPPING Mapping operations carried out under machine control. It is often generalized to include computer-assisted mapping where there may still be considerable human intervention.

AUTOMATIC DIRECTION FINDER (ADF) An aircraft radio navigational receiver operating in the low-frequency bands.

AUTOMATIC LIGHTNING DETECTION SYSTEM (ALDS) *See* Lightning Locator System.

AUTOMIXIS Self-fertilization. *See also* Apomixis.

AUTOROTATION A helicopter flight condition in which the lifting rotor is driven entirely by the action of air when the helicopter is in motion. A means of controlling the rate of descent and flight path of a helicopter that no longer has its engine running.

AUTOSOME A chromosome that has no influence over determining the sex of an organism. It is sometimes called somatic chromosome.

AUTOTROPHIC Any organism that can produce its own organic material from inorganic chemicals and an external source of energy (e.g., plants and specialized bacteria). Autotrophs are producers of matter. *See also* Carnivores; Frugivores; Herbivores; Heterotrophic; Omnivores; Trophic Level.

AUXIN A group of plant hormones related to indoleacetic acid that promote or regulate growth and development. Natural auxins occur in young, actively growing leaves and shoots, where their effects include cell elongation and initiation of root formation. The synthetic auxins 2,4-D and 2,4,5-T were once widely used as herbicides, but concerns about their persistence and fate in the environment have now led to the development of other, less controversial herbicides.

AVAILABLE FOREST LAND In the United States, that portion of the forested land base for which timber production is planned and included within the area contributing to the allowable sale quantity. This includes both lands allocated primarily to timber production and lands on which timber production is a secondary objective.

AVAILABLE FUEL That portion of the total fuel that would actually be consumed under specified burning conditions. Unless otherwise stated, this term is assumed to be just the fuel consumed in the fire front and is used in this context in the models incorporated in the US National Fire Danger Rating System. Although generally ignored, the fuel consumed behind the fire front by intermittent flaming and glowing combustion is also a part of the available fuel and can in some instances comprise a significant portion of the total.

AVAILABLE FUEL ENERGY The amount of heat released per unit area when the available fuel burns. *See also* Energy Release Component.

AVAILABLE WATER *See* Soil Water.

AVALANCHE A large mass of snow and/or ice, sometimes accompanied by rocks and vegetative debris, moving rapidly down a slope.

AVALANCHE CHUTE The track or path formed by an avalanche. *See also* Avalanche Track.

AVALANCHE CONES Cones of debris deposited by snow avalanches; similar to talus cones but with concave longitudinal profiles and gentler slopes.

AVALANCHE TRACK The central channel-like corridor along which an avalanche has moved. It may take the form of an open path in a forest, with bent and broken trees, or an eroded surface marked by pits, scratches, and grooves.

AVERAGE RARITY A diverse plant or animal community in which many species are present, all of which are relatively rare.

AVERAGE RELATIVE HUMIDITY In the US National Fire Danger Rating System, the arithmetic average of the maximum and minimum relative humidities measured at a fire danger station from one base observation time to the next.

AVERAGE TEMPERATURE In the US National Fire Danger Rating System, the arithmetic average of the maximum and minimum dry-bulb temperatures measured at a fire danger station from one base observation time to the next.

AVERAGE WORST DAY In the United States, the average fire danger of the highest 15 per cent of the days occurring in the average worst year.

AVERAGE WORST YEAR In the United States, the third worst fire season in the last ten, as determined by the sum of daily danger or burning indices during the regularly financed fire season. The same number of days are used each year to determine these totals.

AVERAGE YARDING DISTANCE The total yarding distance for all turns divided by the total number of turns for a particular setting.

AVIAN Of or like birds, which are members of the class Aves.

AVICHORE A form of zoochory in which a propagule is dispersed by birds. *See also* Zoochore.

AVIRULENT Not virulent. *See also* Virulent.

AVOIDABLE Typically describes an adverse effect that with better planning or more careful implementation and/or supervision of planned activities might not have occurred or could have been minimized. Many adverse effects are known before they arise, but occur due to inadequate planning, lack of supervision, inadequate education or understanding at the field operator level, or a lack of committed funds to undertake better work. *See also* Unavoidable.

AWL-SHAPED A shape that tapers from the base to a slender, stiff point. *See also* Subulate.

AWN A long, stout, bristlelike appendage. Awns are used to assist the dispersion of plant propagules by sticking them to more mobile species such as birds or animals (i.e., burrs and certain types of grass). *See also* Grass (for illustration).

AXENIC The culture of a single species in the absence of any others (i.e., a pure culture).

AXES **1** The base lines of a standard plot, being the *x* axis and the *y* axis; the plural of axis. *See also* Abscissa; Ordinate. **2** The term used to describe the shape of sedimentary particles. Length is the *a* axis, width is the *b* axis, and depth is the *c* axis.

AXIL The angle or cavity formed at the upper side of the junction of a petiole or stem with its parent stem.

AXILLARY Located or produced in the axil. *See also* Leaf Shape (for illustration)

AXIOMS OF COMMUNITY Those principles without which community cannot thrive. A community in human terms is a moral order and tradition usually bound together by shared spiritual considerations. The four axioms of community are shared values, shared place, shared respect, shared aid.

AXIS The main or central line of development in an organism, from which lateral organs or other parts arise.

AZIMUTH **1** In photogrammetry, the azimuth of the principal plane is the clockwise angle from north (or south) to the principal plane of a tilted photograph. **2** Generally, the horizontal angle, or bearing of a point measured clockwise from true (astronomic) north.

AZIMUTH CIRCLE A circle graduated in 360 degrees in a clockwise direction, with the zero point indicating true north.

AZONAL SOIL A soil profile lacking distinct horizons or other characteristics, due to its immaturity, conditions of relief, or parent soil material that prevent full genesis.

AZYGOSPORE A parthenogenetic zygospore formed by some vesicular-arbuscular mycorrhizal fungi in the family Endogonaceae.

B

BACCATE Berrylike, pulpy, or fleshy in texture.

BACK-BLADING In road construction, backblading involves dropping the blade of a bulldozer onto the rough surface and driving backwards to smooth out the surface.

BACKCOUNTRY **1** An imprecise term typically applied to all those portions of wildlands in which there are usually no permanent, improved, or maintained access roads, or operational facilities such as lumber mills, ski resorts, or settlements with permanent residents. Deteriorating, unused, and unoccupied structures may be present. Those roads that are present typically require four-wheel-drive vehicles and are usually dead-end, rather than continuing through to the other side. Camping and other facilities are generally primitive. Backcountry management objectives typically emphasize off-road, self-propelled recreational activities such as hiking, trail-bike riding, hunting, or fishing. The term is generic and very subjective and has a wide range of legislative objectives around the world.

BACK-COUNTRY BYWAY In the United States, a road segment designated as part of the National Scenic Byway System.

BACKCROSS In genetics, a cross between a hybrid and one of its parents, or to an individual of the same strain as one of the parents. The product of such a cross is also termed a backcross.

BACKCUT The final cut in felling a tree. It is made on the opposite side of the direction of fall.

BACKFIRING A form of indirect attack used in prescribed burning or wildfire control. An extensive fire is set along the inner edge of a control line or natural barrier, usually some distance from the main fire area. The backfire takes advantage of indrafts to consume fuels in the path of the fire, and thereby halt or retard the progress of the fire front by cutting off its fuel supply. *See also* Flank Fire; Ignition Patterns (head fire).

BACKGROUND The distant part of a scene, or landscape, usually as far into the distance as the eye can see and still detect the presence of objects, that imparts harmony and/or contrast

to the view. *See also* Foreground; Middleground.
BACKGROUND LEVEL The ever-present environmental conditions or effects above which a phenomenon must manifest itself in order to be detected. The background level may serve as a baseline against which changes can be judged.
BACK GUY The line behind the spar tree, opposite the main line or skyline, which takes most of the pull when logs are being yarded.
BACKING FIRE A fire spreading or ignited to spread, into (against) the wind or downslope. A fire spreading on level ground in the absence of wind is a backing fire. It is also termed a backburn. *See also* Flank Fire; Heading Fire.
BACKING WIND A wind that changes direction in a counter-clockwise motion.
BACK LINE A boundary line marked by paint or ribbon indicating the limit of the cutting area.
BACKLOG In the administrative sense, work in need of completion, such as forest lands that need restocking to an acceptable standard, or habitats in need of assessing and classifying.
BACKPACK PUMP A portable sprayer equipped with a hand-pump that is fed from a container of liquid fitted with shoulder straps. *See also* Bladder Bag.
BACKSLOPE The geomorphic component that forms the steepest inclined surface and principal element of many hill slopes (e.g., valley sides, ridge sides). In profile, backslopes are typically steep, linear, and may or may not include cliff segments, which are called gravity slopes or free faces. The term mid-slope may be used to designate an element without a cliff. In terms of gradational processes, backslopes are erosional forms produced mainly by mass wasting and running water. The term may sometimes be used as a synonym for dipslope when describing homoclinal ridges. *See also* Hillslope (for illustration).
BACKSWAMP An extensive, marshy, depressed area of floodplains between the natural levee borders of channel belts and valley sides or terraces.
BACTERIUM Plural bacteria. A unicellular microorganism lacking chlorophyll and a true nucleus and multiplying by simple fission.
BADLAND Land that is barren, rough, and usually strongly dissected by erosional gullies. It is typical of semi-arid regions where streams have become entrenched in the softer substrate materials. Land unsuited to grazing or cultivation.
BAFFLE A partitioned wall placed in vehicular or aircraft water tanks to reduce shifting of the water load when starting, stopping, or turning.
BAG LIMIT The number of animals or fish that are allocated for legal harvest by an individual within a specified time period (day, month, year).
BAILEY BRIDGE A prefabricated type of bridge used since the early 1940s. It is constructed from simple components and is a very versatile structure that can be launched from one side of the area to be crossed. Often used as a temporary crossing.
BAITING The use of food, water, semiochemicals, or other attractants to lure animals into a particular area for purposes such as monitoring their distribution or numbers, harvesting them, controlling their movements, or reducing their numbers. *See also* Semiochemicals.
BAJADA A broadly, gently inclined, piedmont slope formed by lateral coalescence of a series of alluvial fans, and having a broadly undulating transverse profile (parallel to the mountain front) resulting from the convexities of component fans. The term is generally restricted to constructional slopes of intermontane basins in the southwestern United States.
BALANCED FOREST USE Within the context of ecologically responsible forest use, a policy of ensuring that all forest users (human and nonhuman) have fair, legally protected land bases that are well distributed throughout the forest, of sufficient size to meet their needs, and permit them to carry out their functions within the ecosystem. *See also* Ecologically Responsible Forest Use.
BALANCED OBJECTIVISM An idealistic point of view that advocates that resource use decisions should be reached in a completely objective manner, not disproportionately influenced by any special interest group pressure tactics, nor special consideration given for any particular segment of society (whether privileged or disadvantaged), nor any of the other planning value determinants (e.g., biophysical, social, economic).

Critics argue that balanced objectivism is conceptually unrealistic because it ignores the political reality of pressure groups, fails to recognize that issues (i.e., value conflicts between resource use advocates) are typically the impetus for any planning effort, and that most value system clashes cannot be satisfactorily resolved by rational arguments. *See also* Alternative Dispute Resolution; Subjective.
BALANOID Having a shape resembling an

acorn. *See also* Fruit (for illustration).

BALLENA A landform comprising distinctively round-topped ridgeline remnants of fan alluvium. The ridge's broadly rounded shoulders meet from either side to form a narrow crest and merge smoothly with the concave backslopes. The perfect example would see the slightly concave footslopes of adjacent ballenas merge to form a smoothly rounded drainageway.

BALLOCHORE *See* Autochore.

BAND **1** To encircle a tree trunk with any material, usually a sticky surface, which protects it against the passage of insects moving up the stem. **2** The application of a pesticide as a spray, dust, or granules, in one or more localized bands around the tree, rather than to the entire ground area. **3** The application of a numbered or otherwise traceable plastic or metal identification band around the leg of a bird, for the purposes of re-identification in subsequent years or at different places, in order to track longevity and distribution.

BAND RATIOS In remote sensing, a method in which ratios of different spectral bands from the same image or from two registered images, are taken to reduce certain effects such as topography, and to enhance subtle differences of certain features.

BANK *See* Stream Bank.

BANKING SNAGS The act of throwing mineral soil around the base of an unlighted snag to prevent its being ignited by a surface fire.

BANK STORAGE The storage of water in stream banks due to infiltration into stream bank material during periods of high flow.

BANNER *See* Standard.

BAR **1** A ridgelike accumulation of sand, gravel, or other alluvial material formed in the channel, along the banks, or at the mouth of a stream where a decrease in velocity induces deposition. Bars tend to obstruct water flows and induce sediment deposition. Bar types are: (1) **braiding**, in which numerous river bars are interconnected with small channels; (2) **dunes**, which are a wave-like bed form common in relatively active sand bed channels; (3) **islands**, or relatively stable bars or land segments within the stream channel, usually vegetated, and normally surrounded by water; (4) **junction bar**, which is a bar formed at the junction of two streams; (5) **lee bar**, or a bar created by eddies and lower current velocities and formed in the lee of large immovable objects such as boulders or logs; (6) **mid-channel bar**, a bar found in the mid-channel zone, but not extending right across the channel; (7) **point bar**, or a bar found on the inside of meander bends; (8) **side bar**, one located at the side of a river channel, usually associated with a slight curve; and (9) **transverse bar**, which is a bar that extends diagonally across the full width of the active stream channel. **2** An elongated landform generated by waves and currents and usually running parallel to the shore, composed predominantly of unconsolidated sand, gravel, cobbles, or stones, and with water on two sides. **3** In meteorology, a unit of atmospheric pressure equal to a pressure of 29.5306 inches (75.006 centimetres) of mercury at 32 degrees Fahrenheit, in latitude 45 degrees at sea level and one atmosphere. The more usual unit is the millibar (10^{-3} bar).

BAR AND CHANNEL The microrelief common to floodplains and relatively young alluvial terraces. Over time, the microrelief becomes subdued as the higher lying bars erode into the channels. The ridgelike bars often consist of accumulations of coarse sediment, while the channels are finer textured. The relief between bar and channel is largely related to the competence of the stream.

BARBED **1** Generally, having sharp points capable of hooking onto or into other surfaces. **2** Botanically, describes bristles or awns having short, stiff, terminal or lateral hairs sharply slanted downward or backward.

BARBELLATE A diminutive of barbed.

BARBER CHAIR A high, slablike splint, resembling a chair back, left standing on a stump above the undercut as a result of faulty felling or the heavy lean of a tree.

BARDON HOOK A hook used with wire rope slings for gripping trees or logs to be skidded.

BARE-ROOT PLANTING *See* Seedling.

BARE-ROOT STOCK *See* Seedling.

BARGAINING Bargaining refers to a process whereby two or more entities reach an accommodation that is acceptable to all involved. The bargain will usually be based on undertakings by one or more of those involved to do or not do certain things.

Bargaining may be implicit. For example, a decisionmaking body may choose to modify its preferred alternative in order to achieve the support (or defuse the opposition) of some other party. While there is no direct exchange of offers and counter-offers, a public agency might modify a planned action in response to opposition voiced in a public hearing. The anticipated result (other half of the bargain) would be the dropping of opposition to the proposed action.

BARK **1** A non-technical term applied to the protective layer of plant tissue external to the wood. **2** More technically, the several types of tissue lying outside of the cambium. These include the phloem, cortex, phellogen, and the phelloderm.

The **cortex** is located between the phloem and outer tissues and in young stems provides food storage and stem support functions. Cortex tissue is usually absent in mature stems. The **phellogen**, or bark cambium, produces the outer bark tissues. It is situated outside the cortex or phloem, and is seen in mature trees. It functions much like the cambium, but produces cork (also called phellem) on the outside and phelloderm on the inside. Not all tree species produce phelloderm. The **phelloderm** and its associated tissues are called the periderm. Species having smooth bark tend to have cortical tissues and epidermal cells, or active phelloderm, that keep pace with the increasing diameter of the stems. Trees with rough bark typically have phelloderm tissues that do not develop right to the stem periphery, hence, as the diameter increases the outer layers of bark stretch and eventually crack, forming very characteristic bark patterns for different species. **3** As a verb, to strip away or peel the bark from a tree. **4** The sound made by certain animals such as dogs, sea lions, or seals.

BARK ALLOWANCE A factor applied to allow for the thickness of bark present, to better determine the exact volume of wood available under the bark. The factor can be measured empirically, applied by convention, or as a statutory deduction, typically as a percentage reduction of the measured overbark volume. For diameter or girth measurements, the more correct term is bark deduction, this being the difference between underbark and overbark measurements. *See also* Bark Gauge.

BARK BEETLES Small, often cylindrical beetles in the family Scolytidae that bore through the bark of host trees to lay their eggs; as larvae, they tunnel and feed in the cambium, or outer sapwood, of living, dying, and recently dead or felled trees. Important genera include *Ips*, *Dendroctonus* and *Scolytus*, and they cause serious damage to trees around the world. Some bark beetles also act as vectors of disease, such as the Dutch elm disease. A few species attack roots, twigs, cones, and solid wood.

BARK CAVITY A space behind layers of peeling bark that permits nesting (small birds) or roosting (bats).

BARK DRILLER Birds that hammer into the surface layers of bark in search of prey.

BARKER *See* Harvesting Machine Classification.

BARK GAUGE An instrument for measuring the thickness of bark. It is used to determine underbark volumes or basal areas.

BARK GLEANER Birds that pick prey or other food from the surface of a tree's bark.

BARKING IRON A tool with a narrow-shaped, curved blade used in removing bark by hand. It is also termed a bark spud.

BARK RESIDUE Strictly, the bark removed from logs, but more usually includes other foreign matter such as sand, grit, or stones that may have been embedded in the bark.

BAROCHORE Gravity dispersed propagule, usually heavier than an anemochore. May also be dispersed by animals. *See also* Anemochore; Autochore; Hydrochore; Propagule; Zoochore.

BAROGRAPH A barometer that produces a graphical trace on a chart – the barogram. *See also* Anemograph.

BAROMETRIC PRESSURE *See* Atmospheric Pressure.

BARREN Land devoid of trees or having only very stunted trees. Typical of extreme climatic conditions, such as very dry regions, whether deserts or sub-polar, or very windy regions.

BARRIER *See* Physical Barrier.

BARRIER BEACH A narrow, elongate sand ridge rising slightly above the high-tide level and extending generally parallel with the shoreline, but separated from it by a lagoon or marsh. It is seldom more than several kilometres long. Also termed offshore barrier, offshore beach, or bar beach.

BARRIER FLAT A relatively flat area, often occupied by pools of water, separating the exposed or seaward edge of a barrier from the lagoon behind it.

BARRIER ISLAND A long, narrow, sandy, coastal island, representing a broadened barrier beach that is above high tide and parallel to the shore, and that typically has dunes, vegetated zones, and swampy terrains extending lagoonward from the beach. It could also refer to a long series of barrier beaches.

BASAL In plants, at the base.

BASAL AREA The cross-sectional area of a tree's bole measured at a predefined point above ground, usually breast height, and expressed as a ratio of bole area to land area (e.g., M^2/hectare). The basal area of stands or forests is the cross-sectional area of all the trees (usually determined by sampling). Assuming a round tree trunk and diameters measured in inches or centimetres, the formulas for calculating basal area are:

Imperial:

$$\text{basal area (ft}^2) = \frac{\pi dbh^2}{4(144)} = 0.005454\ dbh^2$$

Metric:

$$\text{basal area (m}^2) = \frac{\pi dbh^2}{4(10{,}000)} = 0.00007854\ dbh^2$$

See also DBH.

BASAL AREA FACTOR Refers to the factor applied to an angle gauge. It is the basal area or stem area per unit area corresponding to the angle of projection. *See also* Point Sampling.

BASAL BARK TREATMENT A treatment designed to kill trees and shrubs by applying a band of herbicide to the bark, encircling the tree close to the ground.

BASAL CUP The cup-like remnant of a dwarf mistletoe infection that remains on the bark long after disintegration of an aerial shoot.

BASAL FLARE The rapid increase in diameter that occurs at the junction of the trunk and root crown, associated with stem and root tissues.

BASAL SHOOT SCAR *See* Basal Cup.

BASAL TILL Material that accumulates underneath a glacier from basal ice, including lodgement till and basal meltout till.

BASE In road construction, the layer of load-bearing material that distributes the weight of the traffic over the formation. The underlying lighter layer, placed to prevent the entry of moisture into the base from the formation, is called the sub-base. *See also* Formation.

BASE AREA In the US National Fire Danger Rating System, an area representative of the major fire problems on a protection unit. Base fuel model and slope class are chosen from the base area.

BASE FLOW The typical flow rate for a given stream at a particular time of year. Usually, the contribution that groundwater flow makes in sustaining water yields in a watercourse during periods of no rainfall.

BASE FUEL MODEL In the US National Fire Danger Rating System, a representation of the vegetative cover and fuel in a base area. It is used in the calculation of fire danger ratings.

BASE-HEIGHT RATIO A map that displays basic planimetric information (drainage and cultural features) and that is used as a base for the forest map. Base maps are usually compiled from topographic or planimetric maps, or aerial photographs. *See also* Planimetric Map; Topographic Map.

BASE LINE In surveying, a line of known length and position, from which further triangulation work can proceed. *See also* Baseline.

BASELINE **1** The starting point for analysis. This may be the conditions at a point in time (e.g., when inventory data are collected) or it may be the average of a set of data collected over a specified period of time. *See also* Impact; Scope. **2** In prescribed burning, the initial line of fire, usually set as a backing fire along a barrier or control line, which serves to contain subsequent burning operations.

BASELINE DATA The data gathered as a part of the baseline inventory assessment.

BASE MAP A map displaying basic planimetric information constructed from original surveys of observable phenomena, not interpreted or analyzed, such as drainage and cultural information, which can be used as a base for other forms of resource planning, such as forestry and terrain mapping. The base map is typically compiled from existing topographic or planimetric maps or aerial photographs.

BASE OBSERVATION TIME In the US National Fire Danger Rating System, the time established to take the fire danger observations. These should be at the same time of day when fire danger is normally the highest. It is also termed basic observation time.

BASE OF A FIRE *See* Forest Fire.

BASIC FOREST MANAGEMENT **1** A concept that promotes the protection of the forest from fire and insects, with artificial regeneration used where needed. **2** Management activities required by law. *See also* Basic Silviculture; Extensive Forest Management; Intensive Forest Management; Intensive Silviculture.

BASIC SILVICULTURE **1** An administrative term describing the practices necessary to establish regeneration of the desired species at specified densities and stocking, free from competing vegetation, and within a certain time limit. **2** Silvicultural activities required by law. *See also* Intensive Silviculture.

BASIDIOCARP A fruiting body bearing or containing basidia in fungi belonging to the Basidiomycotina.

BASIDIOMYCETE A fungus found in the phylum Basidiomycota in the kingdom Fungi, a phylum containing over 14,000 species. These organisms typically have septate mycelia and produce spores (basidiospores) externally in clublike reproductive structures called basidia. The class Heterobasidiomycetae encompasses the jelly fungi, rusts, and smuts. The class Homobasidiomycetae includes mushrooms, puffballs, and earthstars. Members are of economic importance as a food source and also as disease (rusts and smuts) and decay organisms (e.g., dry rot in wood).

BASIDIOSPORE *See* Basidiomycete.

BASIDIUM Plural basidia. A tiny, club-shaped structure formed at the tip of a hypha of a basidiomycete fungus and bearing four (sometimes eight) sexually formed basidiospores.

BASIFIXED Anthers are basifixed when they are joined at the base and are unable to move independently. *See also* Androecium (for illustration); Dorsifixed.

BASIN A depressed area having no, or very limited, outlets for surface waters; for example, a closed depression in a glacial till plain, a lake basin, or a river basin. *See also* Watershed.

BASIPETAL Developing from an apical or distal point toward the base. Opposite of Acropetal. *See also* Acropetal.

BAST The fibrous parts of bark.

BATESIAN MIMICRY A mimicry system developed by animals and insects, in which at least one distasteful model species is mimicked by one or more edible species to avoid predation.

BATHOLITH A massive intrusion of igneous rock caused by upwelling magma and covering large areas of land, typically more than forty square miles, dome shaped, and forced up into the surrounding rocks (see illustration). Contact metamorphism may occur along the boundaries of the intrusive rock and its surroundings. *See also* Dyke; Laccolith; Sill.

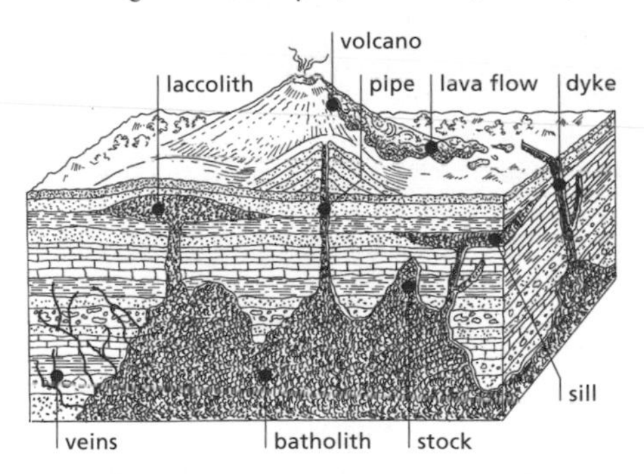

BATHYMETRY The science of mapping the contours of ocean floors or lake beds.

BATTER The sloped surface of an earth bank or retaining wall, expressed as one unit of horizontal measurement to so many units of vertical measurement (e.g., one in three), or as a slope in degrees, or as a slope in per cent.

BAULK Generally, a large piece of sawn or hand-hewn timber, usually square, suitable for resawing. Some countries have specific dimensions to describe a baulk.

BAY(S) OF A FIRE *See* Forest Fire.

BEACH The unconsolidated material that covers a gently sloping zone, typically with a concave profile, extending landward from the low-water line to the place where there is a definite change in material or physiographic form (such as a cliff) or to the line of permanent vegetation. The temporary accumulation of loose, water-borne materials that is actively moved along, or deposited on, the shore zone between the limits of low and high water.

BEACH RIDGE A low, essentially continuous, mound of beach or beach and dune material heaped up by the action of waves and currents on the backshore of a beach, beyond the present limit of storm waves or the reach of ordinary tides, and occurring singly or as one of a series of approximately parallel deposits. The ridges are roughly parallel to the shoreline and represent successive positions of an advancing shoreline.

BEACH TERRACE A landform consisting of a wave-cut scarp and wave-built terrace of well-sorted sand and gravel of marine or lacustrine origin. It may also occur on a lower piedmont slope in some places.

BEAK **1** In plants, a prolonged, more or less slender tip on a thicker organ, such as a seed or fruit. **2** In birds, the upper and lower mandibles of the mouth, consisting of bony structures covered with keratin. It is also referred to as the bill.

BEARDED **1** A long awn or bristlelike hair (e.g., the inflorescence of certain grasses). **2** A tuft line, or area of pubescence on a plant. *See also* Inflorescence.

BEARING A compass direction on the ground, or on a map, defined by the clockwise angle measured from a datum point, usually north, which can be magnetic north, true north, or grid north.

BEARING TREE A tree marked to identify the nearby location of a survey corner or similar marker. It is also termed a witness tree.

BEAUFORT WIND SCALE A system of estimating and reporting wind speeds (see table). In its present form for international meteorological use, this scale equates: (1) Beaufort force (or Beaufort number); (2) wind speed; (3) descriptive term; (4) visible effects upon land objects or sea surface.

Beaufort Wind Scale

Scale no.	Wind	Force (m.p.h.)	Observed effects
0	calm	0	Smoke rises vertically
1	light air	1-3	Wind direction shown by smoke drift, but not by vane
2	light breeze	4-7	Wind felt on face; leaves rustle; vane moves
3	gentle breeze	8-12	Leaves and small twigs in motion; a flag is extended
4	moderate breeze	13-18	Raises dust; small branches move
5	fresh breeze	19-24	Small trees sway; small crests on waves on lakes
6	strong breeze	25-31	Large branches in motion; wind whistles in telephone wires
7	moderate gale	32-38	Whole trees in motion
8	fresh gale	39-46	Breaks twigs off trees
9	strong gale	47-54	Slight structural damage to houses
10	whole gale	55-63	Trees uprooted; considerable structural damage
11	storm	64-75	Widespread damage
12	hurricane	> 75	Devastation

BED **1** To level and buffer the ground along the line on which a tree is to be felled in order to minimize the shattering of the timber. **2** The load-bearing part of the chassis structure in a truck. **3** The more or less flat and horizontal face of the undercut when falling a tree. **4** The ground on which any body of water lies, limited laterally by a bank or shore. **5** A single layer of sediment or rock, separated from layers above and below by more or less well-defined boundary planes.

BEDDING **1** The mechanical mounding of soil to provide a well-drained ridge upon which seedlings can be planted. A site preparation method common to the southeastern United States. **2** In the nursery, the planting out (bedding) of small seedlings so they can develop in less crowded conditions. **3** The flattened vegetation used by animals sleeping on the ground. **4** In terrain analysis, a collective term signifying the existence of beds or laminae (layers). **Well bedded** indicates beds are immediately apparent, clearly defined, and can be easily traced across the deposit. **Poorly bedded** means beds are only discernible after careful scrutiny, or bedding planes are discontinuous. **Moderately bedded** is intermediate between the two.

BEDLOAD Stream-transported materials, such as sediments and small rocks, transported along the stream bed in the lower layers of streamflow by dragging, rolling, or saltation. *See also* Dissolved Yield; Saltation; Sediment Yield; Suspended Sediment.

BED PLATE **1** *See* Anvil. **2** A large piece of horizontal timber on which rest the posts or stringers forming part of the abutment of a wooden bridge.

BEDROCK Solid rock, usually older than Quaternary (except rock formed by cooling of lava); either exposed at the land surface or underlying surficial deposits or regolith of varying thickness.

BEETLE A member of the insect order Coleoptera, characterized by the adults having hardened leathery forewings (elytra) and chewing mouthparts. They undergo complete metamorphosis, and the larvae (grubs) also have well-developed mouthparts.

BEHAVIOURAL PATTERNS A relatively uniform series of overt activities that can be observed with some regularity.

BELIEF An unmeasurable and unprovable assertion based on one or more fundamental assumptions. *See also* Attitude; Opinion.

BELT WEATHER KIT A type of portable fire weather station. It includes a sling psychrometer, water bottle (for saturating the wick of the wet-bulb thermometer), psychrometric slide rule or tables, hand-held windmeter, compass, pencil(s), and a booklet of weather report forms, all of which are carried in a canvas case with fitted pockets and that can be attached to a person's belt.

BENCH *See* Structural Bench.

BENCHMARK A survey reference point, used to signify a starting point. Benchmarks are typically defined by exact latitude, longitude, and elevation measurements.

BENEFICIAL USE In the United States, and from water use law, the reasonable use of water for a purpose consistent with the laws and interests of the people of the state. Such uses include, but are not limited to, the following: instream, out of stream, and groundwater uses; domestic, municipal, industrial water supply; mining; irrigation; livestock watering; fish and aquatic life; wildlife; fishing; water contact recreation; aesthetics and scenic attraction; hydropower; and commercial navigation.

BENEFICIATION **1** A process used to upgrade wood chips, making them more acceptable for pulp and paper manufacture. Upgrading is accomplished by separating the acceptable from the unacceptable chips. **2** In mining, the reduction of ores.

BENEFIT-COST ANALYSIS An analytical technique to assess the balance of quantifiable benefits versus costs over a known planning period. Costs are goods, services, and resources (tangible and/or intangible) that are consumed in the project in order to produce its potential benefits. Benefits are goods and services produced by the project. Benefits and amenities foregone may be seen as costs, and costs avoided may be seen as benefits. Costs and benefits may be intangible or tangible. *See also* Opportunity Cost.

BENEFITS Typically, the gross gains made by taking or avoiding an action, plan, or program of activities. An important part of assessing benefits is: (1) their ease of quantification; (2) the time over which they occur; (3) issues of equity over the affected population or environment. Some benefits are intergenerational and thus accrue over very long periods of time to people as yet unborn. Assessment of such long-term benefits incurs increasing levels of uncertainty. *See also* Costs; Intangibles.

BENTHIC Any process, material, or organism associated with the benthos.

BENTHIC INVERTEBRATES The community of invertebrate species associated with the living portion of the benthos, and forming a vital part of the food chain for higher order autotrophs. In marine biology, associated with ocean floors. In freshwater biology, associated with streams and streambed environments.

BENTHOS Animal or plant life living in direct association with the substrate of a lake, river, or sea at any depth of water (freshwater, estuarine, marine). *See also* Nekton; Neuston; Plankton.

BERGER-PARKER INDEX (*d*) An index of diversity that measures dominance by expressing the proportional importance of the most abundant species:

$$d = \frac{N_{max}}{N}$$

where

N_{max} = number of individuals in the most abundant species

N = number of individuals.

The reciprocal form of the Berger-Parker Index ($1/d$) may be used to ensure that the index value increases with increasing diversity.

BERGMANN'S RULE Warm-blooded animals have larger body sizes in colder climates than in warmer climates. Less energy is expended in thermo-regulation if the volume-to-surface area ratio is larger. The opposite holds true for cold-blooded animals in warmer climates.

BERM It is also called a bund in some areas. **1** The outside or downhill side of a ditch or trench. **2** A raised or level fill area by the shoulder of a road to act as a counterweight beside the road fill to reduce the risk of foundation failure. **3** A raised bank of soil or rock constructed in the path of flowing water to divert its direction. **4** A levee, shelf, or bench along a stream bank that may extend laterally into the channel to partially obstruct the flow, or parallel to the flow to contain the flow within its stream banks. May be natural or manufactured. **5** In marine biology, a nearly horizontal deposit of beach material accumulated by wave action near the water's edge. **6** In fire suppression, a ridge of soil and debris along the edge of a fire line, resulting from line construction. It may be created on the downhill side to stop rolling material.

BERRY An indehiscent, pulpy fruit, with one or many seeds. Berries develop from a single compound pistil. *See also* Fruit (for illustration).

BEST MANAGEMENT PRACTICES (BMP) Methods, measures, or practices designed to prevent or reduce water pollution. Not limited to structural and nonstructural controls, and procedures for operations and maintenance. Usually, BMPs are applied as a system of practices rather than a single practice.

BETA DIVERSITY *See* Diversity.

BIAS **1** The difference between the expected value of the estimate and the true value being estimated. A systematic error that affects all measurements in a similar manner. *See also* Mean Square Error. **2** The predisposition of an individual or group toward a particular set of values (e.g., an industry bias, a fibre bias, a wilderness bias). *See also* Accuracy; Precision.

BIAURICULATE Having two auricles.

BIENNIAL Growing over two seasons from germination to death, usually developing vegetative growth the first year, and flowering, fruiting, and dying in the second year.

BIFID A shape ending in two distinct clefts or forks with two points, such as the apices of certain leaves or petals.

BIFOLIATE A compound leaf having two leaves. *See also* Leaf Shape (for illustration).
BIFOLIOLATE Having two leaflets per leaf.
BIFURCATE Forked or forking into two branches.
BIG GAME Large mammals, fish, or birds that are hunted by humans for sport. Examples include elk, black-tailed deer, black and grizzly bears, mountain goats, cougars, Dall's sheep, marlin, swordfish, and wild turkeys.
BIG STICK LOADER A steel frame located either midway on the bed of a bobtail pulpwood truck or directly behind the cab. A short rotatable horizontal boom attached to a centre post mounted on a pulpwood truck.
BILABIATE Two-lipped.
BILATERAL SYMMETRY An animal or plant structure capable of being divided along its longitudinal axis into two halves each being a mirror image of the other. The plane of division typically separates the dorsal (upper) surface from the ventral (lower) surface. The higher invertebrates, including the Platyhelminths, the Annelids, and the Arthropods, and all vertebrates exhibit bilateral symmetry. All of these organisms have a distinct anterior (head) and posterior (tail) end, with the anterior end containing the main collection of sensory cells, which is the brain in the vertebrates. Having an end that normally leads movement, a phenomenon termed cephalization, is an important evolutionary trait of actively mobile animals. *See also* Symmetrical; Zygomorphic.
BILLET A short piece of round or partly round wood, usually smaller in cross-section than a block or bolt. A billet may be further cut to form a peeler bolt, a shingle bolt, a stave bolt, or a pulpwood bolt.
BILTMORE STICK A straight wooden stick calibrated for the direct measurement of DBH (diameter at breast height). The stick is held horizontally against the tree at breast height at a known distance from the observer's eye. The scale is graduated by the following formula:

$$\text{DBH graduation on the stick} = \sqrt{\frac{AD^2}{A+D}}$$

where

A = fixed distance from the observer's eye to the stick in inches

D = any selected tree diameter in inches.

The Biltmore stick provides measurements of variable accuracy due to the difficulty of keeping the eye-to-stick distance constant.
BIMODAL DISTRIBUTION A statistical distribution between two statistical modes (i.e., a distribution of quantities showing divergence into two separate distributions). In the illustration, the abundance of a species along a soil moisture gradient shows a bimodal distribution.

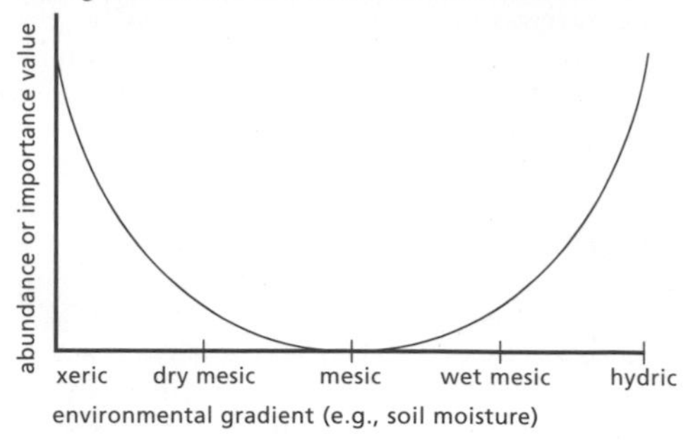

BIND **1** Usually, to get a saw stuck when falling or bucking a tree due to the sides of the cut pinching in. Wedges are used to remedy the situation. **2** To get a long log stuck in a sharp curve of a flume.
BINDER **1** A chain or wire rope used to bind logs or secure them on a truck. It is also termed a chain hook. **2** A glue or bonding agent capable of binding wood, wood particles, or wood fibres together into a cohesive whole, or a substance that binds together aggregates such as gravel, cement, and water to form concrete.
BINOMIAL NOMENCLATURE The basis of naming individuals and groups of organisms in a taxonomic classification. The system was devised by the Swedish botanist Linnaeus in 1753. Every species is given two names: a generic name (the genus), which has the first letter capitalized (unless it is being used as a common noun), and a specific name (the species). Both genus and species are always either underlined or more commonly, italicized. Finally, the author of the name is often quoted (e.g., the ponderosa pine is *Pinus ponderosa* Douglas). No two species can have the same specific name. Many of the genus and species names are derived from Greek or Latin origins and are descriptive of certain features. The system is used in all parts of the world and avoids the confusion caused by adoption of local names that have no meaning elsewhere. *See also* Systematics; Taxonomy; Appendix 1: Classification of Organisms.
BINUCLEATE Having or containing two nuclei.
BIOACCUMULATION/BIOMAGNIFICATION **1** The gradual increase in the concentration of a persistent substance in an aging organism. **2** A cumulative increase in the concentration of a persistent and toxic substance in successively higher trophic levels of the food chain. These substances (e.g., DDT and heavy metals) are ingested and retained either directly from the

environment, or through the consumption of food containing the chemicals, eventually reaching biologically harmful levels.

BIOCHEMICAL OXYGEN DEMAND (BOD) The amount of molecular oxygen in water that is consumed by microorganisms during the process of decomposition. Higher amounts of organic matter in the water require higher amounts of oxygen. BOD is used as an indicator of water pollution from organic wastes, and is measured in parts per million (milligrams per litre) of dissolved oxygen consumed. The water sample is kept in the dark at twenty degrees Celsius with oxygen levels measured at the start and end of a five-day period. It is also called biological oxygen demand.

BIOCIDE **1** A toxic material with the potential of causing lethal damage to metabolic systems, and producing effects in all forms of living organisms in a more or less comparable range of exposure. **2** In general, a substance potentially lethal to an organism, but not necessarily to all organisms.

BIOCLIMATIC UNIT A definable stratum of land with distinguishing climate, plant, animal, and microbial communities.

BIOCOENOSE *See* Community.

BIODEGRADABLE Any substance that is capable of being broken down by living organisms and biological processes into inorganic or organic compounds.

BIODIVERSITY (BIOLOGICAL DIVERSITY) The variety, distribution, and abundance of different plants, animals, and microorganisms, the ecological functions and processes they perform, and the genetic diversity they contain at local, regional or landscape levels of analysis. Biodiversity has five principal components: (1) genetic diversity (the genetic complement of all living things); (2) taxonomic diversity (the variety of organisms); (3) ecosystem diversity (the three-dimensional structures on the earth's surface, including the organisms themselves); (4) functions or ecological services (what organisms and ecosystems do for each other, their immediate surroundings, and for the ecosphere as a whole (i.e., processes and connectedness through time and space); and (5) the abiotic matrix within which the above exists (the unity of the soil, water, air, and organisms, with each being interdependent on the continued existence of the other). *See also* Diversity.

BIOECONOMIC ANALYSIS An analysis combining biological production factors and economic valuation.

BIO-ENERGY The kinetic energy released from biomass when it is eaten, burned, or converted into fuel. The potential energy embodied in the biomass.

BIOENGINEERING A multidisciplinary applied science that uses living plant material as a component of site engineering and landscape construction in order to stabilize and conserve soils. Modern applications include riverbank engineering, stabilization of steep slopes, erosion control, and other earthworks. One example of bioengineering is wattling, the partial burying of plant stakes cut from live willows (*Salix* spp.) in exposed or altered riverbanks. When the plant stakes take root, they both re-vegetate and stabilize the riverbank slope. The illustration shows an example of wattling, using live plant stakes to stabilize a slope. A dormant stake with live buds is pushed into the soil (A). The soil is backfilled (B), and the stake sets roots and leaves and eventually grows into the slope.

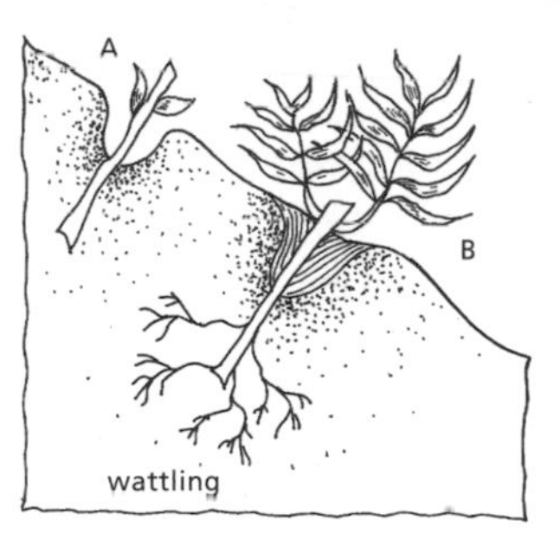

BIOGENOUS Refers to sediments or other materials produced in the oceans as a result of biological activity. *See also* Terrigenous.

BIOGEOCHEMICAL CYCLES The cycling of elements such as carbon, nitrogen, oxygen, hydrogen, calcium, sodium, sulphur, phosphorus, and other elements, between the abiotic and biotic components of the environment, including the atmosphere, terrestrial, aquatic, and vegetative systems, by the processes of production, assimilation, and decomposition.

BIOGEOCLIMATIC CLASSIFICATION A multilevel, integrated system of ecological classification utilizing climate, vegetation, and soils data to produce a classification of ecosystems. The system develops a detailed vegetation classification utilizing the Braun-Blanquet system. Then, integrating the ecological concepts of zonal and climax ecosystems, a hierarchy of classification units is produced. Ecosystem units are recognized and classified at both regional and local levels of classification. Biogeoclimatic classification is widely used in British Columbia for forest and wildlife management.

BIOGEOCOENOSIS A plant community (phytocoenosis) together with its environment. *See also* Ecosystem.

BIOGEOGRAPHIC PROVINCE Large, landscape-level tracts of land having biota that are distinct from other similar-sized tracts of land (e.g., boreal forest). *See also* Biome.

BIOGEOGRAPHY The study of the geographical distribution of living or dead organisms.

BIOLOGICAL CONTROL **1** The deliberate regulation of a pest species to acceptable levels by conservation and/or augmentation of the natural enemy complex of this pest species, or by introduction of exotic natural enemies. **2** In plant pathology, biological control has been defined more broadly as the reduction of the amount of inoculum, or of disease-producing activity of a pathogen, through manipulation of the environment and/or antagonistic organisms, or mass introduction of one or more antagonists. Some pathologists feel that manipulation of the environment should be considered 'cultural' rather than 'biological' control. *See also* Chemical Control; Manual Control; Mechanical Control; Silvicultural Control.

BIOLOGICAL CORRIDOR A habitat band linking areas of similar management and/or habitat type.

BIOLOGICAL GROWTH POTENTIAL The average net growth of trees in a fully stocked natural forest stand.

BIOLOGICAL LEGACIES Large trees, logs on the ground, snags, and other components of the forest that are left after a disturbance and contribute to maintaining site productivity and providing structures and ecological functions in the subsequent stands.

BIOLOGICAL OPINION In the United States, the document resulting from formal consultation that states the opinion of the US Fish and Wildlife Service or National Marine Fisheries Service about whether or not a federal action is likely to jeopardize the continued existence of listed species or results in destruction or adverse modification of critical habitat.

BIOLOGICAL PESTICIDE A pesticide in which the active ingredient is a living organism, such as a virus, bacterium, or nematode. The pesticide is applied in a manner similar to a conventional pesticide. *See also* B.t.; Microbial Pesticide.

BIOLOGICAL PRODUCTIVITY **1** The production of biomass. **2** The capacity to produce biomass under a given set of conditions.

BIOLOGICAL RESOURCES The living natural resources of the planet Earth, including plants, animals, and microorganisms, plus the environmental resources to which species contribute. Biological resources are the focus of biodiversity conservation activities and are renewable if conserved, but can be destroyed completely if not conserved.

BIOLOGICAL ROTATION *See* Rotation.

BIOLOGICAL SPECIES CONCEPT A concept that species can be considered as groups of natural populations that are reproductively isolated from other such groups. *See also* Phylogenetic Species Concept.

BIOLOGICAL UNIT MANAGEMENT In the US Forest Service, any unit for management of a particular species or any unit of intensive or special management. The term includes any big-game management unit as recognized by a cooperating state, even though it may not strictly be a herd unit. For fisheries management, the term may include a drainage system.

BIOLOGY The study of living organisms.

BIOMAGNIFICATION *See* Bioaccumulation.

BIOMARKER The variation, induced by a substance foreign to the body, in cellular or biochemical components or processes, structures, or functions that is measurable in a biological system or sample.

BIOMASS The total mass (at any given time) of living organisms of one or more species per unit of space (species biomass) or of all the species in a biotic community (community biomass).

BIOMASS PRODUCTION The rate and yield of biomass produced by plant or animal regardless of function or use. *See also* Yield.

BIOME A major regional ecosystem, characterized by its distinctive vegetation, a particular plant formation, and associated animals, microbes, and physical environment (life zone) (e.g., grasslands, tundra, savanna). A biome is a subdivision of a continent on the basis of major differences in the life form of the vegetation, where life-forms reflect the regional climates and soils.

BIOPHYSICAL The naturally occurring objects and processes in an area. The term implies that everything can be classified as abiotic or biotic. *See also* ABC Planning.

BIOPHYSICAL HABITAT CLASSIFICATION *See* Ecological Land Classification.

BIOPHYSICAL HABITAT MAPPING A mapping system that integrates those elements of the natural environment that are relevant to wildlife, including terrain, soils, and vegetation.

BIOREGIONAL, BIOREGION, and BIOREGIONAL MOVEMENT Refers to a philosophy that our cultures must arise from an ecologically meaningful context. It is predicated on the notion that if humans dwell in the same place for centuries, they identify with those places and their songs, stories, and sense of identity. Consequently, they are intertwined with those places to such an extent that they spontaneously protect, care for, and defend them.

BIOSPHERE That part of the planet that supports life, from the deepest oceans to the upper atmosphere. It consists of the hydrosphere, the lithosphere, and the lower atmosphere. *See also* Hydrosphere; Lithosphere; Troposphere.

BIOSPHERE RESERVE A management model proposed by the United Nations Man and the Biosphere program, in which a core area is preserved free from human disturbances, surrounded by buffer zones, which then lead into more intensive areas of disturbance and human activity. The concept has intrinsic merit because it recognizes that finite boundaries on a nature reserve have little or no ecological value. The traditional approach of nature reserve designation has been to assume that on one side of a fence nature could be left alone, while on the other side, it could be exploited. The biosphere reserve approach explicitly recognizes that ecosystems cannot be chopped up and still expected to function well. By advocating gradual changes around a central undisturbed core, the functional processes are much less severely disturbed, and thus, have a higher chance of successfully retaining the important components desired.

The illustration shows the concept of a biosphere reserve located along a coastline. The core of the protected area is surrounded by a buffer zone, which extends beyond the coastline, in which limited human activities are permitted. A transition area outside of the buffer zone permits more intensive human activities and habitation.

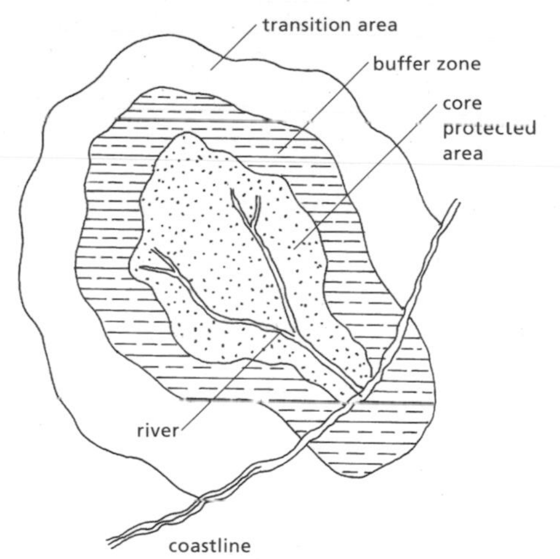

BIOSTASY One of two concepts characterizing alternative processes for landscape formation. Biostasy describes an interval in geological time when the predominant landscape (geomorphological) process was the deposition of organic and inorganic matter through biological and geochemical transformations. The Mesozoic era is representative of a period of biostasy. *See also* Rhexistasy.

BIOTA All of the living organisms (plants, animals, fungi, and microorganisms) found within any one area.

BIOTERRAIN MAPPING Terrain mapping with criteria slightly modified to emphasize or include those elements of the landscape that are relevant to wildlife habitat, such as soil moisture conditions, aspect, and vegetation characteristics.

BIOTIC Any living aspect of the planet, especially population or community characteristics.

BIOTIC POTENTIAL The theoretical maximum number of young that a female can produce under ideal environmental conditions (no limiting factors).

BIOTOPE The smallest geographical unit of land or habitat in which environmental conditions (soil and climate), and the associated organisms dwelling there, are uniform.

BIOTROPHIC An organism that is entirely dependent upon another for its nutritional needs.

BIOTYPE **1** Those members of a species having an identical genotype. **2** A biological strain of a species that may be morphologically indistinguishable from other members of the species and/or exhibits distinctive physiological characteristics, particularly in regard to its ability to successfully utilize a pest-resistant host (i.e., it is a pathotype), or to act as an effective beneficial species. **3** A subgroup within a species usually characterized by the possession of a single or a few features in common.

BIPINNATE Twice pinnate; where the primary pinnae or leaflets are further divided into secondary leaflets. *See* Compound Leaf (for illustration).

BIPLOT A one-, two-, three-, or higher dimensional diagram constructed from the results of an ordination analysis. The biplot consists of two types of stand data such as species composition and environmental variables, hence the prefix 'bi.' The direction of change in a variable (species or environment) is indicated in the biplot by an arrow that begins at the centroid of the plot and ends at the point of maximum correlation. Depending on the ordination technique used, arrows may represent the species or the environmental variables. *See also* Ordination.

BIRD A warm-blooded, feathered vertebrate of the class Aves, which has the following characteristics: (1) forelimbs modified as wings for flying; (2) mandibles in the form of a bill or beak without teeth; (3) internal fertilization; and (4) incubation of calcareous-shelled eggs outside the body. *See also* Amphibian; Mammal; Reptile.

BIRDDOG AIRCRAFT An aircraft carrying the birddog officer, who supervises and directs one or more airtankers in a fire-bombing operation.

BIRTH-PULSE POPULATION A population assumed to produce all of its offspring at an identical and short-duration point during the annual cycle, as opposed to species that reproduce at various times of the year.

BIRTH RATE The ratio of the number of live births to total population, usually within one year. For humans, it is expressed as births per thousand persons per year. *See also* Death Rate.

BISERIATE In botany, describes items placed in two rows or series.

BISEXUAL A flower having both stamens and pistils present and functional within the same flower; plants with perfect (hermaphrodite) flowers.

BISTRATOSE Plants having cells in two layers, sometimes seen on the leaves.

BIT In computer science, an abbreviation of binary digits, and one of the two digits (either 0 or 1) used in binary notation. It is generally considered to be the smallest possible unit of information. *See also* Byte.

BITERNATE *See* Ternate.

BITTERLICH METHOD/SAMPLE *See* Point Sampling.

BIVOLTINE The condition in which an organism, such as an insect, produces two generations in one year. *See also* Multivoltine; Univoltine.

BLACK BOX PLANNING An unknown and/or unknowable system of rendering decisions in which only the inputs and outputs are visible. The means, or criteria, used to render the decision are hidden from public view and, in some cases, may be based on one person's intuitive sense of what he or she feels is or is not right and desirable. Black box planning is characteristic of organizations that assume only people who are inside the organization have the necessary knowledge, skills, or technical competence to make 'correct' decisions. More open planning and decisionmaking by transparent means may be an uncomfortable experience, especially if the decisionmaking criteria in use are demonstrably flawed or biased.

BLACK CHECK **1** A dark stain in the sapwood and heartwood surrounded by abnormal formation of wood. Caused in conifers by bark maggots, pitch moths, and possibly bark moths. In oaks, it is caused by roundheaded borers. **2** A small, resin-filled pocket in wood, formed as a result of insect injury. *See also* Black Streak.

BLACK FLECK Small, dark flecks running parallel to the grain of decayed wood, characteristic of the activity of certain fungi (e.g., *Fomes annosus*).

BLACK HEART A condition not necessarily associated with decay, in which a black or dark brown zone or core develops in a tree, simulating heartwood in species (mostly in hardwoods) that do not normally differentiate it.

BLACKLINE The preburning of fuels, either adjacent to a control line before igniting a prescribed fire, or along a roadway or boundary as a deterrent to human-caused fires. Blacklining is usually done in heavy fuels adjacent to a control line during periods of low fire danger to reduce pressure on holding forces. A blackline denotes a condition in which there is no unburned fine fuel remaining.

BLACK STREAK A small, dark pocket, tangentially extended, from which a thin, narrow, dark streak extends in both directions longitudinally. It is found chiefly in western hemlock and often associated with infestation by bark maggots. It is also called black check.

BLACK-TOP **1** The condition of a dead tree after all the needles have fallen. **2** In the case of a bark beetle infestation, a tree two or more years after the beetles primarily responsible for its death have left it. It is also termed grey attack. **3** Generic term for asphalt paving.

BLADDER BAG A collapsible backpack pump made of neoprene or high-strength nylon fabric.

BLADE **1** The expanded part of a leaf or petal, excluding the petiole. *See also* Fern; Grass (for illustration); Leaf. **2** The metal cutting edge on earth-moving equipment, such as a bulldozer.

BLANKET A mantle of surficial material, thicker than about one metre, that reflects the topography of the bedrock or older surficial material upon which it rests, although minor details of that topography may be masked.
BLANKET BOG Large upland areas, typically in cold, wet climates, where extensive accumulations of undecomposed peat cover waterlogged, nutrient-poor ground. Blanket bogs derive their nutrient inputs from precipitation. In the United Kingdom, it is termed blanket mire.
BLAZE To permanently mark trees by cutting away a pronounced slab or chunk of bark and cambial tissue. Used to delineate trails, boundaries, or directions.
BLEEDING The exudation of natural gum, oil, resin, etc., from trees or converted timber following wounding. *See also* Resinosis.
BLIGHT A general term for any plant disease that causes rapid infection, death, or dieback of plants. Sometimes applied to specific parts of the plants, such as leaf blight, needle blight, bud blight. Characterized by sudden dying of shoots, foliage, or blossoms. Needle blight may continue through the summer and can destroy older as well as the current year's foliage. Can be very widespread and a serious economic pest (e.g., the chestnut blight or fire blight). *See also* Needle Cast; Wilt.
BLIND AREA The ground or the vegetation growing thereon, that is not visible to a fire lookout and lies more than a specified depth below the line of sight, or that lies at the limit of visibility from the lookout point and lacks a good background. *See also* Indirectly Visible Area; Seen Area.
BLIND CONK A pronounced swelling around a knot resulting from the tree's attempt to heal over an abortive conk, or the point from which an old conk has dropped. The affected knot may be partially covered by sound wood.
BLISTER **1** A small cavity formed in the bark or leaves by the separation and raising of the surface layers. Sometimes caused by insects or fungal attack. **2** Any disease characterized by this symptom, such as those caused by the fungi in the genus *Taphrina* on elm, and poplar, or by *Cronartium ribicola* (white pine blister rust).
BLOCK **1** A pulley used in wire rope logging to change the direction of the cable or to increase pulling power. **2** In the production of veneer, a log cut to a designated length, usually four to eight feet long, or a log cut to a designated length for use as pulpwood. It is also termed a bolt. **3** In statistics, a set of items or experimental units under treatment or observation that have been grouped to minimize initial differences between items or units, with respect to the variable under study. **4** In computer science, words, characters, or digits treated as logical units of data (e.g., data is transferred between memory and peripheral units, in discrete blocks). **5** The geographic area of trees or vegetation that is distinct from surrounding conditions. Block size may vary considerably. **6** The geographic area of trees scheduled for harvest or other treatment (e.g., cut block, spray block).
BLOCK CUTTING PATTERN A felling pattern started along the timber's front face next to the roadside. The felling machine works back and forth along the face and when sufficient timber has been felled to allow skidding, the cutting machine begins a second pass along another side of the block.
BLOCK FIELD A level or gently sloping area covered with angular blocks derived from underlying bedrock or drift by weathering and/or frost heave and having undergone no significant downslope movement; characteristic of periglacial regions. It is also termed felsenmeer.
BLOCK PLAN **1** A detailed prescription for treating a specified burning block with fire. **2** A detailed plan of a harvesting unit delineating the actual boundaries of cut blocks.
BLOCKS Angular rock fragments with intermediate diameter greater than 256 mm.
BLOOM **1** A relatively high concentration of phytoplankton that is readily visible and rapidly proliferates in a short period of time during favourable growing conditions generated by nutrient or sunlight availability (e.g., algal bloom). *See also* Eutrophication; Nutrient. **2** A fine, often waxy powdery coating on some leaves, stems, fruits, or other plant organs, typically whitish, greyish, or blueish, that is easily rubbed off. **3** A very general term for a flower.
BLOTCH A large, irregularly shaped necrotic or discoloured area on a leaf, shoot, or stem, or any disease with these symptoms.
BLOWDOWN *See* Windthrow.
BLOW OUT A general term for a small saucer-, cup-, or trough-shaped hollow or depression formed by wind erosion on a pre-existing dune or other sand deposit.
BLOW-UP A sudden, and sometimes unexpected, major increase in the rate of spread and

frontal fire intensity that is sufficient to upset overall fire suppression action or plans. Blow-ups can result from small or large fire situations, and may be accompanied by violent convection currents. *See also* Conflagration; Extreme Fire Behaviour; Flare-up.

BLUESTAIN A deep-seated fungal discolouration, predominantly bluish, but sometimes grey, black, or brown, confined mostly to sapwood. It does not cause a loss of structural strength. It is often associated with bark beetle or ambrosia beetle attack and may degrade the lumber value. It is also termed blue sapwood stain. *See also* Brownstain; Sapstain.

BLUFF A steep, precipitous slope of great lateral extent compared to its height.

BOARD FOOT Used to describe the measurement of lumber or timber, one board foot is the amount of wood contained in an unfinished board 1 inch thick, 12 inches long, and 12 inches wide; one twelfth of a cubic foot. Timber and lumber is sold in many parts of the world based on increments of one thousand board feet.

BOARD OF REVIEW A committee selected to review the results of fire suppression action within a given area, or the specific action taken on a given fire to identify reasons for either effective or ineffective action, and to recommend or prescribe ways and means of doing a more effective and efficient job in the future. It is synonymous with fire post-mortem.

BOBTAIL Describes a two-axle truck, usually used for hauling smaller loads of wood.

BOD *See* Biochemical Oxygen Demand.

BOG A wetland ecosystem made up of in-situ accumulations of peat, either moderately or only slightly decomposed, derived primarily from sphagnum moss. Bog water is acidic, usually at or very near the surface, and unaffected by the nutrient-rich groundwater found in the adjacent mineral soils. Vegetative cover is typically dominated by ericaceous shrubs, sedges, and peat moss, but trees may also be present. *See also* Fen; Marsh; Swamp; Wetland.

BOLE The stem of a tree once it has grown to substantial thickness, and is generally capable of yielding sawtimber, veneer logs, large poles, or pulpwood. Seedlings, saplings, and smaller poles have stems rather than boles. *See also* Stem.

BOLE SCAR A large, elongated, diamond-shaped scar on the stem of a tree. May be due to injury, or severe dwarf mistletoe, or rust infection.

BOLSON An internally drained, intermontane basin with two major landform components: the basin floor and the piedmont slope. The basin floor includes nearly level alluvial plains and playalike depressions. The piedmont slope comprises slopes of erosional origin adjoining the mountain fronts (pediments) and complex constructional surfaces (bajadas) composed mainly of individual and/or coalescent alluvial fans. A regional term restricted to the southwest United States.

BOLSTER *See* Bunk.

BOLT *See* Block.

BONE DRY TON Wood pulp or residues that weigh 2,000 pounds at 0 per cent moisture content. It is also termed an ovendry ton.

BONE DRY UNIT Wood residue that weighs 2,400 pounds at 0 per cent moisture content.

BONEYARD **1** A storage yard for old, used, or worn-out equipment or machinery. **2** In fire suppression, a mop-up term used to indicate an area cleared to the mineral soil for piling unburned fuels. To 'bone yard' a fire is to systematically work the entire area, scraping embers of remaining fuels, feeling for heat with the hands, and piling unburned materials in areas cleared to the mineral soil.

BOOLEAN SEARCHES A specialized form of searching databases for information, Boolean searches offer immensely powerful capabilities by being able to string together conditions for the search. Typically, these conditions offer a series of filters such as 'and,' 'or,' and 'not and,' which permits the operator to screen out records and fields easily. Thus, a Boolean search of this dictionary might be set up to look for all records containing the word 'tree' but then tell the search to reject any phrases with the words 'tree height,' but accept any phrases with the words 'total tree height.' This ability to execute complex search commands is essential in writing algorithms for GIS databases, where many layers of interrelated data can be questioned at one time to portray a range of 'what if' scenarios. (E.g., how many, and what is the total volume, of all Douglas-fir trees more than age class 6 existing within 2.8 kilometres of all class 2 roads in a defined area, excluding those that are reserved for aesthetic reasons or already scheduled for harvest in the next two years?)

BOOM **1** A pole, timber, or metal arm (the jib) protruding from a machine (e.g., the boom on a loading machine). Upwards and downwards motion is termed luffing or derricking, while side-to-side motion is termed swinging or slewing. **2** A string of logs called the boom sticks, which are tied together by boom chains or cables to contain other logs floating in the water. The boom may be in the form of a flat raft, or a loose bag of logs in the water, or if the logs are bound together in bundles within the boom, a bundle boom.

BOOSTER PUMP An intermediary pump for supplying additional lift in pumping water uphill past the capacity of the first pump.

BORDERLINE TREE A tree sufficiently close to the boundary of a sample unit of which more accurate measurements are required to establish whether the tree is inside or outside the unit.

BOREAL **1** A derivation from the Latin word for 'north' or 'of the north,' as opposed to austral, meaning 'south' or 'of the south' (i.e., *aurora borealis* versus *aurora australis*). It is also a truncation of Boreal Biogeographic Region, which is a climatic zone where the winters always have snow, and the summers are usually short. **2** A climatic period extending from about 7500 to 5500 BC, when the climate is believed to have been dry with cold winters and warm summers, as indicated by the development of a pine-hazel flora. *See also* Boreal Forest.

BOREAL FOREST A major global biome and the most extensive forest type in the world, the boreal forest is circumpolar in the northern hemisphere. It consists of a vegetation type dominated by coniferous trees, especially black and white spruce, balsam fir, or larch, interspersed with deciduous broad-leaved species, such as aspen and birch. It is the dominant forest type in tundra regions, and often includes peaty and swampy landscapes. It is also termed the northern coniferous forest, the spruce-fir forest, or taiga. Recent research points to the importance of the boreal forest as the single most important biome on Earth for maintaining planetary climatic systems. Apparently the albedo effect of having this area covered with trees as opposed to ice, snow, or something white or light coloured, is what helps prevent the formation of permafrost at lower latitudes.

BOREHOLE A hole drilled into the Earth, commonly to great depth, as a prospective well for water or oil, or for exploratory purposes.

BORER A beetle or other insect, usually in its larval state, that bores holes.

BORING **1** Starting a cut in the centre of the log using the tip of the saw blade. It is also termed a plunge cut.

BORING DUST **1** The frass caused by wood-eating insects. **2** Fine, light-coloured, powdered wood, cast out of tunnels made by insects, such as bark beetles, ambrosia beetles, and carpenter ants. Often an early sign of attack by these insects. *See also* Frass.

BORROW PIT An small quarry or excavation beyond the limits of road or dam construction, which provides material for use in the construction project.

BOSTRYX *See* Helicoid Cyme.

BOTTLENECK **1** A physical constriction in the landscape that forces concentration of organisms moving from one place to another (e.g., canyon). **2** A temporary decrease of a population to only a few individuals, thereby passing only a sample of genetic resources to subsequent populations.

BOULDERS *See* Substrate Particle Sizes.

BOUNDARY The edge between differing habitats. If the boundary is distinct, it can be considered a separate edge or Ecotone. Boundaries that are readily crossed by an organism are termed **permeable**, while those that are crossed reluctantly, are termed **semipermeable**. Boundaries that are not crossed are termed **impermeable**.

BOUNDARY DISCRETENESS A measure of the abruptness in change between adjoining landscape components.

BOUNDARY LAYER The air in immediate contact with a distinct surface, such as a fuel particle, the ground, or the surface of a leaf. *See also* Planetary Boundary Layer.

BOW The gradual curve of a stem or branch.

BOWLES BAG A neoprene tank designed for attachment to the landing skid frame of a helicopter, with a capacity of eighty to one hundred gallons (US) of water or fire retardant. Also termed monsoon bucket. *See also* Helitak.

BOX *See* Notching.

BP An abbreviation for Before Present. Used with radiocarbon age estimates. AD 1950 is the standard zero point. *See also* Radiocarbon Age; Tree-Ring Corrected.

BRACKET Refers to the bracket or shelf-like basidiocarp of some fungi, laterally attached to the trunk of a tree. It is typically associated with wood-decaying fungi.

BRACKISH WATER Water having salinity greater than fresh water (>0.5 per cent) but lower than saltwater (35 per cent).

BRACT A foliar organ, usually a leaf subtending a reproductive structure, such as a flower. Typically, the leaf is specialized and often dissimilar to the foliage leaves.

BRAIDED A stream or river pattern formed by a network of interlaced stream channels separated from each other by islands or bars of bedload material.

BRAIDING CHANNEL Refers to streams where the active channel zone is occupied by many diverging and converging channels separated by bars.

BRAKE PACK An internal brake on a skidder or machine transmission.

BRANCH A secondary division of a tree or shrub trunk. A small branch is referred to as a branchlet.

BRANCH ANGLE The angle of attachment between two stems (e.g., trunk and lateral branch), measured at or near the point of attachment. Branch angle is sometimes measured as the angle between the stem and the end of the branch. This will be less accurate if the branch is bowed.

BRANCH ATTACHMENT The structural linkage of branch to stem.

BRANCH BARK RIDGE The swelling of bark tissue on the uppermost side of the branch junction. It is a normal pattern of development, unlike embedded or included bark. *See also* Included Bark.

BRANCH COLLAR The wood that forms around a branch attachment, frequently more pronounced below the branch. *See also* Collar; Root Collar.

BRAND **1** A log mark used to identify the origin or owner of logs. **2** A distinctive mark or sign that is burnt into the hide of animals to identify ownership.

BRANDING AXE A specialized axe used to brand logs.

BRASH WOOD A type of reaction wood that is weaker than normal due to thin cell walls and decreased fibre content. Its presence may indicate an increased likelihood of failure. Brash wood tends to fail in a characteristic manner, normally as if sheared quite cleanly across the grain with little or no tearing along the primary axis. *See also* Reaction Wood.

BRAUN-BLANQUET COVER-ABUNDANCE SCALE A simple system for estimating the quantities of plant species in a stand, based on a scale of 1 to 5, with additional symbols for few and solitary individuals where: *5* represents any number of individuals in a species, with cover more than 75 per cent of the stand (greater than 75 per cent); *4* represents any number of individuals in a species with 50 to 75 per cent cover in the stand; *3* represents any number of individuals in a species with 25 to 50 per cent cover in the stand; *2* represents any number of individuals in a species with 5 to 25 per cent cover in the stand; *1* represents numerous scattered individual plants in a species with cover up to 5 per cent; + represents few individual plants in a species with little cover; *r* represents solitary plants with little cover.

BREAK A gap or sudden change in landscape structure.

BREAK A LINE To insert a gate valve or some other device into a hose line.

BREAK-EVEN POINT A point in the life of a company, or the operation of a machine or other piece of equipment, where the operating costs exactly equal the revenues derived. In a financial analysis, the break-even point defines the intersection of income and expenditures, beyond which profit can occur.

BREAK LEFT or RIGHT To turn left or right. Describes an aircraft in flight, usually on the retardant drop pass. When given as a command to the pilot, prompt compliance is implied.

BREAKOVER A fire edge that crosses a control line intended to control a going fire, or the resultant fire. It is synonymous with slopover.

BREAK-UP The period of time in spring when melting snow or thawing ground creates soft soil conditions and high water in streams. Logging and hauling are usually curtailed at this time.

BRECCIA Sedimentary rock composed mainly of coarse, angular fragments that are cemented together by calcite, iron oxide, or silicates. *See also* Agglomerate; Conglomerate.

BREEDING BIRD CENSUS In North America, a census program of the National Audubon Society that uses the spot-mapping method during the breeding season. *See also* Common Birds Census.

BREEDING BIRD SURVEY In North America, a cooperative program between the US Fish and Wildlife Service and the Canadian Wildlife Service for monitoring population changes in North American breeding birds by using point counts along roads.

BREEDING DISPERSAL The movement of individuals that have reproduced between successive breeding sites.

BREEDING PARASITISM *See* Brood Parasitism.

BREEDING SEASON The time of year when animals mate. *See also* Rutting Season.

BRIDGE A structure erected across a road, ravine, or watercourse to permit passage of people and/or machines to the opposite side.

The basic components of a bridge are shown in the illustration.

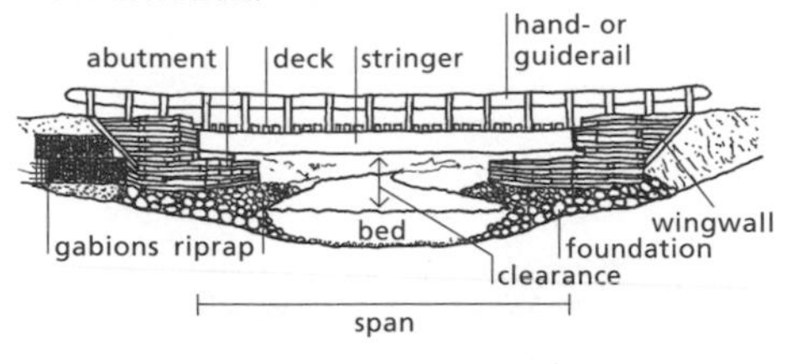

BRIDGE FUELS *See* Ladder Fuels.

BRILLOUIN INDEX (*HB*) An index of diversity used when the randomness of a sample cannot be guaranteed. For example, when a complete census is taken by measuring every individual, or when sampling techniques favour the collection or measurement of certain species over others. The value of the Brillouin Index is usually less than 4.5 and is calculated as:

$$HB = \frac{ln\ N!\ \ -\Sigma ln\ n_i!}{N}$$

where

ln = log normal
n_i = number of individuals in each species
N = total number of individuals
$N!$ = factorial of the total number of individuals.

BRITISH THERMAL UNIT (BTU) A measure of the amount of heat required to raise one pound of water one degree Fahrenheit. The amount of latent heat available to be released when a substance undergoes combustion.

BROADCAST BURNING A type of prescribed burning in which a controlled fire is allowed to burn over a designated area within well-defined boundaries to achieve clearly defined management objectives (e.g., reduction of fuel hazard), as a silvicultural treatment (e.g., in site preparation), or both. The fuels to be burned are as found and not piled or windrowed. Sometimes used to sanitize an area infested by pests (e.g., bark beetles, slash-infesting insects, or mistletoe) in residual trees. *See also* Spot Burning; Windrow Burning.

BROAD-LEAVED By widely accepted convention, the term refers to the shape of leaves on angiosperm plants, most of which are characterized by a broad, flat surface with net venation throughout. Broad-leaved trees are more common in warm temperate, subtropical, and tropical parts of the world, but extend into the Boreal Forest. Most broad-leaved trees are deciduous, but there are exceptions. Timber from broad-leaved species is typically called hardwood. *See also* Conifer; Evergreen; Needle-Leaved.

BROOD **1** All the progeny of the same female produced within a certain period (e.g., a clutch of bird's eggs, a honey bee brood in one season or year, or the progeny of one female bark beetle). The term is used mainly with reference to birds, insects, reptiles, amphibians, and mammals. **2** All the individual insects that hatch at about the same time from eggs laid by the preceding generation and which normally mature at about the same time (e.g., a bark beetle brood developing under the bark of trees).

BROOD BODY In plants, detachable cells or organs with the capability of vegetatively producing new plants. *See also* Gemma.

BROOD PARASITISM (INTERSPECIFIC) The laying of eggs by an individual of one species in nests of other species. The parasite young are cared for by the hosts. It is also termed breeding parasitism and nest parasitism.

BROOD TREE **1** A tree that is actively infested, for example, by bark beetles. **2** A tree from which the next generation of bark beetles will emerge.

BROOM **1** An exotic imported plant in certain parts of the world with the capacity to seriously alter ecosystems. **2** *See* Witches' Broom.

BROW LOG A large log laid beside the track or road at a log dump or landing to prevent logs from swinging or kicking back against the railroad cars or logging trucks.

BROWN AND BURN A vegetation management technique in which an oil or desiccant herbicide is applied in midsummer to green vegetation, especially hardwoods and brush. After allowing ten to twenty days for the brush to dehydrate, the area is then burned. *See also* Desiccant.

BROWN ROT A light to dark brown decay caused by fungi that attack the cellulose and associated carbohydrates in wood. The residue, which is mainly lignin, is friable and splits along regular planes in the advanced stages of decay. It is also termed brown cubical rot. *See also* White Rot.

BROWNSPOT CONTROL The use of prescribed fire to control fungal infection (brown spot disease) of longleaf pine in the small seedling stage.

BROWNSTAIN A dark brown stain, confined mainly to the sapwood, caused by fungi and possibly by other microorganisms. It occurs mainly in pines. *See also* Bluestain; Sapstain.

BROWSING **1** Refers to animals eating the tender current growth (and occasionally older growth) or bark of woody plants as a food source. Browse (when used as a noun) is the generic term for the food source. *See also* Forage; Grazing. **2** In GIS work, the ability to be able to select and quickly examine on a monitor part of a map or a database to check for features or data of interest. Usually, no analysis or manipulation is involved.

BRUSH Woody vegetation including shrubs and scrub trees of non-commercial height and form, often seen in the initial stages of succession following a disturbance. Brush often grows in very dense thickets that are impenetrable to wild animals and serve to suppress the growth of more desirable crop trees. However, brush can also serve an important function as desirable habitat for a range of bird, animal, and invertebrate species, and often provides a good source of browse and cover for larger wildlife. It adds structural diversity within the forest and is important in riparian zones. It is also termed scrub.

BRUSH BLADE A bladelike attachment with long teeth specially designed for ripping and piling brush with a minimum inclusion of soil. The blade mounts on the front of a bulldozer or angledozer and replaces the standard earth-moving blade.

BRUSH CONTROL The activity of suppressing or eliminating vegetation that competes for space, light, moisture, and nutrients with seedlings or crop trees, also known as brushing (see below). Control methods include chemical (herbicide), manual (saw, axe, or brushsaw), grazing (usually sheep), or mechanical (machinery chipping, shredding, or flailing).

BRUSH HOOK A heavy cutting tool with a wide blade, generally curved to protect the blade from being dulled by rocks. It is designed to cut brush at the base of the stem.

BRUSHING The removal of brush competing with more desirable crop trees, using mechanical means, either by cutting manually or by using machinery for crushing, rolling, flailing, or chipping it, or by chemical means (herbicides), or a combination of these.

BRYOPHYTE Primitive plant in the plant phylum Bryophyta, lacking a vascular system and typically growing in moist habitats (e.g., mosses, hornworts, and liverworts).

B.t. (*BACILLUS THURINGIENSIS*) A bacterial pathogen of insects, particularly the larvae of mosquitoes and moths. B.t. is used as a microbial insecticide against agricultural pests, mosquitoes, and some forest defoliators, such as the spruce and pine budworm.

BTU *See* British Thermal Unit.

BUCCAL Pertaining to the mouth cavity.

BUCKER The person who saws up felled logs into specified lengths, such as logs, bolts, or sticks. *See also* Harvesting Machine Classification.

BUCKER/SLASHER *See* Harvesting Machine Classification.

BUCKING *See* Harvest Functions.

BUCKLE GUY A line attached to the middle of a spar tree or steel tower to prevent bending of the spar when under load.

BUD An undeveloped leafy shoot or flower.

BUD BLAST A developed bud that appears to have died suddenly. The dead buds may be partially opened.

BUDDING A grafting technique where a bud (also called an 'eye') with a small amount of tissue at its base is inserted into a slit in the bark or epidermis of a rootstock. After union, the portion of the rootstock above the bud is removed, leaving the new shoot to develop from the grafted bud.

BUD TRACE The microscopic vascular connection between stem and bud.

BUDWORM A moth, which in its larval stage feeds on buds and shoots early in the season and later feeds on the expanded foliage. Budworms, such as the spruce budworm, are important forest defoliators and account for significant losses of timber.

BUFFER ZONE or STRIP Used in several contexts. **1** In protecting critical nesting habitat areas, the buffer is an area of forest land that reduces the impacts of adjacent activities on the critical area. The dangers associated with adjacent disturbances might include windthrow or wind damage to nest trees and young birds in nests, increased predation, and loss of interior forest conditions. **2** A strip of land between two areas under different management regimes. Pesticide buffer zones are used to limit the possible drift, run-off, or leachate of pesticide from a site into other areas, such as water bodies or creeks. Streamside buffers are used to limit the effects of logging on creeks, such as siltation, loss of shading, loss of nutrient inputs from trees, and degradation of riparian zones. The size and composition of the buffer zone depends on its intended function. *See also* Biosphere Reserve; Set-backs; Streamside Management Zones. **3** An area maintained around a sample or experimental plot to ensure that the latter is not affected by any treatment applied to the area beyond the buffer. **4** In GIS work, a new polygon computed on distance from a point, line, or existing polygon. **5** In managing biosphere reserves, an area or edge of a protected area that has land-use controls that only allow activities compatible with the objectives of the protected area. Examples of compatible activities might include tourism, forestry, agroforestry, etc. The objective of the buffer zone is to provide added protection for the core reserve area.

BUG **1** A very loose and derogatory term for any insect and certain other arthropoda. **2** In the correct technical sense, any insect in the order Hemiptera, and a few in the order Homoptera. Characterized by the presence of piercing/sucking mouthparts, a triangular scutellum, two pairs of wings, and gradual metamorphosis.

BUILDUP **1** The cumulative effects of those fire weather elements that cause drying of forest fuels and thereby heighten fire danger. **2** The accelerated spreading of a fire with time.

BUILDUP INDEX **1** *See* Canadian Forest Fire Weather Index System (FWI). **2** In the United States, a relative measure of the cumulative effect of daily drying factors and precipitation on fuels within a ten-day timelag.

BULB An underground leaf bud modified to serve as a storage organ. It consists of a short, thick stem and is covered with fleshy scales or leaf bases. *See also* Corm.

BULBIL A small, bulblike reproductive structure, often located in a leaf axil, or replacing a flower.

BULK DENSITY A measure of mass per unit of bulk volume (e.g., kilograms per cubic metre) of a material at a specified moisture content. In pedology, bulk density is the weight of dry soil per unit of bulk volume before drying to constant weight. Porosity, bulk density, and particle density are related as follows:

$$\text{porosity} = \frac{\text{bulk density}}{\text{particle density}}$$

It is useful in assessing soil compaction, and reflects the soil composition, structure, and porosity. For soils of similar composition (e.g., low organic matter content), higher bulk densities mean more compacted soils, which (if extreme) translates into poor drainage, poor soil aeration, and impeded root growth and root function, but good ability to support loads.

BULLATE Describes a bubble or knoblike swelling.

BULL BLOCK The main line block in high-lead logging, which has sufficient size to permit butt rigging to pass through.

BULLDOZER A crawler tractor that has a steel blade mounted across the front of the machine, with the capability of being raised and lowered, but not angled side to side (an angledozer), so all pushing or dragging is straight forward or backwards. An angledozer can move the blade up, down, and angled from side to side. The standard blade can be replaced with a toothed blade, termed a brush blade, capable of clearing and piling small trees and vegetation.

BUNCHING *See* Harvest Functions.

BUND *See* Berm.

BUNDLE SCAR One or more dotlike scars within a leaf scar, indicating the location of the vascular conducting tissues prior to leaf fall.

BUNDLING The binding together of logs or pulp bolts with wire cables or steel strapping to facilitate handling and transportation.

BUNK The cross member on a log-hauling truck, trailer, or log car on which the logs sit. It is also termed a bolster. The bottom layer of logs is termed the bunk load.

BURIED VALLEY A valley that has been filled by unconsolidated deposits, such as glacial drift.

BURL A woody excrescence on a bole, branch, buttress, or rhizome, having a slightly contorted grain. Burls are more or less rounded in form, and usually result from the entwined growth of a cluster of adventitious buds. It is also called a burr. *See also* Adventitious; Galls.

BURN or BURNED AREA Any unit of land over which a fire of any kind has spread. *See also* Fire Size Class.

BURNING BAN A declared ban on all open-air burning within a specified area, usually due to sustained high fire danger.

BURNING BLOCK In prescribed burning, an area having sufficiently uniform conditions of stand and fuel to be treated uniformly under a specified burning prescription. The size ranges from the smallest area that allows an economically acceptable cost per unit area, up to the largest that can be conveniently treated in one burning period.

BURNING BOSS The person responsible for managing a prescribed fire, from the ignition stage through to mop-up.

BURNING CONDITIONS The state of the combined components of the fire environment that influence fire behaviour and fire impact in a given fuel type. Usually specified in terms of such factors as fire weather elements, fire danger indices, fuel load, and slope. *See also* Fire Danger.

BURNING INDEX A relative number related to the contribution that fire behaviour makes to the amount of effort needed to contain a fire in a specified fuel type. Doubling the burning index indicates that twice the effort will be required to contain a fire in that fuel type, if all other factors are held constant.
BURNING INDEX METER A device used to determine the burning index for different combinations of burning-index factors.
BURNING OFF A fire suppression operation where fire is set to consume islands of unburned fuel inside the fire perimeter during mop-up operations.
BURNING OUT A fire suppression operation where fire is set along the inside edge of a control line or natural barrier to consume unburned fuel between the line and the fire perimeter, thereby reinforcing the existing line and speeding up the control effort. It is generally a small-scale routine operation as opposed to backfiring.
BURNING PERIOD That part of each twenty-four-hour day when fires are generally the most active. Typically, this is from mid-morning to sundown, although this varies with latitude and time of year.
BURNING PRESCRIPTION A written statement and/or list defining the objectives to be attained from prescribed burning, as well as the burning conditions under which fire will be allowed to burn, generally expressed as acceptable ranges of the various parameters, and the limit of the geographic area to be covered.
BURNING PRIORITY RATING A system of rating slash to indicate the treatment objective, whether or not burning is required to meet that objective, the fuel treatment necessary to achieve successful burning, and the time of year burning should occur.
BURNING ROTATION The planned number of years between prescribed fires on a specified area.
BURNING TORCH Any flame-generating device used to ignite forest fuels. Typically a container of diesel (kerosene) with a wick system that allows lighted fuel to be dribbled onto the ground, or it can also be a flame-throwing system. *See also* Drip Torch.
BURN-OUT TIME The duration of active flaming and smouldering combustion at a given point in the ground, surface, and crown fuel layers, expressed in convenient units of time. *See also* Residence Time.
BURR **1** A woody protuberance on a trunk, branch, buttress, or rhizome that has a very contorted grain within. Highly valued by wood workers for their interesting grain patterns. It is also called a burl. **2** The permanent base from which deer antlers grow annually. **3** In plants, a means of enhancing dispersal. *See also* Awn.
BURROW A cavity or tunnel made in the ground by a bird or mammal that serves as a nesting or denning site.
BURROW-NESTER A bird that excavates a burrow among tree roots on forested islands for its nest (e.g., ancient murrelet, rhinoceros auklet, fork-tailed storm petrel).
BUST (FIRE) *See* Multiple Fire Situation.
BUTT The base of a tree or the larger end of a log.
BUTTE An isolated, usually flat-topped, upland mass characterized by summit widths that are less than the heights of the bounding erosional scarps. It is typically produced by differential erosion of nearly horizontal, interbedded weak and resistant rocks, with the latter making up the caprock layers. As the summit area increases relative to height, buttes become transformed into mesas. *See also* Mesa.
BUTTERFLY An insect in the order Lepidoptera, which has the following characteristics (which have no taxonomic status): (1) mainly diurnal; (2) clublike antennae (see illustration); and (3) wings fold vertically above the abdomen when resting. Butterflies are subdivided into two superfamilies: (1) the Papilionoidea, which are the butterflies that tend to have narrow bodies, long antennae, and colourful wings; and (2) the Hesperioidea (skippers), which are distinguished by having stocky, compact, and hairy bodies and short wings that are usually brown, black, grey, or orange-brown. *See also* Lepidopteran.

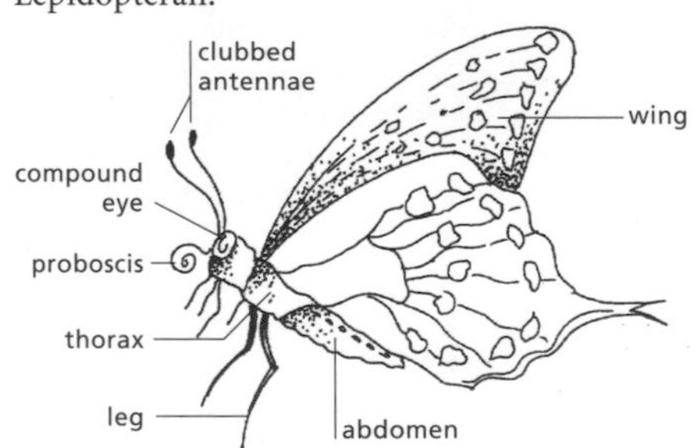

BUTT HOOK The heavy hook on the butt rigging (cable logging) or dragline (ground logging) to which the chokers are attached. It is also termed the bull hook.

BUTT LOG The first log cut off the tree above the stump.
BUTTRESS The ridge of wood developing in the angle between a lateral root and the butt of the tree, which may extend up the trunk to considerable heights. Common in tropical woods and trees in wetlands, buttresses may also be seen on stems and roots.
BUTT RIGGING A system of swivels, links, shackles, and clevises that permit connections between the haul-back and main lines without kinking and tangling. It can also define the point of attachment for the chokers.
BUTT ROT A rot that characteristically develops in the root crown or lower bole of a tree and is confined to that area. In practice, many fungi occur in the roots and in the butt and are less easily separated into root and butt rots.
BYRAM'S FIRELINE INTENSITY *See* Fireline Intensity.
BYTE In computer science, a storage unit equivalent to a character of information, consisting of a group of bits. A byte is usually eight bits. *See also* Bit; Word.

C

CABLE LOGGING (YARDING) The yarding of logs from the stump to a landing using an overhead system of winch-driven cables, to which the logs are attached with chokers.
CABLE SKIDDER *See* Harvesting Machine Classification.
CABLEWAY A system of steel cables strung across a setting to permit the partial or full suspension of logs off the ground during yarding. The load of logs can travel along the cable on a carriage (usually a skyline system), or with the cable as it moves (usually a high-lead system). *See also* Ground-Lead Logging; High-Lead Logging; Skyline Logging.
CADASTRAL MAP A map portraying the legal location of land and property boundaries, often in conjunction with topographic and cultural features. *See also* Planimetric Map; Topographic Map.
CADASTRAL SURVEY A survey undertaken to define the legal locations of land and property boundaries.
CADUCOUS Falling or dropping early (e.g., the caducous sepals in poppies fall away when the flower opens).
CAEOMA Plural caeomata. A diffuse aecium without period cells and with or without paraphyses. *See also* Paraphysis.
CAEOMOID Having a shape resembling a caeoma.
CAESPITOSE Growing in tufts.
CALCAR A spurlike cartilage on the hind foot of bats that projects from the inner side of the hindfoot into the interfemoral flight membrane.
CALCARATE Having a spur.
CALCAREOUS SOILS Soils high in calcium or magnesium carbonate, derived from limestones. Detected by fizzing when cold hydrochloric acid is added. Often leached out in acidic soils, the absence of calcium or magnesium leads to chlorosis and stunting of plant growth.
CALCICOLE A plant that grows best on limestone or calcareous soils. *See also* Calcifuge; Calciphile.
CALCIFORM Looking like a calyx.
CALCIFUGE A plant seldom found or unable to grow upon limestone or calcareous soils. *See also* Calcicole; Calciphile.
CALCIPHILE A plant that occurs in, and is tolerant of, calcareous habitats. *See also* Calcicole; Calcifuge.
CALCULATION OF PROBABILITIES **1** A calculation to estimate the probability that a known event will occur within a known period of time. The longer the period of time, the less reliable the estimate due to the likelihood that unknown or unplanned factors will influence the calculation. **2** In fire suppression, the evaluation of all factors pertinent to the probable future behaviour of a going fire and of the potential ability of available forces to perform fire suppression operations on a specified time schedule.
CALDERA A large, basin-shaped, volcanic depression, more or less circular or cirquelike in form, the diameter of which is many times greater than that of the included volcanic vents, regardless of the steepness of the walls or the form of the floor. Three main types are recognized: (1) explosion, (2) collapse, and (3) erosion.
CALIBRATED AIRSPEED The indicated airspeed of an aircraft, corrected for position and instrument error. It is equal to the true airspeed in a standard atmosphere at sea level.
CALIBRATION **1** The act or process of determining certain specific measurements in a camera, instrument, or device by comparison with a standard. Once calibrated, the instrument is then capable of producing valid measurements if used correctly. Correct calibration still requires that the instrument be used in a

precise and accurate manner to obtain the best results possible. **2** The adjustment of generic models of complex biological processes for use in specific places.

CALIPERS An instrument to measure the diameter of trees or logs. It consists of a graduated rule with two arms, one fixed at right angles to the zero end of the rule, the other sliding on the rule parallel to the fixed arm.

CALLED SHOT A water or fire retardant drop technique in which the air attack boss or the air coordinator triggers the drop by voice signal to the airtanker pilot.

CALLICHE A general term for a prominent zone of secondary carbonate accumulation in surficial materials of warm, subhumid to arid areas, formed by geologic and pedologic processes. Finely crystalline calcium carbonate forms a nearly continuous surface coating and void-filling medium in the parent rocks. Cementation levels can vary from weak in nonindurated forms to very strong in indurated forms.

CALLOSE The amorphous, hardened carbohydrate component of plant cell walls that typically develop after injury.

CALLOSITY A leathery or hard thickening or protuberance, a callus, but not formed in response to wounding.

CALLOW ADULT Also called a teneral adult. A newly moulted adult insect, after ecdysis but before the new exoskeleton has hardened completely. Usually pale in colour, the term refers mainly to beetles or ants.

CALLUS A mass of undifferentiated tissue, or organized tissues (including xylem, phloem, and periderms) that proliferate on or at the edges of wounded or infected parts of a tree and gradually cover the affected area. The ridge of new tissue formed is sometimes called the callus roll.

CALYCULATE **1** Having a calyculus. **2** Resembling a calyx.

CALYCULUS A whorl of small bracts or bractlets, resembling a calyx and usually subtending the true calyx or involucre.

CALYPTRA A caplike or lidlike structure, particularly the cap or hood of a moss capsule, or the united and circumscissile calyx lobes and petals of a Eucalyptus flower. *See also* Moss (for illustration).

CALYX The outer part of a flower, like a cup, composed of united or separated sepals. *See also* Flower (for illustration).

CAMBER **1** The vertical rise in profile, or hump, such as in the centre of a culvert bedding, which allows for the anticipated downward deflection. **2** The tilt or pitch of a road at ninety degrees to the alignment, designed to allow faster passage of traffic on curves by counteracting the tendency of centripetal forces acting on the vehicle to pull it off the road.

CAMBIUM A layer of actively dividing cells situated between the xylem and phloem. As the cells develop, they add a new layer of woody material on the inner side of the root or stem (mainly xylem) and a new layer of bark (phloem and associated tissues) on the outer side. It is also known as vascular cambium. *See also* Phloem (for illustration).

CAMERA STATION The point in space occupied by the camera lens at the moment of exposure. It is also called air station or exposure station. *See also* Air Base.

CAMPAIGN FIRE A fire of such size, complexity, or priority that its extinction requires a large organization, high resource commitment, significant expenditure, and prolonged suppression activity. It is synonymous with project fire.

CAMPANULATE Bell-shaped. *See also* Flower or Pileus (for illustration).

CAMPYLOTROPOUS An ovule that is curved by uneven growth so that its axis is approximately at right angles to its supporting stalk (funiculus).

CANADIAN FOREST FIRE BEHAVIOUR PREDICTION (FBP) SYSTEM A subsystem of the Canadian Forest Fire Danger Rating System. The FBP system provides quantitative outputs of selected fire behaviour characteristics for certain major Canadian fuel types and topographic situations. For example, head fire rate of spread, which can be adjusted for the mechanical effects of slope, is expressed in metres per minute. The system depends partly on the Canadian Forest Fire Weather Index System components as inputs.

CANADIAN FOREST FIRE DANGER RATING SYSTEM (CFFDRS) The national system of rating fire danger in Canada. Before 1976, it was termed the Canadian Forest Fire Behaviour or Behaviour Rating System. The CFFDRS includes all guides to the evaluation of fire danger and the prediction of fire behaviour, such as the Canadian Forest Fire Weather Index System and the Canadian Forest Fire Behaviour Prediction System.

CANADIAN FOREST FIRE WEATHER INDEX (FWI) SYSTEM A subsystem of the Canadian Forest Fire Danger Rating System, previously referred to by several names, including Canadian Forest Fire Weather Index, Canadian Fire Weather

Index, and Canadian Forest Fire Weather Index Tables. The components of the FWI System provide numerical ratings of relative fire potential in a standard fuel type (e.g., a mature pine stand) on level terrain, based solely on consecutive observations of four fire weather elements measured daily at noon (1200 hours local standard time or 1300 hours daylight saving time) at a suitable fire weather station. The elements are dry-bulb temperature, relative humidity, wind speed, and precipitation. The system provides a uniform method of rating fire danger across Canada.

The FWI System consists of six components. The first three are fuel moisture codes that follow daily changes in the moisture contents of three classes of forest fuel; higher values represent lower moisture contents and hence greater flammability. The final three components are fire behaviour indices representing rate of spread, amount of available fuel, and fire intensity; their values increase as fire weather severity worsens.

The six standard codes and indices of the FWI System are as follows. (1) **Fine Fuel Moisture Code** (FFMC) is a numerical rating of the moisture content of litter and other cured fine fuels. This code indicates the relative ease of ignition and flammability of fine fuel. (2) **Duff Moisture Code** (DMC) is a numerical rating of the average moisture content of loosely compacted organic layers of moderate depth. This code indicates fuel consumption in moderate duff layers and medium-sized woody material. (3) **Drought Code** (DC) is a numerical rating of the average moisture content of deep, compact organic layers. This code indicates seasonal drought effects on forest fuels, and the amount of smouldering in deep duff layers and large logs. (4) **Initial Spread Index** (ISI) is a numerical rating of the expected rate of fire spread. It combines the effects of wind and FFMC on rate of spread, but excludes the influence of variable quantities of fuel. (5) **Buildup Index** (BUI) is a numerical rating of the total amount of fuel available for combustion that combines DMC and DC (referred to as the Adjusted Duff Moisture Code or ADMC between 1969 and 1975). (6) **Fire Weather Index** (FWI) is a numerical rating of fire intensity that combines ISI and BUI, It is suitable as a general index of fire danger throughout the forested areas of Canada.

CANADIAN HERITAGE RIVERS SYSTEM The Canadian Heritage Rivers System (CHRS) was established in 1984 by the Canadian Parks Service in order to provide national recognition and protection for rivers or segments of rivers that meet one or more of the following criteria: (1) **natural heritage** are rivers that are significant examples of the Canadian natural environment, including its geology, vegetation, and wildlife; (2) **human heritage** are rivers that played an important role in Canadian history and contain historical or archaeological artifacts or were an important route for exploration or trade; and (3) **recreational value** is the term for rivers that offer outstanding wildland recreation opportunities.

A river is nominated for CHRS protection by the political jurisdiction through which it flows (territorial, provincial, or federal). In addition, a river or river segment must meet size (length) and water quality integrity standards in order to maintain a wild, scenic, or recreational environmental quality.

CANALICULATE Having a longitudinal channel or groove.

CANDIDATE SPECIES In the United States, this refers to plants and animals that are included in the Federal Register 'Notices of Review' that are being considered by the Fish and Wildlife Service for listing as threatened or endangered. Two categories that are of primary concern are the following. (1) Taxa for which there is substantial information to support proposing the species for listing as threatened or endangered. Listing proposals are either being prepared or have been delayed by higher priority listing work. (2) Taxa information indicates that listing is possibly appropriate. Additional information is being collected.

CANDLE or CANDLING **1** *See* Fire Behaviour; Torch. **2** The growing terminal shoot of certain conifers, especially pines, where the silvery-white bud scales or a secretion of waxy white cuticle give it the appearance of a white candle.

CANESCENT Greyish-white pubescence, hoary, densely covered with short, fine white or grey hairs.

CANINE TEETH In carnivores, the prominent teeth situated between the incisors and molars. The canine teeth are often referred to as 'fangs.'

CANKER A sharply defined necrotic lesion, often swollen or sunken in the bark and cambium of the stem, branch, or root. The host plant may react to produce an overgrowth of the infected area by the surrounding tissues. It is also the scar left after shedding of bark tissues killed by localized disease or environmental injury. There are five forms of canker. (1) **Annual canker** is one that enlarges only once and does so within an interval briefer than the growth cycle of the plant, usually less than one year. (2) **Diffuse canker** is one that enlarges without characteristic shape or noticeable callus formation at the margins. Diffuse cankers usually grow more rapidly than the radial growth of the tree, and may girdle the tree after several years (e.g., in a tree infected with white pine blister rust). (3) **Hip canker** occurs on one side of the bole (typical on pine trees) and may be partly or almost completely grown over. (4) **Perennial canker** is one that enlarges in more than one year, and the intermittent activity of the pathogen, and the host's responses over a period of years, prevent complete healing. (5) Perennial cankers tend to have concentric rings of callus tissue and are sometimes called **target cankers**.

CANONICAL CORRESPONDENCE ANALYSIS (CCA) CCA is a canonical ordination technique that explores the patterns of species occurrences in stands as they are directly related to environmental variables. CCA requires both species data and environmental data to be supplied for each sampled stand.

Canonical ordinations attempt to explain the species responses by constructing ordination axes that are constrained to be linear combinations of supplied environmental variables for each stand. Statistically this is accomplished through the integration of regression and ordination techniques into multivariate direct gradient analysis. CCA is a powerful tool for determining non-linearity, and it is able to detect unimodal relationships between species and environmental variables. *See also* Ordination.

CANONICAL VARIABLES The simultaneous analysis of many variables, using multivariate statistics to produce a set of transformed axes that have been generated by linear discriminate functions on which individual scores can be plotted. It is sometimes called canonical variates.

CANOPY Typically the uppermost continuous layer of branches and foliage in a stand of trees or shrubs, but can also refer to middle and lower layers in stands with multiple storeys.

CANOPY CLOSURE The degree to which the canopy foliage overhead blocks sunlight or obscures the sky. It can only be determined accurately from measurements taken under the canopy, to account for openings between branches and tree crowns. *See also* Leaf-Area Index.

CANT A log squared on two or more sides. *See also* Slabs.

CANYON A deeply incised, steep-walled valley, typically in bedrock.

CAP **1** A cone of sheet-iron or steel, with a hole in the apex through which a chain passes, fitted over the end of a log to prevent it catching on stumps during skidding. **2** The top of a fungus with a stem. *See* Pileus.

CAPABILITY The potential of an area of land or water to produce resources, supply goods and services, and allow resource uses. Capability is determined by the current vegetation conditions, and by site conditions such as climate, slope, landform, soils, and geology. In the case of water, capability is affected by ambient temperature, pollution inputs, buffering (dilution) capacity, and biochemical oxygen demand. Capability is also affected by season. Capability can be of two forms. (1) **Intrinsic capability** is the land's capability as it stands without further modification by human activities. (2) **Managed capability** is the potential capability that is anticipated after human-induced changes have been implemented.

CAPILLARY FRINGE An area above the water table where water is held between particles of soil by capillarity, and can be utilized by plants.

CAPITAL **1** One of the main factors of production, consisting of property in money or in kind, from which a monetary income can be derived. **2** The present or expected future monetary value of assets, discounted to the present at a given rate of interest. **3** In forest management, forest capital includes the nutrient capital of the soil, which determines in part the fibre capital contained in the standing trees (the growing stock), the capital values of the many other outputs possible from the forest as a whole, and the physical improvements (roads, buildings, drains, fences, etc.) that make up the forest estate.

CAPITALIZATION **1** The process of determining the value, at one point in time, of a series of values arising at subsequent points in time. **2** In accounting procedures, the addition of certain types of expenditures (costs) into the capital account for the purposes of depletion (capitalizing the costs).

CAPITATE A shape having a knob or headlike form, or a dense aggregated cluster of these.

CAPITULUM A flower head; an inflorescence composed of a dense cluster of usually sessile flowers (e.g., clover).

CAPSULE **1** In angiosperms, a dry, dehiscent fruit made up of two or more united carpels. There are several types of capsules: pyxis, septicidal, and poricidal. *See also* individual terms as defined; Dehiscence; Fruit (for illustration). **2** In cryptogams, a stalked, thin-walled structure containing the spores.

CAPTIVE BREEDING Breeding under captive conditions, as opposed to breeding in the wild.

CAPTURE-RECAPTURE METHOD A procedure involving the distinctive marking of individuals and their subsequent recapture (or sighting) to estimate population size and other population parameters. It is also termed mark-recapture.

CARBONATE ROCK A rock composed of carbonate minerals, most commonly limestone or dolomite; a sedimentary rock composed of more than 50 per cent by weight of carbonate minerals.

CARBONIFEROUS PERIOD A period of geological time lasting from about 360 to 286 million years ago, also called the Age of Coal, falling in between the Devonian and Permian periods of the Palaeozoic era. It encompasses the North American terms Mississippian and Pennsylvanian periods. The period is sometimes divided into the Lower and Upper Carboniferous at about 325 million years BP. During the Upper Carboniferous period, much of the prevailing vegetation was transformed into coal. Amphibians were the most common vertebrate animals, but it also marks the emergence of the reptiles. *See also* Appendix 2: Geological Time Scales.

CARBON RESERVOIR An area where carbon has accumulated in appreciable amounts, as a result of past or present activities of a carbon sink.

CARBON SINK An area where the rate of carbon uptake by living organisms exceeds the rate of carbon release. The surplus carbon is actively sequestered into organic or inorganic forms.

CARDINAL ALTITUDES 'Odd' or 'even' thousand-foot altitudes. It is synonymous with Cardinal flight levels.

CARDINAL DIRECTIONS North, south, east, west (unmodified, as in southeast, northwest, etc.). It is used for giving directions and information from the ground or air in describing the location of a fire (e.g., the west flank or east flank, rather than the left or right flank).

CARDINAL VALUES *See* Measurement.

CARGO CHUTE A parachute designed and rigged for dropping equipment and supplies from an aircraft, sometimes modified for use as a cargo net for use in sling loading.

CARGO DROPPING The dropping of equipment or supplies from an aircraft in flight, with or without a parachute.

CARGO HOOK A mechanically and electronically operated hook attached to the bottom of a helicopter to which a sling load is attached.

CARGO NET A net attached to the cargo hook of a helicopter, used to carry cargo. It is also termed cargo sling.

CARGO RACK An externally mounted rack on a helicopter for transporting supplies or cargo.

CARGO SLING *See* Cargo Net.

CARINATE Boat-shaped, or more commonly, keeled, or provided with a projecting central longitudinal line or ridge.

CARNASSIAL TEETH In carnivores, carnassial teeth are the fourth upper premolar and the first lower molar. These teeth are an adaptation for flesh-shearing.

CARNIVORES Any heterotrophic organism that feeds on (consumes) animal matter. Taxonomically, a member of the animal kingdom in the order Carnivora, such as wolves, bears, weasels, raccoons, and cats, and having large, well-developed incisor and canine teeth for tearing flesh. *See also* Autotrophic; Carnivorous Plants; Frugivore; Herbivore; Omnivore; Trophic Level.

CARNIVOROUS PLANTS A plant that supplements its nutrient requirements by trapping and digesting insects. Many such plants are common in wet and nutrient-poor soils, where elements such as nitrogen are difficult to obtain. Examples include sundew, Venus fly trap, bladderwort, and pitcher plant. Some authorities consider such plants to be insectivores.

CAROTIFORM Shaped like a carrot.

CARPEL The female sporophyll; a simple pistil or one comprising a compound pistil bearing an ovule (see illustration).

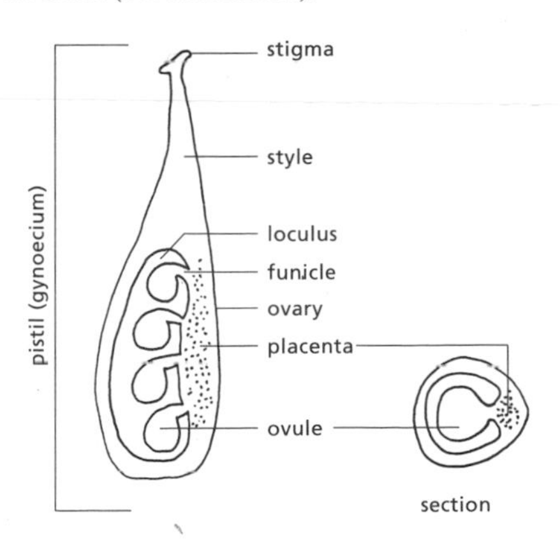

CARPELLATE Possessing or composed of carpels.

CARPOPHORE **1** A slender stalk forming the axis for a carpel or carpels. **2** A wiry stalk that supports each half of the dehiscing fruit in the Umbelliferae. **3** The fruiting body (spore-producing organ) of a mushroom.

CARRIAGE The mechanical assembly from which logs are suspended, that moves along the skyline. In multispan skylines, the carriage is open on one side to permit it to pass by the intermediate support jack.

CARRIER **1** An individual with a recessive gene capable of causing a genetic disorder, such as hemophilia, that can be transferred to their offspring. **2** A host harbouring a parasite without showing any symptoms of the parasite's presence and which may or may not act as a source of infection for other hosts. **3** An inert material serving as a vehicle for the active ingredient or toxicant in a pesticide formulation.

CARRYING CAPACITY **1** The concept of carrying capacity (ecological, visual, recreational, psychological) in resource management involves the specification of several key aspects. These are (1) a level of use that (2) will allow for the long-term maintenance of (3) some level of environmental quality within (4) some predefined level of management activity determined by the costs of maintaining the resource quality at (5) a level that will provide resource user satisfaction.

Any level of use greater than zero will result in change, thus it is incorrect to imply that ecological carrying capacity is the same as a 'no change' regime. Ecological carrying capacity can only be determined after the acceptable levels of change have been set, preferably as measurable thresholds that can be readily monitored. It is imperative that a baseline value be determined in order to have an effective or meaningful monitoring program. **2** The number (or weight) of organisms of a given species and quality (in terms of health) that can survive in a given ecosystem without causing its deterioration, through the least favourable environmental conditions that occur within a stated interval of time. For example, in wildlife management, it indicates the maximum number of organisms that can be supported in a given area of habitat at any given time. **3** Psychological carrying capacity is that level of use beyond which the sensory and conceptual quality of the resource starts to deteriorate for one or more user groups as a result of overcrowding (i.e., the number of simultaneous users has become too high and the quality of the individual experience declines).

CARTILAGINOUS Tough, hard, but flexible, like a cartilage.

CARTOGRAPHY The art and science of expressing graphically, by maps and charts, the known physical features of Earth, or of another celestial body. Cartography can be used to display many different attributes including abiotic, biotic, and cultural features.

CARYOPSIS An achene derived from a superior ovary, with the pericarp united to the seed wall. Normally, restricted to grasses.

CASCADE A stream habitat characterized by swift currents, exposed rocks and boulders, high gradient, and considerable turbulence and surface agitation, in a series of stepped drops down the channel.

CASCADING **1** The flow of water over one or more well-defined drops, such as a waterfall. **2** Free-fall dropping of uncontained, liquid fire retardant or suppressants, not in spray form.

CASE The hollowed-out and silk-lined portion of a needle used as a protective covering by certain insects during one or more stages of their life cycle (e.g., the larch casebearer *Coleophora laricella*).

CASE-HARDEN Wood that has been dried in severe conditions undergoes case hardening, caused by compression in the outer layers of wood and tension in the core (e.g., wood that has been burned on the outside).

CASH FLOW The difference between the dollar value of income received and the expenditures paid in any one period (e.g., annually, quarterly, or monthly).

CASTING **1** The characteristic mould of fine soil particles excreted by worms. **2** The premature loss of abscised leaves or twigs resulting from stress due to injury or ill health.

CATADROMOUS FISH Fish that are born and rear in saltwater, move to freshwater to grow and mature, and return to saltwater to spawn. *See also* Anadromous Fish.

CATASTROPHIC EVENTS Any event that originates from a sudden and unusually severe disturbance, usually of calamitous proportions (high intensity but low frequency) (e.g., windstorms, wildfires, floods, avalanches, mass wasting, earthquakes, and insect epidemics). Catastrophes typically cause a sudden decrease in population size and, in some cases, may eliminate entire subpopulations.

CATCHMENT The total area draining into a given

reservoir or impoundment area. Usually refers to water stored prior to release for other purposes, such as hydroelectricity generation, flood control, potable water storage, or irrigation.

CATEGORY DAY In the United States, a numerical index related to the ability of the atmosphere to disperse smoke. Different agencies use different scales (e.g., in South Carolina, the current scale is based on the ventilation factor and ranges from (1) poor to (5) excellent).

CATENA A group of adjacent soils originating from the same parent material at about the same time, but with differing characteristics due to variations in relief and drainage patterns.

CATENULATE Shapes occurring in chains or in end-to-end series (e.g., most aeciospores of rusts).

CATERPILLAR The larvae of butterflies and moths (Lepidoptera) and sawflies (Hymenoptera). *See also* Grub; Larva; Maggot.

CATFACE **1** A defect on the surface of a tree or log resulting from a wound that the tree has not been able to properly heal. **2** A well-defined healing or healed wound on the bole of a tree, usually at the base. **3** A deformation in fruit, induced by insect feeding during development of the fruit.

CATION A positively charged ion. *See also* Anion.

CATION EXCHANGE CAPACITY The total number of cation charges that a soil can adsorb, per unit mass of soil solids. The Cation Exchange Capacity of many soil constituents is affected by soil pH. It is used as a measure of the following: (1) the soil's ability to retain nutrients; (2) the clay composition of soils; and (3) the engineering characteristics of the soil, such as swelling and shrinkage.

CATKIN A type of inflorescence, typically a soft, flexible and scaly spike or raceme of small apetalous unisexual flowers. It is characteristic of willows, birches, and oaks. The catkin normally falls from the plant as a single unit. It is also called an ament. *See also* Inflorescence (for illustration).

CAUCUS The members of a negotiation process representing a common set of interests. For example, those who come from a primarily conservation perspective, or a group representing industrial interests. When these members are meeting among themselves, they are said to be caucusing.

CAUDATE Bearing a tail-like appendage or appendages (e.g., the apex of certain leaves, the spadix of some Araceae, or the base of the anther in some Compositae).

CAUDEX **1** The basal portion of a plant comprising both stem and root. **2** The stem of a palm tree or palmlike plants. **3** A stout, enlarged or swollen simple stem from which smaller stems, leaves, or flowers arise.

CAULESCENT Possessing a well-developed stem above ground.

CAULICOLOUS Growing on a stem.

CAULINE Pertaining to, or attached to, a stem.

CAUSAL AGENT The organism or abiotic agent that induces a given disease. It is different from the disease itself, which includes a host response. It is sometimes called the disease agent. *See also* Pathogen.

CAUSES OF FIRES *See* Fire Cause Class.

CAVITY An open wound, typically in a tree trunk or larger branches, characterized by the presence of extensive decay, which results in a hollow.

CAVITY EXCAVATOR A bird species that digs or chips out cavities in wood to provide a nesting, roosting, or foraging site.

CAVITY NESTER Wildlife species, usually birds, but can include mammals, that require cavities in trees for nesting and reproduction.

CAVITY-NESTING BIRDS Birds that nest in holes in trees.

CEILING The height above the Earth's surface of the lowest layer of clouds, or obscuring phenomena, that is not classified as a thin layer or partial observation, and which when taken together with all lower clouds or obscuring phenomena covers more than half the sky as detected from the point of observation. *See also* Cloudy; Dense Cloud Layer; Variable Ceiling.

CELL **1** The basic structural and functional unit of all living organisms. The cell is enclosed in a membrane that contains the cytoplasm, one or more nuclei, and other structures. Cell size is limited by physical constraints and has a characteristic size and shape in certain tissues or organs. **2** In meteorology, centres of high or low pressure. *See also* Locule. **3** In a grid mapping system, a defined geometric shape which stores data or defines an area that is labelled in a mapping system. The cell is the smallest addressable unit of space.

CELLULOSE The main structural and chemical component of cell walls in plants (approximately 50 per cent of the chemical constitution of wood). Cellulose is a complex carbohydrate polymer of glucose with the empirical formula $(C_6H_{10}O_5)_n$, built up into long, chainlike polymers. The cellulose and hemicellulose (simpler sugar molecules) component of the plant form the carbohydrate fraction of wood and this is the main component of paper and rayon. *See also* Lignin.

CELL WALL The protective, resistant, but permeable rigid structure, composed primarily of cellulose, which is secreted by the cell protoplasm on the outside of a cell membrane in plants, fungi, and bacteria. Older cells sometimes produce a thicker secondary cell wall, containing lignin, inside the primary cell wall. These cells typically die after production of the secondary wall (e.g., xylem vessel cells).

CELSIUS A temperature scale with 0 degrees as the freezing point and 100 degrees as the boiling point of water at sea level. It is also, incorrectly, called centigrade.

CENSUS **1** As a noun, a complete (to the extent possible) inventory of every member in a population within a specified period. **2** As a verb, the counting of all individuals in a specified area within a specified period in order to estimate density or total population for that area.

CENSUS EFFICIENCY The proportion of actual population density that is captured by a census.

CENTINELIAN EXTINCTION Extinctions of species before their discovery by science.

CENTIPOISE A standard unit of viscosity in imperial units, equal to 0.01 poise (e.g., water at 68 degrees Fahrenheit has a viscosity of 1.002 centipoise (cP).

CENTRE FIRING *See* Ignition Pattern.

CENTRE OF ACTIVITY **1** The area where an animal spends most of its time, within the total area encompassed by its home range. **2** Used in wildlife research to indicate the nest site of a breeding bird or animal or the primary roost area of a territorial species (e.g., spotted owls).

CENTRIFUGAL A force or phenomenon developing at the centre and progressing outwards to the periphery or margins. *See also* Centripetal.

CENTRIFUGAL PUMP A pump that expels water by centrifugal force through the ports of a circular impeller rotating at high speed. This type of pump allows the discharge line to be shut off while the pump is running.

CENTRIPETAL A force or phenomenon developing at the periphery or margins and progressing toward the centre. *See also* Centrifugal.

CENTROID Describes the geographic centre or the average of the *x* and *y* values making up the perimeter points of polygons. The centroid is used to locate a polygon and its label. The term has sometimes been generalized to mean that the point (centroid) may occur at any point in the polygon. *See also* Label Point.

CENTROMERE The area on a chromosome associated with the formation of spindle fibres, used to move chromosomes to the poles of dividing cells in mitosis and meiosis.

CENTRUM The six factors that directly determine an animal's ability to survive and breed. The factors are hazards, predators, diseases, genetics, resources, and humans.

CEPHALIUM A woolly growth at the apex of the stem of certain cacti, on which flowers are borne.

CEPHALODIUM Warty outgrowths found on or in a lichen thallus, containing cyanobacteria.

CEREBROID A form or surface having convolutions of folds resembling the cerebrum of a brain.

CERNUOUS Drooping or nodding; usually applied to flowers with drooping or curved pedicels that are attached to a straight or upright inflorescence axis.

CESPITOSE/CAESPITOSE Growing in tufts, dense mats, or dense clumps.

CHAFF A small, dry, membranous scale or bract; in particular, the bracts among the florets on the surface of the receptacle in flowerheads of Compositae.

CHAFFY Having a texture similar to the chaff from a threshing machine. *See also* Paleaceous.

CHAIN An imperial unit of measure used in land surveys, equal to 66 feet (80 chains equal 1 mile). It is commonly used to report perimeters and other distances (10 square chains equal 1 acre). In Canada, most areal measurements are expressed in hectares, although agricultural land is still measured and sold in chains and acres.

CHAINING **1** A method of extracting bundles of pulpwood by wrapping a chain around the bundles and dragging them diagonally downhill. It is used mainly on steep, snow-covered slopes. **2** A technique to knock over undesirable trees and brush by dragging a cable between two tractors with the centre of the cable weighted down by a concrete cylinder or similar large weight. **3** The activity of measuring distances on the ground using a calibrated steel or plastic chain. One chain equals 20.1168 metres.

CHAIN LIGHTNING Lightning occurring in a long zigzag or apparently broken line.

CHALAZA The basal part of an ovule, where it is attached to the funiculus.

CHANCE Describes an area or unit of forest land being logged. It also indicates the topographical difficulty of the logging chance.

CHANGE DATA The periodic and quantitative information describing forest resource dynamics, including: (1) depletions to the forest in terms of area and fibre volume due to harvesting, windthrow, wildfire, and insect or disease attack; (2) accruals to the forest in terms of area and fibre volume due to ingrowth; (3) management activities undertaken to protect or enhance the timber resource, or other resource values (silviculture, habitat enhancement, etc.); and (4) changes in land ownership and status that affect the utilization of the resources.

CHANNEL A discernible waterway that continuously or periodically contains moving water within a defined bed and banks.

CHANNEL CONFINEMENT The extent to which the lateral alignment of a river or stream channel is limited by adjacent topography (e.g., by valley walls or terraces).

CHANNELIZATION The straightening or dredging of a stream to make it deeper, straighter, or shorter.

CHANNEL PATTERN The plan view of a stream as it relates to curvature. Patterns include: (1) **straight**, with very little curvature in any one reach; (2) **sinuous**, with slight curvature within a belt of less than approximately two channel widths; (3) **irregular**, having no repeatable pattern; (4) **irregular meander**, having a repeated pattern vaguely present in the channel plan, where the angle between the channel and the general valley trend is less than ninety degrees; (5) **regular meander**, characterized by a clearly repeated pattern; and (6) **tortuous meander**, having a more or less repeated pattern characterized by angles greater than ninety degrees.

CHANNEL WIDTH The horizontal width of the channel between high-water marks (mean or annual), or the rooted vegetation on the banks, measured at right angles to the direction of flow. Multiple channel widths are summed to represent total channel width.

CHAPARRAL A vegetation type characteristic of mild temperate regions that have long dry summers and cool moist winters. Chaparral consists of thickets of drought-resistant sclerophyllous shrubs and small trees. Typical of the Mediterranean or coastal California regions, chaparral is maintained by periodic fires that prevent succession into a forest type. *See also* Hard Chaparral; Soft Chaparral.

CHARACTERISTIC LANDSCAPE The established landscape within an area being viewed. This does not necessarily mean a naturalistic character; it could refer to an agricultural setting, an urban landscape, a primary natural environment, or a combination of these types. *See also* Landscape.

CHARCOAL PHASE OF COMBUSTION *See* Combustion.

CHARGED LINE A line of fire hose filled with water.

CHARTACEOUS Describes leaves or bracts having a papery or tissuelike texture, usually not green.

CHASMOGAMOUS Where pollination takes place in the expanded flower. *See also* Cleistogamous.

CHECK **1** A longitudinal fissure in a log or tree caused by drying following cutting or after death due to disease or insect attack. Wood with these characteristics is said to be checked, or in the process of checking. **2** The condition where plant growth is arrested or drastically reduced through competition with other plants for light, nutrients, or water; by the state of the soil; or by disease. Individual stands or trees in this condition are said to be in check, or checked, or stagnant.

CHECK DAM A small dam structure constructed in a ditch in the path of the flowing water to reduce the water's energy and thus reduce erosion potential. It may also help to aerate the water flowing by. The water flows over the check dam, which is usually made with an erosion-resistant, spill-over section. The check dam can be a sophisticated structure or a simple depression or hole in the ditch. In both cases, it will also serve to collect silt and other erosion debris as the water slows down and, consequently, require regular maintenance to function effectively. It is also termed a silt trap.

CHECKED **1** *See* Stagnant. **2** The splits and cracks that develop along the length of a tree trunk or a board when it dries out.

CHECKERBOARD OWNERSHIP **1** In the US, a land ownership pattern in which every other section (square mile) is in particular ownership as a result of early federal land grants.

CHECKPLOT *See* Control.

CHECK SCALER A person who rescales logs in order to detect errors in the initial scale.

CHECK VALVE A valve that permits the flow of liquid through a hose or pipe in one direction but prevents a return flow. It is used with a positive displacement pump to prevent backflow of water on uphill hose lays.

CHELATION A process in which organic compounds in the soil form new compounds containing metal atoms in a new bond. Some chelates prevent metals from being fixed in the soil, making them available for plant uptake. Others hold metals so tightly that they contribute to nutrient deficiency in some soils.

CHEMICAL CONTROL The planned use of a chemical pesticide to control a pest population. *See also* Biological Control; Manual Control; Mechanical Control; Silvicultural Control.

CHEMICAL PULPING The process in which wood fibres are separated by removing the lignin and certain other wood components through the use of chemicals.

CHEMOSYNTHESIS An autotrophic process used by some organisms to derive energy from chemical reactions without requiring sunlight for photosynthesis.

CHEMOSYSTEMATICS A taxonomic approach that uses the chemical attributes of organisms as a basis for establishing the order and relationship of the taxa.

CHERNOZEM A soil descriptor commonly used in Europe to describe a mature soil grassland of semi-arid climates, usually developed from loess, and characterized by a surface horizon of good crumb structure, deep permeation by dark organic matter, and a zone of accumulation of secondary calcium carbonate below.

CHEVRON IGNITION *See* Ignition Pattern.

CHIASMATA The point at which two chromatids cross over and may exchange segments during the first prophase of meiosis.

CHIMERA **1** Botanically, a plant or plant organ consisting of tissues of more than one genetic composition and origin; typically a graft or mutant form. **2** A fish common in Jurassic times. **3** A DNA molecule that has nucleotide sequences from more than one different organism.

CHIP A small piece of wood used to make pulp. Chips are made either from wood waste in a sawmill or pulpwood operation, or from pulpwood specifically cut for this purpose. Chips are larger and coarser than sawdust.

CHIP-N-SAW A registered trade name for a machine that makes small logs into cants, converting part of the outside of the log directly into chips without producing any sawdust. The cants are then sawn directly into lumber as a part of the same operation. The chips are recovered for use as pulpwood.

CHIPPER *See* Harvesting Machine Classification.

CHIPPING *See* Harvest Functions.

CHI-SQUARED TEST Any test of significance based on the χ^2 distribution. It is often a test of agreement between expected and observed frequencies; a test of goodness of fit.

CHITIN The semitransparent substance forming the rigid exoskeleton of insects, the shells of crustaceans, and a major component of some fungal cell walls. Chitin is a polymer based on the molecule complex of polyacetylglucosamine.

CHLAMYDOSPORE A thick-walled, nondeciduous, and asexual spore that arises by the rounding-up of one or more hyphal cells. It is typical of soil-borne fungi.

CHLOROPHYLL The green pigments, mainly chlorophyll a and b, found in most plants exposed to sunlight. These pigments absorb light energy from the sun, making photosynthesis possible. They are contained in the chloroplasts.

CHLOROPLAST An organelle of plants containing chlorophyll and the site of photosynthesis.

CHLOROSIS A pronounced yellowing of normally green tissue due to the destruction or reduced production of chlorophyll. It is often a symptom of mineral deficiencies, disease, feeding by sucking insects, root or stem girdling, or serious light deficiencies. Plants in this condition are said to be chlorotic. *See also* Etiolation.

CHOKED A condition in which a log is attached to the skidding unit by means of a wire rope or chain choker.

CHOKER A short length of flexible wire, rope, or chain terminating in a choker hook, used to attach logs to a winch line or directly to a tractor.

CHOKER HOOK The fastening device at the end of a choker that permits a noose to be formed around the log to be skidded.

CHORIPETALOUS *See* Polypetalous.

CHOROPLETH MAP A map showing discrete areas, such as counties, soil units, vegetation types. These units are considered to be uniform with respect to the statistics collected within them.

CHRISTMAS BIRD COUNT An annual project of the National Audubon Society, involving a one-day bird count throughout the Americas. Undertaken in December, it involves counting all the individuals of all bird species observed within a circle that is fifteen miles (twenty-four kilometres) in diameter.

CHROMATID One of a pair of duplicated chromosomes that have recently been replicated and are joined at the centromere. Eventually, the pairs separate to become the chromosomes of each new daughter cell.

CHROMATOGRAPHY A process used to separate

constituent parts of a substance by utilizing the individual molecular properties of each constituent as a means of differential migration across an inert substance. The range and spread of each part is compared to the migration patterns of known chemicals, permitting identification of the constituents.

CHROMOSOME The coiled structure seen in the nucleus of eukaryote cells, containing DNA (deoxyribonucleic acid) organized in a linear sequence. The genetic material making up genes. The genes determine the heritable characteristics of the organism.

CHROMOSOME NUMBER The number of chromosomes characteristic of any one organism; seen in pairs in diploid organisms, or singly in haploid organisms (such as fungi and many algae). Humans have forty-six chromosomes.

CHRONIC SYMPTOMS Symptoms of disease or other disorders that persist over a long time.

CHRONIC TOXICITY Toxicity of long duration that produces an adverse effect on organisms. The end result of chronic toxicity can be death, but more usually the effects are sublethal, that is, they inhibit reproduction or growth patterns. These sublethal effects are reflected in the productivity and population dynamics of any one community and usually require long-term studies to elucidate.

CHRONOSEQUENCE The sequential set of changes in structure and composition of a forest stand, or for determining the stratigraphic sequences in peat layers, sediments, and rock formations. *See also* Stratigraphic Position.

CHRYSALIS The pupa of a butterfly. *See also* Pupa.

CHUTE A narrow, confined channel through which water flows rapidly; a rapid or quick descent in a stream, usually with a bedrock substrate. A short, straight channel that bypasses a long bend in a stream and is formed by the stream breaking through a narrow land area between two adjacent bends.

CILIA **1** Small, hairlike projections on specialized cells (e.g., in the bronchial tubes in mammals). **2** Whiplike filaments of protoplasm that give locomotion to microorganisms, to spores of some algae, and to sperms of ferns, cycads, ginkgos, etc. **3** Botanically, marginal hairs on a leaf or other flattened organ. **4** Another term for eyelashes on mammals. The term cilia is the plural of cilium, which is seldom used.

CILIATE Fringed with hairs.

CINCINNUS *See* Scorpioid Cyme. *See also* Inflorescence.

CINDER CONE A steep-sided, conical hill formed by the accumulation of cinders and other pyroclastic deposits around a volcanic vent; normally of basaltic or andesitic composition.

CINEREOUS Ash-coloured or light grey.

CIRCINATE Rolled or coiled from the top downward (e.g., the young, coiled leaf of a fern or cycad).

CIRCUMBOREAL Occurring throughout the boreal biome and circling the northern (or boreal) hemisphere of Earth.

CIRCUMSCISSILE An opening or splitting open where the entire top comes off as a lid (e.g., eucalyptus seed capsule and some mosses).

CIRQUE A steep-walled, amphitheatre-like bowl at the head of a glaciated valley or a rounded recess in a mountain. Cirques are formed by frost wedging, weathering, and glacial erosion. Typically, they have steep head and side walls and a relatively gently-sloping floor, which is commonly a basin with a small lake and terminated downvalley by a convex break of slope. Cirques range in diameter from a few hundred metres to several kilometres.

CIRRHOUS/CIRROSE Said of leaves, where the midrib continuation forms a coiling or spiralling tendril.

CIRRUS (CIRRHUS) **1** Plural cirri (cirrhi). A mass of spores resembling a ribbon or tendril, forced from the fruit body of a microfungus. **2** High cloud resembling curling fibres or tendrils.

CITES An acronym for the Convention on International Trade in Endangered Species (CITES) of Wild Flora and Fauna signed in 1975 by 103 nations to restrict international trade and administered by the United Nations Environment Programme. It currently lists 675 species that cannot be traded commercially as live specimens or as wildlife products because they are endangered or threatened with extinction. While a conceptually useful tool, it lacks a simple means of enforcement, it is totally dependent on the political will of the signatories, and has many exceptions that limit its global effectiveness.

CLADE The set of species that are descended directly from a single ancestral species.

CLADISTICS A classification scheme for plants and animals in which organisms are ordered and ranked based on their recent origins from a common ancestor. Like a family tree, the system focuses on the branching of the tree rather than on the differences within it. Ancestral forms are shown at the bottom of the tree, recently diverged forms at the top. A system not favoured by evolutionary taxonomists who place greater emphasis on the absolute differences and less on the exact lineage.

CLADODE *See* Cladophyll.

CLADOGENESIS The splitting of an evolutionary line into lineages; the portrayal of which is shown in a cladogram.

CLADOGRAM *See* Cladogenesis.

CLADOPHYLL A flattened stem having the form and function of a leaf but arising in the axil of a minute, bractlike, often caducous, true leaf.

CLAMBERING Trailing over the ground without support from twining stems or tendrils.

CLAM BUNK SKIDDER *See* Harvesting Machine Classification.

CLAMP CONNECTION A clamplike hyphal outgrowth that at cell division connects the resulting two cells by fusing with the lower one. It is characteristic of fungi in the Basidiomycotina.

CLASPING Botanically, partially or completely surrounding the stem, such as the base of certain leaves.

CLASS A taxonomic category, beneath phylum, and above order. A class is a group of related orders. *See also* Genus; Order; Phylum; Species; Taxon.

CLASSIFICATION **1** Generally, the systematic grouping of entities into categories based upon shared characteristics, such that data can be readily evaluated and manipulated for the purposes of analysis. **2** In remote sensing, two forms of classification are recognized.
(1) **Supervised classification** is a computer-implemented process through which each measurement vector is assigned to a class according to a specified decision rule, whereby the possible classes have been defined on the basis of representative areas of known identity.
(2) **Unsupervised classification** is a computer-implemented process through which each measurement vector is assigned to a class according to a specified decision rule, whereby the possible classes have been based on inherent data characteristics rather than on training areas.
3 Ecological classification techniques are used to statistically group or cluster artificial or natural sampling units based on their resemblances to each other in order to define, describe, and demonstrate the relationships of the sampling units to each other.

Ecological classification takes several forms. **Hierarchical** in which groups at any lower level of a classification are considered exclusive subgroups of those groups at higher levels. **Reticulate** in which the classifications define groups separately and are linked together in a weblike network, rather than being hierarchically ordered. **Divisive** in which the final groupings are determined by dividing and redividing the entire suite of sampling units. Divisions are based on similarities in sampling units. **Agglomerative** in which individual sampling units are combined and recombined successively to form larger groups of sampling units. **Monothetic** in which the similarity of any two sampling units is based on the value of a single variable, such as presence or absence of a single species. **Polythetic** in which the similarity of any two sampling units is based on their overall similarity as measured by numerous data variables, such as species abundances.

Cluster analysis is an example of a polythetic, agglomerative classification technique. Two-way Indicator Species Analysis (TWINSPAN) is an example of a hierarchical, polythetic, divisive classification technique. Association-analysis is an example of a monothetic, divisive classification technique.

The first stage in the classification of ecological communities involves collecting qualitative and quantitative data from the sampling units. These data typically include species presence lists and/or some indication of species abundance (density, frequency, per cent cover, or biomass), and environmental factors. The second stage is to determine ecological resemblance by quantifying the similarity or dissimilarity between all pairs of sampling units using Q-mode analysis. Finally, the sampling units are grouped or clustered according to their resemblances. *See also* Q-mode Analysis; R-mode Analysis.

CLASS OF FIRE *See* Fire Size Class.

CLAST An individual particle of a detrital sediment or a sedimentary rock, initially produced by the disintegration of a larger mass of bedrock; classified according to size as sand, gravel, pebbles, boulders, etc.

CLASTIC Of or pertaining to fragments. Sedimentary deposits of rock fragments derived from the accumulation, compression, and consolidation of terrestrial detritus. *See also* Nonclastic.

CLAVARIFORM Club-shaped. It is also termed clavate or clavoid.

CLAVATE Club-shaped, with a long body tapering toward the top; shaped like a baseball bat.

CLAW Botanically, the narrow stalk at the base of a petal, or a sepal in some flowers.

CLAY **1** *See* Substrate Particle Size. **2** A rock or mineral fragment of any composition having a diameter less than 1/256 millimetres (four micrometres) (Wentworth scale). **3** A finely crystalline, hydrous silicate of aluminum, iron, manganese, magnesium, and other metals belonging to the phyllosilicate group, such as kaolinite, montmorillonite, bentonite, and vermiculite, collectively known as clay minerals. *See also* Sand, Silt.

CLEANING The selective removal of unwanted trees in a stand that has not yet passed the sapling stage in order to free the crop trees from competition.

CLEARCUT LOGGING A silvicultural system in which the entire stand of trees is cleared from an area at one time, regardless of their potential utility on or off the site. It is usually used as a simple means of obtaining wood fibre, but may also be used as a means of removing low-quality standing timber in order to regenerate a new forest. Clearcutting results in the establishment of a new even-aged stand of trees, which can be naturally or artificially created. Clearcutting can be implemented in blocks, strips, or patches. *See also* Selection Cutting; Selective Cutting.

CLEFT Indented half way or nearly half way to the middle of a midrib or the base of an organ.

CLEISTOGAMOUS Where self-pollination takes place in the unexpanded, closed flower. *See also* Chasmogamous.

CLEISTOTHECIUM Plural cleistothecia. An ascocarp that lacks an opening. It is typical of powdery mildew fungi.

CLEVIS A U-shaped metal fitting with a pin connecting the two ends, used for connecting cables and rigging.

CLIMATE The prevailing environmental conditions resulting from the interactions of wind, water, and temperature. Climate is the main determinant of terrestrial ecosystems. *See also* Continental Climate; Maritime Climate.

CLIMATE CHANGE The actual or theoretical changes in global climate systems occurring in response to physical or chemical feedback, resulting from human or naturally induced changes in planetary terrestrial, atmospheric, and aquatic ecosystems.

CLIMAX The culminating, self-replacing seral stage in plant succession that is relatively stable and persists for long periods relative to other seral stages. The climax succession theory remains a subject of debate.

CLIMAX FOREST The culminating stage in plant succession for any given site where, in the absence of catastrophic disturbances, the vegetation has reached a highly stable condition and undergoes change very slowly. The climax forest is seen as an endpoint in succession, heavily influenced by climate. There are divergent opinions about the validity of the theory supporting the idea of a climax seral stage. Three main theories exist: (1) monoclimax theory; (2) polyclimax theory; and (3) climax pattern hypothesis.

To overcome some of the debate about climax successional theories, the phrases 'potential vegetation' or 'late successional vegetation' are often seen in place of 'climax forest.'

CLIMBER **1** A plant that grows up any vertical support (tree trunk, wall, lattice, etc.) either by twining around the support or by attaching itself to the support by means of tendrils, hooks, or aerial roots. Larger climbing woody stems are usually termed lianas. **2** The person who climbs a tree to install rigging for cableway systems or to effect pruning and other forms of tree surgery within the tree canopy.

CLINE **1** A geographic gradient in a measurable character, such as altitude or latitude. **2** A gradient in gene, genotype, or phenotype frequency. **3** A gradual change in population characteristics along an environmental gradient.

CLINOMETER *See* Hypsometer.

CLIPPING **1** Describes the smooth, oblique, scissorlike cut made on woody shoots by animal browsing. **2** The mechanical removal of pest-infested or otherwise damaged leaders or branches to eradicate the developing pest brood (e.g., spruce or pine weevil broods).

CLOACA The terminal portion of the gut in most vertebrates, except the higher mammals, forming the internal receptacle for ducts from the kidneys and from the digestive and reproductive systems, which then leads to one posterior opening via a vent.

CLONE A population of individuals all originating asexually from the same single parent and, therefore, genetically identical. Clones are named with non-Latin names preceded by the abbreviation 'cl.'

CLOSED AREA An area in which specified activities or entry are temporarily restricted by agency legislation to reduce the risk of human-caused fire. In some jurisdictions, a closed area is called a restricted travel zone, or a restricted fire zone.

CLOSED SAPLING or POLE STAGE A stand of trees where the trees are at the end of a sapling stage and in the early pole stage, characterized by a closed tree canopy and minimal ground cover. Canopy closure is more than 60 per cent and may be 100 per cent.

CLOSELY ASSOCIATED SPECIES A species is designated as 'closely associated' with a forest successional stage if the species is found to be significantly more abundant in that forest successional stage compared to other successional stages, if it is known to occur almost exclusively in that successional stage, or if it uses habitat components that are usually produced at that stage.

CLOSURE A legal restriction, but not necessarily elimination, of specified activities that might cause fires in a specified area (e.g., smoking, camping, entry). It is synonymous with forest closure.

CLOUD A visible cluster of minute water or ice particles in the atmosphere. *See also* Cirrus; Cumulonimbus Cloud, Cumulus Cloud.

CLOUDY An adjective describing the degree to which the sky is obscured by clouds. In weather forecast terminology, expected cloud cover of about 0.7 or more warrants use of the term. In the US National Fire Danger Rating System, cloud cover of 0.6 or more is termed 'cloudy.' *See also* Ceiling.

CLUMP **1** A group of trees, isolated from their neighbours. **2** The group of stems emanating from the same root, rhizome system, or stool. It is applied particularly to grasses and bamboos.

CLUSTER **1** In the context of owl research, a cluster is an area containing habitat capable of supporting three or more breeding pairs of spotted owls with overlapping or nearly overlapping home ranges. **2** In landscape ecology, refers to several ecosystem types (landscape elements) found within a few hundred metres of a point. **3** In statistics, a sample unit comprising two or more sample elements (subplots).

CLUSTER ANALYSIS A polythetic, agglomerative statistical technique that classifies sampling units based on the quantitative abundance data of species. Sampling units with similarities or overall resemblance to one another are grouped or 'clustered,' and arranged in a hierarchical, treelike structure called a dendrogram. *See also* Classification.

CLUSTERING **1** In remote sensing, the analysis of a set of measurement vectors to detect their inherent tendency to form clusters in multidimensional measurement space. **2** In harvesting, the arrangement of cut blocks in a pattern to minimize disruption of other landscape features. **3** In statistics, the division of a sample population into heterogeneous groups or clusters from which samples are then derived. Sampling strategies can be single-stage cluster samples or multistage cluster samples. Cluster sampling is commonly used in social surveys to reduce the costs of data collection. *See also* Sampling.

CLYPEUS **1** A sclerite (face plate) on the head of an insect, above the mouthparts. **2** A band of tissues around the mouth of the perithecium in certain fungi, also called a shield.

CO-ADAPTATION The process in which genes having similar positive and/or synergistic effects become established in a population through natural selection.

COARSE (BROAD) SCALE In mapping or landscape assessments, when the ratio of the map length to the true ground length is small. Coarse scale assessments cover a large area. *See also* Fine Scale.

COARSE FILTER ANALYSIS An analysis of aggregates of elements within the whole (e.g., the cover type or plant community). *See also* Fine Filter Analysis.

COARSE-FILTER MANAGEMENT Conservation of land areas and representative habitats with the assumption that the needs of all associated species, communities, environments, and ecological processes will be met. *See also* Fine-Filter Management.

COARSE FUELS *See* Heavy Fuels.

COARSE-GRAINED **1** The feel or appearance of a surface that looks or feels rough. **2** In ecology, the qualities of an environment that occur in large patches with respect to the activity patterns of an organism. It results in the organism's ability to select usefully from among a range of qualities. *See also* Fine-Grained.

COARSE WOODY DEBRIS Typically, sound or rotting logs, stumps, or large branches that have fallen or been cut and left in the woods, or trees and branches that have died but remain standing or leaning. *See also* Fine Woody Debris; Large Woody Material.

COBBLE *See* Substrate Particle Sizes. **1** A rock fragment between 64 and 256 millimetres intermediate diameter (Wentworth scale). **2** Rounded and subrounded rock fragments between 62 and 256 millimetres intermediate diameter.

COCCUS One of the separable parts of a lobed, sometimes leathery or dry, fruit with one- and, occasionally, two-seeded cells.

COCHLEATE Coiled like a snail's shell.
COCOON The silken case spun by an insect larva, in which it subsequently pupates.
CODOMINANT **1** Genetically, alternative alleles in a gene, both of which are phenotypically expressed equally within the individual. **2** In trees, *see* Crown Class.
CODON The group of three adjacent nucleotide bases in DNA or messenger RNA (ribonucleic acid) that are the code for a specific amino acid in the synthesis of proteins. It is also called a triplet.
COEFFICIENT OF DETERMINATION: R^2 In statistics, the square of the correlation coefficient, and in regression analysis, the proportion of the total sum of squares attributable to an independent variable(s) in the model tested. *See also* Correlation Coefficient.
COEFFICIENT OF NONDETERMINATION In statistics, the coefficient of nondetermination is determined by $1 - R^2 = K^2$ and is the basis of an error given by the unexplained proportion of the total sum of squares.
COEFFICIENT OF VARIATION In statistics, a relative measure of variation in contrast to the standard deviation, used to facilitate the comparison of variability. It is defined as the sample standard deviation expressed as a percentage of the sample mean and, being a ratio of two averages, is independent of the unit of measurement used.
COENOCLINE Also termed community gradient. A sequence of biotic communities along an environmental gradient. *See also* Complex Gradient.
COENOCYTIC Cell nuclei that are not separated by cross walls and are non-septate.
CO-EXISTENCE Adult plants whose physiological requirements and tolerances may be very similar may continue to co-exist in the same community if they differ in the factors that control their regeneration.
COFFERDAM A temporary enclosure built in a watercourse and pumped dry to permit work on bridge abutments or piers, thus separating the work area from the surrounding water.
COHERENT Botanically, united or fused, as in a corolla tube. Usually referring to the joining of similar parts or organs. *See also* Adherent.
COHESION **1** The capacity of particles to stick or adhere together. **2** A descriptor of community referring to the degree of attraction among the elements, both individuals and groups, of a spatial area. It often reflects shared beliefs, perceptions, or activity patterns.
COHORT Individuals all resulting from the same birth-pulse, and thus all of the same age.
COINCIDENCE In mapping, the occurrence of two or more map features in the same location (e.g., a road alignment that is right on a property line).
COL A low point on a ridge between two summits, or where the headwalls of two cirques intersect.
COLD FRONT *See* Front.
COLD TRAILING *See* Fire Suppression.
COLEOPTILE The single cotyledon of a grass seedling, which develops a sheath surrounding the plumule.
COLIFORM A group of bacteria found in the large intestine of humans and other warm-blooded animals. Coliform counts are used to determine the degree to which water has been polluted by sewage.
COLLAR In grasses, the part of the outer, lower side of a leaf blade that occurs at the junction of the sheath and blade. *See also* Branch Collar; Grass (for illustration); Root Collar.
COLLIMATE In photogrammetry, to adjust the fiducial marks of a camera so that they define the principal point. *See also* Calibration.
COLLIMATING MARKS The marks on the stage of a reduction printer or projection equipment, with which a negative or diapositive is oriented. *See also* Fiducial Marks.
COLLOID Very small soil particles, mainly clay or humus, with charged surfaces capable of attracting cations or capable of being suspended in water without rapid settlement. The upper limit of colloid size is commonly taken as one micrometre.
COLLUVIAL FAN A fan-shaped mass of sediments deposited by colluvial processes, most commonly debris flows.
COLLUVIAL PROCESSES *See* Mass Movement and Slope Processes.
COLLUVIUM Materials that have reached their present positions as a result of direct, gravity-induced mass movements. No agent of transportation, such as water or ice, is involved, although the moving material may have contained water or ice. It includes talus, landslide debris, and debris flow deposits. In some cases, it may also include deposits resulting from slope wash. *See also* Alluvium.
COLONIZATION **1** The process by which a newly exposed bare ground area acquires a vegetative cover (e.g., after a landslide or fire). **2** The establishment of a species in an area not currently occupied by that species. Colonization

often involves dispersal across an area of unsuitable habitat. *See also* Emigration; Immigration; Migration. **3** The location of a suitable host tree by bark beetles, followed by the aggregation of sufficient numbers of beetles on the tree to overcome its defences, and the establishment of an egg population in brood galleries under the bark. **4** The establishment of a saprophyte, a facultative parasite, or a parasite on or in a particular substrate, such as a tree stump. *See also* Infection; Infestation.

COLONY **1** A group of organisms of the same species living together, or in proximity, and sometimes forming an integrated society, such as ants or termites. **2** A recently established group of individuals in a new area. **3** A collection of individual microorganisms, such as bacteria or yeasts, or a group of fungal hyphae growing together, often derived from a single cell or spore.

COLUMELLA The persistent axis of a fruit composed of several carpels.

COLUMN **1** In plants, the structure formed by the union of the style and stamens in the *Orchidaceae*, or of the staminal filaments in the *Malvaceae*. **2** In analyzing trees for decay and structural weaknesses, the assessor may encounter a 'column' of internal decay, the extent of which directly affects the tree's strength.

COMA **1** A tuft of soft hairs attached to the testa of a seed, which aids in wind dispersion. **2** A tuft of leaves or bracts at the apex of an inflorescence. **3** A leafy crown or head, as typified in many palms.

COMBINATION In describing plants, the name of a taxon below the rank of genus, consisting of a combination of the name of the genus, the specific epithet, and any infraspecific epithets (e.g., Scots pine *Pinus sylvestris*). *See also* Epithet.

COMBUSTION A chemical oxidation-type process in which heat is produced (i.e., a substance is combined with oxygen). In the case of forest fires, living and dead fuels are converted to mainly carbon dioxide and water vapour, and heat energy is released very rapidly. Flaming combustion is characterized by the movement of a visible flame through the fuel bed. By contrast, smouldering or glowing combustion is generally associated with the residual burning of forest fuels following flaming combustion.

Combustion actually consists of three more or less distinct but overlapping phases: (1) **preheating phase** in which unburned fuel is raised to its ignition temperature and gaseous vapours begin to evolve; (2) **distillation or gaseous phase** in which the flammable gases escaping from the fuel surface are ignited in the presence of oxygen; energy in the form of heat and light is produced; and (3) **charcoal or solid phase** in which the presence of combustible vapours above the fuel is too low to support a persistent flame. The residual solid fuel or char burns away slowly.

COMBUSTION PERIOD The total time required for a specified fuel component to be completely burned.

COMBUSTION RATE The rate of heat release per unit of burning area per unit of time. It is synonymous with reaction intensity or fire line intensity.

COMMENSALISM A relationship between two organisms, where one (the commensal) lives in or on the other, to the benefit of one without harm or benefit to the other (e.g., epiphytes). Commensalism lies in between mutualism and parasitism. *See also* Parasitism; Symbiosis.

COMMENSURABLE VALUES Values or resource yields that have common units of measurement and can therefore be compared (e.g., dollars, kilograms, or cubic metres).

COMMERCIAL FOREST LAND Forest land assigned to the production of timber crops and not withdrawn from production for other uses. The definition may also include a minimum productivity threshold of so many cubic metres of wood per hectare per year (or equivalent units).

COMMERCIAL THINNING *See* Thinning.

COMMERCIAL TREE SPECIES Any conifer or broad-leaved species that forms a part of the allowable cut calculations, or has commercial value.

COMMISSURE The place or surface where two plant bodies or parts meet (e.g., the face along which one carpel meets or is united with another).

COMMODITY A transportable resource product with commercial value. The resultant products of resource extraction and processing that are utilized in commerce.

COMMON BIRDS CENSUS (UK) In the United Kingdom, a program of the British Trust for Ornithology designed to census birds using the spot-mapping method. *See also* Breeding Bird Census.

COMMONS Areas of land with control vested in local communities. Land available for use by anyone within community-defined guidelines.

COMMUNITY **1** In an ecological sense, the living organisms in a particular ecosystem: the plants, animals, fungi, and microbes of a given seral stage, typically interacting within a framework of horizontal and vertical linkages such as competition, predation, and mutualism. **2** In a geographic sense, the sense of place defined by human activities, such as a village, neighbourhood, or region. Such areas may have distinctive ethnic or cultural characteristics, or may be more psychological within the area residents. **3** The area of land occupied by people within the larger (unoccupied) landscape.

COMMUNITY DEVELOPMENT A planned and deliberate effort to promote socio-cultural change within a community as a means of enhancing the community infrastructure, well-being, sense of pride, or economic stability. Generally, the goals include an improved quality of life by improving skills, facilities, access to resources, and social empowerment.

COMMUNITY FOREST **1** In arboriculture, the collection of trees in streets, parks, and private ownership that, taken together, form the urban forest. *See also* Urban Forestry. **2** Around the world, the forested lands surrounding or considered to be a part of the community. In a 'developing world' context community forests are a source of fuelwood, fodder, grazing and agriculture, and typically the most vital means of community survival. *See also* Agroforestry. In the developed world, community forests are less well defined and encompass many forms of tenure to achieve many different purposes, including recreation, aesthetics, timber supply, fish and wildlife enhancement, and watershed protection. However, as in the developing world, most forms embrace the concepts, in varying degrees, of local benefits for local people, local control of local resources, and one or more intensive forms of management to provide a wide array of outputs from the forested lands.

COMMUNITY STABILITY The capacity of a town, village, or any other form of defined community, to absorb, cope with, and adapt to change, without suffering major hardship to institutions or groups within the community during the process of change.

COMOSE Bearing a coma, in any sense of its definition; comate.

COMPACTION **1** In stream morphology assessments, the relative density of bed material, usually caused by sedimentation, mineralization, or imbrication. **2** The crushing force that collapses soil and other aggregate particles into a smaller volume, typically by reducing the pore space between particles. Soil compaction is desirable for engineering practices, since the compacted soil will support heavier loads (e.g., along roads or under foundations). It is undesirable for plant growth since the compacted soil has insufficient pore space to allow effective diffusion of gases and liquids necessary to permit or maintain root development and nutrient uptake in plants. Compacted soil is a major cause of tree death or decline and severely inhibits establishment and effective growth of replacement trees. *See also* Soil Compaction.

COMPANION CELL A specialized cell adjacent to the sieve tubes in the phloem.

COMPARATIVE PHILOSOPHY Philosophizing that involves the study of different philosophies and worldviews as they have arisen historically and in places outside the context of Western culture. A form of cross-cultural and transhistorical analysis and reflectiveness driven by a quest to understand life and its complexity more fully.

COMPARTMENT The basic territorial unit of a forest under management. The compartment is permanently defined for the purpose of location, description, record-keeping, and as a basis for the planning and management of all forest activities.

COMPARTMENTALIZATION A natural process inside trees that serves to isolate wounded or diseased tissues and thus slow or stop the spread of pathogens within the tree. The xylem cells next to the wound react and build cell walls around the wound area by the formation of chemically and anatomically specialized tissue.

The process has been given the acronym CODIT (Compartmentalization Of Decay In Trees), which provides a model of the inner processes taking place after a wound takes place. The CODIT model identifies four distinct surfaces or walls forming after a wound and in two distinct parts; part 1 includes walls 1, 2, and 3, while part 2 includes wall 4.

Wall 1 involves the plugging of the xylem vessels in angiosperms, or tracheids in gymnosperms, above and below the wound, thus providing resistance to vertical spread of pathogens from the wound. Wall 2 provides resistance against inward spread, while wall 3 provides resistance to lateral spread. Wall 4, also called the barrier zone, separates the wood present at the time of wounding from the wood formed after wounding. Note that the model and its four walls are theoretical constructs and not biological features.

COMPATIBLE **1** A relationship between a host and a pathogen in which disease can develop. **2** Substances or organisms having the capability to interact together. Chemicals are said to be compatible when neither one affects the actions of the other. *See also* Antagonism; Incompatibility; Synergism.

COMPATIBLE DATA Two or more mutually exclusive data sets that, for the purposes of combination, are using the same standards and definitions.

COMPENSATORY MITIGATION A design and planning process used to create biophysical capacity of a particular type of ecosystem where the ecosystem did not previously exist as a substitute for biophysical capacity of the ecosystem lost at another site.

COMPENSATORY MORTALITY Any factor (typically hunting) that replaces natural mortality factors such as predation, disease, etc.

COMPETENCE The largest size of particle that a stream or air flow can carry, and dependent on flow velocity.

COMPETITION The demand for a common resource, including space or other conditions, by two or more organisms, in an environment where resources or desired conditions are actually or potentially limited (competitive exploitation). It is also, an interaction between organisms for resources or conditions that creates interference of one organism's existing habits even though the resources or conditions are not limited. Competition negatively affects the fitness-related characteristics of at least one of the competing species. Positive competition occurs when species populations fluctuate in unison in response to limited resources.

COMPETITIVE EQUILIBRIUM The long-term coexistence of two or more competing species.

COMPETITIVE EXCLUSION The elimination of one or more species from an area by another species. Not all species can occupy exactly the same niche at the same time because one species will always outcompete the other for the same resources. A negative interspecific association occurs when interference between species produces exclusion.

COMPILOSPECIES A species that incorporates genes and characteristics from other species through hybridization.

COMPLANATE Flattened together; compressed in one plane.

COMPLETE A flower having sepals, petals, stamens, and carpels.

COMPLETE FERTILIZER Any fertilizer that has a balance of nitrogen, phosphorus, and potassium.

COMPLETE METAMORPHOSIS *See* Holometabolous.

COMPLEX A group of similar and related species of fungi or other organisms, commonly designated as a group because species differences have not yet been resolved by taxonomists.

COMPLEX DISEASE A plant disease condition induced by the interaction of two or more pathogens, abiotic agents, or a combination of these factors.

COMPLEX GRADIENT The assemblage of physical environmental factors changing along a coenocline. *See also* Coenocline.

COMPOSITE **1** Composed of many distinctly individual parts. **2** Any plant in the family Compositae (e.g., sunflowers, asters). **3** An image created by carefully piecing together smaller component parts. *See also* Mosaic.

COMPOSITE LIFE TABLE The development of a life table based on data collected over two or more periods using mark-and-recapture techniques.

COMPOSITION The component tree species and age classes in a stand, usually assessed in descending order of occurrence (major through to minor), or expressed as a percentage of either the total number, basal area, or volume of all tree species in a stand.

COMPOUND **1** A substance created by the chemical combination of two or more elements, the resultant material having chemical and physical properties different from its constituent parts. **2** As a verb, to increase (e.g., compound interest or compounding a problem). **3** Botanically, having two or more similar component parts.

COMPOUND LEAF A leaf composed, typically, of two or more leaflets. Occasionally there may be only one (e.g., citrus), when the lateral leaflets have been lost in the course of evolution and only the terminal one remains. A leaf is **digitately** or **palmately compound** when three or more leaflets arise from a common point at the end of the petiole. It is **pinnately compound** when one or more pairs of leaflets are arranged along the sides of the axis, with

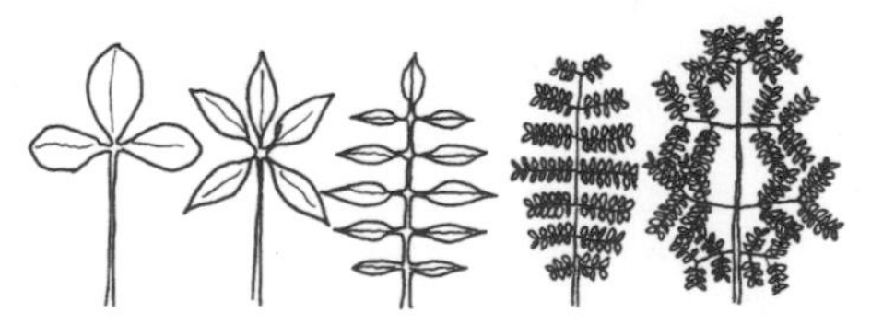

(odd-pinnate) or without (even-pinnate) a terminal leaflet. It is **ternately compound** when the leaflets or the divisions of the leaf occur in threes and **trifoliate compound** when the leaf is comprised of three leaflets (see illustration).

COMPOUND PISTIL A pistil or ovary produced by the partial or complete union of two or more carpels. The number of cells or locules within the ovary may or may not indicate the number of carpels. A pistil in which the ovary has more than one cell or locule is almost always compound. A pistil having a one-celled ovary, but more than one placenta or style or stigma, or with a combination of these duplications, may be presumed to be compound.

COMPREHENSIVE PLANNING The traditional planning approach, relying on science and quantitative analysis to provide the 'answers' to guide planning activities. It is also termed synoptic, or rational comprehensive planning, advocates promote it as an objective and impartial approach that can be systematically evaluated. Planners using such an approach are essentially technical analysts. Some of the weaknesses of such an approach are that it assumes impartiality and objectivity in the methods chosen for analysis (but who chooses and what are their preferences?), it assumes there will be one 'correct' answer, and it assumes that there will be a unitary preference among those affected when, in fact, disparate views and preferences are the norm. As with many other forms of planning, it is subject to political influence and, because of its comprehensive approach, the final answers or solutions being debated are often gross over-simplifications of very complex realities. *See also* Incremental Planning; Strategic Planning.

COMPRESSED Botanically, a plant organ or part that is flattened, especially laterally.

COMPRESSION A squeezing or crushing force. **1** In soils and geology, the process by which soils or loosely piled sediments become consolidated due to the compressive forces of the overlying material. **2** The way in which a grass floret is flattened to a glume, either lateral or dorsal (see illustration). *See also* Glume.

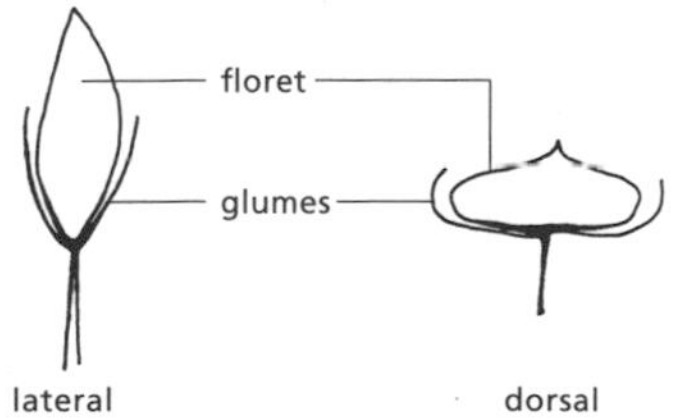

COMPRESSION WOOD *See* Reaction Wood.

COMPUTED GROSS WEIGHT Describes the calculation of permissible payload for helicopters. The computed gross weight is the maximum computed gross weight, from performance charts, at which a helicopter is capable of hovering in ground effect or hovering out of ground effect at a stated density altitude. The computed gross weight for hovering out of ground effect is less than that for hovering in ground effect. *See also* Equipped Weight; Gross Weight; Payload.

CONCEPTUAL MODEL A hypothetical model that describes ideas in a qualitative, abstract manner.

CONCERN A point of dispute, or public apprehension, that a proposed land-use, policy, decision, or management activity might produce specific or vaguely defined undesirable results.

CONCILIATION Conciliation is used in several ways. It may refer to attempts to settle disputes without bringing the disputing parties into joint session, with the conciliator acting as broker. It is also used by some authors to describe the initial attempts to convene the parties, with the 'conciliator' becoming a 'mediator' at the point when the joint sessions begin.

CONCOLOROUS Having the same colour.

CONDITION The state of being or health of an abiotic or biotic material or system (e.g., fertile soil, healthy vegetation, well-sorted gravel). In nursery practice, seedlings are prepared for transplanting into the field by 'conditioning' them to adapt to the harsher outside conditions.

CONDITIONAL LETHAL MUTATION A mutation that is fatal within one environment but not in another.

CONDITION OF HERBACEOUS VEGETATION The proportion, expressed as a percentage, of the cured and/or dead materials in the vegetation component of surface fuels. Herbaceous plants within a fuel type may consist of grasses, herbs, forbs, and ferns, but not woody-stemmed upright or trailing shrubs.

CONDUCTION *See* Heat Transfer.

CONDUCTIVITY A measure of how easily heat or electricity flows through a material. Electrical conductivity reflects the concentration of ionized substances in solution. Conductivity is the reciprocal of resistivity.

CONDUPLICATE Folded once lengthwise, such as many orchid leaves. Conduplicate cotyledons in the seed are folded lengthwise with one enfolded within the other, with the radicle lying in the fold of the inner one. *See also* Accumbent; Incumbent.

CONE **1** A reproductive structure having a main axis bearing sporophylls (cone scales) and sometimes, bracts, that forms a detachable unit. Some cones are short-lived, such as male pine cones, while others have a long duration and are often woody, such as female pine cones. *See also* Strobile. **2** A mountain, hill, or other landform shaped like a cone, having relatively steep slopes and a pointed top. **3** A sector of a cone with a straight or concave long profile and slopes generally steeper than 15 degrees (26 per cent). It includes talus cones and avalanche cones.

CONE CUTTING **1** The removal of cones from trees by squirrels. **2** The slicing of a cone in order to evaluate its seed content, potential viability, and to check for seed insects, and thus determine by sampling, the potential of the tree or stand as a seed source.

CONE RAKE A device attached to a helicopter that is lowered over the tree. As the rake is lifted up, it removes cones and small branches, which are then sorted out on the ground.

CONFIDENCE INTERVAL The range, bounded by confidence limits, in which the population parameter is expected to occur at a given probability.

CONFIDENCE LEVEL The probability that the true value for a parameter is included within the confidence interval calculated for a sample parameter.

CONFIGURATION The shape or outline of forest stands or plant communities. The degree of irregularity in the edge between stands or communities, ranging from simple to mosaic. *See also* Edge; Mosaic.

CONFLAGRATION A popular term for a large, fast-moving wildfire exhibiting many or all of the features associated with extreme fire behaviour. *See also* Blow-up; Fire Storm.

CONFLAGRATION THREAT The likelihood that a wildfire capable of causing considerable damage will occur.

CONFLICT RESOLUTION *See* Alternative Dispute Resolution.

CONFLUENT Merging, running into one another.

CONGELIFRACTION *See* Frost-Churning.

CONGELITURBATION *See* Frost-Churning.

CONGENERIC Belonging to the same genus.

CONGESTED In botanical descriptions, tight, closely spaced, crowded. It is the opposite of lax.

CONGLOMERATE Sedimentary rock composed of rounded pieces of rock, such as boulders and pebbles, with finer material, cemented together by calcite, iron oxide, or silica. *See also* Breccia.

CONGLUTINATE Glued together.

CONIDIOPHORE In fungi, a specialized hypha that bears or produces the conidia. *See also* Conidium.

CONIDIUM Plural conidia. The asexual spore of a fungus usually borne exposed at the tip or side of a specialized hypha. *See also* Conidiophore.

CONIFER A wide range of tree species within the order Gymnospermae, typically evergreen, bearing cones, and having needle-shaped or scalelike leaves. Conifer timber is termed softwood. *See also* Broad-Leaved.

CONIFER LEAVES The leaves of conifers are typically needle-shaped, and have distinct characteristics. Some needle clusters are borne on a peg or sterigma (e.g., sessile on a peg, as with *Picea*), petiolate on a peg (*Tsuga*), petiolate without a peg (*Pseudotsuga*). Pegs are located on the leaf side of the abscission layer and stay with the needles following dehiscence. The scale, linear, and subulate leaves of several conifer species are attached to the stem and may extend down it below the point of divergence, yielding a decurrent leaf base. The cluster of needles, called the fascicle (typically one to five needles per cluster), is usually on a short stem located in the axil of the primary leaf. Thus the needles themselves are actually secondary leaves. *See also* Fascicle; Hard Pines; Soft Pines; Sterigma.

CONIFEROUS Cone-bearing plants; pertaining to plant members in the class Gymnospermae.

CONK **1** A large, protruding, firm sporophore of a wood-decaying basidiomycete fungus, usually bracketlike or resupinate in form. Typically found on the external surface of tree trunks, branches, or stumps; a sterile growth that resembles such a sporophore. **2** In the lumber trade, the term conk refers to rot found in manufactured products.

CONNATE United, joined, grown together or attached. In particular, it describes like or similar structures joined into one body or organ, such as sepals in plants. *See also* Adnate.

CONNATE-PERFOLIATE Describes opposite, sessile leaves that are connate by their bases, the axis seemingly passing through the joined bases. *See also* Leaf Shape (for illustration).

CONNECTEDNESS The structural links between habitat patches in a landscape. It can be described from mappable features.

CONNECTIVITY A measure of how well different areas (patches) of a landscape are connected by linkages, such as habitat patches, single or multiple corridors, or 'stepping stones' of like vegetation. The extent to which conditions among late successional/climax forest areas provide habitat for breeding, feeding, dispersal, and movement of late successional- or climax-dependent wildlife and fish species. Natural landscapes often tend to be better connected than those that have been heavily influenced and disturbed by human activities. Consequently, there is a body of opinion that the best way to avoid fragmentation of landscapes is to maintain, or re-establish, a network of landscape linkages. At a landscape level, the connectivity of ecosystem functions and processes is of equal importance to the connectivity of habitats. *See also* Corridor; Forest; Fragmentation.

CONNIVENT Coming in contact or converging, but not fused.

CONSANGUINITY A genetic origin sharing at least one recent common ancestor. Reproduction between such closely related individuals is termed consanguineous.

CONSENSUS A decisionmaking process in which all parties involved explicitly agree on the final decision. Consensus decisionmaking does not mean that all parties are completely satisfied with the final outcome, but that the decision is acceptable to all because no one feels that his or her vital interests or values are violated by it.

CONSERVATION **1** The management or control of human use of resources (biotic and abiotic) and activities on the planet, in an attempt to restore, enhance, protect, and sustain the quality and quantity of a desired mix of species, and ecosystem conditions and processes for present and future generations. **2** The process or means of achieving and maintaining conservation objectives. Conservation is explicitly concerned with the temporal distribution of use; that is, carefully considered use now so that some (more, less, or the same amount) will still exist for use later on. The use in question could be consumptive (harvesting of a resource) or non-consumptive (retention of ecological reserves). There are many varied definitions of conservation in different fields. Most encompass the notion of judicious use by humans over time, which in some instances may mean no use at all or use that serves to enhance, rather than deplete, resources.

CONSERVATION AREA Designated land where conservation strategies are applied for the purpose of attaining specific conservation objectives. These should include cultural and biological aspects.

CONSERVATION BIOLOGY A branch of the biological sciences that studies biodiversity, species abundance, scarcity, and extinction, and the relationships of these to natural processes, habitat conditions, and population changes in response to human-induced disturbances. *See also* Biology.

CONSERVATION STRATEGY A management plan for a species, group of species, or ecosystem that prescribes standards and guidelines that, if implemented, would provide a high likelihood that the species, groups of species, or ecosystem, with its full complement of species and processes, will continue to exist as a viable population within a planning area.

CONSISTENCE An assessment made in the field of the degree to which a soil sample exhibits consistency. This is generally taken to be the soil's resistance to deformation or rupture or, conversely, the degree to which the soil particles exhibit cohesion and adhesion. Terms used to describe consistence are based on soil moisture. **Wet soil** occurs when the soil moisture is at or slightly above field capacity. Its consistence can be defined in terms of (1) stickiness (capability of sticking to other objects) ranging from nonsticky, slightly sticky, sticky, to very sticky and (2) plasticity (capability of being moulded) ranging from nonplastic, slightly plastic, plastic, to very plastic. **Moist soil** occurs when the soil moisture is between field capacity and dryness. Its consistence is defined as loose, very friable, friable, firm, very firm. **Dry soil** occurs when soil is air dry. Its consistence can be defined as loose, soft, slightly hard, hard, very hard, and extremely hard. **Cementation** occurs in some soils when they are cemented and therefore brittle. Cemented soils are tested for consistence in dry and wet (one hour after soaking) conditions and can be defined as weakly cemented, strongly cemented, indurated. In engineering work, soil consistency describes the condition of the soil in place as soft, firm or medium, stiff, very stiff, and hard.

CONSISTENCY In the US under the Federal Land Policy and Management Act, the adherence of Bureau of Land Management resource management plans to the terms, conditions, and decisions of officially approved and adopted resource-related plans or, in their absence, with policies and programs of other federal agencies, state and local governments, and Native tribes, so long as the plans are also consistent with the purposes, policies, and programs of federal laws and regulations applicable to the Bureau of Land Management Lands. Under the Coastal Zone Management Act, the adherence to approved state management programs, to the maximum extent practicable, of federal agency activities affecting the defined coastal zone.

CONSOCION Any layer of vegetation that has patches of dominant species that alternate with each other.

CONSOLIDATION **1** In engineering, the gradual reduction in volume of a soil mass resulting from an increase in compressive stress; involves removal of pore water and a decrease in void ratio. **2** Used to describe the density of surficial materials, especially those that contain silt and clay. A material that is highly consolidated means it has high density and low void ratio.

CONSPECIFIC Belonging to the same species.

CONSTANT **1** An ecosystem or species within that system that maintains a constant density of plants or animals over long periods of time. **2** A quantity or parameter that has a constant value while other variables change.

CONSTANT DANGER The resultant outcome of all fire danger factors that are relatively unchanging in a specific area (e.g., resource values at risk, topography, fuel type, exposure to prevailing wind).

CONSTANT EFFORT MIST-NETTING A capture method, standardized over space and time, used to count the number of birds captured in mist nets.

CONSTRAINT The restriction, limiting, or regulation of an activity, quality, or state of being to a predetermined or prescribed course of action or inaction. Constraints can be a result of policies, political will, management direction, attitudes, and perceptions; or budget, time, personnel, and data availability limitations; or more typically, a complex interaction of all these factors.

CONSTRUCTIONAL In geomorphology, a landform owing its origin, form, position, or general character to depositional (aggradational) processes, such as accumulation of sediments, to form an alluvial fan or terrace.

CONSULTATION Consultation processes are often part of a regular decision-making process, but the locale of the decision remains with the established decisionmaker and the degree to which the decision is influenced is at the discretion of the decisionmaker.

Consultation is the basis of a variety of procedures referred to by such terms as public consultation, public participation, and public involvement. Methods range from public hearings and requests for written submissions to more interactive techniques, such as workshops and advisory committees.

Consultation processes may be conducted by public agencies, developers, or by consultants engaged by such entities.

CONSUMER SURPLUS In economics, the difference between the price that a consumer pays for a good or service and the amount the consumer would be willing to pay rather than be deprived of the good or service. In economic analysis, consumer surplus is a consideration when the output of the project causes the market price of the product to fall. Those consumers previously paying the higher old price (what they were willing to pay), will reap a benefit (consumer surplus) from the lower new price, which must be added to the benefits accruing to the new consumers.

CONSUMPTION The amount of a specified fuel type or strata that is removed through the fire process, often expressed as a percentage of the preburn weight. It includes available fuel plus fuel consumed after the fire front passes.

CONSUMPTIVE USE Use of resources that diminish the available total stock or flow (i.e., consumes it). The term makes no distinction between consumption of renewable or non-renewable resources. *See also* Non-consumptive Use.

CONTACT **1** In wildlife census work, a single field record of an individual by sight or sound. It is also termed detection, cue, registration, or observation. **2** The surfaces that separate a stratigraphic unit from overlying and underlying units; may be sharp or gradational, horizontal or inclined, planar or wavy. *See also* Stratigraphic Unit.

CONTACT HERBICIDE A herbicide designed to kill plant tissue by direct contact, as opposed to being effective only after it has been translocated through the plant. *See also* Herbicide; Systemic Pesticide.

CONTACT INSECTICIDE An insecticide designed to kill insects by direct contact with the cuticle, as opposed to being effective only after it has been ingested. *See also* Insecticide; Systemic Pesticide.

CONTAGIOUS DISEASE The transmission of disease between animals by direct or indirect means.

CONTAINER SEEDLING *See* Seedling.

CONTAINMENT The completion of a control line around a fire and any associated spot fires that can reasonably be expected to stop the fire's spread.

CONTAMINATION The introduction of any foreign, undesirable physical, chemical, or biological substance, often human-made, into the environment.

CONTEXT **1** Generally, the correct usage of a word, term, or phrase (i.e., in its proper context). **2** The inner or body tissue of a fruit body that supports the fruiting surface.

CONTIGUOUS Botanically, plant parts that are touching or in contact, without fusion.

CONTIGUOUS HABITAT Habitat distributed continuously or nearly continuously across the landscape, with boundaries that make contact but do not overlap with other habitats, and is capable of supporting the life needs of species.

CONTINENTAL CLIMATE A climate that is characteristic of the interior of a land mass of continental size, marked by large annual, diurnal and day-to-day ranges of temperature, low relative humidity, and irregular precipitation. *See also* Climate; Maritime Climate.

CONTINUOUS FOREST INVENTORY *See* Inventory.

CONTINUOUS VARIATION Variation among specific phenotypic traits that cannot be seen as clearly distinct classes because the differences are small, thus yielding a range of forms, usually as a bell-shaped distribution curve.

CONTINUUM **1** An abstract concept used to describe the ordering or gradual change of plant and vegetation distributions. Plant species have different environmental requirements. Since these environmental factors vary continuously in time and space, vegetation can be described as a continuous variable. Plant distributions form a continuum of variability, not discrete communities. **2** A gradual change in species composition, or other ecosystem attributes, along an environmental gradient. A relative assessment of continuity through time and space.

CONTOUR FELLING Timber that is felled parallel to the ground contour line, usually to try and reduce breakage and shatter.

CONTOUR LINE The line on a map representing an imaginary line on the ground where the elevation above sea level is the same along its entire length. Contour lines are an abstraction but serve to delineate the shape of the landscape and its relative heights. The distance on the map between contour lines, the **contour interval**, can be used to determine slope steepness. The closer the contour lines, the steeper the slope, and vice versa. The pattern of the contour lines can be used to determine the shape of the land. The scale of the map determines the contour interval.

CONTRAST **1** In photography, the actual difference in density between the highlights and the shadows on a negative or positive. Contrast is not concerned with the magnitude of density, but only with the difference in densities. Contrast also refers to the rating of photographic material corresponding to the relative density difference that it exhibits. **2** *See* Edge Contrast.

CONTRAST STRETCHING A technique used in remote sensing to improve the contrast of images by digital processing. The original range of digital values is expanded to utilize the full contrast range of the recording film or display device.

CONTROL **1** In mapping, a system of points with established positions or elevations, or both, which are used as fixed references in positioning and correlating map features. Three basic forms are recognized. (1) **Basic control** implies both horizontal and vertical control determined in the field and permanently marked or monumented, which is required to control subordinate surveys. (2) **Geodetic control** takes into account the size and shape of the earth. It implies a reference spheroid representing the geoid, horizontal, and vertical control-datums. (3) **Ground control** is established by ground surveys as distinguished from control established by photogrammetric methods. The term control usually implies geodetic control or basic control. **2** In photogrammetry, the control established by photogrammetric methods, as distinguished from control established by ground control. **3** In statistics, the control is part of the experimental design and provides a sample plot, area, or attribute that is as similar as possible to the other experimental units to be treated in some way. The control plots, areas, or attributes are left untreated for later comparison with those that have been treated. In field work, it is sometimes called a checkplot.

CONTROL A FIRE To complete a control line around a fire, any spot fires emanating from it, and any interior island(s) to be saved; burning out any unburned areas adjacent to the fire side of the control lines; burning off any unwanted island(s) inside the control lines; cooling down all hot spots that are immediate threats to the control line until the control lines can be expected to hold under foreseeable conditions. The stages of control are listed. **Out of control** describes a wildfire not responding or only responding on a limited basis to suppression action such that perimeter spread is not being contained. **Being held** indicates that with currently committed resources, sufficient suppression action has been taken that the fire is not likely to spread beyond existent or predetermined boundaries under prevailing and forecasted conditions. It is synonymous with partial control (but this term is not universally recognized). **Being observed** indicates a wildfire currently not receiving suppression action, due to agency resource management objectives and/or priorities. **Under control** indicates a wildfire having received sufficient suppression action to ensure no further spread of the fire. **Being patrolled** indicates a wildfire in a state of mop-up, being walked over and checked. **Out** indicates that the fire has been extinguished.

CONTROLLED MOSAIC *See* Aerial Photograph Mosaic.

CONTROL LINE A comprehensive term for all constructed or natural fire barriers and treated fire perimeters used to control a fire. *See also* Fire Guard; Fire Line.

CONTROL POINT **1** In photogrammetry, any station in a horizontal and vertical control system that is identified on a photograph and used for correlating the date shown on that photograph. The term is usually modified to reflect the type or purpose. **2** In inventory work, a point located by ground survey with which a corresponding point on a photograph is matched as a check for use in the production of photo mosaics.

CONTROL TIME *See* Elapsed Time.

CONVARIETY A group of similar cultivars within a variable species or interspecific hybrid. Archaic usage, the term now replaced by Group. *See also* Group.

CONVECTION **1** In meteorology, vertical atmospheric motion in a predominantly unstable atmosphere, in the absence of wind (contrast to advection), which results in the vertical transport and mixing of atmospheric properties. **2** The transfer of heat by the movement of a gas or liquid. Convection, conduction, and radiation are the three principal means of energy transfer.

CONVECTION COLUMN The definable plume or column of hot gases, smoke, fly ash, firebrands, particulates, and other by-products produced by, and rising above, a fire. The column has a strong vertical component indicating that the buoyant forces override the ambient surface wind. More than one convection column may be present on multiple-headed fires. *See also* Smoke.

CONVECTIVE ACTIVITY A general term describing manifestations of atmospheric convection, particularly the development of convective clouds and their resulting weather phenomena.

CONVECTIVE BURNING *See* Ignition Pattern (centre fire ignition).

CONVECTIVE-LIFT FIRE PHASE The phase of a fire when most emissions are entrained into a definite convection column.

CONVENIENCE SAMPLE The units being sampled are those that are readily available regardless of statistical validity. It is not a good sampling technique. *See also* Sampling.

CONVENOR A person who assembles or brings together a group of people to resolve a conflict by consensus. The convenor usually lays out terms of reference and may look after the basic funding for the process.

CONVERGENCE ZONE The area of increased flame height and fire intensity produced when two or more fire fronts burn together. It is synonymous with junction zone.

CONVERGENCY LINE A line corridor separating two types of landscape elements, thus providing three types (the two adjoining plus the transition zone) in proximity. A transition zone where ecosystem types converge to provide higher than average habitat diversity. *See also* Edge.

CONVERGENCY POINT A location where three or more types of landscape elements intersect. *See also* Edge.

CONVERGENT EVOLUTION The independent origin of similar features in different evolutionary lines due to similar adaptive pressures.

CONVERSION **1** The transformation of roundwood forest products into sawn lumber or other products. Primary conversion involves topping, branch trimming, cutting to initial log lengths, and initial cutting into boards. Secondary conversion is the subsequent resawing, milling, planing, and finishing into final products. **2** The transformation of a forest from one species or type into another.

CONVOLUTE Rolled up or twisted together lengthwise. It typically describes plant organs, such as leaves or petals in the bud.
COORDINATES Linear or angular quantities that designate the position that a point occupies in a given reference frame or system. It is also used as a general term to designate the particular kind of reference frame or system, such as plane rectangular coordinates or spherical coordinates. (1) **Plane rectangular coordinates** are used to describe a position on a horizontal plane with respect to a specific origin by means of two distances perpendicular to each other. The merit of a rectangular coordinate system is that positions of points, distances, and directions on it can be computed by the use of plane trigonometry. (2) **State Plane and Universal Transverse Mercator** (see UTM) **coordinate systems** are plane rectangular systems commonly used to describe locations in a Geographic Information System. (3) **Grid coordinates** describe the position within a plane rectangular coordinate system based on, and mathematically adjusted to, a map projection so that geographic positions in terms of latitude and longitude can be readily transformed into plane rectangular coordinates. (4) **Geographic** and **Geodetic coordinates** describe a position on the Earth in terms of latitude and longitude.
COPPICE As a verb, to reproduce vegetatively from stumps or root suckers. As a noun, the numerous small-diameter stems resulting. Coppicing was widely used in the past as a source of materials for fencing, stakes, poles, firewood, and fodder. In stands actively managed as coppice, the stump is usually called a stool. Typical coppice species include hazel, sweet chestnut, and oak. In some cases, the coppice is intermingled with an overstorey of mature or semi-mature trees (the standards), typically oak, ash, or larch (species not casting a heavy shade) that have been allowed to grow on from the coppice stage, a silvicultural system termed coppice with standards. *See also* Pollarding.
COPROPHAGE An animal that eats the feces of other animals.
CORD A stack of wood measuring 4 feet high, 4 feet deep, and 8 feet long, with a theoretical volume of 128 cubic feet of wood. In practice, the volume of wood in a cord is typically about 60 to 70 cubic feet, the balance being air space. Used for pulpwood or firewood measurement. Note that firewood is sometimes measured in face cords, which are 4 feet high, 8 feet long, but only as deep as the length of the firewood pieces, typically about 16 inches. A face cord is about one-third the volume of a standard cord.
CORDATE Shaped like a heart; often used to describe the base of a plant organ, such as a leaf. *See also* Leaf Shape (for illustration).
CORDUROY ROAD A road supported by numerous logs placed at ninety degrees to the line of the road. It is commonly used as a cheap subgrade in swampy areas.
CORDWOOD Wood that is cut in short lengths, usually measured in cords and used as fuelwood or pulpwood.
CORE **1** The wood remaining after a veneer peeling operation; also termed a spin-out. **2** The central part of a wire rope. **3** The cylindrical piece of wood extracted by an increment borer.
CORE AREA That area of habitat essential in the breeding, nesting, and rearing of young, up to the point of dispersal of the young. An area of land that has vital attributes necessary for the survival of one or more species, or ecosystem functions, and that is considered an essential component of a broader management plan. Core areas are typically designated to be left alone, rather than actively managed. *See also* Biosphere Reserve.
COREMIUM Plural coremia. *See* Synnema.
CORE SHAMANISM Refers to a distillation of the core techniques, ceremonies, rituals, and practices of shamanic journeying and healing. For shamanism, reality has three main levels: (1) the upper world, wherein dwell the ancestor and god spirits; (2) a lower world, wherein dwell animal, tree, and other spirit beings; and (3) a middle world, which is daily life.

It is possible to use shamanic journeying techniques to travel in all of these worlds, as in the middle world one communicates with another shaman hundreds of miles away without the aid of technological devices. One becomes a shaman through initiation and study, as well as through spontaneous visionary experience and accumulation of spiritual power and integration through journeying in the wilderness (vision quests), or in the ceremonial setting with the drum, chanting, and other means. Most primal peoples practice shamanism. Shamanism respects the integrity of each person, and there is no such thing as a centralized doctrine. Each person's stories and experiences are listened to with respect. Remnants of shamanism are found in all major world religions.

CORE TABLE The primary data table in a relational database and that is linked to all other data tables; contains data that is not replicated in any other tables.
CORIACEOUS Having a leathery texture, yet smooth and flexible.
CORK A part of the periderm on the outside of tree trunks and roots, composed of dead cells that are relatively impermeable to water and gases. It protects the inner living tissues against insect and fungal attack, desiccation, and mechanical injury. Often formed in response to wounding. *See also* Bark; Phloem (for illustration).
CORM The solid, swollen part of an underground plant stem, in which food is stored. It is sometimes wrapped in one or more membranous layers. *See also* Bulb.
CORNICLES The dorsal tubular appendage on the abdomen of some aphids, used to secrete wax.
CORNICULATE Bearing or terminating in a small, hornlike protuberance.
CORNUTE Describes an aecia that is hornlike, pointed, with the peridium made up of characteristically marked cells.
COROLLA The inner whorl of floral parts, normally the petals. If these parts are separate, they are petals and the corolla is said to be choripetalous or polypetalous. If the parts are united to some degree, the corolla is said to be gamopetalous or sympetalous, in which case the parts may be seen only as teeth or lobes on the rim of a corolla, cup, or tube, or they may be entirely undifferentiated. Basic corolla shapes shown in the illustration are: rotate, companulate, funnel form, urceolate, salverform, biabiate, ligulate, papilionaceus, and tubular. *See also* Flower.

rotate

campanulate

funnelform

urceolate

salverform

tubular

bilabiate

papilionaceous

ligulate

CORONA In plants, a set of petal-like structures or appendages between the corolla and androecium.
CORRELATION Statistically, the interdependence between quantitative or qualitative data. In particular, the relationship between measurable random variables, where a change in the value of one variable is accompanied by a measurable change in the value of one or more other variables. Correlation values close to 1 mean strong positive association, while values close to −1 mean strong negative association; 0 indicates no association at all.
CORRELATION COEFFICIENT: *R* In statistics, a measure that demonstrates the degree to which two or more variables influence or are associated with each other. Two forms are seen: (1) **simple correlation coefficient**, a measure of the linear relationship between two variables, for bivariate data; and (2) **multiple correlation coefficient**, a measure of the closeness of association between the observed *Y* values, and a function of the independent values used in the model. *See also* Coefficient of Determination.
CORRESPONDENCE ANALYSIS (CA) **1** *See* Detrended Correspondence Analysis. **2** The term reciprocal averaging is used as a synonym for CA. *See also* Ordination.
CORRIDOR **1** A physical linkage, connecting two areas of habitat and differing from the habitat on either side. Corridors are used by organisms to move around without having to leave the preferred habitat. A linear habitat patch through which a species must travel to reach habitat more suitable for reproduction and other life-sustaining needs. Many corridors, linking several patches of habitat, form a network of habitats. The functional effectiveness of corridors depends on the type of species, the type of movement, the strength of the edge effects, and its shape. *See also* Physical Barrier; Filter. **2** An area of uniform width bordering both or one side of a lineal feature, such as a stream or route. **3** In GIS work, **corridor analysis** is the manipulation, measurement, analysis, and output of data within a corridor. **Corridor generation** is a process to automatically outline a corridor along a defined lineal feature.
CORRIDOR SKIDDING A logging procedure using cable yarders in which narrow clearcuts are made through a stand. Cables are strung in these clearcut corridors to transport logs from the woods to the landing. Between corridors, only a portion of the trees in the stand are removed, and these harvested trees are skidded to the corridor.
CORRUGATED MORAINE Terrain crossed by a

series of subparallel, small, regularly spaced morainal ridges that are oriented transverse to the ice movement. Collectively they resemble a washboard.

CORTEX The outer primary tissue of a stem or root between the primary phloem or endodermis and the epidermis, composed mainly of parenchyma cells. In lichens, the cortex consists of fungal hyphae. In mosses and liverworts, the cortex is the outermost layer or layers of cells on the stem. *See also* Bark.

CORTICAL STRANDS The radiating strands of mistletoe tissue that grow through the cortex and secondary phloem of the parasitized tree stem.

CORTICOLOUS Growing on bark.

CORYMB A broad, almost flat-topped indeterminate flower head with the outer flowers opening first. *See also* Inflorescence (for illustration); Umbel.

CORYMBOSE Having flowers in a corymb or similar structure.

COSEWIC An acronym for the Committee on the Status of Endangered Wildlife in Canada. COSEWIC lists and designates plants and animals in Canada according to their relative abundance at a national level. Individual provinces and some regional jurisdictions have their own comparable listings of plants and animals. The six COSEWIC categories are as follows. (1) **Rare** indicates an indigenous species of flora or fauna that, because of its biological characteristics or because it occurs at the fringe of its range, or for some other reasons, exists in low numbers or in very restricted areas in Canada but is not a threatened species. (2) **Extinct** indicates any indigenous species of fauna or flora formerly indigenous to Canada no longer known to exist elsewhere. (3) **Extirpated** indicates any indigenous species of fauna or flora no longer known to exist in the wild in Canada but existing elsewhere. (4) **Endangered** indicates any indigenous species of fauna or flora that is threatened with imminent extirpation or extinction throughout all or a significant portion of its Canadian range. (5) **Threatened** indicates any indigenous species of fauna or flora that is likely to become endangered in Canada if the factors affecting its vulnerability do not become reversed. (6) **Vulnerable** indicates any indigenous species of fauna or flora that is particularly at risk because of low or declining numbers, occurring at the fringe of its range or in restricted areas, or for some other reason, but is not a threatened species.

COSTA **1** Riblike structures, which in plants form the primary veins or midribs of the leaf. Less commonly, the rachis of a pinnately compound leaf. *See also* Moss (for illustration). **2** Less commonly, the rachis of a pinnately compound leaf. *See also* Moss (for illustration). **3** In animals, the costa is a rib, while in insects, the costae are the primary veins on the wings. In certain amphibians, costal grooves form riblike vertical indentations or grooves along the side of the body.

COST-BENEFIT ANALYSIS *See* Benefit-Cost Analysis.

COST EFFECTIVENESS The usefulness of specific inputs (costs) to produce specified outputs (benefits). In measuring cost effectiveness, some outputs, including environmental, economic, or social impacts, are assigned in physical terms. *See also* Technical Efficiency.

COST OF CAPITAL The price of a return on capital. The cost of borrowing financial assets.

COST-REVENUE ANALYSIS An analysis designed to provide information about the government costs incurred in supplying public improvements and services to urban land areas, and relating these costs to the revenues existing or anticipated as a result of these improvements and services.

COSTS **1** Typically, an expression related to the dollar (or equivalent currency) value of what monies need to be invested, or will be lost, if an action is pursued. An important part of assessing costs is the time over which they occur, and to whom they accrue. **2** The negative or adverse effects caused by an activity, policy, or program. Costs can be monetary, social, physical, psychological, or environmental in nature. Many such costs are often hidden or are difficult to evaluate and assess. *See also* Benefits; Intangibles.

COTYLEDONS The first leaves to develop in an embryo. They may or may not emerge from the seed upon germination. Flowering plants and many gymnosperms usually have two cotyledons, but some members of the pine family have as many as seventeen. Plants with two cotyledons are termed dicotyledonous, while those typically having one cotyledon are monocotyledonous. *See also* Germination (for illustration).

COTYPE *See* Type.

COUNCIL OF ALL BEINGS A process-oriented program that invites participants to engage in imaginative and other cognitive and affective sharing with other beings beyond the human realm. It involves facilitating removal of self-imposed blocks to our feelings and acknowledgment of the pain associated with the environmental crisis, such as self-deception, denial, repressed grief, and so on. Adoption of the concepts promoted are believed to permit human beings to 'think like a mountain' and 'feel as a tree.'

COUNT **1** As a noun, the act or process of enumerating, or the number or sum total obtained by counting. **2** As a verb, to record the number of individuals or groups present in a population or population sample. *See also* Census; Index.

COUNTER FIRE A type of suppression fire. Emergency firing to try to stop, delay, or split a fire front, or to steer a fire. *See also* Burning Out.

COUPLETS A pair of sedimentary layers in lake deposits that represent related deposits. In the case of charcoal and ash deposits in a sediment core, the couplets represent the settling out of heavier particles before the finer particles from a single fire event.

COUPLING A device that connects the ends of adjacent hoses or other components of a hose lay.

COURSE **1** The intended direction of an aircraft in horizontal flight. **2** The path or flow of water. **3** Describing a rough texture of a surface or structure of a substance, such as soil particles.

COVARIANCE In statistics, the measure of how two variables change in relation to each other. If larger values of Y tend to be associated with larger values of X, then covariance will be positive. If larger values of Y tend to be associated with smaller values of X, the covariance will be negative. A covariance matrix is a table of paired covariance values for the variables in the data set.

COVE A sheltered bay lying between two headlands or valley sides.

COVER **1** Vegetation used by wildlife as protection from predators, or to mitigate weather conditions, or to reproduce (e.g., thermal and hiding cover). Also refers to the protection of the soil and the shading provided to herbs and forbs by vegetation. **2** In aquatic ecology, the plants, rocks, and other materials (including organic debris) used by fish for shelter from adverse conditions and predation, feeding, or resting. Cover can be instream or overhead. *See also* Hiding Cover. **3** The vertical projection of the crown or shoot area of a species to the ground surface, expressed as a fraction or per cent of a stand.

COVERAGE In remote sensing and mapping, the area covered by aerial photographs or maps. **Stereoscopic coverage** is possible when the area is covered by aerial photographs with sufficient overlap for any point to appear on at least two photographs in a manner suitable for stereoscopic viewing.

COVER CROP **1** Generally, a natural or planted crop used to protect the land from erosion. **2** A subsidiary crop of low plants introduced in the earlier stages of a timber plantation to protect the forest floor and help to suppress weeds.

COVER-FORAGE AREA RATIO The ratio, in per cent, of the amount of area in forage condition to that area in cover condition. It is the usual criterion by which potential use of an area by deer and elk is judged.

COVERT **1** *See* Convergency Line. **2** In wildlife management, an area of vegetation, typically limited in extent such as a thicket, that provides natural shelter and perhaps some food supply for wildlife.

CRAB **1** A crustacean. **2** In remote sensing, any turning of an airplane, usually in a crosswind, which causes its longitudinal axis to vary from the track of the airplane. It is also the condition caused by failure to orient the camera with respect to the track of the airplane as indicated in vertical photography by the edges of the photographs not being parallel to the air base lines.

CRACK A split in the stem of a tree, involving the bark, cambium, and xylem. It may be horizontal or vertical. Depending on the species, location, and magnitude of the crack, it may be important in assessing a tree for hazard. *See also* Growth Crack.

CRAG AND TAIL A streamlined hill consisting of a knob of resistant bedrock (the crag) and a elongate tail of drift, usually till, pointing in the direction of glacier flow.

CRANIAL BREADTH The greatest width of the brain case.

CRAWLER The active crawling stage of an immature stage of an adelgid or scale insect.

CREEP The imperceptibly slow, more or less continuous downhill movement of soil or rock on slopes. The movement is essentially a flow of a highly viscous medium under shear stresses sufficient to produce deformation but too small to produce shear failure, as in a landslide. *See also* Flow; Slide; Slump.

CREEPING A plant that is trailing along on top of or under the ground, and rooting at intervals.

CREEPING FIRE *See* Fire Behaviour.

CREMOCARP A dry, two-seeded fruit of the Umbelliferae, separating at maturity into two mericarps borne on hairlike carpophores. A schizocarp.

CRENATE Botanically, having shallow, rounded to blunt teeth, or scalloped. *See also* Leaf Margin.

CRENULATE Having small crenations. *See also* Leaf Margin.

CREPUSCULAR Any organism whose most active period is at dawn or at dusk. *See also* Diurnal; Nocturnal.

CREST The typically linear top of a ridge, hill, mountain, or other landform.

CRESTED Having an elevated and irregular or toothed ridge or ridges.

CREVASSE A fissure formed in the brittle, upper part of a glacier or ice sheet due to glacier flow.

CRIB A pen or stack of short logs assembled in cabin style. The crib is often filled with rocks to serve as a pier to support certain types of bridges.

CRISPATE Describes leaves or hairs that are curled, ruffled, or irregularly twisted on the margin. *See also* Leaf Margin.

CRITERIA **1** A set of predetermined rules, measurements, quality levels, or thresholds for ranking alternatives in order of desirability to facilitate and expedite the decisionmaking process. **2** A scientifically based threshold value upon which a defensible judgment can be made concerning the suitability of a resource to meet required uses. Note that criteria, unlike standards, are resource quality levels that have been determined by the accumulation of scientific data showing the relationship between levels of quality and damage to the resource. Criteria should be capable of quantitative evaluation and be acceptable analytical procedures. They should also be capable of definitive resolution (i.e., their controlling relationship to acceptable quality levels should not be clouded by possible synergisms, antagonisms, or other effects).

CRITICAL BURNOUT TIME The total time a fire can burn and continue to feed energy to the base of a forward-travelling convection column.

CRITICAL HABITAT In conservation biology, part or all of an ecosystem occupied by wildlife species, or a population of such species, that is recognized as essential for the maintenance and long-term survival of the population. In the US, critical habitat is defined under the Endangered Species Act as: (1) the specific areas within which the geographic area occupied by a federally listed species on which are found physical and biological features essential to the conservation of the species, and that may require special management considerations or protection; and (2) specific areas outside the geographic area occupied by a listed species, when it is determined that such areas are essential for the conservation of the species.

CRITICAL LINKAGES Geographic areas between definable physiographic provinces, representing the most likely avenues of dispersal for a species, provided that the habitat conditions are conducive for such movement. *See also* Corridor.

CRITICAL PATH METHOD (CPM) The Critical Path Method and the Program Evaluation and Review Technique (PERT) are both network analysis models. Each has its own modelling language, but they differ in only one fundamental respect. CPM seeks to determine the expected times of completion of the total project and times of completion of the subprojects of which it is composed. PERT goes further and seeks to estimate variances associated with these expected times of completion.

CRITICAL WINTER RANGE Any habitat, usually composed of stands of shrubs, windswept open grasslands, or mature or old-growth conifers, that provides the resources essential for the survival of any or a given animal species during severe winters.

CROCHETS **1** A locomotory hook on the foot of the prolegs of lepidopterous larvae. **2** A balancer in larval salamanders.

CROOK **1** A short length of naturally curved timber. **2** A defect in trees and logs consisting of an abrupt bend. May be a result of insect-induced topkill and subsequent recovery by a lateral branch. *See also* Shepherd's Crook.

CROP TREE Any tree selected to become, or forming a component of, the final crop in a stand.

CROSS-BEARINGS The intersecting lines of sight from two or more points on the same object. They are used to determine the location of a wildfire from a lookout. It is also termed cross-shots. *See also* Bearing.

CROSSBEDDING The arrangement of sets of inclined beds or laminations between the main horizontal plains of stratification of a deposit; present in fluvial sands and gravels and aeolian sands.

CROSS-DATING A dendrochronological technique used to compare annual ring sequences in ancient pieces of timber with those of more recent pieces in order to produce a chronological pattern extending back into ancient times that can permit more exact dating estimates.

CROSS-DITCH A shallow channel laid diagonally across the surface of a road so as to lead water off the road and prevent soil erosion. It is also termed a water bar.

CROSSHAULING The technique of loading logs onto a vehicle by rolling them up a ramp by means of cables or chains, one end of which is made fast to the vehicle and the other passed under and round the log(s) to a winch or other source of traction. The space cleared for the operation is termed the crosshaul. It is also termed parbuckling.

CROSSING OVER The physical breakage and reunion of parts of homologous chromosomes during meiosis, in which non-sister chromatids are exchanged, thus producing recombination and genetically different cells.

CROSSING-THE-LEAD Felling timber across rough terrain or across other felled timber. It is a major cause of breakage in large timber.

CROSS-POLLINATION In angiosperms, the transportation of pollen from the stamens of one plant to the stigmas of a flower in another plant. In gymnosperms, the transportation of pollen from a pollen cone (male) to a seed cone (female).

CROSS-PROTECTION Where one pathogen is antagonistic to another pathogen in the same host tissue.

CROSS-SECTION **1** In graphics usage, a two-dimensional pictorial representation method that shows the characteristics and relationships between land (or water) characteristics that would be observed in a vertical slice through that portion of the earth. **2** In land-use planning, cross-sections frequently only show land surface conditions (soil, soil moisture, vegetation type distributions, elevations, slope steepness, etc.), though they may also be used to illustrate subsurface geological structures, groundwater relationships, etc.

The vertical scale of projection is frequently exaggerated in relation to the horizontal to emphasize topographic relationships (e.g., while the scale of horizontal projection may be 1 centimetre in 10 metres, the vertical projection scale may be 1 centimetre in 1 metre). Thus slopes will appear steeper and elevation changes more rapid than they truly are.

This graphical method is frequently used to analyze or show the impacts that would result from potential land uses or use practices on an area by superimposing over the natural profile the changes in land surface (and/or subsurface) conditions. *See also* Profile View.

CROSS-SUPPORT A lateral line used to provide intermediate support for a multispan skyline. It is also termed the support line or jack line.

CROTCH The point (or angle) at which two branches, or branch and leader, or trunks meet. A very narrow crotch impedes normal bark and cambium development and creates a structural weakness, subject to splitting. *See also* Included Bark.

CROWN **1** The upper part of a tree or other woody plant that carries the main system of branches and the foliage. **2** The raised, usually curved surface of a road in cross-section. The centre part of the road is higher and slopes off to the edges by about 4 per cent to permit free drainage of water into the ditches.

CROWN AREA The area covered by the vertical projection of a tree crown to a horizontal plane. Crown area may be determined in the field from crown-diameter measurements, or from aerial photographs by dot grids or digitizers.

CROWN CLASS Refers to groups of trees in a forest with crowns of similar development and occupying a similar position in the canopy. Crown classes are generally defined as follows. **Open crown** defines trees with crowns receiving full light from all sides due to the openness of the canopy. **Dominant** defines trees with crowns extending above the general level of the main canopy of even-aged groups of trees, receiving full light from above and partial light from the sides. **Codominant** defines trees with crowns forming the general level of the main canopy in even-aged groups of trees, receiving full light from above and comparatively little from the sides. **Intermediate** defines trees with crowns extending into the lower portion of the main canopy of even-aged groups of trees, but shorter in height than the codominants. These receive little direct light from above and none from the sides, and usually have small crowns that are crowded on the sides. **Suppressed** or **over-topped** define trees with crowns entirely below the general level of the canopy of even-aged groups of trees, receiving no direct light either from above or from the sides.

CROWN CLEAN PRUNING A pruning that removes all the dead, dying, diseased, rubbing, and structurally unsound branches from within the crown area.

CROWN CLOSURE **1** That point in stand development when all the available crown space has been occupied with live foliage. **2** An assessment of the degree to which the crowns of trees are nearing general contact with one another. The percentage of the ground surface that would be covered by a downward vertical projection of foliage in the crowns of trees.
CROWN CLOSURE CLASS The assessment of the proportion of the ground covered by the canopy foliage overhead (when projected vertically downwards).
CROWN DENSITY The amount, compactness, or depth of foliage of the crowns of trees and/or shrubs.
CROWN DIAMETER The horizontal distance between two extremities of the crown on opposite sides of the tree. Crown diameter is often an average of two measurements (maximum and minimum), and can be measured on aerial photographs or in the field.
CROWN FIRE *See* Forest Fire.
CROWN FUELS *See* Aerial Fuels.
CROWN GALL A pronounced, but localized, tumourlike swelling, which usually occurs on roots or the root crown (root collar). It is caused by the action of pathogenic bacteria. *See also* Gall.
CROWNING *See* Fire Behaviour.
CROWN LAND In Canada, any land deemed to be the property of the Crown. Federal Crown land includes lands in the Northwest Territories including the Arctic Archipelago and the islands in Hudson Strait, Hudson Bay, and James Bay; lands in the Yukon Territory, ordnance and admiralty lands, national parks and national historic parks and sites, forest experiment stations, experimental farms, Indian reserves and, in general, all public lands held by the several departments of the federal government for various purposes connected with federal administration. Provincial Crown land is any land owned and under the administration of a provincial government, which can include municipal lands.

In the United States, the rough equivalent is federal or state land.
CROWN LENGTH The vertical distance from the top of a standing tree to the base of the crown, measured either to the lowest live branch-whorl or to the lowest live branch.
CROWN OUT *See* Forest Fire.
CROWN RAISE PRUNING A pruning technique where the lower branches are removed, thus raising the overall height of the crown from the ground.
CROWN REDUCTION PRUNING Removal of large branches and/or cutting back to large laterals to reduce the height or width of the crown. It is often called 'drop crotch pruning' or 'natural pruning.'
CROWN RESTRUCTURE PRUNING The restoration of natural and/or structurally sound form to a tree that has been previously topped or damaged. It is also called crown restoration.
CROWN SCORCH The browning of needles or leaves in the crown of a tree or shrub caused by the heat rising above a surface fire as a result of convection.
CROWN THINNING *See* Thinning.
CRUCIFORM Cross-shaped.
CRUDE BIRTH RATE The annual number of live individuals born per thousand persons within a predetermined population and area, in the middle of the year.
CRUDE DEATH RATE The annual number of individuals dying per thousand persons within a predetermined population and area, in the middle of the year.
CRUDE DENSITY The population of animals or biomass of plants counted per unit area regardless of what the area contains (good or bad habitat, roads, buildings etc.).
CRUISE **1** The systematic measurement of a forested area designed to estimate, to a specified degree of accuracy, the volume of timber it contains, by evaluating the number and species of trees, their sizes, and conditions. Cruise data can also include an assessment of habitat conditions, environmentally sensitive areas, and a tally of important features that have to be considered in an integrated resource management plan. **2** A quantified sample that determines the quality and quantity of timber to be sold, as well as providing information regarding stand productivity for estimating stumpage value, and data for management, protection, and silvicultural decisions.
CRUISE LINE A line of travel along which data are recorded, either continuously or at predetermined intervals. *See also* Cruise Strip; Line Plot Cruise; Point Transect; Quadrat; Strip Transect Method; Transect.
CRUISE STRIP A long, narrow plot of specified width along which the recording of data is continuous.
CRUISING RADIUS The distance travelled in one day by an animal searching for food and cover.

CRUSTACEOUS Having a hard, brittle texture.

CRUSTOSE A growth form of lichens, where the thalli grow in intimate contact with the substrate and lack a lower cortex. *See also* Foliose; Fruticose.

CRYOPLANATION The reduction of land surfaces by processes associated with frost action.

CRYOTURBATION Heaving, churning, and sorting of soil and surficial materials due to repeated freezing and thawing; results in the development of convoluted and flamelike structures in the soil and in patterned ground, such as stone stripes and sorted polygons.

CRYPTIC COLORATION The protective coloration or pattern that conceals or camouflages an animal or insect. It is also termed apatetic coloration.

CRYPTIC SPECIES Describes animals that live in holes in trees or rocks and are usually hidden from view, or small inconspicuous plants that grow in generally unseen places.

CRYPTOGAM A plant reproducing by spores instead of seeds (e.g., ferns, mosses, algae, and fungi). *See also* Phanerogam.

CUBICAL CRACKING The characteristic of wood in an advanced stage of brown rot, where the decayed wood breaks up into distinct cubes.

CUCULLATE Hooded or hood-shaped, with a slit on one side.

CUESTA An asymmetric, homoclinal ridge, capped by resistant rock layers of slight to moderate dip (less than 10 degrees, or 16 per cent), produced by differential erosion of interbedded resistant and weak rocks. A long, gently sloping to sloping face, roughly parallel to the inclined beds, and opposing the relatively short and steep scarp or face cut across the tilted rocks. *See also* Hogback; Mesa.

CULL **1** All or part of a tree that, due to defect, is considered to be unmerchantable. **2** To reject all or part of a log, or to weed out seedlings or animals considered to be of substandard or marginal quality.

CULL FACTOR An estimate of the percentage of a standing tree's gross volume rendered unmerchantable by defects.

CULM The stem of grasses, sedges, and bamboos, usually hollow except at swollen nodes. *See also* Grass (for illustration).

CULMINATION AGE The age at which the mean annual increment of a stand reaches its maximum. This age is generally used as the rotation age if the management objective for the stand is maximization of wood volume. *See also* Pathologenic Rotation Age.

CULTIGEN A plant or plant group known only in cultivation, and which presumably originated under domestication. For example, the pumpkin (*Cucurbita maxima*) and corn (*Zea mays*) are considered to be cultigens. A term not synonymous with 'cultivar.'

CULTIVAR An acronym for cultivated variety. A genetically distinct plant variety, selected and propagated because it has significant horticultural, agricultural, or silvicultural characteristics. *See also* Variety.

CULTIVATION The practice of growing and nurturing plants outside of their wild habitat (i.e., in gardens, nurseries, arboreta).

CULTURAL CHANGE The modification of an established culture by innovation, invention, discovery, or by the introduction of these through contact with other cultures.

CULTURAL DIVERSITY The variety and variability of human social structures, belief systems, and strategies for adapting to biological situations and changes in different parts of the world.

CULTURAL LANDSCAPE The use and physical appearance of the land as it is seen today, resulting from modifications caused by human activity over time. *See also* Landscape.

CULTURAL LEGACIES The results of past planned or unplanned human activities that form, enhance, or destroy a culture. In the natural resource management context, the health, stability, and likely sustainability of whole societies or individual communities that are determined by the manner in which natural resources have been exploited in the past or are being exploited in the present.

CULTURALLY MODIFIED TREE A tree bearing the marks of traditional human uses; abbreviated as CMT.

CULTURE **1** A laboratory-produced association of organisms, typically growing on an artificial medium and under controlled conditions. Usually, but not always, of one species or strain, especially fungi or bacteria. **2** A complex body or assemblage of human beliefs, art, morals, customs, religion, and laws, which has evolved historically and is handed down through the generations as a force that determines the behaviour and standard social characteristics of a society.

CULVERT A corrugated steel or plastic pipe used to convey water under a road (see illustration). The pipes are joined together with couplers. Larger culvert structures (greater than 1.8 metres or 6 feet in diameter) are made with multiple plates that are assembled in the field by bolting them together to make the required shape and length.

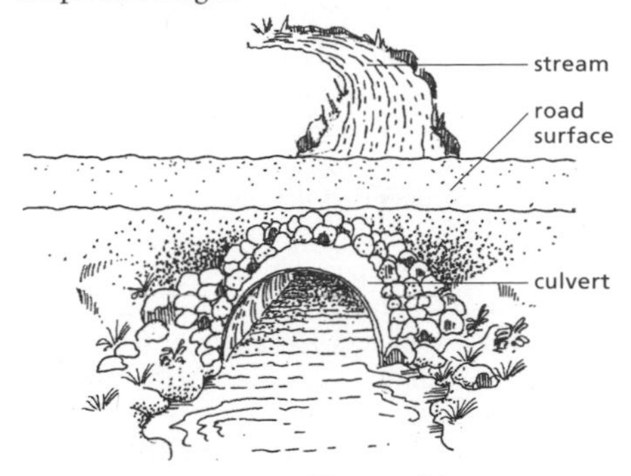

CUMULATIVE EFFECTS The resulting outcomes of many different effects (positive or negative) acting together additively, antagonistically, or synergistically. Effects may be large or small, long or short term, widespread or isolated in occurrence, known or unknown, and may or may not have been anticipated. While cumulative effects may develop without prior consideration, they are also an important outcome of integrated planning, in which many different activities are planned and implemented in order to achieve management goals and objectives. The geographical boundaries and time frames used in analyzing cumulative effects may influence the predicted outcomes.

CUMULATIVE RELATIVE FREQUENCY *See* Empirical Distribution Function.

CUMULATIVE SEVERITY INDEX (CSI) *See* Keetch-Byram Drought Index.

CUMULATIVE USE The sum of individual resource demands over time. The term does not encompass rate of use. *See also* Rate of Use.

CUMULONIMBUS CLOUD The ultimate growth of a cumulus cloud into an anvil-shaped cloud with considerable vertical development, usually with fibrous ice crystal tops, and usually accompanied by lightning, thunder, hail, and strong winds. *See also* Cloud.

CUMULUS CLOUD A principal low-cloud type in the form of individual cauliflower-like cells of sharp nonfibrous outline and less vertical development than cumulonimbus clouds. *See also* Cloud.

CUNEATE Wedge-shaped, triangular, with the narrow end of the triangle at the point of attachment (e.g., some leaves or petals). *See also* Leaf Shape (for illustration).

CUNIT A pulpwood measurement term; one cunit equals one hundred cubic feet of solid wood.

CUPOLA *See* Lookout Cupola.

CUPULE A small cuplike structure, often seen at the base of some fruits, formed by coalescent bracts (e.g., the cup of an acorn) or by dry, enlarged floral envelopes (e.g., in some palms). Some plant and spore shapes resemble the cupule and are termed cupuliform or cupulate.

CURB WEIGHT The weight of an empty truck (no payload or driver), ready to drive, including a full fuel tank, cooling system, crankcase, tools, spare wheel, and all other equipment specified as standard. *See also* Gross Vehicle Weight.

CURRENT ANNUAL INCREMENT The growth increment added in the past year, or in the past few years, in which case, it would be a periodic annual increment. *See also* Mean Annual Increment.

CUSHION PLANT A plant that forms a low-growing mat of vegetation that hugs the ground. Individual plants spread vegetatively at the outer edge of the mat, sometimes rooting at nodes or branch tips.

CUSP An abrupt, sharp, rigid point.

CUSPIDATE Botanically, a shape that terminates in an abrupt, sharp point or cusp, with the sides concave as they approach the tip. *See also* Leaf Shape (for illustration).

CUTANEOUS Pertaining to the skin.

CUTBLOCK An area defined on the ground and planned for harvest, usually in one season.

CUTICLE **1** The non-cellular outer layer of the body wall of an insect or other arthropod, usually made up of three layers: the epicuticle, exocuticle, and endocuticle. **2** A thin, continuous waxy layer on the surface of leaves that helps to prevent desiccation. *See also* Palisade Layer (for illustration).

CUTOVER An area of forest land from which some or all of the timber has been recently cut.

CUTTING CYCLE **1** The planned interval between selective cuts in an uneven-aged stand. **2** In a multi-pass logging system, the interval between passes, also called the 'green-up' period. *See also* Green-up Period.

CUTTINGS In plant propagation, young shoots or stems removed for the purpose of growing new plants by vegetatively rooting the cuttings.

CYANOBACTERIA A group of organisms related to the true bacteria and belonging in the kingdom Monera. It is also called Cyanophyta or the blue-green algae.

CYBERNETICS The study of information systems, how they are organized, how they work, and how to construct artificial ones with the aim of controlling natural and other systems through the information flow, both content and form. When people talk about the cybernetic revolution, they usually have in mind the introduction of computer systems and 'information highways.' The term was originally introduced by Norbert Wiener.

CYCAD A member of the Cycadophyta. A gymnosperm bearing palmlike or fernlike leaves, naked seeds in cones (gynostrobili), and found only in tropical or subtropical regions. They are dioecious and date back to the Mesozoic period. Less than thirty cycad species still exist on the planet and, of these, almost half are found in Australia.

CYCLIC **1** Occurring in well-defined cycles. **2** Botanically, plant parts or organs arranged in whorls or circles.

CYME A broad, almost flat-topped, determinate inflorescence, with the inner flowers opening first. *See also* Inflorescence (for illustration).

CYMOSE Bearing flowers in cymes, or arranged in or similar in structure to a cyme.

CYPHELLA A recessed pore.

CYSTOLITH A microscopic mineral concretion, usually of calcium carbonate, occurring in some cells of leaves or other organs in certain groups of plants.

CYTOKININ Any of a group of plant hormones related to zeatin that promote cell division.

CYTOLOGY The study of cells, their structure, function, reproduction, and development.

CYTOPLASM The living contents of a cell, other than the nucleus.

CYTOTYPE Any variety of a species having a chromosome complement that is different, quantitatively or qualitatively, from the standard complement of that species.

D

DAILY ACTIVITY LEVEL In the US National Fire Danger Rating System, the daily activity level is a subjective estimate of the degree of activity of a potential human-caused fire source relative to that which is normally experienced. Five activity levels are defined as none, low, normal, high, and extreme.

DAMAGE The temporary or permanent ecological and physical effects of pests, diseases, or other biotic or abiotic factors on forest growth, structure, and productivity. The temporary or permanent reduction or impairment in the financial, aesthetic, or ecological value of forest trees, or other biotic or abiotic attributes and functions of a forested landscape.

DAMAGE APPRAISAL **1** In pest management, an estimation of the amount and severity of damage caused by a particular pest or disease, typically expressed in terms of lost timber volumes or the dollars that these represent. More generally, an estimation of the amount and severity of damage caused by any factor, and some sense of what the costs of clean-up might be, plus the lost revenues, plus the costs to restore the attribute(s) damaged to their pre-damaged state, and the time necessary to accomplish these aspects. **2** A method of determining financial or other losses resulting from a wildfire. *See also* Fire Damage.

DAMPING-OFF The decay of seeds in the soil, or the collapse and death of young seedlings, often due to fungal infection at or below the soil line. Different fungi cause pre- or post-emergent damping-off.

DANGER CLASS *See* Fire Danger Class.

DANGER INDEX *See* Fire Danger Index.

DANGER TREE In assessing wildlife trees for possible retention, a live or dead tree whose trunk, root system, or branches have deteriorated or have been damaged so as to be a potential danger to forest workers in the vicinity of the tree. *See also* Hazard Tree.

DATA A collection of raw facts and figures that can be processed into information. Each datum can be precisely defined. Three types of data are common: (1) **agreeable data**, that is, data derived from two or more mutually exclusive data sets, using the same standards and definitions, for the purposes of combining the data sets into one new data set; (2) **comparable data**, where there are two or more data sets using the same standards and definitions for purposes of comparison; (3) **universal data**, which are data that are basic to many uses and from which many other types of information can be derived.

DATABASE A collection of data stored in a systematic manner, such that information can be readily retrieved. Most databases are now computerized, and consist of fields and records. One complete record contains all the information entered for datum point. Each aspect of the data collected can be stored in separate fields, which can then be linked together to allow complex search-and-compare routines (e.g., tree height, diameter, species, and age might comprise four fields in any one record). The number of fields and the manner in which they are cross-linked defines the structure of the database. Fields can contain letters (characters) or numbers or both. To make the database more powerful, the records are often structured into sets, so that various attributes are clearly related; this is termed a relational database.

DATA COMPRESSION A computer process that reduces the amount of memory required by computer files, regardless of content. Compressed files are typically said to be archived (or in archival format) and need to be uncompressed (unarchived) before they can be used again.

DATUM **1** Any numerical or geometrical quantity or set of such quantities that may serve as a reference or base for other quantities. **2** In geodesy, a geodetic datum is uniquely defined by five quantities: latitude, longitude, and geoid height are defined at the datum origin. The adoption of specific values for the geodetic latitude and longitude implies specific deflections of the vertical at the origin. A geodetic azimuth is often cited as a datum parameter, but the azimuth and longitude are precisely related by the laplace condition, so there is no need to define both. The other two quantities define the reference ellipsoid: the semi-major axis, and flattening of the semi-major axis and semi-minor axis. **3** In levelling work, the datum is a level surface to which elevations are referred, usually, mean sea level, but may also include mean low water, mean lower low water, or an arbitrary starting elevation(s).

DAUBENMIRE COVER SCALE Named for Professor Rexford Daubenmire. A simple system for estimating the quantities (cover) of plant species in a stand, based on a scale of 1 to 6, where: *6* represents species with a range of 95-100 per cent cover in the stand; *5* represents species with a range of 75-95 per cent cover in the stand; *4* represents species with a range of 50-75 per cent cover in the stand; *3* represents species with a range of 25-50 per cent cover in the stand; *2* represents species with a range of 5-25 per cent cover in the stand; *1* represents species with a range of 0-5 per cent cover in the stand.

DBH An abbreviation for diameter at breast height. The international metric standard is 1.3 metres above ground (above the point of germination in Canada). In the United States, DBH is measured at 1.4 metres (4.5 feet) above ground, or on the uphill side for sloping ground. Diameter is measured overbark, or underbark, depending on the degree of accuracy required and custom. *See also* Bark Allowance.

DDT A synthetic insecticide introduced after the Second World War that has gained widespread notoriety. DDT (dichlorodiphenyltrichloroethane) is an organochlorine that is very persistent and bioaccumulates. Its use in North America is now banned, but it is still used in other parts of the world, primarily for mosquito control.

DEAD FUELS Fuels with no living tissue in which moisture content is governed almost entirely by atmospheric moisture (relative humidity and precipitation), dry-bulb temperature, and solar radiation. *See also* Living Fuels.

DEADHEADS Logs that are floating in a channel, lake, or ocean, with most of the log submerged or just at the surface. A hazard to boat traffic. *See also* Floaters; Large Organic Debris.

DEADMAN *See* Anchor Log.

DEADMAN'S CURVE The in-flight condition, as depicted on a height velocity curve, in which a helicopter does not maintain the speed or altitude required to make a safe autorotation in the event of an engine malfunction or failure.

DEATH (MORTALITY) RATE **1** The ratio of the number of deaths to the total number of individuals in a specific population during one year. For humans, it is expressed as deaths per thousand persons per year. **2** The percentage of a population dying in any one year. *See also* Birth Rate.

DEBARKER *See* Harvesting Machine Classification.

DEBARKING **1** An injury to trees caused by falling timber or extraction, or bark-stripping by animals (e.g., bears, porcupines, deer, rodents). Extreme debarking may lead to girdling and death of the tree, while less extreme damage makes the tree potentially susceptible to frost or fungal injury. **2** The deliberate loosening or removal of bark by humans for a planned use of the bark or the exposed tree surface. **3** The removal of bark from trees that are infested with bark beetles in order to expose and thus kill the developing beetle broods. Also, to remove the infested bark and prevent further spread of the pest when the logs are being transported. *See also* Harvest Functions.

DEBRIS Organic or inorganic materials scattered about or accumulated by either natural processes or human influences.

DEBRIS AVALANCHE Rapid downslope movement on steep slopes of saturated soil and/or surficial material, commonly including vegetative debris; a very rapid to extremely rapid debris flow.

DEBRIS FALL Descent of a mass of soil and/or surficial material by falling, bouncing, and rolling.

DEBRIS FLOW Rapid flow of a slurry of saturated debris, including some or all of soil, surficial material, weathered rock, mud, boulders, and vegetative debris. A general designation for all types of rapid downslope flow, including mudflows, rapid earthflows, and debris torrents.

DEBRIS FLOW TRACKS The paths followed by debris flows; marked by features such as levees, gullies, lack of vegetation or immature vegetation, and debris flow deposits.

DEBRIS LOADING The quantity of debris located within a specific reach of stream channel, due to natural processes or human activity.

DEBRIS SLIDE Downslope sliding of a mass of soil or surficial material; initial displacement is along one or several surfaces of rupture (shear planes); debris may continue to slide downslope over the ground surface, or movement may be transformed into a debris flow.

DEBRIS TORRENT Sudden and rapid fluid-like movement of inorganic and/or organic surficial materials that are supersaturated with water. Debris torrents leave long, linear tracks, scoured clean of all vegetation and loose materials in the main transport zone. As the slope gradient decreases, vast amounts of material are deposited. Rates of movement can be very high (often several metres per second) and damage can be extensive. They occur naturally or as a result of human activity.

DEBT SWAPS A mechanism used to purchase part of the external debt of a nation at a discount, and then sell it back to the government in local currency, with the proceeds being used for conservation purposes.

DECADENT A term used to describe trees or a stand of trees, usually in a pejorative sense, that are deteriorating due to age. Normally used in the context of timber management. Note that decadence does not necessarily equate to overmaturity, since some very old and technically overmature trees are still quite sound. From a wildlife and habitat creation perspective, decadence offers many advantages, such as cavity nest sites, roosting and perching opportunities, and the creation of microhabitats for smaller organisms. *See also* Overmature.

DECAY **1** The disintegration of plant tissue. *See also* Necrosis. **2** The process by which sound wood is decomposed by the action of wood-destroying fungi and other microorganisms, resulting in softening, progressive loss of strength and weight, and often changes in texture and colour. **Incipient decay** refers to the early invasive stages of decay. **Final decay** refers to the more advanced terminal stages where wood structure is almost completely broken down. The terms decay and rot are used interchangeably, although rot generally implies a more advanced and obvious stage. As it is often used to designate both causal organism and its effect, rot is the key term for specifying types of decay (e.g., dry rot, soft rot). *See also* Advanced Decay; Incipient Decay; Intermediate Decay; Rot.

DECIDUOUS Plants whose leaves or flower petals are not persistent and fall off at the end of a defined growing season or during a period of temperature or moisture stress. It typically refers to leaves on broad-leaved trees, but some conifers are also deciduous (e.g., larch).

DECIMATING FACTOR Any factor located in the centrum of an animal that can kill directly, such as a predator, disease, or hazard.

DECISION ANALYSIS MODEL An organized system that policy-makers and managers can use to select a course of action; often, but not necessarily, a formal model.

DECISION SUPPORT SYSTEM A set of decision-making rules built into computer models to assist the computer as it resolves complex problems. These rules tell the computer when to accept or reject data and options, and how to proceed as the changes are made.

DECK A pile of logs between the stump and the landing. If the logs are left for any length of time, it is termed a cold deck. If the logs are piled for immediate haulage onto the landing or beyond, it is called a hot deck.

DECLINATE/DECLINED Bent downward or forward. *See also* Recurved; Reflexed

DECLINATION *See* Magnetic Declination.

DECLINE The gradual reduction in health and vigour as a tree is in the process of dying slowly.

DECLIVITY Describes the truncated or scooped-out termination of the wing covers (elytra) of bark beetles. These features play an important role in bark beetle identification.

DECOMMISSION The planned removal of parts of a road in order to stabilize it while not in use, and prevent, reroute, or stabilize any surface drainage that could pose slope stability or siltation problems. In the US, the term 'hydrologic obliteration' is also used.

DECOMPOSER An organism that utilizes dead plant or animal material for nutrients and energy and, in the process, breaks them down both physically and chemically into simpler organic molecules. The process leads to the recycling of organic and inorganic materials in the ecosystem. Decomposers include earthworms, mushrooms and other fungi, and bacteria.

DECOMPOSITION The breakdown of complex organic materials into simpler materials by other organisms. *See also* Detritivore.

DECOMPOUND Compound, more than once (e.g., bipinnate, tripinnate, triternate). *See also* Compound.

DECORTICATE Areas of a plant where the cortex has been lost, or areas of a log where the bark has been removed.

DECREASER PLANT A plant that decreases in number, and therefore ground cover, as a result of grazing pressure. *See also* Increaser Plant.

DECUMBENT Botanically, a growth habit that is reclining or lying down, but with the growing tips ascending.

DECURRENT Botanically, extending down along and adnate to the stem (e.g., some leaf bases at the point of attachment). *See also* Excurrent; Plant Form.

DECURRENT PLANT FORM *See* Apical Control; Plant Form.

DECUSSATE Arranged in opposite pairs, each pair being at right angles to the last pair, giving four vertical rows along the axis.

DEEP ECOLOGY MOVEMENT Widely espoused as a grassroots, worldwide, political movement that embraces radical environmentalism. Supporters of the Deep Ecology Movement argue the following: (1) humanity cannot go on with business as usual; (2) human numbers and technology are destroying ecological systems; and (3) we must make fundamental changes in our values and practices, which requires recognizing that there are values inherent in nature, and thinking, speaking, and acting ecocentrically.

People support this platform from a number of different ultimate philosophies or religions. Supporting the principles leads to different sorts of practical actions depending on one's own context.

DEEP-SEATED FIRE A fire burning far below the surface in duff or other combustibles, as opposed to a surface fire. *See also* Forest Fire (Ground Fire).

DEFECT Any irregularity in a tree, log, or wood product that reduces the volume of sound wood available, or lowers its durability, strength, or quality. Defects may be caused by fungal or insect attack, growth conditions, harvesting practices, or manufacturing or seasoning processes.

DEFICIENCY A chromosome lacking one or more genes.

DEFINITION **1** The commonly accepted meaning of a word or term, or the alternative meanings being attributed to the more common meaning. **2** In statistics, concepts and experimental hypotheses are defined in order to permit more detailed analysis. The **theoretical definition** defines a concept in terms of other concepts that are already believed to be more fully understood. Propositions involving theoretically defined concepts cannot be empirically tested. The **operational definition** includes procedures for classifying and measuring these concepts. However, operational definitions are usually imperfect indicators of the underlying concept and are, therefore, more commonly used as indices. In many cases, there is no simple way to determine if an operational definition adequately measures the theoretically defined concepts, so operational definitions are used instead as a measure of any one concept (working on the premise of what seems to reasonably fit between observations and theoretical predictions).

It is possible to find more than one operational definition to apply to any one theoretical definition, which may yield very different results in an analysis. The task of sorting out which measure has more validity will be influenced by training, attitudes, and beliefs, but some basic tests would include: (1) What was studied? (2) Can the concept(s) be measured directly? (3) If not, what was actually measured? (4) What assumptions had to be made to get back to the underlying concept? (5) Are these assumptions acceptable? (6) If not, what assumptions would be acceptable and how would these change the results? *See also* Measurement; Sampling.

DEFLATION The erosion of non-cohesive particulate material, chiefly sand and silt, by wind.

DEFLECTION The vertical distance between an imaginary straight line (the chord) between the skyline spar and the tail spar, and the actual curvature of the skyline cable, measured at mid-span. It is usually expressed as a percentage of the horizontal span length.

DEFLEXED Bent downward and outwards. *See also* Reflexed.

DEFOLIANT A chemical which, when applied to a plant, causes the leaves to drop off.

DEFOLIATION An unseasonable reduction in the foliage cover of a plant due to attacks by insects or fungal disease, or as a result of other factors such as drought, storms, or chemicals in the atmosphere. A distinct loss of leaves outside the normal natural period of leaf shedding. *See also* Needle Cast.

DEFOLIATORS Insects that feed on foliage and act to remove some or all of the foliage from a tree, shrub, or herb.

DEFORESTATION The long-term removal of trees from a forested site to permit other site uses. Cutting of trees followed by regeneration is not deforestation.

DEGLACIATION The uncovering of an area from beneath glacier ice as the result of melting (wasting).

DEGRADATION **1** The erosional removal of materials from one place to another, which lowers the elevation of streambeds and floodplains. **2** Any process or activity that removes or lessens the viability of ecosystem functions and processes, and hence biological diversity.

DEGRADED FOREST STAND A forest stand that has suffered damage to natural composition, structures, and functions to such an extent that population levels and diversity of organisms have been changed in an unnatural manner, or where structures required for ecological processes and populations in later temporal phases have been removed and/or will not be regenerated due to human disturbance.

DEGRADING The steady decrease of structure, structural complexity, and/or biomass in a system. *See also* Aggrading.

DEGREES OF FREEDOM In statistics, the number of independent deviations from the mean in a frequency distribution sample.

DEHISCENCE Describes the method or process by which fruiting bodies of fungi or seed capsules in plants open at maturity. Several forms are recognized in plants: (1) **circumscissile dehiscence**, in which the organ splits around the circumference and the top comes off like a lid; (2) **loculicidal dehiscence**, in which the organ splits open at the back, directly into a locule; (3) **poricidal dehiscence**, in which the organ opens by pores or small holes, which may have flaplike valves; and (4) **septicidal dehiscence**, in which the organ splits into the interior septa or partitioning walls and not directly into a locule. *See* Fruit for illustration.

DELAYED AERIAL IGNITION DEVICE (DAID) An incendiary device producing an exothermic chemical reaction that, when dropped from a flying aircraft, will ignite after a predetermined time has elapsed. *See also* Aerial Ignition Device.

DELAY PERIOD The time period between a stand disturbance (logging, windthrow, fire) and the start of regeneration, often called regeneration lag.

DELIGNIFICATION The chemical, usually enzymatic, removal of lignin from the xylem, leaving a cellulosic residue.

DELIMBER *See* Harvesting Machine Classification.

DELIMBER-BUNCHER *See* Harvesting Machine Classification.

DELIMBER-SLASHER *See* Harvesting Machine Classification.

DELIMBER-SLASHER-BUNCHER *See* Harvesting Machine Classification.

DELIMBING *See* Harvest Functions.

DELIQUESCENT **1** Physically, melting away or dissolving. **2** In some plants, the transformation of certain plant parts from a solid to semiliquid. **3** A growth form in which the stem loses its identity through repeated branching. *See also* Excurrent; Plant Form.

DELPHI METHOD A technique developed to arrive at a consensus regarding the issue being examined. The technique consists of a series of structured questionnaires given to individuals whose opinions or judgments are considered valuable. After the initial series of questions, the results are compiled and resubmitted with a second questionnaire to the same individuals. Each individual is encouraged to reconsider his or her response in light of the previous replies and, if appropriate, change that reply. After a series of such iterations, a consensus sometimes emerges on what is the best course of action.

DELTA An accumulation of stream-transported sediments deposited where a stream enters a body of water. The landform is flat or very gently sloping, triangular or fan-shaped in plan, and consists of fluvial (alluvial) gravel, sand, silt and/or clay.

DELTA DIVERSITY *See* Diversity.

DELTATE/DELTOID Shaped like an equilateral triangle, with the broad side at the point of attachment. *See also* Leaf Shape.

DEMAND The functional relationship between the price being paid for a commodity and the quantities being demanded. *See also* Supply.

DEMATIACEOUS Pigmented (e.g., the dark-spored fungi associated with sooty mould).

DEME A local population or interbreeding group within a larger population.
DEMERSAL Found or living in deep water, or close to the bottom of the ocean. *See also* Pelagic.
DEMOGRAPHIC MODEL A model that predicts the future state of a population based on its age and sex structure and birth and death rates.
DEMOGRAPHIC PARAMETERS Fecundity and mortality parameters used to predict population changes, such as the number of eggs laid per clutch, the frequency at which clutches are laid, the survivorship of eggs and young in the nest and to the age of first reproduction, and the subsequent survival of adults through their lifetime.
DEMOGRAPHIC RANDOMNESS The degree of random variation in individuals' chances of dying or reproducing.
DEMOGRAPHIC STOCHASTICITY Random fluctuations in birth and death rates.
DEMOGRAPHIC VIGOUR The population's vital statistics and dynamics expressed as a factor of population growth.
DEMOGRAPHY Population dynamics; the quantitative analysis of population structure and trends in size, growth rate, and distribution.
DENDRITIC PATTERN A branching pattern of streams in a form resembling tree branches.
DENDROCHRONOLOGY The study of growth ring patterns in trees to determine the age and prevailing environmental factors that affected the specimen during its lifetime. The technique is widely used by archaeologists as a means of dating sites, and by climatologists as a means of analysing past climatic patterns.
DENDROCLIMATOLOGY The study of climatic variations through time by analyzing the pattern and density of annual growth rings in trees.
DENDROGRAM A hierarchical, treelike structure used to display groups of similar sampling units identified through the use of multivariate data analysis techniques. The illustration shows a twinspan dendrogram dividing 140 dry dune slack stands into three levels of four groups. *See also* TWINSPAN.
DENDROLOGY The study, identification, and systematic classification of trees.
DENDROMETER Any instrument designed to measure the diameter of a standing tree from the ground, although some dendrometers can also be used to measure tree heights. An optical dendrometer uses optics to enlarge the image and improve measurement accuracy (e.g., the Barr and Stroud dendrometer and the telerelaskop).
DENSE CLOUD LAYER A layer of clouds in which the ratio of dense sky cover to total sky cover exceeds one half. *See also* Ceiling; Cloudy; Thin Cloud Layer.
DENSE SKY COVER Sky cover that prevents detection of higher clouds or the sky above it. *See also* Ceiling; Cloudy; Thin Sky Cover.
DENSITY **1** Mass per unit volume of a material, measured in kilograms per cubic metre. **2** Any measure, normalized on the basis of length, area, or volume (e.g., charge density), expressed in charges per square metre. **3** The number or size of a population (trees, species, etc.) in relation to some unit of space. It is usually expressed as the number of individuals or the population biomass per unit area or volume. In silviculture, stand density is measured as the amount of tree biomass per unit area of land. This can be measured as the number of trees, the basal area, wood volume, or foliage cover. *See also* Stand Density; Stocking.
DENSITY ALTITUDE The altitude as determined by pressure altitude and existing air temperature. Density altitude is used as an index to aircraft performance characteristics, such as take-off distance and rate of climb. *See also* Downloading; Pressure Altitude.

dendrogram

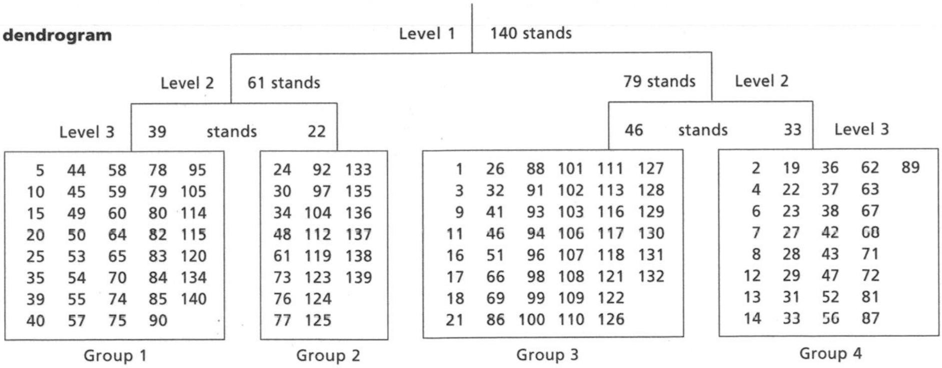

Level 1 — 140 stands

Level 2 — 61 stands | 79 stands

Level 3 — 39 stands 22 | 46 stands 33

Group 1

5	44	58	78	95
10	45	59	79	105
15	49	60	80	114
20	50	64	82	115
25	53	65	83	120
35	54	70	84	134
39	55	74	85	140
40	57	75	90	

Group 2

24	92	133
30	97	135
34	104	136
48	112	137
61	119	138
73	123	139
76	124	
77	125	

Group 3

1	26	88	101	111	127
3	32	91	102	113	128
9	41	93	103	116	129
11	46	94	106	117	130
16	51	96	107	118	131
17	66	98	108	121	132
18	69	99	109	122	
21	86	100	110	126	

Group 4

2	19	36	62	89
4	22	37	63	
6	23	38	67	
7	27	42	68	
8	28	43	71	
12	29	47	72	
13	31	52	81	
14	33	56	87	

DENSITY-DEPENDENT FACTOR A factor that affects a population's ability to increase, and is itself affected by the population density.

DENSITY-INDEPENDENT FACTOR A factor that affects a population's ability to increase regardless of population density.

DENTATE Botanically, having sharp, spreading teeth directed outwards, often perpendicular from the margin. *See also* Leaf Margin (for illustration).

DENTICULATE Having a margin that is minutely dentate. *See also* Leaf Margin (for illustration).

DEOXYRIBONUCLEIC ACID (DNA) A complex nucleic acid molecule that is the information-storing part of genetic material. These molecules, found in most organisms, consist of a series of nucleotides, and control the structure of proteins and, therefore, influence all enzyme-related reactions. The basic model of DNA is a double helix shape, having two polynucleotide chains joined at various stages. *See also* Ribonucleic Acid.

DEPARTURE In the US, a timber sale level that deviates from sustainable sale levels through a planned temporary increase or decrease in the allowable sale quantity. The departure must be economically and biologically justified. The concept of departures relates to an even flow of timber volumes by dint of the theoretical annual allowable cut calculations.

DEPAUPERATE An area that has relatively few plant and animal species, or is low in nutrients. A forest stand with sparse ground covering vegetation due to: (1) a tree overstorey density that precludes sufficient light for understorey plant growth; (2) a deep restrictive litter or duff layer; and (3) a combination of limiting site factors.

DEPENDENCY In database management, any set of data that depends on another set of data to fully describe its characteristics.

DEPENDENT VARIABLE A variable that 'depends on' another variable (i.e., a variable that is predicted by another variable). *See also* Dummy Variable; Independent Variable; Nominal Variable.

DEPLETION The use or consumption of a resource at a rate greater than the resource can be replenished within a defined time period. The notion of time is important, since many renewable resources can be restored if consumption is halted. Rates of depletion can be gradual or rapid.

DEPOSIT An accumulation of earth material, including organic and inorganic matter, resulting from naturally occurring physical, chemical, or organic processes.

DEPOSITION ZONE In hillside erosion processes, the final destination for soil and rock matter that has eroded on the hillslope and been transported to lower elevations. *See also* Erosion; Hillslope (for illustration).

DEPRESSED A botanical term meaning: (1) sunken into the surface; and (2) flattened endwise or from above.

DEPRESSION A circular or irregular enclosed hollow separated from the surrounding area by a distinct slope break.

DEPTH OF BURN The reduction in forest floor thickness due to consumption by fire.

DEPTH OF FIELD The distance between the points nearest and farthest from the camera that are imaged with acceptable sharpness. The general relation is a shallower depth of field at large apertures, and a deeper depth of field at narrower (smaller) apertures.

DESCRIPTIVE STATISTICS Techniques used to organize and summarize data.

DESICCANT **1** Generally, a material that when applied to another material, living or dead, dries it out. **2** In forest management, a chemical that when applied to a living plant, causes or accelerates the drying of its aerial parts. It is used to facilitate the burning of living vegetation by substantially lowering the fuel moisture content within a few hours. *See also* Brown and Burn.

DESICCATE To dry up.

DESIGNATED AREA An identifiable geographic unit of land or water, often with an associated, legally binding mandate, that requires a specific combination of resource management practices to adequately protect important resource values.

DETECTABILITY A measure of the conspicuousness of a species equal to the proportion of actual units (individuals, territorial males, etc.) observed on a given area.

DETECTION **1** The discovery, identification, and delineation of pest or fire outbreaks. **2** The hearing or sighting of a bird or animal during population surveys.

DETECTION AIRCRAFT An aircraft deployed for the express purpose of discovering, locating, and reporting wildfires. *See also* Aerial Detection.

DETECTION DISTANCE The distance from the observer at which the individual or cluster of individuals is seen or heard. The distance is equal to the radius in point counts and the lateral or perpendicular distance in transect counts.

DETERMINATE Describes inflorescences in which the central or terminal bud opens first. *See also* Cyme.
DETERMINISTIC A quantitative empirical model in which relationships are fixed and there can be only one outcome (i.e., they are not determined by chance).
DETERRENT **1** A substance that inhibits any normal behaviour, such as feeding, mating, or oviposition by an organism. **2** A potential fine or procedure that exists to deter specific types of behaviour, or a physical obstacle to deter entry or passage of certain forms of traffic (e.g., bollards preventing trail bikes on pedestrian trails).
DETRENDED CORRESPONDENCE ANALYSIS (DCA) A non-linear, indirect ordination technique based on a modification to reciprocal averaging (RA). In RA, the species ordination scores are weighted averages of the stand scores, and the stand ordination scores are weighted averages of the species ordination scores. A series of weighted-averaging operations (iterations) takes place in order to ordinate stands and species simultaneously until two or more axes are extracted. Problems noted with RA include the 'edge effect,' in which the ends of the first axis are compressed relative to the centre of the axis, and the 'arch effect,' in which the scores of the second axis create a spatial distortion caused by the quadratic relationship with the scores of the first axis.

DCA is considered superior to RA because it eliminates both the edge effect and the arch effect. The results are more reliable when used to explore and infer indirect environmental relationships or gradients. The ordination axes of DCA are scaled in units representing standard deviations (sd) that have a precise meaning. A full turnover of the species composition of stands is expected to occur in about 4 sd, while one half change, or a 50 per cent change in stand composition will occur in approximately 1.2 sd. *See also* Correspondence Analysis; Ordination.
DETRITIVORE Any organism that feeds on dead organic matter, including scavengers. *See also* Decomposition.
DETRITUS **1** Freshly dead or partly decomposed plant or animal matter (component parts or the entire organism). **2** A collective term for loose rock or mineral matter that is worn off or removed directly by mechanical means; especially fragmented material such as sand, silt, and clay, moved away from its place of origin. *See also* Litter.
DEUTEROMYCETE **1** A fungus in the class Deuteromycotina. **2** The conidial spore stage of certain ascomycetes.
DEUTEROMYCOTINA The asexual or imperfect fungi. One of the major classes of the Fungi kingdom.
DEUTOGYNE A reproductive stage of certain eriphydid mites. A distinct female that characterizes one of the alternate generations. *See also* Protogyne.
DEUTONYMPH The third instar of false spider mites, spider mites, and tarsonemid mites.
DEVELOPMENT **1** The advancement of the management and use of natural resources to satisfy human needs and improve the quality of human life. For development to be sustainable, it must account for the social, ecological, and economic factors of the living and nonliving resource base, and of the long-term and short-term advantages and disadvantages of alternative actions. **2** In embryology, the process where eggs, embryos, or young organisms progress toward maturity.
DEW POINT or DEW-POINT TEMPERATURE The temperature to which air must be cooled to reach saturation at a constant atmospheric pressure. The Dew Point is always lower than the wet-bulb temperature, which in turn is always lower than the dry-bulb temperature. The only exception to this occurs when the air is saturated (i.e., relative humidity is 100 per cent), in which case all three are equal. The recommended SI unit is degrees Celsius.
DEW-POINT SPREAD The difference between dry-bulb temperature and the dew point.
DIADELPHOUS Describes stamens when they are arranged in two sets. It is commonly applied to the pea family, where nine of the ten stamens are coalesced in one bundle, the tenth being by itself. *See also* Adelphous; Monadelphous; Syncarp.
DIALYPETALOUS Polypetalous, the corolla being composed of separate and distinct petals.
DIAMETER Several measurements of diameter are used in inventory work, the most common being diameter at breast height (DBH), which is a standard point of measurement for all forest inventory work. Diameter can be measured overbark or underbark, depending on the degree of accuracy required. The international metric standard for DBH is overbark at a point 1.3 metres above ground (above point of germination in Canada). In the US, DBH is measured at 4.5 feet above ground. **Top diameter** is the diameter underbark at the smallest end of

the uppermost merchantable log. **Diameter class** is any interval into which a range of stem diameters of trees or logs is divided for classification and use, and the trees or logs that fit into any one diameter class. **Log diameter** is usually measured as the diameter underbark at the smallest end of the log. **Quadratic mean diameter** is the diameter of the tree with average (for a given stand) basal area at reference height, usually DBH.

DIAMETER CLASS Any interval into which the range of stem diameters of trees or logs is divided for classification and use. Also, the trees or logs falling into such an interval.

DIAMETER LIMIT The minimum, and occasionally maximum, diameter to which trees or logs are to be measured, cut, or used. The limits generally refer to the stump, the top, or breast height.

DIAMETER LIMIT CUTTING The removal of all trees in a stand above a certain minimum diameter, which may vary by species. Originally conceived as a means of ensuring that some trees would remain for continuing development, a diameter limit cut can have detrimental effects, including the removal of trees that, although above the minimum diameter, should really be left to further develop and add more value. In some cases, diameter limit cuts can leave very poor stands of suppressed or stagnant growth that will not perform well in the future.

DIAMETER TAPE Also termed a DBH tape, a specially graduated tape that allows overbark diameters to be read directly from a tree by wrapping the tape around the circumference of the stem.

DIAMICTON A textural term applied to nonsorted sediments consisting of sand and larger particles in a matrix of silt and/or clay; particle size distribution is bimodal, with modes in the silt/clay and sand/gravel fractions.

DIANDROUS Possessing two perfect stamens.

DIAPAUSE A resting stage of an insect in which growth and development are arrested and metabolic processes are low. It is induced by a combination of inherent and environmental factors. *See also* Aestivation; Dormancy; Hibernation.

DIASPORE *See* Propagule.

DIASTEMA In mammals, the space without teeth found between the canine and premolar teeth.

DIATOM Freshwater and marine microscopic unicellular algae. Diatoms are found in the phylum Bacillariophyta in the kingdom Protista. They accumulate silica on the surfaces of their two-part shells, called valves, that fit together like the lid on a box.

DIATOMACEOUS EARTH The naturally occurring marine deposits of fossil diatoms that form a fine-grained material used in industrial processes, such as filter manufacture and polishes, as well as a soil amendment. The material is also used as an abiotic insect control, where the fine and very sharp particles are picked up by passing insects. It slowly abrades their exoskeleton and causes them to desiccate.

DIATREME A volcanic fissure, usually a vertical pipe or neck, that, as a result of upwelling of magma, has become filled with angular rock fragments. Diatremes may contain valuable diamond deposits.

DICHASIAL CYME A falsely dichotomous cyme, in which the axis bears a terminal flower between two more or less equal branches, the branches repeating the process one or more times (in a compound dichasial cyme), or bearing each only a terminal flower (in a simple dichasial cyme). The lowermost flower, terminating the primary axis, opens first. *See also* Cyme.

DICHOGAMY In plants, flowering that occurs in a female-male sequence. *See also* Duodichogamy; Heterodichogamy.

DICHOTOMOUS Forking regularly and repeatedly, the two branches of each fork being equal.

DICHOTOMOUS KEY A system for identifying organisms based on the presence or absence of key characteristics. At each step, there is a choice between two (dichotomous) possibilities. The choice selected leads to the next step where another choice is made between two possibilities. This process is repeated by eliminating the absent characteristics until a positive identification is made.

DICOTYLEDONOUS *See* Cotyledons.

DIDYNAMOUS **1** Divided into two lobes. **2** Fruits found in pairs. **3** Having four stamens in two pairs, the pairs being often of unequal length.

DIEBACK The progressive dying from the tips downward or inward of shoots, twigs, tops, branches, or roots. It may or may not lead to death.

DIFFERENTIAL HOST A host having varying reactions to isolates of a pathogen derived from different physiological races. The reactions can thus be used to distinguish among the races.

DIFFICULTY OF CONTROL The amount of effort

required to contain and mop-up a fire based on its behaviour and persistence as determined by the fire environment. *See also* Resistance to Control; Resistance to Fire Guard Construction.

DIFFUSE **1** As a verb, the process of dispersion or mixing together. **2** As a noun, not concentrated. **3** Botanically, spreading widely by frequent branching; having an open growth habit.

DIFFUSION A movement of materials from a region of high concentration to one of lower concentration. A process of spreading out.

DIGGER LOG *See* Large Organic Debris.

DIGITAL CLASSIFICATION In remote sensing, the use of one or more algorithms to group pixels of a multispectral image with similar characteristics. It is a process by which information labels may be attached to pixels on the basis of their spectral reflectance characteristics. *See also* Algorithm; Pixel; Spectral Reflectance Curve.

DIGITAL ENHANCEMENT In remote sensing, the filtering of data and other processes (which may or may not be statistical) to manipulate pixels to produce an image that accentuates features of interest for visual (i.e., manual) interpretation.

DIGITAL TERRAIN MODEL The computerized portrayal of a landform in three dimensions. It involves translating contour lines into digital format for use in the computer. It is also called digital elevation model.

DIGITATE Having a form resembling a finger.

DIGITIZE The transformation process by which points, lines, and outlines on a plan or map are converted into georeferenced data that can be used on a computer. The process involves a series of decisions about which geometrical information should be digitized and stored, which additional alphanumeric information must be input to describe the digitized features, and the actual input of this information. The process may be manual, semi-automatic, or automatic. In geographic information system work, digitizing is particularly concerned with recording the spatial location of geographic phenomena in real-world coordinates, but also includes the entry of any alphabetic or numeric data that describes these phenomena. Data are usually entered by keyboard or digitizing table. *See also* Geographically Referenced; Geographic Information System; Raster; Vector Format

DIHYBRID A cross between two individuals having two differing sets of characteristics.

DIKARYOTIC A fungus mycelium having two sexually compatible nuclei per cell. *See also* Heterokaryotic.

DILATED A form that is broadened and expanded.

DIMORPHIC Describes a taxon having two distinct types of individuals, differing in form, colour, etc. Dimorphism may be developmental, seasonal, sexual, or geographic (e.g., humans exhibit sexual dimorphism, and several plants, such as eucalyptus trees and ferns, have different leaf shapes between young and mature specimens).

DIOECIOUS A plant having distinct male and female reproductive structures on separate plants. *See also* Autoecious; Heteroecious; Monoecious.

DIOICOUS In mosses, bearing archegonia and antheridia on separate plants. *See also* Autoicous.

DIOXINS and FURANS The common names used to describe two classes of organochlorine compounds, namely the polychlorinated dibenzo-p-dioxins (PCDDs) and the polychlorinated dibenzofurans (PCDFs). Dioxins and furans are formed as byproducts in chemical reactions, such as the chlorine bleaching of wood pulp in the Kraft process.

DIP The angle of inclination away from the horizontal in rock layers or faults. Angle of dip is at ninety degrees to the strike. *See also* Strike.

DIPLOID Having the double number of chromosomes (2n) in one nucleus, or having two haploid nuclei in one cell. *See also* Haploid.

DIPLOSTEMONOUS Having the stamens in two whorls; those in the outer whorl being alternate with the petals, while those in the inner whorl are opposite the petals. *See also* Obdiplostemonous.

DIPSLOPE A slope of land surface conforming to, and dictated by, the underlying bedded rocks (e.g., the long, gently sloping surface of a cuesta). It is also termed a structural backslope.

DIRECT ATTACK *See* Fire Suppression.

DIRECT COMPETITION The exclusion of individuals from resources by aggressive behaviour or the use of toxins.

DIRECT COST Costs immediately attributable to a specific factor of production.

DIRECT DATA ENTRY The direct entry of data from aerial photographs, forest cover maps, or habitat maps, by digitizing or keyboard entry.

DIRECT EFFECT A condition caused by an action or inaction without an intermediary causal agent. An effect characterized by a close causal relationship. It is also termed a primary effect. Direct effects are usually easier to detect and measure with certainty than indirect effects, but they may be either more or less important than indirect effects. *See also* Indirect Effect.

DIRECTIONAL FELLING The planned falling of a tree to control the direction of fall to avoid excessive breakage of the tree or to avoid damage to the ground. Some mechanical shears use a wedge-shaped blade to provide a lever that directs the tree into its lay.

DIRECT JOBS Jobs that are created as a direct result of industrial activity (e.g., millworkers, office staff, or management), as opposed to jobs that are outside the industrial activity, but support it.

DIRECT MANAGEMENT Management that emphasizes regulating people's behaviours; individual choice is restricted and managers aim at directly controlling visitor behaviour with regulations and use requirements. *See also* Indirect Management.

DIRECT PROTECTION AREA That area for which a specified fire protection organization has primary responsibility for attacking an uncontrolled fire and for directing suppression action.

DIRECT SUPPRESSION Any action taken against a pest to reduce its population size (e.g., a pesticide application, sanitation cutting, biological control). *See also* Indirect Suppression.

DIRT A casual and sometimes pejorative description of soil.

DISC/DISK **1** A circular, radially flattened shape. **2** Botanically, a fleshy or elevated development of the receptacle or of coalesced nectaries or staminodes about the pistil. **3** In the Compositae, the central area of the flower head, bearing the florets. **4** In the Orchidaceae, the central area of the lip of the flower. *See also* Disc Flower. **5** A more or less flat apical part of a stroma that protrudes above the bark surface in *Valsa* and related fungi. The exposed fertile portion of an apothecium in Discomycetes.

DISC FLOWER One of the tubular flowers in the central area of the flower head in most Compositae. *See also* Ray Flower.

DISCHARGE Volume of water flowing through a given stream at a given point and within a given time period. Usually measured as volume per unit time (e.g., cubic metres per second).

DISCLIMAX A type of climax community that is maintained by either continuous or intermittent disturbance, such as grazing, burning, logging, to a severity that the natural climax vegetation is altered.

DISCOID **1** Disc-shaped. **2** Having only disc flowers.

DISCOLORATION A change in colour or hue from what is typical.

DISCOUNTED CASH FLOW Used in evaluating investment opportunities, the various costs and benefits anticipated in future years discounted to the present. These values can be expressed by their difference, giving a net present value.

DISCOUNTING The process of estimating the present worth of one or more anticipated costs or revenues by determining the amount of money which, if presently invested and allowed to accumulate at compound interest, will exactly equal the expected costs or revenues at the time when they become due.

DISCOUNT RATE The rate at which an economic agent, such as time preference, converts future values to current values. The social discount rate expresses the preference of society as a whole for present returns rather than future returns, and is used in economic analysis to discount the incremental net benefit stream.

DISCOVERY TIME *See* Elapsed Time.

DISCREPANCY A difference between the results of duplicate or comparable measurements of a quantity. The difference in computed values of a quantity obtained by different processes using data from the same survey.

DISEASE A prolonged impairment of the normal state of a living animal or plant that affects the performance of the vital functions. The causes of disease are biotic and abiotic and include pathogenic microorganisms, nutrient deficiencies or excesses, insects, and air pollutants. Some pathologists consider abiotic factors to be disorders rather than diseases. A disease can be caused by more than one agent, and is said to be virulent when it multiplies so rapidly within the body of an organism that it can overwhelm the organism's immunological system.

DISEASE CYCLE The sequence of events involved in the development of a stage of a disease, including the stages in the life cycle of the pathogen and the symptoms of the disease in the host.

DISINCENTIVE An inducement offered to governments, communities, or organizations to encourage them not to undertake certain actions. Conversely, a mechanism imposed on governments, communities, or organizations that makes it financially, politically, or socially undesirable to proceed with an action.

DISJUNCT Disconnected. Describes populations of the same species that are geographically isolated from each other by large distances.

DISORDER Describes a disease induced by an abiotic factor, rather than by an infectious agent passed from one host to another. It is also termed a noninfectious disease or abiotic disease.

DISPATCHER The person employed to receive reports of discovery and status of fires, confirm fire locations, take action promptly to provide firefighters and equipment likely to be needed to control a fire in initial attack, send them to the proper location, and support them as needed.

DISPERSAL The passive or active movement, usually one way and on any time scale, of organisms from their point of origin to another location where they may subsequently produce offspring (e.g., insect larvae, fungal spores, or plant seeds by wind; insect adults by flight; animals by walking or swimming). Species can have more than one effective means of dispersal. For example, samaras are primarily anemochores, but may become zoochores if a small mammal helps to disperse the seed while foraging.

DISPERSAL CAPABILITY The ability of members of a species to move from their area of birth to another suitable location and subsequently breed.

DISPERSAL DISTANCE A straight-line distance that an individual travels from its birthplace until it stops dispersing (assumed to be a breeding site) or dies.

DISPERSAL HABITAT Habitat that supports the life needs of an individual plant or animal during dispersal. The habitat would satisfy needs for foraging, roosting, and protection from predators, or suitable conditions for growth and development of plants.

DISPERSED RECREATION Outdoor recreation in which visitors are diffused over relatively large areas. Where facilities or developments are provided, they are primarily for access and protection of the environment, rather than for the comfort or convenience of the user.

DISPERSION **1** The spatial distribution of organisms within a population, such as regular, random, or clustered. **2** The nonaccidental movement of individuals into or out of an area or population, typically a movement over a relatively short distance and of a regular nature. **3** The removal (by whatever means) of pollutants from the atmosphere over a specified area, or the distribution of a specified quantity of pollutant throughout an increasing volume of atmosphere.

DISPERSION INDEX In the US, a numerical index reflecting the atmosphere's capacity to disperse smoke from prescribed fires over a 1,000-square-mile area. It is related to the ventilation factor, but also considers the rate of pollutant dispersion.

DISPLACEMENT In photogrammetry. **1** In regard to an image, any shift in the position of an image on a photograph that does not alter the perspective characteristics of the photograph (i.e., shift due to relief or height of the objects photographed, scale change in the photograph, shift due to tilt of the photograph). The opposite of distortion. *See also* Distortion; Rectification. **2** In referring to relief, displacement is the movement of images radially inward or outward with respect to the photograph nadir because the ground objects are, respectively, below or above the elevation of the ground nadir. *See also* Nadir Point.

DISPLAY **1** As a noun, in computer science or remote sensing any device that is capable of producing a visual representation of the data set in use, normally on a computer monitor. The abnormal activities of birds and animals seen during the courtship and mating season. **2** As a verb, the process of creating the visual image. Birds and animals in the act of courting a mate.

DISPUTE Any clash between opposing or seemingly incompatible ideas, principles, goals, objectives, or factions.

DISRUPTION Describes the effect of artificial release of semiochemicals (such as a pheromone or its analogue) on the communications between insects or other organisms. The artificial semiochemical is used to disrupt communications (e.g., the disruption of mating in moths by atmospheric permeation with a sex pheromone, or the disruption of host selection by bark beetles by the release of an anti-aggregation pheromone).

DISSECTED **1** A valley, floodplain, hillside, or other landform that has been cut down by erosional processes. **2** Botanically, cut or divided into numerous segments. *See* Leaf Shape.

DISSEMINATION The transport or spread of inoculum from its source to healthy plants. *See also* Dispersal.

DISSEMINULE *See* Propagule.

DISSOLVED OXYGEN The concentration of oxygen in water at a specified temperature and atmospheric pressure. It is used as a measure of the water's ability to support aquatic life. Low concentrations do not support fish or similar organisms.

DISTAL Describes the location of a feature on an organism that is the farthest away from the centre or point of attachment to the main structure (e.g., leaves are attached at the distal end of branches; hands are attached at the distal end of the arm). *See also* Proximal.
DISTICHOUS Botanically, arranged in two opposite rows along a branch or stem.
DISTINCT **1** In general, obvious; standing alone; readily distinguishable. **2** Botanically, separate and not united, typically describing similar parts of the same whorl (e.g., petals distinct and not united one to another).
DISTORTION In photogrammetry, any shift in the position of an image on a photograph that alters the perspective characteristics of the photograph (i.e., image distortion caused by motion of the film or camera, differential shrinkage of film or paper, and lens aberration). **Radial distortion** occurs because the camera is not vertically above every point on the photograph, features near the edges appear to lean outward. **Topographic distortion** results from differences in scale related to topography; scale is larger where topography is high and camera-to-ground distance is least, and vice versa. *See also* Displacement.
DISTRESS CONE CROP An unusually heavy cone crop, often of smaller than normal cones, caused by trees growing under conditions of biologically or environmentally induced stress.
DISTRIBUTION **1** The manner, pattern, or relative frequency with which objects, events, activities, or values of a variable are dispersed among a population or over a landscape. Distribution patterns may be described as random, regular, or clustered (see illustration). At habitat scales, most plant species show clustered patterns correlated to specific environmental conditions. **2** The spatial arrangement of a species within its range. *See also* Dispersion.

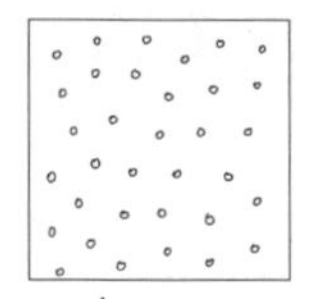
regular

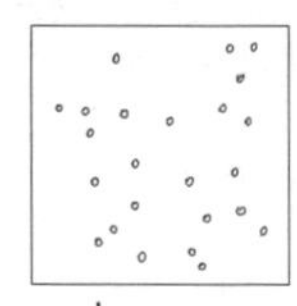
random

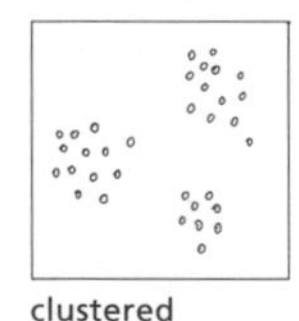
clustered

DISTURBANCE A discrete force that causes significant change in structure and/or composition through natural events such as fire, flood, wind, or earthquake; mortality caused by insect or disease outbreaks, or by human-caused events such as the harvest of a forest. In forests, larger disturbances generally favour colonizing species, while smaller disturbances favour the competitive species. Typically, diversity in the landscape is greater with large disturbances at infrequent intervals. Small but frequent disturbances create high diversity at the stand or ecosystem level.
DISTURBANCE PATTERN The spatial and temporal arrangement of disturbances.
DIURNAL **1** Any organism whose most active period is between dawn and dusk. *See also* Crepuscular; Nocturnal. **2** The daily cycle (changes between daytime and nighttime conditions) of dry-bulb temperature, relative humidity, wind speed, and atmospheric stability.
DIVARICATE Greatly divergent, spreading far apart.
DIVERGENT **1** Generally, differing; not similar (e.g., opinions, pathways). **2** Botanically, spreading broadly from the centre, but not as much as divaricate.
DIVERGENT SPECIES An evolutionary theory that postulates that some species once related, have since evolved along divergent pathways due to long periods of geographical isolation, and thus now possess distinguishing features that clearly separate them.
DIVERSITY Diversity is an assessment of the number of species present, their relative abundance in an area, and the distribution of individuals among the species. Some people consider diversity to be an indicator of ecological complexity or quality, where high species diversity is equated to higher complexity or quality, and declining species diversity is an indication of declining complexity or quality, but this is highly dependent on the potential of the site and the management objectives being used. However, whether increasing diversity as a result of management activities is automatically an indicator of increasing ecological quality remains subject to debate.

Diversity is a measure of the complexity of an ecosystem; newly established communities are low in diversity; older, more stable communities have higher diversity. Indicators of diversity need to include genetic characteristics, species populations, plant and animal communities, ecosystems, special habitats, and the principal landscape level elements. Vegetation is the most widely used indirect indicator of diversity.

The issue of diversity is rapidly gaining social and political recognition. It is generally recognized that hypothetical diversity indices can be used to model diversity, but actually creating and/or maintaining biologically diverse ecosystems is a much more difficult problem, and the transition from theory into effective practice is still evolving. One of the most important aspects of diversity is to retain a diversity of diversities in the landscape, thus leaving many options for the future, rather than maximizing one form of diversity that precludes other forms of diversity, possibly of equal or greater importance in the future.

Thus, the broad goal of maintaining diversity, now increasingly common in management plans, requires a very detailed knowledge and understanding of the structure, functions, and processes of ecosystems and species populations at all levels, and not just the stand or local level as was common in the past.

A problem of equal importance is that the retention of diversity is now seen to require a major change in societal, cultural, and all resource management attitudes. Such a shift, reflecting an increasing awareness of humanity's impacts on planetary ecosystems, poses huge challenges to the established status quo methods of operating.

Diversity can be measured in several ways. **Alpha diversity** is the number of different species in a local area, often called species richness. **Beta diversity** is a measure of the degree of change in species composition, or vertical and longitudinal structure of communities along an environmental gradient – the diversity occurring between habitats or ecosystems. **Delta diversity** is the diversity of entire plant communities within the vegetational mosaic of management units at a landscape level. **Gamma diversity** is the species diversity across a variety of ecosystems. It depends upon alpha diversity in each habitat and beta diversity among them.

The term species diversity has been subsumed in recent years, not always correctly, under the term biodiversity. Other forms of diversity include: Genetic, Habitat, Horizontal, Landscape, Structural, Taxonomic, and Vertical Diversity. *See also* Abundance; Evenness; Shannon-Weiner Index; Species Richness.

DIVERSITY INDEX A number that indicates the relative degree of diversity in habitat per unit area, expressed mathematically as:

$$DI = \frac{TP}{2\sqrt{A\pi}}$$

where

TP = total perimeter of an area plus any edge within the area in metres or feet

A = area in square metres or square feet

π = 3.1416.

DIVIDE In geomorphology, the line of separation between two drainage systems. The highpoint of a summit, gap, or pass or of an interfluve.

DIVIDED An imprecise term meaning deeply incised, cut, lobed, or cleft.

DIVIDENDS Incomes or rents of ecosystem outputs that result from the investments of capital in ecosystem management.

DIVISION In older classification schemes of the plant kingdom, the division and subdivision were used as the equivalent of phylum and subphylum. More modern schemes use phylum regardless of kingdom. *See* also Phylum.

DNA *See* Deoxyribonucleic acid.

DOG **1** A short, heavy piece of steel, bent over at the end to form a sharpened point, with a ring or eye at the other end, to which is attached a chain or cable (e.g., a butt hook). It is used to skid logs through the forest. **2** In sawmilling, one or more toothlike projections that firmly hold the log in place on the carriage as it travels past the sawblade. **3** A sturdy steel projection on the endless chain of a log ladder, which serves to catch or snag logs as they are dragged out of the water and into the mill. **4** The teeth mounted on a chainsaw besides the cutting chain, which serve to help the faller gain extra purchase and a more secure grip of the saw on the wood during felling.

DOLABRIFORM Pick-shaped, attached more or less toward the middle.

DOME A roughly symmetrical upfold, with beds dipping in all directions, more or less equally, from one point. A smooth, rounded landform of domelike shape.

DOMESTICATE The caring, cultivation, or taming of wild organisms to serve human needs.

DOMINANCE **1** The degree to which one or a few species predominate in a community in terms of numbers, crown closure, importance, or biomass. **2** In genetics, the ability of one allele to suppress the phenotypic expression of another allele in the heterozygote. The suppressed allele is then recessive to the dominant allele.

DOMINANT **1** A plant or group of plants which, by their collective size, mass, or number, exert the most influence on other components of the ecosystem. **2** In forest stand evaluations, *see* Crown Class. **3** A trait or allele that has dominance over another.

DOMIN-KRAJINA COVER-ABUNDANCE SCALE A simple system for estimating the quantities (cover and abundance) of plant species in a stand, based on a scale of 1 to 10, with an additional symbol for solitary individuals, where: *10* represents any number of individuals in a species, with complete cover (100 per cent) in the stand; *9* represents any number of individuals in a species, with greater than 75 per cent cover but less than complete cover in the stand; *8* represents any number of individuals in a species, with 50-75 per cent cover in the stand; *7* represents any number of individuals in a species, with 33-50 per cent cover in the stand; *6* represents any number of individuals in a species, with 25-33 per cent cover in the stand; *5* represents any number of individuals in a species, with 10-25 per cent cover in the stand; *4* represents any number of individuals in a species, with 5-10 per cent cover in the stand; *3* represents scattered individuals in a species, with 1-5 per cent cover in the stand; *2* represents very scattered individuals in a species, with less than 1 per cent cover in the stand; *1* represents seldom found species with insignificant cover; and + represents a solitary plant with insignificant cover in the stand.

DORMANCY A period of reduced or suspended physiological activity in plants, animals, or other organisms. Dormancy can be a normal part of the life cycle, or it may be induced by unfavourable environmental conditions, and it may be facultative or obligatory. The term includes hibernation, aestivation, and diapause. It is also used to describe abiotic features that have the potential for sudden and rapid change (e.g., volcanoes). *See also* Aestivation; Diapause; Hibernation.

DORMANT **1** An organism in a state of reduced physiological activity, or an abiotic feature, such as a volcano, that is in between periods of active change. **2** A state in which viable plant seeds exposed to favourable environmental conditions fail to germinate.

DORMANT APPLICATION The application of herbicide as a spray, an injection, or by hack-and-squirt methods, in the late winter or early spring, when buds are starting to swell but have not yet opened. At this time some angiosperm brush types are highly susceptible to treatment, while certain conifers are resistant. Thus, the selectivity of a dormant application treatment is enhanced at this time.

DORMANT SPRAY A chemical applied in winter or very early spring before the treated plants have started active growth.

DORSAL Describes the location of a feature that is on the back of a plant, animal or organ, or on the side farthest from the ground. *See also* Ventral.

DORSIFIXED Anthers are dorsifixed when they are attached at the back. *See also* Androecium (for illustration); Basifixed.

DORSIVENTRAL Flattened and having a distinct dorsal and ventral surface; laminate, such as a leaf blade.

DOT GRID A transparent sheet of film (overlay) with systematically arranged dots, each dot representing a square or rectangular area. Dot grids provide a relatively simple means of determining areas on maps, aerial photographs, plans, and drawings. They provide reasonable accuracy on level terrain with accurate scale, but if used on more variable terrain and photographs where scales vary, a more controlled scale should be employed. Dot grid estimations provide a less accurate measure of area than planimeters.

DOUBLE Botanically, describes flowers that possess or seem to possess more than the usual number of floral envelopes, especially petals. The supernumary petals are often petaloid stamens. Applied to flower heads in the Compositae, the term indicates the conversion of most or all of the normally tubular flowers of the disc to ligulate flowers.

DOUBLE-ACTION SHEAR A mechanized cutting tool for felling trees. It works like a pair of scissors, with one blade slightly offset, but both working against each other. Some work edge to edge.

DOUBLE-CLUTCHING The deliberate removal of one set of eggs from a brooding hen to cause the hen to lay a second clutch.

DOUBLE DRUM WINCH A winch mounted on and powered by a tractor, consisting of two cable drums: one for the dragline and one for the haul-back line.

DOUBLE-HACKING Girdling a tree by means of a double frill cut around the tree trunk, and removal of the chips between the two frills.

DOUBLY ORDERED TABLE A table having two ordinal values.

DOUBLY SERRATE Botanically, margins having primary teeth, each bearing additional secondary teeth. *See also* Leaf Margin.

DOWNLOADING **1** A reduction in aircraft gross weight made to compensate for loss of performance due to increase in density altitude, or due to runway length (or lack of it), or for other reasons. **2** In computing, the transfer of data, often in a compressed format, from one computer to another. Often refers to the transfer of data from a computerized bulletin board system to a remote computer.

DOWN LOG That portion of a tree that has fallen or been cut and left in the woods. *See also* Coarse Woody Debris.

DOWNWASTING OF ICE Lowering of the surface of a glacier or ice sheet due to ablation.

DOWNY Surfaces having soft, weak, short hairs. *See also* Pubescent.

DOYLE RULE Devised around 1825, this log rule tends to underestimate board footage in small logs and overestimate in large logs. The basic formula is:

$$\text{volume (in board feet)} = \left[\frac{D-4}{4}\right]^2 L$$

where

D = log diameter in inches

L = log length in feet.

See also International Log Rule; Scribner Rule.

DRAFT Drawing water from a static water supply into a pump that is above the level of the water supply, accomplished by removing air from the pump and allowing atmospheric pressure to push water through a non-collapsible hose into the pump.

DRAG **1** A simple sled used for hauling logs, where one end of the log rests on the sled, while the other end drags on the ground. **2** A simple means of levelling a rough surface using a large log or a frame of iron dragged behind a tractor.

DRAG LINE **1** The cable or chain that does the actual hauling of logs. **2** A specialized excavating machine in which the bucket is attached to a system of cables and can be swung (thrown) out onto an area, then dragged back in toward the carrier to fill the bucket. Typically used in dredging operations, and can operate from a barge or from dry land. It is also termed a dredge.

DRAINAGE **1** The surface and sub-surface water derived within a clearly defined catchment area, usually bounded by ridges or other similar topographic features, encompassing part, most, or all of a watershed. The size of catchment area will vary by jurisdiction. **2** The passage of water under the influence of gravity through soils, rocks, and other substrates. *See also* Basin; Sub-drainage; Watershed.

DRAPED FUELS Needles, leaves, and twigs that have fallen from above and have lodged on lower branches or brush. Draped fuels are part of aerial fuels.

DRAW SHEAR A carrier-mounted, single-action anvil shear, where the blade is drawn through the tree toward the carrier.

DRAY A squirrel's nest of leaves, twigs, and bark.

DRIFT **1** The movement of pesticide droplets, vapour, or dust by wind or air currents. Drift of pesticide away from the area intended for treatment, known as the target area, is undesirable and is one of the major hazards of pesticide application. Drift can be used to advantage in incremental spraying patterns. *See also* Buffer Zone; Incremental Spraying; Volatility. **2** The voluntary or accidental dislodgement of aquatic invertebrates from the stream bottom into the water column, where they move or float with the current and may become available as a food source for fish. It is also, any detrital material transported in the water current. **3** A general term for sediments or rock materials deposited by glacial ice or glacial meltwaters, usually in areas no longer glaciated. **4** The transportation of sediments in coastal areas by near-shore currents. **5** The movement of plants or animals within or beyond their home range, or the movement of livestock within their range area, unfettered by human controls. **6** The movement of smoke away from a fire source. **7** In aerial photography, the horizontal displacement of an aircraft from its planned course (flight path) due to wind or other causes.

DRIFT PROSPECTING Mineral exploration by sediment sampling and geochemical analysis of sediments such as till, in conjunction with reconstruction of former ice-flow directions.

DRIFT SMOKE *See* Smoke.

DRIPLINE The width of the crown; measured as the outermost point at which a drop of water would fall vertically from the crown foliage, and expressed either as a radial distance from trunk to dripline, or as a diameter of the area encompassed.

DRIP-TIP The term used to describe a plant with leaves that taper to a very narrow, much elongated apex. The technical term for this shape of leaf is aristate. In the tropics, many tree species have drip-tip leaves, which serve several important functions: (1) to clear moisture off the leaf in order to open the stomata; and (2) to clear moisture off the leaf surface in order to prevent algal growth that would otherwise block photosynthesis.

DRIP TORCH A hand-held device for igniting prescribed fires. It consists of a fuel tank dripping lighted liquid fuel at an adjustable rate onto the materials to be burned. The fuel used is typically a mixture of 65-80 per cent diesel and

20-35 per cent gasoline. *See also* Aerial Torch.

DRIVING FORCES Forces that lie beyond forest or other natural resource management policy that cannot readily be changed and that have a major effect on policy development and practice (e.g., international markets and trade agreements, consumer preferences, societal attitudes).

DRIZZLE Precipitation composed exclusively of water drops smaller than 0.5 millimetres (0.02 inches) in diameter.

DROP PATTERN The distribution of an aerially delivered retardant drop on the target in terms of its length, width, and momentum (velocity × mass) as it approaches the ground. The momentum determines the relative coverage level of the fire retardant on fuels within the pattern. *See also* Retardant Coverage.

DROP ZONE *See* Entry.

DROUGHT A period of relatively long duration with substantially below-normal precipitation, usually occurring over a large area. *See also* Drought Index; Ketch-Byram Drought Index.

DROUGHT INDEX A number representing the net effect of evapotranspiration and precipitation in producing cumulative moisture depletion in deep duff or upper soil layers. *See also* Ketch-Byram Drought Index.

DRUM A behavioural pattern of some birds in which a drumming sound is created by tapping on a resonating surface (e.g., woodpeckers), or by a rapid beating of the wings against the body to make a reverberating sound (e.g., grouse).

DRUMLIN A streamlined deposit of glacial till or other drift, shaped like a teardrop in plan view, with the tapered (narrow) end pointing in the direction of glacier movement (see illustration).

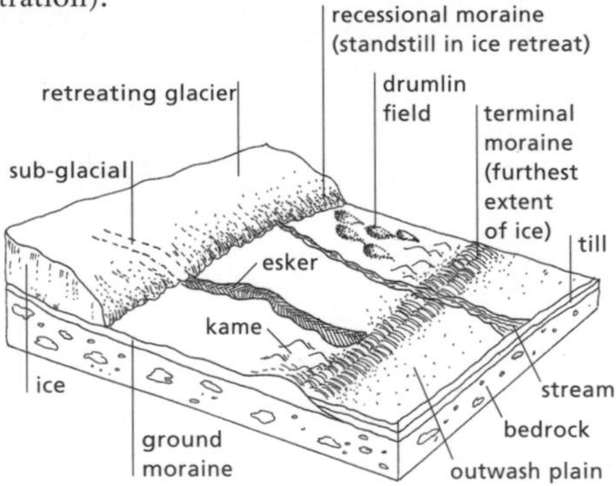

DRUPE A fruit with a fleshy exocarp and a hard (stony) endocarp covering a single seed (rarely two-seeded), such as peach, plum, or cherry.

DRUPELET A diminutive form of drupe. Typically, a cluster of drupelets are clustered to give the appearance of one main fruit (e.g., blackberry or raspberry).

DRY ADIABATIC LAPSE RATE A meteorological term referring to the rate of decrease of temperature with height of a parcel of dry air ascending in the atmosphere without mixing or heat exchange. Numerically, it is equal to about 1 degree Celsius per 100 metres, or 3 degrees Celsius per 1,000 feet. Conversely, dry air descending in the atmosphere warms at the same rate. *See also* Atmospheric Stability; Environmental Lapse Rate; Lapse Rate.

DRY-BULB TEMPERATURE Technically, the temperature registered by the dry-bulb thermometer of a psychrometer. However, it is identical to the temperature of the air and may be used in that sense. It is synonymous with air temperature.

DRY-BULB THERMOMETER In a psychrometer, an ordinary glass thermometer that has a dry bulb and therefore directly measures the temperature of the air. *See also* Wet-Bulb Thermometer.

DRYING REGIME The response of fuel moisture content to cyclically varying temperature/relative humidity combinations.

DRY LIGHTNING STORM A thunderstorm in which negligible precipitation reaches the ground.

DRY ROT A brown rot caused by *Serpula lacrymans* or *Poria incrassata*, fungi that are able to conduct moisture via mycelial strands from an available source and extend their attack to wood previously too dry to decay. It is typically found in buildings.

DRY STORAGE **1** An area where dry powders or granular substances can be stored without them getting wet. **2** In fire-fighting, the storage of dry chemical retardants at air bases and available for use once mixed with water. *See also* Wet Storage.

DUFF LAYER Sometimes just called duff. The layer of loosely compacted, decaying debris underlying the litter layer on the forest floor. Usually, a combination of the litter layer and the less decomposed portion of the humus. It may be equated to the F layer or L + F Layer. *See also* Humus; Litter.

DUMMY RUN A simulated fire-bombing run made on a target by the birddog aircraft to indicate approach and target to the airtanker and to check for flight-path hazards. *See also* Inspection Run; Lead In.

DUMMY VARIABLE In statistics, a variable introduced into a regression analysis that has two or more distinct levels. This contrasts with variables normally used in regression equations that take values over some continuous range.

DUNE **1** A ridge or hill, often transitory in form if not vegetated, created by wind-blown sand. The illustration shows four main dune types. (1) **Barchan or lunate dunes** lie transverse to the direction of wind, with the points trailing downwind. (2) **Stellate or star dunes** have multiple slopes or slip faces that result from winds blowing sand from several directions. These dunes grow vertically rather than expanding by lateral migration. (3) **Seif dunes** occur inland in desert areas and are formed parallel to the direction of prevailing winds that funnel through the depressions between dunes. (4) **Transverse dunes** lie transverse to the direction of prevailing winds, and often occur in series. In coastal areas the oldest dunes are found farthest inland, while the youngest dunes are nearest to the shoreline in direct contact with the prevailing winds. **2** Low mounds or ridges on the bed of a stream consisting of mobile bed material (sand or gravel).

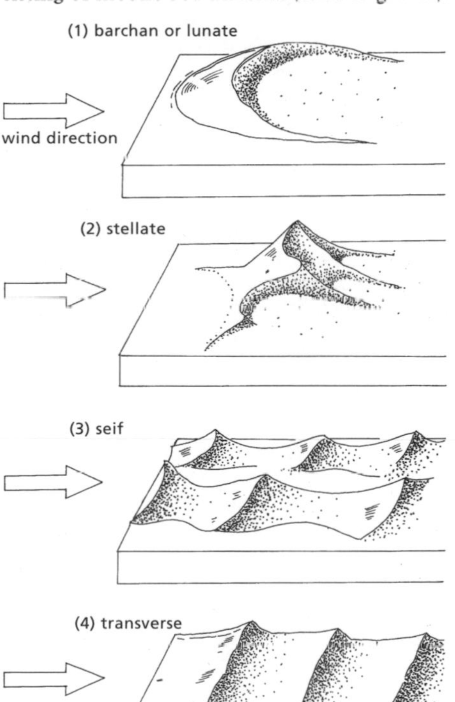

DUNE FIELD An extensive area occupied by wind-formed dunes.

DUNNAGE Lower quality wood products typically used as crating, stacking, or packaging material, or for supporting (wedging, bracing, and containing) loads of higher quality wood during transportation in ships or rail cars.

DUODICHOGAMY In plants, flowering that occurs in male-female-male sequence.

DWARFING The underdevelopment of any organ of a plant. *See also* Atrophic.

DWARF MISTLETOE *See* Mistletoe.

DWARF SHOOT In gymnosperms, such as pines and larches, a lateral shoot consisting primarily of a cluster of needles at the apex of a very short stem. *See also* Shoot.

DYKE Zones of intrusive igneous rock that have filled in cracks existing in the previous rock formations. Dykes can be a few centimetres to kilometres in length. *See also* Batholith (for illustration); Laccolith; Sill.

DYNAMIC EQUILIBRIUM The balance point in a non-static system where opposing activities, processes, or inputs and outputs of energy, counteract each other to yield a period of stability (no change). In ecosystems, the balance point between plant and animal densities.

DYSGENIC Any process that tends to degrade the genetic quality of a population of organisms. In a forestry context, the removal of plus trees and the retention of genetically inferior trees as a seed source would be considered a dysgenic activity. It is also called outbreeding depression. *See also* Eugenic.

DYSTROPHIC Refers to waters containing a high humus content, very low in nutrients, with high acidity and biogeochemical oxygen demand (e.g., bogs). In this combination, organic matter accumulates rather than decomposes, leading to the eventual formation of a swamp. *See also* Eutrophication.

E

E- or EX- In botanical descriptions, a prefix denoting that the object is not something (e.g., edentate [not dentate]), or is pointing out, outward, or beyond (e.g., explanate [flattened out]).

EARLY DROP Fire retardant that lands before (i.e., in front of) the designated target area.

EARLY SERAL STAGE FORESTS The stage in forest development that includes seedlings, saplings, and pole-sized trees.

EARLY WOOD The less dense, larger-celled

portion of an annual growth ring formed during the early part of the growing season. *See also* Late Wood.

EARTH **1** A mixture of soil, surficial materials, and weathered rock, spelled with a lower-case e (earth). **2** The planet upon which we live; spelled with an upper-case E (Earth).

EARTH FIRST! The name of an organization, its publication, and its imperative mission. The exclamation point emphasizes that there is to be no compromise where the well-being of Earth is concerned. Earth Firsters! emphasize that Earth is a common home, which humans share with a multitude of beings, all of which are interdependent.

EARTHFLOW A form of mass wasting in which soil and weathered rock move almost imperceptibly downslope under the influence of gravity over a discrete shear zone. Typical of soils having a high proportion of silt and clay.

EASEMENT **1** *See* Right-of-Way. **2** A legal document noting the rights of the owner(s) to keep the land in a natural state, or some other defined condition, for the purposes of conserving important environmental features. The easement may include specific conditions outlining what is or is not permissible.

EBRACTEATE Without bracts.

ECCENTRIC Morphologically, a form that is off-centre, not radially uniform.

ECDYSIS The periodic shedding of the epicuticle and endocuticle during moulting, typical of reptiles and arthropods. *See also* Moult.

ECDYSOID A synthetic or botanical chemical that mimics the effects of ecdysone.

ECDYSONE A hormone that controls growth and moulting in insects.

ECHINATE Covered with stout, bluntish prickles.

ECHINULATE Covered with small or finely pointed spines.

ECLOSION The act of an adult insect leaving the pupal or the last nymphal skin.

ECOCENTRIC A value system and attitude that sees humans as a part of larger ecological processes and systems. Natural and human communities are folded into one another, and we participate, and cannot avoid doing so, with these communities. Ecocentric attitudes consider *Homo sapiens* as having a primary obligation to take responsibility for themselves and their actions. Past failures to accept this responsibility are seen to be a root cause of contemporary environmental crises. *See also* Anthropocentric.

ECOCLINE **1** A continuous change in ecosystem types or community composition along an environmental gradient. **2** A gradient of changes occurring in different populations of a single species as a result of different selection pressures of different habitat zones. Ecoclines are a continuous gradation of forms, as opposed to a discontinuous gradation of ecotypes. **3** Differences in community composition that reflect changes in topography or global latitudes (e.g., elevations up a hillside or moving from tropical to temperate regions). **4** A continuous pattern of genetically based differences in a species over an environmental gradient. *See also* Cline.

ECOFEMINISM Feminist scholarship and activism focused especially on the ecological dimensions of human activity.

ECOFORESTRY and ECO-AGRICULTURE Examples of putting the prefix 'eco' on words for current practices and studies to emphasize that their starting foundation is an ecological paradigm using ecocentric values. In forest management, it means a rejection of the twentieth-century industrial-agricultural model of large-scale clearcutting of natural forests and their replacement by human-designed plantations of few tree species. Ecoforestry promotes alternative practices based on the management of human activities so as not to interfere with the functioning natural forest ecosystems, and also to restore those damaged by destructive human practices. It is claimed by proponents of ecoforestry, eco-agriculture, ecofishing, etc., that all resource use should be based on the same approach described for ecoforestry. Advocates of eco- practices base all development activities on the wisdom inherent in a place, respecting all values, and aim for ecosophy, that is, ecological wisdom and harmony.

ECOLOGICAL AMPLITUDE The degree to which an organism can tolerate variations in environmental conditions.

ECOLOGICAL APPROACH Resource planning and management activities that assure consideration of the relationships among and between all organisms, including humans, and their environment.

ECOLOGICAL BALANCE A state of dynamic equilibrium within a community of organisms in which genetic, species, and ecosystem diversity remain relatively stable, subject to gradual changes through natural succession.

ECOLOGICAL CONSCIOUSNESS The term is used as a contrast to lack of ecological consciousness, that is, behaviour and thought that ignores ecological realities and has no sense of participating in the larger context of place. Many people believe that the ultimate aim of the environmental movement is to develop ecological consciousness so that our social and cultural lives manifest ecosophy, that is, ecological harmony and wisdom. Ecological consciousness can take many forms, just as there are many forms of ecosophy.

ECOLOGICAL DOMINANT Any organism whose presence can change the environment of other organisms.

ECOLOGICAL INTEGRITY The quality of a natural, unmanaged or managed ecosystem in which the natural ecological processes are sustained, with genetic, species, and ecosystem diversity assured for the future.

ECOLOGICAL LAND CLASSIFICATION A classification scheme used to delineate differing scales of landscape, or ecosystems, based on factors such as climate, physiography, and vegetation. Many schemes have been devised; most are implemented and then refined in light of experience and ease of application. One form of classification system (the Ecosystem Classification System) proposed for use in Canada includes the following categories. **Ecozone** defines large landscapes representing generalized ecological units characterized by interactive and adjusting abiotic and biotic factors. Fifteen ecozones are recognized in Canada: Tundra Cordillera, Boreal Cordillera, Pacific Maritime, Montane Cordillera, Boreal Plains, Taiga Plains, Prairie, Taiga Shield, Boreal Shield, Hudson's Plains, Mixed Wood Plains, Atlantic Maritime, Southern Arctic, Northern Arctic, and Arctic Cordillera. **Ecoprovince** defines a part of an ecozone characterized by major assemblages of structural or surface forms, faunal realms, and vegetation, hydrological, soil and climatic zones. **Ecoregion** defines a part of an ecoprovince characterized by distinctive ecological responses to climate as expressed by the development of vegetation, soil, watercourses, fauna, etc. **Ecodistrict** defines a part of an ecoregion characterized by distinctive assemblages of relief, geology, landforms, soils, vegetation, water, and fauna. **Ecosection** defines a part of an ecodistrict throughout which there is a recurring assemblage of terrain, soils, vegetation, water bodies, and fauna. **Ecosite** defines a part of an ecosection in which there is a relative uniformity of parent material, soil, hydrology, and vegetation. **Ecoelement** defines a part of an ecosite displaying uniform soil, topography, vegetation, and hydrology.

Ecological land classification has many differing applications in forest management. *See also* Biogeoclimatic Classification; Classification; Site Classification; Terrain Classification.

ECOLOGICALLY RESPONSIBLE FOREST USE Human use of the forest that is planned and carried out so as to maintain fully functioning forest ecosystems at all levels, from small forest communities to large landscapes, in both the short and the long term. *See also* Balanced Forest Use.

ECOLOGICALLY SIGNIFICANT Species, stands, or forests considered to be important in maintaining the structure, function, and processes of particular ecosystems or landscapes.

ECOLOGICAL NICHE An organism's actual place within a community, including its tolerances for the physical environment, its interactions with other organisms, and the manner in which the organism utilizes the component parts of its habitat. *See also* Ecological Range.

ECOLOGICAL OPTIMUM The actual set of environmental conditions in which a species normally exists and functions most effectively within the presence of any enemies or competitors. This is synonymous with the concept of 'realized niche.' The performance or fitness of a species is usually determined by measuring growth (see illustration), reproductive success, survivorship, or population size, along an environmental gradient. This environmental gradient may be a single factor (as in the illustration) or multi-dimensional, involving many factors. The point of ecological optimum occurs where there are no factors limiting the growth or performance of the species.

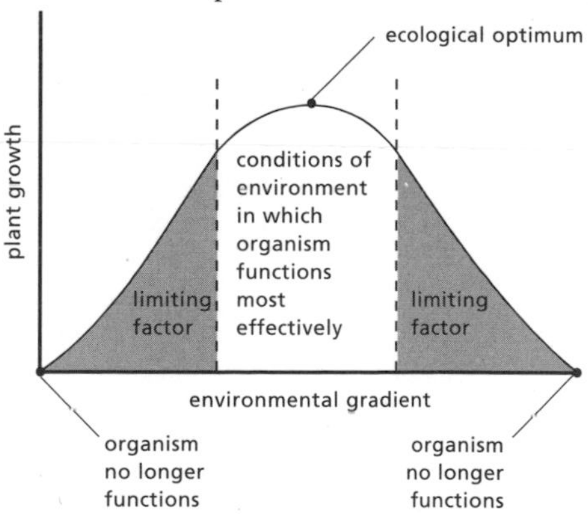

ECOLOGICAL PLASTICITY Any organism having the capability of utilizing a wide range of habitat types and/or utilizing a wide variety of foods.

ECOLOGICAL PRINCIPLES The biological basis for sound ecosystem management through which ecosystem sustainability may be ensured.

ECOLOGICAL PROCESS The actions or events that link organisms (including humans) and their environment, such as disturbance, successional development, nutrient cycling, carbon sequestration, productivity, and decay.

ECOLOGICAL RANGE For every organism there is a range of environmental conditions within which it can live, thrive, and survive. These limiting factors define the ecological range and ecological tolerance of a species. In the diagram, the shape of the curve describes the ecological tolerance of a species to certain conditions. The curves of some species can overlap with others. A mesokurtic curve shows moderate tolerance for a condition, a platykurtic curve shows broad tolerance, and a leptokurtic curve shows narrow tolerance.

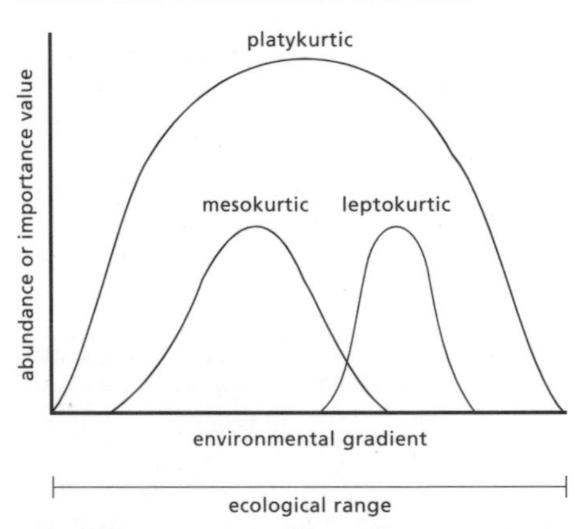

ECOLOGICAL RANGE EXPANSION The invasion, settlement, and population growth of a species into a region where it was formerly absent. Range expansion may be brought about because of: (1) intrinsic factors affecting the original population such as overcrowding or other dynamics or; (2) extrinsic factors offering favourable conditions at the new region such as resource availability, lack of competition, or climate modification. *See also* Dispersal.

ECOLOGICAL RESERVES In Canada, a legally protected natural area where human influence is minimized, functioning primarily for the preservation of genetic resources and for scientific research. Change, itself a natural phenomenon, is not interfered with but is allowed, as far as is possible, to proceed uninterrupted by humans.

Ecological reserves area a category of protected natural areas. The Ecological Reserve Programme was started in 1964 under the International Biological Programme (IBP) to locate, document, and seek protection for major natural ecosystems throughout the world. Since that time, most provincial jurisdictions have established legislation to set up a system of ecological reserves, and the system continues to evolve. *See also* Research Natural Areas.

ECOLOGICAL RISK ASSESSMENT A process that evaluates the likelihood that adverse ecological effects may occur or are occurring as a result of exposure to one or more stressors. Ecological risk assessment may evaluate one or more stressors and ecological components.

ECOLOGICAL RISK CHARACTERIZATION A process that uses the results of the exposure and ecological effects analyses to evaluate the likelihood of adverse ecological effects associated with exposure to a stressor.

ECOLOGICAL ROTATION *See* Rotation.

ECOLOGICAL SELF The larger self of which each of us is a part. In most spiritual traditions, it is recognized that the natural process of maturation takes us beyond narrow identification with our own self-interest to a larger sense of obligation, to family, to neighbourhood, to place, to the larger community, etc. The widest extent of love and caring is love for the ecos as a whole with its many beings. This is ecocentrism realized as ecosophy, ecological harmony, and the wisdom to dwell with unconditional love for a place. Thus the realization of the Ecological Self is held to be the flourishing of compassion and relationships that are spontaneously supportive and caring, rather than enforced from a system of rules and codes of ethics. The Ecological Self is the wider context; the egoself is the separate, small, boundaried self.

ECOLOGICAL SITE CLASSIFICATION A system originated by Angus Hill's hierarchical land classification system used in Ontario, and based on perceivable features of physiography (landform and climate) significant to production. The categories in the system include the following. **Landtype** is an area of land within a specific climatic region with particular soil texture and bedrock geology (e.g., a loam over bedrock). **Physiographic site** is a subdivision of landtype based on characteristics of soil moisture, depth of rooting zone, and relief (e.g., a shallow loam upland over limestone bedrock). **Physiographic site classes** are subdivisions of landtype established by characteristics of soil moisture, depth, and climate (e.g., a dry site class has some moisture but may vary in depth and local climate). **Physiographic site type** indicates the moisture, soil, and local climate gradients that are used to subdivide a landtype (e.g., moderately shallow, dry sites with with hot and dry local climate). **Physiographic site unit** is a subdivision of a site type based on any physiographic feature of significance in land-use planning.

ECOLOGICAL TIME The time period used to describe ecological changes (e.g., plant succession). Often measured as approximately ten generations of an organism's life span. *See also* Geological Time Scale.

ECOLOGY The science that studies the interrelationships, distribution, abundance, and contexts of all organisms and their interconnections with their living (biotic) and nonliving (abiotic) environment, in addition to the processes that determine ecosystem function, change over time, and response to disturbances. Ecology takes two main forms: (1) **systems ecology**, which relies heavily on computer modelling and inventory data; and (2) **field ecology**, which studies organisms and communities in their natural settings.

Ecology is a word now used in many contexts, and most disciplines have a branch that uses the word ecology or a prefix that is a contraction for it (e.g., socioecologists study human ecology).

ECONOMETRICS The testing and quantification of economic theories and the solution of economic problems by their conversion to mathematical forms, using mathematical processes and statistical analysis.

ECONOMICALLY ACCESSIBLE Resources located where not all the economic rent possible is dissipated in the costs of gaining access. *See also* Benefit-Cost Analysis.

ECONOMIC BASE The sum of all activities that result in the receipt of income, in any form, by a city's (or other type of region's) inhabitants. The analysis of an economic base distinguishes between basic economic activities, which create goods and services for export, and non-basic or service enterprises, whose products serve only the home area and result in no additional income flowing in from outside of the city (or region).

ECONOMIC RENT The value realized in excess of the production costs, and including an acceptable return on the investment necessary to achieve production.

ECOPHENE A direct modification of plant form resulting from environmental influences that is not heritable.

ECOPHILOSOPHY A branch of philosophy that goes further than environmental philosophy. It is philosophizing as if nature matters. The aim of ecophilosophy is to bring philosophy to the larger context that includes the natural world. An ecophilosopher is dedicated to understanding the spiritual and philosophical dimensions of environmental problems, and to contributing to positive understanding and creation of new ecological paradigms and ecocentric values that involve ecosophic practices. The ultimate aim of ecophilosophy is practical realization of **ecosophy**.

ECOSOPHY Literally, the wisdom of the household place. It implies the wisdom to dwell harmoniously and nondestructively in a place. It involves being receptive and responsive to the needs of a place and the wisdom that nature has enfolded into that place with its many beings and their communities of organization. Communities that live ecosophically evolve practices of forest and land use that are called **vernacular technologies**. For example, if shelters are built ecosophically, they reflect the places they grow out of and take full advantage of the natural heating and cooling characteristics of a place. Thus, they minimize the need for consumption and they maximize aesthetic fit.

ECOSPHERE **1** That part of Earth's atmosphere that is able to support life. **2** In philosophy, the total living community and all systems of the Earth and sky. Each whole entity is nested within a larger system that has features of being whole, such as self-reproduction, self-organization, and self-perfection (e.g., we are embedded in a human community, it is embedded in a larger society, which in turn is embedded in a bioregion, which is embedded in a larger ecoregion, and so on).

ECOSTATE Lacking a costa.

ECOSTERY A term made of two word parts: *ecos,* which means place, and *stery* from the word monastery, suggesting a sacred community. Hence, an ecostery is a place where ecological wisdom and harmony are learned, practised, and taught. It can refer to an individual or family dwelling and its place, a community and its place, when these are intentionally developed to be based on the aim of realizing and teaching ecosophy. The term can be used metaphorically, the ecostery serving as a model for our daily lives. It also applies to actual intentional communities that have nature sanctuaries and shrines, as well as educational programs aimed at practising, teaching, and living ecosophy.

ECOSYSTEM **1** A complex system of living organisms (plants, animals, fungi, and microorganisms), together with their abiotic environment (soil, water, air, and nutrients) that function together to circulate nutrients and create a flow of energy which creates biomass, a trophic structure in the living community, and a change in ecosystem form and function over time. **2** A unit of land or water comprising populations of organisms considered together with their physical environment and the interacting processes between them; for example, marsh, watershed, or lake ecosystem. Any one ecosystem has relative uniformity in the composition, structure, and properties of both the biotic and abiotic components and their interactions. Ecosystems do not have boundaries fixed in time or space, since their component parts are in a constant state of flux and can change rapidly or slowly, depending on prevailing environmental factors.

While many definitions tend to emphasize the component parts present, it is the processes acting on and/or initiated by the component parts that make the ecosystem function. Without the vital processes, the system is dysfunctional or, worse still, non-functional.

ECOSYSTEM CLASSIFICATION SCHEMES The basis of many different planning and management decisions, there are many different ecosystem classification schemes in use. Each one is designed to answer one or more questions, at one or more scales. In using a classification scheme, it is important to consider the following: (1) the purpose of the scheme and how the information derived will be used in practice; (2) the scale and its applicability (national, regional, local, site-specific), and if the data can be used at other scales as well; (3) Is the classification based on one or several components of the ecosystem? Which ones dominate? Do they include both abiotic and biotic factors? (4) Who carries out the assessments in the field? Geologists, biologists, foresters? Are their data gathered in such a way that they can all contribute to a broader understanding of the area (very desirable) or, are all data incompatible with other data sets (undesirable)? (5) Is the classification scheme static or can it be readily improved as new or better data become available?

Most of the classification schemes used in ecosystem management involve one or more of the following components: climate, physiography, soils, and vegetation. Vegetation is commonly used in most schemes, but has important limitations: (1) it is complex and may require identification and inclusion of entire ecosystems to be useful; (2) it is highly sensitive to disturbance, making a good understanding of site history essential; (3) it varies considerably in distribution, biomass, and association; (4) it has structural complexity both vertically and horizontally that may be of more importance than species composition for some planning activities; and (5) it is in a state of constant flux (succession), and thus different sites will have myriad different patterns of vegetation. Some of these difficulties are overcome by using climax or potential natural vegetation communities as the best indicator of any one ecosystem. *See also* Ecological Land Classification; Geographic Information Systems.

ECOSYSTEM FUNCTIONS The many and varied biotic and abiotic processes that make an ecosystem functional, changing, and interactive (e.g., biogeochemical processes, nutrient cycling, decomposition, regeneration, and succession).

ECOSYSTEM MANAGEMENT A management practice and philosophy aimed at selecting, maintaining, and/or enhancing the ecological integrity of an ecosystem in order to ensure continued ecosystem health while providing resources, products, or non-consumptive values for humans. An integral part of ecosystem management is the maintenance of ecologically significant structure and processes within the ecosystem. The actions taken reflect the management goals and range from protection from human influence through to an increasing intensity of interventions to serve human needs.

ECOTAGE Derived from the idea of ecological sabotage, the term reflects the actions taken by some radical environmentalists to dramatize concerns for particular places or nature as a whole. For example, these might include spiking trees to prevent their being cut and then advertizing that this has been done, or sabotaging equipment to prevent road building. *See also* Earth First!

ECOTHEOLOGY Theology practised and developed as if creation matters. It is claimed, in critique of traditional Christian theology, that it is anthropocentric in the sense of bias. Ecotheology holds that the Earth was created solely for humans by the Heavenly Father, God.

We can use it as we desire, for it is His gift to us. Only we have souls, for we are created in God's image, the rest of the Earth's beings do not. Most major religions have at least an implicit ecotheology. From the standpoint of ecocentrism, ecotheology can be destructive anthropocentrism in that it is thought to legitimize destruction of the natural world and its mastery and control by humans.

ECOTONE The transition zone where two structurally different plant communities meet. *See also* Edge.

ECOTOPIA A place that is ecologically balanced and harmonious, where the human dwellers in their communities have created life-forms that blend with natural processes and are thus nondestructive. An ecotopia is based on thinking of all beings, not just humans, as part of the community. A utopia is the ideal place for humans, but it need not consider the well-being of other creatures, whereas an ecotopia must.

ECOTYPE A genetic subdivision of a species (a subspecies) with distinct morphological and/or physiological characteristics, adapted to local or regional environmental conditions and that has resulted from genetic selection in response to local environmental factors.

ECTOPARASITE A parasite that lives on the outside of its host and gains nourishment by means of penetrating feeding structures, or by causing exudation of host tissues or fluids. Ectoparasites include some nematodes and many beneficial (to humans) insects that parasitize other insects.

ECTOPHYTE A plant growing on the outside of another plant in a parasitic relationship and deriving its nutrients from the host plant (e.g., dwarf mistletoe). *See also* Endophyte; Epiphyte.

ECTOTHERM *See* Homeotherm.

EDAPHIC The biological influence of soil conditions, such as moisture or texture, on the surrounding natural plant community.

EDDY A circular current of water, sometimes quite strong, diverging from and initially flowing contrary to the main current. Usually formed at a point at which the flow passes some obstruction or on the inside of river bends. It often forms backwater pools or pocket water in riffles. *See also* Pool; Riffle.

EDGE **1** The point at which dissimilar plant communities (different vegetation types, successional stages, or vegetative conditions) meet. Two principal forms of edges are: (1) **inherent edge**, or an edge created by a soil or topographical feature of the site; and (2) **induced edge**, where there are short-term effects created by changes in vegetation caused by natural or human-induced disturbances. *See also* Covert; Ecotone; Edge Contrast; Interspersion; Tension Zone.

EDGE CONTRAST A qualitative measure of the difference in structure of two adjacent vegetated areas (e.g., low-, medium-, or high-edge contrast). A low change in structure across the edge equates to low contrast, and vice versa.

EDGE EFFECT **1** The penetration of wind, light, and humidity creating differences in microclimate (air and soil temperature, wind, light, humidity), as well as sound, predation, and visibility, beyond and into vegetation bordering a zone of disturbance. The distance of edge effect penetration varies with the vegetation condition of the forest and the adjacent opening, as well as aspect and topography. Edge effects can drastically reduce the area of a vegetated 'island' that can function as 'interior' forest, thus creating important habitat modifications for a wide range of species. Edge effects also play an important role in the selection of sampling or experimental plots and must be accounted for in the experimental design and sampling strategy. **2** The increased richness of flora and fauna resulting from the mixing of two communities where they join. *See also* Edge; Interior Forest Conditions.

EDGE ENHANCEMENT In remote sensing, the use of analytical techniques to emphasize transition in imagery.

EDGE MATCHING In GIS work, a process to overcome the line mismatches that sometimes occur between adjoining map sheets or photographs.

EDGE SPECIES/EDGE SPECIALIST A species that is adapted to or successfully exploits the interface between two habitat or vegetation types. *See also* Edge.

EDGE TREE A tree on the edge of a stand and therefore growing under conditions of light and exposure that differ from those prevailing within the stand. Trees standing on a newly formed edge, as a result of harvesting, are often subject to windthrow or other stress factors as a result of sudden microclimatic and structural changes in the canopy and at the ground level. The form of edge trees reflects their past history: tall, high crowns with few lower branches indicate a tree that was once part of a larger stand. More fully formed crowns with branches extending well down toward the ground on the open side of the tree indicates that the tree has always been an edge tree.

EDGETYING *See* Edge Matching.

EDITING The modification of an existing data set to a more desirable (updated) or more correct (error correction) format (e.g., in GIS work, the addition, deletion, or modification of polygons, lines, points, and associated labels).

EFFECTIVE AREA OF AERIAL PHOTOGRAPH That central part of the photograph delimited by the bisectors of overlaps with adjacent photographs. On a vertical photograph, all images within the effective area have less displacement than their corresponding images on adjacent photographs. *See also* Displacement.

EFFECTIVE POPULATION SIZE The size of an ideal population, which when contrasted to the population under study, would possess the same rate of increase in inbreeding, or decrease in genetic diversity due to genetic drift.

EFFERENT Leading, or conducting away from an organ or location (e.g., blood vessels conducting fluids away from a specific organ). *See also* Afferent.

EFFICACY The effectiveness of a planned action to achieve the desired results (e.g., the effectiveness of a pesticide to kill or greatly impair the targeted pest).

EFFICIENCY The ratio of outputs to inputs. All processes, whether physical, chemical, or biological, use some of the energy inputs to drive the actual process. Consequently, energy inputs (resources of any kind) never equal energy outputs (products). A highly efficient process uses up very little energy (resources), while a very inefficient process absorbs most of the energy (resource) inputs for little gain in outputs. Efficiency is an important aspect of all systems. In ecosystems, the term includes: (1) **utilization efficiency**, the proportion of primary producer energy exploited by the primary consumer trophic level relative to the total energy produced; (2) **assimilation efficiency**, the ratio of energy digested and assimilated by a consumer trophic level relative to the overall energy inputs to that level; (3) **tissue growth efficiency**, the ratio of energy used to develop net production relative to the total energy assimilated; (4) **ecological growth efficiency**, the ratio of energy ingested relative to the energy converted into net production; and (5) **trophic efficiency**, the ratio of net production in one trophic level to net production in the previous tropic level.

EFFIGURATE An organism having a definite shape or outline. *See also* Effuse.

EFFLUENT STREAM **1** A stream intersecting and gaining water from the water table. **2** Liquid waste products entering the environment from sewage or industrial processes. *See also* Influent Stream.

EFFUSE The shape of bacterial cultures; spreading out loosely or flat. *See also* Effigurate.

EFFUSED-REFLEXED Describes the shape of a sporophore that is spread out over the substratum and turned back at the margin.

EGALITARIANISM A belief or philosophy that advocates the elimination of social, political, and economic inequalities, and promotes the notion that all people are of equal intrinsic worth and should have equal access to the rights and privileges of their society.

EGG SCAR A plant wound where an insect has laid its eggs; the scar left after an insect has oviposited in a plant.

EIGENANALYSIS The process of extracting characteristic roots from a transposed data matrix using matrix algebra.

EIGENVALUE In eigenanalysis, the variance accounted for by a new axis is represented by its eigenvalue. An eigenvalue has a value between 0 and 1. The sum of all the eigenvalues equals the 'trace' or total variance, which is equal to the number of variables in a transposed matrix. *See also* Principal Components Analysis.

EIGENVECTOR Eigenvectors are a product of eigenanalysis. Associated with each eigenvalue is an eigenvector, which represents the correlation of variables with each axis. The value of each eigenvector represents the ordination scores for the stands. The ordination diagram thus consists of a scatter plot of the eigenvector scores. *See also* Principal Components Analysis.

ELAIOSOME A small protuberance of nutritious tissue attached to a seed that attracts ants and facilitates dispersal of the seed. Examples of plants with elaiosomes include the Bloodroot (*Sanguinaria canadensis*), Trilliums (*Trillium* spp.), Twinleaf (*Jeffersonia diphylla*), and Bleedinghearts (*Dicentra* spp.). *See also* Myrmecochore.

ELAPSED TIME **1** The total time required to complete an operation from start to finish. **2** In fire-fighting operations, it is usually divided into the following phases. **Discovery time** is the period from the start of a fire (estimated or known) until the time of discovery. **Report time** is the period from discovery of a fire until the first person charged with initiating suppression action is notified of its existence and location. **Get-away time** is the period from receipt of a report of a fire by the first person responsible for suppression until departure of the initial attack force. **Travel time** is the period between departure of the initial attack force for a fire and its arrival at the fire. **Attack time** is the period from receipt of the first report of a fire to the start of actual fire-fighting, including get-away and travel time. **Control time** is the period from initial attack until the fire is controlled. **Mop-up time** is the period from achievement of control until enough work has been done to ensure the fire can not rekindle. **Patrol time** is the period from completion of mop-up until the fire is declared out.

ELAPSED TIME STANDARDS The maximum amounts of time allowed by agency policy for given steps of fire suppression.

ELATOR A small, unicellular, threadlike structure found in the spores of liverworts and other cryptogams.

ELECTROMORPHS Proteins that have been isolated by electrophoresis and can thus be distinguished.

ELECTROPHORESIS In genetics research, a technique in which related enzymes can be separated by means of an electric field. The results give an indication of how closely (if at all) certain substances are matched and by extension, possibly related.

ELEMENTS **1** The principal chemicals found naturally, or artificially created, on the earth. Elements are incapable of decomposition into simpler substances by normal chemical or physical methods. **2** A substance or phenomenon (wind, water, fire) in its simplest, least adorned state (i.e., elemental). **3** The main structural components of an ecosystem or landscape.

ELEVATION The vertical distance from a datum, typically mean sea level, to a point or object on the Earth's surface. Elevation may not necessarily be the same as altitude, which is the vertical distance above the Earth's surface.

ELEVATION LOSS In hydraulics, the pressure loss caused by raising water through a hose or pipe to a higher elevation (roughly equal to one psi for every two-foot increase in elevation above the pump). *See also* Head.

ELFIN FOREST High-elevation forest in moist temperate regions characterized by stunted trees and covered in epiphytes.

ELICITOR The production, by a host or pathogen, of a molecule that induces a response (e.g., the production of a phytoalexin) in the host.

ELLIPTICAL Shaped like an ellipse; oblong with regularly rounded ends. *See also* Leaf Shape.

ELUVIATION The removal of soil components (such as clay) or nutrients in solution or suspension from one or more soil horizons by percolating water. The process involves mobilization and translocation of the materials. That part of the soil is then said to be eluviated or is an eluvial horizon. *See also* Illuviation (for illustration); Leaching.

ELYTRON Plural elytra. The hard or leathery forewings of beetles that cover the membraneous hind wings when the insect is not in flight.

EMARGINATE Having a shallow notch at the apex. *See also* Leaf Shape.

EMBEDDED BARK *See* Included bark.

EMBEDDEDNESS The degree to which larger particles (boulders or gravel) are surrounded or covered by fine sediment. It is usually measured in classes according to the percentage of coverage of the larger particles by fine sediments.

EMBER TRANSPORT *See* Heat Transfer.

EMBRYO **1** The new plant, enclosed in a seed, comprising an axis and attached cotyledon, plus young secondary leaves. Embryos of pteridophytes and nonvascular plants are not enclosed in seeds and have no resting stage. **2** In animals, the stage following cell cleavage and up to the point of being born or hatching from an egg.

EMBRYOPHYTES Plants forming embryos (e.g., bryophytes and vascular plants).

EMBRYOTEGA A disclike callosity on the seed coat near the hilium.

EMERGENCE **1** The act of an adult insect leaving the host tissue in which it has developed (e.g., bark beetles emerging from a brood tree). *See also* Eclosion; Hatching. **2** The appearance of a developing aerial part of a plant, particularly of a plant that has just germinated above the surface of the soil.

EMERGENCE HOLE *See* Exit Hole.

EMERGENCE PERIOD The time period between the first and last appearance of adults of a generation or brood of insects.

EMERGENCY LOCATOR TRANSMITTER (ELT) A radio transmitter attached to an aircraft structure that operates from its own power source on 121.5 megahertz and 243 megahertz, transmitting a distinctive downward-sweeping audio tone for search-and-rescue teams to home in on. It is designed to function without human action after an accident.

EMERGENT VEGETATION Plants that have their roots in shallow water, with the remaining structures (stems and leaves) above the water (e.g., cattails). *See also* Submergent Vegetation.

EMERSED Above water.

EMIGRATION Permanent movement of individuals of a population away from the area occupied by that population to a new area. *See also* Colonization; Immigration; Migration.

EMINENT DOMAIN The legal right or power of government or public agencies to claim private property for public use, usually in return for a level of compensation negotiated or offered to the landowner.

EMISSION FACTOR The amount of pollution released to the atmosphere per unit weight of dry fuel consumed during combustion.

EMISSION RATE **1** The mass of a specific pollutant released to the atmosphere per unit mass of dry fuel consumed per unit time. **2** The quantity of pollutant released to the atmosphere per unit length of fire front per unit time.

EMPIRICAL DISTRIBUTION FUNCTION Also termed the cumulative relative frequency. The proportion of responses up to and including a specified response category.

EMPIRICAL MODEL A model that is based on observational (qualitative), or experimental (quantitative) data.

EMPIRICAL YIELD TABLE *See* Yield Table.

EMPTY WEIGHT The weight of a helicopter including the structure, powerplant, all fixed equipment, all fixed ballast, unusable fuel, undrainable oil, and total quantity of hydraulic fluid. *See also* Equipped Weight.

ENATION An outgrowth, usually virus-induced, from the surface of a plant organ, such as a stem or leaf.

ENDANGERED SPECIES ACT In the US, an act passed in 1973 and subsequently amended several times. The legislation places the conservation of listed species above almost all other considerations. It provides for identifying (listing) endangered and threatened species or distinct segments of species, monitoring candidate species, designating critical habitat, preparing recovery plans, consulting federal agencies to ensure that their actions do not jeopardize the continuing existence of listed species or adversely modify critical habitats, restricting importation and trade in endangered species or products made from them, and restricting the taking of endangered fish and wildlife. *See also* COSEWIC.

ENDEMIC **1** Native; indigenous to a particular area; not introduced and often with a limited geographical range. Many tropical forest species are endemic, whereas most species of northern forests have broad geographical and habitat ranges. *See also* Exotic Species. **2** Describes a disease that is permanently established and occurs with little variation in severity within a particular area. *See also* Enphytotic; Enzootic; Epidemic; Epiphytotic; Epizootic.

END MORAINE A ridge of glacial till (less commonly, other drift) formed at the terminus of a valley glacier or at the margin of an ice sheet when it is in balance (i.e., the rate of advance is equal to the rate of melting), and thus a ridge of material accumulates. The term includes terminal moraines and recessional moraines. *See also* Drumlin (for illustration).

ENDOBIOTIC Living or growing inside another living organism.

ENDOCARP In fruit, the inner part of the pericarp.

ENDOCONIDIOPHORE A conidiophore that produces conidia within itself.

ENDOCONIDIUM A conidium produced within its conidiophore. Endoconidia are extruded from the tips of their conidiophores.

ENDOCYCLIC Describes rusts having a life cycle with spermogonial and aecial spore states only, in which the aeciospores function as teliospores.

ENDOPARASITE A parasite that lives inside its host.

ENDOPHLOEDAL Located within the bark.

ENDOPHYTE A plant growing within the tissues of another plant in a parasitic or a symbiotic relationship (e.g., a fungus). *See also* Ectophyte; Epiphyte.

ENDOPHYTIC SYSTEM Refers to mistletoes and is that part of the parasite that grows within the host; the cortical strands and sinkers.

ENDOSPERM A layer of cells in the immature seeds of flowering plants containing starch and oil. It is sometimes termed the albumen.

ENDOTROPHIC The fungal development of mycorrhizae inside the cell walls of a root.

ENDOZOOCHORE *See* Zoochore.

ENDPOINT **1** A characteristic of an ecological component that may be affected by exposure to a stressor. **2** A characteristic of valued environmental entities that are believed to be at risk. Two forms of endpoint have been recognized: (1) **assessment endpoint**, which is an explicit expression of the actual environmental value that is to be protected; and (2) **measurement endpoint**, which is a measurable response to a stressor that is related to the valued characteristics chosen as the assessment endpoints.

END WEIGHT The concentration of foliage at the distal end of branches, leading to potentially excessive levering forces on the entire branch, which may cause failure.

ENERGY BALANCE An energy balance represents the energetic state of a system at any given time. For example, the energy balance equation for a leaf in bright sunlight is:

$$R + \lambda E + C + S + G + P = 0$$

where

R = net heat gained through radiative exchanges, allowing for the absorption of both downward and upward components of long and shortwave radiation

E = evaporation rate multiplied by the latent heat of vaporization (λ), in order to express the evaporation rate in energy units

C = heat lost by convection

S = rate at which heat goes into storage within the leaf

G = conduction of heat down the petiole

P = rate at which energy is being trapped in chemical bonds by photosynthesis.

ENERGY RELEASE COMPONENT The computed total heat released per unit area within the fire front at the head of a moving fire. *See also* Available Fuel Energy.

ENERGY RELEASE RATE The rate of heat released within the fire front at the head of a moving fire.

ENHANCEMENT The alteration of environmental attributes in order to provide improvements. It is usually the result of planned or unplanned human activities in an attempt to mitigate undesirable aspects. Natural events also yield variable and constantly changing attributes. The concept of enhancement is subjective, and depends on context, point of view, and to a large extent, an anthropocentric attitude.

ENHANCEMENT BURN A prescribed fire for recreation and aesthetic purposes (e.g., to maintain parklike stands of trees and increase number and visibility of flowering annuals and biennials).

ENPHYTOTIC A plant disease that is constantly present in a given area and causes about the same amount of damage every year. *See also* Endemic; Enzootic; Epidemic; Epizootic; Epiphytotic.

ENSIFORM Sword-shaped with an acute tip.

ENTIRE Botanically, having a continuous unbroken margin, lacking teeth or indentations; smooth. *See also* Leaf Margin.

ENTOMOLOGY The scientific study of insects.

ENTOMOPHAGOUS Insect-eating organisms, usually invertebrates. *See also* Insectivorous.

ENTOMOPHILOUS Insect-pollinated. *See also* Anemophilous.

ENTRANCE COURT The point of invasion of a disease organism into its host.

ENTROPY The degree of chaos or disorder within a system. In thermodynamics, entropy is related to the portion of the energy contained in a system that can be converted to usable work.

ENVIRONMENT The combination of climatic, physical, chemical, and biotic conditions that may affect the growth and welfare of an organism or group of organisms.

ENVIRONMENTAL CHARACTERIZATION The prediction or measurement of the spatial and temporal distribution of a stressor and its co-occurrence or contact with the ecological components of concern.

ENVIRONMENTAL ETHICS A subdiscipline of values studies in philosophy; an applied area of ethics. Ethics is the disciplined study of moral values and the good. Environmental ethics has two main forms. (1) The first is based on axiology, that is, the development of a system of 'thou shalts' and 'thou shalt nots,' or a code, usually supported by an ethical theory. (2) The other form involves the realization that values are embedded in nature and that one cannot separate moral values from the whole spectrum of values.

ENVIRONMENTAL GRADIENT *See* Gradient.

ENVIRONMENTAL IMPACT ASSESSMENT (EIA) The actual technical assessment work that leads to the production of an environmental impact statement. In some countries, the term is used synonymously with environmental impact statement. The technical methodologies used must be scientifically sound, and explainable and defensible in a court of law. The scope of the assessment is typically outlined at the start of the project so that the project has some well-defined boundaries. These may include physical, temporal, political, cultural, and financial limits within the project mandate.

ENVIRONMENTAL IMPACT STATEMENT (EIS) A report required by law in many countries around the world, outlining the project being proposed, its anticipated effects, and environments likely to be affected, as they relate to human and nonhuman environments. The report must be systematic and interdisciplinary, integrating the natural and social sciences, as well as the design arts, in planning and in decisionmaking. The report must identify: (1) the environmental impact of the proposed action; (2) any adverse environmental effects that cannot be avoided should the proposal be implemented; (3) alternatives to the proposed action; (4) the relationship between local, short-term uses of man's environment and the maintenance and enhancement of long-term productivity; and (5) any irreversible and irretrievable commitments of resources that would be involved in the proposed action should it be implemented.

ENVIRONMENTAL LAPSE RATE The rate of decrease of temperature with elevation, determined by the vertical distribution of temperature at a given time and place. It is distinguished from process lapse rate, which is applied to an individual air parcel. *See also* Dry Adiabatic Lapse Rate; Lapse Rate.

ENVIRONMENTALLY SENSITIVE AREA (ESA) A term often used loosely (sometimes meaninglessly) to mean a site or area that has environmental attributes worthy of retention or special care. ESAs are important in the management of all landscapes and require tight definition to be defensible. A more exacting definition is: An environmentally sensitive area is any parcel of land, large or small, under public or private control, that already has, or with remedial action could achieve, desirable environmental attributes. These attributes contribute to the retention and/or creation of wildlife habitat, soils stability, water retention or recharge, vegetative cover, and similar vital ecological functions.

Environmentally sensitive areas range in size from small patches to extensive landscape features. They can include rare or common habitats, plants, and animals. Taken together, a well-defined and protected network of environmentally sensitive areas performs necessary ecological functions within urban and rural landscapes. This network makes a very important contribution to the overall quality of life for all species living in and around the area, and plays a particularly important role in maintaining or enhancing the health and livability of city and urban landscapes.

The delineation of ESAs must be achieved on the basis of defensible and measurable criteria, so that inventory data can be sieved to yield a list showing importance and environmental sensitivity of the areas under consideration. Suggested criteria are as follows: (1) The area provides habitats for rare or endangered indigenous species that are endangered regionally, provincially, or nationally. (2) The plant and/or animal communities of the area are identified as unusual, or of high quality locally within the municipality, the province (state), or country. (3) The ecological function of the area is vital to the healthy maintenance of a natural system beyond its boundaries, such as serving as a water storage or recharge area, or being an important wildlife migratory stopover or concentration point. (4) The area has an unusually high diversity of biological communities and associated plants and animals due to a variety of geomorphological features, soils, and associated vegetation and microclimatic effects. (5) The location of the area, combined with its natural or cultural heritage features, make it particularly suitable for scientific research and heritage conservation education purposes. (6) The area is an unusual habitat with limited representation in the municipality, province, or country, or is a small remnant of particular habitats that have virtually disappeared within the municipality. (7) The combination of landforms and habitats is identified as having high aesthetic value, in the context of the surrounding landscape, and any alteration would significantly lower its value. (8) The area represents a distinctive and unusual landform within the municipality, province, or country. (9) The area is large, potentially affording a habitat for species that require extensive blocks of suitable habitats. (10) The area provides a linkage of suitable habitat between natural biological communities. (11) The area, while not representing particularly rare or sensitive landforms, habitats, or species, does by its relatively undisturbed nature, represent a good example of features that are common but usually occur in disturbed landscapes. (12) The area is already set aside due to the presence of on-site or nearby hazard lands (geological hazards, floodplains, etc.) that would suffer unwanted degradation if the area were to be further disturbed.

ENVIRONMENTAL MODIFICATION SPECTRUM A concept that describes a continuum of settings that range from the totally modified landscape of a modern city to those remote and pristine reaches of a country. *See also* Recreational Opportunity Spectrum; Wilderness Opportunity Spectrum.

ENVIRONMENTAL PHILOSOPHY A division of applied philosophy that focuses on the environment and seeks to answer such questions as: What are our underlying assumptions about the nature of the world and our relationship to nature? What values are embedded in the modern Western world view? What role do our values play in shaping our actions toward the natural world?

ENVIRONMENTAL QUALITY A subjective and experiential attribute assigned by humans to a wide array of qualities that we deem desirable. These can be environmental attributes that are deemed essential to human health and safety, such as clean air or water, or spiritual attributes, such as the availability of wilderness or healthy forests with abundant wildlife. The qualities also involve psychological traits emanating from the surrounding natural and built environments. All of these qualities or attributes may exist without human designation, but it is only humans that make or assign values to these attributes, either as individuals or as groups. The notion of 'quality' is usually a separate reality for each person and is based on that person's beliefs and value judgments.

Ideally, assessment of environmental quality would be based on a set of measurable thresholds or indicators that would serve as a standard against which increasing or decreasing environmental quality could be judged. While some surrogate indicators can be used in this way (e.g., lichens as indicators of air quality, or benthic invertebrates as indicators of water quality), it is seldom feasible to use just one or two indicators to assess the quality of complex ecosystems.

ENVIRONMENTAL RESOURCE Resources, such as clean air, clean water, and scenic values, that are not considered assets in an assessment. Consequently, most interest is focused on activities that use these resources and to the ways in which the actions of some users affect the well-being of others. *See also* Biological Resources.

ENZOOTIC A disease of an insect or other animal that is permanently established in a particular area and occurs with low, relatively constant, severity and frequency. The animal equivalent of endemic for humans. *See also* Endemic; Enphytotic; Epidemic; Epiphytotic; Epizootic.

ENZYME A protein molecule produced in living cells that acts as an organic catalyst. They are sensitive to pH and temperature.

EOLIAN (AEOLIAN) Small soil particles transported or deposited into unconsolidated formations (such as sand dunes) by wind. They may include loess and sand. *See also* Loess.

EON The longest unit of geological time. Four eons are generally recognized: (1) the Phanerozoic eon (the eon of visible life), dating from the present back to about 580 million years ago; (2) the Proterozoic eon, dating from about 580 back to 2,400 million years ago; (3) the Archean eon, dating back from 2,400 to approximately 3,800 million years ago; and (4) the Pre-Archean eon, dating from 3,800 to 4,600 million years ago. Eons are divided into eras, periods, and epochs. *See also* Appendix 2: Geological Time Scales.

EPHEMERAL Lasting for brief periods of time (e.g., flowers lasting a few days).

EPHEMERAL STREAM *See* Stream.

EPICALYX A calyxlike involucre of bracts outside and below a true calyx; a false calyx.

EPICENTRE **1** The geographic location in which a pest outbreak originates or is first detected. **2** The point on the surface of the Earth where an earthquake is first detected; directly on top of the focus of an earthquake.

EPICHILE The terminal part of the lip in certain orchids.

EPICLASTIC Any clastic rock or sediment that is not pyroclastic in origin. Its constituent fragments are derived by weathering and erosion, as opposed to direct volcanic forces.

EPICORMIC SHOOT A shoot that develops from a dormant or adventitious bud, often in response to a pathogen, severe defoliation by an insect, or to the opening up of a stand of trees. Epicormic shoots may also be an indicator of internal decay or stress in certain species. Two types of epicormic growth are found. (1) **Watersprouts** develop on older wood located above the ground or above the graft union of landscape trees. They are rarely well-attached to the existing wood and, once they reach a large size, almost always fail by ripping out of the branch or tree trunk. (2) **Suckers** develop from roots below the ground, or from the trunk part below the graft union. As with watersprouts, they are not well-attached. Suckers on a grafted tree are of the original root stock and thus very different from the main grafted tree.

EPICOTYL The stem or axis of a germinating seedling above the cotyledons. *See also* Germination (for illustration).

EPIDEMIC A widespread, and often rapidly built up, unusually high level of incidence of an insect, or disease, or other pest problem in a human population. It is often applied loosely to such incidences in populations of other organisms. *See also* Endemic; Enphytotic; Enzootic; Epiphytotic; Epizootic; Outbreak.

EPIDEMIOLOGY The scientific investigation of the causes, distribution, control, and the factors influencing the spread of infectious diseases.

EPIDERMIS The outermost layer of cells in a plant. *See also* Palisade Layer (for illustration).

EPIGEAL Seed germination, where the cotyledons are borne above ground and form the first foliage leaves of the plant. *See also* Hypogeal.

EPIGYNOUS Specifically, borne on or arising from the ovary. More typically, the sepals, petals, and stamens appearing to be on the ovary, but actually growing from the edge of the floral cup or tube, which is adnate to the ovary and free above it. An epigynous flower has its floral cup adnate to the ovary. *See also* Hypogynous; Perigynous; Receptacle (for illustration).

EPINASTY In the strictest sense, a downwards curving of leaves or stems due to the cells on the upper sides elongating more rapidly than those of the lower sides. It is often used incorrectly to describe any curling or twisting of a plant organ caused by uneven growth patterns. Epinasty may be a symptom of damage due to exposure to a synthetic growth regulator type of herbicide, such as 2,4-D. *See also* Hyponasty.

EPIPARASITE An organism that is parasitic on another organism, that in turn parasitizes a third organism.

EPIPELAGIC The surface layer of oceans.

EPIPETALOUS Borne on or arising from the petals or corolla.

EPIPHYLLOUS Growing on the upper, adaxial surface of leaves or needles.

EPIPHYTE A plant growing on the outside of another plant in a nonparasitic relationship. Most of the plant's necessary moisture and nutrients are derived from the atmosphere, or from throughfall and stemflow, nutrients that the host plant has already lost (e.g., bromeliads, moss, orchids). *See also* Ectophyte; Endophyte; Saprophyte.

EPIPHYTOTIC A widespread and destructive outbreak, at epidemic levels, of a plant disease. *See also* Endemic; Enphytotic; Enzootic; Epidemic; Epizootic.

EPISQUAMOUS Growing on scales, particularly the scales of seed cones.

EPISTASIS The interaction of genes at different loci leading to one gene interfering with the expression of another. The suppressing gene is called the epistatic gene, while the suppressed gene is the hypostatic gene.

EPITHET In describing plants, any word (in the name of a taxon below the rank of genus) following the name of the genus and not denoting rank (e.g., in the name *Pinus sylvestris,* the word *sylvestris* is a specific epithet).

EPIZOOTIC An epidemic disease in an insect or other animal population. *See also* Endemic; Enphytotic; Enzootic; Epidemic; Epiphytotic.

EPOCH In geological time scales, a subdivision of a period. *See also* Eon; Era; Period.

EQUILIBRIUM A system that is in balance, with inputs and outputs matching; a condition of stasis.

EQUILIBRIUM MOISTURE CONTENT **1** The moisture content that a fuel element would attain if exposed for an infinite period in an environment of specified constant dry-bulb temperature and relative humidity. When a fuel element has reached its equilibrium moisture content, it neither gains nor loses moisture as long as conditions remain constant. **2** That moisture content within a piece of wood at which it neither gains nor loses moisture when exposed to a constant set of temperature and humidity conditions. *See also* Air-dried Wood; Fibre Saturation Point; Kiln-Dried Wood.

EQUILIBRIUM TURNOVER The change in species composition of an area when immigration rate equals extinction rate.

EQUIPPED WEIGHT The empty weight of a helicopter plus the weight of the equipment required for the mission, plus the weight of oil. *See also* Payload.

EQUITABILITY **1** In ecology, the evenness relative to any specific standard or model of species abundance. The uniformity of abundance in an assemblage of species. Equitability is greatest when all species are equally numerous. **2** The relative distribution of goods or services among a population through time.

EQUITANT Describes conduplicate leaves that overlap one another in two ranks, to form a fan or row (as in iris).

ERA In geological time scales, a subdivision of an eon. For example, the Phanerozoic eon is made up of the Cenozoic, Mesozoic, and Paleozoic eras. A detailed breakdown is provided in Appendix 2: Geological Time Scales. *See also,* Eon; Epoch; Period.

ERADICANT **1** A fungicide that is used to control disease after infection has occurred. **2** A fungicide that kills the attacking organism at the surface of its host, or at its source before it

can reach a host (e.g., infected leaves lying on the ground). *See also* Fungistatic; Protectant.
ERADICATION **1** The complete elimination of a particular organism from a specific area. Contemporary pest management is not based on the concept of pest elimination, but rather on the concept of containment to acceptable levels. However, in some circumstances, complete elimination may be a goal (e.g., for newly introduced pests in a limited geographic area, household pests, or pests infesting trees of historical or special value). **2** The control of a disease by elimination of the pathogen after it is already established. This may refer to the removal of infected parts of one host, or to the removal of infected individuals from a host population (e.g., by sanitation thinning, destruction of infected residual trees in cutover stands, or pruning of infected branches). *See also* Extermination.
ERICACEOUS Plants in or related to the heather family (Ericaceae), typically found on acidic soils (e.g., Arbutus, Rhododendron, *Vaccinium* spp.).
ERINEUM A gall composed of tiny plant hairs with round beads. The gall develops in the form of a velvety and sometimes glossy pad. They are caused by eriophyid mites.
EROSE Irregularly jagged and having the look of being gnawed or eroded.
EROSION **1** The wearing away of the land surface by running water, wind, ice, or other geological agents, including such processes as gravitational creep. The following terms are used to describe different types of water erosion. **Accelerated erosion** is much more rapid than normal, natural, or geological erosion, occurring primarily as a result of the influence of human activities, or occasionally, animals. **Geological or natural erosion** is normal or natural erosion caused by geological processes (water, wind, ice) acting over long geological periods under conditions of natural vegetation and climate undisturbed by humans. **Gully erosion** is a process in which water accumulates in narrow channels and, over short periods, removes the soil from this narrow area to considerable depths, ranging from 0.5 metres to as much as 25 to 30 metres. **Interill erosion** is the removal of a fairly uniform layer of soil on a multitude of relatively small areas by splashes due to raindrop impact or film flow. **Normal erosion** is the gradual erosion of land used by humans which does not exceed geological/natural erosion. **Rill erosion** is the process in which numerous small channels of only several centimetres deep are formed, and is mainly found on recently cultivated soils. **Sheet erosion** is the removal of soil from the land surface by rainfall and surface runoff; often interpreted to include rill and interill erosion. **Splash erosion** is the detachment and airborne movement of small soil particles caused by the impact of raindrops on soil. On hillslopes and steep terrain, an erosion zone can occur on the shoulder, footslope, and toeslope. *See also* Hillslope (for illustration). **2** The detachment and movement of soil or rock by water, wind, ice, or gravity. The following terms are used to describe different types of water and wind erosion. **Saltation** is (1) the bouncing or jumping action of soil particles (usually 0.1 to 0.5 millimetres in diameter, but occasionally much larger) by wind, usually at a height less than 15 centimetres above the soil surface, for relatively short distances; (2) the bouncing or jumping action of mineral particles, including gravel or stones, affected by the energy of flowing water; or (3) the bouncing or jumping movement of material downslope in response to gravity. **Surface creep** is the rolling of dislodged soil particles 0.5 to 1.0 millimetres in diameter by wind along the soil surface, or the movement of soil particles downhill under the influence of gravity. **Suspension** is the movement of soil particles, usually less than 0.1 millimetres in diameter, through the air, usually at a height of greater than 15 centimetres above the soil surface, for relatively long distances. The term also applies to sediments suspended in water (e.g., suspended sediment).

In a forestry context, erosion is an important factor in the integration of timber management with other values, such as retention of fishery habitats. The accumulated duff, litter, and humus on the forest floor dissipates the energy of falling rain, minimizes overland water flows, and protects erodible soils. The root systems of the vegetation bind soil together and reduce water transport capability. The removal or severe disturbance of the litter and duff layer or root systems increases the potential for severe erosion and damaging siltation downstream.
EROSIONAL A landform, position, or general character that owes its origins to wearing down processes, such as removal of weathered rock debris by any mechanical or chemical processes that then form a new feature (e.g., a pediment or valley side).
EROSION PAVEMENT A layer of gravel or coarse

fragments that are left behind on the surface after the finer sediments have been eroded by wind or water.

ERRATIC **1** Boulders or smaller clasts of rock types that are dissimilar to underlying bedrock and transported to their present location by glacier ice. **2** An irregular, unpredictable course of action or pathway.

ERROR **1** In statistics, the difference between an observed or computed value of a quantity and the ideal or true value of that quantity. Errors are defined by types or by causes. Anticipation of errors is an essential part of modelling and hypothesis-building. A **Type I** error is committed if the Null Hypothesis is rejected, when in fact it is true (rejecting assumptions when they are in fact true). The probability that a Type I error will be made is termed the level of significance of the test and is denoted by α. A **Type II** error is committed if the Null Hypothesis is accepted when in fact it is false (failing to reject assumptions when they are actually false). In any given test, the probabilities of Types I and II errors are inversely related, that is, the smaller the risk of a Type I error, the greater the probability of a Type II error. **2** In measurement, derivation of an incorrect result arising from inaccurate measurement or collection of the raw data; imprecise measurements; bias in the measurements, sampling strategies, or data compilation; and computational errors due to incorrect arithmetic. *See also* Null Hypothesis; Significance.

ERUMPENT Fungal hyphae that break through a surface; bursting forth.

ESCAPE **1** An exotic or cultivated plant or animal that breaks away from the original population and colonizes elsewhere as a wild population. **2** The failure of an inherently susceptible plant to become diseased because it did not become infected. **3** A prescribed burn, or a wildfire previously under control, that breaks away from the main fire area to start a new fire, or breaks out of the control lines and expands the size of the original fire.

ESCAPED FIRE A wildfire (or prescribed fire that has burned beyond its intended area) that remains out of control following initial attack.

ESCAPED FIRE ANALYSIS The process of deciding what action to take on an escaped fire. This involves a review and analysis of the threats to public safety, values-at-risk, resource management objectives, probable fire effect(s), existing fire load, present and anticipated fire behaviour, availability of fire suppression resources, probability of successful control, and feasible fire suppression methods to minimize costs and reduce fire damage(s) and/or maximize fire benefits. The decision may be to maintain, increase, decrease, or discontinue the fire suppression effort. *See also* Fire Suppression; Limited Action Fire.

ESCAPEMENT The number of adult fish that avoid being caught by fishing gear and manage to migrate upstream to their spawning grounds.

ESCAPE ROUTE A preplanned route leading away from a dangerous area in a fire, or from the base of a tree being felled.

ESCARPMENT A steep slope that is usually of great lateral extent compared to its height, such as the risers of river terraces and steep faces associated with stratified rocks. Escarpments are produced by differential erosion or faulting of the bedrock.

ESKER A sinuous ridge of sand and gravel resulting from deposition by meltwater in a tunnel beneath or within a glacier or ice sheet. The ridges generally trend at right angles to a glacier margin, and the sand and gravel may be covered by till or glaciolacustrine sediments.

ESTABLISHED **1** Describes an introduced organism, which may be exotic or a reintroduction, that survives and develops a new population over time in its new location. **2** Describes a plantation that is adequately stocked, free of competing vegetation, safe from normal adverse conditions such as frost, drought, or animal damage, and vigorous enough to allow some anticipated volume yields in the future. Sometimes applied to naturally regenerated stands.

ESTABLISHMENT PERIOD The time elapsing between initiation of regeneration and its acceptance at a free-to-grow status.

ESTIMATOR A function of sample data that describes or approximates a parameter.

ESTIPULATE Without stipules.

ESTRUS Also spelled Oestrus. The period during which female animals are sexually responsive to males. It is synonymous with 'heat' and 'breeding period.' *See also* Rut.

ESTUARY A semi-enclosed body of water that has a free connection with the open ocean and within which sea water is measurably diluted with fresh water derived from land drainage. They can also be a drowned river mouth created by the subsidence of land near the coast, or by the drowning of the lower portion of a nonglacial valley due to a rise in sea level.

Estuaries are found at the mouths of rivers and streams and are subject to tidal conditions. They include five main habitat types. (1) **Upland** includes vegetated areas above the tidal reach under forest, woodland, or grassland. (2) **Freshwater** includes rivers and streams leading into the estuary and free from saltwater influences. (3) **Intertidal zone** includes marshland (upper intertidal) and mudflats (lower intertidal). (4) **Subtidal zone** is the area located below the low tide zone. (5) **Saltwater** includes oceans or bays subject to constant tidal influence.

Estuaries are extremely productive sites for benthic invertebrates due to the constant flushing action of the tides, which mixes freshwater and saltwater organisms and nutrient loads. They provide abundant sources of food for fish and larger organisms. They are also extremely sensitive, often unstable ecosystems, with limited diversity of plant and animal life, and can easily be destroyed or severely damaged.

ETHNICITY **1** The characteristics of a large group of people classed according to common traits or customs. **2** The condition of people belonging to a particular cultural group.

ETHNOBOTANY A branch of botanical study concerned with the ways in which people utilize plants, including plant lore, agriculture, medicinal, and religious uses.

ETIOLATION The whitening (yellowing) of foliage and the resultant lack of chlorophyll production. It is normally due to a lack of light or infection with a pathogen. Other symptoms include abnormally small leaves and elongation of stems. Etiolation is normally associated with lack of light, while chlorosis, producing similar symptoms, is due to some other cause. *See also* Chlorosis.

ETIOLOGY **1** The examination and/or determination of the causes of a disease, including the predisposing factors, the biotic or abiotic pathogens, and the interactions of hosts, pathogens, or parasites and the environment over time.

EUGENIC Any process that tends to improve the genetic quality of a population of organisms. In a forestry context, the retention of trees having genetically superior characteristics as a source of seed, would be considered a eugenic activity. *See also* Dysgenic.

EUKARYOTE Any organism with cells having a distinct nucleus surrounded by a membrane and several distinct organelles. Includes all higher unicellular and multicellular organisms, except bacteria, the blue-green algae, and actinomycetes. An organism with these traits is said to be eukaryotic. *See also* Prokaryote.

EUPHOTIC ZONE The upper portion of a water body penetrated by sunlight.

EUPLOID A cell having a chromosome number that has one or multiples of the same chromosome set. A condition called euploidy. *See also* Aneuploid.

EUSTATIC Pertaining to worldwide changes of sea level that affect all the oceans. **Glacio-eustacy** refers to changes in sea level brought about by the interchange of water between oceans and ice sheets.

EUTROPHICATION The natural, but more commonly, human-induced addition of nutrients (especially nitrogen and phosphorus) to a body of water, resulting in high organic production rates that may overcome the natural self-purification processes. Eutrophication produces several undesirable effects, including algal blooms, seasonally low oxygen levels, and reduced survival opportunities for fish and invertebrates. Excessive nutrient inputs are frequently derived from sources of pollution on the adjacent lands. Water bodies in this state are said to be eutrophic. *See also* Bloom; Dystrophic; Nutrient; Oligotrophic.

EVALUATION A determination of the worth, quality, significance, amount, degree, or condition of something by careful appraisal and study.

EVALUATION INTERVAL/CYCLE The period of time between evaluations.

EVANESCENT An organ or part thereof that is only slightly developed and soon disappears.

EVAPORATION The loss of molecules as a liquid changes into a gaseous phase.

EVAPOTRANSPIRATION The movement of water from the soil, an individual plant, or plant communities to the atmosphere by evaporation of water from the soil and transpiration of water by plants.

EVEN-AGED A crop or forest containing examples that are all within a narrow band of ages, or within one age class. *See also* All-Aged.

EVEN-AGED STAND A stand of trees in which the age differences among trees are small, usually less than 10 to 20 years, or 30 per cent of the rotation age in stands more than 100 years old. Even-aged stands result from disturbances occurring at one point in time, such as wildfires, a clearcut, a seed tree cut, or a shelterwood cut, or coppicing.

EVEN-AGED MANAGEMENT A planned sequence of treatments designed to maintain and regenerate a forest stand with one age class. The range of tree ages is usually less than 20 per cent of the rotation.

EVENNESS The extent to which all species in a community are equally abundant, rather than one or two species greatly exceeding the others in abundance. It is the opposite of dominance in a community. *See also* Diversity.

EVERGREEN Trees with green leaves or needles that are retained throughout the season with no marked period of leaf shedding. As a result, the tree is capable of year-round photosynthesis and may have a competitive advantage over other species – an evolutionary factor that partly explains the great success of conifers around the world. Some evergreens have adapted leaf forms to assist in water conservation (e.g., conifers have needles, while broad-leaf evergreens, such as arbutus, laurel, and holly, have very waxy leaves). *See also* Deciduous.

EVOLUTION A cumulative genetic change in a population of organisms related by descent, over time. It is typically the result of natural selection but can also be due to random genetic drift. Evolution has no determined endpoint.

EXCIPLE The portion of the apothecium surrounding the hymenium and that forms the margin of the apothecium.

EXCLOSURE Structures, usually fences of some kind, designed to keep grazing animals out of certain areas.

EXCLUSION **1** The prevention of the entry of infected or infested plants into an area free of a pest, usually by means of quarantine enforcement. **2** The use of a physical barrier or similar measure to prevent pest damage to a plant.

EXCRESCENCE A gall or abnormal growth that disfigures a plant. It is akin to a tumour.

EXCURRENT Botanically: **1** Projecting or extending beyond a margin or apex, such as a midrib extended into a mucro or awn. **2** Having a growth habit where the main axis is dominant and remains clearly identifiable, with the branches secondary to it. *See also* Apical Control; Decurrent; Plant Form.

EXCURRENT PLANT FORM *See* Apical Control; Plant Form

EXFOLIATE The casting or flaking off of bark, or the spalling off of loose sheetlike layers of rock in concentric circles due to physical and chemical weathering.

EXFOLIATING Peeling off in thin strips, flakes or plates. It describes certain types of tree bark, weathered rock formations, or corroding metals.

EXHUMED In geology, a previously buried landform, geomorphic surface, or paleosol that has become re-exposed by erosion of the overlying materials.

EXINE/EXTINE The outer coat of a pollen grain.

EXISTENCE VALUE The external benefit that accrues to individuals having no intention of ever visiting or using the site or environment in question. These individuals are willing to give up resources simply to know that the area, feature, or good exists in a particular condition.

EXIT HOLE The hole made by an insect, usually the young adult, as it leaves the plant tissue (wood, bark, fruit, etc.) in which it developed. It is also called the emergence hole.

EXOCARP The outer layer of a fruit, or the fleshy part of a peach, or the husk of a walnut or hickory nut.

EXOSKELETON The hard, external covering of insects and other arthropods, which is periodically shed during moulting to allow for growth. The discarded skeleton is sometimes improperly referred to as a 'skin' or, more properly, 'exuviae.' *See also* Ecdysis; Moult.

EXOSTOME The outer layer of the peristome in mosses having two layers. Technically, the peristome layer with teeth, having two tiers of cells when viewed from the outside.

EXOTIC SPECIES A species accidentally or purposefully introduced into an area (reintroductions, transplants, restocking, or accidental releases) where it did not formerly occur. The concept of exotic versus native species depends on the temporal and spatial context of analysis, and if extended back to the last ice age, can be quite complicated. Exotic species often, but not always, have undesirable effects on native species and the ecological integrity of the native ecosystem. *See also* Native Species.

EXOZOOCHORE *See* Zoochore.

EXPECTATIONS The expectations of participants in a dispute resolution process about both what costs or benefits can be expected by participation, and how the process used to achieve these will happen. Issues of process may be as important as the actual outcomes.

EXPERIMENT A systematic process of testing something unknown. There are two main reasons for experimentation: (1) to see if a process works as expected; and (2) to try to find out how it works the way it does. In natural resource management there is often a reluctance to try something new because the image of experimentation is perceived to be one of uncertainty by the public. In fact, unless new ideas and techniques are tested experimentally, little progress can be made. This is especially true in most matters relating to ecology, where the interactions between theory and practice serve as a basis for experiments that will yield practical results which can be used to adapt the theory in light of better understanding. In all experiments, it is essential to remember that results perceived as failures are just as important, perhaps even more important, than results judged as successes. Both outcomes reveal greater insights into the nature of the problem under study, and new ideas raise new problems. Ultimately, the acid test of ecological success in natural resource management is always determined by the results on the ground, and carefully designed experiments are an essential part of this.

EXPERIMENTAL PLOT An area of ground defined as part of an experiment to determine the effects of certain treatments. Examination of such effects may be short or long term. *See also* Experimental Unit.

EXPERIMENTAL UNIT The basic unit of experimental material, which could be an area of ground, a tree, a colony of insects, or a community of plants. The units selected are as homogeneous as possible so that any effects recorded can be attributed to the experimental factors being manipulated rather than other factors inherent in the experimental unit.

EXPLANATE Spread out flat.

EXPLOITATION **1** The consumptive use of resources in order to provide benefit either individually or for a wider range of individuals. In a pejorative sense, the consumptive use is considered to be selfish, that is, of benefit to a few at the expense of many. **2** In wildlife management, the removal of individuals or biomass from a population by predators or parasites.

EXPLOITATION COMPETITION Competition in which two or more organisms consume the same limited resource. *See also* Competition; Exploitation; Interference Competition.

EXPONENTIAL GROWTH Growth that increases by a fixed percentage of the whole in a given time period. Can refer to an increase in numbers or mass. The rate of growth is expressed as e^n, where ^{n} is the exponent.

EXPOSURE **1** Property that may be endangered by a fire burning in another structure or by a wildfire. In general, property within twelve metres (forty feet) of a fire may be considered to involve exposure hazard. **2** *See* Aspect. **3** The general surroundings of a site, with special reference to openness, winds, and sunshine.

EXPOSURE LATITUDE The range of photographic exposure that results in an acceptable image.

EXPOSURE TIME The time a specified point in a burn is subjected to elevated temperatures, generally above a threshold of 60 degrees Celsius. It is synonymous with fire duration.

EXPRESSIVITY The intensity of phenotypic expression attributable to the effect of any one gene, which may be affected by genotype and environment.

EXSERTED Botanically, projecting and not included (e.g., the stamens exserted from a corolla). *See also* Included.

***EX SITU* CONSERVATION** Transfer of organisms (plant or animal) from one site (e.g., in the wild) to another site (e.g., seed banks, zoos), for the purpose of maintenance or breeding as a means of conserving the organism. *See also In Situ* Conservation.

EXSTIPULATE Without stipules.

EXTANT Now in existence.

EXTENDED ATTACK SITUATION A situation in which a fire cannot be controlled by the initial attack crew within a reasonable period of time. The fires usually can be controlled by additional resources within twenty-four hours after commencing suppression action. *See also* Escaped Fire.

EXTENSIVE Used to refer to spatial extent of disturbance by fire or logging. A disturbance that is widespread. The term has no implications about the intensity of disturbance. *See also* Intensity.

EXTENSIVE FOREST MANAGEMENT The protection of the forest from fire and insects, and relying on natural regeneration for provision of the next forest. *See also* Basic Forest Management; Intensive Silviculture.

EXTERMINATION The elimination of a particular organism from a structure or area. *See also* Eradication.

EXTERNALITY Affects (costs) generated by one person that create costs for someone else but are not paid for by the person generating them (e.g., downstream pollution or sedimentation caused by logging affecting fishery resources). In economic analysis, externalities result when production or consumption activities of one economic unit have a direct economic affect on the well-being of a separate production or consuming unit. Externalities are detrimental if the results deplete the spectrum of opportunities available for the separate unit. Beneficial externalities result when the separate unit gains opportunities without having to pay for them. Once the externalities to either party have been evaluated and included in the economic analysis, they become internalized.

EXTERNAL YARDING DISTANCE The slope distance from the landing to the farthest point within the cutting unit boundary.

EXTINCT In the narrowest sense, a species that no longer exists anywhere. The term is sometimes used in a regional rather than global setting.

EXTINCTION The termination of a species caused by failure to reproduce and death of all the remaining members of that species. Can be natural or human-induced.

EXTINCTION RISK The risk that a species may face premature extinction, defined in terms of the probability of extinction within a specified time period. It is based on the theory of extinction times for single populations and on meaningful time scales for conservation action. Three categories are recognized on the basis of decreasing probabilities of extinction risk over increasing periods of time: (1) **critical species**, having a 50 per cent probability of extinction within 5 years or 2 generations, whichever is longer; (2) **endangered species**, having a 20 per cent probability of extinction within 20 years or 10 generations, whichever is longer; and (3) **vulnerable species**, having a 10 per cent probability of extinction within 100 years. *See also* COSEWIC.

EXTINCTION VORTEX The genetic and demographic processes that occur when a population becomes small and isolated. The genetic problems of inbreeding depression and lack of adaptability can further reduce the population size, which in turn reduces the chances of finding a mate and successfully breeding. Thus, the population declines further, more inbreeding takes place, and genetic diversity is lost. The population tends to spiral downward at an ever-increasing rate, toward extinction.

EXTINGUISHING AGENT A substance used to put out a fire by cooling the burning material, blocking the supply of oxygen, or chemically inhibiting combustion. *See also* Fire Retardant; Foam; Inhibitor; Suppressant; Viscous Water.

EXTIRPATION The elimination of a species or subspecies from a particular area, but not from its entire range. *See also* COSEWIC; Locally Extinct.

EXTRACTION **1** A general term covering the removal of forest products from the forest to a loading point, for transportation elsewhere. It may include all operations of logging (falling, yarding, decking). **2** More specifically, the chemical or physical removal of one or more items or attributes from their source (e.g., delignification to extract cellulose from wood fibre, or stump extraction).

EXTRACTIVE RESERVES Conservation areas that permit certain kinds of resource harvesting on a (theoretically) sustainable basis.

EXTREME FIRE BEHAVIOUR A level of fire behaviour that often precludes any fire suppression action. It usually involves one or more of the following characteristics: (1) a high rate of spread and frontal fire intensity; (2) crowning; (3) prolific spotting; (4) presence of large fire whorls; and (5) a well-established convection column. Fires exhibiting such phenomena often behave in an erratic, sometimes dangerous manner. *See also* Blow-up; Conflagration; Fire Storm.

EXTRINSIC VALUES Resources of human origin, or recreational features resulting from human activity, which can be clearly contrasted with resources of natural origin (nonhuman). *See also* Intrinsic Values.

EXTRORSE Facing or directed outward. *See also* Introrse.

EXTRUSIVE Igneous rocks, derived from deep with the molten magma of Earth's crust, that have risen to the surface, including volcanically, and cool *in situ*. *See also* Intrusive.

EXUDATE The metabolites diffusing from plant roots into the soil or, the oozing or seeping of sap or gums from above-ground parts of a tree.

EXUVIAE The epi- and exocuticle material cast off by moulting insects in the process of ecdysis.

EYE Botanically, **1** the centre of a flower differentiated from the rest in colour. **2** A bud on a tuber. **3** A single lateral bud stem cutting.

F

FABRIC The attitude of clasts within a sediment or sedimentary rock; recorded as the trend and plunge of clast long-axes.

FACE **1** The side of a hill or mountain being logged. **2** One side of a tree, log, or cant. **3** The standing timber adjacent to an area already logged.

FACIES **1** A stratigraphic unit of rock or sediment distinguished by its composition or other characteristics, such as lateral changes in aspect. The sum of all primary lithologic and paleontologic characteristics exhibited by a sedimentary rock and from which its origin and environment of formation can be inferred. **2** In the Braun-Blanquet plant classification scheme, a local modification of an association, usually of small extent, characterized by great (sometimes temporary) abundance of one species.

FACILITATION Refers to the task of managing discussions in a joint session. A facilitator may be used in any number of situations where parties of diverse interests or experience are in discussion, ranging from scientific seminars to management meetings to public forums. A mediator will serve as a facilitator as part of his or her broader role.

FACT-FINDING Similar to arbitration, except that the fact-finder's findings are advisory. Underlying this process is the assumption that the judgment of an independent and respected but non-involved person will bring pressures to bear on the parties resulting in their accepting a compromise or accommodation on that judgment. The fact-finding process is usually less formal than an arbitration hearing. Fact-finding may also be termed 'non-binding' or 'advisory' arbitration.

FACTOR A circumstance affecting the results of an observation or experiment. **1** Used in describing a set of related treatments in an experiment; each treatment of the set is a different state or level of the factor (e.g., different varieties of the same plant species, different levels of fertilizer application, or different methods of cultivation). **2** In experimental design, randomization is often built into the design to permit separation of the effects attributable to controlled factors from those attributable to the uncontrolled factors.

FACTOR ANALYSIS A family of statistical techniques designed to represent a set of (interval-level) variables in terms of a smaller set of hypothetical values.

FACTORIAL EXPERIMENT An experiment in which all levels of two or more treatments or factors are applied singly and in combinations, so that differential effects can be observed.

FACTORS OF PRODUCTION The resources essential for production: land, labour, capital, and the entrepreneur to match all of these together productively.

FACULTATIVE SPECIES Refers to organisms able to survive in a wide range of environments, roles, modes of life, or environmental processes outside their normal or typical lifestyles. Thus facultative parasites can function as either parasites or saprophytes (e.g., the honey fungus *Armillaria mellea*). Facultative anaerobes are normally aerobic but can exist in anaerobic conditions. Facultative plants can occur in two or more distinct regimes, such as wetlands or uplands. *See also* Obligate Species.

FADE To change foliage colour slightly in the early process of dying. It usually occurs from a dark green toward a lighter grey green.

FAIRLEAD A device containing pulley wheels or rollers, used so that a winch can pull in a cable from any direction without damaging the cable as it spools on the drum.

FALCATE Sickle-shaped.

FALL BLOCK A block which, in tight-skyline systems, can be lowered to pick up loads on the ground and then raised as required for hauling them onto the landing. The block is long and narrow, with the pulley wheel(s) at the top, and balanced so that most of the weight is at the bottom.

FALL DOWN EFFECT A reduction in the allowable cut resulting from overharvesting the existing growing stock prior to accurately establishing sustainable harvest levels at a lower level. A reduction in the annual allowable cut under a sustained yield management regime due to pests, fires, and withdrawals of land creating reductions in the timber inventory or growth capacity of the remaining sites. A reduction in the allowable cut resulting from replacement of old-growth forests with second-growth forests having younger trees and smaller volumes per unit area at harvest.

FALLER A person who fells trees; also known as a feller.

FALLING WEDGE In tree-falling, one or more wedges hammered into the backcut of a tree to help direct the falling tree in the desired direction.

FALSE COLOUR In remote sensing, the use of one colour to represent another. For example, the use of red emulsion to represent infrared light in infrared film.

FALSE HEART Wood that has been discoloured by natural causes such as fungus, frost, or abnormal conditions of growth, such that it simulates normal heartwood. Typically very irregular in shape when viewed across the log.

FALSE SMOKE *See* Smoke.

FAN **1** An accumulation of detrital material in the shape of a low-angle cone, usually at the point where a stream emerges from a canyon onto a plain. **2** A sector of a cone with a gradient not steeper than fifteen degrees. *See also* Alluvial Fan; Colluvial Fan.

FAN APRON A sheetlike mantle of relatively young alluvium covering part of an older piedmont (and occasionally, alluvial fan) surface. At some point, it buries a pedogenic soil that can be traced to the edge of the fan apron where the soil emerges as the land surface, or relict soil. No buried soils should occur within a fan-apron mantle; instead, they separate the mantles.

FAN PIEDMONT The most extensive major landform of piedmont slopes, formed by the lateral coalescence of mountain-front alluvial fans downslope into one generally smooth slope without the transverse undulations of the semi-conical alluvial fans, and by accretion of fan aprons.

FAN TERRACE A relict alluvial fan, no longer a site of active deposition, incised by younger and lower alluvial surfaces. An abandoned former fan surface.

FARINACEOUS/FARINOSE **1** Starchlike, or containing starch. **2** Botanically, covered with a granular or mealy coating.

FARM FOREST The aggregation of trees, hedgerows, windbreaks, orchards, plantations, forests, agroforests, and their associated activities that typify the rural landscape on farm and range lands. *See also* Forest.

FASCIATION Bundled together; a malformation of plant stems, which become enlarged and flattened, as if by the fusion of several shoots. *See also* Witches' Broom.

FASCICLE **1** A bundle or cluster of stems, leaves, flowers, or other plant organs. **2** The point of attachment for needle clusters in conifers. The fascicle is usually wrapped by overlapping bud scales at its base (the fascicle sheath). These may drop off as the needles develop (soft pines) or they can persist (hard pines).

FASCICULATION Clustering or bundling of plant organs such as roots, twigs, or fruits about a common point. Often arises from adventitious development caused by pathogenic aggravation. *See also* Witches' Broom.

FASTIGIATE Plants having leaves or branches more or less parallel and pointed upward.

FAULT A fracture zone in the surface or underlying geological strata resulting from movements in the Earth's crust. A normal fault dips to the downthrow side, while a thrust fault or reverse fault, dips to the upthrow side. *See also* Plate Tectonics.

FAUNA The animal community found in one or more regions.

FAVOURABLE GRADE Describes a highway grade that is a downhill haul for a loaded log truck. Generally, a gradient that slopes downhill in the direction of log haul.

FEASIBILITY STUDY A preliminary survey undertaken to determine the practicality of undertaking a project prior to committing large amounts of money or other resources. The concept of practicality may include short- and long-term political, social, environmental, and financial aspects.

FEATURED SPECIES A species of fish or wildlife for which specific management guidelines have been written. These guidelines aim to coordinate all timber and wildlife habitat management efforts in an attempt to fulfil the needs of the selected species.

FECUNDITY **1** In general terms, the ability to reproduce prolifically. **2** The potential rate of production of viable offspring of an organism or a population, measured by the number of gametes or asexual propagules. It is often expressed as the number of female young produced annually per adult female in the population of interest. *See also* Fertility; Parthenogenesis.

FEEDBACK A system in which one component affects a second component that in turn affects the first component. The feedback can be positive (reinforcing) or negative (detracting).

FEELING FOR FIRE Examining burned material after the fire is apparently out and feeling with the bare hands to find live embers. *See also* Fire Suppression (cold trailing; mop-up).

FEE SIMPLE OWNERSHIP Ownership that may last forever and may be inherited by the heirs of an owner. Ownership that has no limitation, qualification, or condition affecting it and is the maximum possible ownership in real estate under the system of property rights founded on English Common Law.

FELDSPAR An important and widespread group of rock-forming crystalline minerals, common in igneous rocks, consisting of aluminum silicates in combination with potassium, calcium, sodium, and barium.

FELLER *See* Harvesting Machine Classification.

FELLER-BUNCHER *See* Harvesting Machine Classification.

FELLER-CHIPPER *See* Harvesting Machine Classification.

FELLER-DELIMBER *See* Harvesting Machine Classification.

FELLER-DELIMBER-BUNCHER *See* Harvesting Machine Classification.

FELLER-DELIMBER-SLASHER-BUNCHER *See* Harvesting Machine Classification.

FELLER-DELIMBER-SLASHER-FORWARDER *See* Harvesting Machine Classification.

FELLER-FORWARDER *See* Harvesting Machine Classification.

FELLER-SKIDDER *See* Harvesting Machine Classification.

FELLING *See* Harvest Functions.

FELSENMEER *See* Block Field.

FEN A landscape of low-lying peat land, made up of partly to well-decomposed sedge (occasionally moss) materials, where the water is at or near the surface and fed by relatively fast-moving, nutrient-rich groundwater that is usually neutral or alkaline, and rich in calcium. Surface vegetation is dominated by sedges, occasionally with trees present. *See also* Bog; Marsh; Swamp; Wetland.

FENESTRATE Botanically, a surface that is perforated with windowlike openings or transparent areas.

FERAL An animal that has escaped from domestication and returned to a wild state (e.g., feral horses, goats, pig, cats, and dogs). Feral individuals may be descendants of the original escapees.

FERN A leafy plant in the phylum Pterophyta. Leaves may be undivided or divided several times into leaflets (pinnae) as shown in the illustration. The fern life cycle consists of two main stages. In the gametophyte stage, a spore germinates and develops into a small (usually less than one centimetre wide), inconspicuous, and typically heart-shaped structure known as the gametophyte or prothallus. When mature, the male (antheridia) and female (archegonia) sex organs develop. After fertilization, an embryo begins to develop, eventually forming the sporophyte, and the gametophyte dies off. In the sporophyte stage, the fern consists of recognizable leafy fronds, rhizomes, roots, and sporangia (capsules). Spores are produced within the sporangia, which may consist of a single unit or, as multiple units in clusters, cones (strobili), or sori. Typically, ferns develop sori on the back of the pinnae. The sori consists of a sporangium or sporangia surrounded by an indusium. Inside a sporangium, spores are produced by meiosis and, when dispersed, begin the life cycle again by developing into independent gametophytes. *See also* Sorus.

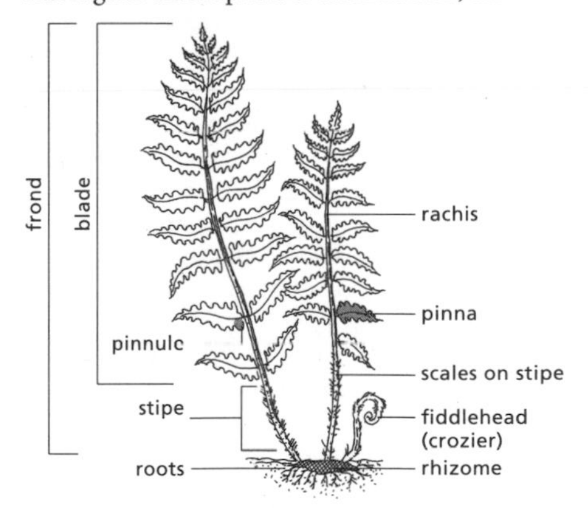

FERRALLITIC **1** A well-drained soil originating from basic igneous rocks, consisting mainly of hydrated oxides of iron and aluminum with a low silica dioxide content. **2** Generally, almost any soil made up of kaolinite, iron, aluminum oxides, and silica dioxide, but lacking weatherable minerals, free carbonates, or clays of the montmorillonite or illite groups. Such soils are often termed lateritic. *See also* Allitic; Ferruginous; Fersiallitic; Siallitic.

FERRUGINOUS **1** Describes a rust-coloured surface. **2** Minerals having iron in their composition. **3** A soil containing large quantities of iron compounds, especially the oxides. *See also* Ferrallitic.

FERRULE The metal band or socket in which the terminal end of a wire or wire rope is fastened securely.

FERSIALLITIC A soil whose clay fraction, generally kaolinite, contains appreciable amounts of siliceous clays, as well as free iron oxides and weatherable minerals. *See also* Ferrallitic; Siallitic.

FERTILE **1** An organism, typically female, having the capability to produce offspring as a result of sexual reproduction. **2** Botanically, stamens bearing functional pollen, flowers with functional pistils, or fruits containing viable seeds. **3** Shoots bearing flowers.

FERTILITY **1** In ecological studies, fertility is the reproductive performance of an organism or population measured by the number of viable offspring produced in a given period. *See also* Fecundity. **2** A measure of the nutrient status of soil and thus its capacity to grow plants.

FERTILIZATION The successful union of male and female gametes, resulting in the creation of a new individual cell, the zygote.

FERTILIZER Any organic or inorganic material of natural or synthetic origins (excluding liming materials) that is added to a soil to supply one or more elements essential to the growth of plants. Organic fertilizers contain carbon and one or more plant nutrients, in addition to hydrogen and/or oxygen. Inorganic fertilizers do not have carbon as a major component of the main chemical structure. Urea is often considered to be an inorganic fertilizer due to its rapid hydrolysis to form ammonium ions in the soil. Fertilizer can be added to the soil through surface applications or by mixing it in with the soil. In an urban setting, fertilizer is sometimes applied as a foliar spray or injected into the base of a tree from small capsules.

FETCH Wind-generated waves on the surface of a water body.

F_1 GENERATION The first filial generation (the children) from a cross between two parents.

F_2 GENERATION The second filial generation (the grandchildren), resulting from a cross between two members of the F_1 generation or, in plants, self-pollination of the F_1 members.

FIBRE SATURATION POINT The moisture content at which all free moisture has been removed from wood, but at which the cell walls are still saturated. It is typically seen at moisture contents of about 25 to 30 per cent based on oven dry weights. *See also* Equilibrium Moisture Content.

FIBRIC MATERIAL A textural descriptor applied to organic materials. The least decomposed organic material, it consists largely (>40 per cent) of fibres that are readily identifiable as to botanical origin and retain their character upon rubbing.

FIDDLEHEAD An unexpanded fern frond. It is also referred to as a crozier. *See also* Fern (for illustration).

FIDUCIAL MARKS The index marks, usually four, that are rigidly connected with the camera lens through the camera body and which form images on the negative and usually define the principal point of the photograph. It is also four marks in any instrument that define the axes whose intersection fixes the principal point of a photograph and fulfils the requirements of interior orientation. *See also* Collimating Marks.

FIELD In computer science, fields are one logical element of data within a record or collection of subfields. A field may be a number, or numbers, or a collection of characters. Field sizes and data types are dependent on the format of the record. *See also* Database.

FIELD CAPACITY *See* Soil Water.

FIELD CHECK Refers to the observations and written description of conditions at a particular site in a terrain polygon. Used to verify the correctness of air photo interpretation and to collect information that cannot be obtained by air photo interpretation.

FIELD RESISTANCE The resistance to natural infection by a pathogen. It is a type of resistance that is sometimes seen under field conditions, but is not detected in standard laboratory tests for resistance because it is expressed at low inoculum densities and is usually sensitive to environmental factors. Horizontal resistance is commonly of this type, but the terms are not synonymous, since field resistance conveys no information about interactions between various host and pathogen races. Field resistance is often polygenic, but again, the term carries no implications regarding the mechanism or inheritance of the observed resistance.

FIGURE The patterns or marking on a piece of wood, usually one that has been worked to some extent. Often mistakenly called the grain, figure reflects the structure of the wood and is of economic importance in several species that have characteristic figure (e.g., fiddleback maple, bird's eye maple).

FILAMENT **1** A threadlike organ. **2** Botanically, the stalk that bears the anther in a stamen. *See also* Androecium or Flower (for illustration).

FILAMENTOUS Threadlike (e.g., the hyphae of fungi).

FILAMENTOUS FUNGUS Any fungus producing hyphae that do not organize into discrete fruiting or resting structures.

FILE In computer usage, a file is the collection of one set of records (numerical, text, or both) within a section of memory, having discrete starting and ending points, and a unique file-identifying name.

FILIFEROUS Having threadlike appendages.

FILIFORM Threadlike. *See also* Leaf Shape (for illustration).

FILL **1** The localized deposition of material eroded and transported from other areas, resulting in a change of stream bed elevation. It is also the deliberate placement of inorganic materials in a stream, usually along banks or margins, to reduce erosion or scour. *See also* Scour. **2** The placement of excavated materials necessary to raise a low point in a road alignment up to the required grade line.

FILL PLANTING The planting of trees in small areas of a replanted or naturally regenerated forest that are considered to be understocked. It is also called interplanting.

FILTER In the landscape ecology sense, a dispersal route with a narrow range of habitats that acts as a filter for species movement, allowing some but not all species to pass through. *See also* Coarse Filter Analysis; Fine Filter Analysis.

FIMBRIATE Fringed, or with the margins finely torn.

FINAL DECAY An ultimate stage, sometimes recognized specifically, in which destruction of wood substance has progressed very far, with partial or complete collapse of the wood structure. *See also* Decay.

FINAL RUN A live fire-bombing run where the pilot is intending to drop the load.

FINANCIAL ROTATION *See* Rotation.

FINANCIAL YIELD In forest management, the income realized on money invested (i.e., on the forest) over a period, taking into account all items of expenditure (both direct and capital) and of income, during the same period.

FINE FILTER ANALYSIS An analysis of components of aggregates (e.g., plant communities) within a cover type or species within a plant community. *See also* Coarse Filter Analysis.

FINE-FILTER MANAGEMENT Specific management for a single or a few species rather than broad management for a habitat or ecosystem. *See also* Coarse-Filter Management.

FINE FUEL MOISTURE The measured or estimated moisture content of fast-drying fuels that have a timelag of one hour or less. This includes grass, leaves, ferns, tree moss, draped-pine needles, and small twigs. These fine fuels are also termed flash fuels. *See also* Heavy Fuels; Medium Fuels.

FINE FUEL MOISTURE CODE *See* Canadian Forest Fire Weather Index System.

FINE FUELS Fuels that ignite readily and are consumed rapidly by fire (e.g., dry grass, leaves, twigs, and needles). Dead fine fuels dry very quickly and present a higher fire hazard. It is also termed flash fuels because the fire does not last long.

FINE-GRAINED **1** The feel or appearance of a surface that looks or feels smooth. **2** In ecology, the qualities of an environment that occur in small patches with respect to the activity patterns of an organism. It results in the organism's inability to distinguish usefully from among a range of qualities. *See also* Coarse-Grained.

FINES In aquatic ecology, bed or bank materials less than two millimetres in diameter, including silt, clay, and fine organic materials. *See also* Substrate Particle Size.

FINE SCALE In mapping or landscape assessments, when the ratio of the map length to the true ground length is high. Fine scale assessments cover a small area. *See also* Coarse Scale.

FINE TEXTURE *See* Soil Texture.

FINE WOODY DEBRIS Sound or rotting parts of trees that have fallen or been cut and left in the woods. Typically, the smaller branches, twigs, leaves, and roots. *See also* Coarse Woody Debris.

FINGERLING A young fish, usually in its first or second year and generally between two and twenty-five centimetres long. *See also* Fry; Parr.

FINGERS OF A FIRE *See* Forest Fire.

FINITE RATE OF INCREASE The rate of change (lambda) of population size that is the ratio of the total number of animals in one year to the total number of animals the next year.

FIORD A glacial trough with a floor below sea level, appearing as a long, narrow arm of the sea flanked by steep mountainsides and hanging valleys. Fiords are commonly characterized by great depth.

FIRE **1** The simultaneous release of heat, light, and flame, generated by the combustion of flammable material. **2** In a general sense, any outbreak of fire. *See also* Forest Fire; Wildfire.

FIRE ATLAS An ordered collection of fire maps, charts, and statistics used as a basis for fire management planning.

FIRE BEHAVIOUR The manner in which fuel ignites, flame develops, and fire spreads and exhibits other related phenomena, as determined by the interaction of fuels, weather, and topography. Some common terms used to describe fire behaviour include the following. **Smouldering** indicates a fire burning without flame and barely spreading. **Creeping** indicates a fire spreading slowly over the ground, generally with a low flame. **Running** indicates a fire spreading rapidly and with a well-defined head. **Torch** or **Torching** indicates when the foliage of a single tree or a small clump of trees ignites and flares up, usually from bottom to top. It is also termed candle or candling. **Spotting** indicates a fire producing firebrands carried by the surface wind, a fire whirl, and/or convection column that fall beyond the main fire perimeter and result in spot fires. *See also* Heat Transfer. **Crowning** indicates a fire ascending into the crowns of trees and spreading from crown to crown. Note the three classes of crown fire defined under forest fire. *See also* Forest Fire.

FIRE BEHAVIOUR FORECAST The prediction of

probable fire behaviour, in support of fire suppression or prescribed burning operations.

FIRE BEHAVIOUR TRIANGLE An instructional aid in which the sides of an equilateral triangle represent the three interacting components of the fire environment that are responsible for fire behaviour (i.e., fire weather, fuels, and topography). It is synonymous with fire environment triangle. *See also* Fire Triangle.

FIRE BENEFITS The effects of fire that have positive monetary, social, or emotional value, or that contribute, through changes in the resource base, to the attainment of organizational goals. *See also* Fire Damage; Fire Effects; Fire Impacts.

FIRE BOMBER *See* Airtanker.

FIRE BOSS *See* Fire Overhead.

FIREBRAND A piece of flaming or smouldering material capable of acting as an ignition source.

FIREBREAK *See* Fuelbreak.

FIRE CAUSE CLASS Fires are grouped for statistical purposes into broad fire cause classes. In the US, these are lightning, campfire, smoking, debris burning, incendiary, equipment use, railroad, children, and miscellaneous. In Canada, these are: (1) **lightning**, when a wildfire is caused directly or indirectly by lightning; (2) **recreation**, when a wildfire is caused by people or equipment engaged in recreational activity (e.g., vacationing, fishing, picnicking, non-commercial berry-picking, hiking, etc.); (3) **resident**, when a wildfire results from activity performed by people or machines for the purpose of agriculture, or an accidental fire is caused by activity associated with normal living in a forested area; (4) **forest industry**, when a wildfire is caused by people or machines engaged in any activity associated with forest products production; (5) **other industry**, when a wildfire is caused by industrial operations other than forest industry or railroads. It includes municipal, provincial, or federal works projects whether employees, agents, or contractors; (6) **railroads**, when a wildfire is caused by any machine, employee, agent, or contractor performing work associated with a railway operation, or a passenger on a train; (7) **incendiary**, when a wildfire is wilfully started for the purpose of mischief, grudge, or gain; (8) **unknown**, when the cause of a wildfire is not determinable; and (9) **miscellaneous**, when a wildfire of known cause cannot be properly classified under any of the other standard classes listed above.

FIRE CLIMATE The composite pattern or integration over time of the fire weather elements that affect fire occurrence and fire behaviour in a given area.

FIRE CLIMAX A plant community maintained at a certain seral stage by the periodic presence of fires (e.g., tall grass prairie).

FIRE CONCENTRATION A situation in which numerous fires are burning in a locality, or more specifically, the number of fires per unit area or locality for a given period, usually one year. *See also* Fire Frequency; Fire Occurrence.

FIRE CONTROL *See* Fire Suppression.

FIRE CONTROL LINE *See* Control Line.

FIRE CONTROL PLAN *See* Fire Suppression Plan.

FIRE CYCLE The number of years required to burn over an area equal to the entire area of interest. *See also* Fire Frequency; Fire Interval.

FIRE DAMAGE Any effects of fire that are detrimental or damaging in terms of the attainment of forest management and other land-use objectives. *See also* Fire Benefits; Fire Effects; Fire Impacts.

FIRE DANGER A general term describing an assessment of both fixed and variable factors of the fire environment that determines the ease of ignition, rate of spread, difficulty of control, and fire impact. *See also* Burning Conditions; Fire Hazard; Fire Risk.

FIRE DANGER CLASS A segment of a fire danger index scale identified by a descriptive term (nil, very low, low, moderate, high, very high, or extreme), or by a numerical value (I, II, III, IV, or V), and/or a colour code (green, blue, yellow, orange, and red). The classification system may be based on more than one fire danger index (e.g., the Buildup Index is sometimes used in addition to the Fire Weather Index).

FIRE DANGER INDEX A quantitative indicator of one or more facets of fire danger, expressed either in a relative sense or as an absolute measure. It is often used as a guide in a variety of fire management activities (e.g., to judge day-to-day preparedness and suppression requirements as a basis for providing information on fire danger to the general public) in fire prevention as an aid to prescribed burning.

FIRE DANGER METER A device for combining ratings of several variable factors into numerical classes of fire danger. The process of integration is termed fire danger rating.

FIRE DANGER RATING The process of systematically evaluating and integrating the individual and combined factors influencing fire danger represented in the form of fire danger indices.

FIRE DANGER RATING AREA A geographical area within which climate, fuel, and topography are relatively homogenous, hence fire danger can be assumed to be uniform.
FIRE DANGER STATION *See* Fire Weather Station.
FIRE DEATH A human casualty that is fatal or becomes fatal within one year of the fire and resulting from the fire.
FIRE DETECTION A system for, or the act of discovering, locating, and reporting wildfires.
FIRE ECOLOGY The study of the relationships between fire, the physical environment, and living organisms.
FIRE EDGE Any part of the boundary of a going fire at any given moment. It may apply to any portion of the fire perimeter (the entire boundary of the fire) as distinct from the different segments defined under the term Forest Fire.
FIRE EFFECTS Any changes on an area attributable to a fire, whether immediate or long term, and on or off site. They may be detrimental, beneficial, or benign from the standpoint of forest management and other land-use objectives. *See also* Fire Benefits; Fire Damages; Fire Impacts.
FIRE ENVIRONMENT The surrounding conditions, influences, and modifying forces of topography, fuel, and fire weather that determine fire behaviour.
FIRE EQUIPMENT CACHE A supply of fire-fighting tools and equipment in planned quantities or standard units at a strategic point for exclusive use in fire suppression. It is synonymous with fire tool cache or tool cache.
FIRE FINDER A device or instrument used to determine the horizontal bearing and sometimes the vertical angle of a fire from a lookout.
FIRE FINDER MAP A map situated on a fire finder and used to establish the location of forest fires from a lookout.
FIRE FLAIL *See* Fire Swatter.
FIRE FLAP **1** A general term connoting high levels of fire suppression activity, or continuing detection of new fires that is creating additional activity. **2** *See* Fire Swatter.
FIRE-FLOOD CYCLE The greatly increased rate of water run-off and soil movement from steep slopes that may follow removal of the surface vegetation after burning.
FIRE FREQUENCY The average number of fires that occur per unit time at a given point. *See also* Fire Cycle; Fire Incidence; Fire Interval.
FIRE FRONT The strip of primarily flaming combustion along the fire perimeter; a particularly active fire edge. Fine fuels typically produce a narrow fire front, whereas dry heavy fuels produce a wider zone or band of flames. In ground fires, the fire front may be primarily smouldering combustion. It is synonymous with flaming front. *See also* Flame Depth.
FIRE GUARD **1** A strategically planned barrier, either manually or mechanically constructed, to stop or retard the spread of a fire, and from which suppression action is carried out to control a fire. The constructed portion of a control line. *See also* Fire Line; Fuelbreak. **2** A general term for a fire fighter, lookout, patrol, prevention guard, or other person directly employed for the prevention and/or detection and suppression of fires.
FIRE HAZARD A general term to describe the potential fire behaviour, without regard to the state of weather-influenced fuel moisture content, and/or resistance to fire guard construction for a given fuel type. This may be expressed in either the absolute sense (e.g., cured grass is a fire hazard), or the comparative sense (e.g., clearcut logging slash is a greater fire hazard than a deciduous cover type). Such an assessment is based on physical fuel characteristics (e.g., fuel arrangement, fuel load, condition of herbaceous vegetation, presence of ladder fuels). *See also* Fire Danger; Fire Risk.
FIRE HAZARD ZONES Those wildland areas where the combination of vegetation, topography, weather, and the threat of fire to life and property create difficult and dangerous problems.
FIRE HEEL *See* Forest Fire.
FIRE HISTORY The study and/or compilation of evidence (e.g., historical documents, fire reports, fire scars, tree growth rings, charcoal deposits) that records the occurrence and effects of past wildfires for an area. *See also* Fire Cycle; Fire Frequency; Fire Incidence; Fire Interval; Fire Occurrence.
FIRE IMPACTS The immediately evident effect of fire on the ecosystem in terms of timber losses or biophysical alterations such as crown scorch, mineral soil exposure, depth of burn, fuel consumption. *See also* Fire Benefits; Fire Damage; Fire Effects.
FIRE INCIDENCE The average number of fires started in a designated area during a specified time. *See also* Fire Concentration; Fire Frequency; Fire Occurrence.
FIRE INTENSITY *See* Fire Line Intensity.
FIRE INTERVAL The average number of years between the occurrence of fires at a given

point. The size of the fire area must be clearly specified. *See also* Fire Cycle; Fire Frequency.

FIRE INVESTIGATION An evaluation to determine, at a minimum, when, where, and how one or more fires were started, and by whom or by what.

FIRE ISLAND *See* Forest Fire.

FIRELAMP In the US, a multi-resource computer model (standing for Fire and Land Management Planning) that simulates the effects that naturally caused prescribed fires have on the future production of natural resources, such as timber, forage, wildlife, recreation, and water.

FIRE LANE A cleared path wide enough to permit single-lane vehicular access into a remote area for the purpose of fire-fighting activities or prevention.

FIRE LINE **1** That portion of the fire upon which resources are deployed and are actively engaged in suppression action. In a general sense, the working area around a fire. *See also* Control Line; Fire Guard. **2** Any cleared strip of land used to control a fire. Loosely synonymous with fire guard.

FIRE LINE INTENSITY The rate of heat energy release per unit time per unit length of fire front. Flame size is its main visual manifestation. Frontal fire intensity is a major determinant of certain fire effects and difficulty of control. Numerically, it is equal to the product of the heat of combustion, quantity of fuel consumed per unit area in the flaming fire front, and linear rate of spread of the fire. Measured in kilowatts per metre or BTU per second per foot of fire front. In the US, it is termed Byram's Fireline Intensity or Line-fire Intensity. *See also* Flame Length.

FIRE LOAD **1** In the US, the number and size of fires historically experienced on a specified unit over a specified period (usually one day) at a specified index of danger. **2** In Canada, the number and magnitude (i.e., fire size class and frontal fire intensity) of all fires requiring suppression action during a given period within a specified area.

FIRE LOAD INDEX A numerical rating of the maximum effort required to contain all probable fires occurring within a rating area during the rating period.

FIRE LOOKOUT *See* Lookout.

FIRE MANAGEMENT The activities concerned with the protection of people, property, and forest areas from wildfire and the land use of prescribed burning for the attainment of forest management and other land-use objectives, all conducted in a manner that considers environmental, social, and economic criteria.

Fire Management represents both a land management philosophy and a land management activity. It involves the strategic integration of such factors as a knowledge of fire regimes, probable fire effects, values-at-risk, level of forest protection required, cost of fire-related activities, and prescribed fire technology into multiple-use planning, decisionmaking, and day-to-day activities to accomplish the stated resource management objectives. Successful fire management depends on effective fire prevention, detection, and presuppression, having an adequate fire suppression capability, and consideration of fire ecology relationships.

FIRE MANAGEMENT AREA One or more parcels of land having a common set of fire management objectives.

FIRE MANAGEMENT IMPROVEMENTS All structures built and used primarily for fire management (e.g., lookout towers, telephone lines, firebreaks, access roads).

FIRE MANAGEMENT OBJECTIVE The planned, measurable result derived from fire protection and use based on land management goals and objectives.

FIRE MANAGEMENT PLAN A statement of policy and prescribed actions with respect to forest fires (prescribed fires and wildfires) for a specific area. The plan may include maps, charts, and statistical data. *See also* Fire Suppression Plan; Pre-attack Plan.

FIRE MANAGEMENT PLANNING The systematic, technological, and administrative management process of determining the organization, facilities, resources, and procedures required to protect people, property, and forest areas from fire, and to use fire to accomplish forest management and other land-use objectives.

FIRE OCCURRENCE The number of fires started in a given area over a given period of time. *See also* Fire Frequency; Fire Incidence.

FIRE OCCURRENCE MAP A map showing, with symbols, the ignition points of all fires for a specified area and period.

FIRE OVERHEAD A collective term for all fire supervisory positions. The following is a summary of the key fire line positions used in the Canadian Interagency Forest Fire Centre's National Fire Command System. Some agencies use a slightly different fire overhead organization, or use synonymous terms for some positions. Note that specialist and support positions have not been defined. Instead, general descriptions of the main support functions are given. **Fire boss** is the person responsible and accountable for conducting all direct suppression and logistical activities consistent with an agency policy, given fire, or zone of fires. Depending on the size of the fire and the complexity of operations, the fire boss may carry out all duties directly or may assign line and staff duties to subordinates. The term is synonymous with fire foreman or fire superintendent. **Suppression boss** is the person responsible to the fire boss for supervising, directing, and auditing the suppression effort on the entire fire line. The term is synonymous with line boss and line foreman. **Division boss** is the person responsible to the fire boss or suppression boss, depending on the degree of organization required, for the conduct of all suppression work on a division; supervises two or more sector bosses. The term is synonymous with division foreman. **Sector boss** is a first-line supervisor responsible and accountable to a division boss, suppression boss, or fire boss, depending on the degree of organization required, for directing and controlling the total suppression effort on one sector of a fire. Generally supervises two or more crew bosses. **Crew boss** is the person responsible to a sector boss or fire boss, depending on the degree of organization required, for the supervision of fire-fighting crews on the fire line. Synonymous with Crew Foreman. **Plans function** is the part of the fire suppression organization (reporting to the fire boss) that is responsible for the gathering, compiling, and recording of all fire intelligence information required to formulate the daily fire suppression action plan. **Service function** is the part of the fire suppression organization (reporting to the fire boss) that is responsible for the procurement, maintenance, and distribution of personnel, equipment, and supplies at the time and place called for in the fire suppression action plan. It may involve record keeping, accounting, provision of food and lodging, safety and first-aid, and transportation.

FIRE PERIMETER The entire outer edge or boundary of a fire. *See also* Fire Edge.

FIRE PLOUGH A heavy-duty plough of either the share or disc type, designed solely for constructing fire guards or fuelbreaks.

FIRE POCKETS *See* Forest Fire.

FIRE PRESUPPRESSION Those activities undertaken in advance of fire occurrences to help ensure more effective fire suppression. It includes overall planning; recruitment and training of fire personnel; procurement and maintenance of fire fighting equipment and supplies; fuel treatment; and creating, maintaining, and improving a system of fuelbreaks, roads, water sources, and control lines.

FIRE PREVENTION All activities directed at reducing fire occurrence. It includes public education, law enforcement, personal contact, and reduction of fire hazards and risks.

FIRE PROGRESS MAP A map maintained on a large fire to show at specified times the location of the fire perimeter, deployment of suppression forces, and the progress of suppression. It is synonymous with fire status map.

FIRE-PROOFING A procedure aimed at reducing the flammability of fuels by coating them with fire retardant.

FIRE PROTECTION PLAN *See* Fire Suppression Plan.

FIRE-RESISTANT TREE A species with morphological characteristics, such as thick, platy, or corky bark, or buds protected by long needles, that give it a lower probability of being injured or killed by fire than a fire-sensitive tree.

FIRE RETARDANT Any substance other than plain water that by chemical or physical action reduces the flammability of fuels, or slows down their combustion rate. A slurry applied aerially or from the ground during fire suppression. *See also* Extinguishing Agent; Foam; Inhibitor; Long-term Retardant; Short-term Retardant.

FIRE RISK The probability or chance of fire starting determined by the presence and activities of causative agents (i.e., potential number of ignition sources). *See also* Fire Danger; Fire Hazard.

FIRE RUN A term normally associated with the rapid advance of a wildfire characterized by a marked increase in the rate of spread and a corresponding increase in frontal fire intensity with respect to that noted before and following the event.

FIRE SCAR **1** An injury or wound on a tree caused or accentuated by fire. **2** A scar on the landscape caused by a fire.

FIRE-SCOUTING The reconnaissance of a fire and its surroundings by any means to obtain fire intelligence information.

FIRE SEASON The period(s) of the year during which fires are likely to start, spread, and do damage to values-at-risk sufficient to warrant organized fire suppression. A period of the year set out and commonly referred to in fire prevention legislation. The fire season is usually further divided on the basis of the seasonal flammability of fuel types (e.g., spring, summer, and fall).

FIRE-SENSITIVE TREE A species with morphological features, such as thin bark, which has a relatively high probability of being injured or killed by fire. *See also* Fire-Resistant Tree.

FIRE SEVERITY The degree to which a site has been altered or disrupted by fire. Loosely, the product of fire intensity and the residence time. *See also* Light Burn; Moderate Burn; Severe Burn.

FIRE SIMULATOR A training device that imposes simulated fire and smoke and depictions of fire suppression measures on a projected landscape scene to instruct fire management personnel in different fire situations and fire suppression techniques.

FIRE SITUATION MAP A map used by fire management personnel to locate and plot wildfires reported, burning, or out.

FIRE SIZE CLASS The assignment of a wildfire to a category according to its size (from the smallest to the largest). The following clarifications are used for reporting national wildfire statistics.

Class number	Class letter	In Canada (hectares)	In the U.S. (acres)
1	A	up to 0.1	up to 0.25
2	B	0.11-1.0	0.25-10.0
3	C	1.10-10.0	10+-100
4	D	10.1-100	100+-300
5	E	100.1-1,000	300+-1,000
6	F	1,000.1-10,000	1,000+-5,000
7	G	10,000.1-100,000	5,000 or more
8	H	over 100,000	

FIRE STORM A large continuous area of intense burning characterized by violent, fire-induced convection resulting in gale-force indraft surface winds near and beyond the fire perimeter, a towering convection column, and the occurrence of large fire whirls. *See also* Conflagration; Extreme Fire Behaviour.

FIRE SUPPRESSION All activities concerned with controlling and extinguishing a fire following its detection. It is synonymous with fire control. Methods of suppression include the following. **Direct attack** is a method whereby the fire is attacked immediately adjacent to the burning fuel. **Parallel attack** is a method whereby a fire guard is constructed as close to the fire as heat and flame permit, and burning out the fuel between the fire and the fire guard. **Indirect attack** is a method whereby the control line is strategically located to take advantage of favourable terrain and natural breaks in advance of the fire perimeter and the intervening strip is usually burned or backfired. **Hot spotting** is a method used to check the spread and intensity of a fire at those points that exhibit the most rapid spread or that otherwise pose some special threat to control of the situation. This is in contrast to systematically working all parts of the fire at the same time, or progressively, in a step-by-step manner. **Cold trailing** is a method of determining whether or not a fire is still burning, involving careful inspection and feeling with the hand, or by use of a hand-held, infrared scanner, to detect any heat source. **Mop-up** is the act of extinguishing a fire after it has been brought under control. It involves extinguishing or removing burning material along or near the control line, felling snags, or trenching logs to prevent rolling. *See also* Control a Fire.

FIRE SUPPRESSION PLAN A document containing the essential elements of actions necessary to save human life and property, and minimize fire damage. It may also apply to an overall fire suppression program for a broad area, but is usually for site-specific situations. It is synonymous with fire control plan or fire protection plan. *See also* Fire Management Plan; Pre-attack Plan.

FIRE SUPPRESSION STRATEGY **1** Preparedness. In a broad organizational sense, the determination of when, where, and what level of resource deployment is required to meet anticipated fire incidence. **2** When dealing with active fires, it is the determination of the potential control problems based on a calculation of fire probabilities and development of an appropriate action plan that will best utilize the assigned resources in the control effort. It is generally a command and planning decision as opposed to a line function. *See also* Fire Suppression Tactics.

FIRE SUPPRESSION TACTICS Determining exactly where to establish control lines, what to do along these lines, and how best to utilize each fire-fighting resource group to cope with site-specific conditions and fire behaviour at the moment. A line function. *See also* Fire Suppression Strategy.

FIRE SWATTER A fire-suppression tool, sometimes improvised, used in direct attack for beating out flames along a fire edge. It may consist merely of a green bough or wet sacking, or it may be a manufactured tool, such as a flap of belting fabric attached to a long handle.

FIRE-TOLERANT SPECIES Plant species that have evolved to survive various types of fire disturbances.

FIRE TOWER *See* Lookout Tower.

FIRE TRAP **1** An accumulation of highly combustible material, rendering fire-fighting dangerous. **2** Any situation in which it is highly dangerous to fight fire.

FIRE TRIANGLE An instructional aid in which the sides of an equilateral triangle represent the three factors necessary for combustion and flame production (i.e., oxygen, heat, fuel). When any of these factors is removed, flame production is not possible or ceases.

FIRE TYPE A particular cover type that commonly follows or is otherwise dependent on fire.

FIRE WEATHER Collectively, those weather parameters that influence fire occurrence and subsequent fire behaviour (e.g., dry-bulb temperature, relative humidity, wind speed and direction, precipitation, atmospheric stability, winds aloft).

FIRE WEATHER FORECAST A prediction of the future state of the atmosphere prepared specifically to meet the needs of fire management in fire suppression and prescribed burning operations. Two types are most common. (1) **Zone** or **area weather forecast** is issued on a regular basis during the fire season for a particular geographical region and/or one or more fire weather stations. These regions are delineated on the basis of fire climate and/or administrative considerations. (2) **Spot weather forecast** is issued to fit the time, topography, and weather of a specific campaign fire location or prescribed fire site. These forecasts are issued on request and are more detailed, timely, and specific than zone or area weather forecasts.

FIRE WEATHER INDEX *See* Canadian Forest Fire Weather Index System.

FIRE WEATHER STATION A meteorological station equipped to measure fire weather elements. A primary weather station is one at which sufficient weather observations are taken to compute fire danger indices. A secondary weather station does not provide this level of information but, rather, provides supplementary data on weather conditions. *See also* Remote Automatic Weather Station.

FIRE WEATHER STATION NETWORK A grid of specifically designated weather observation sites from which operational fire weather data are collected on a daily basis.

FIRE WHIRL/WHIRLWIND A spinning vortex column of ascending hot air and gases rising from a fire and carrying aloft smoke, debris, flame, and firebrands. These whirls range in size from less than one metre to several hundred metres in diameter. They may involve the entire fire area or only the hot spots within or outside the fire perimeter.

FIRING TECHNIQUE A general term used to differentiate between ground and aerial ignition, between line and point source ignition, or to reflect the type of fire resulting from one or more ignitions (e.g., backing fire, flanking fire). *See also* Ignition Pattern.

FIRST LAW OF THERMODYNAMICS Matter is neither created nor destroyed. In effect, when energy or matter is transformed from one state to another, the overall amount of energy or matter remains constant. *See also* Entropy.

FIRST-YEAR BIRD A bird in its first twelve to sixteen months of life, or until its second prebasic moult. *See also* After-Hatching Year Bird; Hatching-Year Bird.

FISH **1** In a narrow sense, a vertebrate living in water and breathing through gills. **2** In an all-encompassing sense, such as in the Canadian Fisheries Act, or the US Fisheries Act, fish is defined to include all the life stages of fish, shellfish, crustaceans, marine animals, and marine plants.

FISHERIES SENSITIVE ZONES Aquatic environments deemed important for the life history of fish, including areas that may not be defined as streams. Fisheries sensitive zones may include side and flood channels, valley wall ponds, swamps, seasonally flooded depressions, lake littoral zones or spawning areas, estuaries, and recreationally fished areas.

FISH LADDER An inclined waterway, commonly an artificial channel or stepped pools, designed to permit migrating fish to pass over or around a dam, waterfall, or other barrier to movement.

FISTULOSE Cylindrical and hollow.

FITNESS The relative survival value and reproductive capability of an allele or genotype to following generations, relative to other alleles or genotypes. It may be either an absolute value, measured by the number of progeny per parent, or it may be relative to some reference genotype. Thus, members within the population carrying genes that ensure greater reproduction success and survival are said to be more fit than those not having these genes.

FIX A geographical position determined by visual reference to the surface, by reference to one or more radio navigational aids, by celestial plotting, or by any other navigational device.

FIXATION **1** The process by which substances in the atmosphere or soil are converted into a form usable by plants (e.g., nitrogen or potassium fixation). **2** In genetics, an allele for which, at that locus, no alternative alleles are found within the population (i.e., that allele has only one form (monomorphic) in the population).

FIXED COSTS Operational costs that remain constant for an economic activity, regardless of level of production. They include the initial costs of purchase.

FIXED-DISTANCE METHOD *See* Point Count; Strip Transect Method.

FIXED-POINT DETECTION The detection of fires from lookout towers or semi-permanent locations, as distinguished from roving ground patrols or aerial detection.

FIXED VALUES Values of the variable are fixed in advance of data collection.

FLABELLATE/FLABELLIFORM Fan-shaped, or broadly wedge-shaped (e.g., Ginkgo leaves). *See also* Leaf Shape.

FLACCID Weak, limp, lacking turgor. It is characteristic of plants that have recently undergone stress due to lack of water.

FLAG A dying or nearly dead leafy twig or branch that contrasts in colour with the normal green foliage of the living tree.

FLAGGING **1** The occurrence of conspicuous dead shoots or branches, with the foliage still present and discoloured. **2** The loss of rigidity, and drooping of leaves and tender shoots preceding the wilting of a plant.

FLAGSHIP SPECIES **1** A species that is used to galvanize political and public awareness, and thus facilitate conservation research and action for a broader range of species (e.g., tigers, California condors, or spotted owls). **2** A highly charismatic species, typically a large-bodied mammal or bird, that is in some peril of extirpation and that can be managed so as to also provide habitats and resources for other species (e.g., grizzly bear, sockeye salmon). *See also* Indicator Species; Keystone Species; Umbrella Species.

FLAME A mass of gas undergoing rapid combustion, generally accompanied by evolution of sensible heat and incandescence.

FLAME ANGLE The angle between the flame at the leading edge of the fire front and the ground surface, expressed in degrees.

FLAME DEPTH The width of the zone within which continuous flaming occurs behind the edge of a fire front.

FLAME HEIGHT The average maximum vertical extension of flames at the fire front. Occasional flashes that rise above the general level of flames are not considered. This distance is less than the flame length if flames are tilted due to wind or slope.

FLAME LENGTH The length of flames measured along their axis at the fire front. The distance between the flame height tip and the midpoint of the flame depth at the ground surface. Flame length is an approximate indicator of frontal fire intensity.

FLAME-THROWER A device for throwing a stream of flaming liquid to facilitate rapid burning in suppression firing or in prescribed burning.

FLAMING COMBUSTION PHASE The luminous oxidation of gases evolved from the rapid decomposition of fuel. This phase follows the pre-ignition phase and precedes the smouldering combustion phase, which has a much slower combustion rate. Water vapour, soot, and tar comprise the visible smoke. Relatively efficient combustion produces minimal soot and tar, and white smoke. A high fuel moisture content also produces white smoke.

FLAMING FRONT *See* Fire Front.

FLAMMABILITY The relative ease with which a substance ignites and sustains combustion.

FLANK FIRE A fire spreading, or set to spread, at roughly 90 degrees to the prevailing wind direction. *See also* Backfiring; Ignition Pattern (head fire).

FLANK FIRE IGNITION *See* Ignition Pattern.

FLANKING In fire suppression, working along the flanks of a fire, whether simultaneously or successively, from a less active or anchor point, toward the head of the fire in order to contain it.

FLANKS OF A FIRE *See* Forest Fire.

FLARE-UP Any sudden, localized acceleration in the rate of spread or intensity of a fire or part of a fire within or along the fire perimeter requiring a temporary adjustment in suppression action in order to avoid a possible blow-up condition. Unlike a blow-up, a flare-up is of relatively short duration and does not radically change existing control plans. *See also* Blow-up.

FLARK The elongate pools of water that form perpendicular to the direction of water flow and alternate with the drier strings in patterned fens.

FLASHBACK **1** The translocation of poison, through natural root-grafting, from a chemically treated tree or plant to an untreated one, causing the latter's injury or death. **2** The accidental, almost instantaneous ignition of a flammable vapour and its source (liquid or gaseous), usually due to unsafe practices or poor equipment design, often resulting in an explosion. It applies to aviation or automobile fuels, which have low flash points and high volatility. Aerial ignition equipment, especially drip torches, have a built-in flashback-arresting loop in the fuel lines to minimize the risk.

FLASH FUELS *See* Fine Fuels.

FLASHOVER The rapid combustion and/or explosion of trapped, unburned gases. It usually occurs in poorly ventilated areas. The flashover phenomenon is usually associated with structural or urban fires. However, it can occur in forest fires (although rare) when gases are trapped in topographic pockets or accumulate over a broad area when there is a temporary lull in air movement.

FLECK A minute spot, often white or translucent, and often composed of necrotic tissue (a necrotic fleck). *See also* Pith Fleck.

FLEDGING PERIOD The time interval for a bird between hatching from the egg and successful flight.

FLEDGING SUCCESS **1** The average number of offspring fledged (i.e., raised until they leave the nest) per female. **2** The percentage of hatchlings that fledge.

FLEDGLING An immature bird capable of flight. *See also* Nestling.

FLEXUOSE/FLEXUOUS Botanically, a shape that is wavy, curved, or bent in a zigzag pattern.

FLIGHT LINE A line drawn on a map or chart to represent the actual or proposed track of an aircraft in remote sensing work. It is also the line connecting the principal points of overlapping vertical photographs representing the approximate flight line followed.

FLIGHT PERIOD The period or periods, within a day or year, during which adult insects fly, usually involving dispersal or selection of a new host or habitat.

FLIGHT RANGE The maximum distance over which dispersing adult insects of a particular species generally fly.

FLIGHT VISIBILITY The average forward horizontal distance from the cockpit of an aircraft in flight at which prominent unlighted objects may be seen and identified by day, and prominent lighted objects may be seen and identified by night. *See also* Ground Visibility; Instrument Flight Rules; Visual Flight Rules.

FLITCH A large piece of lumber sawn or hewn on two or more sides, which has been cut from the side of a log and is intended for further conversion.

FLOATERS **1** In ecology, nonbreeding or nonterritorial adults and subadults that move and live within a breeding population, often replacing breeding adults that die; nonterritorial individuals. **2** In timber management, logs that float at or on the surface of the water. *See also* Deadheads; Sinker.

FLOATING MARK In photogrammetry, a mark seen as occupying a position in the three-dimensional space formed by the stereoscopic fusion of a pair of photographs and used as a reference mark in examining or measuring the stereoscopic model.

FLOCCOSE Covered with tufts of soft, woolly hairs that are easily rubbed off.

FLOCCULATION The process that causes colloidal solids, suspended in a liquid, to clump or flocculate together to form larger particles, which then precipitate out. It is used as a means of removing fine solids from a liquid, especially in mineral extraction and sewage treatment.

FLOOD A surface water flow that exceeds the capacity of the stream or channel, and flows out onto the floodplain.

FLOOD BASIN The largest absolute floodplain ever likely to occur within any one drainage.

FLOOD CHANNELS Stream channels that usually contain water only when mainstream water levels are higher than normal.

FLOODPLAIN Flat land bordering a stream or river onto which a flood will spread. The underlying materials are typically unconsolidated and derived from past stream transportation activity. The extent of the floodplain varies according to the volume of water, and is thus defined by a specified flood size (e.g., a fifty-year-old floodplain would be defined by the largest flood that would, on average, occur once within a fifty-year period, estimated from historic stream flow records. *See also* Flood Basin.

FLOOR A generic term describing the nearly level, lower part of a basin or valley, or the bed of any body of water.

FLORA **1** The plant species found in one or more regions, or eras. **2** A botanical manual containing key information for the identification of plants.

FLORAL CUP A cuplike structure in flowers, bearing on its rim the sepals, petals, and stamens. The cup originates as: (1) a hypanthium; (2) a calyx tube formed by coalescence and adnation of the bases of the sepals, petals, and stamens; or (3) a perianth tube where the sepals and adjacent petals are adnate edge to edge. *See also* Floral Tube (for illustration).

FLORAL ENVELOPE *See* Perianth.

FLORAL TUBE An elongated floral cup formed by the union of perianth parts and sometimes other organs (see illustration). It is occasionally used in the sense of hypanthium. *See also* Perigynous.

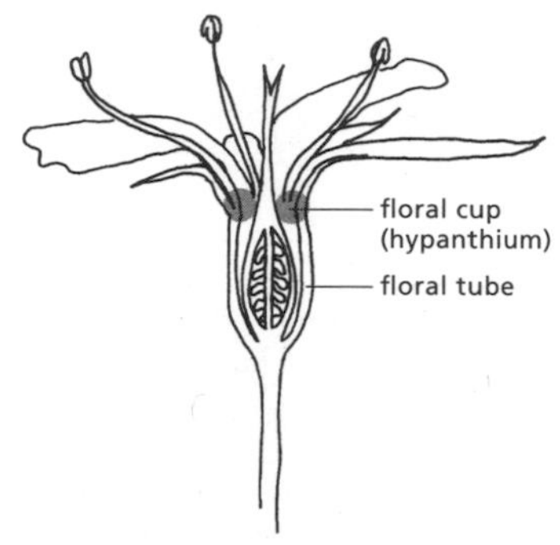

FLORET **1** A very small individual flower that forms part of a dense inflorescence. It is typical of flowers in the Compositae family. **2** The flower of a grass (Gramineae), comprising the lemma, palea, lodicules, and the enclosed flower itself. *See also* Grass (for illustration).

FLORICANE A biennial shoot or cane, especially on brambles, during its second year, when producing flowers and fruits. Brambles or raspberries (*Rubus* spp.) are examples of plants with floricanes. *See also* Primocane.

FLORIFEROUS Bearing flowers.

FLORISTICS The study of the species composition of plant associations in any one flora. *See also* Flora.

FLOTSAM Natural or human-made debris floating on the surface of water bodies that tends to collect in eddies or is transported downstream. *See also* Jetsam.

FLOW **1** The movement of a fluid (water or air) from place to place. The fluid itself as it moves, or the volume of fluid passing a given point in a given period of time (e.g., litres per second). Flows are classified into several types. **Base flow** is the portion of the stream discharge that is derived from natural storage (i.e., groundwater outflow and the draining of large lakes and swamps or other sources outside the net rainfall that creates surface runoff). It is also called sustaining, normal, ordinary, or groundwater flow. **Flushing flow** is a discharge (natural or human-induced) of sufficient size and duration to scour and remove fines from the stream bed gravel, and thus maintain intragravel permeability. **Improvement flow** is a discharge that will improve on the existing aquatic habitat and related activity by correcting for water quality deterioration and/or utilization pressures. **Intragravel flow** is that part of the surface water that infiltrates the stream bed and moves through the substrate pores. **Laminar flow** is that type of flow in a stream of water in which each particle moves in a direction parallel to every other particle. **Low flow** is the lowest discharge recorded over a specified period of time. It is also called minimum flow. **Natural flow** is the flow of water as it occurs under natural, unregulated conditions at any given location. **Peak flow** is the highest recorded discharge over a specified time period. **Subsurface flow** is that portion (part or all) of the water that infiltrates the stream bed and moves horizontally through and below it. It may or may not return to the stream channel at some point downstream. **2** A type of mass-wasting process where water-saturated materials move downslope in the form of a viscous material. *See also* Creep; Slide; Slump.

FLOW CONDITIONER Chemical powders that will, in very small quantities, impart freeflowing qualities to other powders and tend to prevent them from caking and flocculating. They are used with fire retardant chemicals.

FLOWER A complex strobilus formed at the end of a branch or other axis, bearing one or more pistils, or one or more stamens, or both. When bearing only pistils, it is a **pistillate flower** (female). When bearing only stamens it is a **staminate flower** (male). When bearing both stamens and pistils it is a **perfect flower** (bisexual or hermaphroditic). When a perfect flower is surrounded by a perianth representing two floral envelopes (inner envelope or corolla; outer envelope or calyx), it is a **complete flower**. The illustration shows the parts of a complete flower. *See also* Inflorescence.

FLOW TILL Formed when saturated supraglacial debris (ablation till) on melting ice moves downslope as a debris flow and comes to rest on an adjacent lower, stable surface. It is common in stagnant ice deposits and typically interlayered with glaciofluvial and glaciolacustrine sediments.

parts of a flower

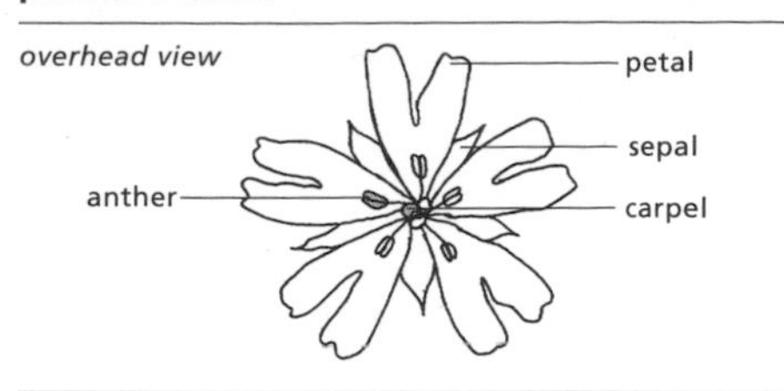

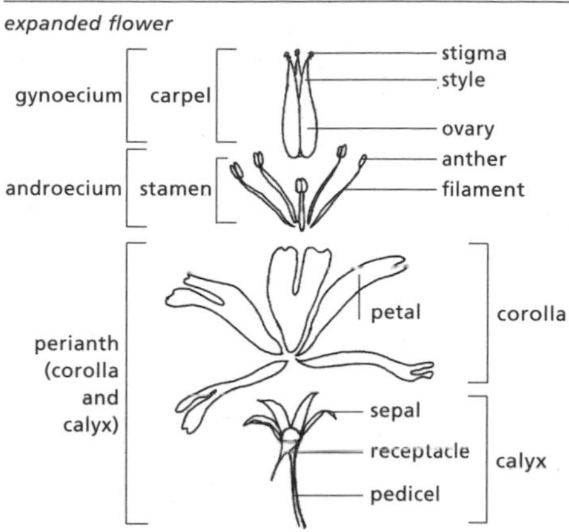

FLUSH **1** A periodic and temporary increase in water volumes along a watercourse that serves to move (flush) sediments and other accumulated solids further downstream. **2** The area adjacent to a spring or small stream that is kept moist by the presence of moving water. **3** The fresh growth of foliage or blossom in plants, usually occurring in a short period of time.

FLUSH CUT A pruning technique where both branch and stem tissue are removed by cutting off a branch exactly flush with the stem. It is considered to be poor pruning practice. *See also* Natural Target Cut.

FLUTED Channelled or furrowed, as along the main axis of a column.

FLUTINGS **1** Smooth, straight furrows, parallel to ice-flow direction, and formed in bedrock by glacial abrasion. **2** Smooth, straight, shallow furrows, parallel to ice-flow direction, in till or other drift.

FLUVIAL A comprehensive term for several stream or river processes, involving the transport and deposition of materials by water. Fluvial systems are divided into three main parts: (1) **drainage basin** or **sediment production zone**, where water and sediment loads are derived; (2) **transfer** or **transportation zone**, where materials are moved downstream; and (3) **zone of deposition** or **sink**, where the materials are deposited.

Sediments can be stored, eroded, transported, and produced within each zone, but typically, each zone is dominated by one single process. As a complete system, it is in a state of flux, with constant inputs, throughputs, and outputs of energy and materials.

FLUVIAL TERRACES *See* River Terrace.

FLUX **1** The flow of energy in one or more forms, from a source to a sink. It can be continuous or a series of defined changes. **2** The rate of flow or change of a liquid, gas, or radiation across the landscape.

FLY A member of the insect order Diptera, characterized by complete metamorphosis, wormlike larvae (maggots), and adults with one pair of membranous wings.

FLY ASH Particulates emitted by a fire, larger than ten microns in diameter with a consequently short residence time in the atmosphere.

FLYCATCHING A feeding method in which a bird flies from a perch, catches an insect in flight, and returns to the same perch. *See also* Hawking.

FLYING DRIP TORCH *See* Helitorch.

FLYWAY The geographic migration route for birds, including the breeding and wintering areas that the flyway connects. Most species follow the same migration routes in spring and autumn, but some use one flyway southward-bound and another flyway on the route northward. In the Americas (New World), migration occurs in autumn (southward), and spring (northward). The following southward flyways are recognized for autumn migration. **Pacific Flyway** generally follows the coast of the Pacific Ocean from Alaska and the Yukon Territory to Central America. **Great Plains Flyway** is the central flyway across the Great Plains and prairies to the western side of the Gulf of Mexico coast and further south from the Canadian Arctic to Central and South America. **Mississippi Flyway** follows the course of the Mississippi River to the central portions of the Gulf of Mexico coast and further south from the Canadian prairies to Central and South America. **Atlantic Flyway** collects together tributary streams of migrants from across central and eastern Canada and follows the coast of the Atlantic Ocean to Florida, the Caribbean islands and South America. **Appalachian Flyway**, after detouring from the Atlantic Flyway, follows the wooded ridges of the Appalachian mountain range and overwinters there.

The following northward flyways are recognized for spring migration. **Pacific Flyway** is the reverse of the Pacific Flyway described above. **Gulf Coast Flyway** is the reverse of the Great Plains Flyway described above. **Trans-Gulf Flyway** is the reverse of the Mississippi Flyway described above. **West Indian Flyway** is the reverse of the Atlantic Flyway described above.

The flyway routes vary slightly between northward and southward migrations, reflecting the differences in prevailing winds at the different times of the year. On the European continent, migration from Europe to Africa generally tends to avoid lengthy sea routes by crossing the Mediterranean Sea at its narrowest points: (1) the Straits of Gibraltar; (2) the 'boot' of Sicily; and (3) from Greece and Eastern Europe across the Marmara Denizi and along the eastern coast of the Mediterranean to Egypt and points south.

FOAM A chemical fire extinguishing mixture. When applied, it forms bubbles that greatly increase the mixture volume. The foam adheres to the fuel and reduces combustion by moistening and cooling, and excluding oxygen. It also provides gradual release of water and retards evaporation.

FOCAL LENGTH The distance measured along the optical axis from the rear nodal point of the lens to the plane of critical focus of a very distant object.

FOG **1** A jet of fine water spray discharged by spray nozzles, used to extinguish fires, and generally considered most efficient at nozzle pressures of about 100 pounds per square inch. High-pressure fog is water spray delivered through gun-type nozzles attached to small hoses supplied by pumps discharging at pressures greater than 250 pounds per square inch, the normal maximum pressure for standard ground tankers. **2** A suspension of minute water droplets extending vertically from the ground to at least twenty feet, reducing horizontal and vertical visibility. *See also* Ground Fog; Haze.

FOLD A curve or bend of a planar structure such as rock strata, bedding planes, foliation, or cleavage. Two of the major types of folds are shown in the illustration. Along with monoclines, synclines and anticlines may fold back on themselves, becoming overturned folds. *See also* Anticline; Monocline; Syncline.

FOLIACEOUS Leaflike. Particularly describes sepals, calyx lobes, or bracts that resemble leaves in texture, size, and colour.

types of folds

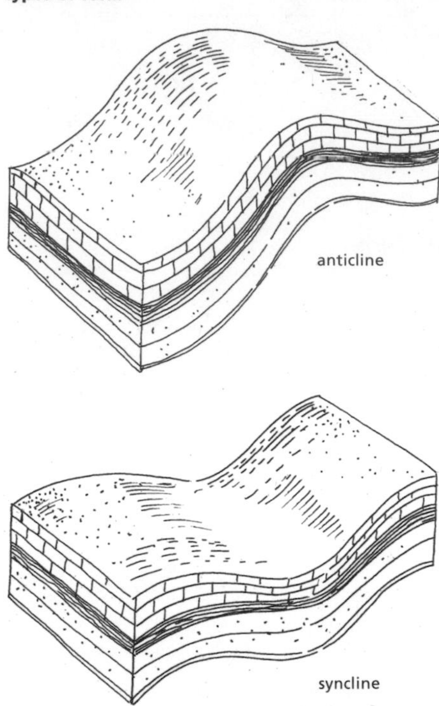

FOLIAGE GLEANER Birds that pick food from the surface of vegetation.

FOLIAGE HEIGHT DENSITY An index of the complexity of the structure of the above-ground vegetation. Increasing numbers of layers and/or more species lead to higher index values.

FOLIAR APPLICATION The application of a pesticide to the leaves or foliage of plants.

FOLIAR DIAGNOSIS The analysis of plant foliage to determine mineral nutrient deficiencies; based on chemical composition of foliage, its colour, and growth patterns.

FOLIICOLOUS Growing or occurring on foliage.

FOLIOSE A lichen growth form, bilaterally symmetrical, leaflike with an upper and usually a lower cortex. *See also* Crustose; Fruticose.

FOLLICLE A dry, dehiscent, one-carpelled fruit with usually more than one seed and opening along its ventral suture. *See also* Fruit (for illustration).

FOLLOW-UP The act of supporting or increasing the efforts of initial attack forces by increasing suppression resources and commitment to control.

FOOD CHAIN The hierarchy of trophic levels or feeding sequences in an ecosystem through which energy flows (e.g., algae, phytoplankton, and plants to herbivores to carnivores, plus fungi, saprophytes, etc.). Within the food chain, organisms that are interrelated in their feeding habits, feed upon organisms that are lower in the chain and in turn are fed upon by organisms higher in the chain. Food chains consist of two main energy pathways. The grazing pathway comprises the larger organisms above ground or in the water, while the detritus pathway comprises the smaller organisms existing on or in the soil. *See also* Trophic Level.

FOOD WEB The interlocking network of food chains, each interconnected by one or more trophic levels. A conceptual way of outlining energy and material flows through an ecosystem. *See also* Food Chain.

FOOTHILLS A steeply sloping upland with hill relief (up to 300 metres) that fringes a mountain range or high plateau escarpment.

FOOTSLOPE The geomorphic component forming the inner, gently inclined surface at the base of a hillslope. The surface profile is dominantly concave. In terms of gradational processes, it is a transition zone between upslope sites or erosion (backslopes) and the downslope sites of deposition (toeslope). *See also* Hillslope.

FORAGE Woody or herbaceous plant material utilized by animals as food, either by browsing, grazing, or as harvested material. *See also* Browsing; Grazing.

FORAGING SUBSTRATE The surface from which food is acquired.

FORB A herbaceous plant with broad leaves, excluding the grasses and grasslike plants (e.g., buttercup, sunflower).

FORECAST A prediction of future conditions and occurrences based on the perceived functioning of the system being examined. The accuracy of a forecast depends on a proper understanding of the system; hence the highly variable nature of forecasts involving natural resources, which are typically very complex and seldom fully understood. Note that a forecast differs from a 'projection.' A projection is also a prediction of anticipated future conditions, but it is based on an extrapolation of past trends. The distinction between the two terms is sometimes imprecise.

FOREDUNE A coastal dune or dune ridge oriented parallel to the shoreline, occurring at the landward margin of the beach along the shoreward face of a beach ridge, or at the landward limit of the highest tide, and more or less completely stabilized by vegetation.

FOREGROUND In visual resource management, the foreground is technically described as that part of the landscape immediately in front of the viewer. It can be seen with clarity and in detail for distances of approximately zero to one-quarter mile, depending on the complexity of the landscape. *See also* Background; Middleground.

FOREST **1** In the narrow technical sense, a vegetation community dominated by trees and other woody shrubs, growing close enough together that the tree tops touch or overlap, creating various degrees of shade on the forest floor. The amount of understorey vegetation depends on the forest type and its successional stage. It is also an area of standing trees that is being managed or otherwise maintained to produce benefits such as timber, recreation, wildlife habitat, etc. Many types of forest are recognized around the world, including ancient, boreal, climax, commercial, community, elfin, farm, high, low, managed, natural, non-commercial, normal, old-growth, production, protection, second-growth, traditional, urban, and virgin. *See* specific terms for more detail. **2** In the historical sense, forests were quite distinct from woods. In medieval times, woods were areas of forested land not reserved for the pleasure of the nobility. Forests, by contrast, were areas reserved for the nobility within which they could enjoy hunting, and such areas were very strictly controlled under a system of laws and regulations. The etymological derivation of the word forests is thought to be quite literally, a place designated by the King for the rest of wild animals (from the latin *fera* and *statio,* meaning a safe abode or sanctuary for animals). It is believed that this was later compounded to *foresta.* Later on, the meaning of forests changed as the emphasis shifted away from retention of wildlife for hunting to more utilitarian wood values. A new era emerged in the late eighteenth century with the concept of a forest being an entity in need of management, and this attitude has evolved almost continuously through to the present day. Almost all of the current controversies surrounding forests, virtually anywhere in the world, still hinge on the schism between the forest as sanctuary and the forest as utilitarian resource.

FOREST BIRD A bird that dwells in the forest, especially to breed. Some species utilize different environments on different continents, and thus might not be considered as forest birds in all places.

FOREST CANOPY The cover of branches and foliage formed collectively by the crowns of adjacent trees and other woody growth.

FOREST CAPITAL The value represented by the land, the growing stock on the land, and the physical improvements made, such as roads, buildings, drains, fences, etc., that, taken as a whole, make up the forest estate.

FOREST CLOSURE *See* Closure.

FOREST COVER All the trees and other plants (including ground cover) occupying the forest site.

FOREST DWELLERS **1** The people that live in and rely on forest ecosystems to maintain their livelihood, social structure, cultural identity, and traditional knowledge, which must be safeguarded and respected. **2** In a broader sense, all the organisms, including people, living in the forest.

FOREST ENTOMOLOGIST A professional person engaged in the study and/or management of insects in a forest environment. *See also* Entomology.

FOREST FIRE Any wildfire or prescribed fire that is burning in forested areas, grass, or alpine tundra vegetation. **1** There are the following main types of forest fires. **Ground fire** is a fire burning primarily on or in the ground, consuming organic material on the forest floor and burning into the soil itself (e.g. on peatlands). Ground fires are less subject to the influence of wind than surface fires. **Surface fire** is a fire that burns in the surface fuel layer, excluding the crowns of the trees, as either a head fire, flank fire, or backfire. **Crown fire** is a fire that advances through the crown fuel layer, usually in conjunction with the surface fire. Crown fires can be classified according to the degree of dependence on the surface fire phase. **Intermittent crown fire** is a fire in which trees discontinuously torch, but the rate of spread is controlled by the surface fire phase. It is synonymous with passive crown fire. **Active crown fire** is a fire that advances with a well-defined wall of flame extending from the ground surface to above the crown fuel layer. Probably most crown fires are of this class. Development of an active crown fire requires a substantial surface fire and thereafter the surface and crown phases spread as a linked unit. It is synonymous with dependent crown fire. **Independent crown fire** is a fire that advances in the crown fuel layer only. It is synonymous with running crown fire. **2** The anatomical parts of a forest fire are classified as follows. **Bay** is a marked indentation in the fire perimeter usually located between two fingers. It is synonymous with pockets. **Finger** is an elongated burned area projecting from the main body of the fire resulting in an irregular fire perimeter. **Flanks** are those portions of the fire perimeter that are between the head and the back of the fire which are roughly parallel to the main direction of spread. This term is synonymous with sides. **Head** is that portion of the fire perimeter having the greatest rate of spread and frontal fire intensity which is generally on the downwind and/or upslope part of the fire. It is synonymous with front. **Back** is that portion of the fire perimeter opposite the head. The slowest spreading part of the fire, it is synonymous with base, heel, and rear. **Islands** are one or more areas of unburned fuels located within the fire perimeter. **Point of origin** is the location within the fire perimeter where ignition first occurred. It is synonymous with origin of a fire.

FOREST FLOOR **1** A general term encompassing the layer of undecomposed organic matter (leaves, twigs, and plant remains in various stages of decomposition) lying on top of the mineral soil. **2** Technically, the organic horizons (over 0.17 kilograms of organic carbon per kilograms of solids) at the surface of forest soil.

FOREST FRAGMENTATION The change in the forest landscape from extensive and continuous forest cover to a mosaic of smaller patches separated by open areas or very young stands of forest. The process of reducing the size and degree of connectivity of the stands that make up the forest, leading to varying degrees of isolation of the remaining patches. Can also refer to the elimination of continuous forest cover by changes in adjacent land uses (e.g., conversion of forest lands to agriculture).

FOREST HEALTH As a specific condition, the term refers to a growing forest having many or all of its native species of plants and animals. As a management objective, it refers to maintaining or restoring the capacity of a forest to achieve health.

FOREST LAND **1** In the timber management sense, forest land is that land designated as being capable of, and presently intended for, the growth and harvest of trees. In this sense, forest land is usually classified as productive (i.e., capable of growing trees of the desired species and within a desired time frame) or non-productive (i.e., not capable of producing a timber crop of the desired species within a desired time frame). **2** In the forest management sense, forest land is land currently, or in the recent past, or intended to be in the near future, under a forest cover of some type and successional stage, regardless of the functions possible or intended. Forest land in this sense has the capability of supporting many different functions and outputs, including recreation, aesthetics, wildlife habitat, water quality and quantity regulation, hunting and gathering opportunities for indigenous peoples, and maintenance of a wide array of ecological functions and processes, in addition to the narrower sense of provision of timber. *See also* Forest.

FOREST MANAGEMENT The practice of applying scientific, economic, philosophical, and social principles to the administration, utilization, and conservation of all aspects of forested landscapes to meet specified goals and objectives, while maintaining the productivity of the forest. Forest management includes the subset of activities known as timber management, but also involves planning and managing forested landscapes for fish and wildlife, biological diversity, conservation measures, parks, wilderness, recreation, and aesthetic values. Forest management is an all-encompassing activity and is not to be confused with the more restrictive activities associated with timber management. *See also* Timber Management.

FOREST MANAGEMENT UNIT An area of forest land managed as a unit for fibre production and/or other renewable resources. The unit's size can be an entire province (state), a provincial (state) management subdivision, an industrial licence area, etc.

FOREST MAP A base map showing factors such as the location of the forest, its management units, the species types, age classes, topography, wildlife habitats, and management history. A complete set of forest maps completed over many decades (centuries in many parts of Europe and Scandinavia) offers the reader a complete historical picture of what was done in the past that created the forest of today, and what should be done today to create the forest for tomorrow.

FOREST MENSURATION The measurement of volume, growth, and development of individual trees and stands, and the various products obtained from them.

FOREST PATHOLOGIST A professional person engaged in the study and/or management of diseases and pathogens of forest trees.

FOREST PEST MANAGEMENT The planning, conduct, and evaluation of activities needed to protect forest resources, products, and facilities from unacceptable damage or loss due to the activities of pests.

FOREST PROTECTION That branch of forestry concerned with the prevention and control of damage to forests arising from the action of people or livestock (especially unauthorized felling, fires, grazing and browsing), of pests (including insects, diseases and weeds), and abiotic agents (including avalanches, fires, storms, frost, and other climatic factors).

FORESTRY **1** A profession embracing the science, business, and art of creating, maintaining, and managing forested landscapes and their many component parts to produce consumptive and/or nonconsumptive outputs for use by humans or other species in a manner that does not cause ecosystem degradation. **2** A loosely used term to describe timber management, and associated activities such as silviculture and forest protection. It is often used erroneously, purporting to mean forest management when in fact describing timber management alone. *See also* Forest; Forest Management; Timber Management.

FOREST TREE IMPROVEMENT **1** The application of genetics to produce trees or a source of seed to create trees with specific desirable traits based on their phenotypic and genotypic characteristics. In some cases, the improved trees can be cloned by growing genetically identical trees from a limited source of germ plasm. **2** The improvement or enhancement of wood quality, volume, and growth rates using a combination of genetic improvement and silvicultural activities, such as fertilization and pruning.

FOREST TYPE A group of forested areas or stands of similar composition that differentiates them from other such groups. Forest types are usually separated and identified by plant species composition and often by height and crown closure classes. In detailed typing, age, site, and other classes may be also be recognized. The delineation of forest types is normally done on aerial photographs and may be supplemented by field data. Type symbols and boundaries are marked on the photographs and then transferred to the forest map. With the advent of GIS technology, the capability to update and validate this information has greatly improved.

FOREST USE Any use made of the forest by any organism, human or nonhuman. Forest use is not limited to economic or income-producing activities. It may also include fish and wildlife habitat, water purification and production, air purification, climate modification, food and herb gathering, trapping, recreation, tourism, research, education, spiritual renewal, traditional uses by indigenous people, wilderness, ecological reserves, domestic grazing, and timber-cutting.

FORK The bifurcation of tree trunks or branches, usually equal in size and occurring at a narrow angle. Sometimes incorrectly termed the crotch. *See also* Crotch.

FORM Plural formae; the singular is officially (by international acceptance) forma, but form is more common. A description below the subspecies or variety level but is still distinguishable morphologically. The lowest rank usually noted by botanists, it designates a very small variation, such as differences in flower colour or leaf lobing.

FORMA SPECIALIS In certain fungi, an infraspecific population of a plant pathogenic species, distinguished by host preference usually at the genus level, but scarcely or not at all by morphological criteria.

FORMATION **1** The surface of the ground, following all preparatory work such as excavation, filling, and shaping, on which the road base will be placed. *See also* Base. **2** In geology, the basic unit of lithostratigraphy. Formations are combined into groups or subdivided into members. The formation is the body of rock (typically a sedimentary stratum or strata, but could also be igneous or metamorphic rocks) that is generally characterized by some degree of internal lithologic homogeneity, or distinctive features (such as chemical composition, structure, texture, or fossils), by a prevailing (but not necessarily tabular) shape, and by its mappability at the Earth's surface (at a scale of about 1:25,000), or by its traceability in the subsurface. **3** An obsolete term for a widespread, naturally occurring vegetation type, similar in scale to the more contemporary term, biome. **4** The major unit of vegetation according to the monoclimax theory of vegetation succession.

FORM CLASS Any of the intervals into which the range of form quotients of trees or logs is divided for classification and use. Also the trees or logs falling into such intervals. In general, the clarification of trees according to their taper. *See also* Form Quotient; Taper.

FORM DISTORTION LOSS The reduction in merchantable timber due to topkill and recovery, or other pest-caused damage that has resulted in multiple leaders, forks, etc. The wood above these distortions is often not usable for sawtimber. *See also* Increment; Mortality.

FORM FACTOR The ratio of the inside-bark volume of a tree and the volume of a cylinder having the same diameter and height. Three different form factors are defined, the difference being related to the point on a tree at which the diameter is measured: (1) **absolute form factor**, in which the cylinder diameter is equal to the stump diameter; (2) **breast height form factor**, in which the cylinder diameter is equal to the diameter at breast height (the usual factor used); and (3) **normal form factor**, in which the cylinder diameter is equal to a diameter measured at a distance above ground having a fixed ratio to tree height.

FORM GENUS Generally, a genus whose species are not always related to a common ancestor (e.g., the Deuteromycotina class of fungi (asexual fungi).

FORM POINT A point in the crown of a tree estimated by eye to be the centre of wind pressure or the geometrical centre of the crown.

FORM QUOTIENT The ratio of any two overbark diameters of a tree stem. The absolute form quotient is the ratio of half the tree height above breast height to the diameter at breast height, and is used to develop tree volume tables.

FORMULATION **1** A chemical preparation containing pesticide and ready for application in the field. The formulation is a mixture of active ingredients, diluents, emulsifiers, spreaders, synergists, and/or other materials. **2** An analytical process of making a mathematical analogue of a real world situation in order to attempt to use the model to predict change in the real world.

FORWARDER *See* Harvesting Machine Classification.

FORWARDING *See* Harvest Functions.

FORWARD-LOOKING INFRARED (FLIR) A hand-held or aircraft-mounted device designed to detect heat differentials and display their images on a video screen. FLIRs have thermal resolution similar to infrared line scanners, but their spatial resolution is substantially less. They are commonly used to detect hot spots and flare-ups obscured by smoke, evaluate the effectiveness of firing operations, or detect areas needing mop-up. *See also* Infrared Imagery.

FOSSORIAL A burrowing animal adapted for living completely underground, for example, moles (family Talpidae).

FOUNDATION The base upon which a structure sits (e.g., a bridge or pier), retaining wall, or road grade. The strength of the foundation determines its ability to resist sinking under load, lateral shear forces, and vibratory motion, and thus directly affects the short- and long-term stability of the structure that it supports. The foundation can be bedrock, compacted soil, or concrete, or a combination of these.

FOUNDER EFFECT Occurs when the founding members of a new population do not carry a completely representative sample of the total genetic variability seen in the parent population.

FOVEOLATE Marked with one or more shallow pits.

FRACTAL DIMENSION An index of the complexity of spatial patterns.

FRACTAL GEOMETRY A method to study shapes that are self-similar over many scales.

FRAGILITY **1** In a general sense, the quality of being easily broken, damaged, or destroyed, or of being unable, or barely able to endure the normal day-to-day demands of existence without harm. **2** In resource management, the relative ability of resources to tolerate sustained use without degradation of the resource base. The term is context-dependent, and thus a resource may be fragile for one set of uses, but quite durable under a different set of uses. **3** Forested lands where harvesting would result in reduced future site productivity, or where the ecosystem would take a long time to return to its original condition after disturbance. Fragility is related to soil structure and composition, geology, topography, and groundwater regimes. *See also* Rotation.

FRAGIPAN A loamy subsurface horizon with high bulk density and mechanical strength, but low organic content. Fragipans have a hard consistency when dry but become weakly brittle when wet, and slake if immersed in water. They are sometimes mottled, semi-permeable or impermeable to water, and are considered to be root-restricting horizons. It is found in cultivated or virgin soils but not in calcareous material.

FRASS The solid excrement of insects, particularly larvae. For bark beetles, a loose definition combines excrement and boring dust into the term frass.

FRAYING The abrasion of bark and wood from tree stems caused by deer seeking to remove the velvet from their antlers or as a means of demarcating breeding territory.

FREDLE INDEX An index of the quality of spawning gravel obtained by dividing the geometric mean diameter of particle size by the sorting coefficient. *See also* Sorting Coefficient.

FREE Botanically, plant parts that are separate, not fused or adnate to other organs. It is usually used to describe the separateness of dissimilar organs or parts, such as filaments free from the corolla, but may also be used in the sense of distinct.

FREE-BURNING A general term describing the condition of a fire or portion of a fire perimeter that is unaffected by natural or man-made barriers to fire growth and or any suppression measures taken.

FREE FLOW The maximum rate of water flow a fire pump will attain when there are no restrictions at the pump outlet or losses due to friction loss or head.

FREE-LIVING Any organism living independently, rather than symbiotically (e.g., an insect able to move about as opposed to living within a gall or in a leaf mine).

FREE LOG *See* Large Organic Debris.

FREE MOISTURE In wood, the moisture contained in the cell cavities and intercellular spaces, held by capillary forces only.

FREE-TO-GROW That point when a newly established stand of trees meets the following criteria: (1) it meets or exceeds the minimum stocking levels; (2) it has the desired species composition; (3) it meets or exceeds a minimum height requirement; and (4) it is free from any vegetative competition that would hinder further growth.

FREIGHT ON BOARD (FOB) A term used to acknowledge that the quoted price includes the costs of loading the product being purchased onto the carrier delivering the product, but not the costs of delivery beyond the loading point.

FREQUENCY **1** In statistics, the number of observations assigned to any of an arbitrary set of classes. **2** The number of plots, stations, counts (visits), or intervals in which a species is detected. When expressed as a fraction of the total sampled, it becomes relative frequency. It can be measured by visual estimation to produce loosely defined categories, such as very abundant, abundant, frequent, occasional, rare, or very rare. *See also* Density.

FREQUENCY-DEPENDENT SELECTION Where the intensity of natural selection is dependent on the frequency of genotypes or phenotypes within the population.

FREQUENCY DISTRIBUTION A graphical, tabular, or mathematical representation of the manner in which the frequencies of a continuous or discrete random variable are distributed over the range of its possible values.

FRESHET A sudden and rapid rise in the level of a stream or river due to heavy rains or rapid snowmelt.

FRIABLE A term describing the ease with which a soil sample crumbles. *See also* Consistency.

FRICTION LOSS A loss of pressure caused by the turbulent movement of water or solution against the interior surface of fire hose, pipe, or fittings. It is normally measured in pounds per square inch per 100 feet of hose or pipe. *See also* Friction-Reducing Agent.

FRICTION REDUCING AGENT A water-soluble substance that reduces frictional drag of solutions and dampens turbulent flow while being pumped through the pipe or hose.

FRIGID **1** Generally, freezing temperatures. **2** A soil temperature regime that has mean annual soil temperatures greater than 0 degrees Celsius but less than 8 degrees Celsius, with a greater-than-5-degree-Celsius difference between mean summer and mean winter soil temperatures at 50 centimetres below the surface.

FROND The leaf blade of a fern. It is also used more generally to describe a large compound leaf, such as a palm leaf. *See also* Fern (for illustration).

FRONT In meteorology, the boundary between two air masses of different density. A cold front represents the leading edge of colder air replacing warmer air. The reverse of this is a warm front.

FRONTAL RECESSION The retreat of an ice sheet or a glacier terminus by melting back upvalley against the direction of ice flow. It is the common mode of retreat of valley glaciers.

FRONT OF A FIRE *See* Forest Fire (head).

FROST Crystals of ice formed and deposited like dew, but at a temperature below freezing.

FROST-CHURNING A term describing the all-inclusive actions of frost in the ground that leads to stirring, churning, modification, and similar disturbances of the regolith and other earth materials. It includes heaving, solifluction, and differential mass movements, and leads to patterned ground. It may also be termed congeliturbation, cryoturbation, and frost stirring.

FROST CRACK Radial splitting along the grain in the stem and branches of a tree as a result of internal stresses set up by freezing temperatures. Such cracks may open to the surface or remain internal. Frost crack is an indicator of hidden defects due to the entry of wood-destroying fungi.

FROST HEART A type of false heart in which a coloured zone or series of zones develops, simulating heartwood in species that do not normally differentiate it. It is often ascribed to the action of severe frost on standing timber. *See also* Black Heart.

FROST HEAVE The pushing up of a surface by the accumulation of ice in the underlying soil structure. Boulders, rocks, and newly planted trees are often heaved up by the action of frost.

FROST-SHATTERING The mechanical disintegration, splitting, or breakup of a rock or soil caused by the great pressure exerted by the freezing of water contained in cracks or pores, or along bedding planes. It is also termed congelifraction, frost-splitting, frost-riving, frost-bursting, frost-weathering, frost-wedging, gelivation, or gelifraction.

FRUCTICOLOUS Growing on fruit.

FRUCTIFICATION *See* Fruiting Body.

FRUGIVORE Any animal that eats fruit for all or a part of its diet. *See also* Carnivore; Herbivore; Omnivore; Trophic Level.

FRUIT The fertilized and ripened ovary with its enclosed seeds. The seed-bearing organ. There are two principal types of fruit. (1) **Fleshy fruits** fall into three categories: (a) those derived from a single flower with a syncarpous gynoecium, such as berry, drupe, hesperidium, and pepo (see illustration); (b) those formed from the receptacles or floral cup (hypanthium), such as pomes and hips; and (c) those resulting from the union of many separate carpels of a single flower (aggregate berry) or by the fusion of several fruits of separate flowers (multiple berries). (2) **Dry fruits** fall into two categories: (a) those that are indehiscent and single-seeded, such as achenes, caryopsis, nuts, and nutlets, samaras, and utricles; and (b) those that are dehiscent and having several to many seeds, such as capsules, follicles, legumes, loments, silicles, and siliques (see illustration).

FRUITING BODY A complex fungi structure that contains or bears spores. It may be annual, functioning for at most only one season; or perennial, seasonally active for two or more years. The term includes mushrooms and conks.

FRUTESCENT Shrubby, or eventually becoming so.

FRUTICOSE **1** A lichen growth form that is

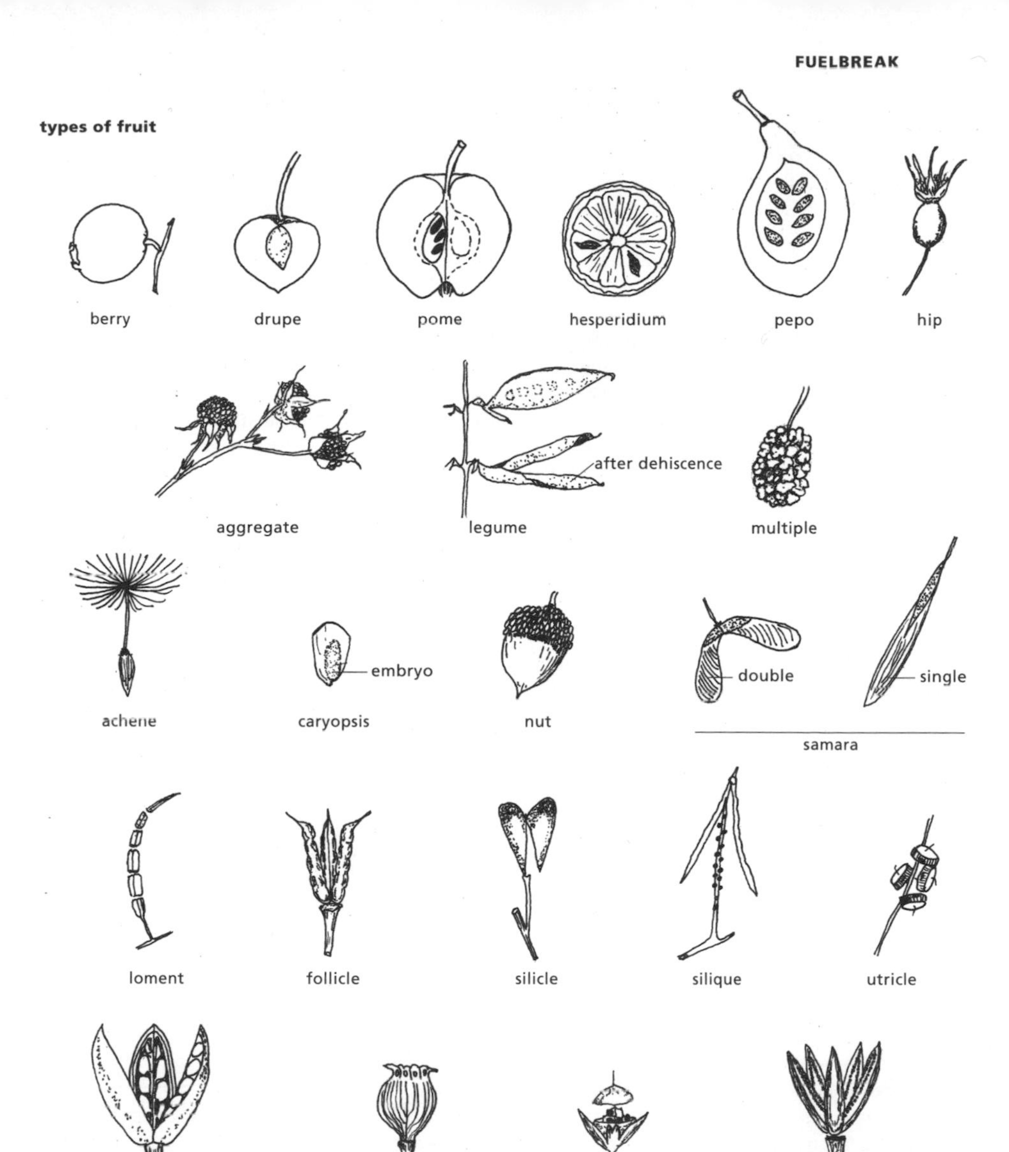

radially symmetrical, tufted, stalked or pendent and surrounded by a cortex. *See also* Crustose; Foliose. **2** Having a shrubby form, with many woody stems and branches but no obvious main trunk.

FRY The life stage of fish between full absorption of the yolk sac and less than one year old, or a more arbitrarily defined fingerling or parr stage in the case of salmon and trout, and which is generally reached by the end of the first summer. *See also* Fingerling; Parr.

FUEL ARRANGEMENT Describes the horizontal and vertical distribution of all combustible materials within a particular fuel type.

FUELBREAK An existing barrier or change in fuel type (to one that is less flammable than that surrounding it), or a wide strip of land on which the native vegetation has been modified or cleared, that acts as a buffer to fire spread so that fires burning into them can be more readily controlled. They are often selected or constructed to protect a high value area from fire. In the event of fire, the fuelbreak may also serve as a control line from which to carry out suppression operations. It is synonymous with Firebreak. *See also* Control Line; Fire Guard.

FUEL BULK DENSITY The dry weight of combustible materials per unit volume. Numerically, it is equal to the fuel load divided by the depth of the particular fuel layer (e.g., duff, tree crown foliage); measured in grams per cubic centimetre or kilograms per cubic metre (0.1 grams per cubic centimetre is equivalent to 100 kilograms per cubic metre).

FUEL CLASS A group of fuels possessing common characteristics. Dead fuels are grouped according to time lag after death (1-, 10-, 100-, and 1,000-hour time lag), and living fuels are grouped as herbaceous (annual or perennial) or woody.

FUEL CONDITION The relative flammability of fuel as determined by fuel type and environmental conditions.

FUEL CONTINUITY The degree or extent of continuous or uninterrupted distribution of fuel particles (surface or aerial) in a fuelbed, thus affecting a fire's ability to sustain combustion and spread.

FUEL ENERGY *See* Available Fuel Energy.

FUEL INVENTORY An inventory of the fuels available on the forest floor or in the canopy, by type (species) and size class, including fine (less than one centimetre) and coarse (greater than one centimetre) materials.

FUEL LADDER *See* Ladder Fuels.

FUEL LOAD The ovendry weight of combustible materials per unit area. Expressed in kilograms per cubic metre, tonnes per hectare, or tons per acre.

FUEL MANAGEMENT The planned manipulation and/or reduction of the flammability and resistance to control of living or dead fuels for forest management and other land-use objectives (e.g., hazard reduction, silvicultural purposes, wildlife habitat improvement). This is achieved by use of prescribed fire, mechanical, chemical, or biological means, and/or changing the stand structure and species composition.

FUEL MOISTURE CONTENT The amount of water present in fuel, generally expressed as a percentage of the substance's weight when thoroughly dried at 100 degrees Celsius.

FUEL MOISTURE STICKS A specially prepared wooden device of known weight that when periodically weighed after being continuously exposed to the weather elements indicates changes in the moisture status and relative flammability of certain dead fuels.

FUEL TREATMENT Any manipulation or removal of fuels to reduce the likelihood of ignition and/or to lessen potential damage and resistance to control (e.g., lopping, chipping, crushing, piling, and burning).

FUEL TYPE An identifiable association of fuel elements of distinctive species, form, size, arrangement, continuity, or other characteristics that will cause a predictable rate of spread or resistance to control under specified weather and burning conditions.

FUELWOOD Trees of sufficient size and quality to yield firewood, and the logs that these trees produce. In some parts of the world, branch materials are the main source of fuelwood.

FUGACIOUS Falling or withering away early.

FUGITIVE COLOUR A colouring agent used in fire retardants that permits high visibility at the time of use, but which fades rapidly following use to minimize the long-term visual impact of use.

FULL-SIB FAMILIES In a tree (or other plant) improvement program, a group of offspring where the genotype of both parents is known or anticipated, and pollination is artificial and therefore controlled. *See also* Half-Sib Families.

FULL TREE HARVESTING Extraction of the complete tree, including top and branches, from the stump out to the landing. The top and branches are then removed at the landing and either piled and left to rot, or disposed of by chipping, burning, or other forms of redistribution back to the cutover area. It is sometimes termed whole tree harvesting.

FULLY FUNCTIONAL FOREST ECOSYSTEM A forest ecosystem where the full natural range of ecological functions, including change and disturbance, is maintained at both the stand and the landscape level.

FULLY STOCKED *See* Stocking.

FUMIGATION The planned application of chemicals in the form of volatile liquids or gases to kill pests. It is used as a means of disinfecting an enclosed area such as a greenhouse, or as a soil sterilant where the ground has been covered with an impermeable cover (tarpaulin or plastic).

FUNCTIONAL RESPONSE The change in an individual predator's rate of exploitation of prey as a result of a change in prey density.

FUNDATRIX A parthenogenic, often wingless female that develops from an egg. One of several adult forms of an adelgid or aphid.

FUNGICIDE A chemical or biological substance applied to kill or inhibit fungal growth and the production of spores.

FUNGI IMPERFECTI Fungi in the class Deuteromycetes. An artificial group consisting of those fungi in which production of spores by meiosis is not known to occur. Sexual forms have been identified for many fungi originally placed in this group. Many Ascomycetes are referred to in the literature by names given to either the imperfect form or the sexual form without mentioning the other. Fungi assigned to this group are often called imperfect fungi or simply imperfects.

FUNGISTATIC A treatment applied to prevent the growth of a fungus without killing it. *See also* Eradicant; Protectant.

FUNGUS Plural fungi. A group of organisms belonging to a distinct kingdom known as the Fungi. Usually, a multicellular organism with chitin-containing cell walls, but lacking flagella and chlorophyll. Typically composed of hyphae with well-defined nuclei, fungi obtain nutrition by absorbing nutrients digested by secreted exoenzymes, and usually reproduce by spores. There are five phyla within the kingdom: (1) Zygomycota (bread moulds and fly fungi); (2) Ascomycota (yeasts and sac fungi); (3) Basidiomycota (mushrooms, smuts, rusts, puffballs, and stinkhorns); (4) Deuteromycota (imperfect fungi); and (5) Mycophycophyta (lichens). Note that the slime moulds, slime nets, chytrids, and oomycetes are now considered to be members of the kingdom Protista. The illustration shows the different parts of a Basidiomycete fungus.

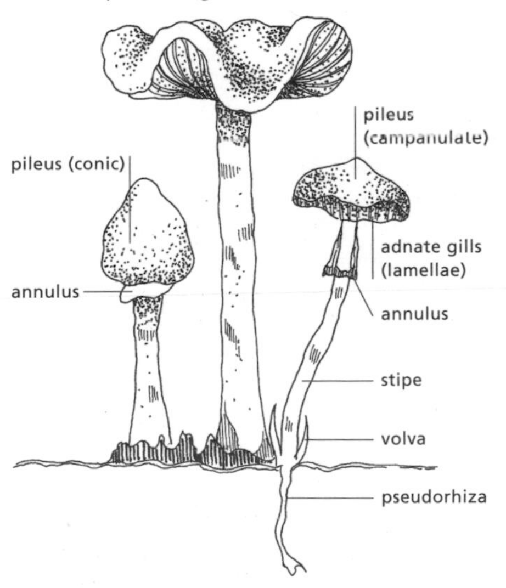

FUNGUS MAT A dense, leathery mass of fungus mycelium often formed in decayed wood by certain wood-rotting fungi.

FUNICLE/FUNICULUS The stalk or thread by which an ovule is attached to the placenta in the ovary. *See also* Carpel (for illustration).

FUNNELFORM Having a tube that gradually widens upwards and into the limb.

FURANS *See* Dioxins and Furans.

FUR BEARER Any mammal whose pelt has commercial value (e.g., fox, bobcat, coyote, marten, beaver).

FURCATE Forked.

FURFURACEOUS Covered with soft, branlike scales.

FURROWED Having longitudinal grooves.

FUSCOUS Smoky dark in colour; greyish brown or blackish.

FUSIFORM Describes a canker shape or swelling that is spindle-shaped and tapered at both ends. It is sometimes called a spindle-shaped swelling.

FUTURES **1** An all-inclusive description of what it is believed the area being planned for will be like if a proposed plan or course of action is followed. *See also* Scenario. **2** An attempt to examine and analyze where existing trends will lead if they continue. Once these are better understood, they provide a context for action taken now and in the future. Lacking this understanding may lead to important planning options being neglected.

G

GABION A woven wire basket that is filled with rocks and stones large enough so that they do not pass through the wire mesh. The individual baskets are laid and stacked in place like building blocks and form a durable retaining wall that is erosion-resistant, relatively cheap, and simple to install. Gabions are used to stabilize banks, prevent erosion, or alter stream flow patterns as a part of stream or riparian area enhancement activities. *See* Bridge (for illustration).

GAIA HYPOTHESIS The idea that the Earth is like a living organism composed of all living organisms on the planet and the abiotic environment, and that the Earth is dependent on these biotic and abiotic components and the ecological processes associated with their interactions. The Gaia Hypothesis suggests that humans should think of ecological processes and human participation with them as involving these living systems. When we do, we have a much deeper sense of connection with the Earth as a whole; moreover, we understand the degree to which the whole Earth environment has been created and is maintained by a multitude of living beings, which cooperate to create a larger living entity, much as the cells of our bodies together form a larger, whole, and living system. The word Gaia comes from the ancient Greek name for the Earth as a Goddess.

GALEA A hood formed from part of the perianth. Derived from, for example, the two uppermost petals coalescent indistinguishably into one.

GALL A pronounced but usually localized swelling on a woody plant, caused by the proliferation of greatly modified plant tissue. This leads to a permanent swelling, or outgrowth. Galls are induced by certain fungi, bacteria, insects, mites, or nematodes. Galls associated with certain organisms have a characteristic shape and location on the plant.

GALL APHID An aphid, commonly in the genera *Adelges* or *Pineus* (Adelgidae), that induces galls in the host tissue, twig die-back, and defoliation, during feeding.

GALL MIDGE A small fly of the family Cecidomyiidae, with pink or yellowish larvae (maggots) that cause many kinds of galls on plants, generally on leaves, roots, cones, seeds, or twigs. Some gall midges give rise to pockets of resin in the bark of conifers.

GALLERY A passage, burrow, tunnel, or mine excavated by an insect in plant tissues for feeding, oviposition, or shelter. Bark beetle galleries are constructed in the inner bark, often etching the surface of the wood. The form and layout of galleries is characteristic for particular genera and most species. *See also* Pupal Chamber.

GAME **1** Animals (mammals, birds, or fish) habitually hunted for food and/or particular products, and/or sport, including trophies. **2** Animals defined under legislation for the purposes of some form of management.

GAMETE A specialized cell (haploid) that is capable of fusing with another gamete of the opposite sex to form a zygote cell (diploid), which is then capable of development into a new individual. The process of fusion in simple organisms is called isogamy; in more complex organisms it is termed oogamy. Where oogamy occurs in animals, the male cells are sperms and the female cells eggs. In plants, the male gametes originate in the pollen grain, while the female gametes are the egg cells found in the embryo sac.

GAMETOPHYTE The stage or generation in plants that produces gametes. In ferns, the gametophyte is a very small thalluslike body bearing archegonia (female gametes) and antheridia (male gametes). In angiosperms, the gametophyte is the pollen tube that develops from a pollen grain and produces male gametes, and the embryo sac that develops in the ovule and produces a female gamete.

GAMMA DIVERSITY *See* Diversity.

GAMODEME A group of individuals within a species that are able to interbreed.

GAMOPETALOUS With petals united to one another by their margins, and at the least, basally. *See also* Apetalous; Polypetalous.

GAMOPHYLLOUS Having leaves or leaflike organs (e.g., bracts, petals, or sepals) united to one another by their margins. *See also* Aphyllous.

GAMOSEPALOUS With sepals united to one another marginally, and at the least, basally. *See also* Aposepalous; Polysepalous.

GAP **1** An opening in the forest canopy. It is typically associated with the death, blowdown, or other removal of one or more dominant trees. Gaps are characterized by high structural and species diversity due to growth of understorey species and colonization by new species, which are facilitated by the microclimatic conditions (temperature, light, humidity) of the gap. **2** A hole or missed area in a fire retardant drop. *See also* Opening.

GAP ANALYSIS A methodology used to assess important components of biodiversity to determine which components already occur in protected areas, those that are underrepresented within these areas, or those that are unprotected from potentially destructive or irreparable activities.

GEITONOGAMY Cross-fertilization between flowers on a single plant. Genetically, the same as autogamy.

GELIFRACTION *See* Frost-Churning.

GELIVATION *See* Frost-Churning.

GEMMA Plural gemmae. A small body of cells that form an asexual, budlike reproductive body in some crytogams. *See also* Moss (for illustration).

GENE A specific sequence of DNA nucleotides within a segment of the DNA molecule, coded to produce specific proteins which then determine the attributes characteristic of a species. The basic unit of heritable characteristics in the chromosome, which can be transmitted between cells and thus between generations.

GENE BANK A place where germ plasm is kept

for use in *ex situ* conservation work.

GENE FLOW The exchange of genetic traits between populations by movement of individuals, gametes, or spores.

GENE POOL The total of all the genes of all breeding individuals available within a population at any one time.

GENERALIST A species with broad food or habitat preferences, or both. *See also* Specialist.

GENERAL RESISTANCE Resistance to more than one pest or disease. The term is often used to mean resistance to all races of a particular pathogen, but for this, the term race non-specific resistance is considered preferable. *See also* Field Resistance; Horizontal Resistance.

GENERATION **1** A group of offspring descending from common parents, or a group of parents. **2** The period of time between the birth of one generation and that of the next. **3** The period of time required to complete the life cycle of an organism from birth to reproduction. **4** All those individuals of an organism that are separated from a common parent or ancestor by an equal number of reproductive cycles.

GENERATION TIME The average age at which a female produces offspring, or the average time for a population to increase by a factor equal to the net reproductive rate.

GENET A new plant formed as a result of sexual reproduction. The production of seed.

GENETIC DIVERSITY The genetic variability within a population or a species. The number and relative abundance of alleles. This is the foundation of all diversity, and loss of genetic diversity within species is increasingly recognized as an important and largely undocumented problem, at least as serious as loss of entire species. Genetic diversity can be assessed at three levels: (1) diversity within breeding populations; (2) diversity between breeding populations within any one geographic area; and (3) diversity within the species. *See also* Biodiversity.

GENETIC DRIFT A change in the genetic composition of a population resulting from random events over a long period of time. Typically, a loss of alleles from the population as a result of random change. Genetic drift is more pronounced in small populations and those that are reproductively isolated from other populations of the same species.

GENETIC GAIN An improvement in the mean genotypic value of a selected character, obtained as a result of breeding. The gain is the product of the degree of heritability and the selection differential for that character.

GENETIC MATERIAL **1** The genes comprising an organism. Specific genes, containing desirable characteristics, can be used to clone new organisms with the same or a new combination of desirable traits. **2** Refers to land classification schemes in which the surficial materials are classified according to their mode of formation (genesis) (e.g., erosion, transportation by wind or water, mass wasting, weathering, and weather fracturing).

GENETIC RESOURCE Genetic resources are the heritable characteristics of a plant or animal of real or potential benefit to people. The term includes modern cultivars and breeds; traditional cultivars and breeds; special genetic stocks (breeding lines, mutants, etc); wild relatives of domesticated species; and genetic variants of wild resource species. A 'wild genetic resource' is the wild relative of a plant or animal that is already known to be of economic importance. The reasons for conserving such a resource include the provision of direct and indirect economic benefits. However, the conserved genetic material must be made available to the people who require it to improve the productivity, quality, or pest resistance of utilized plants or animals.

GENETICS The science of heredity, dealing with the causes of resemblances and differences among organisms related by descent.

GENICULATE Abruptly bent, like a knee.

GENICULUM A kneelike, often thickened joint, at which an organ is bent (e.g., the joint in the petiole of some Araceae, or a node in the stem of some Graminae).

GENOME **1** The genetic complement of an individual. **2** All of the DNA sequences in a single (haploid) set of chromosomes. The genetic material inherited from either parent.

GENOTYPE The genetic make up of an organism, this being the sum total of all the genetic information in the organism. In analysis of the genetic constitution of a few gene loci, the genotype is all the characteristics on the chromosome, even if they are not expressed in the phenotype. *See also* Phenotype.

GENTLE SLOPE *See* Slope.

GENUS Plural genera. A division in the classification of plants and animals, consisting of a group of related species (occasionally just one species; e.g., Ginkgo). A taxonomic rank below family and above species. The genus name always starts with a capital letter. *See also* Class; Order; Phylum; Species; Taxon.

GEOCHEMICAL ANALYSIS Laboratory analysis to determine chemical and/or mineralogical composition of earth materials.

GEOCODING In GIS work, the transformation or typing in of digitized coordinates and labels to a map coordinate system (e.g., six degrees UTM).

GEODETIC SURVEY *See* Survey.

GEOGRAPHICALLY REFERENCED Refers to the condition of data for which 'positional' information is available, enabling the geographical position of the data to be established and communicated. The normal functioning of a geographic information system requires the existence of geographically referenced data in a spatial database and a means of manipulating these data. *See also* Spatial Database.

GEOGRAPHIC INFORMATION SYSTEM (GIS) The use of a computer system to overlay large volumes of spatial data of different kinds. The data are referenced to a set of geographical coordinates and encoded in computer (digital) format so that they can be sorted, selectively retrieved, statistically and spatially analyzed. The different data planes can be overlain in virtually any order, and can be used to test a variety of questions and 'what if' scenarios in modelling possible outcomes from different management regimes, or disturbances in the landscape at an infinite number of scales. *See also* Spatial Database.

GEOGRAPHIC ISOLATE *See* Subspecies.

GEO-GRID A soil-reinforcing material made up of a polythene grid in a two-metre wide roll. The material is laid out to form part of the subgrade and then acts to bind this layer together.

GEOLOGICAL PROCESSES **1** *See* Geomorphological Processes. **2** Those dynamic actions or events that take place below the Earth's surface, and result in effects such as earthquakes and volcanism, as well as geomorphological processes.

GEOLOGICAL STRUCTURE The three-dimensional arrangement of geological contacts and discontinuities, such as bedding, stratification, joints, faults, dykes, plutons, folds.

GEOLOGICAL TIME SCALE The periods of time that accord with changes in the Earth, and the plant and animal history that subsequently evolved. *See also* Appendix 2: Geological Time Scales.

GEOMETRIC MEAN DIAMETER A measure of the central tendency of particle size composition of substrate materials, sometimes used as an index of the quality of spawning gravels. It is also called the D50 size.

GEOMETRIC REGISTRATION In remote sensing, the process of geometrically aligning two or more sets of image data so that resolution cells for a single ground area can be digitally or visually superimposed. Data being registered may be of the same type, different kinds of sensors, or collected at different times.

GEOMETRIC ROAD STANDARD A set of engineering parameters that define the geometry of a road's cross-section, alignment, and profile grade. Higher standards typically allow for higher usage rates and vehicle weights, and higher travel speeds.

GEOMORPHIC SURFACE A surface representing an episode of landscape development that consists of one or more landforms. The mappable portion of the land surface that is defined in terms of morphology (relief, slope, aspect) and the stability of its component landforms.

GEOMORPHOLOGICAL HISTORY The evolution of landforms and landscapes, surface materials, and changes with time in geomorphological processes.

GEOMORPHOLOGICAL PROCESSES Dynamic actions or events that occur at the Earth's surface due to application of natural forces resulting from gravity, temperature changes, freezing and thawing, chemical reactions, seismic shaking, and the agencies of wind and moving water, ice and snow. Where and when a force exceeds the strength of the earth material, the material is changed by deformation, translocation, or chemical reactions.

GEOMORPHOLOGY The study of the origin of landforms, the processes whereby they are formed, and the materials of which they consist.

GEOPHYTE Plants that have their perennating buds (rhizomes, bulbs, tubers) below ground level. *See also* Hemicryptophyte; Life-Form (for illustration).

GEOTEXTILE FABRIC A synthetic fabric composed of a woven blanket of fibres usually in rolls four metres wide. The material is laid out below the final grade material, which is then spread out on top of it and compacted in the normal manner. The geotextile serves to reinforce the subgrade, but also allows free drainage of water through the fabric, while at the same time preventing mud and fine silt particles from pumping up into the finished grade. The latter property is especially useful for road construction work in areas of deep mucks or silty subgrades.

GEOTROPISM The response of plants to the forces of gravity. A **negative** response occurs when the plant grows away from the Earth's centre of gravity (most plant stems), and is **positive** when the response is toward the pull of gravity (most roots).

GERMINATION The start of growth in a mature, generally dormant, seed, spore, or pollen grain. Germination is characterized by the rupture of the seed coat or of the spore or pollen grain wall, and the emergence of a root, shoot, thallus, or hypha. In the field, germination is usually measured as the percentage of seeds in any given sample that germinate and produce a seedling, regardless of subsequent seedling survival. The illustration shows the germination of *Celtis*

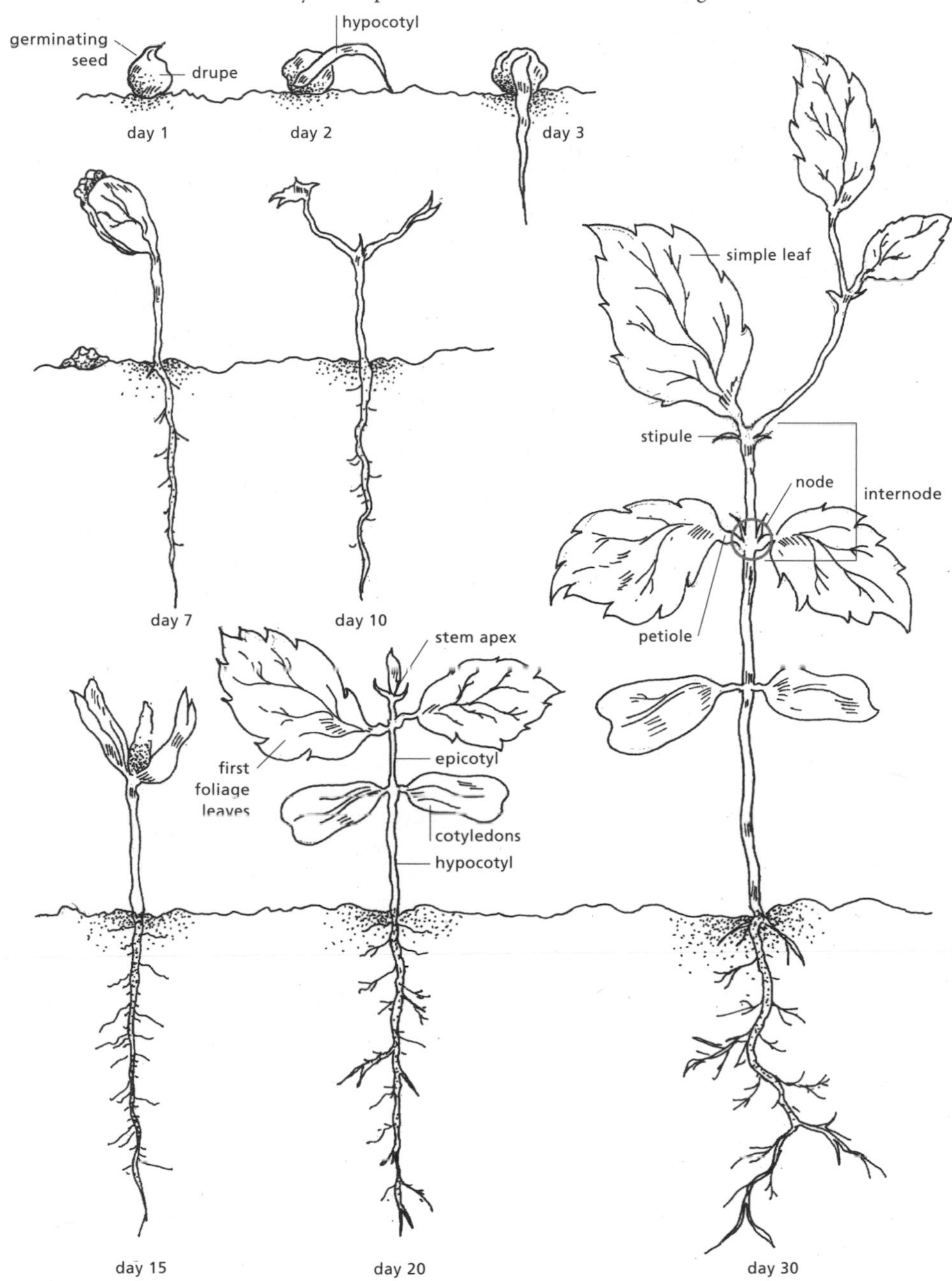

tenuifolia, the Dwarf Hackberry, and its development during the first month of growth.

GERMINATIVE CAPACITY The total percentage of seeds potentially capable of germinating. It is one measure of seed viability, but has less use in estimating the potential production of seedlings from a seed lot, because only those seeds that germinate rapidly will usually have sufficient stamina to develop into healthy and vigorous seedlings later on. *See also* Germinative Energy.

GERMINATIVE ENERGY The percentage of seeds in a well-mixed sample that will germinate under optimum conditions during the period of most active germination. It is a useful measure of the potential production of healthy seedlings from any one seed lot. *See also* Germinative Capacity.

GERM PLASM The genetic material of an individual organism contained in the seed, pollen, sperm, eggs, or embryos, which constitutes the heritable characteristics of the organism. The plasm is stored in carefully controlled conditions for future breeding, genetic engineering, derivation of pharmacological products, or conservation of species. Germ plasm can be stored in seed banks, sperm banks, or gene banks.

GERM TUBE The early growth of mycelium produced by a germinated fungus spore.

GET-AWAY TIME *See* Elapsed Time.

GIARDIASIS An intestinal disease affecting mammals, including humans, caused by the protozoan pathogen, *Giardia lamblia*, which has become common in wilderness waters over the past thirty years. It is commonly called Giardia or 'Beaver Fever,' since it was once thought that beavers were the main vector.

GIBBOUS Botanically, swollen on one side, typically at the base. *See also* Ventricose.

GILGAI The microrelief of soils produced by expansion and contraction as moisture levels change. It is typical of soils having significant clay content, which swells or shrinks as it gets wet or dries out. Gilgai usually consists of a succession of microbasins and microknolls in nearly level areas, or of microvalleys and microridges parallel to the direction of the slope.

GILL FUNGI Those fungi with mushroom-shaped fruiting bodies that bear gill-like plates on the underside of the cap.

GILLS **1** In fish and amphibians, the organ used for breathing underwater; **2** In certain fungi, the bladelike, spore-bearing structures on the lower surface of the fruiting bodies.

GIRDLE **1** To destroy the conducting bark tissues (phloem) all the way around a trunk, stem, branch, or root, thus preventing the movement of fluids bearing nutrients and photosynthetic products up or down the tree, causing death of the affected part. When the trunk of a tree is girdled, nutrient depletion may cause the roots to die, cutting off the water supply to the crown, thus killing the tree top as well. Many deciduous trees can repair girdling damage and survive, a phenomenon useful in the successful application of bark grafts. Girdling damage may be caused by bark beetles, weevils, rodent gnawing, or fungal infections (natural girdling), as well as the deliberate use of girdling to kill unwanted trees (mechanical girdling). **2** A technique used to kill live trees without cutting them down. It involves the severing (by cuts) of a continuous band of cambial tissue around the tree. Chemical or poison-girdling involves the addition of a herbicide to the cuts. *See also* Hack-and-Squirt.

GIRDLER **1** An animal, usually an insect, that in feeding or mining in or on a plant, girdles the main or secondary stems. **2** A mechanical device used to girdle trees by physically stripping the bark down to the cambial tissues.

GIRDLING ROOT A root that encircles and constricts the stem or roots of a plant causing death of the phloem and/or cambial tissue. Girdling roots often arise during nursery production, typically due to the use of potted containers where the roots extend to the walls and then start to grow around them, thus forming a compact circle of roots that do not change once the tree is planted.

GIS *See* Geographical Information System.

GLABRATE/GLABRESCENT Nearly glabrous, or becoming glabrous with age.

GLABROUS Lacking hairs; smooth; not pubescent.

GLACIAL Of or pertaining to glaciers (or ice) and their associated activities, such as movement and erosion; the distinctive features and materials they produce; or to an ice age or region of historical glaciation.

GLACIAL ABRASION The scouring action of particles embedded in glacier ice.

GLACIAL DRIFT Rock debris that has been transported and deposited by glacial ice or meltwaters.

GLACIAL FLOUR Rock material that has been ground down to silt and clay particles by the action of glaciers and ice sheets.

GLACIAL GROOVE A pronounced, generally

straight furrow or depression, larger and deeper than a striation, and produced by glacial abrasion of bedrock, or erosion or compression of drift.

GLACIAL HISTORY The time-sequence of glaciations, including glacial advances and recessions.

GLACIAL LAKE **1** A lake that derives much or all of its water from the melting of glacier ice (i.e., fed by meltwater). **2** A lake that is dammed by a glacier or resting on glacial ice.

GLACIAL LINEATION A collective term for linear features that indicate former ice-flow directions.

GLACIAL TILL *See* Till.

GLACIAL TROUGH A valley with a U-shaped cross-profile due to erosion by a valley glacier.

GLACIER A body of ice formed by the compaction and recrystallization of snow that has definite lateral limits, and with motion in a definite direction. *See also* Drumlin (for illustration).

GLACIER OUTBURST FLOOD A catastrophic flood that results from the collapse of an ice-dam and rapid drainage of a glacial lake.

GLACIOFLUVIAL Pertaining to the channelized flow of glacier meltwater (meltwater streams), and deposits and landforms formed by meltwater streams.

GLACIOFLUVIAL DEPOSITS Material moved by glaciers and subsequently sorted and deposited by streams flowing from the melting ice. The deposits are stratified and may occur in the form of outwash plains, deltas, eskers, and kame terraces. *See also* Drumlin (for illustration).

GLACIOFLUVIAL MATERIALS Sediments that exhibit clear evidence of having been deposited by glacial meltwater streams, either directly in front of, or in contact with, glacier ice; most commonly sands and gravels.

GLACIOLACUSTRINE Pertaining to glacial lakes.

GLACIOLACUSTRINE MATERIALS Sediments deposited in or along the margins of glacial lakes; primarily fine sand, silt, and clay settled from suspension or from subaqueous gravity flows (turbidity currents), and including coarser sediments (e.g., ice-rafted boulders) released by the melting of floating ice; also includes littoral sediments (e.g., beach gravels), accumulated as a result of wave action.

GLACIOMARINE Pertaining to processes, sediments, and landforms associated with glacier termini in marine waters, such as receding glaciers in fiords and ice shelves.

GLACIOMARINE DRIFT Sediments deposited in a glaciomarine environment; includes well-sorted clays, silts, sands and gravels, stony muds, and diamictons.

GLACIOMARINE MATERIALS Sediments of glacial origin laid down from suspension in a marine environment in proximity to glacier ice, and deposits of submarine gravity flows, including particles released due to the melting of floating ice and ice shelves; primarily fine sand, silt, clay, and stony muds. Marine shells or shell casts may be present.

GLAEBULE A space in the parent rock or soil material occupied by another material having clearly different fabric or chemical composition, or a distinct boundary with the adjacent materials. *See also* Nodules.

GLAND A distinct organ that secretes substances to the outside of the organ via a duct or, in animals, sometimes directly into the bloodstream. The gland may be an individual cell in some organisms.

GLAUCOUS Covered with a white or bluish bloom, often waxy, that is easily rubbed off. *See also* Bloom.

GLEANING The act of picking food from a surface.

GLEYING A soil characteristic caused by poor soil aeration in saturated soils, leading to a soil that is typically grey in colour interspersed with yellow, orange, or rusty brown mottles or streaks. The colours result from alternating oxidation or reduction of iron materials in the soil as the soil is aerated or waterlogged. Such soils are termed gleys.

GLIDE In stream ecology, a slow-moving, relatively shallow stream section with calm water flowing smoothly and gently, having a moderately low velocity (ten to twenty centimetres per second) and little or no surface turbulence, reflecting a relatively smooth and stable stream bed.

GLOBAL CHANGE The large-scale planetary alterations in climate, patterns of land and water use, environmental chemistry, etc., and especially alterations related to human activities.

GLOBAL FARM, THE A concept that expands on the global village concept to focus attention on the interdependence between people, nations, and nature. The speed of information exchange now enables the world's people to manage, use, and share their biological heritage with each other. Joint stewardship to sustain the world's biological diversity and biological productivity, as the means to ensure intergenerational fairness for all species, recreates the world in the image of a global family farm. The global garden and the global village are integral parts of the global farm.

GLOBAL POSITIONING SYSTEM (GPS) A navigation and positioning system with which the three-dimensional geodetic positions and the velocity of a user at a point on or near the Earth can be determined in real time. The system consists of a constellation of satellites that broadcast on a pair of ultrastable frequencies. The user's receiver tracks the satellites from any location at any time, thus establishing position and velocity.

GLOBAL VILLAGE, THE The new electronic interdependence recreates the world in the image of a global village. In the electronic environment of information, transmitted at the speed of light, all events on this planet become almost simultaneous, with no time or space separating events. This enables us to live not just in one region or nation, but in many cultures and worlds simultaneously.

GLOBAL WARMING A projected increase in atmospheric temperatures caused by release into the atmosphere of the gaseous by-products (principally carbon dioxide) of fossil-fuel consumption (greenhouse gases), which trap long-wavelength radiant energy.

GLOBOSE Shaped like a globe or sphere.

GLOCHID A minute barbed spine or bristle, commonly seen in tufts on the areoles in many Cactaceae.

GLOMERATE Occurring in a dense or compact cluster or clusters.

GLOWING COMBUSTION PHASE The oxidation of solid fuel accompanied by incandescence. All volatiles have already been driven off and there is no visible smoke. This phase follows the smouldering combustion phase and continues until the temperature drops below the combustion threshold value, or until only noncombustible ash remains. *See also* Combustion.

GLUMACEOUS Resembling a glume in texture, or in appearance.

GLUME A small chaff-like bract, typical of the Gramineae and related plants. An **empty glume** is one of two sterile bracts at the base of a grass spikelet that are usually referred to as the glumes. A **fertile** or **flowering glume** is another term for a lemma. A **sterile flowering glume** is a lemma whose flower is staminate or obsolete. At maturity, the floret containing the ripe fruit separates from the plant in one of two ways (see illustration): *A*, either the glumes disperse with the floret (articulation below the glumes) or *B*, the glumes remain attached to the plant (articulation above the glumes). *See also* Grass; Lemma.

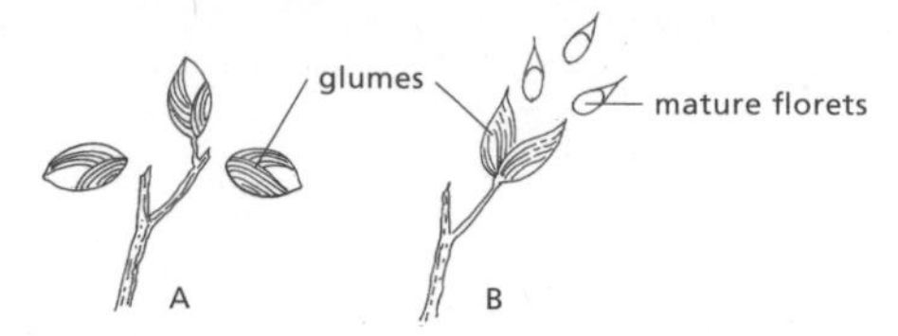

GOAL An ideal; a desired endpoint; frequently defined in abstract terms. Goals are qualitative and are achieved by means of objectives. *See also* Objective; Policy.

GOING FIRE The state of a fire during the period between its ignition and extinction.

GONADS The male or female reproductive organs.

GORGE A narrow, deep valley with nearly vertical rocky walls, enclosed by mountains; smaller than a canyon, and with steeper sides than a ravine. It can be the steep-walled section of a canyon.

GPS Acronym for Global Positioning System, a surveying and locating method utilizing satellite technology.

GRADE **1** The slope of the road alignment in degrees or per cent; more correctly termed gradient. **2** The completed base of a road (e.g., subgrade and final grade). **3** To reduce a surface to a level and/or sloped surface. **4** The quality of lumber in a grading scheme designed to classify products according to defect and allowable end-product use. **5** In genetics, a group of organisms having similar levels of phenotypic organization, typically a series of closely related branches rather than a single line.

GRADED BEDS An arrangement of sediment layers in which each layer displays a gradual change in particle size, usually from coarse at the bottom to fine at the top.

GRADED STREAM Streams extending over long reaches, in a state of equilibrium between the rate of sediment transport and the rate of sediment supply. It is also called a mature stream.

GRADIENT **1** The rate of change of a measurable characteristic (slope, temperature, wind speed, etc.) per unit of distance (e.g., a stream or road gradient is the rate of vertical slope change per unit of stream or road length). **2** A gradual change, over distance, in some environmental or biological condition. Normally refers to an environmental gradient, such as latitude, elevation, climate, temperature, or soil moisture. Organisms may be distributed along the gradient in distinct groups (associations or communities) or as a continuum of species.

GRADIENT WIND The result of the balance between pressure gradient forces and rotational forces associated with the Earth's rotation and the rotation inherent in the wind itself. Any horizontal wind tangent to the contour line of a constant pressure surface (or to the isobar of a geopotential surface) at the point in question. *See also* Local Winds; Surface Wind.

GRADING **1** An engineering term pertaining to the degree of sorting by size of particles in a clastic sediment or sedimentary rock; sandy and gravelly materials with a wide range of particle sizes are termed **well graded;** material with a small range of sizes is **poorly graded**. Note that these terms are the reverse of the geological expressions 'well sorted' and 'poorly sorted.' **2** The process of creating a relatively flat surface across and along the axis of a road. **3** The sorting of lumber into categories based on strength, visual appearance, and similar factors. The grades are based on a series of grading rules.

GRADUAL METAMORPHOSIS A type of insect development in which immature stages (nymphs) resemble the adult in general form and in which there is no pupal stage preceding the adult. *See also* Hemimetabolous; Holometabolous; Metamorphosis.

GRAFT **1** As a noun, a plant that has had the upper part of one plant (the scion) joined to the lower part (the rootstock) of another plant, the point of joining being the graft or graft union. **2** As a verb, the act of joining the two plants together; a form of vegetative propagation.

GRAFT-HYBRID A hybrid plant derived from horticultural grafting of two different species.

GRAIN **1** In conservation biology, refers to two or more resources distributed in such a way that a consumer species encounters them either in the same proportion as they actually occur (fine-grained) or a different proportion (coarse-grained). **2** In wood science, the cell structure. **3** In lumber manufacturing, the characteristic wood texture of any one species of wood.

GRANIVORE Any organism that feeds exclusively or predominantly on seeds, or grains. *See also* Trophic Level.

GRANULE A rock particle two to four millimetres in size; larger than sand but smaller than pebbles.

GRAPPLE A hinged, clawlike mechanism capable of being opened and closed by hydraulics or cables, used to grip logs during yarding and loading. Some grapples can also swivel and tilt to assist in the loading of logs.

GRAPPLE-SKIDDER *See* Harvesting Machine Classification.

GRAPPLE-YARDER *See* Harvesting Machine Classification.

GRAPPLE-YARDING A cable yarding system that uses a grapple rather than chokers to yard the logs to the landing.

GRASS Plants in the family Gramineae, whose characteristics include stems that are jointed at nodes, are hollow (culms), have sheathing leaves, and inflorescences surrounded by glumes. *See* illustration of *Agropyron repens* (Quack grass). Grass roots may be fibrous, rhizomatous, or stoloniferous. Many grasses have basal meristems, unlike other plants that have apical meristems.

GRASSLAND An ecosystem where the tallest stratum is dominated by grasses.

GRATICULE The network of intersecting parallels and meridians (the lines of latitude and longitude) superimposed on a map. These lines may be straight or curved, depending on the projection employed in making the map. *See also* Map Projection.

GRAVEL *See* Substrate Particle Size. **1** An accumulation of rounded pebbles. **2** An accumulation of rounded particles that includes at least two of the size classes represented by pebbles, cobbles, and boulders. It may include interstitial sand.

GRAVITY FLOWS (SUBAQUEOUS) Downslope flow of a dense mixture of water and sediment; commonly generated by subaqueous slumping of deltas.

GRAVITY LOGGING Any cable system that depends on the force of gravity for downhill travel of the carriage.

GRAZING Herbivorous animals eating grasses or non-woody plants (e.g., cows, sheep, geese, or ants). Controlled grazing by domestic livestock, especially sheep, can be an effective tool in vegetation management in some cases. The deliberate use of domesticated animals in this manner is controversial because it has the potential to disturb existing indigenous animal populations, especially the carnivores, as well as introducing ectoparasites and vectoring diseases. Uncontrolled grazing is a traditional management problem in many parts of the world and leads to major shifts in vegetation patterns. *See also* Browsing; Forage.

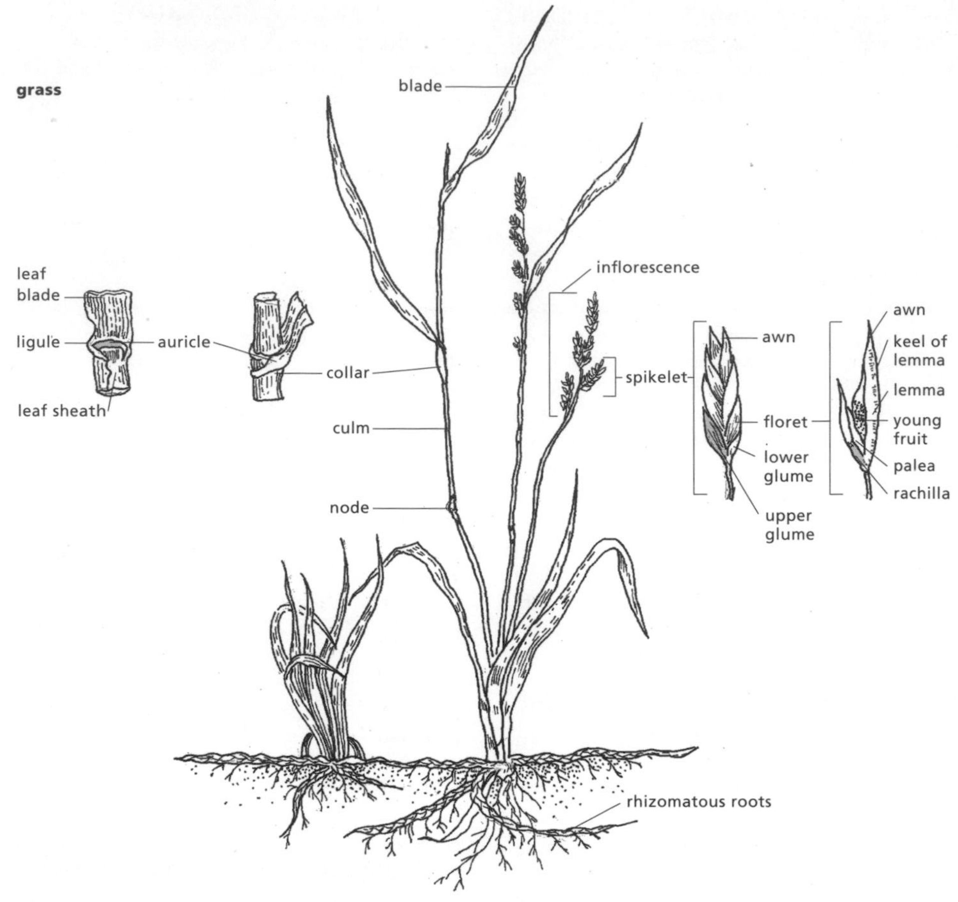

GRAZING CAPACITY A measure of the number of grazing animals that can be maintained on a range without depletion of the range and its forage. The determination of grazing capacity is based on herbage and browse-to-weight ratios:

$$\text{Grazing capacity per unit area} = \Sigma \frac{x}{y}$$

where

Σ = dry weight per unit area for each plant species

x = species use factor

y = animal unit requirement.

GREEN **1** Living wood or wood that has recently been felled and thus has a moisture content above the fibre saturation point. **2** A loosely applied term to any professional lacking depth of experience. **3** A loosely applied term denoting environmental awareness and greater consideration for environmental aspects of management.

GREEN ATTACK Describes a beetle attack code assigned to a tree that is infested by bark beetles but still has green foliage. Boring dust may be found in bark crevices and pitch tubes may be seen on the bole. The inner bark contains beetles in their characteristic egg, larval, or pupal galleries. *See also* Green Strip Attack; Grey Attack; Red Attack.

GREENBELT **1** An irrigated, landscaped, and regularly maintained fuelbreak, usually put to some additional use, such as a golf course, park, or playground. **2** A planning designation that mandates the setting aside of otherwise developable lands for the purpose of creating natural or semi-natural open spaces. Greenbelts are usually linear parkways, tracts, or belts of land running through or around urban conurbations.

GREENHOUSE EFFECT The warming of the Earth's atmosphere caused by the increasing concentration of atmospheric gases, such as water vapour and carbon dioxide. These gases absorb radiation emitted by the Earth, thus slowing down the loss of radiant energy from the Earth back to space. The effect has been present for millions of years, but recent human activities are thought to be accelerating the effect. Some of the theoretical implications include elevated global temperatures, rising sea levels, and changing climates, all of which may alter the manner in which all living organisms develop and reproduce or even their ability to do so.

GREEN POLITICS The overall political activity of environmentalists working to end what they perceive to be an environmental crisis and to save natural landscapes. It also refers to the emergence of green parties (politically) that believe that ecocentric values must be the basis for our actions.

GREEN STRIP ATTACK Describes an attack code assigned to a tree infested by bark beetles. Such trees are infested in a strip on the lower bole where broods either failed or succeeded in completing their development, but the attack has not killed the tree. *See also* Green Attack; Grey Attack; Red Attack.

GREEN TREE A live and growing tree.

GREEN-TREE RETENTION A stand management practice associated with the emerging North American silvicultural practice called 'New Forestry.' It is a stand management practice in which live trees, as well as snags and large downed wood, are left as biological legacies within harvest units to provide habitat components over the next management cycle. Two levels are defined as follows. (1) **High Level** is a regeneration harvest designed to retain the highest level of trees possible while still providing enough disturbance to allow regeneration and growth of the naturally occurring mixture of tree species. Such harvest should allow for the regeneration of intolerant and tolerant species. Harvest design would also retain cover and structural features necessary to provide foraging and dispersal habitat for mature forest-dependent and old-growth-dependent species. (2) **Low Level** is a regeneration harvest designed to retain only enough green trees and other structural components (snag, coarse woody debris, etc.) to result in the development of stands that meet old-growth definitions within 100 to 120 years after harvest entry, considering overstorey mortality.

GREEN-UP PERIOD The time needed to re-establish vegetation after a disturbance such as wildfire or logging. Specific green-up periods may be established for visual constraints, hydrological requirements, or as a means of ensuring re-establishment of vegetation (for silviculture, wildlife habitat, or hydrology reasons) before adjacent stands can be harvested.

GREEN WOOD The wood of a live tree or a very recently cut tree with similar moisture content.

GREGARIOUS Describes a species in which individuals tend to gather in groups.

GREX A collective term for cultivars of the same hybrid origin, which in some cases may be divisible into groups. It is usually used to describe orchid hybrids.

GREY ATTACK Describes a beetle attack code assigned to a tree infested by bark beetles. Such trees have been dead for two or more years and have little or no foliage left. The boles of trees that have been dead for longer may have loose bark and checking. Pitch tubes on the bark of the lower bole, and/or galleries under the bark, may still be discernible. *See also* Black-Top; Green Attack; Red Attack.

GREY TONES The various shades of grey that appear on an air photo; any density or shade between and including absolute white and absolute black that is registered by the land surface on a non-coloured air photo or photographic negative.

GRIBBLE A wood-boring marine crustacean in the genus *Limnoria*, which causes damage to pilings. *See also* Teredo.

GRID A systematically laid out group of observation or measurement points covering an entire stand or block, usually in the form of a series of squares or rectangles formed by equally spaced intersecting transect lines perpendicular to baselines and at right angles to each other. *See also* Dot Grid.

GRID IGNITION TECHNIQUE *See* Ignition Pattern.

GRID INTERVAL The fixed distance between transect lines in a grid.

GRID-PROBE A strip-cruise within a pre-specified width on either side of a compassed line. It is often used to tally forest attributes, such as the attack stage of infested trees.

GROSS DOMESTIC PRODUCT The total value at current prices of goods produced and services rendered by the people and enterprises of a country during a given period, usually one year. If the value of foreign investments is added in, it yields gross national product. Deducting depreciation gives net domestic or net national product.

GROSS NATIONAL PRODUCT *See* Gross Domestic Product.

GROSS SCALE The total volume of wood without deduction for defects.
GROSS VEHICLE WEIGHT (GVW) The weight of the vehicle plus maximum allowable payload.
GROSS WEIGHT The maximum allowable cargo in an aircraft in a calm, standard atmosphere. *See also* Downloading; Equipped Weight; Payload.
GROUND APPLICATION The application of a pesticide from the ground by a person wearing a backpack sprayer, fogger, or similar equipment mounted on a machine. *See also* Aerial Application.
GROUND CHECKING *See* Field Check.
GROUND CONTROL POINT Control points, established by ground surveys, used to fix the attitude and/or position of one or more aerial photographs for mapping purposes.
GROUND COVER **1** The understorey of a multistoried forest, or simply the lowest stratum of vegetation covering the ground. **2** In erosion control, the ground cover is established to control water and wind from eroding the underlying soil. **3** In landscape design work, a ground cover is often used to control soil moisture regimes around other vegetation, especially trees, or to reduce the extent of grassed areas, which demand more water and maintenance.
GROUND EFFECT The reaction of a helicopter's rotor downwash against the ground surface, forming a 'ground cushion' of compressed air that increases the lifting capability of that parcel of air. It is sometimes called Hovering In Ground Effect (HIGE). Once the helicopter is a certain distance above the ground's surface, ground effect is lost. Hovering Out of Ground Effect (HOGE) requires more engine power for the same payload.
GROUND FIRE *See* Forest Fire.
GROUND FOG Fog that extends vertically to less than six metres (twenty feet).
GROUND FORAGER A bird (or other organism) that feeds primarily upon the ground or forest floor.
GROUND FUELS All combustible materials below the litter layer of the forest floor that normally support smouldering or glowing combustion associated with ground fires (e.g., duff, roots, buried punky wood, peat). *See also* Aerial Fuels; Ladder Fuels; Surface Fuels.
GROUND-LEAD LOGGING A cable yarding system in which the main line lead block is hung on a stump, and the logs being skidded are not lifted off the ground. *See also* Cableway; High-Lead Logging; Skyline Logging.
GROUND LENGTH The extent to which the ground around a tree is broken by ridges, gullies, swells, rock outcrops, or sharp slope changes.
GROUND MORAINE **1** A plain or very gently undulating area underlain by till. **2** A deposit of rock debris dragged along, in, on, and underneath a glacier and emplaced by processes including basal lodgement and release from downcasting stagnant ice (as a result of ablation).
GROUND PRESSURE The weight of a vehicle under specific conditions, transmitted to the ground and computed for the per-unit area of contact between the ground and the wheels or track shoes.
GROUND PROBE A specialized nozzle used to penetrate deep-seated combustible fuels to extinguish ground fires.
GROUND SKIDDING The skidding of logs parallel to and right on the ground without using an arch or fairlead to raise the forward end off the ground.
GROUND SPEED The velocity of an airplane along its track in relation to the ground. It is calculated as the result of the heading and air speed of the airplane and the direction and velocity of the wind. *See also* Air Speed.
GROUND-TRUTHING **1** In inventory work, checking on the ground at the site observed and/or measured, data and observations made from aircraft, satellites, other aerial platforms, aerial photographs, or maps. The aim is to verify that what has been observed is actually what exists on the ground. Ground-truthing is usually undertaken by sampling points on the image and correlating these to ground conditions. Ground-truthing helps to refine and amend image interpretation.
GROUND VISIBILITY The horizontal visibility observed at the ground (i.e., surface or control-tower visibility). *See also* Flight Visibility; Fog; Ground Fog; Haze.
GROUNDWATER The water that moves down into the soil and underlying geological strata from the upper soil layers following rainfall. Groundwater is stored in aquifers, and the boundary between aquifers and overlying unsaturated soils is the water table. Groundwater may move underground by streams and seepage.
GROUP **1** A collection of closely related species. **2** In its semi-technical use in the nomenclature of cultivated plants, a group is an assemblage of similar cultivars within a species or interspecific hybrid.

GROUP FELLING A felling technique in which the butts of trees are oriented together to facilitate subsequent skidding.

GROUP SELECTION CUTTING *See* Regeneration Method.

GROUP SPECIES A cluster of populations of similar appearance but biologically distinct, known by the same name and not differentiated by normal taxonomic criteria.

GROWING DEGREE-DAYS The equivalent of 1 degree of temperature maintained for 24 hours above or below any specified base temperature (e.g., 2 degrees for 12 hours or 1/2 degree for 48 hours). It is used to relate plant and arthropod growth and maturation to environmental air temperature. The base temperature is considered to be the point at which growth can be initiated and maintained.

GROWING SEASON The frost-free part of any one year. Most continental regions are divided into zones based on the number of frost-free days.

GROWING STOCK The trees growing in a forest or stand, usually measured as number of trees or volume per unit area.

GROWTH CRACK A longitudinal split in the bark due to normal expansion of cambium and xylem. It is not considered a defect in assessing trees for hazard. *See also* Crack.

GROWTH FORM The typical shape, appearance, and mode of growth of plants, as opposed to size or colour (e.g., pyramidal, erect, bushy, procumbent).

GROWTH LOSS Reduced tree growth caused by harmful or destructive agents, such as insects, disease, weather.

GROWTH REGULATOR *See* Insect Growth Regulator; Plant Growth Regulator.

GROWTH RING *See* Xylem.

GRUB Generally, the soft, broad-shaped larva of beetles. *See also* Caterpillar; Larva; Maggot.

GRUB OUT To dig out, or otherwise remove a stump or root system by exposing and cutting the roots.

GRUS The fragmental products of *in situ* granular disintegration of coarse crystalline rocks, especially granitic rocks.

GUIDELINES A set of recommended or suggested methods or actions that should be followed in most circumstances to assist administrative and planning decisions, and their implementation in the field. Guidelines may consist of policy statements, procedures, or checklists. They are provided as a broad framework of recommended actions to be taken and, therefore, provide some flexibility for decisionmaking. Note that guidelines cannot, by definition, be mandatory; such actions are prescribed by regulations or rules. *See also* Standard.

GUIDING RATE OF RETURN The rate attached to the use of capital that guides a company in its choice of investments. In general, investments that promise a rate of return less than the guiding rate are rejected.

GUILD A set of species that shares a common habitat (such as old-growth forests), that use the same resources (such as foods), or that use resources in the same manner (such as mode of foraging). A group of organisms having similar ecological niches and/or lifeforms. Competition is expected to be important within guilds.

GUILD INDICATOR *See* Indicator Guild.

GUILLOTINE SHEAR A type of carrier-mounted, single-action, anvil shear used in mechanized cutting, where the blade is pushed through a stem and away from the carrier, instead of being pulled, as in the draw shear.

GULCH A small stream valley, narrow and steep-sided in cross-section and larger than a gulley. The term seems to be restricted in use to arid regions. A more general term is ravine.

GULLY A small valley or ravine, longer than wide, typically from a few metres to a few tens of metres across, having steep sides cut by running water and through which water normally runs only after a period of rain or snowmelt. A gully is usually too large for a vehicle to cross and cannot be repaired by ploughing over it. *See also* Erosion.

GUM A collective term describing the non-volatile, viscous exudates of many plants and especially trees, which either dissolve or swell up when in contact with water. Gums are highly polymerized carbohydrates.

GUMMOSIS **1** The exudation of gum from a plant in response to adverse environmental conditions, wounding, or the presence of a pathogen. **2** The partial or complete destruction of cells, accompanied by the formation of gum, which occludes the newly formed cavity and occasionally the cells adjacent to it. *See also* Resinosis; Wound Gum.

GUST A sudden brief increase in wind speed that lasts for less than one minute.

GUTTER TRENCH A ditch dug to the mineral soil on a slope below a fire to trap rolling firebrands, such as cones and logs.

GUY A rope, chain, or rod attached to a structure to brace, steady, or guide it.

GYMNOSPERM Plants that bear naked seeds, usually within cones. In modern plant-kingdom classification schemes these are represented by the four phyla of Coniferophyta, Cycadophyta, Ginkgophyta, and Gnetophyta. In older classification schemes these four phyla were placed within a phylum termed spermatophyta. *See also* Appendix 1: Classification of Organisms.

GYNADROUS Having the stamens adnate to the pistil (e.g., Orchidaceae).

GYNANDRIUM A structure formed by adnation of the stamens to the pistil (e.g., as in orchids).

GYNOBASE An elongation or enlargement of the receptacle in a flower, on which the pistil (or pistils) is raised.

GYNOBASIC Describes a style that is attached at its base to an elongation of the receptacle between the carpels.

GYNODIOECIOUS Having perfect (bisexual) flowers on some plants, and only pistillate (female) flowers on others.

GYNOECIUM The female element of a flower. A collective term describing the pistil or several pistils of a single flower when described as a unit. When only one pistil is present, the terms pistil and gynoecium are synonymous. *See also* Androecium; Carpel (for illustration).

GYNOPHORE The stalk under a pistil that raises it above the level of the receptacle.

GYROSE Convolutedly ridged, folded many times across the surface.

GYTTJA Sedimentary peat consisting mainly of plant and animal residues precipitated from standing water.

H

HABIT The characteristic appearance, shape, posture, and mode of growth of an organism, as opposed to the organism's size or colour. In plants, the form of arrangement of stem, roots, and branches, or of the entire plant. It is also termed growth form. Such features are typically possessed in common by a given species in a given habitat.

HABITAT **1** Those parts of the environment (aquatic, terrestrial, atmospheric), often typified by a dominant plant form or physical characteristic, on which an organism depends, directly or indirectly, in order to carry out its life processes. **2** The specific environmental conditions in which organisms thrive in the wild.

HABITAT BLOCK An area of land covered by a relatively homogeneous plant community in essentially a single successional stage or condition.

HABITAT COMPONENT A simple part, or a relatively complex entity regarded as a part, of an area or type of environment in which an organism or biological population normally lives or occurs.

HABITAT DIVERSITY The number of different types of habitats within a given area. *See also* Diversity.

HABITAT FRAGMENTATION The alteration or breaking up of habitat into discrete or tenuously connected islands as a result of modification or conversion of the landscape by management activities.

HABITAT GENERALIST Any species capable of exploiting a broad range of habitats or niches.

HABITAT ISLAND Any geographically patchy or isolated habitat. These can be naturally occurring (e.g., islands, mountaintops) or human-caused (e.g., remnant patches of forest surrounded by extensive disturbances such as logged areas, or lands converted to agriculture or urban uses). Resident organisms may or may not be able to move away, depending on the species and the connectivity of the habitat island within the broader landscape. 'Islands' of mature forest surrounded by younger forest differ from true islands because the edges are different in character from the water/land edge of an island, and they change in character over time.

HABITAT PATCHES Areas distinguished from their surroundings by environmental discontinuities. Patches are organism-defined (i.e., the edges or discontinuities have biological significance to an organism).

HABITAT RICHNESS The relative degree of ability to produce numbers of species of either plants or animals. The more species produced, the richer the habitat. The alpha diversity of a habitat.

HABITAT SELECTION Species showing a preference for certain habitats.

HACHURES The lines of maximum slope sketched on a map from visual observation in order to portray general relief of the area.

HACK-AND-SQUIRT A method of killing undesirable trees by making one or several overlapping axe cuts into the sapwood, and then applying herbicide into the fresh wound. *See also* Girdle; Stubbling.

HAFT Botanically, the narrow, constricted base of an organ (e.g., the haft of a fall sepal in an Iris flower).

HALF-SIB FAMILIES In a tree (or other plant) improvement program, a group of offspring that have the genotype of one parent in common. *See also* Full-Sib Families.

HALLUCINOGENIC Any substance capable of producing hallucinations when ingested.

HALOPHYTE Plants growing (by requirement or by tolerance) where salt levels in the ground or atmosphere are high, usually near or just inland from the ocean. *See also* Hydrophyte; Mesophyte; Xerophyte.

HAMATE Hooked at the tip.

HAND LINE A fire line constructed with hand tools.

HANGER A partially attached but clearly broken branch, or an unattached branch, lodged in the crown of a tree but with the potential to fall down and cause damage and/or injury.

HANGING VALLEY A tributary valley whose floor is higher than that of the trunk valley in the vicinity of their junction; most commonly applied to glacial troughs.

HANGOVER FIRE *See* Holdover Fire.

HANG-UP **1** In tree falling, a tree that catches on another and lodges there without falling all the way to the ground. **2** In skidding, a log (or logs) that gets stuck or caught on an obstruction. **3** It occurs when one or more planned actions get temporarily stopped or delayed due to an unexpected occurrence, component failure, or intervention.

HANZLIK FORMULA *See* Annual Allowable Cut.

HAPLOID Having the single number of chromosomes (n) in one nucleus. Characteristic of gametes, some sporozoa, individuals that originated by parthenogenesis, and the spores and gametophytes of many plants. *See also* Diploid.

HAPLONT A fungus or other plant in its haploid phase.

HARD CHAPARRAL Dense stands of tough, upright, woody shrubs, such as manzanita (*Arctostaphylos* spp.), *Ceanothus* spp., scrub oak (*Quercus* spp.), chamise (*Adenostoma* spp.). *See also* Chaparral; Soft Chaparral.

HARDENING-OFF A nursery process in which young plants are prepared for their final location outside by exposing them to a period of gradual change in water, light, and temperature regimes. Hardening-off usually takes place before the young plants are lifted and transplanted to another location.

HARDNESS **1** The physical property of minerals that describes their resistance to scratching and abrasion. It is determined by the strength of bonding within the mineral. **2** The total concentration of dissolved calcium and magnesium ions in water.

HARDPAN A distinct layer of soil, nearly impermeable, formed by the cementation of soil particles with organic matter, silica, calcium carbonate, or iron oxides. The hardness of the soil does not change when wet, and fragments do not slake in water.

HARD PINES Pines with two or three needles per cluster, of the subgenus *Pinus* (Diploxylon). Usually with two vascular bundles in cross-section. *See also* Soft Pines.

HARDWOOD **1** Typically refers to the wood of broad-leaved trees, most of which are Angiosperms and deciduous. Hardwood timbers have a more complex cell structure than softwoods, including the presence of vessels, and are considered to be a more highly evolved plant form. *See also* Broad-Leaved; Deciduous. **2** In countries having few coniferous species of commercial value, the term is applied more literally based on the physical hardness of the woods, their durability, and resistance to decay; the 'hard' wood being harder, more durable, and more decay-resistant.

HARVEST The cutting and removal of physically mature trees of commercial value, in contrast to cutting and removal of immature trees, which are thinnings, or merely the cutting of immature trees as a thinning treatment without their removal.

HARVESTABLE SURPLUS The number of game animals or fish that can be removed from a population, typically for hunting or fishing, that will not cause the population to unduly decline. Sustainable harvest surplus is the number that can be removed every year or every harvest season for an indefinite period of time.

HARVESTER *See* Harvesting Machine Classification.

HARVEST FUNCTIONS A group of activities that is collectively termed harvesting. **Bucking** is cutting up a tree or log into shorter lengths. It is also called slashing. **Bunching** is the skidding and assembly of two or more logs at a time, either at a landing or at an intermediate deck from where they are forwarded to the landing, prior to loading and hauling. **Chipping** is the breaking or cutting of trees or parts of trees into pieces of wood, usually in a set size range. **Debarking** is the removal of the outer bark from the trees or logs. **Delimbing** is the removal of the branches. **Felling** is the cutting down or uprooting of standing trees. **Forwarding** is the movement of forest products from the stump to the landing, where they are decked for further transportation. It is typically used to move shorter log lengths of small- to medium-diameter trees on level to moderately sloping ground. **Loading** is picking up trees or logs from the ground (landing or deck) or from another vehicle (forwarder) and loading them onto a vehicle capable of transporting them to the point of manufacture, or to an intermediate transfer point for further transportation. **Piling** is picking up tree-length logs or bolts and depositing them in large piles so that the logs are horizontal and parallel to each other and the ends are approximately in the same vertical planes. **Skidding** is the removal of trees or logs from the stump to a deck or landing by trailing or dragging them along the ground. **Topping** is cutting off the top of a tree at a predetermined minimum diameter. **Yarding** is the initial hauling of a log from the stump to a collection point. Yarding can be by means of ground skidding or a cable system.

HARVESTING MACHINE CLASSIFICATION Many types of machine are used in the harvesting stage of timber management. Self-propelled or mobile machines are classified according to their function. Many of the functions described below can be combined in one machine having multiple functions (e.g., feller-delimber-slasher-buncher, feller-buncher, feller-skidder). There are many colloquial terms for almost all of these machines, although their basic functions are the same.

Single-function machines include the following. **Bucker-slasher** is a mobile machine designed to cut felled trees to a predetermined length with a shear or saw. **Chipper** is a machine designed to chip whole trees or parts of trees on the site. **Debarker** is a machine that removes bark and comes in two forms. (1) A drum debarker is used primarily to remove the bark from pulpwood. The bolts tumble together forcibly and repeatedly in their passage through a large drum, rubbing off bark as they roll against each other and against the corrugated interior of the drum. The drum's corrugated interior keeps the bolts tumbling as the drum rotates, while gravity and the force of additional incoming bolts force the wood through. (2) A ring debarker is used primarily to remove bark from saw logs and veneer bolts. An infeed conveyor belt advances the log longitudinally into the feed rollers, which automatically centre the log in the rotating mechanical ring. The ring has five crescent-shaped fingers that open automatically as the feed rollers force the log against them and the log advances through the rotating mechanical ring. **Delimber** is a self-propelled or mobile machine designed to remove all limbs from trees with flailing chains or knives. **Feller** is a self-propelled machine designed for felling standing trees. **Forwarder** is a self-propelled machine, usually self-loading, designed to transport trees or parts of trees for the purpose of piling or loading. **Loader** is a self-propelled or mobile machine with grapple and self-supporting structure designed to pick up or discharge trees or parts of trees for the purpose of piling or loading. The operation may be swing-to-load, slide-to-load, or travel-to-load. It is also termed a hydraulic loader or knuckleboom if it swings-to-load and has hydraulically activated boom members. **Mobile yarder** is a self-propelled or mobile machine designed to perform cable logging with the use of a tower that may be integral to the machine or a separate structure. **Skidder** is a self-propelled machine designed to transport trees or parts of trees by trailing or dragging them along the ground. **Clam bunk skidder** is a skidder using an integrally mounted loader to assemble the load and a clam or top-opening jaws to hold it. **Cable skidder** is a skidder using a main winch cable and cable chokers to assemble and hold the load. **Grapple skidder** is a skidder using a grapple, or bottom-opening jaws to assemble and hold the load. **Swath cutter** is a self-propelled harvesting machine capable of continuous movement while simultaneously felling multiple stems across a six- to eight-foot-wide swath.

Multiple function machines include the following. **Delimber-buncher** is used to delimb trees and arrange logs in piles on the ground. **Delimber-slasher** is used to delimb and slab trees. It is also known as a delimber bucker. **Delimber-slasher-buncher** is used to delimb and slash trees and arrange logs in piles on the ground. **Feller-buncher** is a self-propelled machine designed to fell standing trees and arrange them in bunches on the ground. May travel-to-bunch or swing-to-bunch. **Feller-chipper** is used to fell and chip whole trees. **Feller-delimber** is a self-propelled machine designed to fell and delimb trees. **Feller-delimber-buncher** is a self-propelled machine designed to fell, delimb, and arrange trees in bunches. **Feller-delimber-slasher-buncher** is a self-propelled machine designed to fell, delimb, and slash trees and arrange tree parts in piles on the ground. **Feller-delimber-slasher-forwarder** is a self-propelled machine designed to fell, delimb, and slash trees and carry tree parts to a landing. **Feller-forwarder** is a self-propelled, self-loading machine designed to fell standing trees and transport the stems by carrying them completely off the ground. **Feller-skidder** is a self-skidder, self-loading machine designed to fell standing trees and transport them by skidding. **Harvester** is a self-propelled multifunction machine that may be capable of operating as a swath cutter but also performs chipping and/or forwarding functions in addition to felling. **Limited-area feller-buncher** is a feller-buncher with a shear mounted on a knuckleboom, allowing the machine to reach and fell several trees while remaining stationary. **Processor** is a multifunction machine that does not fell trees but handles two or more subsequent functions. **Slasher-buncher** is used to cut logs to predetermined lengths and arrange them in piles on the ground.

HARVESTING METHOD The cutting method by which a stand is harvested. The emphasis is placed on meeting logging requirements rather than silvicultural objectives.

HASTATE Having the shape of an arrowhead, but with the basal lobes turned outward from the stalk. *See also* Leaf Shape; Sagittate.

HATCHING SUCCESS The percentage of eggs that hatch. It is also termed hatching rate.

HATCHING-YEAR **1** A bird capable of sustained flight and known to have hatched during the calendar year in which it was branded or seen. **2** A bird in its first basic plumage in its first calendar year.

HAUL-BACK BLOCK The block used to guide the haul-back line.

HAUL-BACK LINE The cable used to haul the main line and the chokers back to the point where the logs are to be attached in the setting.

HAUSTORIUM Plural haustoria. In plant-parasitic fungi, the haustorium is a hyphal branch within a host cell that is specialized for the absorption of nutrients. In mistletoes and other parasitic plants, it is a multicellular, usually highly branched structure that differentiates in the cortex and/or secondary phloem of the host, and provides anchorage and a means of nutrient absorption.

HAWKING A feeding method employed by birds in which they capture (by mouth) insects in flight (e.g., swallows). *See also* Flycatching.

HAZARD **1** Any action or substance that has a potential to create an adverse effect without reference to the probability of the potential actually occurring (which is defined by risk assessment). **2** The condition of stands, trees, and the prevailing environmental conditions, which are conducive to the creation of a hazard (e.g., very dry fine fuels for a fire; stressed trees for insect or disease attack). *See also* Risk.

HAZARD RATING A system of identifying and ranking individual stands in terms of the vulnerability to becoming conducive for the creation of a hazardous condition. The rating system is used to project the likely course of the hazard if it were to occur (e.g., the direction of fire spread, the movement and infestation patterns of insects). The rating can also be used to schedule priorities for hazard abatement plans, such as harvesting to break up fuel continuity, or the use of trap trees to reduce pest levels. It can be further used to schedule remedial treatments to restore forest cover once the hazard has run it course.

HAZARD REDUCTION **1** The treatment of living or dead forest fuels to diminish the likelihood of a fire starting, and to lessen the potential rate of spread and resistance to control. It is synonymous with fuel control. **2** In arboriculture, the treatment of a hazard tree to reduce or eliminate the hazard.

HAZARD TREE In arboriculture, a hazard tree is any tree or part of a tree that if it were to fall, might hit a target, usually people or property. Hazard-tree assessment requires careful assessment of the standing tree for signs of structural weakness caused by growth habit, disease, or decay, and an assessment of whether or not a target exists in the potential fall zone. If no target exists, the tree is automatically not a hazard tree. *See also* Danger Tree.

HAZE Fine dust or particles in the atmosphere that diminish visibility. *See also* Smoke.

HAZE METER An instrument for measuring the dependable range of distance at which a standard smoke column can be detected by the unaided eye under existing haze conditions.

HEAD **1** A short, dense cluster of flowers grouped on a common receptacle; a capitulum. The overall shape may be flat or approximately globose. *See also* Inflorescence. **2** The difference in the depth of a liquid at two different points in a body or column of fluid. The resulting pressure of the fluid at the lower point is termed pressure head.

HEAD FIRE IGNITION *See* Ignition Pattern.

HEADING **1** The compass direction in which the longitudinal axis of an aircraft points. **2** A pruning technique where the cut is made to a bud, weak lateral branch, or stub.

HEADING FIRE A fire spreading, or set to spread, with the wind (upslope in the absence of wind). *See also* Backfiring; Flank Fire.

HEADLAND **1** The irregular, and usually higher, cliff face that juts out from a coastline into a lake or ocean. **2** The high ground around a cove. **3** The steep crag or cliff face of a promontory.

HEAD OF A FIRE *See* Forest Fire.

HEADRIG The main saw in a sawmill operation, used for initial breakdown of logs by sawing along the grain. The logs are first cut into cants on the headrig before being sent on to other saws for further processing. It is also termed the head saw.

HEAD SAW The first saw in a sawmill, used to cut up the raw log into smaller component parts, which can then be resawn by other saws of differing size and capacity.

HEAD SPAR The spar tree or tower at the landing of a skyline logging operation. It is also termed a head tree.

HEADWALL The steep slope at the head of a valley, and particularly, the rock cliffs at the back of a cirque.

HEALTHY ECOSYSTEM An ecosystem in which the structure and functions permit the maintenance of the desired condition of biological diversity, biotic integrity, and ecological processes over time.

HEART ROT A decay characteristically confined to the heartwood, often beginning in the living tree via infection of wounds or branch stubs, known as infection courts.

HEARTWOOD The inner layers of wood situated farthest away from the vascular cambium. In the growing tree, the heartwood has ceased to conduct nutrients or water, contains no living cells, the reserve materials (e.g., starch) have been removed or converted into more durable substances, and the cells have become infiltrated with various organic compounds, such as gums, resins, and tannins. Heartwood is generally darker (but not always) in colour than sapwood, more durable, less easily attacked by decay-producing organisms, and is less penetrable to preservatives and other liquids. It has an important structural function in the early years, but with age, the heartwood column may decay with no immediate loss of strength in the overall tree. *See also* Sapwood.

HEAT OF COMBUSTION The potential heat energy available for release by the combustion process. In frontal fire intensity calculations, the heat of combustion value is used subject to several possible reductions, chiefly because of the presence of moisture in the fuel. A quantity is generally specified for a particular fuel on a per unit weight basis. Measured in kilojoules per kilogram or calories per pound.

HEAT TRANSFER The process by which heat is imparted from one body or object to another. In forest fires, heat energy is transmitted from burning to unburned fuels by a number of methods. **Convection** is the transfer of heat by the movement of masses of hot air. The natural direction is upwards in the absence of any appreciable wind speed and/or slope. **Radiation** is the transfer of heat in straight lines from warm surfaces to cooler surroundings. **Conduction** is the transfer of heat through solid matter.

Note that in forest fires, the transmission of heat may also take place by solid mass or ember transport. This is the transfer of heat resulting from firebrands being transported ahead of a fire by the wind, gravity (e.g., rolling downhill), or by being carried aloft in the convection column or by a fire whirl (i.e., spotting).

HEATH An open, uncultivated landform covered with low vegetation, often coarse grasses, heathers, gorse, or broom, and a few scattered trees, if any, growing on sandy to gravelly soils; dryer than moors.

HEAVY FUELS Large-diameter woody or deep organic materials that are difficult to ignite and burn more slowly than fine or medium fuels. It is synonymous with coarse fuels.

HEAVY HELICOPTER A helicopter capable of carrying fifteen to twenty-six passengers. *See also* Light Helicopter; Medium Helicopter.

HEAVY METALS Those metals having densities greater than 5.0 milligrams per cubic metre. They are typically toxic in low concentrations, persist in the environment, and can accumulate to levels that stunt or preclude plant growth and damage animal life. Heavy metals include lead, cadmium, silver, arsenic, chromium, mercury, copper, iron, manganese, cobalt, zinc, and nickel. However, some of the heavy metals are also vital micronutrients for plants and their absence will also affect plant growth.

HECTARE A metric unit of area, 100 metres by 100 metres (10,000 square metres) or 2.471 acres.

HEEL BOOM A loading boom with tongs that have a steel plate set on the underside against which one end of the log can be placed to serve as a fulcrum point for raising the log into a loading position.

HEELING-IN In the nursery or as a temporary measure on site, planting stock that is being moved can be stored in a trench of moist soil that is as deep as the seedling roots are long.

HEEL OF A FIRE *See* Forest Fire (back).

HEEL TACKLE The system of lines and blocks used to tighten the skyline.

HEIGHT Height is measured at various points on a tree depending upon the purpose of the measurement. There are various standards of measurement. **Breast height** is set at 1.3 metres above ground and is the standard point at which the diameter of a standing tree is measured in Canada and other countries adhering to the standards set out by the International Union of Forest Research Organizations (IUFRO). In British Columbia, it is 1.3 metres above the point of germination on the ground. In the United States, it is defined as 4.5 feet above ground. Unless otherwise specified (as in British Columbia), breast height on sloping ground is normally taken from the uphill side of the tree. **Merchantable tree height** is the vertical distance between stump height and a point on the standing tree having a specified utilization limit (usually expressed as a diameter underbark). **Stand height**, in mensuration work, is the average height of dominant and codominant trees of the main species forming the stand. In remote sensing, the average height of all dominant and codominant trees in a stand. **Stump height** is the vertical distance between ground level and the top of a stump. On slopes, ground level is generally taken on the upper side of the stump. Stump height may be the actual height of a cut stump or some arbitrarily selected standard. In rainforests and mountainous terrain, the point of germination is used in place of ground level. **Top height** is the mean height of 100 trees per hectare of the largest diameter at breast height. From five to fifteen trees in a particular stand will be measured, depending on the uniformity and size of the stand. **Tree height** is the distance between the uppermost shoot of a tree and the ground level or point of germination, if that differs from ground level.

HEIGHT CLASS Any interval into which the range of tree or stand heights is divided for classification and use, and the trees or stands falling into such an interval.

HELD LINE All of the control line that still contains the fire when it is declared under control.

HELIBUCKET A specially designed rigid or collapsible container slung by a helicopter and used for picking up and dropping suppressants or retardants on a fire. The size of the bucket load is compatible with the size of the helicopter. It is synonymous with bucket or water bucket.

HELICOID Coiled spirally like a spring; a helix spiral.

HELICOID CYME An inflorescence coiled in a bud and superficially resembling a raceme, with the lowermost flower opening first and flowers all developing on the same side of the apparent axis. In reality, however, the inflorescence is determinate, since the lowermost flower terminates the main axis, and each succeeding flower similarly terminates a branch that arises from the axil of the next lowest flower, with the branching always being in the same direction. *See also* Inflorescence; Scorpioid Cyme.

HELICOPTER RAPPEL CREW *See* Rappel Crew.

HELICOPTER SOUNDING The determination of the vertical temperature profile based on observations of a helicopter's free-air thermometer and corresponding altimeter readings. *See also* Minisonde Observation; Rawinsonde Observation.

HELIJUMP A technique for deploying firefighters from helicopters when there is no helispot near the fire. This method, which requires special training for helijumpers and pilots, involves a freefall in a protective suit from very a low altitude above ground, typically from a hovering helicopter. It is also termed a hover jump.

HELIPAD The prepared surface at a heliport where a helicopter actually lands (the surface where the skids are placed).

HELIPORT A permanent landing area for helicopters where fuel, service, and supplies are generally available. A fully equipped heliport usually has a wind sock, and the landing ground is permanently marked to indicate the north direction either with an arrow pointing north or by placing the long legs of the letter H in a north-south alignment.

HELISPOT A temporary area prepared to facilitate helicopter landings.

HELITACK Initial attack on wildfires involving the use of helicopters and specially trained crews, deployed as a complete unit.

HELITACK CREW An initial attack crew specially trained in the tactical and logistical use of helicopters for fire suppression.

HELITANK A specially designed tank fitted to a helicopter and used for transporting and dropping suppressants or retardants.
HELITANKER A helicopter equipped with a helitank. *See also* Airtanker.
HELITORCH A specialized drip torch, using a gelled fuel, slung and activated from a helicopter. It is synonymous with flying drip torch. *See also* Aerial Ignition Device.
HELOPHYTE A herbaceous marsh plant having overwintering buds lying in the mud. *See* Life-Form.
HEMIBIOTROPHIC An organism that feeds on living tissues in the early stages of infection and dead tissues later on.
HEMICRYPTOPHYTE Plants with their perennating buds at ground level. The above-ground plant parts die back during unfavourable conditions. See also Life-Form (for illustration).
HEMIMETABOLOUS An insect life cycle characterized by incomplete metamorphosis, in which there is no pupal stage but a distinct change in body form between the immature and adult stages (e.g., dragonflies). *See also* Holometabolous.
HEMIZYGOUS Describes genes present only once in the genotype (i.e., have only one allele of a gene rather than two).
HERB **1** Any seed-producing plant whose above-ground parts are composed of non-woody tissue and are not persistent; includes forbs and grasses. Such plants are said to be herbaceous. **2** The leaves, flowers, or roots of a plant that are or were historically used for food, seasoning, medicine, or fragrance. **3** A plant member of the Compositae family.
HERBACEOUS Vegetation that is usually forbs, grasses, or leafy plants.
HERBAGE All species of browse, forbs, and grasses produced in any one area.
HERBARIUM A collection, systematically organized, of dried plants and fungi.
HERBICIDE Any chemical substance applied to plants (forbs, grasses, woody plants, and their seeds) as a means of killing them or inhibiting their growth.
HERBIVORE Any heterotrophic organism that feeds (consumes) exclusively on plant matter. *See also* Carnivore; Frugivore; Omnivore; Trophic Level.
HERITABILITY The genotypic variance (as distinct from variance due to environmental influences) of any one feature of an organism as a percentage of the total variance in the same feature. In progeny tests (based on sexually propagated material), heritability is described as **narrow sense** and is the ratio of the additive genetic variance to the total (genetic + environmental = phenotypic) variance of a character. In clonal tests (based on vegetatively propagated material), it is described as **broad sense** and is the ratio of the total genetic variance to the total (phenotypic) variance of a character.
HERITAGE A tangible object, an idea, a process, or an activity that is passed down through generations, or remains from past societies, and is considered worthy of preserving for the enjoyment and learning of present and future generations. Heritage can be cultural (crafts, folklore, rituals, tools, techniques, customs, language, dialect, songs, legends, etc.) or natural (land, water, air, rocks, fossils, plants, fungi, animals, habitats, etc.).
HERITAGE CONSERVATION The understanding, appreciation, and preservation of natural elements in a landscape, as well as objects, ideas, activities, or processes that are considered to be an important part of a society's culture and history.
HERMAPHRODITE **1** A plant that produces male and female gametes. A flowering plant that has male and female organs within each flower. **2** An animal containing both male and female reproductive organs.
HESPERIDIUM A type of berry having a thick, leathery rind, and many internal radial sections (e.g., an orange). *See also* Fruit (for illustration).
HETEROBLASTIC CHANGE A transition from the juvenile to the adult stage with an abrupt change in morphology.
HETERODICHOGAMY In plants, flowering where the flowers are either all female or all male.
HETEROECIOUS In rust fungi and aphids, a life cycle requiring two or more distinct and unrelated host species for completion. The opposite of Autoecious. *See also* Autoecious; Dioecious; Monoecious.
HETEROGAMETIC Describes the sex that has gametes with different types of sex chromosomes. Human males are heterogametic (*XY*), while human females are homogametic (*XX*).
HETEROGENEOUS Any system whose composition or structure is not uniform. *See also* Homogeneous.
HETEROKARYOTIC A fungus mycelium containing two or more genetically distinct nuclei. *See also* Dikaryotic.
HETEROMORPHISM One structure having many

possible forms (e.g., the many different shapes of leaves).

HETEROPHYLLY A plant having two or more different leaf forms on the same plant.

HETEROSIS *See* Hybrid Vigour.

HETEROSTYLIC In plants, refers to the styles of different lengths in the flowers of different individuals.

HETEROTROPHIC Any organism that depends on the utilization of chemical energy stored in other living organisms. Heterotrophs are consumers of matter already created by Autotrophs. *See also* Autotrophic; Herbivore; Carnivore; Frugivore; Omnivore; Trophic Level.

HETEROZYGOSITY An individual having different alleles in a pair of genes or two different forms of the same gene in all diploid cells. Thus, if gene A is heterozygous, it will have alleles A1 and A2 and the offspring could possess either of the genes. A heterozygous organism can pass on either of the genes and so may not always breed true to type. *See also* Homozygosity.

HIBERNACULUM **1** A silken shelter or shelter made from a leaf or other material in which an insect larva overwinters (such as a cocoon). **2** A sheltered place (habitat niche) where an overwintering animal rests, or a den where snakes hibernate. **3** In plants, a structure that protects the embryo or growing tip during the dormant season (e.g., a bulb or bud).

HIBERNATION A dormant condition characteristic of certain mammals in which greatly reduced metabolic activity is triggered by the onset and duration of winter or a cold spell. *See also* Aestivation; Diapause; Dormancy.

HIDDEN AGENDA A personal expectation or motivation that can affect how that person behaves in a group or feels about a group, but which is not known to others in the group. The person may plan to deliberately steer the discussion in one direction, or the person may not even realize that she or he has a private goal not necessarily identical with the group's goal.

HIDDEN DEFECT A defect in a log that cannot be detected or observed prior to milling.

HIDING COVER Generally, any vegetation used by wildlife for security or to escape from danger. More specifically, any vegetation capable of providing concealment (i.e., hiding 90 per cent of the animal) from the view of humans or other predators. *See also* Cover.

HIERARCHICAL DOMINANCE The 'pecking' order within a social group of animals.

HIERARCHY The systematic ordering or ranking of factors or attributes based on a list of criteria.

HIGHBALL To work at a high rate of speed, usually smoothly and efficiently. A fast, skilled logging show is termed a highball operation.

HIGH FOREST Stands or crops of trees originating from seedlings that have developed into a high, closed-canopy forest of long rotation length, as opposed to coppice forests of shorter rotation length. Silvicultural practices that create high forest conditions are termed high forest systems. *See also* Forest; Low Forest.

HIGH GRADE or HIGH-GRADE **1** The best quality of lumber in the grading scheme. **2** A logging operation in which only the higher value trees (based on species, size, and quality) are removed from the stand, with no consideration for the quality of the remaining trees left behind, often felled but unused. High grading is a policy of 'take the best and leave the rest,' often masquerading under the guise of selective cutting. *See also* Selective Cutting.

HIGH-LEAD LOGGING A wire rope system that involves yarding in logs or trees by means of a rope passing through a block at the top of the head spar, thus enabling one end of the log (the lead) to be lifted off the ground. *See also* Cableway; Ground-Lead Logging; Skyline Logging.

HIGH SEVERITY FIRE A wildfire event with acute ecological impacts; usually, but not always, a fire of high intensity.

HILL A natural elevation of the land surface, rising up to 300 metres (1,000 feet) above the surrounding lands and usually of restricted summit area, with a well-defined profile and slopes greater than 15 per cent. In local usage, the terms hill and mountain may overlap.

HILLSLOPE The steeper part of a hill between its summit and the drainage line, valley flat, or depression floor at the base of the hill (see illustration). In descending order, the geomorphic

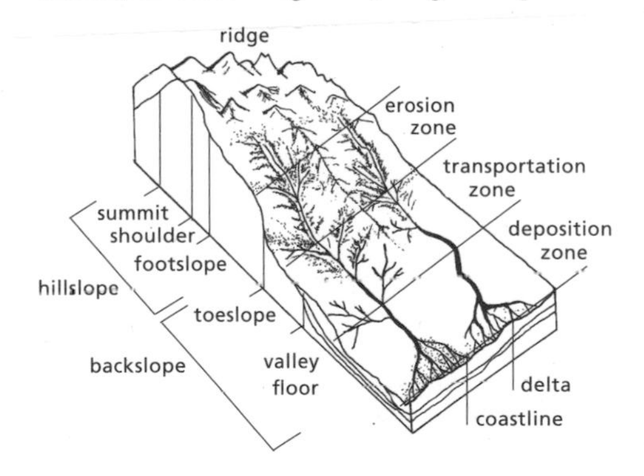

components may include shoulder, backslope, footslope, and toeslope. Complex hillslopes may include several aspects of one or more features. *See also* Erosion.

HILUM The scar or mark showing the point where the funicle was attached to a seed.

HIP The 'fruit' of a rose, made up of a fleshy, hollow floral cup and the achenes enclosed within it. *See also* Fruit (for illustration).

HIP CANKER *See* Canker.

HIPPOCREPIFORM Horseshoe-shaped.

HIRSUTE Having a cover of coarse, stiff hairs; hairy.

HIRTELLOUS Softly or minutely hirsute.

HISPID Covered in rigid hairs or bristles.

HISTOGRAM A graphical representation of the frequency distribution of a variable, using a vertical bar to portray the variation, with absolute amounts plotted along the x-axis and frequency along the y-axis.

HOARY Botanically, covered with a close white or grey-white pubescence.

HOGBACK A sharp-crested, symmetric (homoclinal) ridge formed by highly tilted resistant rock layers. It is produced by differential erosion of the interlayered resistant and weak rocks having dips greater than about 45 per cent.

HOLDING WOOD **1** In tree falling, the part of the tree left uncut, which serves as a hinge, holding the tree in place until the last moment. The width and position of the holding wood assist in getting the tree to fall in the direction desired. **2** The structurally critical wood in a tree trunk or branch, typically under tension, that is preventing the trunk or branch from failing.

HOLDOVER **1** An individual of an insect brood that fails to emerge at the normal time, such as late summer or fall, but which emerges later (e.g., in the following spring). **2** A tree from which a bark beetle brood emerges later than normal. **3** A 'veteran' tree that has escaped logging, windthrow, or fire, and currently occupies a dominant position in the stand.

HOLDOVER FIRE A fire that remains dormant and undetected for a considerable time after it starts (particularly lightning-caused fires). It is synonymous with sleeper fire. *See also* Overwintering Fire.

HOLISM The idea that a whole is more than the sum of its parts. It is also spelled wholism.

HOLOCENE EPOCH The most recent interval of geological time, from approximately 10,000 years ago to the present. Corresponds to the second epoch of the Quaternary period of geologic time. Similar to postglacial time. It is also the corresponding time-stratigraphic series (layers) of earth materials. *See also* Appendix 2: Geological Time Scales.

HOLOMETABOLOUS An insect whose life cycle is characterized by complete metamorphosis, in which an insect develops through four different stages of life form: egg, larva, pupa, and adult. *See also* Gradual Metamorphosis; Hemimetabolous.

HOLOTYPE *See* Type.

HOMEOSTASIS The self-regulation of a biotic community or an individual organism. A process in which communities or organisms, using inherent regulatory mechanisms, constantly adjust to the changing conditions of their physical environment.

HOMEOTHERM Any warm-blooded animal (mammal or bird) able to maintain its body temperature at an approximately constant level, regardless of the prevailing environmental conditions. It is also called endotherm. Other spellings are homoiotherm or homotherm. *See also* Poikilotherm.

HOME RANGE The area that an animal traverses in the scope of normal activities, such as feeding; not to be confused with territory. *See also* Territory.

HOMOCLINAL In structural geomorphology, the strata that dip in one direction with a uniform angle. *See also* Hogback.

HOMOEOLOGOUS CHROMOSOMES Chromosomes that are only partially homologous. It is an indication of a common ancestry.

HOMOGAMETIC Describes the sex that has gametes with the same types of sex chromosomes. Human females are homogametic (*XX*) while human males are heterogametic (*XY*).

HOMOGENEOUS Any system whose composition or structure is uniform. *See also* Heterogeneous.

HOMOLOGOUS A substance, organism or form of similar basic structure and common evolutionary descent. *See also* Analogous.

HOMOLOGOUS CHROMOSOMES Chromosomes having identical genetic loci, carrying codes for the same functions, and being of the same shape and size. They may have different allelic forms. Diploid organisms have chromosomes in homologous pairs (i.e., one member from each parental pair), which themselves become separated during meiosis and migrate to the different gamete being formed. *See also* Homoeologous Chromosomes.

HOMOLOGY Two or more species possessing a

trait from their common ancestor that may or may not have been modified.

HOMONYM A name of a taxon that duplicates a name previously and validly published for a taxon of the same rank, based on a different type.

HOMOPLASTIC SIMILARITY Similar characters in unrelated groups, resulting from convergent evolution.

HOMOZYGOSITY An individual having the same alleles in a pair of genes or two identical forms of the same gene in all diploid cells. Thus, if gene *A* is homozygous, it will have alleles *A1* and *A2*. Two homozygous types of offspring are feasible: *A1/A1* or *A2/A2*. A homozygous organism will produce purebred offspring. *See also* Heterozygosity.

HONEYDEW The sweet, sticky fluid, derived from plant sap and excreted by aphids, certain scales, mealybugs, whiteflies, and some leafhoppers.

HOOF-SHAPED Having a hooflike appearance. It describes the fruiting bodies of certain wood-decaying fungi that are flat on the bottom and rounded on the top and sides.

HOPPERBURN The foliar discoloration, usually brown and at the edge of the leaf, caused by certain leafhoppers.

HORIZONTAL DIVERSITY The distribution and abundance of plant and animal communities and successional stages across an area of land. The greater the number of communities, the higher the degree of horizontal diversity. *See also* Structural Diversity; Vertical Diversity.

HORIZONTAL RESISTANCE It is also termed race non-specific resistance. A type of resistance, usually polygenic, in which the ranking of all host varieties by degree of resistance (but not necessarily by the actual level of resistance), remains constant against all pest genotypes. It is generally quantitative in effect (e.g., characterized by increased incubation times, decreased rate of pathogen reproduction, or slowed rate of spread of an epidemic). *See also* Field Resistance; General Resistance; Monogenic Resistance; Polygenic Resistance; Vertical Resistance.

HORMONE A chemical secreted in trace amounts by cells in one part of an organism that exerts an effect on the activities in another part of the organism. *See also* Insect Growth Regulator; Plant Growth Regulator.

HORNING A pattern of social display in ungulates, involving the rubbing and thrashing of antlers on vegetation.

HOSE LAY The arrangement of connected lengths of fire hose and accessories on the ground beginning at the first pumping unit and ending at the point(s) of water delivery.

HOST **1** The plant or animal on which an insect feeds. **2** The organism on or in which a parasite lives and obtains its food, to the detriment of the host. A host is termed **definitive** when the parasite lives in it during the adult stage of the parasite's life cycle, when it may reproduce sexually. A host is termed **intermediate** when the immature forms of a parasite, or adult parasites in a resting stage between times on the definitive host, live on it. Parasites may reproduce asexually on the intermediate host. **3** An organism that is attacked or susceptible to attack by a pathogen or insect.

HOST RANGE All the hosts that any one insect or parasite may attack.

HOST SELECTION The location of a susceptible host individual by a phytophagous or entomophagous insect. *See also* Pioneer Beetle.

HOST SPECIFICITY The degree to which an organism is restricted to a particular type of host. *See also* Host Range; Monophagous; Oligophagous; Stenophagous.

HOST SUSCEPTIBILITY RATING **1** Generally, a measure of the ability of a tree species to resist attack by a particular pest. **2** A classification system used in British Columbia to describe the susceptibility of various tree species to dwarf mistletoes. It is based on a determination of an infection factor (i.e., the percentage of trees of the species in question that are infected within six metres of heavily infected principal hosts). The five host-susceptibility classes based on these infection factor percentages are as follows. (1) **Principal host** is the main host of a particular taxon. The infection factor is at least 90 per cent and usually nearly 100 per cent. Although some trees may show little infection within the six-metre zone, uninfected trees are seldom found unless they are very suppressed. A dwarf mistletoe may have several principal hosts. (2) **Secondary host** indicates that the infection factor ranges from 50 to 90 per cent. (3) **Occasional host** indicates that the infection factor ranges from 5 to 50 per cent. (4) **Rare host** indicates that the infection factor is more than zero but less than 5 per cent. (5) **Immune host** indicates the trees that are not infected even in stands where the dwarf mistletoe in question is common. The infection factor is zero. It is also called a non-host.

Many undefined, subjective terms (e.g.,

common, principal, main, uncommon, or rare hosts) have been used to describe relative susceptibility of trees to dwarf mistletoes without quantification. The above system provides a less subjective system. Other pest problems may use similar approaches as a means of assessing areas that are most in need of pest control.

HOT SPOT **1** A particularly active part of a fire. *See also* Fire Suppression (hot spotting). **2** A small area of smouldering or glowing combustion, which may be exhibiting smoke, located on or within the fire perimeter. A term commonly used during the mop-up stage of a fire. It is synonymous with smudge. *See also* Fire Suppression (cold trailing).

HOVERING/HOVER GLEANER A bird that feeds from a surface while hovering in place (e.g., hummingbirds).

HUMAN-CAUSED RISK SCALING FACTOR In the US National Fire Danger Rating System, a number relating human-caused fire incidence to the ignition component in a fire danger rating area. It is based on three to five years of fire occurrence and fire weather data that adjusts the prediction of the basic human-caused fire occurrence model to fit local experience. *See also* Lightning Risk Scaling Factor.

HUMAN DIMENSION An integral component of ecosystem management that recognizes a range of factors, including: (1) people are a part of ecosystems (not separate from them); (2) people's pursuits of past, present, and future desires, needs, and values (including perceptions, beliefs, attitudes, and behaviours) have and will continue to influence ecosystems; and (3) ecosystem management must include consideration of the physical, emotional, mental, spiritual, social, cultural, and economic well-being of people and communities.

HUMANISTIC BOTANY Botanical research that examines the ways people use plants, and the affects of plants on the culture's civilization and history.

HUMIC A textural descriptor applied to organic materials; refers to material at an advanced stage of decomposition. It has the lowest amount of fibre, the highest bulk density, and the lowest saturated water-holding capacity of the organic materials. Fibres that remain after rubbing constitute less that 10 per cent of the volume of the material.

HUMIFICATION The transformation of carbon in organic residues (plant or animal) into humus.

HUMMOCKS Steep-sided hillocks and hollows, non-linear and chaotically arranged and with rounded or irregular cross-profiles; slopes are between 15 and 35 degrees (26-70 per cent) on surficial materials and between 15 and 90 degrees (more than 26 per cent) on bedrock.

HUMMOCKY MORAINE A moraine consisting of an apparently random assemblage of knobs, kettles, hummocks, ridges, and depressions. *See also* Ablation Moraine.

HUMUS In the narrow sense, humus is amorphous organic material (plant or animal) that has decayed beyond the point of recognition, and lies beneath the litter layer and above the mineral soil. A rich component of soil containing humic and fulvic acids, humus forms the main organic layer on the forest floor, but can also be found in water. In the broader sense, humus may refer to the whole forest floor and organic matter within the mineral soil. *See also* Mature Forest Floor; Moder; Mor.

HUSK The outer covering of some fruits, usually derived from the perianth or involucre.

HYALINE Clear and colourless or appearing white; transparent or translucent.

HYALODERMUS In sphagnum mosses, a cortex of large, empty, colourless cells.

HYBRID The offspring of two genetically different parents (species, varieties, or breeds).

HYBRIDIZATION The breeding of individuals from genetically different strains, populations, or species. Occasionally, interbreeding between species (e.g., the mule being a cross between a horse and a donkey).

HYBRID SWARM A population consisting of hybrids, backcrosses, and successive generations.

HYBRID VIGOUR The increase in vitality and productivity of offspring resulting from a cross between two inbred lines. It is also termed heterosis.

HYDATHODE A tiny gland at the edge of a leaf or other plant organ, from which droplets of water may issue.

HYDRAULIC BARKING The removal of bark and debris from roundwood, such as logs, bolts, or billets by high-pressure jets of water as the pieces are mechanically rotated in a closed chamber.

HYDRAULIC GRADIENT **1** The slope of the water surface. **2** The drop in pressure head per length of stream, in the direction of flow. It is also called hydrologic gradient.

HYDRIC Characterized by considerable moisture. *See also* Mesic; Xeric.

HYDROCHORE A plant seed or a spore dispersed by water. Characteristics of hydrochory include buoyancy and floatation. The classic example is the coconut. *See also* Anemochore; Avichore; Barochore; Propagule; Zoochore.
HYDROGENIC SOIL Soil that developed under the influence of water standing within the profile for long periods of time. It is found mainly in cold, humid regions.
HYDROGRAPH A graph showing, for a given point on a stream, the discharge, stage, velocity, or other property of water with respect to time.
HYDROLOGIC CYCLE The naturally occurring, solar-driven cycle of evapotranspiration, condensation, precipitation, and runoff of water. The cycle involves the movement of water between the atmosphere and terrestrial, aquatic, or ocean environments.
HYDROLOGIC FEATURES (LOCAL) Refers to water-related features visible at the land surface, such as stream channels, seepage zones, springs, and soil moisture, including soil moisture characteristics as deduced from vegetation characteristics.
HYDROLOGY The science of water, its properties, and movement (cycling) over and under land surfaces.
HYDROLYSIS The chemical weathering process in which minerals are changed by chemical reaction with water, involving the splitting of a water molecule. Hydrolysis is usually associated with acids, but can take place with alkalis.
HYDROPHOBIC SOILS Soils that can repel water due to the presence of dense fungal mycelial mats, lipid-covered plant or animal residues, or hydrophobic substances that have been vaporized and then, due to heating and cooling, condensed on soil particles (e.g., during a fire).
HYDROPHYTE Plants growing in water or on very wet soil moisture regimes deficient in oxygen at least part of the time. *See also* Halophyte; Mesophyte; Xerophyte.
HYDROSEEDING A mechanical seeding technique in which a mixture of seed and water is sprayed onto slopes too steep for hand broadcasting or drilling, followed by raking and harrowing. Fibrous material is sometimes added to the mix to help hold the seed to the soil surface and act as a mulch.
HYDROSERE Plant succession patterns originating in habitats with abundant water, usually growing on the submerged substrate. *See also* Biosphere; Lithosphere; Sammosere; Troposphere.
HYDROSPHERE The oceans, lakes, and water bodies; atmospheric water; and subsurface water of the planet.
HYGROGRAPH A continuous-recording hygrometer.
HYGROMETER An instrument for measuring the water vapour content of the air. *See also* Psychrometer.
HYGROPHANOUS Becoming watery when moist.
HYGROPHYTE A plant typically restricted to growth in or on moist sites.
HYGROSCOPIC A substance having the ability to expand or contract in the presence or absence of water.
HYGROTHERMOGRAPH An instrument that records automatically and continuously both air temperature and relative humidity. It is synonymous with Thermohygrometer. *See also* Thermograph.
HYMENIUM A layer of spore-producing cells in or on a fungal fruiting body.
HYPANTHIUM A ringlike, cuplike, or tubular structure on which appear to be borne the sepals, petals, and stamens. In fact, the structure is usually formed by the fusion of the lower parts of these organs and is sometimes called the floral cup. *See also* Epigynous; Floral Cup; Floral Tube (for illustration); Perigynous.
HYPERPARASITE A parasite that parasitizes another parasite. *See also* Multiple Parasitism; Primary Parasite.
HYPERPLASIA The enlargement or overgrowth of organs or tissues in plants or animals due to an increase in the number of cells, usually as a result of disease. *See also* Hypertrophy; Hypoplasia.
HYPERTONIC A fluid that has a greater osmotic pressure than another, allowing water to move from the hypertonic fluid to the hypotonic. *See also* Hypotonic; Isotonic; Osmosis; Plasmolysis.
HYPERTROPHY The enlargement or overgrowth of organs or tissues in plants or animals due to an increase in the size of the cells, often as a result of increased functional activity resulting from disease. *See also* Hyperplasia; Hypoplasia.
HYPHA Plural hyphae. A fine, threadlike and often branched string of fungal cells that make up the mycelium, or the fruiting body of a fungus.
HYPHOPODIUM Plural hyphopodia. A short branch of one or two cells in the epiphytic mycelium of a black mildew fungus.
HYPOCOTYL The part of a plant embryo in a developing seed just below the cotyledons, from which the primordial root develops. *See also* Germination (for illustration).

HYPODERMIS **1** The layer of tissue immediately under the epidermis of plant stems. **2** A layer of transparent cells beneath the epidermis of leaves, particularly well developed in pine needles.

HYPOGEAL **1** Seed germination in which the cotyledons remain underground and develop within the seed coat. The young shoot and root both grow out of the seed. **2** Fruiting bodies that mature within the soil. *See also* Epigeal.

HYPOGEOUS Below the ground.

HYPOGYNOUS In flowers where the perianth and androecium are borne on the receptacle and below the ovary. *See also* Epigynous; Perigynous; Receptacle (for illustration).

HYPONASTY An upward curving of leaves or stems due to the cells on the lower sides elongating more rapidly than those of the upper sides. *See also* Epinasty.

HYPOPHYLLOUS Growing on the lower, abaxial surface of leaves or needles.

HYPOPLASIA The underdevelopment of cells, organs, or tissues in plants or animals due to underproduction of cells as a result of disease or nutrient deficiency. *See also* Hyperplasia, Hypertrophy.

HYPORHEIC ZONE The area under the stream channel and floodplain that contributes to the stream.

HYPOTHALLUS Plural hypothalli. A layer of fungal tissue (usually black) next to the substrate and below the thallus proper, often appearing between areoles of crustose lichen, or forming a marginal zone around the thallus.

HYPOTHECIUM Plural hypothecia. The tissue layer immediately below the hymenium, usually expanded into a cone between the exciple and hymenium.

HYPOTHESIS An abstract postulation designed to explain a phenomenon based on limited observations of the phenomenon. Hypotheses are used in designing experiments to prove or better understand the manner in which systems or phenomena function. If the hypothesis stands up to rigorous experimental testing, it could become a theory. *See also* Null Hypothesis.

HYPOTHESIS TEST A type of statistical inference that involves comparison of an observed value (or values) with a value (or values) derived from probability theory.

HYPOTONIC A fluid that has a lower osmotic pressure than another, allowing hypertonic fluids to penetrate through osmosis. *See also* Hypertonic; Isotonic.

HYPOTROPHY The condition in which cortical tissues on the underside of a horizontal plant organ develop more thickly; the formation of stipules or buds.

HYPSITHERMAL Early to mid-Holocene warm interval; also referred to as 'xerothermic interval' and 'climatic optimum' (about 6000 to 2500 BP), during which climatic conditions are thought to have been warmer than earlier or later times.

HYPSOMETER A class of instrument designed to measure tree heights from the ground using trigonometric principles. The observer takes a sighting on the top and the base of the tree from a known distance. For accurate results, trees must not lean more than five degrees from the vertical, and the horizontal distance must be measured rather than estimated. If the level of the observer's eye is above the base of the tree, the top and bottom readings are added. If the level of the eye is below the base of the tree, the tree height is the difference between the two readings.

HYSTEROTHECIUM Plural hysterothecia. A specialized fruiting body of needle cast fungi that is usually elongate and covered, and opens at maturity by a long slit.

I

ICE-CONTACT Pertains to sediments deposited against, on top of, or in tunnels underneath a glacier or ice sheet.

ICE-DISINTEGRATION MORAINE A moraine resulting from the accumulation of ablation till and other drift on top of stagnant ice. It is similar to hummocky moraine and ablation moraine.

ICE-RAFTED STONES Stones dropped into glaciolacustrine and glaciomarine sediments from melting icebergs.

ICE SHEET A continental-scale, more or less continuous cover of land ice that spreads outward in all directions and is not confined by underlying topography.

ICE SHELF A floating tabular mass of ice at the margin of and attached to an ice sheet.

ICE-WEDGE CASTS Infilled cavities formerly occupied by ice wedges; cavities are vertical and taper downward; width at the top is typically between a few centimetres and a metre, and the vertical dimension of most cavities is greater than their width. They are used as indicators of former periglacial conditions.

IDEAL POPULATION A theoretical, diploid, sexually reproducing population that meets the following criteria. (1) Individuals in an ideal population mate at random and their generations do not overlap. (2) In order to make the 'ideal population' fit mathematical constructs, the additional restrictions include the following assumptions: (a) there is no migration into or out of the population; (b) there is no selection; and (c) there are no mutations occurring.

Such a population definition permits certain manipulations of data and probabilities that assist biologists in determining likely trends and effects in natural populations.

IDLE TIME *See* Machine Time.

IGNEOUS ROCK Rock formed by cooling and crystallization from a molten or partially molten state. Major varieties include plutonic and volcanic rocks. *See also* Metamorphic Rock; Sedimentary Rock.

IGNITION The beginning of flame production or smouldering combustion. The start of a fire.

IGNITION PATTERN The manner in which a prescribed burn, backfire, or burnout is set, determined by weather, fuel, ignition system, topographic and other factors having an influence on fire behaviour and the objective of the burn. Several methods are commonly used. **Angled strip ignition** is the setting of a number of lines of fire on an area at an angle to the wind. The effect is to create lines of fire with attributes of both a head fire and a flank fire. Somewhat similar to maple leaf ignition, except that the angled strip method is normally used on flat or uniform terrain, whereas the maple leaf method is intended for hilly areas. **Area ignition** is the setting of a number of individual fires throughout an area either simultaneously or in quick succession and so spaced that they soon coalesce, influence, and support each other to produce a hot, fast-spreading fire throughout the area. **Area grid ignition** is the setting of a number of individual fires throughout an area so spaced that they will spread independently over most of the area before finally reinforcing one another. It is sometimes referred to as spot ignition. **Backfire ignition** is the setting of a line of fire so that it will burn away from a control line against the wind or downhill. **Centre fire ignition (centre firing)** is the setting of fires in the centre of an area or concentrated to create a central convection column, with additional fires set progressively and less concentrated near the outer control lines. As indrafts develop, they draw the fire toward the centre. It is synonymous with convection burning. **Flank fire ignition** is the setting of a line of fire along a line parallel to the wind, with the fire spreading at right angles to the wind or across a slope. It is sometimes called single strip flank fire. **Head fire ignition** is the setting of a line of fire so that it will burn with the wind or upslope away from a control line. It is sometimes called single strip head fire. **Maple leaf ignition** is the setting of lines of fire progressively from the apex of a ridge point and proceeding uphill. It is used in hilly areas to burn knolls or ridges where slope is the main influence on fire spread. It is also termed radial strip flank fire or chevron ignition. **Perimeter fire ignition (perimeter firing)** is the setting of a series of fires or a line of fire around the perimeter of an area and allowing the fire(s) to burn toward the centre of the area. May or may not involve centre firing. Typically, fires are set first on the downwind side to produce a backfire, then along the sides of the area to produce flank fires, and then on the upwind side to produce a head fire. **Strip fire ignition** is the setting of successive parallel strips of fire (progressing outward toward the perimeter of the area), each one burning adjacent to the strip previously burned. May be used for backfires, flank fires, or head fires. It is also termed multiple strip backfire, multiple strip flank fire, or multiple strip head fire.

IGNITION PROBABILITY The chance that a firebrand will cause ignition when it lands on receptive fuels.

IGNITION TEMPERATURE The minimum temperature at which ignition can take place and sustained combustion can occur. It is synonymous with kindling point.

IGNITION TIME The time between application of an ignition source and self-sustained combustion of a fuel.

ILLEGITIMATE NAME In botany, a scientific name validly published but in some way outside the rules established by the International Code of Botanical Nomenclature or the Code of Nomenclature for Cultivated Plants, and is therefore not an acceptable name.

ILLUVIATION The deposition from percolating water of soil components such as clay, organic matter, or sesquioxides, translocated from a higher to a lower soil horizon (see illustration). *See also* Eluviation; Leaching.

IMAGE In remote sensing, the permanent record of the likeness of any natural or manufactured features, objects, and activities. Images

illuviation

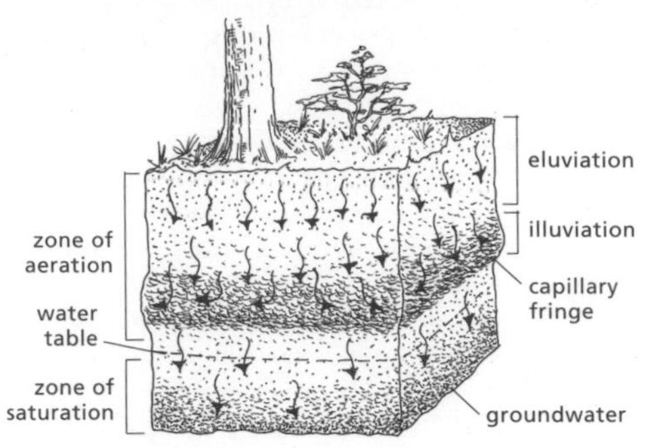

can be acquired directly on photographic materials using cameras, or indirectly if non-imaging types of sensors have been used in data collection.

IMAGE ENHANCEMENT *See* Digital Enhancement.

IMAGE MOTION In aerial photography, the blurring of images on an aerial photograph due to the relative movement of the camera with respect to the ground during exposure.

IMAGO The adult, sexually mature form of an insect, having completed all the stages of metamorphosis.

IMBRICATION **1** Plants having a pattern of overlapping scales on buds or cones. **2** Geologically, a phenomenon in which wedges of rock pile up against and over each other as a result of overthrust in the Earth's crust. The rocks are thrust out in slices showing no signs of folding, with each slice being separated by a thrust plane. **3** A distinct pattern seen in sedimentary deposits, especially pebble beds and conglomerates, resulting from a strong river current aligning the long axes of these materials along the current flow, to be subsequently cemented in that position.

IMMATURE Trees or stands that have grown beyond the regeneration stage but are not at the mature stage.

IMMATURE SOIL A soil without definable horizons due to incomplete development by weathering or biological processes.

IMMIGRANT POPULATION In pest management, a population of insects in a particular locality that have arrived there by dispersal from another locality. *See also* Resident Population.

IMMIGRATION Movement of individuals into a population. *See also* Colonization; Emigration; Migration.

IMMOBILIZATION **1** The assimilation and conversion of inorganic compounds into an organic form in plant materials. **2** The assimilation of nutrients by soil microorganisms. *See also* Mineralization.

IMMUNITY The state of being exempt from infection by a given pathogen. *See also* Resistance; Susceptible; Tolerance.

IMMUNIZATION The development of induced resistance to disease as a result of previous infection. This may be inherited, or it may result from acquired resistance developed as a result of exposure to the disease.

IMPACT Describes a positive or negative change in the environment through space or time as a result of human, nonhuman (natural), or abiotic activity. In Canada, 'effect' is often used synonymously. The general term 'environmental impact assessment' (EIA) is widely used around the world and can include assessments of social, economic, cultural, biophysical, technological, and policy aspects. Impacts can be additive (the outcome equals the sum of the individual impacts), subtractive (the outcome is less than the sum of individual impacts because some have cancelled each other out), or synergistic (the final impact is greater than the sum of the individual impacts). *See also* Baseline; Scope; Significance.

IMPARIPINNATE Odd-pinnate; having leaflets in pairs along the axis and terminating in a single terminal leaflet or tendril. *See also* Paripinnate.

IMPEDED DRAINAGE *See* Soil Drainage.

IMPELLER The rotating part of a centrifugal pump that imparts energy to the liquid to be moved.

IMPERFECT **1** Flawed in some way and therefore not perfect. **2** A flower with only one sex (i.e., unisexual). *See also* Perfect.

IMPERFECT FUNGUS *See* Fungi Imperfecti.

IMPERFECT STAGE or STATE A phase of the life cycle of a fungus in which asexual spores, such as aeciospores and urediniospores, are produced.

IMPERVIOUS Generally, a surface incapable of being penetrated by liquids, gases, or physical activity such as plant roots.

IMPOVERISHMENT A process that results in diminished number of species or other measure of diversity. It may result in reduced environmental quality.

IMPRESSED Botanically, sunken into the surface.

IMPROVEMENT CUTTING A cutting made in a stand past the sapling stage primarily to improve composition and quality by removing less desirable trees of any species.

INBREEDING Mating or crossing of individuals

more closely related than average pairs in the population. Used to try to fix (establish or stabilize) economically beneficial characteristics in a population, typically in plants and animals used in agriculture. It can lead to undesirable characteristics, particularly with normally outcrossing species like many forest trees. *See also* Outbreeding.

INBREEDING DEPRESSION The result of inbreeding, leading to reduced fitness or vigour for the species due to increased homozygosity.

INCENDIARY FIRE *See* Fire Cause Class.

INCENTIVE Any action that incites or motivates one or more people to adopt desirable behaviour or activities. Incentives can be financial, political, or social.

INCIDENCE The number of occurrences of a given phenomenon over time. *See also* Intensity.

INCIDENT The occurrence or event (including wildfires), either human-caused or natural phenomena, that requires action by emergency service personnel to prevent or minimize loss of life or damage to property and/or natural resources.

INCIDENTAL ASSOCIATION The accidental, unpredictable, or noncompelling association of a wildlife species with a habitat, as opposed to an association that is strong, predictable, and mandatory. *See also* Primary Association.

INCIDENTAL TAKE 'Take' of a threatened or endangered species that is incidental to, and not the purpose of, the carrying out of an otherwise lawful activity.

INCIPIENT DECAY An early stage of decay in which discoloration of the wood may be the only visible symptom. An initial phase of this stage, in which wood is invaded but no visible change has occurred, is sometimes referred to as the invisible or hidden stage.

INCIPIENT INFECTION An infection that is actively developing but has not yet reached a stage at which it is apparent. *See also* Latent Infection.

INCISED Botanically, a shape being sharply, deeply, and irregularly cut. An indeterminate form between toothed and lobed.

INCISOR In mammals, the front or foremost teeth in the skull, which are used for cutting.

INCLUDED Botanically, not projecting, not exserted; enclosed within (e.g., the stamens included in the corolla).

INCLUDED BARK Bark formed in a pronounced ridge at the junction of two or more trunks, or stems in a tree, due to being pushed inwards rather than outwards. Included bark is an indicator of potentially weak points of attachment between the trunks or stems. It is also called embedded wood. *See also* Branch Bark Ridge; Occlusion.

INCOMPATIBILITY **1** The inability of substances (such as pesticides) in solution emulsion, or suspension, to mix without causing undesirable reactions, such as physical reactions (coagulation, congealing, or precipitation) or chemical reactions (e.g., detoxification). The substances are said to be mutually antagonistic. **2** A phenomenon in plants or animals where the main body rejects transplanted tissues (animal organs or plant grafts). **3** The inability to achieve fertilization between one flower (or algae or fungus) and other flowers on the same or genetically similar plants. *See also* Antagonism; Compatible; Synergism.

INCOMPATIBLE HOST A host infected by a disease that leads to an abnormal parasitic relationship. In dwarf mistletoe, pronounced swellings may develop, with few if any shoots produced. Incompatible hosts are usually, but not always, rare hosts. *See also* Host Susceptibility Rating.

INCOMPLETE A flower lacking one of the four whorls (calyx, corolla, androecium, gynoecium).

INCOMPLETE METAMORPHOSIS *See* Hemimetabolous.

INCREASER PLANT A plant that increases in number, percentage ground cover, or biomass with increasing grazing pressure because other more desirable plants are consumed first. *See also* Decreaser Plant.

INCREMENT The amount of new wood fibre added to a tree or trees in a given period, normally one year. Increment can be measured on one tree or across a whole stand as an increase in diameter, basal area, height, volume, quality, or value. Typically, increment is measured in terms of volume per year. The assessment of increment plays a fundamental role in determining many different aspects of forest management. **Current Annual Increment (CAI)** is the amount of new biomass added in the current year. Because this amount may vary from year to year, some assessments seek a more average value, determined by a **Periodic Annual Increment (PAI)**, which is the total biomass accumulated over a number of years divided by the number of years in that period, usually five or ten years. An extension of this is to seek the **Mean Annual Increment (MAI)**, which is the amount of biomass accumulated to date divided by the total age. Because age must be known, MAI can only be determined in even-aged stands or for trees of known age (planting date or year of regeneration).

The relationship between CAI or PAI and MAI is shown in the illustration. In an even-aged stand, the mean annual increment reaches a peak, known as the maximum mean annual increment (MMAI), when the tree reaches a point where it is accumulating biomass at its maximum rate per year. At that point, the PAI will be the same.

Two other aspects of increment are important. **Gross increment** is the total biomass produced over the life of the tree or stand, even though some of that biomass may not be present at the end of the life span. **Net increment** accounts for the biomass present after losses due to self-thinning or for other reasons. Additionally, biomass production may include all the below-ground matter, such as roots and root hairs, and this may be more in total than the above-ground production.

patterns of volume increment in an even-aged stand

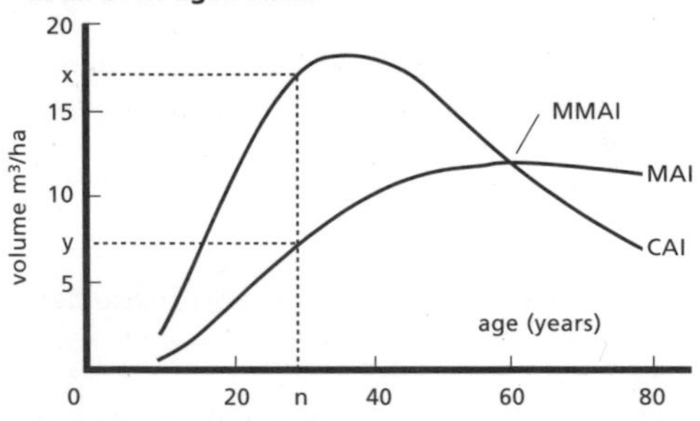

INCREMENTAL DROP An airtanker drop in which the tank doors are opened in sequence so that fire retardant cascades continuously. It is synonymous with string drop, trail drop, and train drop. *See also* Salvo; Split Drop.

INCREMENTAL PLANNING Also termed disjointed incrementalism or the science of muddling through. Where comprehensive planning is seen to be all-encompassing and, therefore, rather slow to yield usable results, incremental planning is founded on the perceived need for negotiated solutions in which the players can derive a more acceptable solution at a local level without the need for centralized decision-making. However, the issue of who can negotiate, and with what backing, can introduce discrepancies in the power distribution, and the broader 'public interest' might not always be served by such an approach. Moreover, a common condition of negotiations is that some decisions are made in secret and thus outcomes are less readily scrutinized, and the data supporting these outcomes may be harder to evaluate and challenge. A final problem is that an incremental approach runs the risk of losing track of the larger context within which small problems are being addressed.

In reality, most planning activities do not adopt any one approach all the time, but tend to mix approaches as the needs dictate. *See also* Comprehensive Planning; Strategic Planning.

INCREMENTAL SILVICULTURE *See* Intensive Silviculture.

INCREMENTAL SPRAYING A pesticide application method in which successive passes by the spray aircraft, flying in a constant cross-wind, result in a layering of deposits downwind, thus providing sufficient coverage of the target area. *See also* Drift.

INCREMENT BORER A hollow metal auger, used to drill into a tree and extract a core or cylinder of wood.

INCREMENT CORE The core or cylinder of wood extracted by an increment boring tool. It is used to determine the annual increment and age of a tree by counting growth rings, or to determine the internal condition of the tree by assessing the uniformity of the core.

INCUBATE The process by which a bird, through sitting upon its eggs, maintains suitable conditions (typically temperature and humidity) for the development and hatching of fertilized eggs.

INCUBATION PERIOD In plant pathology, the interval between penetration and infection (or inoculation) of a host by a pathogen, and the first visible evidence of infection (or inoculation) symptoms on the host. *See also* Lag Period; Latent Period.

INCUMBENT Folded inward and lying or leaning upon another organ (e.g., an incumbent anther is turned inward and lies against the inner face of its filament). Incumbent cotyledons in the seed are face to face, with the back of one lying against the radicle. *See also* Accumbent; Conduplicate.

INCURSION **1** In general, the progression of an activity from one area into another across a boundary. **2** In pest management, the usually predictable spread of a pest infection or infestation into an area of forest or range across a boundary from another land jurisdiction.

INDEHISCENT Fruit bodies that remain closed or do not open along regular lines. *See also* Fruit (for illustration).

INDEPENDENT CROWN FIRE *See* Forest Fire.
INDEPENDENT VARIABLE A variable that can be used to predict another variable. *See also* Dependent Variable.
INDETERMINATE **1** Of uncertain cause or origin. **2** In morphology, a shape that is not terminated definitely; without definite margin or edge. **3** An inflorescence in which the elongation of the main axis is not stopped by the opening of the first flowers. **4** Of indefinite growth where the size or numbers of organs produced is not predetermined.
INDEX **1** A ratio or some other number derived from a series of observations that is used as an indicator or measure of conditions, properties, phenomena, or trends. **2** A composite numerical value for some environmental attribute for which there is more than one indicator. **3** A number used to indicate change in magnitude of some variable, such as cost, price, or volume of production, as compared with its magnitude at some specified time, usually taken as having an index number of 100. **4** A systematic, usually alphabetical, collection of key words that permits easy access for search and retrieval of stored data. **5** In ecology, the proportional relation of counts of objects or signs associated with a given species to counts of that species on a given area. **6** In bird surveys, counts of individuals (e.g., at a feeding station) reflecting changes in relative abundance on a specified or local area. **7** A single number derived from two or more indicators that quantify an environmental or social condition in its simplest and most essential form.
INDEX MAP A map showing the location and numbers of flight lines and aerial photographs.
INDEX METHOD A counting method involving sampling that yields measures of relative abundance rather than density values.
INDICATOR A single quantity derived from a single variable that describes or measures an environmental or social condition.
INDICATOR GUILD A set of species sharing a common habitat or resource use characteristic for which management guidelines can be directed. All species of an indicator guild are sometimes assumed, erroneously, to respond identically to management activities and environmental conditions.
INDICATOR PLANT **1** A plant that is considered to be representative of a particular region, locality, or habitat type and thus, by its presence, indicates that region, locality, or habitat type. **2** In pest management, a plant species or variety that reacts to a particular pathogen or environmental factor by the development of obvious symptoms and is used to detect the presence of the pathogen or environmental factor.
INDICATOR SPECIES A species that is closely correlated with a particular environmental condition or habitat type such that its presence or absence can be used as an indicator of environmental conditions. A species whose population size and trend is assumed to reflect the population size and trend of other species associated with the same geographic area and habitats. *See also* Indicator Species Management.
INDICATOR SPECIES MANAGEMENT A fish or wildlife management scheme in which planning and management guidelines are prescribed for a particular species on the assumption that the welfare of this selected species will indicate the welfare of other species. *See also* Featured Species; Keystone Species.
INDICATOR SPECIES SYSTEM Analogous to featured species management in wildlife management. In plant ecology, the use of plant species to indicate special environmental factors or plant community types.
INDICATOR VARIABLE *See* Dummy Variable.
INDIFFERENCE CURVE A graphical delineation of all combinations of two goods or services with which an individual would be equally pleased (i.e., indifferent between them).
INDIFFERENCE MAP A two-dimensional graph of a combination of indifference curves denoting an individual's preference system to various combinations of two goods or services. Each line of the family of curves represents equally desirable mixtures of the quantities in question. With different curves representing differing levels of satisfaction, it is possible to determine what quantities an individual will consume when faced with different prices and incomes.
INDIGENOUS A species of plant, animal, or abiotic material that is native to a particular area (i.e., occurs naturally in an area and is not introduced). *See also* Exotic Species.
INDIRECT ATTACK *See* Fire Suppression.
INDIRECT COMPETITION The exploitation of a resource by one individual that reduces the availability of that resource to others.
INDIRECT EFFECT **1** A condition caused by an action or inaction through intermediary causal agents. An effect for which the causal linkages to the action or inaction are not readily apparent. Note that this is not a measure of impor-

tance, but merely a classification by causal linkages. *See also* Direct Effect. **2** The impact on a species caused by affecting the species' competitors, predators, or mutualists. **3** The impact of toxic chemicals on a species by directly affecting interactions between species. Examples are disruptions in food resources or habitat changes that affect competitive interactions, biomagnification up the food chain, and impacts on populations' parasites, symbionts, pollinators.

INDIRECT JOBS Employment opportunities that result from the development of the many and various demands created by the creation of direct jobs (e.g., mill workers [direct jobs] requiring groceries, fuel, or hardware [indirect jobs]). *See also* Direct Jobs.

INDIRECTLY VISIBLE AREA Ground, or the vegetation growing thereon, that is not directly visible to a fixed point lookout but lies at not more than a specified depth (commonly 300 feet) below the lookout's line of sight. *See also* Blind Area; Seen Area.

INDIRECT MANAGEMENT Management that emphasizes modifying people's behaviour by managing factors and situations that influence their decisions; visitors retain their freedom to choose. A 'light-handed' approach to wilderness management. An example would be retaining a low-standard access road to help limit use of a popular wilderness trailhead. *See also* Direct Management.

INDIRECT SUPPRESSION The suppression of a pest population by altering the stand or other conditions that favour it. *See also* Direct Suppression.

INDIVIDUAL SELECTION A selection pressure that acts differentially on different genotypes within a population, thus affecting their contribution to subsequent generations.

INDUCED DIVERSITY INDEX A number that indicates the relative degree of induced diversity in habitat per unit area produced by edges formed by the junction of successional stages or vegetative conditions within plant communities. It is expressed mathematically as:

$$\text{Induced DI} = \frac{TE_s}{2\sqrt{A\pi}}$$

where

TE_s = total length of edges between successional stages or conditions within plant communities

A = area

π = 3.1416.

See also Edge; Inherent Diversity Index.

INDUMENT/INDUMENTUM A dense covering of hairs, scurf, or scales.

INDUPLICATE Rolled or folded inwards.

INDURATE A hardened and tough surface.

INDURATION **1** The formation of brittle hardpan layers within a soil. **2** The hardening of a geological material by heating, compaction, or cementation.

INDUSIATE Having an indusium.

INDUSIUM The membranous covering extended over a spore cluster in ferns.

INEQUILATERAL *See* Oblique.

INFECT The start or continuance of an interactive relationship between a parasite or pathogen and its host, which is then said to be infected.

INFECTED RESIDUAL An infected tree remaining after logging or a natural catastrophe, such as a fire or windstorm. It often refers to trees infected with dwarf mistletoe. *See also* Residual.

INFECTION **1** The entry and subsequent interaction of an organism or virus into a host and the establishment of a parasitic or pathogenic relationship. **2** That process in which dwarf mistletoes successfully penetrate host tissue and initiate establishment of the endophytic system. **3** The whole mistletoe plant (aerial shoots and endophytic system) developing from a single seed, plus the associated host symptoms.

INFECTION AGE The length of time since the infection of a host individual by a particular pathogen. Often used in reference to dwarf mistletoe. It is usually determined by counting the number of infected rings and adding one or two years to account for the period before xylem stimulation.

INFECTION CENTRE A localized concentration of disease originating from one point of origin, such as an infected stump. There is a characteristic distribution of infected trees: (1) dead trees in the centre; (2) a fringe of recently killed trees; and (3) infected but still living trees around the perimeter. The infection centre gradually increases in radius as the pathogen spreads from tree to tree. *See also* Epicentre.

INFECTION CLASS A system used to determine the severity of a pest infestation, typically used in assessing dwarf mistletoe. *See also* Infection Rating System.

INFECTION COURT The site where infection or inoculation might occur, or already has occurred (e.g., wounds or stomatal openings).

INFECTION RATING SYSTEM A system for rating the intensity of attack by a pest. Individual trees are visually divided into portions (stem, top, middle, bottom, crown thirds). The degree of infection, defoliation, or other indication of attack is assessed for each portion, and the ratings for the portions are combined to give a rating for the whole tree. A stand is rated by taking the average of the ratings for individual trees within it. *See also* Six Class System.

INFECTIOUS **1** Having the capability of causing an infection. **2** Describes a disease caused by a pathogen that can spread from a diseased host to a healthy one.

INFECTIVE **1** Having the ability to attack a living organism and cause infection. The term is often qualified as 'weakly infective,' 'strongly infective,' etc. **2** Describes a vector carrying a pathogen and capable of transferring it to a host and thus causing infection.

INFERIOR In botany, describes the relative position of an organ (such as an ovary situated below the receptacle) or part of an organ as below, beneath, or lower. *See also* Superior.

INFESTATION **1** Describes an area, one or more organisms, or an abiotic substrate harbouring large numbers of insects, mites, nematodes, weeds, or pathogens. *See also* Infect. **2** The occurrence of one or more pest species in an area or location where their numbers and impact are currently or potentially at intolerable levels. *See also* Outbreak.

INFILTRATION The movement of surface water into soil or rock through cracks and pores.

INFLORESCENCE **1** The flowering part of a plant. Many different types of inflorescences occur including bearded, catkin, cyme, head, panicle, raceme, spike, and umbel. Refer to the illustration and individual terms for more detail. **2** The way in which the flowering parts of a plant are organized.

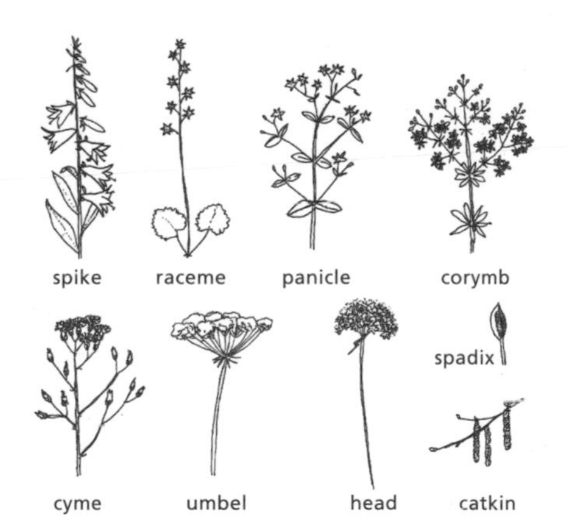

INFLUENCE Used to describe the relationship between different factors (e.g., the topographic influence refers to the forces of change that topography has exerted on the vegetation lying on top of the topography). In some cases, the influence is bidirectional, thus the vegetation could, over longer periods of time, exert some influence on the topography.

INFLUENT STREAM A stream above the water table that loses water by seepage into the streambed. *See also* Effluent Stream.

INFRA- A prefix meaning below (e.g., infraspecific, infrastipular).

INFRAORBITAL FORAMEN In anatomy or zoology, a hole. In mammals, the opening in the maxillary bone immediately below the front corner of the eye. Foramina (plural of foramen) allow for the passage of nerves and other thread- or stringlike structures.

INFRARED Electromagnetic radiation with wavelengths between 0.75 micrometres and 1 millimetre. Infrared radiation (IR) lies just beyond visible red light and is usually classified as near and far infrared. Near IR encompasses the shorter wavelengths from 0.7 micrometres up to 2 or 3 micrometres and emphasizes the radiation reflected from plant materials. It is also called solar IR because it is only available for use in daylight hours. Far IR encompasses the longer wavelengths from 25 micrometres to 1 millimetre, but this is limited in terrestrial survey applications because the atmosphere transmits very little radiation in these wavelengths. Much of the infrared radiation arriving at the Earth's surface is absorbed by water vapour. However, the near IR is used extensively for satellite and low-level flight inventories mapping vegetation, since the condition of the vegetation has different reflectance properties and can be calibrated to vegetative conditions.

INFRARED (IR) IMAGERY Imagery created by optical-electronic equipment utilizing the infrared wavelengths of the electromagnetic spectrum. IR imagery is used in fire suppression through dense smoke, haze, and vegetation canopy to (1) detect the incidence of wildfires in remote terrain, especially following lightning storms; (2) to map the perimeters, hot spots, and spot fires of going fires; and (3) to detect residual heat sources during mop-up. Generally, the first two uses employ IR scanners in aircraft while the third use employs hand-held IR scanners on the ground or in slow-flying helicopters. IR imagery is not cost-effective through fog, rain, or other moisture. It is synonymous with thermal imagery.

INFRASPECIFIC One or more units of classification below the rank of species.

INFRUCTESCENCE The arrangement of fruits on a branch stem.

INFUNDIBULAR Funnel-shaped.

INGEST To eat, or take within the body.

INGRESS The establishment of natural regeneration in an opening. *See also* Ingrowth.

INGROWTH **1** It is the number of trees, or the volume of trees that have grown past a predetermined threshold in a set period. Typically used to refer to the dividing line between seedling to sapling or, sapling to pole stage, or a specific diameter class or merchantability class. Once past the sapling stage, the tree is counted into volume calculations, hence ingrowth can make a very significant difference in the assessment of stand condition. It is also called recruitment. **2** The period after successional growth of a forest stand when it reaches a specified age or structure class (e.g., spotted-owl forage habitat). *See also* Ingress; Recruitment.

INHERENT DIVERSITY INDEX A number indicating the relative degree of inherent diversity in habitat per unit area produced by plant communities to plant community edges. It is expressed mathematically as:

$$\text{Inherent DI} = \frac{TE_c}{2\sqrt{A\pi}}$$

where

TE_c = total edge between plant communities within, or on the perimeter of the area
A = area
π = 3.1416.

See also Induced Diversity Index.

INHIBITION The process of extinguishing a fire by the use of an agent that interrupts the chemical reactions in the combustion process.

INHIBITOR Any agent that retards a chemical reaction (e.g., retardant) or growth processes in plants or animals.

INITIAL ATTACK The first action taken to halt the spread of a fire and before actual fire-fighting begins.

INITIAL ATTACK BASE Any place where initial attack capability has been positioned in readiness for probable fire action. The attack forces must have air and/or ground transport capability on site. It is synonymous with attack centre.

INITIAL ATTACK CREW A crew specially hired, trained, equipped, and deployed to conduct initial attack on wildfires. It is synonymous with shock crew, hotshot crew, suppression crew. *See also* Helitack Crew; Rappel Crew; Suppression Crew.

INJURY Physical, biological, or chemical damage to plants or animals resulting from a long-term process such as disease, or a specific event such as fire, pest attack, etc.

INNER BARK The active layer of tissues (phloem and cambium) between the wood (xylem) and suberized bark. *See also* Suberose.

INNER GORGE A stream reach bounded by steep valley walls that terminate upslope into a more gentle topography. It is common in areas of rapid stream downcutting or uplift.

INOCULATE **1** The planned introduction of material containing or believed to contain, living or killed organisms, generally microorganisms, into a new environment (e.g., soils, a culture media, or another living organism). **2** The deliberate placement of a pathogen in contact with or inside a host, either to test its pathogenicity, or to initiate already-known infection potential.

INOCULATIVE RELEASE The periodic, usually annual, release of a natural enemy of a pest to replenish a population that is severely reduced by unfavourable conditions at certain times but operates effectively against the target pest through the rest of the year. *See also* Biological Control; Inundative Release.

INOCULUM **1** The pathogen, or that portion of it (tissue, spores, mycelial fragments, etc.) that initiates infection of the host. **2** Material containing microorganisms or virus particles to be deliberately introduced into a host or culture medium.

INOCULUM POTENTIAL **1** The energy of growth of a pathogen available for infection of the host at the surface of the host organ to be affected. **2** The density of inoculum, made up of units having certain degrees of virulence and vigour, as affected by environmental factors. Inoculum potential is one of the components that determine whether infection will be successful in any one situation.

INORGANIC A substance that is derived without organic life or its products, typically a mineral or element. *See also* Organic.

INPUT The goods and services taken into or introduced into a process or system as a part of its functioning. The basic resources of land, labour, and capital. The various factors going into production. *See also* Output.

INPUT-OUTPUT ANALYSIS **1** An analysis of the outputs of a system relative to the inputs. **2** A method of measuring and displaying the relationship of each sector of the economy to every other sector of the economy by means of a matrix reporting the inputs and outputs of each sector. **3** In forest economics, a factual study of the technical problems of production, which seeks to determine, having taken into account the interdependence of productive industries and the resources and technology available, the net consumable output of each.

INQUILINE A gall inhabitant that lives in and feeds on gall tissue but is incapable of initiating galls on its own. Some may directly or indirectly kill the gall-maker.

INSECT Any member of the uniramous arthropod class Insecta, characterized by a body divided into three segments: (1) the head, bearing one pair of segmented antennae; (2) the thorax, bearing three pairs of legs and two pairs of wings; and (3) the abdomen. *See also* Uniramia.

INSECT GROWTH REGULATOR **1** An insect hormone that controls growth, moulting, and/or maturation from the pupal stage to the adult. **2** A chemical substance used as a pesticide that disrupts the action of insect hormones controlling such processes as moulting and maturation from the pupal stage to adult. *See also* Ecdysoid; Juvenoid.

INSECTICIDAL SOAP A soap (i.e., a formulation of fatty acid alkali salts) in which the length of the fatty acid chains renders the material relatively toxic to insects and relatively non-toxic to plants. If used operationally in the forest, soaps must usually be registered as pesticides (may vary between jurisdictions).

INSECTICIDE Any chemical or biological substance applied to insects as a means of killing them, or disrupting their development.

INSECTIVORE Any organism that feeds exclusively or primarily upon insects or arthropods.

INSECTIVOROUS Insect-eating plants or animals. The Insectivora belong to a primitive order of placental mammals (Eutheria), which includes shrews and moles.

INSERTED Attached to or placed on, such as a stamen inserted on the corolla. The point of attachment is also called the point of insertion.

***IN SITU* CONSERVATION** Retention, conservation, and propagation of germ plasm resources on the site as a means of continuing the organism or ecosystem in its original habitat or location. *See also Ex Situ* Conservation.

INSOLATION The solar radiation received by the Earth, measured as the amount of radiation falling on a surface of known size, placed perpendicular to the sun's rays over a known time.

INSPECTION RUN A pass over the fire target by an airtanker to assess the flight path and target. Some agencies use the term for the airtanker of the birddog aircraft. In the US, it is termed lead plane. *See also* Dummy Run; Lead In.

INSTABILITY In ecology, a state in which a small environmental change is sufficient to cause a significant change in ecosystem form and function.

INSTANTANEOUS FIELD OF VIEW When expressed in degrees or radians, the smallest plane angle over which an instrument (for example, a scanner) is sensitive to radiation. When expressed in linear or area units, such as metres or hectares, it is an altitude-dependent measure of the ground resolution of the scanner. *See also* Scan Line.

INSTAR **1** The form assumed by an insect during a particular stadium (i.e., any post-egg stage initiated and/or terminated by ecdysis). There are larval or nymphal instars, a pupal instar, and an adult instar. **2** The stage between moults of an insect larva, numbered to designate the various periods (e.g., the first instar is the first stage between the egg and the first larval moult). *See also* Adult; Imago; Stadium.

INSTRUMENT FLIGHT RULES (IFR) Used when flying in weather conditions below the minimum for flight under visual flight rules and therefore requiring the observance of instruments inside the aircraft for controlling flight. The threshold weather conditions are generally considered to be less than 1,000 feet ceiling and three miles horizontal visibility. *See also* Visual Flight Rules.

INTANGIBLE VALUES Those resource yields that are not directly quantifiable or, if quantifiable, cannot be valued by standard market mechanisms. Examples include aesthetic, scientific, educational, historical, recreational, spiritual, and cultural values.

INTEGRATED LOGGING A logging operation that segregates and delivers a variety of products to the mills and processors, to use them to the best advantage.

INTEGRATED PEST MANAGEMENT (IPM) A systematic approach that uses a variety of techniques to reduce pest damage or unwanted vegetation to economically and socially tolerable levels. IPM techniques may include the use of natural predators and parasites, genetically resistant hosts, environmental modifications and, when necessary and appropriate, chemical pesticides or herbicides.

INTEGRATED RESOURCE MANAGEMENT The management of two or more resources in the same general area and period of time (e.g., water, soil, timber, grazing, fish, wildlife, and forests). The process of setting planning and management goals, objectives, strategies, and policies in a cooperative framework among all resource users.

INTEGRITY An assessment of a system and the degree to which it is unimpaired, sound, or complete. Such an assessment requires knowledge of what the unimpaired baseline looks like so that integrity can be judged in a defensible context.

INTEGUMENT **1** In plants, the covering of an organ, particularly the outer layer of tissue covering the ovule, which hardens to become the seed coat. **2** In insects, the cuticle.

INTENSIFICATION Any increase in the numbers of a pest species in a particular locality or stand.

INTENSITY **1** The degree of pest attack upon an individual tree or stand. **2** The magnitude and severity of a fire.

INTENSIVE Refers to the degree or severity of disturbance (e.g., fire, logging) or management activity. *See also* Extensive.

INTENSIVE FOREST MANAGEMENT **1** A management concept promoting basic forest management in combination with juvenile-stand improvement and/or the use of artificial regeneration to ensure reasonably uniform stand establishment and stocking. **2** Any management action beyond those required by law. *See also* Basic Forest Management; Extensive Forest Management.

INTENSIVE SILVICULTURE **1** Also called incremental silviculture. Any silvicultural practices designed to accelerate stand development and improve the stand value and final yields in stands that are well established. The practices included in the definition vary by jurisdiction. The baseline case is often the historical natural yield of wild, untouched stands. **2** Any silvicultural practice beyond those required by law. *See also* Basic Silviculture.

INTER- A prefix meaning between or among. *See also* Intra-.

INTERACTIVE In computer usage, the ability of the machine and the operator to communicate on a real time or continuing basis to solve problems. It is especially important in activities such as data input and editing, updating operations, and the retrieval of data.

INTERCALARY MERISTEM A meristem located between differentiated tissues at the base and top of the plant (e.g., blades of grass originate from intercalary meristems, and dwarf mistletoe sinkers elongate by growth from a meristem near the base of the sinker). *See also* Apical Meristem; Meristematic Tissue.

INTERCELLULAR Changes or processes occurring between or among cells. *See also* Intracellular.

INTERCEPTION The retention of precipitation on vegetation, from which it is subsequently evaporated without ever reaching the ground.

INTERCORTICAL Lying or developing between or among the (host) cortex.

INTERCOSTAL Situated between the ribs or veins of (host) leaves or fronds.

INTERDISCIPLINARY TEAM A group of individuals with varying areas of expertise, working together to solve a problem or perform a task. The team is assembled in recognition of the fact that no one scientific discipline is sufficiently broad enough to adequately analyze the problem and propose actions.

INTEREST The price paid for borrowed or invested money (the principal sum). Simple interest is calculated on the principal sum alone, being paid out at regular intervals. Compound interest is calculated on the combined total of the principal sum plus accumulated interest, the latter not being paid out. Both are expressed as a percentage per annum.

INTERFEMORAL MEMBRANE The thin membrane that stretches between the hindlegs of bats, joining the hindlegs and tail.

INTERFERENCE COMPETITION Competition in which one species prevents the other species from having access to a limiting resource. *See also* Competition; Exploitation.

INTERFLUVE The elevated region between two fluves (drainageways) that sheds water to them.

INTERGLACIAL The periods of time between episodes of glacier development, maximization, and recession.

INTERIOR FOREST CONDITIONS The environmental conditions typical of the central or interior part of a habitat patch. They are usually relatively stable and uninfluenced by the changing climatic conditions and other variables (noise, wind, sunlight, temperature, moisture) associated with edge conditions.

INTERIOR SPECIES Species of plants or animals that are adapted to and depend upon the conditions associated with a closed-canopy forest ecosystem unaffected by edge conditions. Forest interior birds tend to require large tracts of forest habitat for nesting and foraging. *See also* Edge Effect.

INTERLOCKING YARDER A device that allows the main and haul-back drums to be operated together as a single unit to maintain running line tension.

INTERMEDIATE AXIS *See* Shape of Clasts.

INTERMEDIATE DECAY A stage of decay in which some breakdown of the normal wood structure is inevitable, but does not yet have the characteristics of an advanced stage of decay. *See also* Advanced Decay.

INTERMEDIATE SUPPORT A spar tree or cable sling located between the head spar and tail spar to which a tree jack is attached to support a multispan skyline.

INTERMEDIATE SUPPORT SPAR A spar tree located between the head spar and the tail spar to support a multispan skyline.

INTERMEDIATE TREATMENTS (TENDING) A collective term for any treatment designed to enhance growth, quality, vigour, and composition of a forest stand after establishment of regeneration and prior to final harvest.

INTERMEDIATE TREES Describes trees growing in an even-aged stand. Intermediate trees are shorter than the dominant or codominant classes, and have crowns below or extending into the crown cover of the taller trees.

INTERMITTENT Periodic interruptions in a normal pattern or process.

INTERMITTENT CROWN FIRE *See* Forest Fire.

INTERMITTENT SMOKE *See* Smoke.

INTERMITTENT STREAM *See* Stream.

INTERNAL CUSPS In mammals, the prominent points on the inside edge of the crowns of teeth. Unicuspid teeth are teeth with only a single cusp or point on the crown.

INTERNATIONAL BIOLOGICAL PROGRAMME (IBP) A worldwide study of biological productivity of terrestrial, freshwater, and marine communities; conservation; and human adaptability. The program was operated from 1964 to 1974 by the nongovernmental International Council of Scientific Unions, which comprised over forty participating countries. *See also* Ecological Reserves.

INTERNATIONAL LOG RULE Devised in 1906, this is a formula rule that includes a fixed taper allowance of 1/2 inch for each 4 feet of length, an allowance of 1/4 inch for saw kerf, and a 1/16 inch shrinkage for each inch of board thickness. The main rule used by the USDA Forest Service. For a 16-foot log, the basic formula is:

$$\text{Volume (in board feet)} = 0.8\,(D-1)^2$$

where

D = log diameter in inches.

See also Doyle Rule; Scribner Rule.

INTERNODE **1** The region of a plant stem between any two nodes (i.e., the point at which leaves are attached). Buds are commonly borne at nodes in the axils of leaves (i.e., the upper angles between leaves and stems). **2** In forestry, the distance between successive terminal buds in a shoot or branch, which is often assumed to represent one year of growth in height or length. The distance between successive whorls of branches is commonly taken to be an internode in this sense. Such usage may lead to incorrect measurements since more than one whorl of branches may be produced in a given year.

INTERORBITAL BREADTH In mammals, the narrowest portion between the eye-sockets, measured across the top of the skull.

INTERPLANTING **1** The deliberate planting of a different species in an established sapling stand as a means of changing species composition. *See also* Fill Planting; Underplanting.

INTERPOLATE To determine intermediate values between given fixed values.

INTERPRETATION *See* Photo Interpretation.

INTERRUPTED Discontinuous; the interruption of an otherwise symmetrical pattern or arrangement.

INTERSECTION LENGTH The length of that portion of a transect line through a stand which passes through a root rot infection centre. *See also* Intersection Length Method.

INTERSECTION LENGTH METHOD An estimation of the total area of root rot infestation within a stand by determining the linear proportion of one or more straight transect lines that pass through infection centres.

INTERSPECIFIC A process or activity occurring between two separate species. *See also* Intraspecific.

INTERSPECIFIC ASSOCIATION The affinity for coexistence between two species, which may be positive, negative, or absent. Three factors may result in an interspecific association: (1) both species select or avoid the same habitat or components of the same habitat; (2) both species have the same general ecological requirements; and (3) one or both of the species has an affinity for the other that is manifested as an attraction or repulsion. *See also* Competition; Competitive Exclusion; Mutualism; Predation.

INTERSPECIFIC COMPETITION The competitive

interaction between two or more species that are using a resource that is in short supply or, if the resources are not in short supply, the condition that occurs when the organisms seeking that resource nevertheless harm one or the other in the process. Competition usually is confined to closely related species that eat the same sort of food or live in the same sort of place. Competition typically results in ultimate elimination of the less-effective organism from that ecological niche.

INTERSPERSION The spatial and temporal distribution and intermixing of different ecosystem types and their associated edges within a broader landscape matrix. Interspersion determines the amount of edge and habitat diversity found in any one area.

INTERSTADIAL The warmer substage (interstade) of a glacial episode marked by a temporary retreat or standstill of glacial ice.

INTERSTITIAL The spaces between solid bodies, such as streambed gravels.

INTERTIDAL A coastal environment occurring in the shore area between the mean high and mean low tides.

INTERVAL SCALES *See* Measurement; Ordinal Scale.

INTRA- A prefix meaning within or inside. *See also* Inter-.

INTRACELLULAR Processes or activities occurring within cells.

INTRACORTICAL Typically, refers to higher plants. It describes the location of an infection occurring within the cortex.

INTRAGRAVEL FLOW The water moving through the substrate pore of a streambed.

INTRASPECIFIC A process or activity occurring within a single species. *See also* Interspecific.

INTRASPECIFIC COMPETITION The competitive interaction between the same species within a population that are using a resource that is in short supply. Such competition results in a differential ability to survive and reproduce, the less-effective members being less vigorous.

INTRINSIC PROCESSES The amelioration or preparation of severe or biologically barren sites by pioneering species and their eventual elimination by the less hardy climax species through competition, invasion, succession, and displacement.

INTRINSIC RATE OF NATURAL INCREASE The rate at which a population increases, assuming that the age and sex ratios of the population remain stable and that the intrinsic rate is independent of the natural events that would normally affect survival.

INTRINSIC VALUES Those actions, states, beings, conditions, relationships, etc., that are valued for their own sake, not for what they lead to or produce. Hence, a person can value backcountry hiking for its own sake, not because it conditions the body, not because it gets him or her somewhere, but simply for its inherent goodness. *See also* Extrinsic Values.

INTRODUCED ORGANISM *See* Exotic Species.

INTROGRESSION Also termed introgressive hybridization. A flow of genes from one species to another across a fairly strong barrier to interbreeding by means of hybridization and backcrossing.

INTRORSE Facing or directed inwards. *See also* Extrorse.

INTRUSIVE Igneous rocks derived from molten matter that has invaded pre-existing rocks and then cooled beneath the surface of the Earth. *See also* Extrusive.

INTUMESCENCE Generally describes the swelling up of liquids. In fire-fighting, the swelling up of a foam or other retardant after application, usually associated with long-term retardants.

INUNDATE To flood or cover with water.

INUNDATION REGIME A regime that exhibits periodic flooding, characterized by submergence and subsequent emergence of the land surface and supported vegetation.

INUNDATIVE RELEASE The release of large numbers of a natural enemy of a pest over a large area. The released organism is not intended to become established in the area, nor it is anticipated that it would affect subsequent generations of the target pest. *See also* Biological Control; Biological Insecticide; Inoculative Release.

INVENTORY As a verb, the collection of information about what exists. As a noun, the materials found to be existing. Several important forms of inventory exist and are required in resource management. **Continuous forest inventory** is an inventory system in which permanent sample plots distributed throughout the whole forest management unit are repeatedly remeasured at regular intervals to determine total volume, growth, and depletion. **Forest inventory** is a survey of a forest area to determine such data as area by condition, timber volume, species of trees, wildlife and habitat types, environmentally sensitive areas, and critical habitats, for the purposes of planning, purchase, evaluation, management, and/or harvesting. **Integrated inventory** is an inventory or system of inventories designed to meet multifacility, multilevel, multiresource, or temporal needs. Inventory work usually proceeds from a general to a more detailed level. **Reconnaissance inventory** is an exploratory, extensive forest inventory with no detailed estimates given, no formal sampling scheme used, and no precision estimates. This is usually the initial stage of inventory. **Management inventory** is a detailed, intensive forest inventory across areas managed as one unit to assist in management planning. Individual forest types are usually mapped in detail with area and volume estimates given for each type. A precision estimate is given for total timber inventory volume. **Operational inventory** is an intensive forest inventory of a small area for harvesting purposes. Individual stands are mapped, with estimates given for each stand. **Regional inventory** is a detailed, but extensive forest inventory for planning purposes at a regional or provincial (state) level. Major forest types and landforms are mapped and estimates derived for each forest type. Precision estimates are given for total timber inventory volume. Regional inventories are usually initiated as an extensive inventory (a top-down approach), but as more detailed work is undertaken, they can then be refined by aggregation of the more detailed work (a bottom-up approach).

INVERSION **1** The atmospheric condition in which temperature within a vertical layer of air increases with altitude, resulting in a very stable atmosphere. This is contrary to the usual situation in which temperature decreases with height. The term 'inversion' may also be applied to other meteorological properties. However, in fire management, its usage is generally restricted to a temperature inversion based at the Earth's surface, a common occurrence in the early morning hours during the fire season. **2** An aberration in a chromosome where the linear sequence of the genes is reversed in one part of the chromosome.

INVERTEBRATE Animals without backbones. In aquatic ecology, insects, crustaceans, shellfish, and worms. It includes all animals except those in the phylum Chordata.

***IN VITRO* STORAGE** The storage of plant or animal germ plasm in tissue-culture in glass containers.

INVOLUCRAL Pertaining to an involucre.

INVOLUCRE One or more whorls or close spirals of small leaves or bracts standing close beneath a flower or an inflorescence.

INVOLUTE Describes a flattened organ, such as a leaf, that is rolled inwards or toward the uppermost side. *See also* Revolute.

IRREGULAR CHANNEL Refers to streams with an irregularly sinuous channel that displays irregular turns and bends without repetition of similar features.

IRREGULAR FLOWER **1** A zygomorphic flower. **2** An asymmetrical flower.

IRREGULAR UNEVEN-AGED STRUCTURE Stands that have three or more distinct age classes that do not occupy approximately equal areas. Distribution of diameters is unbalanced. *See also* Regular Uneven-Aged Structure.

IRREVERSIBLE IMPACT Used in the US to connote the results of an action or inaction that cannot be reversed within a reasonable period of time.

IRRIGATION The deliberate addition of water to a soil.

IRRUPTIVE SPECIES Any species that undergoes dramatic population fluctuations, usually in response to availability of food (e.g., snowy owls, snowshoe hares, ruffed grouse).

ISIDIUM A tiny, wartlike outgrowth of a lichen, having a cortex and containing algae. It functions as a vegetative propagule.

ISLAND Commonly, a piece of land surrounded by fresh or saltwater. In forestry, it has been proposed that an isolated patch of terrestrial habitat that is not connected to similar habitat types nearby is a form of island, but this is widely debated. *See also* Colonization; Forest Fragmentation; Habitat Island.

ISLAND BIOGEOGRAPHY THEORY The study and analysis of the distribution patterns of animals on true islands (i.e., land surrounded by water), which gave rise to the development of the Theory of Island Biogeography by MacArthur and Wilson in 1967. Their theory was based primarily on the following three observed patterns: (1) that larger islands usually have more species (*see* Species-Area Curve); (2) that smaller, remote islands will have fewer species (*see* SLOSS); and (3) that when islands are colonized by new species, these appear to replace existing species that become extinct (species turnover).

The central idea of the theory was that an equilibrium in the number of species on an island is achieved over time, because immigrations from the nearest continental landmass are balanced by local species extinctions. These ideas were used to explain why the fauna of some remote oceanic islands were depauperate. In the 1970s, island biogeography theory was embraced by nature-reserve designers and managers and applied to developing priorities and strategies for preserving continental islands or habitat fragments left over after the original landscape had been modified by human uses. There continues to be considerable debate about the applied aspects of the theory of island biogeography, mainly because there is insufficient empirical data to support what was originally proposed.

ISOBAR A line of equal or constant atmospheric pressure displayed on a synoptic chart.

ISOCHRONS **1** Time zones spaced around the globe at intervals of fifteen degrees longitude. **2** A concentric set of lines, each of which joins distances with equal travel times from some central reference point of concern.

ISOGONIC CHARTS Charts of the Earth showing points of equal magnetic declination from the north magnetic pole. The lines connecting such points are termed isogons. The point of zero declination (neither east nor west) is termed the agonic line. In North America, the agonic line is currently moving westward at about one minute per year.

ISOHYETAL LINE A line drawn on a map joining points that receive the same amount of precipitation.

ISOLATE **1** To separate a microorganism from its substrate and bring it into pure culture. **2** A single spore, or a culture made by direct isolation from an infected host or other natural substrate, and the subcultures derived from it. **3** The term used to indicate collections of a pathogen made at different times. **4** In conservation biology, a population that is isolated.

ISOLATION **1** The process of placing an organism in pure culture (i.e., on a laboratory medium without any other microorganisms present). **2** The separation of a pathogen from its host, followed by culture on a nutrient medium. **3** The absence of energy flows, or genetic crossing, among populations because of distance or geographic barriers, thus precluding colonization into or out of an island of habitat. Isolation of populations may lead to genetic differences among the population to form subspecies. Factors affecting isolation include climate, cover, predation, distance between islands of suitable habitat, and the species' life cycle needs. Isolation is considered to be the ultimate form of landscape fragmentation. *See also* Island Biogeography Theory; Subspecies.

ISOPLETH A line indicating points of the same numerical value in any one set of data (e.g., contours, mean annual rainfall, seasonal temperatures). The line is plotted on a map to indicate the geographic location of the data.

ISOSTACY The condition of equilibrium of the lithosphere above the asthenosphere. A gradual depression or elevation of the Earth's surface due to the addition or removal of ice sheets is termed glacio-isostacy.

ISOTHERM A charted line connecting points of equal temperature.

ISOTHERMAL LAYERS A layer through which temperature remains constant with elevation.

ISOTONIC Solutions having the same osmotic pressure. *See also* Osmosis.

ISOTROPIC A body or shape having some characteristic that shows uniformity in all directions.

ISOTYPE *See* Type.

ISOZYME/ISOENZYME An alternative enzyme form within an individual or population, each form being coded by different alleles at the same locus. *See also* Allozymes.

ITEROPARITY Production of offspring in distinct events, occurring two or more times throughout the lifespan of the individual. *See also* Polycarpic; Semelparity.

J

JACCARD INDEX(C_j) An index of community similarity that qualitatively measures beta diversity in pairs of sites. All species are counted equally, and abundances are not taken into account.

$$C_j = \frac{j}{(a + b - j)}$$

where

a = species in site A

b = species in site B

j = number of species common to both sites.

In this index, a value of 0 would indicate there is no similarity (no identical species) between the two communities. A value of 1.0 would indicate that the two communities have an identical species composition. *See also* Morisita-Horn Index; Sørenson Index; Sørenson Quantitative Index.

JACK **1** A device for suspending a loading-line lead block from a skyline. **2** A young salmon, usually a male, that matures precociously, generally after one year at sea.

JAMMER A lightweight, two-drum yarder usu-

ally on a truck with a spar and boom. It may be used for short-distance yarding and loading.
JAMMER LOGGING A cable logging system generally restricted to one skidding line and used for winching logs up to 300 feet from the cutting area to a collection point.
JETSAM Human-made materials that wash up along shores and beaches. *See also* Flotsam.
JETTISON *See* Abort.
JOINT In geology, a surface of actual or potential fracture or parting in a rock, without displacement. The surface is usually plane and often occurs with parallel joints to form part of a joint set.
JOINTED Having distinct nodes, or real or apparent points of articulation.
JOYSTICK A hydraulic control lever that can be operated in up to four directions, controlling a number of functions through one hydraulic valve.
JULACEOUS Shoots rendered smoothly cylindrical by closely and evenly imbricate leaves.
JUMP FIRE *See* Fire Behaviour; Spot Fire.
JUMP SPOT A selected landing area for smokejumpers or helijumpers.
JUMPSUIT An approved protection suit worn for smokejumping or helijumping operations.
JURISDICTION A geographical area for which a single agency or administrative unit of an agency has responsibility.
JUVENILE **1** A plant is considered juvenile when it does not flower, even if it has favourable environmental conditions. The apical meristems and associated tissues may change from juvenile to mature, while the rest of the plant may retain characteristics of juvenility. **2** An animal that has not yet reached sexual maturity. *See also* Juvenile Wood; Mature.
JUVENILE HORMONE An insect hormone that determines the life-stage that will follow a given moult. High levels of juvenile hormone maintain the juvenile stages, while low levels interact with the growth and moulting hormone ecdysone to allow the change to pupal or adult stage.
JUVENILE SPACING *See* Thinning (precommercial thinning).
JUVENILE WOOD An inner layer of xylem surrounding the pith, in which the cells are smaller and/or less structurally developed than those of the outer xylem. The period during which it is formed is termed the juvenile period, and it varies between individuals and with species and environmental conditions. Because juvenile wood has differences in cell structure and size, wood density, and growth-ring width, it is typically weaker than wood laid down in later life.

The term is misleading and widely misused because it implies wood characteristics associated with age. More rigorous terms are crown-formed wood and stem-formed wood. Young trees produce crown-formed wood because they have nothing but crown at an early age. Later, they develop crown and stem wood. However, ancient trees can produce juvenile wood in their crowns. Generally, crown-formed wood equates to juvenile wood, while stem-formed wood equates to mature wood. *See also* Compression; Reaction Wood.
JUVENOID A juvenile hormone analog. A synthetic or botanical chemical that mimics juvenile hormone action and can thus be used as an insecticide.

K

KAIROMONE An interspecific semiochemical that induces a response favourable to the perceiving species. *See also* Allelochemic; Allomone; Pheromone; Synomone.
KAME An irregular or conical hillock composed chiefly of sand and gravel, formed by deposition of meltwater-transported sediments in contact with (against, within, or upon) stagnant glacier ice; a type of glaciofluvial deposit. *See also* Drumlin (for illustration).
KAME-AND-KETTLE TOPOGRAPHY Hummocky topography with enclosed depressions, commonly resulting from ice stagnation, and underlain by ablation till and ice-contact glaciofluvial materials.
KAME DELTA A delta of sand and gravel constructed in contact with (against or on top of) glacier ice. It is commonly a conspicuous terracelike landform bounded by a steep ice-contact face or by hummocky collapsed ground – a type of glaciofluvial deposit.
KAME TERRACE A terrace of drift, chiefly sand and gravel, deposited by meltwater in a depression between a melting glacier and the adjacent valley side, and left as a terrace when the glacier melted. The terrace is commonly irregular or fragmentary, and shows topographic and stratigraphic evidence of collapse – a type of glaciofluvial deposit.
KARST Describes landforms and processes associated with dissolution of soluble rocks, such as limestone, marble, dolomite, or gypsum;

characterized by underground drainage, caves, and sinkholes.

KARST DEPRESSION A depression resulting from solution of bedrock and/or collapse of the land surface into underground cavities.

KARST PROCESSES Processes associated with the solution of carbonate bedrock and other soluble rock. It includes surface and underground weathering and collapse and subsidence.

KATABATIC WINDS Also known as cold air drainage, katabatic winds are a downhill air flow created when air passes over a slope with a much cooler temperature. The air mass cools as it flows over the slope, and the colder, denser air mass slides downhill under the influence of gravity. Usually occur later in the day as surface temperatures decrease. Katabatic winds can be very strong where extensive cold surfaces exist, such as mountains and icefields, and at the polar icecaps. *See also* Anabatic Winds.

KEEL **1** A central, longitudinal ridge on the underside of a leaf, bract, petiole, petal, or sepal that looks like the keel of a boat. **2** The two united lowermost petals of a papilionaceous flower. **3** In grasses, a ridge on the back of a lemma or on the back of a leaf blade, usually along the midrib. *See also* Grass (for illustration).

KEETCH-BRYAM DROUGHT INDEX A commonly used drought index developed specifically for fire management applications, with a numerical range from 0 (no moisture deficiency) to 800 (maximum drought). It is used mainly in the US. It is synonymous with cumulative severity index.

KERF The width of cut made by the sawblade.

KETTLE A closed depression or hollow in glacial drift that has resulted from the melting of a buried or partly buried mass of glacier ice. It is common in glaciofluvial deposits. The illustration shows the progression from an open kettle to a kettle bog habitat.

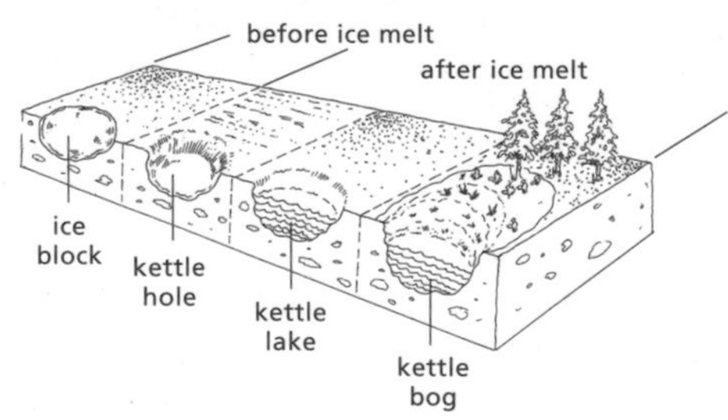

KETTLED OUTWASH Outwash plain with kettles.

KEY FACTOR ANALYSIS A statistical treatment of population data designed to identify factors most responsible for change in population size.

KEY-SPECIES MANAGEMENT **1** In range management, the most palatable and common plant species used by livestock. Typically, the plants on whose status livestock management decisions are based. **2** In wildlife management, the selection of a specific animal species for which habitat alterations are directed.

KEYSTONE SPECIES Species that are dominant in function and possibly (but not necessarily) in structure within any one ecosystem. They hold a crucial role in supporting the integrity of the entire ecosystem, and therefore affect the survival and abundance of many other species in the same ecosystem. *See also* Flagship Species.

KEY WATERSHED *See* Watershed.

KILN-DRIED DENSITY The density of wood that has been dried under the controlled conditions of a kiln, normally to a specified range of moisture content. *See also* Air-Dry Density; Equilibrium Moisture Content.

KILN-DRIED WOOD Wood that has been dried in a kiln to a specific equilibrium moisture content. *See also* Air-Dried Wood; Equilibrium Moisture Content.

KILOPASCAL (kPa) A unit of pressure measurement in the metric system that is equal to 0.145 pounds per square inch.

KINDLING POINT *See* Ignition Temperature.

KIP A unit of weight or force equivalent to 1,000 pounds.

KIT **1** A kitten. **2** A young beaver.

KLENDUSITY The failure of a susceptible host to become infected in the presence of a pathogen because it possesses characteristics that prevent or interfere with the activities of the vector of that pathogen.

KNICKPOINT **1** Any interruption or break in a slope. **2** A point of abrupt inflection in the longitudinal profile of a stream or of its valley.

KNOCK-DOWN **1** The immediate mortality of a target pest following the application of a pesticide. **2** The felling or removal of infected residuals (e.g., for dwarf mistletoe control).

KNOLL A small, low, rounded hill rising above adjacent landforms. It is also termed hillock.

KNOT **1** A unit of wind or ocean travel speed, equal to one nautical mile per hour, or 1.15 miles per hour. **2** The point in a piece of lumber where a branch once grew. Knots can be live or dead (i.e., the branch cambium was or was not still living when the tree was cut). Live knots are tight knots (they do not separate from the surrounding wood during manufacturing), while dead knots tend to be loose (they may separate after manufacture). Loose knots yield lower grades of lumber.

KRUMMHOLZ A German term meaning crooked wood, it refers to stunted, twisted, and scrubby trees that grow in the often harsh, exposed environment at the edge of the alpine zone just beyond the timberline in subalpine forests. *See also* Elfin Forest; Timberline; Tree Line.

K-SELECTION Describes species living in relatively predictable and uniform environments that have high levels of inter- and intraspecific competition. Such species respond to selection pressures by producing fewer but larger offspring with greater competitive abilities; these are called K-strategists. The selection pressures helping to maintain a population close to its carrying capacity (K) include large size, delayed reproduction, iteroparity, limited numbers of offspring, and a high amount of parental attention. *See also* r-Selection; Selection.

KUCHLER VEGETATIVE TYPES The potential natural vegetation of the conterminous United States as classified by Kuchler.

KURTOSIS A measure of the degree of flatness of a frequency distribution, when compared to the normal distribution.

L

LABEL In GIS mapping, alphanumeric data, textural data, or a symbol that describes a polygon, line, or point. It is sometimes called an attribute label, type code, or descriptor.

LABELLUM An orchid petal that differs from the others by having distinctive colour and structure.

LABEL POINT In GIS work, a point in a polygon used to position the label and to reference it to a polygon. *See also* Centroid.

LABIATE **1** Having lips, that is, two opposed structures (e.g., in plants, a calyx or corolla having the parts separated by form or position into opposed upper and lower groups). **2** Any member of the Labiatae (Mint) family.

LABILE A substance capable of adapting or undergoing change; unstable. A substance readily transformed by microorganisms, or one that is readily available to plants.

LACCOLITH Lens-shaped bodies of intrusive igneous rock that can cause an uplifting of the overlying rocks to create a distinct anticline. *See also* Batholith (for illustration); Dyke; Sill.

LACERATE Margins that are torn, irregularly cleft, or cut.

LACINIATE Cut into narrow, pointed lobes.

LACTIFEROUS Producing or containing latex.

LACUNA A cavity, hole, void, or gap.

LACUSTRINE Pertaining to lakes.

LACUSTRINE MATERIALS Sediments that have settled from suspension or underwater gravity flows in lakes; also includes littoral sediments (e.g., beach gravels) accumulated as a result of wave action. Lacustrine clays typically show great variation in organic matter and carbonate content and are poorly drained, but are usually productive soils.

LADDER FUELS Fuels that provide vertical continuity between surface fuels and crown fuels in a forest stand, thus contributing to the ease of torching and crowning (e.g., tall shrubs, small-sized trees, bark flakes, tree lichens). It is synonymous with bridge fuels. *See also* Ground Fuels.

LAG DEPOSIT Residual deposit of coarse material from which the fine fraction has been removed by wind or water; lag gravel.

LAGOON A shallow stretch of water partly or completely separated from a sea or lake by an offshore reef, barrier island, sandbank, or spit.

LAG PERIOD A period of slow growth or inaction in any system or organism, which includes: (1) the latent period following the introduction of bacteria into a culture medium; and (2) the time period occurring between a stimulus and the reaction to a stimulus. *See also* Incubation Period; Latent Period.

LAHAR A mudflow composed mainly of volcaniclastic materials on the flank of a volcano. The debris carried in the flow includes pyroclastic material, blocks from primary lava flows, and epiclastic material.

LAMBDA The finite rate of population change (population size in year 2 divided by the population size in year 1).

LAMBERT CONFORMAL CONIC MAP PROJECTION A conformal map projection on which all geographic meridians (longitude) are represented by straight lines that meet in a common point outside the limits of the map. The geographic parallels are represented by a series of arcs of circles having this common point for a centre. Meridians and parallels intersect at right angles, and angles on the earth are correctly represented on the projection. This type of projection may have one standard parallel along which the scale is held exact, or there may be two standard parallels, both maintaining exact scale. At any point on the map, the scale is the same in every direction. It changes along the meridians and is constant along each parallel. Where there are two standard parallels, the scale between those parallels is too small; beyond them, too large.

LAMELLA Plural lamellae. **1** A green ridge or plate on the midrib or blade of some moss leaves or on the undersurface of lichens. **2** The gills found under the pileus of a basidiomycete fungus. Lamellae radiate from the stalk to the outer edge of the pileus and bear spores. *See also* Fungus (for illustration).

LAMELLATE **1** Composed of many thin, flat sections or plates. **2** Having many cross-partitions, such as lamellate pith.

LAMINA Botanically, a blade, or expanded portion of an organ such as a leaf or petal.

LAMINAE, LAMINATIONS **1** A sedimentary sequence within which most individual beds (the laminations) are thinner than about one centimetre. **2** Decayed wood that readily separates along growth rings. It is characteristic of infection by the root rot *Phellinus weirii.*

LAMINAR FLOW Non-turbulent and non-mixing flow of water in straight paths parallel to the channel alignment.

LAMINATED ROOT ROT *See* Laminae.

LAMMAS SHOOTS An additional whorl of branches or a second flush of leader growth occurring late in the growing season. It is named from Lammas Day, 1 August.

LANATE A woolly covering of long, intertwined, curly hairs.

LANCEOLATE Lance-shaped; much longer than broad, tapering at the ends, widest at about a third of the way up from the base. *See also* Leaf Shape (for illustration).

LAND CAPABILITY The potential ability of the land to support renewable natural resources such as forestry, agriculture, wildlife, recreation, and water production. Although capability does not in the strictest sense depend on utility to humankind (i.e., the land may or may not be capable of supporting a resource regardless of whether humans use it or not), it is usually taken to mean capability relative to management plans imposed by humanity.

LAND CAPABILITY CLASSES Classes used in the Canada Land Inventory to rate the suitability of land for agriculture, forestry, outdoor recreation, ungulates, and waterfowl. For each category, seven capability classes were established to rate the suitability of land for that use. Class 1 has the highest capability or potential, Class 7 the lowest. The maps and information derived from the Canada Land Inventory work are most suited to broad-scale planning, and least suited to fine-scale or site-specific planning.

LANDFORM A segment of the three-dimensional surface of the Earth, consisting of soil and rocks with characteristic shapes produced by natural processes. A landscape unit (element) describing types of land surfaces or features. Landforms have distinctive shapes and positions in the larger landscape that reflect their origins and geological development. These physical attributes are used to classify landscapes.

LANDING The place to which logs are yarded and stored (decked) pending loading and transport to a processing facility. *See also* Deck.

LANDSAT The name of a specific series of satellites designed to obtain images of the Earth's surface and natural resources. A more recent French satellite system, yielding higher resolution images, is known as the SPOT satellite.

LANDSCAPE **1** An expanse of natural or human-made scenery, comprising landforms, land cover, habitats, and natural and human-made features that, taken together, form a composite. The characteristic features of any one landscape form the basis for common classification schemes and can evoke emotional or psychological stimuli through description alone (e.g., mountainous landscapes, grasslands, tundra, agricultural). Some consider the extent of the landscape to be limited to what can be seen in one view by the naked human eye. Others see landscape as ranging in scale from a few hectares to large tracts of land many square kilometres in extent. **2** A mosaic of habitat types occupying a spatial scale intermediate between an organism's normal home-range size and its regional distribution.

LANDSCAPE CHANGE Any alteration in the structure and function of the ecological mosaic of a landscape through time. Changes may be active or passive. Active changes include: volcanoes producing lava flows and pyroclastic debris;

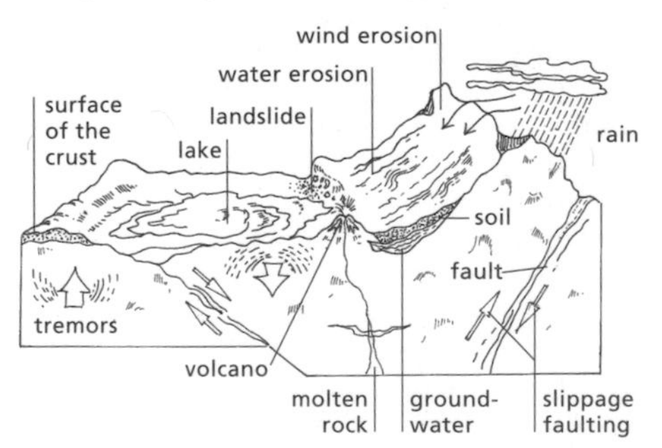

earthquakes causing tsunamis and landslides. Passive changes include: landforms shaped over time by climate (temperature and moisture regimes), erosional processes (wind and water), and mass wasting. The illustration shows some of the factors responsible for landscape change. *See also* Erosion; Hillslope.

LANDSCAPE COMPLEMENTATION Changes in population caused by the relative distributions of habitat patches containing non-substitutable resources in a landscape. For example, increased populations in a portion of a landscape where foraging patches and roosting patches are adjacent, compared with parts of the landscape where these patches are isolated. *See also* Landscape Supplementation.

LANDSCAPE COMPOSITION The spatial arrangement, composition, and relative amounts of the elements within a landscape. **Canopied** means covered or bridged by the uppermost spreading branchy layer of a forest. **Enclosed** means enveloped or surrounded, bounded or encompassed. **Ephemeral** means anything lasting for a brief time. **Feature** means a distinct or outstanding feature or quality that is enduring in the landscape. **Focal** means a feature that provides a focal point in the landscape. **Panoramic** means a continuous series of landscape elements that are varied but blend together to provide a constantly changing scene that can only be absorbed as a wider view (i.e., more than can be absorbed by the eye looking in just one direction).

LANDSCAPE DIVERSITY *See* Diversity.

LANDSCAPE ECOLOGY **1** The study of the development and dynamics of landscape heterogeneity using and applying concepts from the disciplines of ecology, wildlife biology, cultural anthropology, landscape planning, and economics. **2** Assessment and analysis of the spatial and temporal patterns of landscape development; the processes leading to maintenance of the landscape mosaic; and the interactions, fluxes, and influences of these processes on biotic and abiotic components.

LANDSCAPE ELEMENTS In visual assessment work, landscapes can be divided into four major elements. (1) **Form** is the perceived mass or shape of an object that appears unified, and which provides a consciousness of its distinction and relation of a whole to the component parts. (2) **Line** is the real or imagined path, border, boundary, or intersection of two planes, such as a silhouette, that the eye follows when perceiving abrupt differences in form, colour or texture. For example, ridges, skylines, structures, vegetation edges, or individual trees. (3) **Colour** is a visual perception that enables the eye to differentiate otherwise identical objects based on the wavelengths of reflected light. Colour is differentiated by hue (e.g., red, or blue), value (light or dark), chroma (purity of the colour), saturation (the measure of actual colour content), and tint (the degree of brilliance it would have in its spectral hue). (4) **Texture** is the visual 'feel' of a landscape (e.g., hard, smooth, rough, soft, amorphous, etc.).

LANDSCAPE FEATURES/ATTRIBUTES The basic land and water forms, vegetation types, and structures that define a characteristic landscape. The features can be natural or human-caused. At a landscape level of assessment, these features are identifiable on an aerial photograph.

LANDSCAPE FUNCTION The interactions among the spatial elements, that is, the flow of energy, materials, and organisms among the component ecosystems.

LANDSCAPE INDEXES Indexes of landscape structure (pattern), including richness, evenness, patchiness, diversity, dominance, contagion, edges, fractal dimension, nearest neighbour probability, and the size and distribution of patches.

LANDSCAPE PHYSIOGNOMY The features associated with the physical layout of elements within a landscape.

LANDSCAPE STRUCTURE **1** The spatial relationships between distinctive ecosystems, that is, the distribution of energy, materials, and species in relation to their sizes, shapes, numbers, kinds, and configurations of components. **2** The composition and extent of different habitat types (composition) and their spatial arrangement (physiognomy) in a landscape.

LANDSCAPE SUPPLEMENTATION Changes in populations caused by the distribution of habitat patches containing substitutable resources in a landscape. For example, increased population in a small patch found in a portion of the landscape where residents can easily forage in other nearby and similar patches. *See also* Landscape Complementation.

LANDSLIDE A general term for the downslope movement of large masses of earth material and the resulting landforms.

LANDSLIDE HEADSCARP The relatively steep slope, commonly arcuate in plan, that forms the upper part of a landslide scar.

LANDSLIDE HEADWALL *See* Landslide Headscarp.

LANDSLIDE SCAR The part of a slope exposed or visibly modified by detachment and downslope movement of a landslide. It usually lies upslope from the displaced landslide material. It is commonly a steep, concave slope.

LAND SURVEY *See* Cadastral Survey.

LAND-USE PLANNING The iterative process of inventorying and assessing the status, potential, and limitations of a particular geographic area (the landbase) and its resources, with a view to planning and managing these resources to satisfy human needs now and in the future. Traditional land-use planning has emphasized human needs alone, but contemporary resource management plans now include the needs of ecosystem functions and processes, as well as the needs of other species (plant or animal). The distribution of effects through time and space are important to consider since they determine whether or not proposed plans will be sustainable.

LANOSE Woolly.

LANUGINOSE/LANUGINOUS Having a woolly, cottony, or downy surface with the hairs shorter than a lanate surface.

LANULOSE Having a covering of very short, matted hairs.

LANYARD A length of rope or cable used to attach a cargo net or sling load to a helicopter cargo hook.

LAPILLI Volcanic ejecta; typically, small broken fragments or cinders of two to sixty-four millimetres in diameter.

LAPSE RATE The decrease of an atmospheric variable, usually temperature unless otherwise specified, with height. *See also* Dry Adiabatic Lapse Rate; Environmental Lapse Rate.

LARGE FIRE **1** *See* Fire Size Class. **2** A fire burning with such size and intensity that fire behaviour is determined by the interaction between its own convection column and weather conditions above the surface.

LARGE ORGANIC DEBRIS Also called large woody debris. Entire trees, or large pieces of trees, found on the forest floor or within stream channels. Large organic debris in stream channels typically have a diameter greater than ten centimetres and longer than one metre, and provide channel stability and/or create fish habitat diversity. Categories of LOD within stream channels include the following. **Affixed logs** are single logs or groups of logs that are firmly embedded, lodged, or rooted in a stream channel. **Deadheads** are logs that are not embedded, lodged, or rooted in the stream channel, but are submerged and close to the surface. **Digger logs** are logs anchored to the stream banks and/or channel bottom in such a way that a scour pool is formed. **Free logs** are logs or groups of logs that are not embedded, lodged, or rooted in the stream channel. **Rootwad** is the root mass of the tree. **Snag** is a standing dead tree or a fallen submerged tree in larger streams, where the tree top is still exposed. **Sweeper logs** are fallen trees whose bole or branches form an obstruction to floating objects.

Large organic debris in a stream channel can accumulate in several ways, including: (1) **clumps**, or accumulations of debris at irregularly spaced intervals along the channel margin that do not form major impediments to water flow; (2) **jams**, or large accumulations of debris partially or completely blocking the stream channel, creating a major impediment to water flow; and (3) **scattered**, or single pieces of debris at irregularly spaced intervals along the channel.

LARGE PROTECTED RESERVE Within the concept of wholistic forest use, a large watershed or drainage basin (5,000 hectares or more) protected from human use or modification in order to maintain connectivity in the landscape and the full range of biological diversity at all scales. *See also* Wholistic Forest Use.

LARGE SCALE *See* Coarse Scale.

LARGE WOODY MATERIAL In the US, logs on the forest floor in pieces at least sixty centimetres (twenty-four inches) in diameter at the large end. *See also* Coarse Woody Debris.

LARVA Plural larvae. **1** In zoology, the immature form of animals that go though metamorphosis. **2** In entomology, any insect species that undergoes complete metamorphosis. The larva emerges from the egg and is fundamentally different in form from the egg and the subsequent pupal and adult forms. *See also* Caterpillar; Grub; Instar; Maggot.

LATE DROP Fire retardant landing after (beyond) the designated target. *See also* Early Drop.

LATE GLACIAL European term for the final phase of the Pleistocene Era, about 13,000 to 10,200 BP. The period was characterized by a decisive amelioration of the climate and the retreat of ice sheets. *See also* Appendix 2: Geological Time Scales

LATENT BUD A bud that is more than one year old, which has developed enough to be located just below the surface of the bark.

LATENT INFECTION An established infection

that does not show its presence, but which, although inactive, remains viable.

LATENT PERIOD A period of slow growth. *See also* Incubation Period; Lag Period.

LATERAL MORAINE A ridge built up along the side of a valley glacier composed mainly of rock fragments that have been plucked from the valley walls by glacial abrasion or mass wasting.

LATERAL OVERLAP *See* Overlap.

LATERAL SCOUR *See* Pool.

LATERAL SPREAD A type of gravitational (mass movement) process in which movement in dominantly lateral extension accompanied by shear or tensile fractures.

LATERITE A red, or red and yellow residual clay subsoil, common in tropical and subtropical regions, that is hard or capable of hardening on exposure. The soil is rich in hydrated aluminum and iron oxides, and is often seen as an extreme form of weathering. Lateritic materials find widespread use in brick manufacture. *See also* Pedalfer; Pedocal.

LATE SERAL STAGE FOREST A late stage in forest development. It may be the stage before, or the final, climax stage. *See also* Seral Stages.

LATE WOOD The denser, smaller-celled portion of an annual growth ring formed during the latter part of the growing season. *See also* Early Wood.

LATEX A colourless or coloured (typically white or yellow) fluid found in plants, such as milkweeds (*Asclepias* spp).

LATITUDE **1** In general, a linear or angular distance measured north or south of the equator on a sphere or spheroid. **2** In plane surveying, the perpendicular distance in a horizontal plane of a point from an east-west axis of reference. *See also* Longitude; UTM.

LAVA TUBE A hollow space beneath the surface of a solidified lava flow formed when slower-cooling subsurface lava withdraws from the surface crust.

LAW OF DISPERSION An ecological theory, stating that the potential density of wildlife species with small home ranges that require two or more types of habitat is roughly proportional to the sum of the peripheries of those types.

LAW OF INTERSPERSION The number of resident wildlife species that require two or more types of habitat. It depends on the degree of interspersion of numerous blocks of such habitat types.

LAW OF TOLERANCE Any factor that, for any particular species, exceeds the limits of tolerance and becomes a limiting factor for that species.

LAX In botanical descriptions, loose, widely spaced. The opposite of congested.

LAY **1** The position on the ground where a tree will land once cut down. **2** The manner in which the individual strands of wire are arranged in a wire rope.

LAYER **1** In describing vegetation, the life-form (tree, shrub, herb) that defines the characteristic physiognomy of the vegetation being considered at any geographic or classification scale. **2** In geology, the various strata of material laid down over time.

LAYERING A form of vegetative reproduction or propagation, where a branch, still attached to the parent tree, is buried in the organic layer of the soil, and thus induced to develop roots and become independent of the parent tree.

LC50 The median 'lethal concentration.' A statistic indicating the degree of toxicity of a pesticide (or any substance) when dissolved in a solvent (e.g., water), or as a vapour in air. It is expressed as concentration in parts per million of toxicant in air or solvent sufficient to kill 50 per cent of the animals in a test population exposed for a standard period, usually ninety-six hours. It is used to express toxicity toward non-target organisms as well as toward target pests. The lower the LC50, the more toxic the material.

LD50 The median 'lethal dose.' A statistic indicating the degree of toxicity of a pesticide or other substance. It is expressed as milligrams per kilogram of body weight sufficient to kill 50 per cent of the animals in a test population. It is used to express toxicity toward non-target animals as well as toward target pests. An acute LD50 is determined on the basis of single oral doses of the material in question, whereas a chronic LD50 is determined by administering daily doses over a lengthy period of time. The lower the LD50, the more toxic is the substance.

LEACHATE The solution of a material leached from a solid, such as dissolved organic matter leached from fallen leaves, sawdust, or woodchips; or acid mine drainage or other contaminants leached from tailings or other mining activity (e.g., heap leaching). Leachates can be very toxic, and those created by human activity should be carefully contained to avoid stream or groundwater contamination.

LEACHING The mobilization and transportation of soil materials in solution. *See also* Eluviation; Illuvation.

LEAD (Pronounced as leed) **1** A block or series of blocks or rollers attached to a stationary object to guide the cable that drags the load. *See also* Fairlead. **2** The position of the logs relative to the yarding direction.

LEADER The terminal, or the dominant current year's topmost shoot on the main stem, characteristic of the growth of certain plants and trees, especially gymnosperms.

LEAD IN A fire-bombing procedure where a birddog aircraft flies the target run in front of an airtanker on its final run. *See also* Dummy Run; Final Run.

LEAF An appendage attached to the stem of plants by a petiole. The leaf surface is the principle area of photosynthesis. There are numerous types and shapes of leaf, some of which are shown in the illustration.

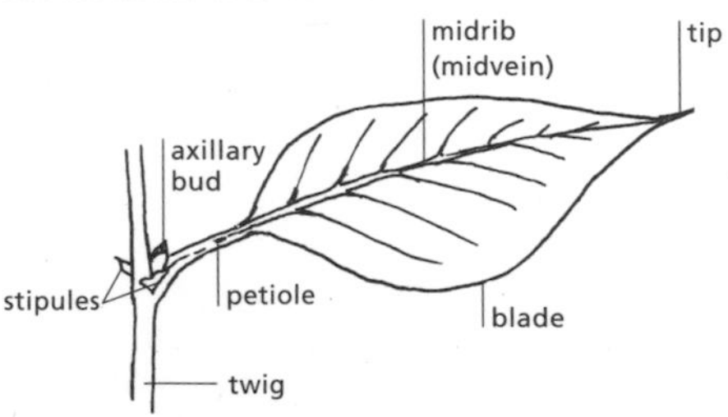

LEAF-AREA INDEX A quantitative assessment of the photosynthetic potential in a plant community. It is based on the ratio of leaf surface area (one side) to ground surface area. Values of this index vary from three to twelve in closed stands, but are ordinarily about five. It provides a measure of the degree of canopy closure and the extent to which lower canopy foliage will be shaded. *See also* Canopy Closure.

LEAF CLASSES A classification system developed by Raunkiaer that assigns plant leaves to six different categories according to leaf size, consisting of: **Leptophylls**, leaves less than 25 square millimetres; **Nanophylls**, leaves 26-225 square millimetres; **Microphylls,** leaves 226-2,025 square millimetres; **Mesophylls**, leaves 2,026-18,225 square millimetres; **Macrophylls**, leaves 18,226-164,025 square millimetres; and **Megaphylls**, leaves greater than 164,025 square millimetres.

LEAFLET Part of a compound leaf.

LEAF MARGIN The appearance of the edge or margin of a leaf is often characteristic for the species, but there may be very wide morphological variation. Basic leaf margin shapes are defined by the extent of incision and division in the leaf margin. When fully expanded, a leaf may fold or roll along the margins (e.g., the leaves of *Ledum groenlandicum* (Labrador tea) are revolute [rolling into the underside of the leaf]). Other types are involute, incurved, and recurved. The most extreme case is terete, where the leaf is rolled tightly to the midrib and the underside is unexposed. Leaf margin types include ciliate, crenate, crenulate, dentate, denticulate, doubly serrate, entire, lobed, lyrate, pinnatifid, revolute, runcinate, serrate, serrulate, sinuate, and undulate. Complex leaf margins might include a combination of types, such as crenate-serrate. Refer to illustration and each term for more detail. *See also* Leaf Shape; Leaf Surface Features.

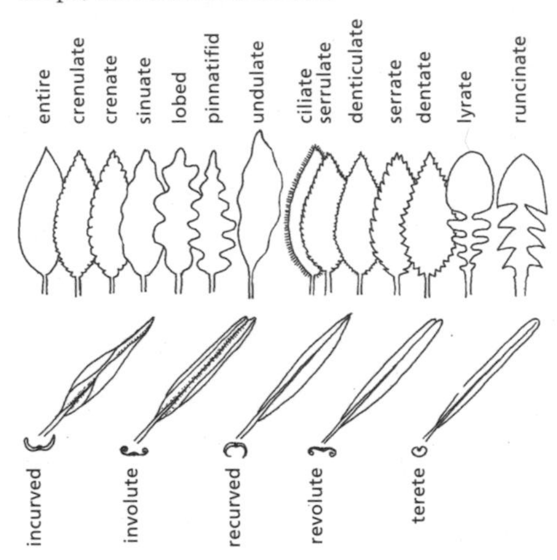

LEAF MINER An insect that lives and feeds as a larva within the inner tissues of leaves or needles. *See also* Leaf Roller.

LEAF ROLLER An insect that rolls the leaf of a plant and lives inside the roll. It is characteristic of moth larvae in the family Tortricidae.

LEAF SCORCH Necrosis, usually at leaf tips or margins, often due to nutrient imbalance or phytotoxicity of a pesticide or other chemical. *See also* Sunscald.

LEAF SHAPE The overall shape of a leaf is often characteristic of the species, although there may be very wide morphological variation. Basic leaf shapes include acicular, deltoid, elliptical, filiform, flabellate, lanceolate, linear, oblanceolate, oblong, obovate, orbicular, oval, ovate, reniform, rhomboidal, scale, spathulate, and subulate. In addition to the overall shape, the top (apex) and bottom (base) of the leaf also have characteristic shapes. Apices include acuminate, acute, aristate, cuspidate, emarginate, mucronate, obtuse, and retuse. Leaf base shapes include attenuate, auriculate, connate-perfoliate, cordate, cuneate, hastate, peltate, perfoliate, oblique, obtuse, rounded, sagittate, and truncate. Refer to illustration and each term for more detail. *See also* Conifer Leaves; Leaf Margin; Leaf Surface Features.

LEAF SPOT A self-limiting, often circular, necrotic lesion on a leaf.

LEAF SURFACE FEATURES Most leaf surfaces (and other plant organs) have distinctive surface features. **Primary relief** is created by the veins or the epidermal cell walls. **Secondary**

leaf shapes

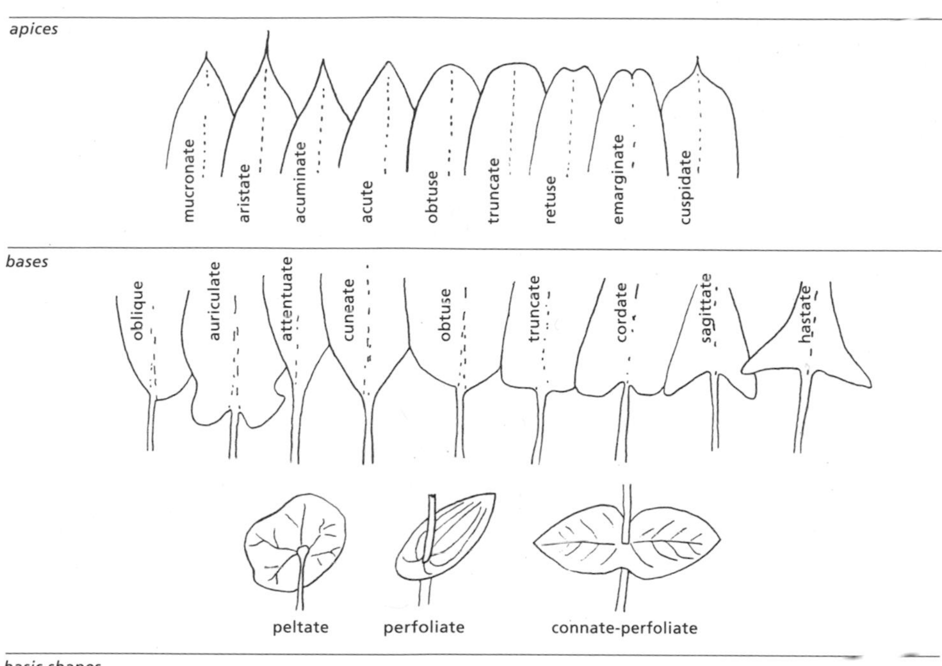

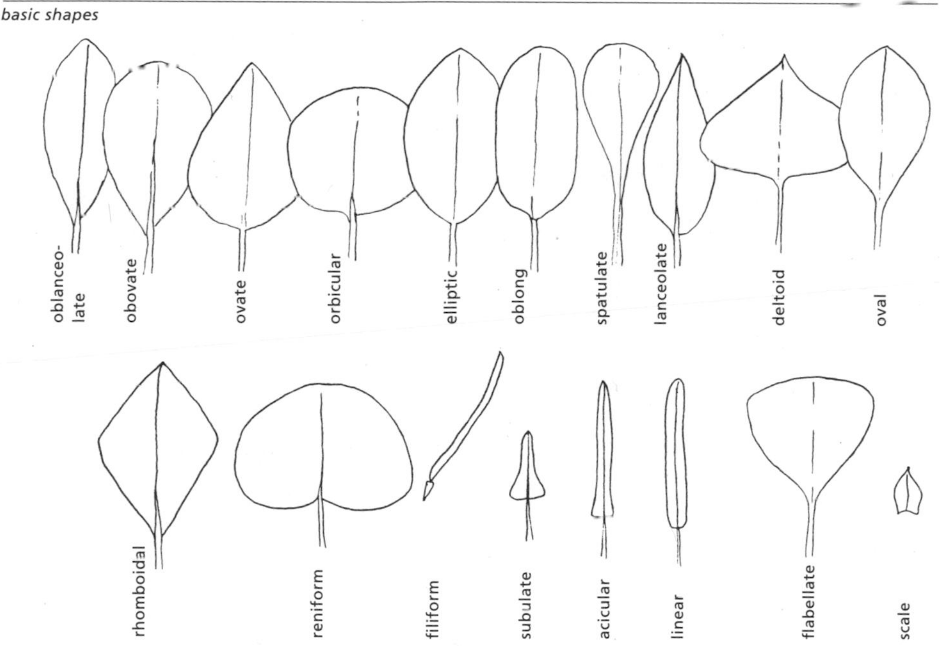

relief includes the projections, striations, and ridges and reflects the surfaces of the epidermis or the cuticle. **Tertiary relief** may be added on top of the cuticle by epicuticular wax. *See also* Glaucous.

Many leaves have surface hairs in varying configurations, including glabrate, glandular, lepidote, puberulent, pubescent, scabrous, stellate, tomentose, and villous. Leaves without hairs have a glabrous surface.

Leaves may also be coriaceous (leathery and thick) or membranous (thin and flexible). Refer to each term for more detail. *See also* Leaf Margin; Leaf Shape.

LEAN The degree and direction that a tree leans from the perpendicular.

LEAVE STRIPS **1** Typically, narrow bands of forest trees that are left along streams and rivers to buffer aquatic habitats from upslope forest management activities. **2** Narrow bands of trees retained along highways to provide a buffer separating the visual effects of forest management activities from highway travellers. **3** Areas of standing timber retained among larger areas of logging activity to satisfy management objectives, such as provision of a seed source, wildlife habitat, or landscape management constraints. *See also* Buffer Zone.

LEAVE TREE A tree planned and marked for retention when other trees are cut. Leave trees are selected to fulfil a variety of management objectives, including provision of seed sources, wildlife habitat, and green-tree retention. *See also* Green-Tree Retention.

LECANORINE An apothecium having a thalline margin, in which both algae and fungi are present.

LECIDEINE An apothecium with a proper margin, in which no algal cells are present. *See also* Proper Margin.

LECTOTYPE *See* Type.

LEDGE A narrow shelf or projection of rock, longer than wide, formed on a rock wall or cliff face by differential erosion processes.

LEE The side of an object that is sheltered from the wind; the downwind side.

LEGEND In mapping, a description, explanation, table of symbols, and other information printed on a map or chart to provide a better understanding and interpretation of it. The title of a map or chart used to be considered part of the legend, but this usage is now considered to be obsolete.

LEGITIMATE SMOKE *See* Smoke.

LEGUME A dry, several-seeded fruit dehiscing along both margins (the midrib and the suture). This fruit only occurs in the pea (Leguminosae) family, whose members are termed leguminous. *See also* Fruit (for illustration).

LEK A location where communal courtship displays take place among birds.

LEMMA In the Gramineae (grasses), the flowering glume – the lower of the two bracts directly enclosing the flower. *See also* Grass (for illustration).

LENTIC Relating to slow-moving water, such as in lakes and bogs. Lentic systems show pronounced vertical gradients in light, temperature, and dissolved gases. In temperate climates, thermal stratification occurs and varies by season, the main layers include the following. **Epilimnion** is a layer of warmer water circulating at the top of the water body in the summer months. **Thermocline** is the layer of water that develops in the summer months, separating the upper and lower layers. Temperature in the thermocline decreases rapidly, and water density increases. **Hypolimnion** is a lower layer of colder, denser water at the bottom of the lake, with less oxygen available in the summer months.

In the fall and winter months, the thermal stratification is less pronounced and a period of vernal overturn takes place as the water density changes in response to temperature changes. This change in density causes circulation of nutrients and oxygen concentrations. *See also* Lotic.

LENTICEL A slightly raised area on the bark of a root or stem, or on the suberous tissue of fruit created by a small pore arising on the epidermis. It is used for gas exchange. *See also* Stoma.

LENTICULAR Lens-shaped; circular, flattened with both sides convex.

LEOPOLD MATRIX *See* Matrix.

LEPIDOPTERAN An insect order (Lepidoptera) containing moths and butterflies. Lepidopterans are characterized by undergoing complete metamorphosis. The adults have four membranous wings largely covered with fine, often highly pigmented scales, a long, coiled proboscis, and slender antennae. Butterflies are typically diurnal, while moths are nocturnal. They encompass a wide range of beneficial (e.g., silk moth) and harmful (e.g., gypsy moth) insects.

LEPIDOTE Covered in small, scurfy scales or hairs.

LESION A localized area of diseased or dead

tissue. A well-defined necrotic area. *See also* Necrosis.

LEVEE (NATURAL) A naturally formed elongate ridge or embankment of fluvial sediments built up alongside a stream channel.

LEVERET A young hare (*Lepus* spp.).

LIANA A general term for woody vines or climbing plants, often tropical, that work their way up tree trunks in order to get better access to the prevailing sunlight.

LIBERATION A release treatment made in a stand not past the sapling stage in order to free the favoured trees from competition with older, overtopping trees.

LICHENS Plants found in the phylum Mycophycophyta in the kingdom Fungi. Lichens are symbiotic organisms created by the association of a fungus (usually an Ascomycete) with a green algae or a cyanobacterium. Lichens live in a very wide range of habitats, from desert to polar plains and the tropics, and can survive in harsh conditions that are too exposed for other plants.

Lichens are very sensitive to air pollution and serve an important role as an indicator species. They are classified on the basis of the growth habit of the thallus: **crustose** being a compact, low crust; **foliose** being a leafy structure; and **fruticose** being a bushy mass. Lichens reproduce by spores.

LIFE CYCLE **1** The series of changes in form (stages) through which an organism develops from spore or fertilized ovum all the way through to the spore or fertilized ovum of the next generation. **2** The length of time taken by a given organism to go through this set of changes.

LIFE-FORM A term coined by Raunkiaer in 1934. A plant classification system based on the position of perennating buds on the plant. The scheme includes the following classifications (see illustration). **Therophyte** are annuals producing viable seeds. **Cryptophytes** are plants with perennating buds beneath the soil or water surface. **Hemicryptophytes** are mostly herbaceous grasses and forbs that bear perennating buds on stolons or runners at the ground surface. **Chamaephytes** are woody or semi-woody perennials that bear their perennating buds close to the ground (but less than twenty-five centimetres from the surface) near a microclimate that offers better protection and growing conditions. **Phanerophytes** are mostly woody perennials (trees and shrubs) that bear their perennating buds in the air at

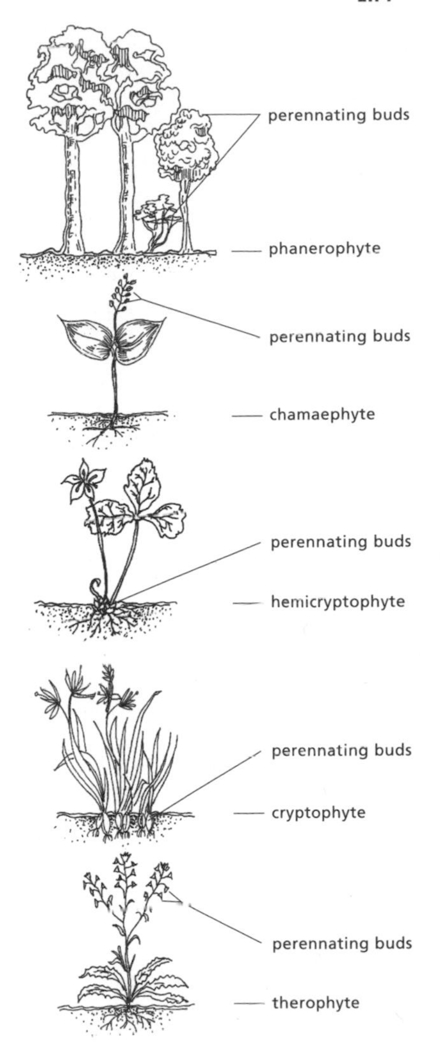

least twenty-five centimetres above the ground and are not protected by soil or the ground surface during winter.

LIFE HISTORY A system of interrelated adaptive traits forming a set of reproductive tactics.

LIFE TABLE The tabulation of mortality and survivorship data for age groups or life stages in a population. The life table displays the changing density of the population through time at any one place. When coupled with information about fecundity, the life table can be used to predict the size of a succeeding generation.

LIFT A stage in the pruning regime needed to create a knot-free sawlog. Typically, three separate lifts are used to obtain a knot-free cylindrical core of wood.

LIGHT BURN A degree of burn that leaves the soil covered with partially charred organic material. Heavy fuels are not deeply charred. *See also* Fire Severity; Moderate Burn; Severe Burn.

LIGHT FUELS *See* Fine Fuels.

LIGHT HELICOPTER A helicopter with a maximum certified gross weight for takeoff and landing of 6,000 pounds or less. *See also* Heavy Helicopter; Medium Helicopter.

LIGHTNING Atmospheric electrical discharges between clouds or from clouds to earth, which allow the electrical charge leaked into the atmosphere to return to earth.

LIGHTNING ACTIVITY LEVEL (LAL) In the US National Fire Danger Rating System, a number on a scale of 1 to 6 that reflects frequency and character of cloud-to-ground lightning (forecasted or observed). The scale is exponential, based on powers of two (i.e., LAL 3 indicates twice the lightning activity of LAL 2). *See also* Lightning Fire Occurrence Index; Lightning Risk.

LIGHTNING FIRE *See* Fire Cause Class.

LIGHTNING FIRE OCCURRENCE INDEX In the US National Fire Danger Rating System, a numerical rating of the potential occurrence of lightning-caused fires. *See also* Lightning Activity Level; Lightning Risk.

LIGHTNING LOCATOR SYSTEM A network of electronic field sensors linked to a central computer to detect, triangulate, plot the location, and record cloud-to-ground lightning flashes in real time over a large predetermined area. In the US, the system is termed an Automatic Lightning Detection System (ALDS).

LIGHTNING RISK (LR) In the US National Fire Danger Rating System, a number related to the expected number of cloud-to-ground lightning strikes to which a protection unit is expected to be exposed during the rating period. The LR value used in the occurrence index includes an adjustment for lightning activity experienced during the previous day to account for possible holdover fires. *See also* Human-Caused Risk; Lightning Activity Level; Lightning Fire Occurrence Index.

LIGHTNING RISK SCALING FACTOR In the US National Fire Danger Rating System, a factor derived from local thunderstorm and lightning-caused fire records that adjusts predictions of the basic lightning fire occurrence model to local experience, accounting for factors not addressed directly by the model (e.g., susceptibility of local fuels to ignition by lightning, fuel continuity, topography, regional characteristics of thunderstorms). *See also* Human-Caused Risk Scaling Factor; Lightning Risk.

LIGHTNING STROKE COUNTER An electronic sensor used to record the number of lightning strokes within a predetermined range over a specified period of time.

LIGHT WIND A wind speed of less than seven miles per hour (six knots) measured at twenty feet above ground. At eye level, light winds are less than three miles per hour (three knots).

LIGNEOUS Woody, as in woody plants containing lignin.

LIGNICOLOUS Growing on decorticated wood, not on living bark.

LIGNIN The non-carbohydrate (non-cellulose) fraction of wood, lignin acts as a binding material in the intercellular layer of plant tissues. It is a complex polymer, and gives woody tissues structural rigidity. Chemically intractable and insoluble, it amounts to 15 to 35 per cent by weight of the cell wall material, and is used mainly as a fuel in the pulping process. *See also* Cellulose.

LIGNITUBER A peglike protrusion, made of lignin or similar materials, covering the host cell wall that is induced by a penetrating fungal hyphae. *See also* Lignotuber.

LIGNOTUBER A woody swelling just above or below the ground, containing adventitious shoots with the potential to develop if the top of the plant is cut or otherwise damaged. *See also* Lignituber.

LIGULATE Strap-shaped, more narrowly so than in lorate. *See also* Lorate.

LIGULE **1** A strap-shaped organ or body, especially a strap-shaped corolla, such as the limb of the ray florets of plants in the Compositae family. **2** A projection from the top of the sheath in grasses, palms, and certain other plants. *See also* Grass (for illustration).

LIKERT SCALES *See* Measurement.

LIMB **1** In animals, an articulated projection used for locomotion (e.g., leg, arm, or wing). **2** In plants, the expanded flat part of an organ, such as a petal, or the expanding part of a gamopetalous corolla. **3** A branch of a tree.

LIMESTONE A sedimentary rock consisting mainly (greater than 50 per cent) of calcium carbonate, typically as calcite. Limestone is formed by a combination of organic and inorganic processes and includes chemical and clastic (soluble and insoluble) constituents. Many forms of limestone contain fossils.

LIMESTONE PAVEMENT A more or less horizontal exposure of limestone, usually coinciding with a bedding plane and consisting of irregular blocks separated by deep clefts formed by the widening of joints by solution.

LIMITED ACTION FIRE A fire that is receiving little or no suppression action, especially beyond initial attack, because of resource management priorities, fire load, or other agency constraints. A fire on which any action taken is less than the agency's normal standard for full suppression. It may involve one or more of the following conditions: (1) a decision to let the fire burn freely; (2) reconnaissance and mapping only; (3) resource staging to await more favourable control conditions; (4) site-specific action to protect a local value; and (5) mop-up of fire perimeter once weather conditions facilitate easy control.

LIMITED ACTION ZONE Any predetermined area within an agency's jurisdiction where fires will be allowed to burn without full suppression effort to control them. These fires may receive initial attack in some cases, but follow-up after escape is always limited. Such a zone is generally established formally to recognize the low values-at-risk or other agency constraints.

LIMITED-AREA FELLER-BUNCHER *See* Harvesting Machine Classification.

LIMITED CONTAINMENT The halting of fire spread at the head or that portion of the flanks of a prescribed fire that is threatening to exceed prescription criteria, and ensuring that this spread rate will not be encountered again. It does not include mop-up.

LIMITED ENTRY HUNT A means of controlling the numbers of hunters allowed to hunt any one species, or the duration in which they are allowed to hunt. Hunting authorization is typically allocated by means of a lottery or similar random selection.

LIMITING FACTOR Any environmental factor or process (physical, chemical, or biological) whose presence, absence, or abundance is the main factor restricting the distribution, numbers, or conditions of an organism. It is also termed the law of the minimum.

LIMITS OF ACCEPTABLE CHANGE (LAC) A planning framework that establishes explicit measures of the acceptable and appropriate resource and social conditions in recreation settings, as well as the appropriate management strategies for maintaining and/or achieving those conditions.

LIMNIC MATERIAL A component common in organic soils made up of inorganic or organic compounds deposited in water by precipitation, or through the actions of aquatic organisms, or derived from underwater and floating aquatic plants and aquatic animals (e.g., marl, diatomaceous earth, and sedimentary peat).

LINCOLN INDEX An animal population estimation technique requiring: (1) the capturing of individuals within a study area over a standard period of time, such as one hour; (2) the marking of captured individuals; (3) their release into the study area; and (4) recapturing individuals in the study area after a standard period of time, such as one day. In Step 4, both marked and unmarked individuals are captured and recaptured. The population may then be estimated by calculating the Lincoln Index formula: population number = (number marked on day 1 × number captured on day 2) ÷ number of marked animals captured on day 2.

LINEAR Long, narrow, with the sides almost parallel. *See also* Leaf Shape (for illustration).

LINEAR PROGRAMMING A mathematical method, deterministic model, or class of programming technique used to analyze and determine allocation between competing demands when both the objective (e.g., profit or cost) and the restrictions on its attainment are expressed as a system of linear equalities or inequalities. Linear programming is used to determine an optimal use of resources to achieve predefined goals when the limitations on available resources can be expressed by simultaneous linear equations.

LINEAR RELATIONSHIP The relationship between a dependent variable and one or more independent variables that can be described by a straight line. *See also* Multiple Regression.

LINEATE A surface bearing, or marked with thin, parallel lines. *See also* Striate.

LINE CUTTER A fire crew member in the progressive method of line construction who cuts and clears away brush, small saplings, vines, and other obstructions in the path of the fire line. This person is usually equipped with an axe or a brush hook.

LINE HOLDING Ensuring that the established fire line has completely stopped fire progress.

LINE IGNITION Setting a fire (e.g., backing fire) as opposed to individual spots.

LINE PLOT CRUISE The collection of field data from sample units typically spaced at regular intervals along straight lines of travel. *See also* Transect.

LINE TRANSECT *See* Transect.

LINGULATE Tongue-shaped.

LINKAGE A physical, biological, cultural, psychological, or policy connection or influence between two or more objects, processes, or policies. It is often used in the tracing of effects (i.e., which object has caused an effect in another object, where was the linkage between the two, and how did it function?).

LINK LABEL A unique polygon label that links graphic features to their associated attribute database.

LION'S TAIL The result of infection by Elytroderma disease, where a severe infection results in so much needle casting that only the current needles remain on the branchlets, thus creating a tufted, 'tail-like' appearance.

LIQUID CONCENTRATE Liquid phosphate fertilizers used as fire retardants, usually diluted three to five times prior to application. *See also* Slurry.

LIRELLA A lichen fruiting body having an elongated disc.

LITHIC CONTACT Any boundary between overlying soil and underlying material that is continuous and has a hardness greater than three on the Moh scale. The underlying material is usually too hard to dig through with a spade.

LITHIFICATION To turn into rock (e.g., the conversion of unconsolidated sediments into solid, coherent rock by processes such as cementation, compaction, desiccation, crystallization, recrystallization, and compression). Lithification can occur with deposition or long afterwards.

LITHOFACIES A unit of sediments or sedimentary rock that contains a record of a particular environment of deposition.

LITHOLOGY The characteristics of a rock. It is commonly used to refer to rock type.

LITHOPHYTE A plant growing on rocks or in very little soil that obtains most or all of its nutritional needs from the atmosphere rather than from the soil.

LITHOSEQUENCE A group of related soils or parent material sequences that differ from one another in some properties, mainly due to their origins from different parent rocks. *See also* Chronosequence; Toposequence.

LITHOSERE Plant succession patterns originating on rock surfaces.

LITHOSPHERE The rocky crust of the Earth. *See also* Biosphere; Hydrosphere; Troposphere.

LITRES-PER-HOUR CONCEPT An initial and supporting fire-bombing operation, with minimum turn-around time for airtankers, involving rapid and repeated dropping of large quantities of water or other short-term retardant, with the objective of holding the fire until complete control is achieved by ground personnel. *See also* One-Strike Concept.

LITTER **1** The top (L) layer of the forest floor, litter is composed of relatively undecomposed organic material in the form of above-ground inputs, leaves, twigs, and branches shed from the trees and below-ground inputs, usually the death of fine root material. In some systems, the below-ground inputs far exceed the above-ground inputs. Litter is the primary source of organic inputs into a forest soil. **2** In animals, the number of progeny produced at any one birth.

LITTLE CHANGE In describing a meteorological forecast, an insignificant change in wind speed, a change of less than five degrees in temperature, and less than five per cent in relative humidity. When used as a general statement in a long-range forecast, all three criteria apply.

LITTORAL Pertaining to the shore of a water body.

LITTORAL ZONE In oceanography, the intertidal zone (between low- and high-water marks). In limnology, the zone between the shoreline of rivers or lakes and a depth of about six metres. *See also* Riparian Zone.

LIVE BURNING The burning of green slash progressively as it is cut.

LIVE CROWN RATIO The percentage of the total stem length covered with living branches. It provides a rough but convenient index of the ability of a tree's crown to nourish the remaining part of the tree. Trees with less than 30 per cent live crown ratio are typically weak, lack vigour, and have low diameter growth, although this depends very much on the tree's age and species.

LIVE SKYLINE A skyline that can be raised and lowered during yarding to facilitate logging.

LIVING FUELS Naturally occurring fuels in which moisture content is physiologically controlled within the living plant. It is synonymous with green fuels. *See also* Dead Fuels.

LOADER *See* Harvesting Machine Classification.

LOAD FACTOR The average load or power output of an engine or machine, expressed as a percentage of its maximum capacity.

LOADING *See* Harvest Functions.

LOADING JACK The rigging suspended from a spar tree guyline immediately above the line of haul and terminating in a loading block.

LOAM A soil containing a mixture of sand, silt, and clay. *See also* Soil Texture.

LOBATE In leaf morphology, broadly, moderately to deeply indented toward the base or

midrib. More restrictively, significantly indented, but less than half-way to the base or midrib.
LOBE A protruding part of an organ, representing a division to or partway to the middle of the organ (e.g., a leaf, corolla, or calyx).
LOBED A leaf is lobed when the blade margin is divided into rounded parts extending one-third to one-half the distance between the leaf margin and the midrib. *See also* Leaf Margin (for illustration).
LOCALIZED INFECTION An infection involving only a limited part of the host. *See also* Systemic.
LOCALLY EXTINCT Elimination of a species in one area but not over its entire range. Local extinctions may aggregate into regional or eventually, global extinctions. *See also* COSEWIC; Extinct; Extirpation.
LOCAL POPULATION A population of animals or plants within a species that is largely genetically isolated from other individuals of the species and has clearly distinguishable genetic and cytological characteristics. It is also called a deme. *See also* Subspecies.
LOCAL VOLUME TABLE *See* Volume Table.
LOCAL WINDS Winds that are generated over a comparatively small area by local terrain and weather. They differ from those that would be appropriate to the general pressure pattern or that possess some other peculiarity. *See also* Gradient Wind; Surface Wind.
LOCULE A chamber or cavity of an ovule, anther, or fruit. *See also* Carpel (for illustration).
LOCULICIDAL In plants, dehiscing lengthwise along the midrib or outer median line of each locule (e.g., *Iris* spp.). *See also* Capsule; Fruit (for illustration).
LODGEMENT TILL Material that accumulates at the base of a moving glacier, typically highly consolidated.
LODICULE One of two or three minute scales below the stamens and adpressed to the base of the ovary in most grasses. Thought to be the rudiments of ancestral perianth parts.
LOESS A homogeneous, nonstratified, not indurated, yellowish- to buff-coloured wind-borne deposit consisting predominantly of silt-sized particles with subordinate amounts of fine sand and clay, porous and permeable, commonly with incipient vertical joints. Typically, loessial soils have large, weatherable nutrient reserves and provide good physical conditions for plant growth. *See also* Eolian.
LOG A fallen tree trunk that may or may not be separated from its root system. *See also* Log Classification (for illustration).
LOG CLASSIFICATION Logs on the forest floor are an important part of the overall ecosystem, providing myriad wildlife habitat opportunities, depending on the size of the log, the species, and its stage of decomposition. Rates of decomposition are determined by the condition of the log, the moisture and temperature prevailing, and the species. A five-class system is used to describe log decomposition (see illustration). (1) In **Class 1**, the trunk is round, bark is intact and maintains texture and original colour, twigs are present, log is elevated above ground on support points of broken limbs. (2) In **Class 2**, trunk is round, bark is intact and maintains original colour, while texture is intact to partly soft, twigs are absent, log is elevated above ground but sagging on support points as broken limbs deteriorate. (3) In **Class 3**, trunk is round, bark remains in traces and original colour has begun to fade, texture is hard and log is in large pieces, twigs are absent, log is sagging near ground. (4) In **Class 4**, trunk is round to oval, bark is absent and original colour has faded to light browns or yellows, texture is soft, log is in blocky pieces, twigs are absent, log is completely on ground. (5) In **Class 5**, trunk is oval, bark is absent and original colour has faded to light yellow or grey, texture is soft and powdery, twigs are absent, log is completely on ground. *See also* Snag Classification; Wildlife Tree.

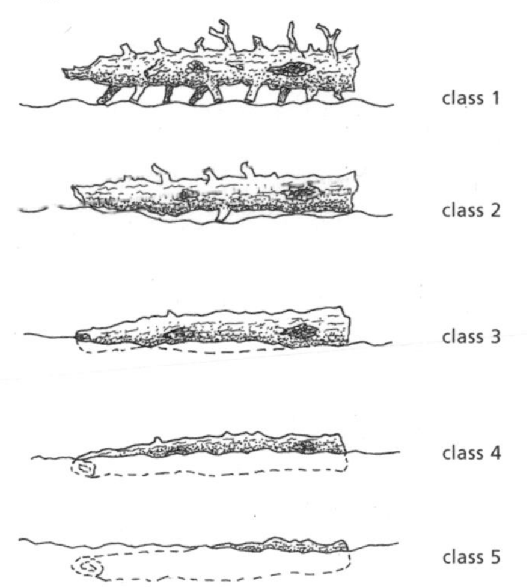

LOGGING The cutting and removal of trees from a forested area.
LOGGING PLAN The plan that defines the areas scheduled for harvest, outlining when, where,

and how harvesting is planned, and the treatments necessary before, during, and after harvesting.

LOGISTIC EQUATION The mathematical expression for a particular sigmoid growth curve in which the percentage rate of increase decreases in linear fashion as population size increases.

LOG JAM *See* Large Organic Debris.

LOG RULES A table of volumes intended to show the amounts of lumber measured in board feet that may be sawn from logs of different sizes under various assumed conditions. The exact formula used depends on log length, as well as tradition or preference according to the forest area. *See also* Doyle Rule; International Log Rule; Scribner Rule.

LOG SCALE The measure of the volume of wood in a log or logs based on the log-scaling rules in effect.

LOG STAIN A stain present in the log before it is sawn into lumber.

LOMENT A leguminous fruit, divided by constriction into a series of segments, each containing one seed, that separate at maturity. *See also* Fruit (for illustration).

LONE WOLF A fire-bombing operation where a fire is attacked by a single airtanker operating without direction from a birddog officer.

LONG-DISTANCE MIGRANTS Bird and insect species that migrate south in the autumn, far beyond their home ranges, and return to their home ranges in the spring (return migration). In remigration, the return leg of a migration is completed by a subsequent generation. This phenomenon occurs, for example, with Monarch butterflies (*Danaus plexippus*).

LONGITUDE A linear or angular distance measured east or west from a reference meridian (usually the Greenwich meridian in Great Britain) on a sphere or spheroid. *See also* Latitude; UTM.

LONGITUDINAL PROFILE A plot of elevation versus length, used to depict stream channel characteristics.

LONG-RANGE FORECAST A weather forecast for a period greater than five days in advance. It is of special interest in fire-fighting.

LONG-RANGE PLANNING The selection or identification of overall, long-range goals and the objectives necessary to attain them. The long-range plan is based on an assessment of what 'might be' in the future based on 'what is' in the present. Various courses of action are analyzed for costs, benefits, and feasibility (political, financial, social, environmental) and a framework for action is then established to guide short-term planning.

LONG-TERM FIRE DANGER The resultant of those factors in fire danger affecting long-term planning. It involves consideration of past records and conditions, and probable future trends. *See also* Short-Term Fire Danger.

LONG-TERM RETARDANT A substance that by chemical or physical action reduces the flammability of combustibles and remains effective after application, even after water content has evaporated. Long-term retardants depend on certain flame-inhibiting chemicals for their effectiveness and may involve other chemical effects, such as film-forming and intumescence.

LONG-TERM SOIL PRODUCTIVITY The ability of a soil to sustain a nondeclining yield of a timber crop in perpetuity and retain the potential for the targeted species to be grown at the same stocking level and growth rate in each successive rotation.

LONG-TERM SUSTAINED YIELD The hypothetical timber harvest that can be maintained indefinitely from a management area once all the stands have been converted to a managed state under a specific set of management activities. In Canada, this is termed the long-run sustained yield.

LONG TON A British (Imperial) measure of weight equal to 2,240 pounds. *See also* Short Ton; Tonne.

LOOKOUT **1** A person designated to detect and report fires from a vantage point; synonymous with towerman. **2** A location and associated structures from which fires can be detected and reported. *See also* Lookout Tower.

LOOKOUT CUPOLA A small building normally constructed with glass walls or windows permitting an unobstructed view on all sides, but not designed for living quarters. It may be located on a lookout tower or other artificial or natural elevation. It is synonymous with tower cupola.

LOOKOUT TOWER A tower built to raise a lookout above nearby obstructions to sight. It is usually capped by a lookout cupola.

LOOPER Also called an inch worm. The larval stage of some Lepidoptera, usually geometrid moths, which have some of the abdominal legs missing, causing the back to arch in a loop when moving. Loopers are further characterized by fast backward movement when touched. They pose a serious economic threat, as epidemic levels can defoliate large tracts of forest.

LOOP ROADS Roads laid out so that they permit

a continuous direction of travel arriving back at the starting point without turning around. They are often used in difficult terrain where there are few opportunities to manoeuvre, or as a simple means of joining up existing roads.

LOPPING **1** A rather crude form of pruning involving the removal of branches from the main stem without concern for stem wounds or correct pruning cuts. Typically used in areas where branchwood is important as a source of fuel or fodder. **2** The chopping up of slash remaining on the ground so that it will lie closer to the ground and thus decay more rapidly. This form of lopping may also involve scattering the resultant debris over a wider area.

LORATE Strap-shaped. *See also* Ligulate.

LOST LINE Any part of a control line that fails to stop the spread of a fire.

LOTIC Relating to flowing water, such as in most streams and rivers. Lotic systems derive their detritus inputs from terrestrial sources. They show a continuum of physical and ecological attributes from their source to the mouth, with a well-defined longitudinal gradient in temperature, depth and width of channel, water velocity, and bed conditions. *See also* Lentic.

LOW-FLOW DISCHARGE The lowest discharge recorded over a specified period of time, usually one year, and typically occurring in late summer or early autumn.

LOW FOREST A forest originating vegetatively from natural sprouts (coppice) or layered branches. *See also* Forest; High Forest.

LOW-LEVEL JET WIND A particular type of wind-aloft condition, evident in the vertical wind profile, in which there is a zone of increasing wind speed near the Earth's surface and then a zone of decreasing velocity above a point of maximum wind speed. Working values for the 'jet point' height and wind speed maximum are roughly 500 metres and 30+ kilometres per hour, respectively.

LOWLAND A general term connoting the differences in soils and vegetation patterns between areas of land that are frequently or occasionally flooded, versus the upland, which are areas of land that are seldom flooded.

LOW THINNING *See* Thinning.

LUMEN The cavity of a cell.

LUNATE Crescent-shaped.

LYRATE Pinnatifid, with the terminal lobe rounded and larger than the lateral lobes. *See also* Leaf Margin (for illustration).

LYSIMETER **1** A device for measuring percolation and leaching losses from a column of soil under controlled conditions. **2** A device for measuring gains (irrigation, precipitation, and condensation) and losses (evapotranspiration of water) by a column of soil. Some lysimeters are designed for collecting water (for chemical analysis) as well as for measurement of flow.

M

MACHINE COST The cost per unit of time for owning and operating a logging machine or some other piece of logging machinery. The cost is composed of **fixed costs**, such as depreciation, loan interest, taxes, and any licence fees; and **variable costs**, such as fuel, lubricants, repairs and routine maintenance, and replacement of parts.

MACHINE TIME Machinery does not operate all the time, yet the costs associated with a machine continue, especially the fixed costs, which are incurred regardless of the amount of time the machine spends in use. Machine time is broken down into several phases of operation, the main distinction being activities that are scheduled and take place either in or out of the normal working shift, and those that occur randomly and are not scheduled. **Scheduled non-operating time** is the time when no productive activity has been scheduled for the machine. Ideally, it is the time in which all servicing, repairs, and maintenance can be undertaken. The time period is broken down into idle time, repair time, and service time. **Scheduled operating time** is the time when a machine is scheduled to do productive work. The time when a machine is on standby as a replacement machine is not considered to be scheduled operating time. When a machine is replaced, the scheduled operating time of the replaced machine is considered as ending when the replacement machine arrives on the job. Scheduled operating time of the replacement machine commences when it starts to move to the location of the machine it is replacing. Extension of the regular shift operation into overtime is considered as scheduled operating time. **Operating time** is the time during this period that can be either productive time or delay time: (1) **productive time** is that part of the scheduled operating time in which the machine is performing one or more functions for which it was scheduled, or it is carrying out productive work other than that which was initially intended;

(2) **delay time** is the sum of the disturbance time, service time, and repair time, defined as follows: (a) **mechanical delay time** is that part of the scheduled operating time spent in repair or service when the machine cannot work. It does not include replacement of oil filters and spark plugs as scheduled in a preventative maintenance program. Servicing includes fuelling, lubricating, and doing the work specified in a scheduled preventative maintenance program. When a machine is being serviced while under repair, the time involved is classified as repair time, not service time. Repair and service time occur in both scheduled operating and nonoperating times, in and out of regular shift times; (b) **repair time** is the sum of active repair time, waiting repair time, and time spent servicing the machine while undergoing repair. Active repair time is the time during which actual repair work is carried out on the machine itself or a dismantled part of the machine. Waiting repair time is the time during which the machine is waiting for a mechanic, spare parts, or repair equipment. It includes time for transporting the machine to and from the workshop; and (c) **service time** is the time allocated for normal service and maintenance plus the time a machine is waiting for service parts, mechanics, or repair facilities. It is a part of the mechanical delay time. **Idle time** is the scheduled nonoperating time during which a machine is not working, moving, under repair, or being serviced. **Non-mechanical delay time** is that part of scheduled operating time during which a machine is not doing productive work for reasons other than repair or service. This time may be subdivided by causes such as weather or terrain conditions, waiting for another phase of an integrated operation, assisting other machines, and an operator talking with visitors. Several categories are: (1) **disturbance time** is the time spent for closing down one operation, towing, detail planning, talking to supervisors, waiting for wood, or waiting for better weather; (2) **in-shift moving time** is that part of nonmechanical delay time during which a machine is moving or being transported. It includes the time taken to move or transport the machine between operating sites or between camp and site, assuming the machine is not under repair or service. It does not include time spent moving between adjacent working positions on any one site; (3) **operational lost time** is that time during which production is halted due to things such as operating conditions, non-availability of auxiliary equipment, or using the machine in a nonproductive manner to assist other machines; (4) **personnel time** is part of non-mechanical delay time in which a machine lacks an operator or any other member of the machine crew; (5) **total time** is the total time elapsed for the period under consideration (e.g., total time for one week is 168 hours (7 days multiplied by 24 hours per day).

All of the above allocations of time yield a better picture of how well the machine is being utilized. This information is then used to determine the following. **Machine availability** is expressed as a percentage of the scheduled operating time during which a machine is not under repair or service. Thus, it is the percentage of the scheduled operating time during which the machine is mechanically fit and is capable of performing productive work. This is expressed by the following formula: availability = (scheduled operating time – mechanical delay time × 100) ÷ scheduled operating time. **Machine down-time** is the time during which a machine cannot be operated in production or auxiliary work because of breakdown, maintenance requirements, or power failure. **Utilization time** is expressed as the percentage of the scheduled operating time that is actually productive. It is computed as: utilization time = (productive time × 100) ÷ scheduled operating time.

The above breakdowns of time are used in time-and-motion studies, and as a means of calculating the efficiency of an operation relative to the costs. Hence, if availability is high but utilization is low, the machine is likely to be expensive relative to the amount of productive work performed. In contrast, high availability and high utilization, with low down-time, is the hallmark of a productive machine that is justifying its costs.

MACROCLIMATE The climate of a major geographic area, usually measured at about 1.5 metres above ground to avoid the influences of the topography, vegetation, and soil. It includes major meteorological factors such as sunshine, relative humidity, wind patterns, temperature, and precipitation. *See also* Mesoclimate; Microclimate.

MACROCYCLIC In rusts and some other fungi, a life cycle involving the aecial, telial, basidial, and typically the spermogonial and uredinial spore states. *See also* Microcyclic.

MACROECONOMICS Economic studies or statistics that consider aggregates of individuals or groups of commodities (e.g., total consumption, regional employment). *See also* Microeconomics.

MACROINVERTEBRATE An invertebrate animal large enough to be seen without magnification.

MACRONUTRIENT Nutrients required by plants in relatively large amounts for healthy development, usually considered to be hydrogen, carbon, oxygen, phosphorus, nitrogen, potassium, calcium, magnesium, and sulphur. *See also* Micronutrient.

MACROPORES Large openings or channels permeating soil horizons, often the result of decayed root structures, that allow rapid movement of water through the soil.

MACROSPORE *See* Megaspore.

MADICOLOUS HABITAT Thin sheets of water flowing over rock faces, found at the edge of stony streams, at the sides of waterfalls, and on rocky chutes.

MAGGOT The legless larva of insects in the order Diptera (true flies). *See also* Caterpillar; Grub; Larva.

MAGNETIC DECLINATION The angle between true (geographic) north and magnetic north (direction of the compass needle). The magnetic declination varies for different places and changes continuously over time. *See also* Isogonic Charts.

MAGNITUDE SCALING A technique used to measure interval-level preferences by use of psychophysical scaling methods. The procedure is based on the premise that sensory perceptions in humans can be weighted numerically according to the strength or intensity of the stimuli observed and the strength or intensity of the observer's response. The technique was developed to try and better gauge people's appreciation for landscapes of varying types.

MAIN HOST *See* Host Susceptibility Rating (dwarf mistletoe).

MAINLINE **1** The principal or primary logging road used for timber extraction in a network of extraction roads. The secondary and tertiary roads all feed into the mainline, which consequently, is usually built to a higher standard and is usually designed as a permanent access road. **2** The line in cable yarding that brings in the logs from the stump to the landing.

MAINSTEM The principal, largest, dominating stream or channel of any given drainage system.

MALACOLOGY In zoology, the study of molluscs.

MAMILLATE Possessing nipplelike protuberances.

MAMMAL A warm-blooded vertebrate of the class Mammalia, characterized by: (1) mammary glands in females that secrete milk used to nourish their young, who are born live, with the exception of the monotremes (duck-billed platypus and spiny anteater); (2) a high metabolic rate combined with hair and sweat glands to control body temperature at a constant level (homoiothermy); (3) efficient respiration systems to provide oxygen to support a high metabolic rate, which includes a diaphragm, intercostal muscles, and the separation of food and breathing passages; (4) the complete separation of blood in the heart to allow circulation of arterial blood under high pressure; (5) three centres of ossification, allowing long periods of bone growth; and (6) a lower jaw, consisting of a single pair of bones, that permits a variety of teeth configurations to serve different purposes (herbivores or carnivores). *See also* Amphibian; Appendix 1: Classification of Organisms; Bird; Reptile.

MANAGED FOREST The term is typically applied to land that is being, or is scheduled to be, harvested and is contributing to an annual allowable harvest calculation. However, under a true forest management regime, a managed forest could be forest land under active manipulation for the production of many different consumable outputs such as water, fish and wildlife, recreation, and where it can be integrated without damage to other resources. *See also* Forest; Timber Management.

MANAGED LANDSCAPE A landscape where human activities have varying degrees of negative or positive (from a human perspective) affect on the ecological processes and functions of the ecosystems present. The managed landscape is in contrast to unmanaged landscapes where both natural and human-induced changes (such as acid rain) take place without direct intervention by humans.

MANAGEMENT ACTIVITY An activity undertaken by humans for the purpose of harvesting, transporting, protecting, changing, replenishing, or otherwise using resources. Management activity is driven (or should be) by management plans.

MANAGEMENT INDICATOR An index or attribute of the landscape that can be quantified to simplify land management planning to determine the success of implementation of planning guidelines. One example is the use of indicator species. *See also* Indicator Species.

MANAGEMENT PRESCRIPTION The management practices and intensity selected and scheduled for application on a specific area to attain predefined goals and objectives.

MANAGEMENT UNIT A defined unit of land that forms the basic area for planning and management purposes. Usually, management units are the basis of detailed plans and actions. They may be further divided into smaller divisions, such as compartments or subcompartments, and are themselves part of a larger planning unit or similar designation.

MANIPULATION In GIS and other forms of data-intensive work, the rearranging or presenting of data without changing the basic data or deriving any new data. *See also* Analysis.

MANUAL CONTROL The use of chainsaws, axes, brushcutters, girdling tools and other hand-held equipment to reduce plant competition by brush and other weed species. *See also* Biological Control; Chemical Control; Mechanical Control; Silvicultural Control.

MAP PROJECTION A method of transforming a spherical representation of the Earth's surface to a non-spherical, usually plane, surface. Transformation of the spherical surface may be accomplished geometrically or mathematically. Map projections most commonly used in resource management are the Universal Transverse Mercator, the Lambert Conformal, and the polyconic, all of which are geometric transformations.

MAPS The Monitoring and Avian Productivity Survivorship program. Coordinated by the Institute for Bird Populations in the US, it utilizes constant effort mist netting and banding and intensive point counts during the breeding season at a continent-wide network of stations.

MAP SCALE Map scale indicates the ratio between the distance travelled between two points on the map and the equivalent true distance that this would represent on the ground. Thus, the ratio 1:50,000 means that one unit of measure on the map represents 50,000 units of measure on the ground. The numerator, usually one, represents the map distance, while the denominator represents the equivalent ground distance. Most maps also include a simple bar scale that permits basic estimations of distance where a high degree of accuracy is not needed.

The level of detail on a map increases as the ratio decreases, thus 1:100,000 covers a large area in coarse detail, while 1:5,000 covers a much smaller area in greater detail. The scale determines the level of accuracy that can be expected. Scale ranges and typical uses are loosely described in table (this page).

MAP SCALE BAR A scaled line in the legend of a map, graduated in equivalent ground distances. In the illustration: A represents an open divided line-scale (e.g., miles); B represents a filled bar-scale (e.g., miles); C represents a time distance bar scale (e.g., miles per hour); and D represents a dual unit line-scale (e.g., kilometres and miles). *See also* Map Scale.

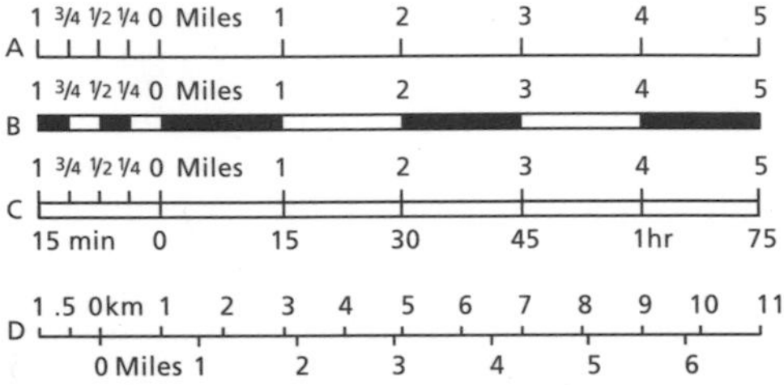

A 1 3/4 1/2 1/4 0 Miles 1 2 3 4 5
B 1 3/4 1/2 1/4 0 Miles 1 2 3 4 5
C 1 3/4 1/2 1/4 0 Miles 1 2 3 4 5
15 min 0 15 30 45 1hr 75
D 1 .5 0km 1 2 3 4 5 6 7 8 9 10 11
0 Miles 1 2 3 4 5 6

MAQUIS Scrubby, dense, shrublike sclerophyllous vegetation characterized by an absence of trees, usually found on infertile and dry soils in the Mediterranean. *See also* Chaparral; Sclerophyllous.

MARCESCENT Plant organs that wither and die, but persist on the plant (e.g., leaves).

MARCOT A branch used in propagation by binding a rooting medium to it and air-layering the combination.

MARGINAL COST The additional cost of increasing output by a small amount (e.g., one).

MARGINAL HABITAT Habitats having few species due to adverse physical or other environmental conditions. Habitats of less than optimum value for a species due to physical or other environmental conditions at or near the limits of the species' adaptation.

MARINE AIR Air that has a high moisture content and temperature characteristics of an ocean surface due to extensive exposure to that surface.

Typical Map Scales and Uses

Scale range	Scale	Typical use
Very large scale	<1:500	Detailed site planning
Large scale	1:500 - 1:10,000	Detailed site measurements
Medium scale	1:10,000 - 1:50,000	Forest inventory mapping
Small scale	1:50,000 - 1:100,000	Reconnaissance and landform studies
Very small scale	>1:1,000,000	Regional overviews

MARINE MATERIALS Sediments deposited in the ocean by settling from suspension and by submarine gravity flows, and sediments accumulated in the littoral zone due to wave action.

MARINE SENSITIVE ZONES Aquatic environments designated as sensitive to disturbance, including fish-spawning areas, shellfish beds, marsh areas, juvenile salmonid-rearing areas, and adult salmon holding areas.

MARITIME CLIMATE A regional climate under the predominant influence of the sea, having high winds, high humidity, and frequent precipitation. *See also* Climate; Continental Climate.

MARKET PLACE A hypothetical construct of economic theory representing the place where all potential buyers and sellers of goods and services come together, express their desires, and offer their wares through bargaining to establish a price structure and complete their transactions. In standard usage, it refers to all locations where economic transactions occur, treated as a single whole.

MARKET VALUE The price at which buyers and sellers conduct business. The price that could be obtained by selling a resource.

MARK-RECAPTURE *See* Capture-Recapture Method.

MARL Soft calcium carbonate, usually mixed with varying amounts of clay and other impurities; may include fossils. Marl is formed mainly under freshwater lacustrine conditions, but can also be associated with marine conditions.

MARSH An area of low-lying land, poorly drained, periodically or permanently inundated with standing or slow-moving, nutrient-rich water, and subject to seasonal fluctuations. Marshes usually have a mineral soil base, as opposed to bogs and fens, which have a peat base. Marshes are dominated by emergent, non-woody vegetation such as rushes, reeds, cattails, and sedges, and exhibit pronounced zonal or mosaic patterns of pools, channels, and clumps of vegetation, surrounded at the fringes by grassy meadows and bands of trees. *See also* Bog; Fen; Swamp; Wetland.

MASKED SYMPTOMS **1** The condition in which a host is infected but does not exhibit disease symptoms because the environment is not favourable for disease development and/or expression. **2** Virus-induced plant symptoms that are absent under certain environmental conditions but appear when the host is exposed to certain conditions of light and temperature.

MASS ATTACK The aggregation of bark beetle adults on one host tree in sufficiently large numbers to overcome the host's defence mechanisms against them.

MASS FIRE A fire resulting from many simultaneous ignitions that generate a high level of energy output. *See also* Conflagration; Extreme Fire Behaviour; Fire Storm.

MASSIVE Rocks or sediments without stratification, bedding, flow-banding, or foliation.

MASS MOVEMENT The downslope movement of masses of rock, soil, and organic matter under the influence of gravity. Mass movements are initiated in five ways (see illustration): (1) **Creep** is a slow, barely distinguishable, downhill movement of soil and surficial materials, lubricated by rainwater, and accelerated by gravity. Exposed roots may show downslope bending. Materials may accumulate against the uphill side of obstacles. (2) **Fall** occurs when bedrock fractures are visible in exposed cliff faces. Fractured blocks and slabs pile up at the base of the cliff and may form a talus slope. Trees are scarred and broken by rock fall. (3) **Flow** occurs when the mass of rock and soil begins movement without fracture or rupture and flows downhill as a cohesive whole, usually in a short period of time. (4) **Slide** is a mass of rock and soil that is displaced by gravity. It may be triggered by seismic activity. Speed is constant throughout the movement. Vegetation and

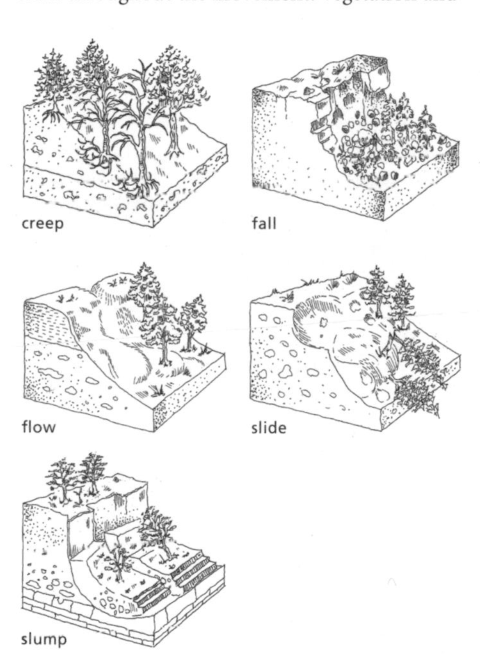

soil are buried beneath the mass when it stops. Vegetation is broken or bent. The resulting surface is typically concave and readily visible. (5) **Slump** is a movement that involves an actual shearing of rocks away from the bedrock, to expose a cliff or bank. The movement is rotational and concave, often uprooting and flipping vegetation back toward the slope. A fresh scar is visible on the hillside. Examples of mass movement include debris slides, debris avalanches, and rockslides. *See also* Zone of Initiation.

MASS TRANSPORT Heat carried ahead of the fire in the storm of firebrands.

MASS TRAPPING The use of baited traps, trees, or logs to attract large numbers of a pest species in an attempt to significantly reduce the size of the breeding population of the pest in a given area and thus reduce subsequent damage.

MASS WASTING **1** A general term for a variety of processes, including weathering and erosion, that together effect reduction of slopes and lowering of the land surface. **2** *See* Landscape Change; Mass Movement.

MASTER FIRE CHRONOLOGY A chronological listing of the dates of fires documented in a designated area, the dates being corrected by cross-dating. The size of the area must be specified.

MASTIGOMYCOTINA Fungi with spores that are motile by means of flagella.

MAST YEAR *See* Seed Year.

MATRIX **1** In mathematical usage, a rectangular array of rows and columns of real numbers. Matrices may be subjected to mathematical operations, such as multiplication of one by another, addition of two or more, and others. Matrices may be manipulated in total in a manner similar to the algebraic manipulation of single numbers, but knowledge of special rules, called matric algebra, is necessary for such manipulation. **2** In impact assessment, a rectangular table showing actions, conditions, resources, effects, values, etc., listed along two perpendicular axes. The matrix structure created corresponds to one element from each axis. By marking or assigning values to the positions in the matrix structure, interactions can be highlighted. It is also called a Leopold matrix. *See also* Measurement. **3** The most extensive and most connected landscape element type occurring in a location; plays the dominant role in landscape functioning. It is also a landscape element surrounding a patch. *See also* Mosaic. **4** In geology, the groundmass in which other materials are embedded.

MATRIX-SUPPORTED Any deposit of sedimentary material where the coarser fraction (gravel and boulders) are not in direct contact with, but are supported by, an underlying matrix of fine sediments. Such deposits are typical of debris flows and debris torrents.

MATTOCK A hand tool with a narrow hoeing surface at one end of the blade and a pick or cutting blade at the other end. It is used for digging and grubbing.

MATURE **1** A plant can be considered sexually mature when it responds to flower-inducing conditions. **2** A tree in a managed forest is considered to be mature when it attains sufficient size to be considered harvestable, as defined under one of several rotation-length criteria. *See also* Rotation.

MATURE FOREST FLOOR Forest floors that, by dint of time, exhibit soil characteristics influenced by the local climate and vegetation. It is typically divided into three main organic layers. (1) **L layer** is made up of recently deposited above-ground litter showing little decomposition or change in form. (2) **F layer**, the decomposition layer, is often rich in fungal mycelia and fine tree roots binding the decomposing litter into a mat. The litter residues have been broken into smaller pieces but their origin is still largely recognizable. (3) **H layer** is well-decomposed material dominated by amorphous humus particles whose origins are unrecognizable, sometimes mixed with the underlying mineral soil, but containing over 0.17 kilograms of organic carbon per kilogram of total solids. *See also* Moder; Mor; Mull; Soil; Solum.

MATURE SOIL A soil that has reached the full developmental stages resulting from weathering and biological processes, typically having well-developed horizons.

MATURE STAND A clearly defined stand of trees for which the annual net rate of growth has peaked. Stand age, diameter of dominant trees, and stand structure at maturity vary by forest cover types and local site conditions. Mature stands generally contain trees with a smaller average diameter, less age class variation, and less structural complexity than old-growth stands of the same forest type. Mature stages of some forest types are suitable habitat for specific bird or animal species. However, mature forests are not always (or necessarily the only) suitable habitat for such species, and the habitat of these species is not always mature forest. *See also* Maturity.

MATURITY **1** Physiologically, the stage at which a tree or other plant has attained full development and is in full seed production. **2** In forest management, the stage at which a tree or stand meets the purposes for which it was managed.

MATURITY CLASS Trees or stands classified by stage of development. Any one maturity class may contain several age classes.

MAXILLARY BONE The upper jaw bone of vertebrates that carries all the cheek teeth, except for the incisors. It is synonymous to Maxilla(e).

MAXIMAX A method of choosing among alternatives by noting the attribute with the highest value for each alternative, and comparing these attributes across alternatives to choose the alternative with the maximum highest value. In order to determine the attribute with the highest value for each alternative and follow this decision rule, a very high degree of comparability is needed between attributes within each alternative and among alternatives.

MAXIMIN A method of choosing among alternatives by noting the attribute with the lowest value or quality standard least met for each alternative, and selecting the alternative with the most acceptable lowest valued attribute or standard. In order to determine the lowest valued attribute or worst met standard, and follow this decision rule a very high degree of comparability is needed between attributes within each alternative and among alternatives.

MAXIMIZATION A process in which the potential gains from one area (or one factor in the planning process) are given the highest rank and weight, such that the greatest possible yield of benefits will result. A maximization strategy inevitably involves a higher degree of discomfort for the supporters of the factors that were not maximized (it may also result in losses being maximized). It is not possible to maximize all forest outputs from any one forest at any one time. *See also* Optimization.

MAYFIELD METHOD A method used to calculate the rate of nesting success based on the number of days that a nest was under observation.

MAZAEDIUM Plural mazaedia. A lichen fruiting body in which a mass of spores and sterile hairs is formed by the disintegration of the club-shaped fruiting bodies of the fungus.

MEAN In statistics, the arithmetic average of the observations in a data set. *See also* Median, Mode.

MEAN ANNUAL INCREMENT The total increment to a given age in years, divided by that age. *See also* Current Annual Increment.

MEANDERING CHANNEL Refers to a stream channel characterized by meanders.

MEANDERS **1** Regular and repeated bends of similar amplitude and wave length along a stream channel. **2** Bends in a stream that have been cut off from the main channel as a result of the water flow shifting its course.

MEAN FIRE INTERVAL The arithmetic average of all fire intervals determined, in years, in a designated area during a specified time period. The size of the area and the time period must be specified. It is synonymous with mean fire-free interval.

MEAN SEA LEVEL (MSL) The average height of the surface of the sea for all stages of the tide over a nineteen-year period. Altitudes are typically taken using the mean sea level as a datum point.

MEAN SQUARE ERROR An unbiased estimate of the true variance about the regression, it is computed as the sum of the squares of the errors divided by the residual (error) degrees of freedom. It is also referred to as residual mean square error (RMS), and the square root of this statistic is called the standard error of estimate. *See also* Precision; Standard Error of Estimate.

MEASUREMENT **1** The determination of the amount or quantity of a substance in terms of length (one dimension), area (two dimensions), volume (three dimensions), and time (four dimensions). Measurement is made by comparison with a known unit of length, usually the metric or SI system, which uses multiples of ten to form millimetres, centimetres, metres, etc., or the Imperial system, which uses the inch as the basic unit of length, increasing to feet, yards, miles, etc. **2** In the design of questionnaires, measurement is used to try to determine the magnitude of response to any one question. Several forms of measurement are possible, each having distinct characteristics that cannot be muddled if the results are to have statistical validity. **Nominal measurement** has no underlying trend in each increase of expressed preference value. Checking any one value (male versus female) merely indicates a category, but the results have no arithmetic utility; they cannot be added to portray overall trends, and the numbers assigned to the list of possible answers are entirely arbitrary. **Ordinal measurement** has an underlying trend in which the lowest number represents a lower level of a continuum of possible answers. The intervals between the numbers assigned bear no relationship to the actual value that may exist between the possible answers. For example:

This book is the best book to be published this year.

Strongly Disagree 1 2 3 4 5 Strongly Agree

The difference of opinion between 2 and 3 may or may not be the same as the difference between 4 and 5. Ordinal measurements merely rank the responses. Ordinal scales of measurement are also known as Likert Scales. **Cardinal measurement** has a distinct numerical value assigned to each variable, which is directly related to a physical property such as height, weight, or temperature. Each number or value has meaning by itself about the property being measured, and hence the values can be arithmetically manipulated with meaning. **Ratio measurement** not only has an underlying trend, but the number assigned represents an actual difference in the response being measured (e.g., a number 5 response might be exactly five times greater than a number 1 response). Ratio measurement permits arithmetic manipulation of the results. *See also* Definition; Sampling.

MECHANICAL CONTROL The use of mechanized equipment to control and manage competing vegetation. *See also* Biological Control; Chemical Control; Manual Control; Silvicultural Control.

MECHANICAL THINNING *See* Thinning.

MEDIAL MORAINE A morainal ridge in the middle of a glacier, parallel to the direction of glacier flow and formed by the union of lateral moraines of two coalescing glaciers.

MEDIAN In statistics, the middle value of a series of observations that are arranged in order of magnitude. The value that divides the ordered observed values into two groups of equal size. *See also* Mean; Mode.

MEDIATION Negotiations with the help of an independent person; the mediator or 'third party.' The relationship between the mediator and the parties involved is critical and has four important aspects. (1) The mediator has independence from the parties and the immediate issues in dispute. (2) The mediator is mutually acceptable to the parties. (3) The focus is on the process, not the substance of the negotiations. (4) The mediator is there to assist in finding a settlement mutually acceptable to the parties. The content of the final settlement is the responsibility of the parties and must be mutually acceptable to them.

In environmental disputes, the mediator usually plays three major tasks: (1) acts as convenor in assisting the parties to define the terms and conditions under which the negotiations will proceed; (2) acts as a broker, representing the interests, concerns, and ideas of one party to another, outside of joint sessions and in caucuses; and (3) acts as a facilitator in joint sessions.

Mediation cannot occur without negotiation, although negotiation does not require mediation. In mediation, the participants are committed to seeking a mutually acceptable resolution of their differences, which they will formally commit themselves to implement and support. Mediation is shared decision-making on a defined set of issues for a specified period of time. It is also based on the understanding that, should the parties fail to reach an agreement within a specified and agreed upon period of time, each party is free to pursue its interests as it sees fit, whether through unilateral decision-making, the political process, the courts, or some other means.

MEDITERRANEAN CLIMATE A type of climate characterized by hot, dry summers and cool, wet winters. It is the opposite of monsoon climate.

MEDIUM FUELS Fuels too large to be ignited until after the leading edge of the fire front passes, but small enough to be completely consumed. It is synonymous with intermediate fuels. *See also* Fine Fuels; Heavy Fuels.

MEDIUM HELICOPTER **1** A helicopter with a maximum certified gross weight for takeoff and landing between 6,001 and 12,500 pounds. **2** A helicopter capable of carrying 6-14 passengers. *See also* Heavy Helicopter; Light Helicopter.

MEDULLA **1** The inner part of a lichen thallus, typically consisting of loosely packed fungal hyphae. **2** The central portion of an animal organ such as the brain.

MEGAGAMETOPHYTE A female gametophyte; usually, the larger gametophyte developing from the megaspore. *See also* Microgametophyte.

MEGALOPS The final developmental stage of crabs or shrimp.

MEGASPORANGIUM A sporangium producing only megaspores. *See also* Microsporangium.

MEGASPORE The larger of two types of spores produced by heterosporous plants. The megaspore develops into a female gametophyte. *See also* Microspore.

MEGASPOROPHYLL A sporophyll containing megaspores. In angiosperms, this is the carpel.

MEIOBENTHOS *See* Meiofauna.

MEIOFAUNA Animals ranging in size from

approximately 0.1 to 0.5 millimetres that live in or on sediments. The size class of transition from micro- to macrofauna, it includes many small invertebrates and larger protozoans. *See also* Mesofauna; Microorganisms.

MEIOSIS The process of nuclear division within the reproductive cells of sexually reproducing organisms. In the process, the cell undergoing meiosis produces four haploid cells from one diploid cell. Meiosis takes place in two distinct and consecutive phases at differing stages of the life cycle in haploid and diploid organisms and has two major functions: (1) it reduces the number of chromosomes from 2n to n, thus preventing a doubling in the chromosome number of each successive generation; and (2) it results in the mixing of genetic material, thus ensuring intergenerational variability (assuming the parent cell has some variability). *See also* Mitosis.

MEIS An acronym for Multi-detector Electro-optical Imaging Scanner, which is a narrow spectral band imager that employs linear array technology to acquire airborne digital data.

MELTOUT TILL Material that accumulates directly by meltout from stationary or stagnant glacier ice. It may accumulate on top of the ice (supraglacial meltout till) or underneath the ice (basal meltout till).

MELTWATER *See* Runoff.

MELTWATER CHANNEL A channel or a valley formed or followed by a glacial meltwater stream; depending upon their position, they are divided into ice-marginal (lateral) channels, subglacial channels, etc.

MEMBRANACEOUS Thin, soft and flexible; like a membrane. It is synonymous with membranous.

MENSURATION *See* Forest Mensuration.

MENTUM A chinlike forward extension of the base of the flower in association with the foot of the column in some orchids.

MENU In GIS and general computer work, a means of encoding data that, instead of relying solely on keyboard entries, uses a list or matrix of options, one of which is selected with a pointing device or by means of arrow keys.

MERCHANTABLE A tree or stand of trees is considered to be merchantable once it has reached a size, quality, volume, or a combination of these that permits harvesting and processing. Merchantability is independent of economic factors, such as road accessibility or logging feasibility.

MERGE **1** In GIS work, the reduction of the number of polygons and labels, once lines have been dissolved during reclassification. **2** In database work, the bringing together of records from two or more different data sets to form one new data set, or the arranging of a data set by restructuring the fields and records to create a new database having all or part of the original data.

MERICARP A one-seeded carpel, one of a pair that split apart at maturity.

MERISTEM Undifferentiated plant tissue with the potential to develop into various organs or tissues (e.g., the apical meristem).

MERISTEMATIC TISSUE The undifferentiated tissues that are actively dividing to form new growth of various plant parts, such as the apical meristems in buds. The cambium and phellogen are meristematic tissues, and it is in these zones of cell division that auxins are produced. *See also* Apical Meristem; Bark; Intercalary Meristem; Root.

MEROMICTIC Lakes that are permanently stratified with distinct epilimnion and hypolimnion layers.

MEROMIXIS The process creating meromictic conditions in a lake.

MESA A broad, nearly flat-topped and usually isolated upland mass characterized by summit widths that are greater than the heights of bounding erosional escarpments. A tableland produced by differential erosion of nearly horizontal, interbedded weak and resistant rocks, with the latter making up the caprock layers. As the summit area decreases relative to height, mesas are transitional to buttes. In some parts of the world, mesas describe broad structural benches and alluvial terraces that occupy intermediate levels in stepped sequences of platforms bordering canyons and valleys. *See also* Butte.

MESIC **1** A term meaning intermediate, often in relation to temperature, moisture, or decomposition. **2** A soil temperature regime that has mean annual soil temperatures of eight degrees Celsius or more, but less than a fifteen-degree-Celsius and greater than a five-degree-Celsius difference between mean summer and mean winter soil temperatures at fifty centimetres below the surface. Isomesic is the same, except the summer and winter temperatures differ by less than five degrees Celsius. **3** Describes an environment that has moderate moisture levels, neither too wet nor too dry; organisms occupying moist habitats. **4** In the Canadian soil classification scheme, mesic describes one of several classes of fibre in organic materials. The mesic fibre material is in an intermediate stage of decomposition, between fibric and humic, with a proportion of the material having identifiable origins. **5** In general, a plant or animal adapted to an area that has a balanced supply of water; neither wet nor dry. *See also* Hydric; Xeric.

MESOCARP The fleshy, middle part of the fruit surrounding the seed and contained by the pericarp.

MESOCLIMATE The climate of small areas of the Earth's surface that may not be representative of the general climate of the district (e.g., small valleys, 'frost hollows,' forest clearings). It is intermediate in scale between macroclimate and microclimate. *See also* Macroclimate; Microclimate.

MESOFAUNA Animals of intermediate size usually considered to be from 200 micrometres to 1 centimetre (e.g., nematodes, oligochaete worms, smaller insect larvae, and microarthropods).

MESOPHYLL The middle or internal components of a leaf. *See also* Palisade Layer (for illustration).

MESOPHYTE Plants growing where soil moisture conditions are average, not excessively dry or wet. *See also* Halophyte; Hydrophyte; Xerophyte.

MESOSPORE A one-celled teliospore found among two-celled ones in rusts having pedicellate teliospores.

METACENTRIC A chromosome having the centromere at or close to the middle. *See also* Acrocentric; Telocentric.

METADATA Data about data, e.g., its source, accuracy, age, etc.

METAMORPHIC ROCK Rock forms derived from existing rocks, but differing from them due to natural geological forces, such as heat and pressure. The original materials could be igneous, sedimentary, or other metamorphic rocks, but the new metamorphic rocks have different physical, chemical, and mineralogical properties. *See also* Igneous Rock; Sedimentary Rock.

METAMORPHOSIS A major change in the shape, structure, and habits of animals as they develop from an egg or embryonic stage into an adult stage (e.g., frogspawn to tadpoles to frogs). Metamorphosis can be complete, gradual or incomplete. *See also* Hemimetabolous; Holometabolous; Neoteny.

META-POPULATION A population comprising several local populations that are spatially separated but linked by migrants, allowing for recolonization of unoccupied habitat patches after local extinction events.

METASTABLE SLOPE A slope that is relatively stable at the present time but may become active if the environmental balance is disturbed by, for example, road construction or removal of vegetation. A metastable slope is often related to base levels of former geomorphic episodes. The regolith is generally moderately deep, may contain stone lines, or relict evidence of slope alluvium. Slope grades usually range between 15 and 45 per cent.

METRIC CAMERA A camera whose interior orientation is known, stable, and reproducible. *See also* Nonmetric Camera.

METRIC CHARACTER In genetics, a trait that is measurable and can be categorized on the basis of measurements, and that varies almost continuously among individuals.

MICROBIAL PESTICIDE A pesticide in which the active ingredient is a microorganism (e.g., a virus or a bacterium such as *Bacillus thuringiensis*), rather than a chemical substance.

MICROCLIMATE The climate in the immediate surroundings. It differs from the macroclimate by dint of local changes in elevation, aspect, vegetation, and soil. Microclimate reflects the small-scale climatic structure of the air space that extends from the surface of the Earth to a height where the effects of the immediate character of the underlying surface no longer can be distinguished from the general local climate (mesoclimate or macroclimate). Generally, four times the height of surface growth defines the level at which microclimate overtones disappear. *See also* Macroclimate; Mesoclimate.

MICROCYCLIC In rusts, a life cycle involving the telial and basidial (occasionally the spermogonial) spore states. *See also* Macrocyclic.

MICROECONOMICS Economic studies or statistics that consider particular individuals, agents, or single commodities (e.g., demand for lumber, forest sector employment). *See also* Macroeconomics.

MICROENVIRONMENT The sum total of all the external conditions that may influence organisms and that come to bear in a small or restricted area.

MICROGAMETOPHYTE The male gametophyte. Typically, the smaller gametophyte developing from the microspore. *See also* Megagametophyte.

MICROHABITATS **1** A specific combination of habitat elements in the place occupied by an organism. **2** A restricted set of distinctive environmental conditions that constitute habitat on a small scale, such as the area under a log.

MICRON Plural micra. A unit of length (μ) equal to one millionth of a metre. In SI units, it is termed a micrometre (μm).

MICRONUTRIENT Nutrients usually required in relatively small amounts for the healthy development of organisms; they may be toxic in higher concentrations. In plants, they include boron, chlorine, copper, iron, manganese, molybdenum, and zinc. *See also* Macronutrient.

MICROORGANISM An organism too small to be seen with the unaided eye (e.g., a virus, bacterium, protozoan, mould, yeast, fungal hypha, etc.). *See also* Meiofauna; Mesofauna.

MICROPYLE The opening in the integument of an ovule through which the pollen tube enters.

MICRORELIEF Small-scale, localized variations in topography caused by knolls, boulders, upturned stump mounds and their associated pits, and gilgai. It is generally less than one metre in amplitude. *See also* Relief.

MICROSCLEROTIUM A microscopic sclerotium. *See also* Sclerotium.

MICROSITE **1** The smallest measurable unit of habitat, a microsite is the specific site occupied by an organism and the special relationship between this organism and its environment. **2** In soil assessments, a microsite is a small area of soil differing in biological or chemical processes from the surrounding soil, such as a pocket of decaying organic residues from a stump, or a small depression that has accumulated deep, organic mucks.

MICROSPORANGIUM A sporangium producing only microspores. In angiosperms, it is usually called the anther sac. *See also* Megasporangium.

MICROSPORE The smaller of the two spore types produced in heterosporous plants, and which develops into the male gametophyte. *See also* Megaspore.

MICROSPOROPHYLL A sporophyll bearing microsporangia. In angiosperms, a stamen bearing anther sacs.

MICRO-TOPOGRAPHY Topography of the surface of the soil as it relates to the successful germination of a seed.

MIDDEN Archaeological remains assembled in one site that occur in associations reflecting their last use, usually a specific kind of activity (e.g., shell mounds, ashes from a fireplace where meals were prepared). Also, sites where refuse or waste material was placed and accumulated.

MIDDLEGROUND Those parts of a scene or landscape that lie in between the foreground and the background. It is at this distance from the viewer that shapes and patterns within the landscape can be clearly discerned and, as a result, the middleground parts are important because they tend to dominate the view and frame the background or more distant scenes. *See also* Background; Foreground.

MIDRIB The central rib or vein of a leaflet or leaf. It is a continuation of the petiole. It is also termed midvein. *See also* Leaf Shape (for illustration).

MIGRATION **1** In genetics, gene flows between populations; often used more generally for broad-scale movement of organisms with or without gene flow. **2** The regular seasonal movement of bird and animal populations to and from different areas, often considerable distances apart (e.g., the downstream movement of young salmon out to the oceans, and the upstream movement of mature salmon into freshwater spawning grounds). Several forms of migration are recognized. **Altitudinal migration** is a vertical pattern of migration in which populations that breed in the alpine or subalpine zones in summer move to lower levels in winter. Inverted altitudinal migration describes organisms that move to higher levels in winter. **Leap-frog migration** is a pattern of migration taken when subspecies of the same species occupy two or more breeding areas (and also wintering areas) in the axis of migratory flight. Subspecies that breed progressively closer to one end of the axis winter progressively closer to the other end. For example, the fox sparrow, of which six subspecies inhabit the Pacific coast of North America. On its migration south, each subspecies flies over winter areas already occupied by the subspecies that breeds south of it. **Long-distance migration** is a pattern of latitudinal migration used by a species that moves from arctic or temperate regions where it breeds, to tropical or subtropical regions for the winter. **Loop migration** is a circular pattern of migration such that the migration pathway in the fall differs from the migration pathway in the spring. **Short-distance migration** is a pattern of latitudinal migration used by species that move within, rather than between, temperate or tropical zones. *See also* Colonization; Emigration; Immigration; Long-Distance Migrants.

MIGRATION CORRIDOR **1** A physical and/or biological feature that acts to concentrate or funnel animals, either during the north-south migration (e.g., birds), or during seasonal altitudinal shifts (e.g., ungulates). **2** A belt, band, or stringer of vegetation that provides a completely or partially suitable habitat and which animals follow during migration.

MIGRATION ROUTE A path or route followed by migrating birds and animals.

MINE **1** As a verb, the act of tunnelling and digging out the ground in order to remove one or more component parts of the mined material (e.g., coal, gold). **2** Also refers to insect larvae that mine their way into leaves or other parts of a plant. **3** As a noun, a mine is a complex of underground tunnels, only a few of which actually connect to the surface, often via a central mine shaft. An **adit** is a tunnel connecting to a mine from a side slope for access or drainage. A **pit** is a hole in the ground, of varying size, that is open to the sky and has been created for the purpose of extracting minerals or aggregates. In some places, an underground mine complex is generically referred to as the 'pit.' Pits may also provide access to tunnels and mines. **Levels** are the varying depths of work in a mine. **4** Refers to tunnels created by leaf-mining insect larvae.

MINERAL A non-technical word more specifically defined by legislation, usually involving one or more of the following: (1) a scientifically recognized inorganic material; (2) a material classified commercially as a mineral; (3) a material derived from the earth that possesses economic value and utility aside from the agricultural purposes of the land surface itself.

Minerals include sand, gravel (common minerals), precious or semi-precious stones, coal, petroleum resources, and natural gas, even though the latter three are not inorganic. Some definitions limit the term to inorganic materials having a distinct chemical composition, characteristic crystalline structure, colour, and hardness.

MINERAL ASH The residue of mineral matter left after complete combustion of wood or other organic matter. It consists largely of oxides, carbonates, and phosphates of calcium, potassium and magnesium, together with other compounds.

MINERALIZATION The transformation of an element from its organic to inorganic form due to microbial activity. *See also* Immobilization.

MINERAL RIGHTS The ownership or rights of access to minerals under a given surface; the legal right to enter the area and mine or otherwise remove them, including clearly defined rights about the extent of the land surface that can be used in the process of removing minerals and, in some cases, the remedial work that must be undertaken to restore the land surface upon completion of the mineral extraction activity. Note that mineral rights are distinct from surface rights.

MINERAL SOIL Any soil composed of mineral materials. The minerals are usually classified as primary or secondary. Primary minerals are formed at high temperatures and/or pressures in igneous and metamorphic rocks and have not undergone chemical modification since crystallization. Secondary minerals are formed at low temperatures and pressures, found at or near the Earth's surface in sedimentary rocks or soils, and originate from the decomposition of primary minerals. Mineral soil characteristics reflect their creation by weathering processes rather than by biological processes. *See also* Mineral; Organic Soils.

MINERAL SUITE A set of minerals that occurs in close association, generally representing a related formation.

MINEROTROPHIC Used to describe wetlands that are nourished by mineral-rich waters. *See also* Ombrotrophic.

MINIMUM FLOW The quantity of water needed to maintain the existing and planned-in-place uses of water in or along a stream channel or other water body, and to maintain the natural character of the aquatic system and its dependent systems.

MINIMUM VIABLE POPULATION The smallest isolated population having an x per cent chance of remaining extant for y years, despite the foreseeable effects of demographic, environmental, and genetic stochasticity and natural catastrophes. The probability of persistence x and y must be socially determined. *See also* Viable Population.

MINISONDE OBSERVATION A method of constructing a vertical temperature profile determined by air temperature data being continuously telemetered to a portable receiver unit at the Earth's surface from a transmitting sensor package that is carried aloft by a free-lift balloon. Winds aloft may also be determined at the same time for the purpose of constructing a vertical wind profile by employing the procedures used for a pilot balloon observation. *See also* Helicopter Sounding; Rawinsonde Observation.

MIRE A peatland. An area having a deposit of organic soil.

MISTLETOE Flowering plants belonging to the Loranthaceae family and which are parasitic on trees and other woody plants. The common mistletoe (including those of Christmastide fame) belongs in the genus *Phoradendron* and occurs throughout the tropics and into the temperate zones. In timber management, the dwarf mistletoe (genus *Arceuthobium*) has no apparent leaves and occurs only on the above-ground parts of conifers, where it causes considerable loss of commercial value. *See also* Host Susceptibility Rating.

MITE A member of the order Acarina in the class Arachnida, characterized by small size and the lack of obvious division of the body into head and thorax. Some species, such as spider mites, may be serious forest pests, while others may be beneficial predators that control other insects.

MITOSIS Nuclear division within a cell producing two daughter cells, but no change in chromosome number. Associated with asexual reproduction in multicellular organisms, mitosis is the basic method by which cell multiplication occurs. It is a continuous process, involving four distinct phases. *See also* Meiosis.

MIXED CONIFER FOREST A forest community that is dominated by two or more coniferous species. *See also* Forest.

MIXED STAND A stand containing two or more species where less than 80 per cent (may vary by jurisdiction) of any one species dominates the main crown canopy. *See also* Pure Stand.

MIXED HARDWOOD FOREST Forest where the species are predominantly deciduous and may number up to fifteen to twenty different species growing codominantly (e.g., Carolinian forest, Great Lakes-St. Lawrence forest, Appalachian forest). *See also* Forest.

MIXEDWOOD FOREST **1** In Canada, stands of trees having a well-mixed composition of angiosperms and gymnosperms, or the woods of such trees mixed together. **2** A forest type in which the softwood component is between 26 and 75 per cent. *See also* Forest.

MIXING HEIGHT A term commonly used in air pollution meteorology to denote the maximum height above the Earth's surface to which relatively vigorous mixing due to convection takes place. Above this layer, a stable atmosphere exists that acts to suppress vertical mixing. The mixing height is dependent on the vertical temperature profile. *See also* Ventilation Index.

MIXMASTER The person in charge of fire retardant mixing operations, with responsibility for quantity and quality of the slurry and for the loading of aircraft in land-based airtanker operations.

MIXOTROPHIC **1** Organisms that can survive using two or more sources of nutrition. **2** Plants that can assimilate carbon dioxide, but also require an organic substrate for nutrition.

MOBILE Describes a machine capable of being moved from one area to another, but not under its own power. *See also* Self-propelled.

MOBILE YARDER *See* Harvesting Machine Classification.

MOBILITY **1** The potential of a species to move about, usually determined by the animal's home range and cruising radius. **2** The ease with which a substance, such as a pesticide, moves over or through soil when in association with water.

MODE In statistics, the value or set of values occurring most frequently in a data set. *See also* Mean; Median.

MODEL An idealized representation of reality developed to describe, analyze, or understand the behaviour of some aspect of it; a mathematical representation of the relationships under study; the quest to find a subset of variables and a function between them that adequately predicts one or more dependent variables. The term model is applicable to a broad class of representations, ranging from a relatively simple qualitative description of a system or organization to a highly abstract set of mathematical equations.

MODER A form of humus on the forest floor. Moders are less acidic than mors and have higher rates of decomposition, lower levels of fungal activity, but higher levels of soil animals and greater mixing between the humus and mineral horizons. In the US classification, many moders would be called 'duff mull.' *See also* Mature Forest Floor; Mor; Mull.

MODERATE BURN A degree of burn in which all organic material is burned away from the surface of the soil, which is not discoloured by heat. Any remaining fuel is deeply charred. Organic matter remains in the soil immediately below the surface. *See also* Fire Severity; Light Burn; Severe Burn.

MOIST ADIABATIC LAPSE RATE The rate of decrease of temperature with increasing height of an air parcel lifted at saturation via an adiabatic process through an atmosphere in hydrostatic equilibrium. The rate varies according to the amount of water vapour in the parcel and is usually between 36 degrees Celsius (2 degrees Fahrenheit) and 41 degrees Celsius (5 degrees Fahrenheit) per 305 metres (1,000 feet).

MOISTURE CONTENT The amount of water present in a material such as wood or soil, and generally expressed as a percentage of the oven-dry weight.

MOISTURE OF EXTINCTION That fuel moisture content beyond which fire will not propagate itself and a firebrand will not ignite a spreading fire. It is synonymous with extinction moisture content.

MOLAR In mammals, molariform teeth are the teeth behind the canines that adapted for grinding and include carnassial teeth, premolars, and molars.

MOLLICUTE A class of Protista, including the Mycoplasmatales. Generally, wall-less prokaryotic, pleomorphic microorganisms. Two broad groups of mollicutes infect plants: (1) **spiroplasmas**, with helical motile cells; and (2) **mycoplasmas**, with nonhelical cells of variable shape. *See also* Mycoplasma; Spiroplasma.

MOLT *See* Moult.

MONADELPHOUS Describes stamens united in one group by connation of their filaments. *See also* Diadelphous.

MONESTRUS Having a single breeding period in a year. It is also spelled Monoestrus.

MONILIFORM Constricted at intervals and appearing like a string of beads (e.g., the fruit of some species of *Acacia*).

MONITORING **1** The process of checking, observing, and measuring outcomes for key variables or specific ecological phenomena against a predefined quantitative objective or standard. It takes place after an event or process has been initiated or is completed to evaluate if the anticipated or assumed results of a management plan have been or are being realized and/or if implementation is proceeding as planned. The results of monitoring are usually compared to a previously known baseline of data, but can themselves become the initial data baseline for future projects. A careful monitoring program permits the defensible documentation of change for the purpose of testing the validity of impact hypotheses and predictions, and the mitigative measures employed or proposed. **2** From a forest management perspective, monitoring is the systematic measurement or analysis of change (e.g., the component parts of the whole system and the processes within or being imposed on the system). Monitoring attempts to determine the effects (outcomes) of planned actions to see how well they comply with anticipated outcomes, or the legal requirements, regulations, and policies in effect and their compliance with stated objectives and standards.

Monitoring is a very important part of environmental impact assessment, but to be truly useful, the monitoring work must be designed so that any results gathered can be compared to an earlier state or condition, known as the baseline data (the condition before change). *See also* Baseline Data.

MONOCARPIC Seed production in plants that takes place only once and is immediately followed by the death of the plant.

MONOCEPHALOUS Bearing only one flower head.

MONOCHASIAL CYME Similar to a dichasial cyme, but with the lateral branches missing, always on the same side, thus giving the branching pattern only one direction.

MONOCHLAMYDEOUS A plant having a perianth of only a single whorl or series.

MONOCLINE A unit of folded strata that flexes from the horizontal in one direction only, and is not part of an anticline or syncline. This structure is typically present in plateau areas where nearly flat strata locally assume steep dips caused by differential vertical movements without faulting. *See also* Anticline; Fold; Syncline.

MONOCOLPATE Pollen grains with a single groove are said to be monocolpate.

MONOCOTYLEDONOUS *See* Cotyledons.

MONOCULTURE **1** The cultivation of forestry or agricultural crops based on individuals of cultivars from one clone or inbred line, or one species, planted over extensive tracts of land. Agricultural monocultures have often proven to be more susceptible to pest and disease infestation than crops having greater species or genetic diversity. Naturally occurring forest monocultures exist (the dominance of one tree species), but these would typically have a wider genotypic variation than plantation monocultures based on a narrow seed source. **2** The term is also used to include human culture (e.g., modern Western industrial culture is considered by some to be a monoculture).

MONOECIOUS **1** Plants having distinct male and female reproductive structures in different flowers on the same plant. **2** Plants having male and female gametes in one organism, typical of mosses and algae. The opposite of dioecious. *See also* Autoecious; Hermaphrodite; Heteroecious.

MONOGAMOUS Any species where a single male and single female pair for the breeding season. *See also* Polygamous.

MONOGENERIC A family, or category of higher rank, composed of a single genus.

MONOGENIC RESISTANCE Resistance to disease controlled by one gene. *See also* Horizontal Resistance; Oligogenic Resistance; Polygenic Resistance; Vertical Resistance.

MONOMORPHIC **1** Having a single form. **2** In genetics, a population where all the individual members have identical alleles of a given gene.

MONOPETALOUS **1** Having a single petal. **2** Gamopetalous.

MONOPHAGOUS An organism that is highly restricted in feeding habits and makes use of only one genus or species as a food source. *See also* Host Specificity; Oligophagous; Stenophagous.

MONOPHYLETIC Being derived from a single ancestral line. *See also* Polyphyletic.

MONOPODIAL A growth habit involving indefinite growth and elongation of the stem or rhizome, typically without branching (e.g., certain orchids). *See also* Sympodial.

MONOTYPIC A genus having only one representative species.

MONSOON BUCKET *See* Bowles Bag.

MONSOON CLIMATE A climate characterized by: (1) a long winter-spring dry season, which includes a 'cold season' followed by a short 'hot season' immediately preceding the rains; (2) a summer and early autumn rainy season, which is usually very wet (but highly variable from year to year); and (3) a secondary maximum of temperature immediately after the rainy season. *See also* Maritime Climate; Mediterranean Climate.

MONTANE Describes species associated with or growing exclusively in mountain areas.

MOOR An open, uncultivated parcel of land, typically having peaty and poorly drained soils, supporting coarse grasses, sedges, heathers and sphagnum mosses, with cotton grasses on the higher elevations. Not as dry as a heath and not as wet as a bog.

MOP-UP *See* Fire Suppression.

MOP-UP TIME *See* Elapsed Time.

MOR A form of humus on the forest floor. It is also called raw humus. Mors develop in cool, moist climates, have more fungi than bacteria, low levels of available nutrients, and slow decomposition. The absence of several kinds of soil animals inhibits mixing of the humus with the mineral soils below. Generally strongly acidic, mors tend to reflect infertile soils and may limit tree growth. *See also* Mature Forest Floor; Moder; Mull.

MORAINE **1** A landform that consists of unstratified glacial drift that is usually till or, less commonly, of other drift. A moraine exhibits a variety of shapes, ranging from plains to mounds and ridges that are initial constructional forms independent of underlying bedrock or older materials. *See also* Drumlin (for illustration); Till. **2** In volcanoes, the solidified volcanic debris borne on the surface of lava flows.

MORAINE RIDGES Refers to major moraines, such as end moraines, lateral moraines, and recessional moraines, and to small moraines, such as washboard moraines. *See also* Drumlin (for illustration).

MORISITA-HORN INDEX An index of community similarity that quantitatively measures beta diversity in pairs of sites. Abundances of species are taken into account. The index is less influenced by species richness and sample size, but highly sensitive to the abundance of the most abundant species.

$$C_{MH} = \frac{2\Sigma(an_i \times bn_i)}{(da + db)aN \times bN}$$

where

aN = number of individuals in site A
bN = number of individuals in site B
an_i = number of individuals in the ith species in site A
bn_i = number of individuals in the ith species in site B

$$da = \frac{\Sigma an_i^2}{aN^2} \text{ and } db = \frac{\Sigma bn_i^2}{bN^2}.$$

See also Jaccard Index; Sørenson Index; Sørenson Quantitative Index.

MORPH A specific form, shape, or structure.

MORPHOLOGICAL MAP A map representing the surface form of the land (e.g., a map showing slope steepness). If the map shows classification information (e.g., underlying geology), it is a morphogenetic map. Note that a contour map is not a morphological map because it only displays elevational relationships.

MORPHOLOGY The form and structure of living organisms or the surficial shape of an object independent of its function. A person who studies morphology is termed a morphologist. *See also* Geomorphology.

MORPHOMETRICS A genetics research technique used to estimate genetic variability in a species on the basis of physical differences between individuals and populations.

MORTALITY **1** Generally, the number of individuals in a population dying in a set time period, usually one year. **2** In timber planning, the death of individual trees, stands, or whole forests due to old age, disease, insect attack, fire, wind, drought, and competition for light, water, nutrients, and space, but excluding harvesting.

MOSAIC **1** In photogrammetry, an assembly of aerial photographs or images whose edges have usually been torn, cut, or overlapped and matched to form a continuous photographic representation of a portion of the Earth's surface. Often called aerial mosaic. Three forms are recognized. (1) **Controlled mosaic** is a mosaic that has been corrected for scale and tilt distortion by the use of ground control points. (2) **Semicontrolled mosaic** is a mosaic partially corrected. (3) **Uncontrolled mosaic** is a mosaic with no correction. **2** The intermingling of plant communities and their successional stages in such a manner as to give the impression of an interwoven design. **3** In landscape ecology, the landscape mosaic is the pattern of different ages and types of ecosystems distributed across the landscape. **4** In genetics, mosaic relates to a mixture of cells in an organism of different genetic composition. **5** In pedology, a mosaic is a group of soils that always occurs in association with each other, regardless of topographical features. **6** In plant pathology, mosaic is a chlorotic mottling of the leaves due to a virus infection.

MOSAIC EDGE An edge between stands or communities that is highly irregular, leading to a relatively large amount of edge per unit area.

MOSS A plant in the division Bryophyta, class Musci. Mosses consist of leafy gametophytes which when mature produce male (antheridia) and female (archegonia) sex organs. After fertilization, a sporophyte develops on an erect stalk and remains attached to, and dependent on, the gametophyte (see illustration). Meiosis and spore production occur within a capsule on the sporophyte. After dispersal of the spores, new gametophytes develop and the cycle starts again. *See also* Bryophyte.

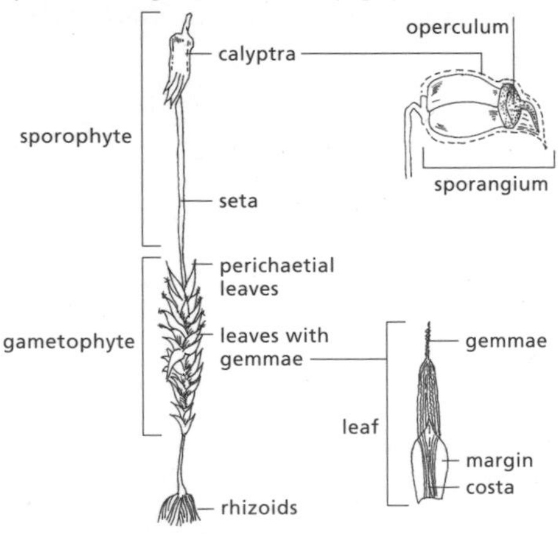

MOTH An insect in the order Lepidoptera that has the following characteristics (which have no taxonomic significance): (1) mainly nocturnal; (2) featherlike antennae; and (3) wings that fold horizontally beside the abdomen when resting. *See also* Lepidopteran.

MOTILITY Any organism capable of moving spontaneously as a whole. Such a creature is said to be motile. *See also* Vagile; Volant.

MOTTLES Spots or blotches of soil of a different colour embedded in the main soil matrix, usually due to localized reducing (anoxic) conditions. Mottles are classified according to (1) **abundance** (few, common, many); (2) **size** (fine, medium, coarse); (3) **contrast** (faint, distinct, prominent).

MOULD **1** Any profuse or woolly fungus growth on damp or decaying matter, or on the surface of plant tissue. **2** Humus-rich soil (e.g., leaf mould).

MOULT/MOULTING The periodic shedding of feathers, fur, hair, skin, insect exoskeleton, or other external layers. It is also spelled molt. *See also* Ecdysis.

MOUND A low, rounded hill of earth, created naturally or as a result of human activity.

MOUNTAIN A natural elevation of the land surface, rising more than 300 metres (1,000 feet) above the surrounding lowlands, which, when compared to a plateau, has a restricted summit area. A mountain generally has steep sides (greater than 25 per cent slope), with or without considerable expanses of bare rock, often with seasonal or permanent snow and ice cover. Mountains are mainly formed by deep-seated Earth movements and/or volcanic action, which have been followed by erosional processes occurring over a geological time scale.

MOUTHPARTS The structures borne by an insect to assist in obtaining food.

MUCILAGINOUS A sticky, gummy, slimy, or gelatinous substance; mucilage.

MUCK Organic soil, darker in colour, and with a higher mineral content than peat, with the organic material decomposed beyond recognition.

MUCRO A short, sharp spur or tip at the end of an organ (such as a leaf) and about the same texture as the organ. A pointed process forming the terminal of a spore.

MUCRONATE Abruptly tipped with a mucro. *See also* Leaf Shape (for illustration).

MUD **1** A soft, wet, sticky or slippery mixture of water and predominantly fine-textured sediments. **2** A textural term used to refer to silt, clay, or a mixture of these.

MUDFLOW A debris flow consisting predominantly of mud.

MUDSTONE Sedimentary rock formed by induration of silt and clay in approximately equal proportions.

MULCH Any material spread out over the ground surface that prevents the soil from eroding by dissipating the energy of raindrops and protects underlying roots from freezing and evaporation. It is also used to reduce competing weed growth.

MULL A form of humus on the forest floor, characteristic of mild, moist climates and fertile soils. Typically, very little surface litter due to rapid and complete decomposition and mixing. The high level of soil animal activity constantly mixes the humus and mineral soil, preventing development of H horizons, and often preventing F horizon development. Bacterial activity is high. Mull soils are high in available nutrients, are alkaline or only weakly acidic, and are characterized by rapid nutrient cycling; they favour rapid tree growth. *See also* Mature Forest Floor; Moder; Mor.

MULTI-AGED STAND A forest stand that has more than one distinct age class arising from specific disturbance and regeneration events at various times. These stands normally have a multilayered structure and an unbalanced distribution of diameters.

MULTILAYERED CANOPY Forest stands with two or more distinct tree layers in the canopy. *See also* Canopy; Multistoried stands.

MULTIPHASE SAMPLING *See* Sampling.

MULTIPLE DISCRIMINANT ANALYSIS (MDA) A multivariate statistical analysis technique that can be used to compare groups of stands, whose species composition have been previously defined using other classification methods, such as TWINSPAN. MDA checks the robustness of these groups in terms of stand environmental data, and can re-allocate stands to other groups depending on the outcome of the results. The best discrimination between groups is produced by projecting them onto a new axis that lies parallel to a line joining the group centroids. This new 'discriminant' axis is a linear function of the groups.

Discrimination between the stand clusters increases as the ratio of the distance between centroids and their common standard deviation increases. If the first two discriminant axes explain a maximum of variance, it is possible to ordinate the results to illustrate differences between the groups and show relationships between stands and their group centroids.

MULTIPLE ENTRY Entering a stand of trees for logging purposes more than once within any one rotation period. Associated with silvicultural systems other than clearcutting. *See also* Single Entry.

MULTIPLE FIRE SITUATION A circumstance of high fire incidence over short periods of time in any administrative unit, usually overtaxing the normal initial attack capability of the unit. It is synonymous with bust or fire bust.

MULTIPLE FRUIT *See* Syncarp.

MULTIPLE PARASITISM The simultaneous infestation of an individual host by two or more species of primary parasites. *See also* Hyperparasite.

MULTIPLE REGRESSION A regression that involves two or more independent variables.

MULTIPLE STRIP BACKFIRE *See* Ignition Pattern.

MULTIPLE STRIP FLANK FIRE *See* Ignition Pattern.

MULTIPLE STRIP HEAD FIRE *See* Ignition Pattern.

MULTIPLE USE A widely used term with differing connotations. **1** The management of land and its associated resources and values to provide a combination of outputs meeting the needs of a wide variety of people, plant, and animal species. **2** Use of land- or water-based resources, in whole or part, in such a manner that the combination of resource uses and users take into account the long-term needs of future human generations for renewable and non-renewable resources, including, but not limited to, recreation, range, timber, minerals, watershed, fish and wildlife, natural, scenic, scientific, cultural, historic, and indigenous values. **3** Harmonious and coordinated management of the various resources without permanent impairment of the productivity of the land or water base, and the quality of the environment.

Multiple use strategies do not maximize one resource output, but strive to achieve an optimal balance of outputs. Thus, a multiple use strategy may not yield the greatest short-term dollar benefits possible, but should yield balanced longer-term dollar benefits. *See also* Single Use.

MULTIPLIER **1** A numerical value that reflects the relative importance being assigned to a resource yield or use-affecting factor when all the values in an assessment cannot be directly and quantitatively compared using one measurement scale. **2** In econometrics, when used in simplified analysis, multipliers are often treated as constants; while in more detailed analysis, multipliers are derived from functions based on levels of, and degrees of change in, some economic activity. **3** In economic theory, multipliers are functions relating a change in some total measure to a change in some component of the total (the derivative of the total with respect to the component). Knowing the multiplier and the amount of a small change in the component, a simple multiplication gives a prediction of the change in the total. This prediction will be accurate if the basic equilibrium equations used to derive the multiplier accurately describe the economic processes involved.

MULTIRESOURCE INTEGRATION The creation of a common data set consisting of one or more variables (universal data) used for two or more different resource functions. It is an attempt to record all or part of the biological and physical conditions of a site regardless of the intended uses of the resource.

MULTISPAN SKYLINE A skyline having one or more intermediate supports.

MULTISPECTRAL IMAGERY Images of the same scene produced simultaneously by two or more sensors responding to different parts of the electromagnetic spectrum.

MULTISPECTRAL SCANNER (MSS) The major sensor system employed on Landsat satellites that generates spectral data in the visible and reflective regions of the light spectrum.

MULTISTAGE SAMPLING *See* Sampling.

MULTISTORIED STANDS Stands that contain trees of various heights and diameter classes and therefore support foliage at various heights in the vertical profile of the stand.

MULTISTRATOSE Having cells many layers deep. *See also* Bistratose.

MULTITYPE SPECIES A wildlife species that uses and requires two or more kinds of habitats or successional stages. *See also* Unitype Species.

MULTIVARIATE Involving two or more variables.

MULTIVOLTINE A condition in which an animal species, such as an insect or nematode, produces many broods or generations in a single year or season. *See also* Bivoltine; Univoltine.

MUNICIPAL LAND Land that is owned by a municipality, or land owned by the federal or provincial (state) government under the direct control of a municipality.

MUNSELL SOIL COLOURS A scheme used to classify the colour of soil on the basis of the following attributes. **Hue** is the dominant spectral colour. **Value** is the lightness or darkness of the soil. **Chroma** is the purity or strength of the spectral colour.

The soil colour reflects the geologic origins, degree of weathering and chemical oxidation/reduction, the organic content, and the presence of eluviation or illuviation. Soil colours vary with soil moisture.

MURICATE A surface that feels rough due to the presence of many short, hardened projections on the surface.

MUSICOLOUS Growing on moss.

MUSKEG A bog formation (usually sphagnum) found in the boreal forest regions. Characteristically found in poorly drained areas, often with permafrost, deep accumulations of peat, and tussock meadows supporting very limited tree growth due to excessive moisture. Two main forms are found. (1) **Clear muskeg** has a tree cover of less than 10 per cent crown closure. (2) **Treed muskeg** has a tree cover of at least 10 per cent crown closure. Percentage crown closure may vary by jurisdiction. *See also* Bog; Wetland.

MUTANT **1** A genetically different variation of a plant or animal, resulting from mutation, that has the capability to pass on the genetic codes for the variation to subsequent generations. **2** A gene within which a mutation has taken place.

MUTATION A change in the makeup of a gene or chromosome in plants or animals that creates an inheritable characteristic of the organism. Spontaneous mutation occurs naturally. Mutations can also be induced by mutagens, such as radiation and other toxic materials.

MUTICOUS Lacking a point; blunt, rounded at the tip.

MUTUALISM The relationship between two or more species; may be positive or negative. Positive mutualism occurs when species enhance each other's survival probabilities. Negative mutualism occurs when habitat requirements overlap and are used exclusively by a species rather than shared. *See also* Parasitism.

MYCANGIUM Plural mycangia. A specialized pocket, found in the exoskeletons of ambrosia beetles, some bark beetles, and other insects, that contains symbiotic fungi. *See also* Mycetome.

MYCELIAL FAN A fan-shaped mass of hyphae, formed between bark layers or between the bark and wood of trees. It is typically found at the base of trees infected with fungi such as *Armillaria* root rot. *See also* Mycelial Plaque.

MYCELIAL FELT A mass of fungus filaments arranged in a flat plane that resembles a thin, feltlike paper or cloth.

MYCELIAL PADS Small mats of compacted mycelia that are often formed by fungi on or in the host.

MYCELIAL PLAQUE A small, thin felt of hyphae, not in a fan shape, formed between bark layers or between the bark and wood of trees. *See also* Mycelial Fan.

MYCELIAL STRAND A water-conducting structure of certain fungi formed by the coalescence of several hyphae (e.g., dry rot). *See also* Rhizomorph.

MYCELIUM The vegetative part of a fungus, made up of interwoven hyphae and usually considered to be distinct from the fruiting body. *See also* Mycelial Fan; Mycelial Plaque; Mycelial Strand.

MYCETOME In insects, the mycetome is an aggregation of specialized cells surrounding symbiotic microorganisms. *See also* Mycangium.

MYCOBIONT The fungal symbiont in a lichen or mycorrhiza.

MYCOPHYCOPHYTA *See* Lichens.

MYCOPLASMA Primitive bacteria, including the genus *Mycoplasma*, lacking cell walls, highly pleomorphic, with complex life cycles and among the smallest independent organisms known. Parasitic in plants and animals and generally termed mycoplasma or mycoplasma-like organisms (MLOs). In the strictest sense, a mycoplasma is a mollicute that can be cultivated and characterized apart from plant or animal hosts. MLOs that are pathogenic to plants are obligate parasites that invade the phloem sieve cells, from where they are translocated around the plant. Susceptible plants die rapidly. Tolerant plants become stunted and may develop witches' broom or become chlorotic. Diseased trees do not recover. Mycoplasma infections are pronounced in elms, leading to elm yellows, and cause serious economic damage in pear and pecan crops. They are believed to be an initiating factor in ash decline.

MYCORRHIZAE A 'fungal root' resulting from a symbiotic relationship between a fungi and the roots of a host plant, in which energy, water, and nutrients flow between the two structures. Many plants perform better when mycorrhizae are present, and in some cases, trees cannot grow, or grow very poorly, without them. The benefits attributed to the presence of mycorrhizae include a greatly increased surface area for absorption of water and nutrients from the soil, increased branching and diameter of infected roots, prolonged root life (endomycorrhizae), and faster absorption of nutrients than is seen in non-mycorrhizal root systems.

Three main groups of mycorrhizae are recognized. (1) **Ectomycorrhiza** in which the hyphae form a compact mantle covering the root surfaces, and the intercellular hyphae have a netlike form in the cortex. The hyphae do not penetrate the cell. Generally formed by basidiomycete fungi, and almost exclusive to trees and woody shrubs (especially the Pinaceae, Betulaceae, and Fagaceae families). Ectomycorrhizae tend to infect the lateral roots and, in conjunction with production of auxins, cause the roots to be shorter, swollen, dichotomously branched, and often devoid of root hairs. It is also termed ectotrophic mycorrhizae. (2) **Ectendomycorrhiza** is similar to ectomycorrhizae but with intercellular and intracellular hyphae. (3) **Endomycorrhiza** is also called vesicular-arbuscular mycorrhizae and are roots with a loose network of hyphae in the soil, with hyphal growth within the root cortex, but without a mantle around the root. Generally formed by phycomycete fungi, the individual hyphae have globular swellings (vesicles) and very small, branched structures (arbuscles), which penetrate the cortical cells. Endomycorrhizae are widespread and abundant, and are found on most angiosperms and gymnosperms. They rarely alter the shape of the infected roots, but prolong root life and serve to enhance nutrient and water uptake. They are especially important for woody plants lacking abundant root hairs. However, infection rates tend to be readily suppressed by high levels of phosphorus and nitrogen. It is also termed endotrophic mycorrhizae.

MYREMECOPHILOUS Plants that afford specialized shelter or food for ants.

MYRMECOCHORE A propagule dispersed by ants. *See also* Elaiosome.

MYTH A story, rationale, or explanation for the belief(s) of a culture, subculture, lifestyle or other social group. In popular usage, myths are regarded as fanciful fiction; beliefs demonstrated to be incorrect. In a sociological sense, the term places emphasis on the critical point that the myth (rightly or wrongly) is or has been believed and therefore can be used to explain people's attitudes, behaviour, and preferences.

N

NADIR POINT In photogrammetry work, the point at which a vertical line through the perspective centre of the camera lens pierces the plane of the photograph.

NAIAD The aquatic nymph stage of a dragonfly or damselfly.

NATAL AREA The location where an animal was born. Thus, in fish biology, natal stream is the stream of birth.

NATALITY The number of new individuals added to as population in any one year.

NATIONAL ENVIRONMENTAL POLICY ACT (NEPA) A US act, passed into law in 1969, that mandated a legislated requirement for environmental assessment of many different aspects of environmental management, and included 'action-forcing' procedures that agencies must observe. Subsequently, additional significant pieces of legislation have been added to clarify the assessment processes and requirements. The introduction of NEPA led to global development of environmental impact assessment policies and procedures.

NATIONAL FIRE DANGER RATING SYSTEM In the US, a multiple index scheme designed to provide fire suppression and land management personnel with a systematic means of assessing various aspects of fire danger on a day-to-day basis.

NATIONAL FOREST MANAGEMENT ACT In the US, passed in 1976 as an amendment to the Rangeland Renewable Resources Act, requiring the preparation of forest plans and regulations.

NATIONAL TOPOGRAPHIC SERVICE (NTS) In Canada, a series of topographic maps covering all of Canada at scales of 1:25,000; 1:50,000; 1:250,000; and 1:1,000,000. The country is divided into a system of large quadrangles, each one (termed a primary quadrangle) representing 4 degrees latitude (north-south) and 8 degrees longitude (east-west). The primary quadrangles are numbered and further subdivided into 16 smaller units labelled A to P. Each of these smaller units is then further divided into another 16 units numbered 1 to 16. Typically, the Universal Transverse Mercator grid system is superimposed on the NTS map sheets so that grid coordinates can be readily plotted and compared for navigational purposes. *See also* UTM.

NATIVE SPECIES Usually, a species known to have existed on a site prior to the influence of humans. It depends on the temporal and spatial context of analysis, since long-established exotic species are often considered to be native by default. *See also* Exotic Species.

NATURAL AREAS In Canada, natural areas are those that fulfil one or more of the following criteria. (1) They are natural or near natural in character and relatively undisturbed, or else in the process of recovery from human disturbance. (2) They are significant regional habitats for either typical or endangered plant or animal species. (3) They encompass one or more regionally characteristic or rare natural ecosystems. (4) They contain typical or unusual geological formations or archaeological sites. (5) They exhibit diverse scenery or other natural physiographic features of scientific, educational, aesthetic, or cultural value.

Natural areas are judged to be very important to the welfare of humanity and are considered to be necessary for the following reasons: (1) they help to maintain the diversity of living organisms through the conservation of wild genetic resources; (2) they offer areas for research on relatively natural vegetation for comparison with managed and utilized vegetation; (3) they are outdoor laboratories for a variety of research programs; and (4) they are living museums to serve outdoor education needs and to inspire an intellectual understanding and aesthetic appreciation of the natural world.

NATURAL BARRIER Any area where lack of flammable material obstructs the spread of wildfires.

NATURAL CAVITY A naturally occurring space within a tree, downed log, rock face, or bank that is used for nesting and/or thermal protection.

NATURAL ECOSYSTEM An ecosystem that is minimally influenced by humans and that is, in the larger sense, diverse, resilient, and sustainable.

NATURAL ENEMIES The parasites, parasitoids, predators, and pathogens associated in nature with a specific wild population of plants or animals.

NATURAL FIRES Any fire of natural origin (e.g., lightning, spontaneous combustion, volcanic activity). *See also* Prescribed Fire; Wildfire.

NATURAL FOREST A forest area that has developed free from the influence of humans and remains largely unaffected by their activities. The natural forest may include, but is not necessarily equivalent to, an old-growth forest. *See also* Forest.

NATURAL FUELS Fuels resulting from a natural process and not directly generated or altered by land management practices. *See also* Activity Fuels.

NATURAL LANDSCAPE An area where human effects, if present, are not ecologically significant to the landscape as a whole.

NATURAL MOISTURE CONTENT The moisture content of soil or surficial material at the time a sample was collected.

NATURAL REGENERATION The renewal of a forest stand by natural rather than human means, such as seeding-in from adjacent stands, with the seed being deposited by wind, birds, or animals. Regeneration may also originate from sprouting, suckering, or layering. *See also* Artificial Regeneration.

NATURAL RESOURCES The term encompasses renewable resources, such as forests, water, wildlife, soils, etc., and non-renewable resources, such as coal, oil, and ores, all of which are natural assets.

NATURAL SELECTION *See* Selection.

NATURAL TARGET CUT A pruning technique where only branch tissue is removed, with removal occurring just beyond the branch collar. *See also* Branch Collar; Flush Cut; Pruning.

NATURAL VARIATION *See* Range of Variability.

NATURE RESERVE An area of land set aside to maintain it in its natural condition. In a North American context, reserves are typically undisturbed or only slightly disturbed lands. In a European context, they can include quite severely disturbed lands. Reserves serve as a baseline for studying ecological baselines of natural change (background effects) and reaction to induced change (direct and active disturbance).

NAVICULAR Shaped like a boat with a deep keel (e.g., the glumes on many grasses).

NECROSIS The death or disintegration of cells or tissues while still part of a living organism, often manifested by the appearance of patches of dead tissue (necrotic) surrounded by living tissue. Necrotic plant tissue is usually darker and can be a symptom of mineral deficiencies or viral disease.

NECROTIC SPOT A dead area on a living plant. It is often caused by biotic and abiotic injury.

NECROTROPHIC Any organism that uses dead plant or animal tissues to meet its nutritional requirements. *See also* Saprophyte.

NECTAR In plants and certain fungi, a secreted sugar solution that attracts insects.

NECTARIVORE Any animal that eats nectar for all or a part of its diet.

NECTARY A nectar-secreting gland, usually seen as a small pit or protuberance.

NEEDLE CAST **1** The premature shedding of needles in conifers, often in May or June. Frequently associated with attack by certain ascomycete fungi, but sometimes caused by non-infectious agents. **2** A disease characterized by these symptoms.

NEEDLE COMPLEMENT The normal or usual number of needles that a conifer of a particular species will bear.

NEEDLE ICE Ice crystals caused by frost-heaving in rocks and soil.

NEEDLE-LEAVED Refers to coniferous trees, where there are many small, needlelike leaves covering the entire tree. *See also* Conifer Leaves.

NEEDLE MINER An insect that lives and feeds as a larva within the inner tissues of coniferous needles.

NEEDLE SPOTTING A needle disease characterized by isolated circular or elongate lesions.

NEEDS The fundamental motivations and requirements of living organisms, as opposed to wants or desires; the latter being requirements that come after basic necessities have been met. In human populations, there is a considerable overlap between the terms 'needs' and 'wants.' Some might argue that needs considered essential in one culture are in fact extravagances in another. Typical basic needs are food, shelter, clothing, potable water, and breathable air.

NEGATIVE FEEDBACK A loop where one component stimulates a second component, but the second then inhibits the first. *See also* Feedback; Positive Feedback.

NEGOTIATION Explicit bargaining. Negotiations occur when two or more entities enter into a direct exchange, typically involving face-to-face meetings, in an attempt to find some resolution to their differences. It is based on the understanding (or assumption) that an agreement will involve a commitment to act within the terms of the agreement. Negotiation is a form of shared decisionmaking (i.e., on a certain set of issues for a period of time, those involved agree to seek an outcome acceptable to all involved). Should the negotiations fail to result in agreement, the participants revert to pursuing their interests as appropriate, whether through unilateral decisionmaking, or attempts to prevent those decisions from being realized through political or legal action or some other means.

NEKTON Aquatic animals that swim actively and may move long distances to feed or breed (e.g., fish, marine mammals, and jellyfish). *See also* Benthos; Neuston; Plankton.

NEMATICIDE A pesticide (usually chemical) or physical agent used to kill or inhibit nematodes.

NEMATODE Non-segmented roundworms in the phylum Nematoda. Nematodes range in size from microscopic to several metres in length, and occupy a very diverse range of feeding habitats, including trees. They can be free-living or parasitic. Some nematodes attack insects and can be used as biological control agents when they parasitize sub-cortical and soil-inhabiting insect pests. Plant-attacking nematodes cause damage by feeding on or in roots or other plant parts, and may induce root-knots on fine feeder roots of trees or seedlings. They may also act as vectors of viruses, fungi, or other pathogenic microorganisms.

NEOGLACIAL INTERVAL, NEOGLACIATION The episode of relatively cool, moist climate during the later part of the Holocene epoch, during which glaciers were more extensive than during the earlier part of the Holocene. *See also* Hypsithermal.

NEOGLACIAL MORAINE Moraines formed during the Neoglacial interval. The term includes the fresh Little Ice Age (late-Neoglacial) moraines that adjoin most modern glaciers.

NEOLITHIC In archaeology, the period in human prehistory characterized by the domestication of plants and animals.

NEOTENY A condition in which a larval stage does not fully metamorphose into the adult form but retains some or all of the juvenile body form, yet is still a sexually mature organism. It is an evolutionary strategy that enhances the likelihood of successful exploitation of environmental conditions and reproduction. This condition is found in amphibians such as frogs and salamanders.

NEOTERIC AREA In the US Forest Service jargon, sites and areas that have been designated as containing outstanding examples of modern human cultural activity, which it is believed will one day become historic property (e.g., buildings that were designed by famous architects).

NEOTROPICAL MIGRANT Any bird that breeds in temperate, boreal, or arctic regions of North America, but 'winters' within the tropics (between the Tropic of Cancer and the Tropic of Capricorn).

NEOTYPE *See* Type.

NEPHELOMETRIC TURBIDITY UNIT (NTU) The measurement of the concentration or size of suspended particles (cloudiness) based on the scattering of light transmitted or reflected by the medium.

NESTED PLOTS The use of plots within larger plots as a means of sampling different plant or animal attributes.

NESTING POPULATION LEVEL The number of individuals or pairs of a nesting species in an area during the breeding season.

NESTING/ROOSTING/FORAGING HABITAT The vegetation with the age class, species of trees, structure, sufficient area, and adequate food source to meet some or all of the life needs of any one species.

NESTLING An immature bird that is incapable of flight and/or has not left the nest. *See also* Fledgling.

NEST PARASITE A bird that lays its eggs in the nest of other species of birds, which then incubate and rear the offspring (e.g., cowbirds, cuckoos).

NEST PARASITISM *See* Brood Parasitism.

NET PRIMARY PRODUCTION (NPP) In a plant community, the energy remaining in plants after respiration and stored as biomass is NPP. NPP represents the total amount of energy produced and stored in plant tissue through photosynthesis, minus the energy consumed during respiration by the photosynthesizing plants. NPP is expressed as grams of plant part per square metre per year ($g/m^2/yr$). *See also* Primary Production.

NET PRODUCTION *See* Net Primary Production.

NET REPRODUCTION RATE (R) The average number of young born per female in each age group.

NET-VEINED Having a network of veins.

NETWORK ANALYSIS A class of GIS functions that operates on networks (e.g., roads or rivers) and their associated attributes.

NEUSTON Minute or microscopic organisms that live on the surface film of water. *See also* Benthos; Nekton; Plankton.

NEUTRAL ATMOSPHERE The condition in which temperature decreases with increasing altitude is equal to the dry adiabatic lapse rate (i.e., the atmosphere neither aids nor hinders large-scale vertical motion). *See also* Atmospheric Stability.

NEW FORESTRY Describes an emerging management approach in North America that seeks to sustain high levels of diversity and long-term productivity in managed forests. It is not ecoforestry. New forestry is founded on landscape ecology and conservation biology principles, and attempts to leave some of the natural system intact while striving to maximize fibre and timber production, as well as selected wildlife species, on forest land. It can be viewed as part of the transition of getting ecological paradigms into more traditional timber management practices.

NEXUS A means of connection. It is typically used in a legal sense to indicate the linkage between a cause (action) and an effect (outcome).

NICHE The unique environment needed to sustain the existence of an organism or species.

NICKPOINT An interruption or break of slope, especially a point of abrupt change or inflection in the longitudinal profile of a stream or its valley, resulting from rejuvenation, glacial erosion, or the outcropping of a resistant bed.

NIGRESCENT Blackish, or becoming black.

NITROGEN CYCLE The process that moves nitrogen within and between ecosystems and throughout the biosphere. Nitrogen typically enters ecosystems from the atmosphere as nitrates or ammonia resulting from lightning, biological fixation, or as precipitation. The cycle is complex and involves a sequence of biochemical changes undergone by the nitrogen in which it is used by a living organism, transformed upon death and decomposition of the organism, and converted ultimately to its original state. Nitrogen makes up approximately 80 per cent of the atmosphere.

NITROGEN FIXATION A process in which nitrogen-fixing bacteria and fungi, working in isolation (free-living) or in association with plants, convert atmospheric nitrogen into nitrogen compounds for use by the same or other plants.

NIVATION Enlargement of hollows occupied by snowbanks due to erosion of bedrock and/or surficial materials by a variety of processes, including freeze-thaw, chemical action of meltwater, solifluction, and snow creep; snow-patch erosion.

NOCTURNAL Any organism whose most active period is between dusk and dawn. *See also* Crepuscular; Diurnal.

NODE **1** In GIS work, a point where digitized segments or arcs join. **2** In vegetation analysis, a distinct and locally (may be at the site level) isolated patch of vegetation, often capable of joining up with other nodes over time to form a continuous vegetative type. **3** A habitat patch leading to or from a landscape linkage, such as a corridor of similar habitat type. It is also an intersection of corridors and a source or sink of plants or animal flows. **4** A slightly enlarged portion of a stem (twig) where leaves and buds arise, and where branches and twigs originate.

NODE SNAP In GIS work, a procedure to close the gap between the end of two lines at a node.

NODOSE Knobby, a term generally used when describing roots.

NODULES **1** Small swellings on plant leaves or roots, often associated with nitrogen-fixing bacteria. **2** A glaebule consisting of undifferentiated rock or soil material. *See also* Glaebule.

NODULOSE A diminutive of nodose.

NOMEN AMBIGUUM A scientific name having multiple meanings, or the same name applied to different taxa.

NOMENCLATURE *See* Binomial Nomenclature.

NOMEN NUDUM A scientific name for a taxon published without a full description.

NOMEN PROVISORIUM A scientific name proposed provisionally but not yet accepted.

NOMINAL SCALE A scale in which things (data) are sorted into homogeneous categories. *See also* Measurement; Ordinal Scale.

NOMINAL VALUES **1** Values that are considered to be of little or no worth; recognized but not considered to be of significance. **2** Values taken as they are encountered and uncorrected for any common impact, such as inflation. *See also* Measurement.

NOMINAL VARIABLE A variable whose numbers are used to simply classify or label different categories. For example, the variable 'sex' is nominal since the numbers one and zero can be used to denote male or female, respectively. *See also* Measurement.

NONCLASTIC Sedimentary deposits in the form of crystalline chemical precipitates (mineral products) (e.g., limestone is a nonclastic sedimentary rock). *See also* Clastic.

NON-COMMERCIAL FOREST LAND Land incapable of yielding a specified volume of wood per unit area of commercial species, or land only capable of producing noncommercial tree species. *See also* Forest.

NON-COMMERCIAL TREE SPECIES Tree species within a stand whose yields, if harvested, would be too small to include in volume assessments. Such species may yield commercial volumes for specialized end uses, such as furniture-grade wood or firewood.

NON-CONSUMPTIVE USE Use of resources in a manner that does not diminish the available total stock; does not consume a resource (e.g., bird-watching). The term makes no distinction between non-consumption of renewable or non-renewable resources. However, non-consumptive uses often still require assessments of carrying capacity and land-use planning (e.g., the effects of birdwatchers on vegetation (trampling), disturbances to nesting birds, and so on) *See also* Consumptive Use.

NON-CONVECTIVE-LIFT FIRE PHASE The phase of a fire when most emissions are not entrained into a definite convection column. *See also* Convective-lift Fire Phase.

NONGAME SPECIES Any species or organism that is not designated as 'huntable' by humans.

NONHYDRIC SOILS A soil that has developed under predominantly aerobic soil conditions. It normally supports mesophytic or xerophytic species.

NONINFECTIOUS DISEASE *See* Disorder.

NONMETRIC CAMERA A camera whose interior orientation is partially unknown. Incorporation of fiducial marks is insufficient to convert a nonmetric camera to metric.

NON-PASSERINE BIRD A bird in any one of the many orders not usually described as songbirds. *See also* Passerine.

NONPATHOGENIC Any substance, process, or organism that is not capable of inducing disease in any other organism.

NON-POINT SOURCE A source of atmospheric, aquatic, or terrestrial pollution in which naturally occurring or human-created pollutants are discharged over a widespread area or from a number of small inputs, rather than from one distinct identifiable source (point source) (e.g., air pollution, large scale acid rain, and erosion from croplands, logged areas, and suburban lands). *See also* Point Source.

NON-RENEWABLE RESOURCES Resources whose total physical quantity does not increase significantly within a human-based timescale. Thus, the resource is finite and each use diminishes the total stock remaining (e.g., oil, coal, gas, and mineral deposits). Biological resources, although technically renewable, can also be considered non-renewable if the populations are decreasing over time without replenishment, and are thus in danger of extinction in the case of species, or eradication in the case of ecosystems.

NON-RESPONSE BIAS In sampling procedures, this occurs when a large number of those selected for a sample do not respond to the questionnaire or interview, thus introducing a bias since the sample may now not fully represent the spectrum of potential respondents.

NON-SELECTIVE HERBICIDE A chemical that is generally toxic to plants without regard to species. The specificity of treatment may be achieved by dosage, or method or timing of application. *See also* Selective Herbicide.

NON-SYSTEMIC INFECTION **1** Generally, a localized or local infection. **2** A dwarf mistletoe infection in which the endophytic system is generally restricted to the swollen portion of the host.

NON-TARGET ORGANISM An organism, including humans, that is not a pest and against which no action is intended, but which is likely to be exposed to a pesticide applied against another organism.

NONVASCULAR Lacking vascular tissue (including xylem and phloem). Nonvascular plants include algae, lichens, mosses, liverworts, as well as the fungi. Because they don't generally have the structural support conferred by vascular tissue, nonvascular plants are essentially non-woody, small, and low-growing. *See also* Vascular.

NON-VIRULENT It describes a variant of a pathogenic organism that is incapable of inducing severe disease. It is also termed avirulent or non-pathogenic.

NORMAL FIRE SEASON **1** The season in which weather, fire danger, and the number or distribution of fires are about average. **2** The period of the year that normally comprises the fire season.

NORMAL FIRE YEAR In the US, the year with the third greatest number of fires in the past ten years.

NORMAL FOREST A conceptual ideal that underpins many aspects of timber management. The normal forest is one in which all age classes are represented on equal areas of equal fertility. If this could be achieved then each year an area of known volume can be felled, and the area regenerated with the certainty that it will develop into a similar equal volume at the time of the next rotation. In the normal forest, the total growing stock is thus predictable and constant.

In practice, it is virtually unattainable for several important reasons. First, the long periods of time needed for most timber management rotations encompass many changing directions in management goals, societal preferences, and legislative requirements, and thus management direction, desired goals, outputs, and practices may be different at the end of the rotation from what was once envisaged. Second, it is extremely difficult to balance perfectly growth with depletion, especially as the area under consideration gets larger. This is because site-specific variations in fertility and other growing conditions introduce greater variability to growth predictions, and unanticipated events such as fire, disease, or windstorms create disruptions in the normal sequence of events that were planned.

There are some forests that after long periods of systematic and very rigorous management could be considered as almost 'normal,' but these are an exception. However, the concept is used as a benchmark against which current conditions can be compared to highlight areas where adaptive management may be needed if contemporary goals are to be met. Striving toward normality is increasingly seen as less important if vital ecological functions, and other aspects such as wildlife habitats, are to be maintained in co-existence with fibre production. *See also* Forest.

NORMAL YIELD TABLE *See* Yield Table.

NORMATIVE Relating to or dealing with norms, that is, the ideal standards of conduct or ethical values that are generally accepted as binding upon the individuals of a group or society and serve to guide, control, or regulate acceptable behaviour.

NOTCHING **1** A type of girdling in which the tree is ringed with notches cut well into the sapwood. **2** The act of making a series of close downward and upward V-shaped incisions into the sapwood. *See also* Girdle.

NOTIONAL COSTS Costs that are imputed but not received in money.

NO-WORK ZONE In wildlife tree assessment, a flagged area on the ground where no worker shall enter except to remove or eliminate hazards.

NOXIOUS PLANT A plant that may or may not be specified by law as being undesirable, troublesome, and difficult to control or eradicate. Typically, noxious plants are shrubs and perennial or annual plants rather than tree species, and have the capacity to readily colonize areas such that they can completely stifle the growth of other plants.

NSR Not Satisfactorily Restocked. *See also* Stocking.

NTS *See* National Topographic Service.

NUCELLAR EMBRYO In plants, an embryo developing from a cell in the nucellus rather than from a fertilized egg. It is genetically identical to the mother plant. *See also* Nucellus.

NUCELLUS The central part of an ovule in which the embryo sac develops; the sporangium.

NUCLEAR POLYHEDROSIS VIRUS (NPV) A viral pathogen of insects, mainly larvae of certain Lepidoptera and Hymenoptera, characterized by the formation of polyhedral bodies in the nuclei of infected cells. Some strains of such viruses are in use as microbial pesticides.

NUCLEUS **1** The protoplasmic organelle in eukaryotic cells, bounded by a nuclear membrane and containing the chromosomes and genetic information that control cell physiology and heredity. *See also* Eukaryote; Prokaryote. **2** In anatomy, an aggregation of nerve cells connected by nerve fibres located in the brains of vertebrates.

NULL HYPOTHESIS In statistics, an assumption that unless results or observations demonstrate otherwise, there is no relationship between two or more groups and that any observed differences are solely a result of chance, as opposed to a systematic cause. *See also* Hypothesis.

NUNATAK An isolated hill, knob, ridge, or peak of bedrock that projects prominently above the surface of a glacier and is completely surrounded by glacier ice.

NUPTIAL CHAMBER A chamber excavated by certain bark beetles under the bark of the host tree, in which mating takes place.

NUPTIAL FLIGHT A mating flight, usually referring to bees, ants, or termites.

NURSE CROP The deliberate use of tree, shrub, or other plant crops to nurture the development and form of more highly valued tree crops during the establishment phase. The nurse crop (or single nurse tree) is used to protect the other crop from the harshness of wind, frost, sun, and the drying effects these have on soils.

NURSE LOG Also Nurse Stump. Typically a fallen log, tree, or stump, that has decayed and become a rooting medium for new trees growing out of and on top of the decaying substrate. The nurse log protects seedlings from environmental factors such as wind, insolation, and frost, and provides the appropriate soil and microclimate for seed germination and development. Often, the resultant trees are not windfirm, and as the substrate further decays, the roots of the new tree form stiltlike structures that may be weak.

NURSE TREE *See* Nurse Crop.

NUT **1** A hard, relatively large, single-celled, single-seeded woody or bony indehiscent fruit. **2** More loosely, a drupe with a thin, fleshy exocarp and a large stone (pyrene), or sometimes, the pyrene itself (e.g., walnut). *See also* Fruit (for illustration).

NUTLET A diminutive of nut. A very thick-walled achene.

NUTRIENT Any element or compound that an organism must take in from its environment either because it cannot produce it at all, or because it cannot produce it fast enough to meet all of its needs. In aquatic systems, nutrients can also be pollutants, especially when they are excessive and when they contain phosphorus or nitrogen that permits high organic growth. *See also* Bloom; Eutrophication.

NUTRIENT BUDGET A schematic budget for any one ecosystem outlining the nutrient sources (pools) and the energy flows (fluxes) through the entire ecosystem. The budget can consider inputs to and outputs from the ecosystem, cycling through the ecosystem, or all three aspects.

NUTRIENT CAPITAL The total amount of available nutrients in an ecosystem.

NUTRIENT CONTENT VERSUS CONCENTRATION Concentration is specific, usually expressed in grams per kilogram or milligrams per kilogram of dry or fresh weight. Nutrient content is usually expressed as weight per unit area (kilogram per hectare). The terms are not synonymous.

NUTRIENT CYCLING Circulation or exchange of elements, such as nitrogen and carbon dioxide, between nonliving and living portions of the environment. Includes all mineral and nutrient cycles involving mammals and vegetation.

NUTRIENT DEPLETION A reduction in the total amount of nutrients in an ecosystem resulting from a change in the rates of input, uptake, release, movement, transformation, or export.

NUTRIENT-SENSITIVE WATERSHED Watersheds where: (1) nitrogen/phosphorous fisheries productivity research is ongoing. Uncontrolled changes are undesirable as they would affect the research; and (2) phosphorous levels have been raised by the introduction of effluent from municipal, industrial, hatchery, agricultural, or other sources creating the potential for a negative impact by the addition of nitrogen fertilizer. Areas with elevated phosphorous levels may be considered for urea fertilization as a means of recovering nutrient balance within the system.

NYMPH The immature stage of an insect that undergoes incomplete metamorphosis. The nymph resembles the adult form except for incomplete wing and gonad development. *See also* Instar.

O

OB- A prefix meaning inversion or reversal of the normal state (e.g., oblanceolate – inversely lanceolate).

OBCOMPRESSED Flattened from the front to the back, rather than from side to side. Flattened at right angles to the primary plane or axis (e.g., the achenes of some Compositae that are flattened at right angles to the radius of the receptacle).

OBCONIC Conical, but attached at the narrow end.

OBCORDATE Inversely heart-shaped, with the notch at the apex.

OBCUNEATE Wedge-shaped, with the broad end at the point of attachment.

OBDELTOID Inversely deltoid, having the narrow end at the point of attachment.

OBDIPLOSTEMONOUS Having the stamens in two whorls, with those in the outer whorl opposite the petals, and those of the inner whorl opposite the sepals. *See also* Diplostemonous.

OBJECTIVE **1** *See* Balanced Objectivism. **2** A quantifiable, measurable, and defined target, capable of attainment within a defined period of time. Objectives are the means by which goals are achieved and should include four main components. (1) They must state the desired outcome (i.e., what is to be accomplished. (2) They must indicate the time period within which the expected outcome is to be achieved. (3) They must include measurement factors, such as quantity, quality, or cost, so that the fulfilment of the objective can be verified. (4) They must indicate who is responsible for achieving the indicated results. Desirable (but not absolutely essential) elements of objectives are a description of how they will be achieved and an indication of who will determine whether the results have been achieved.

Objectives are typically narrower and shorter in range than goals, and serve as milestones toward goal achievement. *See also* Goal; Policy; Subjective.

OBLANCEOLATE Inversely lanceolate, with the broadest width about a third of the way down from the apex, tapering to the base. *See also* Leaf Shape (for illustration).

OBLATE Nearly spherical or globular, but slightly flattened at the poles.

OBLIGATE SPECIES Refers to organisms restricted to one or very few narrowly defined environments (e.g., a tree cavity, rock cave, or wet meadow), roles, modes of life, or processes for survival. Thus, an obligate anaerobe can only live in anaerobic conditions. An obligate parasite can only be a parasite and often only on one specific host. An obligate predator lives off only one species of prey. *See also* Facultative Species.

OBLIQUE In botanical description, slanting with unequal sides. It is also termed inequilateral. *See also* Leaf Shape (for illustration).

OBLONG Longer than broad, having parallel sides. *See also* Leaf Shape (for illustration).

OBOVATE Inversely ovate, broader above rather than below the middle. *See also* Leaf Shape (for illustration).

OBOVOID Inversely ovoid, with the point of attachment at the narrow end.

OBPYRIFORM Pear-shaped, narrowing toward the base end and attached at the narrow end. It is inversely pyriform.

OBSCURING PHENOMENON Any collection of aerosol particles aloft or in contact with the Earth's surface dense enough to be detected from the surface of the Earth.

OBSERVER **1** Any person who studies or scrutinizes an object, population, landscape, etc., in an effort to observe, detect, or analyze occurrences, behavioural patterns, or the interactions between these. **2** In landscape assessments, the relative position of the observer with respect to the landscape being observed. Three main situations are recognized. (1) **Observer inferior** is that visual relationship between viewer and viewed that exists when the location from which something is seen below the level of that object or the dominant visual elements in the surrounding landscape. From the observer-inferior position, features in the foreground (about 0.8 kilometre or 0.5 mile) are most likely to be of maximum visual importance and the middleground (5-8 kilometres or 3-5 miles) is likely to contain the most distant visible elements. (2) **Observer superior** is that visual relationship between viewer and viewed that exists when the location from which something is seen above the level of that object or the dominant visual elements in the surrounding landscape. From the observer-superior position, the maximum extent and expanse of view is expected to be visible with atmospheric conditions and Earth curvature being ultimate distance limitations. (3) **Observer normal** is that visual relationship between viewer and viewed that exists when the location from which something is seen is at (or approximately at) the level of that object or the dominant visual elements in the surrounding landscape. Typically, the viewing position (with respect to a feature or scene) in which a level line-of-sight will generally coincide with the visually dominant elements of the landscape. The observer-normal viewing position generally concentrates visual attention on the solid or water elements of the landscape rather than on the sky.

OBSOLESCENT **1** Botanically, nearly obsolete. It describes a plant part or organ still evident but much reduced and nonfunctional, rudimentary, vestigial. **2** In the process of becoming extinct.

OBSOLETE Botanically, not evident or apparent at its expected location, rudimentary, vestigial.

OBSTRUCTION Any blockage or formation of debris that impedes or blocks waterflow and/or fish migration.

OBTUSE **1** Terminating gradually in a rounded or blunted end. *See also* Leaf Shape (for illustration). **2** An angle greater than ninety degrees. *See also* Acute.

OCCAM'S RAZOR The maxim in scientific evaluations that, in selecting from among various hypotheses or theories, the simplest one that fits the known facts should be used (i.e., use the hypothesis or theory with the least number of assumptions). It is derived from the fourteenth-century English philosopher, William of Occam, who died in 1349. It is also known as the Law of Parsimony.

OCCASIONAL HOST *See* Host Susceptibility Rating (dwarf mistletoe).

OCCLUSION The healing and covering of a tree wound by development of new cambial tissue, which grows over the wound to cover it completely. Complete occlusion of wounds is not a guarantee that the damaged wood lying below the new tissue will be sound.

OCCUPANCY RATE The percentage of inventoried habitat that is estimated to be occupied by breeding pairs of a species.

OCCUPANCY RATING In hazard tree assessments, the level of use of a potential target area and the likelihood that people will be present at the site or target area when failure occurs. The type of use and seasonal variations in use are important aspects of the rating.

OCEANIC CLIMATE *See* Maritime Climate.
OCREA/OCHREA A tubular sheath formed at and around the base of a petiole of a stem by the coalescence of two stipules.
OESTRUS *See* Estrus.
OFF-ROAD VEHICLE (ORV) Any motorized track or wheeled vehicle designed for or capable of cross-country travel on or immediately over land, water, sand, snow, ice, marsh, swampland, or other terrain (e.g., four-wheel-drive trucks, motorcycles, amphibious vehicles, and snowmobiles). It is synonymous with All Terrain Vehicle (ATV).
OLD-GROWTH-DEPENDENT SPECIES An animal species so adapted that it can only exist in old-growth forests.
OLD-GROWTH FOREST Several definitions are possible depending on the forest type under scrutiny. Typically, old-growth forests differ significantly from younger forests in structure, ecological function, and species composition. Typical characteristics of an old-growth forest include: (1) a moderate to high canopy closure; (2) a patchy, multilayered, multispecies canopy with trees of several age classes, but dominated by large overstorey trees with a high incidence of large living trees, some with broken tops and other indications of old and decaying wood; (3) numerous large, standing, dead trees (snags); (4) heavy accumulations of down woody debris; and (5) the presence of species and functional processes that are representative of the potential natural community. Old-growth forests are part of a dynamic but slowly changing ecosystem, and include climax forests, but not sub-climax or mid-seral forests. The age and structure of old-growth forests varies considerably by forest type. Old-growth forests are also typically high in both species and genetic diversity and complex ecosystems and likely contain a number of plant and animal species that are old-growth-dependent.

On the Pacific coast of North America, old-growth characteristics begin to appear in unmanaged forests at 175 to 250 years of age, but this will vary considerably across the continent, depending on the site and forest type. Some definitions of old-growth include the absence of human disturbance, but it is increasingly clear, that few, if any, such places now exist on the planet. *See also* Forest; Second-Growth Forest.
OLEORESIN A type of viscous, soft pitch consisting of a mixture of monoterpenes (e.g., turpentine), resin acids, plant sterols, and other neutral components. The mixture is secreted by the resin-forming cells in pines and certain other trees. When resin canals are severed by bark beetles, oleoresin exudation results in pitch tubes and sometimes pitching out of the attacking beetles. *See also* Resinosis.
OLIGO- A prefix meaning few.
OLIGOGENIC RESISTANCE Resistance controlled by a few genes, the phenotypic effect of which may be large or small. *See also* Monogenic Resistance; Polygenic Resistance; Vertical Resistance.
OLIGOPHAGOUS An organism that is somewhat restricted in feeding habits, making use of only a few kinds of host. *See also* Host Specificity; Monophagous; Stenophagous.
OLIGOTROPHIC Waters that are poor in dissolved nutrients, of low photosynthetic productivity, and rich in dissolved oxygen at all depths. *See also* Dystrophic; Eutrophication.
OMBROTROPHIC A system receiving water and nutrients solely from inputs derived as precipitation. *See also* Minerotrophic.
OMNIVORES Any heterotrophic organism that feeds (consumes) on plant, fungal, and animal matter. *See also* Carnivore; Frugivore; Herbivore; Trophic Level.
ONE-STRIKE CONCEPT In fire suppressing, a fire-bombing operation involving fast initial action and the delivery of enough long-term retardant to achieve the initial attack objective in one trip. *See also* Litres-per-Hour Concept.
ONTOGENETIC Related to or becoming apparent during the course of ontogeny.
ONTOGENY The complete life cycle of an individual member of any one species, or the complete history of development of a tissue or organ. *See also* Phylogeny.
OOGENESIS The process that leads to the production of gamete cells in female diploid cells.
OOGONIUM The female organ producing gametes in thallophytes.
OOLICHAN A small, oily fish. It is also called hooligan or candlefish.
OOSPORE The fertilized female cell in fungi belonging to the Oomycetes, which undergoes a resting stage prior to developing into a sporophyte.
OPENING An opening is represented by the canopy space previously occupied by one or more trees. Openings can be created by natural mortality, by the deliberate removal of selected trees within a stand, or by the removal of all or part of one or more stands within a whole forest. *See also* Gap.

OPENNESS A measure of the horizontal distance visible from a point.

OPEN SPACE Land and water areas retained permanently or semipermanently in a virtually undeveloped condition, or in a condition where land, resource features, ecological functions, and aesthetic values are only slightly modified.

OPERATIONAL CRUISE *See* Inventory.

OPERATIONAL TRIAL A relatively extensive field test of a technological innovation, such as a piece of equipment, a pesticide, or a management procedure, in which the scale of the test is large enough for the innovation's performance and convenience in actual use to be fairly assessed. *See also* Pilot Project.

OPERATIONS RESEARCH The use of analytic methods adopted from mathematics for solving operational problems in an attempt to optimize performance of people, machinery, their interactions, or to discover the best possible course of action. Among the techniques used are mathematical programming, statistical theory, information theory, game theory, Monte Carlo methods, and queuing theory.

OPERATIVE TEMPERATURE The temperature actually experienced by an animal as a result of a combination of environmental effects, such as air temperature, wind speed, solar radiation, and humidity.

OPERCULATE Having a lid or cap.

OPERCULUM **1** A lid or cover at the anterior end of an egg that opens to allow the immature insect to emerge. **2** Botanically, a lid or cap resulting from circumscissile dehiscence. *See also* Moss (for illustration).

OPINION A time-bound judgment or speculation that may fluctuate unpredictably. In contrast to beliefs, opinions express what we believe at a given moment. Opinions are typically short-term impressions or guesses about specific objects, ideas, issues, or events that are usually involved with aspects of public affairs. *See also* Attitude; Belief.

OPPORTUNITY CLASS In recreation management, the opportunity class designates the availability of a particular quality or kind of experience that is appropriate to the condition.

OPPORTUNITY COST The benefit that could result from a course of action but that is foregone when that course of action is not pursued.

OPPOSITE Botanically, having two similar parts occurring at a node on opposite sides of the axis such as in opposite leaves (see illustration). *See also* Alternate; Whorl.

Rhus glabra
(Smooth sumac)

OPTICAL DENDROMETER *See* Dendrometer.

OPTIMAL COVER A combination of vegetative and topographical relief that permits a species to hide from predators and humans (hiding cover), or that permits a species to improve its thermal regulation and survive severely cold winter periods (thermal cover). *See also* Cover.

OPTIMAL HABITAT The best combination of resources that permit a species to successfully survive and breed.

OPTIMIZATION A process whereby potential gains and losses in one or more areas (factors in a planning process) are defined, ranked, weighted, and then amalgamated to yield an outcome that satisfies multiple demands, which might be ecological, social, or political. In forest management, an optimization strategy can yield a mix of benefits concurrently from the same forest at the same time, but many benefits may be at a lower level of yield than is possible under a maximization strategy. *See also* Maximization.

OPTIMUM ROAD SPACING The distance between parallel roads that gives the lowest combined cost of skidding and road construction costs per unit of log volume.

OPTION VALUE The amount an individual would be willing to pay to preserve (or would have to be paid to get him/her to sell) the option to participate in some activity or to use some resource at some future time, whether or not that individual ever actually participates or uses the resource.

ORBICULAR Almost circular. *See also* Leaf Shape (for illustration).

ORDER A division in the classification of plants and animals. It consists of a group of related families or, occasionally, a single family. Intermediate in rank between class and family. *See also* Class; Genus; Phylum; Species; Taxon.

ORDINAL SCALE A scale in which things (data) are sorted into homogeneous categories that are then ordered or ranked with respect to the degree, intensity, or amount of the attribute they contain or represent. *See also* Measurement; Nominal Scale.

ORDINAL VALUES *See* Measurement.

ORDINATE The vertical axis (y) on a graph. *See also* Abscissa.

ORDINATION A term used to describe the use of multivariate data analysis techniques that arrange stands or species in a two-dimensional (or more) space, the end product of which is a graph consisting of several axes. On the graph, similar stands or species are close together, while dissimilar ones are far apart. Outlier stands or species disjunctions are readily visible. There are two kinds of ordination. (1) In **direct ordination**, stands are placed along measured environmental gradients for which data was collected for each stand (e.g., canonical correspondence analysis). (2) In **indirect ordination**, the stands are arranged along the axes according to their similarities and dissimilarities in species composition. Explanation of their ordination positions along the axes in terms of environmental gradients is inferred from an understanding of the ecological requirements of the species and is thus considered to be indirect (e.g., correspondence analysis, detrended correspondence analysis, principal components analysis, and polar ordination). The illustration shows a biplot resulting from an indirect ordination by detrended correspondence analysis (DCA). *See also* Canonical Correspondence Analysis.

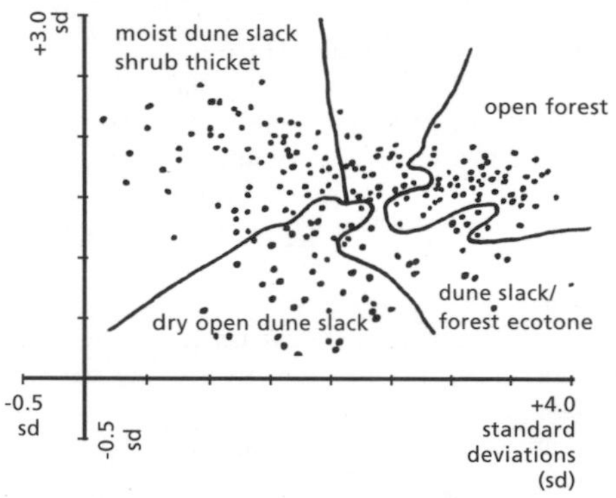

ORGANIC A substance derived from living organisms or their products and involving carbon-based compounds. *See also* Inorganic.

ORGANIC DEBRIS Logs, trees, limbs, branches, bark, and other woody material ranging in size from whole tree trunks down to accumulations of needle or leaf litter and small twigs; accumulates on the forest floor or in floodplains, streams, and other water bodies. The debris performs an important function by dissipating water energy; slowing the transport of gravel and smaller organic materials; creating eddies, pools, and small falls; providing cover for aquatic organisms.

ORGANIC MATERIALS **1** Nonliving material derived from living organisms. **2** In describing stream water, three main types of organic material are recognized. (1) **Coarse particulate organic material (CPOM)** is material having the smallest dimension, at least 1 millimetre to 10 centimetres. It technically includes both living and dead material, but commonly refers to detritus. (2) **Dissolved organic matter (DOM)** or **Dissolved organic carbon (DOC)** is material having the smallest dimension, less than 0.45 micron (i.e., will pass through a 0.45 micron filter). (3) **Fine particulate organic matter (FPOM)** is material having dimensions ranging from 0.45 micron to 1 millimetre.

ORGANIC PAN A layer usually occurring at twelve to thirty inches below the soil surface in coarse-textured soils, in which organic matter and aluminum (with or without iron) accumulate at the point where the top of the water table most often occurs. Cementing of the organic matter slightly reduces permeability of this layer.

ORGANIC SOILS Soils dominated by organic horizons (e.g., peat and muck soils), characteristic of wet sites. It is also termed folisols (consisting of L, F, and H horizons over bedrock or coarse fragments with little or no mineral soil between). *See also* Mineral Soil.

ORGANISM Any living entity from single-cell bacteria, viruses, fungi, to all plants and animals.

ORGANOCHLORINES Also termed chlorinated organic compounds, they are organic compounds containing chlorine, in some cases oxygen, and other elements such as phosphorus. Organochlorines include pesticides, such as dichlorodiphenyltrichloroethane (DDT), Dieldrin, Hexachlorobenzene (HCB), and hexachlorocyclohexane (HCH), as well as industrial chemicals such as dioxins and furans. *See also* DDT; Dioxins and Furans.

ORIENTATION The position of an organism or landscape feature relative to some other larger stable feature or attribute (e.g., relative to stream flow, compass bearing, or the alignment of a valley).

ORIFICE **1** An opening in a plant part, often a gall, for the exit of insects developing inside. **2** The opening at the end of a nozzle in spray equipment. The size of the orifice determines the size of the droplets.

ORIGINS OF A FIRE *See* Forest Fire.

ORNITHOPHILOUS Pollinated by birds (e.g., hummingbird).

OROGENESIS The process that forms mountains.

OROGRAPHIC A process in which air masses are lifted up by mountains or similar obstructions, leading to higher amounts of precipitation on the windward side of the mountain. *See also* Rain Shadow.

OROGRAPHIC RAIN Rain that results from moist winds impinging on and being forced upwards by hills and mountains.

ORTET The original plant from which a clone has been derived.

ORTHOGONAL **1** In remote sensing, meaning at right angles, or rectangularly, in the sense of meeting, crossing, or lying at right angles. **2** In statistics, uncorrelated.

ORTHOPHOTOGRAPH Images based on air photos, but which are true to scale and free of distortion. Orthophotos resemble air photos but, in fact, are maps. *See also* Displacement; Rectification; Rubber Sheeting.

ORTHOPHOTO MAP A controlled mosaic corrected for displacement due to tilt and relief, usually enhanced by drafting of planimetric and other features.

ORV *See* Off-Road Vehicle.

OSMOSIS The diffusion of fluids through a semi-permeable membrane, from a weak to a more concentrated solution. Osmosis balances concentration gradients in solutions on both sides of the membrane. Osmosis is the primary process driving uptake of water and dissolved salts in plants. Fresh water (dilute solution) is drawn into the plant cells (concentrated salts solution) via cells in the roots.

OSMOTROPHS *See* Saprobe.

OSTIOLE A small opening, typically circular, in the fruiting body of a fungus or algae through which spores are discharged (e.g., conceptacle, perithecium) or on a plant part (e.g., stoma, anther sac, etc).

OUTBREAK A sudden increase in destructiveness or population numbers of a pest species (usually in reference to insects) in a given area. *See also* Infestation.

OUTBREEDING Mating in which close relatives do not usually breed. *See also* Inbreeding.

OUTBREEDING DEPRESSION *See* Dysgenic.

OUTCROP That part of a geologic formation or structure that appears at the surface of the Earth.

OUTPUT The result, product, or service that a process or activity actually produces. They can be secondary (induced) (i.e., they are an indirect result of another activity) or primary (i.e., the direct results). *See also* Input.

OUTWASH Glaciofluvial sediments deposited by glacial meltwater downstream from a glacier.

OUTWASH PLAIN A flat or gently sloping landform created by the deposition of well-sorted glacial drift by debris-laden glacial meltwaters. *See also* Drumlin (for illustration).

OVAL Broadly elliptical, having width greater than one half of the length. *See also* Leaf Shape (for illustration).

OVARY The organ that produces female gametes. In plants, it is the basal, ovule-bearing part of the pistil. When borne above the point of attachment of perianth and stamens, or surrounded by a hypanthium that is not adnate to it, it is termed a superior ovary. When located below the apparent point of attachment of these floral envelopes, it is an inferior ovary; when intermediate, it is a half-inferior or subinferior ovary. *See also* Carpel (for illustration); Epigynous; Hypogynous.

OVATE Egg-shaped in outline, having the widest point below the middle. *See also* Leaf Shape (for illustration).

OVERBURDEN **1** Material of any nature, consolidated or unconsolidated, that overlies bedrock or a deposit of useful materials, especially those deposits that are capable of being mined from the surface or by open cuts (e.g., gravel or shale deposits for road construction, ore bodies for mining, rock for quarrying). If these deposits are mined, the overburden may be piled and stored for later use in reclaiming the site. **2** The upper part of a soil or sedimentary deposit that causes the consolidation of the material below.

OVERHEAD COSTS Costs that are not attributable to specific units of production, mainly fixed costs and common costs. It is also the routine cost associated with doing business, rather than the variable costs associated with production (e.g., office administration, business development). *See also* Fixed Costs; Variable Costs.

OVERLAP In remote sensing, the amount by which one image or photograph overlaps another, either in forward or lateral overlap. **Forward overlap** is the overlap along a flight line and is often used synonymously with overlap. **Lateral overlap** is the overlap between flight lines.

OVERLAY A process in which layers of different data are plotted, registered with each other (using common datum points), and stacked to portray the manner in which they interact spatially. In its simplest form, a base map is overlain with a transparent sheet that has another layer of information portrayed. Originally pioneered as a planning and decisionmaking tool by the geographer Ian McHarg (also known as the McHarg process or *Design With Nature*, based on his bestselling book), the overlay process is now an integral part of geographic information systems. Computerization of the data in each separate overlay permits an almost infinite number of data-matching, sorting, and retrieval capabilities.

OVERLOAD A gross vehicle weight in excess of the rated level specified by the manufacturer, or in excess of individual axle ratings or permissible tire and rim loadings.

OVERMATURE A tree or stand that is considered to have gone past the point of maturity. It is usually used in the context of even-aged management regimes. The term is also used synonymously, but incorrectly, with the term decadent. *See also* Decadent; Maturity.

OVERMATURE STANDS In timber management, describes trees of an age at which they decline in vigour and soundness, and thus start to become potentially less useful for lumber.

OVERSTOCKED *See* Stocking.

OVERSTOREY The uppermost layer of foliage in a forest having more than one roughly horizontal layer of foliage.

OVERSTOREY REMOVAL The final harvest in a series of harvests, overstorey removal eliminates the remnant overstorey and permits the regeneration to develop.

OVER-THINNING Excessive pruning of the lateral branches at their point of origin. It is usually associated with removal of large amounts of live tissue. It can lead to premature death if there is not enough foliage remaining to provide sufficient photosynthetic activity to support the plant.

OVERTHRUST A low-angle thrust fault of large scale, with displacement generally measured in kilometres.

OVERTOPPED *See* Crown Class.

OVERWINTERING BROOD The bark beetle brood that passes winter inside the host tree, completing development in spring.

OVERWINTERING FIRE A fire that persists through the winter months until the start of a new fire season. *See also* Holdover Fire.

OVERWINTERING STAGE The stage in which an organism, such as an insect or fungus, endures the adverse conditions of winter.

OVIPOSITOR In female insects, the tubular or valved structure by means of which the eggs are placed. It is usually a protusible organ normally concealed within the body, but sometimes permanently extended far beyond the end of the body. The act of laying eggs through an ovipositor is termed oviposition.

OVISAC An extension of the body wall or specialized structure of a female where certain kinds of insects deposit their eggs.

OVOID Egg-shaped solid bodies.

OVOVIVIPAROUS Eggs with distinct shells that hatch within the maternal body (e.g., some reptiles, fish, and invertebrates).

OVULATE **1** The production of eggs from the ovary. **2** Producing ovules, such as gymnospermous megasporophylls, where the ovules are naked and not enclosed in a pistil.

OVULE The part of a flower that becomes the seed after fertilization. *See also* Carpel (for illustration).

OXBOW A closely looping stream meander having an extreme curvature such that only a neck of land is left between the two parts of the stream. *See also* Oxbow Lake (for illustration).

OXBOW LAKE The curved lake created when a stream cuts through a meander to form a new stream channel (see illustration).

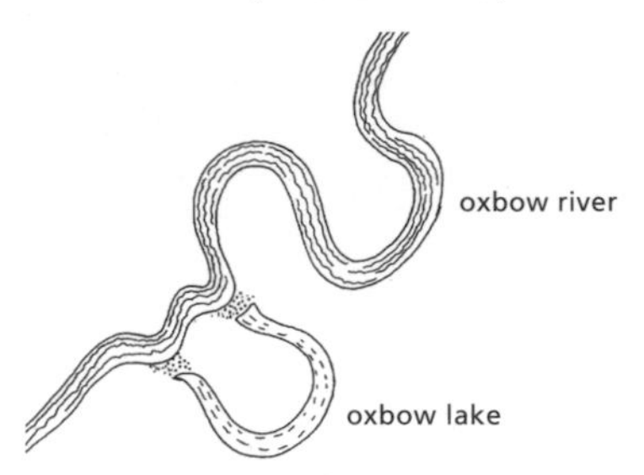

OXIDATION Any chemical process in which one or more electrons are removed from an atom, molecule, or ion. Oxidation of one substance always involves the reduction of another. *See also* Reduction.

OXYGEN SATURATION The maximum concentration of oxygen found in water. It decreases as water temperature increases.

P

PACKING A temporary influx of organisms of various sex and age classes into remaining suitable habitat as previously available habitat is changed to unsuitable conditions.

PALAEO- From Greek, meaning old. It is also spelled paleo-.

PALATE **1** In vertebrates, the roof of the mouth. **2** Botanically, the palate is a rounded prominence on the lower lip, closing or nearly closing the throat of a personate corolla.

PALEA A small, chaffy bract typically seen as:

(1) one of the chaffy scales on the surface of the receptacle of the flower head in many Compositae; and (2) the small, upper (inner) bract (glume) of a pair that encloses the flower in grasses, the lower (outer) pair being the lemma. *See also* Grass (for illustration).

PALEACEOUS **1** Chaffy or chafflike in texture. **2** Bearing paleae.

PALEOCLIMATIC Describing climates of the geologic past.

PALEOECOLOGY The systematic study and analysis of species diversity, distribution, and the interrelationship between prehistoric organisms and their environments by analysis of fossil records found in rocks, soils, and sediments. *See also* Palynology.

PALEOLITHIC From the earlier part of the Stone Age, when primitive stone tools were used by ancient humans. The Paleolithic began about 2.5 million years BP and ended around the end of the last ice age, approximately 10,000 BP, and is divided into three phases: (1) **Lower Paleolithic** is represented by the earliest human forms and the presence of hand-axe industries. It ends approximately 80,000 BP. (2) **Middle Paleolithic** is the era of Neanderthal Man. It ends about 33,000 BP. (3) **Upper Paleolithic** is the era during which modern *Homo sapiens* developed.

PALEONTOLOGY The systematic study of fossilized flora and fauna.

PALEOSOL A soil buried by younger surficial materials. A soil formed on the landscape of the past with distinctive morphological features resulting from a soil-forming environment that no longer exists at the site. The former pedogenic process was either altered because of external environmental changes, or because it was subsequently buried. A paleosol (or one of its component horizons) may be termed a relict if it has persisted in a land-surface position without major alteration of morphology by processes of the prevailing pedogenic environment. An exhumed paleosol is one that was formerly buried and has been re-exposed by erosion of the covering material. Most paleosols have had their diagnostic horizon morphologies affected by varying degrees of modification and profile truncation.

PALISADE LAYER The row of elongated cells in leaves, typically lying just beneath the upper epidermis. They contain many chloroplasts and are the primary location for photosynthesis. The illustration shows a cross-section of a maple (*Acer* spp.) and the location of the palisade layer.

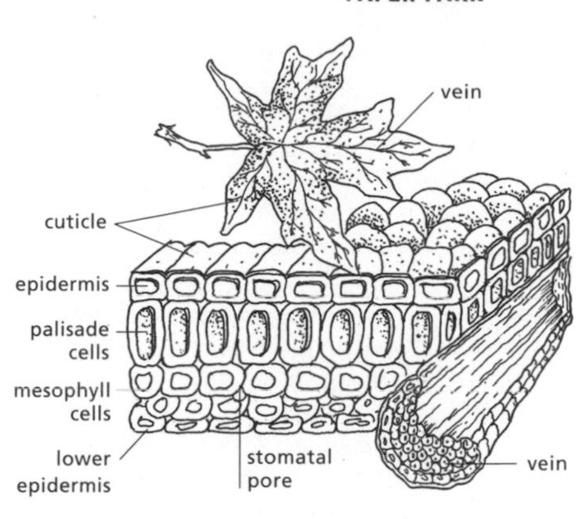

PALMATE Leaves having three or more nerves, lobes, or leaflets radiating fanwise from a common basal point of attachment.

PALMATIFID A leaf cut in the palmate fashion, about halfway to the base.

PALYNOLOGY The study of pollen grains. It is typically derived from sediment sampling to determine which plants were present in past eras of land settlement, and past vegetation patterns and sequences. *See also* Paleoecology.

PANDEMIC An epidemic that occurs over an extended geographical area, or especially one that occurs simultaneously in many parts of the world.

PANDURATE/PANDURIFORM Fiddle-shaped, typically rounded at both ends and constricted in the middle region.

PANGAEA The supercontinent believed to have been the precursor, about 200 million years ago, of the current land masses found around the planet.

PANICLE An indeterminate branching inflorescence, the branches typically being racemose or corymbose. *See also* Inflorescence (for illustration).

PANICULATE Resembling, or formed like, a panicle.

PANNOSE Having a texture similar to felt or being densely covered with woolly hairs.

PANORAMIC PHOTOGRAPH A photograph taken from a lookout point, with azimuth and vertical angle scales, to assist in locating fires with a fire finder.

PANORAMIC PROFILE MAP A panoramic sketch drawn around the circumference of a fire finder map to show topographic profiles as they appear from a lookout.

PAPER PARK A derogatory term describing a designated park of some form, that exists primarily on paper, but has little or no management or protection in reality, or 'on the ground.'

PAPILIONACEOUS Shaped like a butterfly. It typically describes the corolla characteristic of the subfamily Faboideae in the pea family. It is usually seen with five petals, with the uppermost one (the standard, banner, or vexillum) outside and usually largest, the two laterals (the wings) paired and usually clawed, and the two lowermost united along their lower margin and forming a sheath (the keel) enclosing the stamens and pistil.

PAPILLA Plural papillae. A small, nipple-shaped or pimple-like protuberance.

PAPILLATE Having a papilla.

PAPPUS A modified perianth whorl in the flowers of the Compositae, borne at the top of the ovary in the position normally occupied by the calyx in other families. The pappus usually persists into fruit and consists of distinct or united small scales, bristles, and barbed or plumose hairs.

PAR *See* Photosynthetically Active Radiation.

PARADIGM A set of generally accepted assumptions, concepts, and propositions, from which coherent models of thought and action are derived, and which subsequently guide a practice.

PARALLAX In photogrammetry, the apparent displacement of the position of a body, with respect to a reference point or system, caused by a shift in the point of observation. **Absolute parallax** is the algebraic difference, parallel to the air base, of the distances of the two images of an object from their respective principal points. **Differential parallax** is the difference between two absolute parallax values. It is customarily used in the determination of the difference in elevation (i.e., height) of objects. **Photograph parallax** results when the camera position is moved between consecutive overlapping photographs.

PARALLAX BAR A bar-shaped micrometer used with a stereoscope to measure parallax, or to calculate tree heights or differences in elevation of topographic features.

PARALLEL ATTACK *See* Fire Suppression.

PARAMETER **1** Any attribute, variable, or physical property in a set of variables or properties that, taken together, characterize or determine a system's behaviour. **2** A variable, arbitrary constant, or item of information that is used in a mathematical calculation, subroutine, or program, and which can be given a different value each time, and whose values restrict or determine the specific form of the expression.

PARAMETRIC STATISTICS Statistics that assume a parametric model (i.e., a model having finite numerical parameters or facts).

PARAPATRIC Describes geographical contact between separate populations or species without significant overlap or interbreeding. *See also* Allopatric; Sympatric.

PARAPHYLLIUM Plural paraphyllia. A tiny leaflike or threadlike structure borne on the stems and among the leaves of some mosses.

PARAPHYSATE Having paraphyses.

PARAPHYSIS Plural paraphyses. In mycology, sterile filaments, often clavate or capitate, that occur in aecia and/or uredinia of rusts. It is more properly called pseudoparaphyses.

PARASITE An organism that, for at least part of its life cycle, lives on or in, and at the expense of, another living organism (the host), often obtaining nutrients from the host's tissues. Parasites are typically smaller than the host and generally do not kill it. A parasite needs only one or part of one host individual to reach maturity, or to complete a particular stage of development. The terms pathogen and parasite are not interchangeable. Parasite refers to an organism's mode of life, while pathogen refers to its ability to cause disease. Not all parasites are pathogens and not all pathogens are parasites. *See also* Ectoparasite; Epiphyte; Facultative Species; Obligate Species; Parasitoid; Predator; Saprophyte; Symbiosis.

PARASITISM The relationship between a parasite and its host, in which the parasite derives benefits from and at the expense of, the host. *See also* Symbiosis.

PARASITOID An insect that, in its larval stage of development, is parasitic on another insect, destroying the host insect in the process. The adult stage of the parasitoid is free-living.

PARATYPE *See* Type.

PARENCHYMA **1** Botanically, the basic undifferentiated and unspecialized plant tissue making up most of the plant, including the inner tissue of leaves, stem pith, and fruit pulp. Under certain stimuli the parenchyma cells may differentiate into more specialized cells and plant parts. They remain alive at maturity and often have a packing function. **2** Zoologically, the tissue that actually makes the functional parts of an organ, as opposed to the tissue around these.

PARENT ADULT A sexually mature insect that has produced young, particularly a bark beetle or ambrosia beetle that has produced one brood and may attack trees or logs again.

PARENT MATERIAL The unconsolidated and more or less weathered mineral or organic matter from which a soil profile develops. *See also* Matrix.

PARETO OPTIMUM In welfare economics, a concept that sets a condition necessary to maximize the economic wealth of a society. The pareto optimum is said to have been achieved when it is impossible to make any one person better off without making another (or others) worse off.

PARIPINNATE Evenly pinnate, having leaflets in pairs along an axis but lacking a terminal leaflet. *See also* Imparipinnate.

PARR A young salmonid, in the stage between alevin and smolt, that has developed distinctive dark 'parr marks' on its sides and is actively feeding in freshwater. *See also* Fingerling; Fry.

PARTED/PARTITE Cut or cleft almost to the base, into a determinate number of segments.

PARTHENOCARPIC Producing fruits without fertilization.

PARTHENOGENESIS Any organism capable of reproducing by means of an unfertilized ovum. *See also* Apomixis.

PARTIAL CUTTING Removal of selected trees from a forest stand.

PARTICLE SIZE ANALYSIS Determination of the grain size composition of a sediment by laboratory analysis.

PARTICULATE MASS CONCENTRATION The amount of particulate per unit volume of air, expressed in micrograms per cubic metre.

PARTICULATES Short for particulate matter. Air pollutants composed of small liquid or solid particles temporarily suspended in the atmosphere (e.g., dust, pollen, spores, soot, smoke, or spray).

PASSERINE BIRD A group of birds (true songbirds) that have the capability of perching on branches. Passerines have specialized feet adapted for perching, with three of the unlobed toes pointing forward and one pointing backwards. The young are altricial. *See also* Altricial; Non-passerine Bird; Precocial.

PASTURE An area, usually fenced off, devoted to the production of forage and harvested by grazing animals.

PATCH In timber management, a small part of the forest (eight to twenty-four hectares or twenty to sixty acres). The term is often used to indicate a type of clearcutting (patch cutting) associated with the 'staggered setting' approach to distributing harvest units across the forest landscape. In landscape ecology, a small part of the whole landscape, differing from its surroundings. *See also* Staggered Setting.

PATCH CUTTING A modification of the clearcutting system, patch cutting was developed in the Pacific coast region of North America as a means of dispersing logging activities across whole landscapes. Patches of about 5 to 200 hectares are logged as a single setting, separated from adjacent patches (leave blocks) for as long as possible by existing forest (or regenerated forest that is well established). This approach secures an optimum dispersal of seed and avoids the high fire hazard associated with large, continuous areas of slash. However, patch cutting has been seen to be detrimental to wildlife habitats, since it can lead to wholescale fragmentation of the landscape, disruption of connectivity, and loss of interior forest conditions in the remaining forest blocks. *See also* Connectivity; Fragmentation; Green-Tree Retention; Interior Forest Conditions.

PATCHINESS A characteristic of discontinuous and heterogeneous environments consisting of a patchwork of rather different resources, as opposed to homogeneous, or uniform, environments. Sometimes refers to a species distributed in an unexplainable fashion, such that it occurs where the resources would not normally be suitable.

PATENT Botanically, a form that is spreading.

PATERNOSTER LAKES A linear sequence of rock basin lakes and streams formed within a glacial valley. The name alludes to the map view resemblance of paternoster lakes to rosary beads (see illustration).

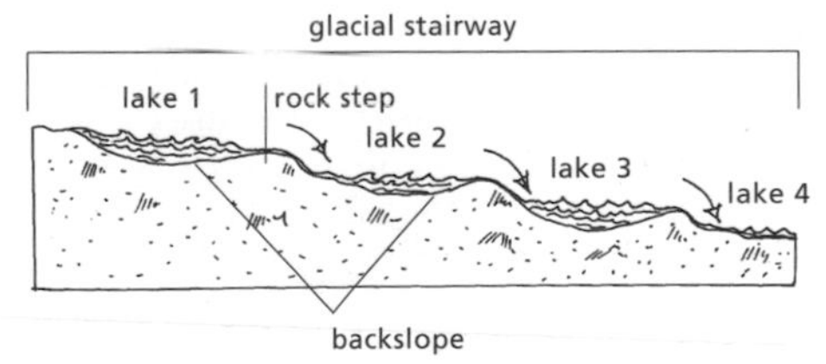

PATHOGEN A disease-inducing organism or abiotic agent.

PATHOGENICITY The capability to cause disease. It may be qualified with a descriptor such as 'high,' 'medium,' or 'low,' but the term virulence is preferable as a means of indicating the degree to which a pathogen is able to induce disease. Pathogenicity may be used to describe a group of organisms, such as a genus or species, while virulence is used to describe the ability of a particular isolate, strain, or other subgroup to cause disease under particular conditions. Thus, it is possible to refer to a non-virulent strain of a pathogenic organism.

PATHOGENIC ROTATION AGE The maximum rotation age through which a stand of trees may be grown without significant loss of volume due to disease (i.e., the rotation age equals that point where volume losses due to disease are equal to annual volume increment).

PATHOLOGY **1** The scientific study of disease, including diseases caused by viruses, bacteria, mycoplasmas, and fungi, and often nematodes. Injury caused by animals and other insects is usually excluded. Disorders of plants due to abiotic factors are frequently but not always considered to be within the sphere of plant pathology. It is also termed phytopathology.

PATHOTYPE *See* Biotype.

PATHOVAR Refers to plant-pathogenic bacteria. An infraspecific population distinguishable mainly or only on the basis of pathogenicity to certain plants.

PATROL **1** In fire suppression, to inspect a section of a control line or portion of the fire perimeter to prevent escape of the fire. **2** To travel (by air or on the ground) a given route to inspect, detect, and suppress fires, or to monitor other aspects of resource management.

PATTERNED GROUND Land surface with distinctive arrangement of stones or microtopography due to the effects of ground freezing and seasonal frost; characteristic of periglacial environments, but some features can also occur in tropical and subtropical areas. The term includes stone stripes, sorted circles, and tundra polygons.

PAYLOAD The weight of passengers and/or cargo being loaded by an aircraft.

PEAK **1** A high point or maximum. **2** A sharp or rugged upward extension of a ridge chain, often at the junction of two or more ridges. **3** The highest point of a summit area.

PEAK FIRE SEASON That period of the fire season during which fires are expected to ignite most readily, burn with the greatest intensity, and create fire damage at an unacceptable level.

PEAK FLOW The highest amount of stream or river flow occurring in a year or from a single storm event.

PEAK MONTHLY AVERAGE The highest monthly average of human-caused fires calculated for a protection unit.

PEAK WIND The greatest five-second average wind speed during the previous hour that exceeded forty miles per hour (thirty-five knots).

PEAT Black or brown, partly decomposed, fibrous vegetative matter that has accumulated in a waterlogged environment, such as a bog.

PEBBLE A rounded rock fragment between two and sixty-four millimetres in intermediate diameter. *See also* Substrate Particle Size.

PECTINATE A shape or margin that is arranged like the teeth of a comb.

PED A unit of soil structure (e.g., aggregate, crumb, prism, block, or granule) formed by natural processes.

PEDALFER A broad category of soils in which calcium carbonate does not accumulate, the soil properties are determined mainly by the presence of aluminum and iron, and leaching is a dominant process. Typical of the humid, middle latitude regions of the world, pedalfers are characterized by an accumulation of silicate clays and iron or aluminum sesquioxides in the B horizon. Includes podsols and the ferrallitic soils. *See also* Pedocal.

PEDATE Describes a palmately lobed or divided leaf in which the two outer side lobes are divided or cleft a second time.

PEDICEL The stalk of a flower (or inflorescence) or a spore. *See also* Flower (for illustration).

PEDICELLATE Borne on, or having a pedicel.

PEDIMENT A gently sloping erosional surface developed at the foot of a receding hill or mountain slope. The surface may be essentially bare, exposing earth material that extends beneath adjacent uplands, or it may be thinly mantled with alluvium and colluvium in transit from the upland front to the basin or valley lowland.

PEDISEDIMENT A layer of sediment eroded from the shoulder and backslope of an erosional slope that lies on and is or was being transported across a pediment.

PEDOCAL A broad category of soils in which calcium carbonate does accumulate and leaching is not a dominant process. Typical of the drier, middle-latitude regions of the world, pedocals are characterized by an accumulation of calcium carbonate in the upper horizons. They include chernozems and rendzinas. *See also* Pedalfer.

PEDOLOGY The scientific study of the general characteristics, origins, and taxonomy of soils.

PEDON **1** A three-dimensional body of soil, ranging in area from one to ten square metres, and in depth from one to two metres, and large enough to permit study of soil horizon shapes and relations. **2** An organism living in or on the substrate of an aquatic habitat.

PEDUNCLE The stalk or stem of a flower cluster or flower borne singly, or the penultimate internode below a single flower.

PEELER A high-grade log from which veneer is peeled on a lathe, for the production of plywood. Peelers are most frequently from old-growth trees. The resulting veneer is usually free of large knots and defects and used on the sanded outer face of the plywood.

PEG *See* Sterigma.

PELAGIC Organisms that swim or drift in oceans or open waters, as opposed to those that live in waters adjacent to land or inland. Pelagic organisms include plankton, many fish species, and oceanic birds (such as albatross). *See also* Demersal.

PELLUCID Almost clear or transparent.

PELTATE A plant organ such as a leaf, almost circular in outline, or shieldlike, and attached by a stalk near the centre of the underside rather than at the edge. *See also* Leaf Shape (for illustration).

PENDENT/PENDULOUS A drooping, hanging downwards, or weeping growth habit.

PENEPLAIN A low, nearly featureless, gently undulating land surface of considerable area, resulting from erosional processes taking place over long time periods. A peneplain may be characterized by gently graded and broadly convex interfluves sloping down to broad valley floors, by truncation of strata of varying resistance and structure, by accordant levels, and by isolated erosion remnants rising above it.

PENETRATION **1** The initial invasion of the host by a parasite or pathogen through natural openings, such as stomata or lenticels, through wounds, or directly through intact host tissues. *See also* Colonization. **2** The degree to which a wood preservative treatment penetrates the wood layers.

PENICILLATE Brushlike; having a tuft of hairs.

PENNINERVED Pinnately nerved.

PENTAMEROUS Having parts in five, or multiples of five.

PEPO A one-celled, many-seeded fruit of the gourd family, having a hard, leathery outer rind and fleshy pulp inside. Typical of pumpkins, squashes, and gourds. *See also* Fruit (for illustration).

PERCENTAGE OF COVER A measure of the degree of dominance, or crown closure, by different plant species or vegetation canopy layers.

PERCENTILE The specific value of a random variable that corresponds to a given cumulative probability.

PERCHED WATER TABLE A water table that is 'perched' or elevated above a layer or lens of impermeable soil such as clay (see illustration). *See also* Water Table.

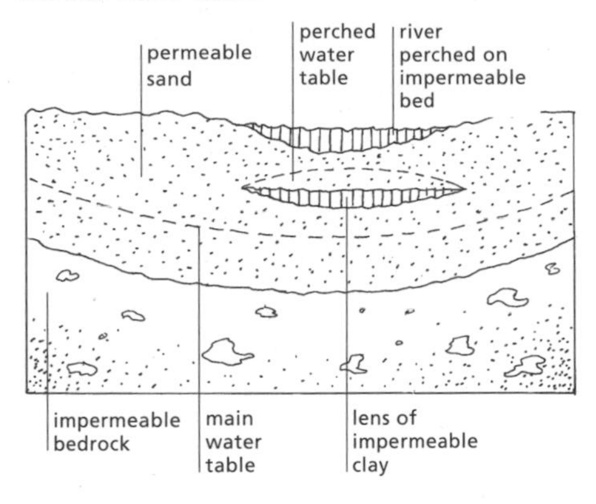

PERCOLATE To move water down in a nearly vertical direction through soil.

PERCOLATION The flow of water or other fluids through soil, rock, or a filter, under the influence of gravity, and in conditions of partial or complete saturation. *See also* Soil Drainage.

PERCURRENT Reaching to the apex, but not beyond (e.g., percurrent costa).

PERENNATE Living or surviving from year to year, typically with a period of greatly diminished activity at one point in the year.

PERENNATING BUD The renewal bud on plants, from which the next season's growth will be made. *See also* Life-Form (for illustration).

PERENNIAL A plant that continues growth from year to year. Many perennial plants are woody, such as trees, shrubs, and some vines, but others include dandelions and daisies, where the above-ground parts die back to leave perennating organs such as tubers, corms, or bulbs underground.

PERENNIAL STREAM *See* Stream.

PERFECT Flowers having both sexes (i.e., bisexual). *See also* Imperfect.

PERFECT SIMPLICITY An area in which no edges occur either on or within the perimeter (i.e., where the diversity index is equal to zero).

PERFECT STAGE *See* Sexual Stage.

PERFOLIATE A sessile leaf or bract, the base of which encircles the stem so that the stem appears to pass through the leaf or bract. *See also* Leaf Shape (for illustration).

PERGAMENTACEOUS Having the look or feel of parchment.

PERIANTH A collective term for the floral envelopes, that is, the calyx and corolla, or both. It is also used to describe a flower where there is no distinction between corolla and calyx. *See also* Flower (for illustration).

PERICARP The wall of a ripened ovary (i.e., the wall of the fruit). Sometimes differentiated into the exocarp (outer layer), the mesocarp (middle layer), and the endocarp (inner layer).

PERICHAETIAL LEAVES In mosses, special leaves surrounding the base of the seta that are often different in size and shape from other leaves of the gametophyte. *See also* Moss (for illustration).

PERICHAETIUM Plural perichaetia. In bryophytes, a special leaf surrounding the female organ (archegonium) at the base of a sporophyte stalk (seta).

PERICYCLE The tissue of a stem or root bounded externally by the cortex.

PERIDERM A protective plant tissue external to the cortex and/or phloem of stems and roots, composed of cork (phellem) on the outside of the cork cambium, the cork cambium (phellogen), and the phelloderm, formed on the inside of the cork cambium. The periderm is more or less impervious to water, solutes, and organisms.

PERIDERMIUM Plural peridermia. In mycology, an aecium with a blisterlike, tongue-shaped, or cylindric peridium. *See also* Peridium.

PERIDIAL Pertaining or belonging to the peridium.

PERIDIUM Plural peridia. In describing rusts, the outer encompassing membrane of the fruiting body, such as aecia and uredinia, of conifer rusts.

PERIGLACIAL **1** Pertaining to processes, conditions, areas, climates, and topographic features found at the immediate margins of former and existing glaciers and ice sheets, and influenced by the cold air of the ice. **2** Pertaining to cold climates, such as in arctic and alpine areas.

PERIGONE In plants, the perianth. Perigone is the term used when the parts are not or are barely differentiated into calyx and corolla. When this is the case, the term used to describe the calyx and corolla is 'tepal.'

PERIGYNIUM The papery sheath or specialized sac that encloses the ovary in sedges (*Carex* spp.).

PERIGYNOUS Borne or arising around the ovary. It describes sepals, petals, and stamens that arise from the upper edge of a hypanthium that is itself attached below the ovary in the form of a floral tube. *See also* Epigynous; Hypogynous; Receptacle (for illustration).

PERIMETER *See* Fire Perimeter.

PERIOD In geological time scales, a subdivision of an era. *See also* Eon; Epoch; Era.

PERIODIC ANNUAL INCREMENT *See* Current Annual Increment.

PERIOD OF ALERT A period when fire-fighters, fire control equipment, and aircraft are kept ready for deployment on short notice, usually when the fire danger reaches a predetermined degree of severity. It may also involve an increase in fire prevention activities and often precedes forest closure. *See also* Standby.

PERIPHERAL **1** A concept or item that lies at the outer edge of thought, action, or a location. **2** In computer science, any input, output, or storage device that operates along with the computer (printers, plotters, digitizers, tape drives, disk drives, mice, digitizing pen, etc.).

PERIPHYTON The complex of plants (algae) and animals (insect larvae and small animals) that grow or move about attached to surfaces submerged in freshwater, such as rocks and plant stems.

PERISTOME The fringe around the mouth of a capsule in mosses and other lower plants.

PERITHECIUM Plural perithecia. **1** A globe- or flask-shaped fruiting body (ascocarp) produced by certain ascomycete fungi, with an opening or pore (ostiole) through which the ascospores are discharged. **2** A flask-shaped fruiting body of a lichen, immersed in the thallus and with a dark and often protruding opening. *See also* Apothecium.

PERITRICHOUS A microorganism having flagella all over the cell surface.

PERMAFROST **1** Technically, material in which temperature has remained below zero degrees Celsius continuously for at least two years, regardless of type of material or water content; a thermal condition. **2** Generally, a perennially frozen layer in the soil, typical of arctic, antarctic, and alpine regions.

PERMANENT FOREST An area of forest that has been designated through land-use policy to be kept permanently under forest cover, rather than available for conversion to other forms of land use. *See also* Forest.

PERMANENT RESIDENT Individual birds or species that remain in the same geographical region all year long, other than seasonal shifts in altitude (non-migratory).

PERMANENT WILTING POINT *See* Soil Water.

PERMEABILITY A measure of the ease with which gases or liquids can penetrate or pass through a porous substance. The permeability of a membrane reflects the degree to which it will permit the passage of compounds in solution. The ease with which plant roots can penetrate soil. In soil analysis, a measure of the rate at which water can pass through a given substrate. Soil permeability is determined by the size, arrangement, and composition of soil particles, and by the degree of compaction (pore space). *See also* Porosity.

PERNICIOUS Any organism that causes destruction or injury.

PERSISTENCE **1** In general, a measure of stability or resistance to change over time, referring to the time period during which a certain characteristic continues to be present at a given level. **2** In toxicology, any chemical compound that does not break down, or breaks down very slowly once released into the environment, is said to be persistent. The classic example is DDT. *See also* Bioaccumulation. **3** In restoration or rehabilitation projects, or as natural phenomena, the state where a plant can maintain itself indefinitely once it has become established. **4** Botanically, a plant part that remains attached shows persistence or is said to be persistent.

PERSONATE Describes a two-lipped corolla in which the throat is closed by a palate (e.g., *Antirrhinum* spp., the snapdragons).

PERSPECTIVE **1** That which suggests the effects of distance upon the appearance of objects. **2** Personal attitudes, or points of view toward a subject under discussion.

PERT Programme Evaluation and Review Techniques. *See* Critical Path Method.

PERVERSE INCENTIVE An action that incites a reaction contrary to the one originally desired. Perversity is subjective and depends on context. *See also* Disincentive; Incentive.

PEST **1** Any organism or damaging agent designated as detrimental to effective resource management. Pests include certain insects, mites, fungi, bacteria, viruses, nematodes, plants, and vertebrates. **2** Any organism or population of organisms (other than microorganisms causing disease in humans, pets, or livestock) that thwarts or constrains resource management objectives, or causes significant harm to people, or loss to their property, or is at least perceived to be doing so. **3** In the Canadian Pest Control Products Act, a pest is defined as, 'Any injurious, noxious or troublesome insect, fungus, bacterial organism, virus, weed, rodent, or other plant or animal pest, and includes any injurious, noxious, or troublesome organic function of a plant or animal.' *See also* Secondary Pest.

PEST CONTROL **1** The reduction of resource losses or pest occurrences to socially, economically, and politically acceptable levels, by direct and immediate application of approved strategies or techniques. **2** The regulation of pest populations to levels below those at which they cause unacceptable harm by human intervention, including the use of chemical, physical, and/or biotic agents. Control, as distinguished from management, often caries the implication of bringing about increased mortality in the population in question. *See also* Pest Management.

PESTICIDE Chemical or biological substances used to deliberately kill unwanted plants or animals. Pesticides include herbicides, insecticides, algicides, and fungicides.

PESTICIDE APPLICATOR An individual qualified to use or apply pesticides.

PESTICIDE-FREE ZONE *See* Buffer Zone.

PESTICIDE RESIDUES The pesticides that remain in food, soil, and water after application. *See also* Bioaccumulation.

PEST MANAGEMENT **1** The application of approved strategies to control or prevent pest infestations and damage. Pest management strategies and tactics include: (1) long-term management to protect forest and range resources; (2) comprehensive silvicultural and harvesting operations; and (3) pest-specific suppression methods. **2** The management of any ecosystem by, or as recommended by professional pest managers, on the basis of defensible information and at acceptable cost, with the dual objectives of preventing or controlling pest-caused harm or loss and avoiding harm to useful organisms. Pest management is one component of forest management and includes the development and implementation of long-term strategies for maintaining pest populations at levels below those causing economically or socially unacceptable damage to the resource. *See also* Integrated Pest Management; Pest Control.

PETAL One of the flower parts forming the corolla or the inner floral envelope of a polypetalous flower, typically coloured and showy. *See also* Flower (for illustration).

PETALOID **1** As an adjective, petal-like, resembling a petal in shape and colour. **2** As a noun, an organ that is petal-like.

PETERSON INDEX *See* Lincoln Index.

PETIOLE The stalk that supports the leaf blade. *See also* Leaf Shape (for illustration).

PETIOLULE The stalk of a leaflet in a compound leaf.

PETROGLYPHS Rock carvings (carved into large rock masses) created by Native peoples to represent ideas, events, or activities.

pH A measure of the concentration of hydrogen ions in a solution, indicating neutrality (pH 7), acidity (less than pH 7), or alkalinity (greater than pH 7).

PHANEROGAM A member of the Spermatophyta. It is a plant reproducing by means of seeds. *See also* Cryptogam.

PHELLEM A tissue produced on the bark side of the phellogen in a stem or root. Normally, it dies soon after formation and forms a waterproof protective tissue with the cell walls composed largely of suberin. *See also* Bark.

PHELLODERM *See* Bark.

PHELLOGEN *See* Bark.

PHENETIC CLASSIFICATION Classification groupings based on the overall similarity of evolutionary relationships. *See also* Cladistics.

PHENOLOGY The study of the timing of periodic phenomena, such as flowering, growth initiation and cessation in plants, especially as they relate to seasonal changes in temperature, photoperiod, etc.

PHENOTYPE The visible physical characteristics of an organism, such as morphology, physiology, biochemistry, and behaviour, resulting from the influence of environmental conditions on its genetic constitution. *See also* Genotype.

PHENOTYPIC PLASTICITY Variation in characteristics that are nonheritable.

PHEROMONE A complex biochemical substance produced by an organism that stimulates a specific behavioural or physiological response by other individuals of the same species (e.g., sex pheromones). *See also* Allelochemic; Allomone; Kairomone; Synomone.

PHI The annual probability of survival of adult females.

PHLOEM A specialized tissue in vascular material that conducts food and growth regulators. The tissue is characterized by the presence of vascular bundles containing sieve tubes, companion cells, fibres, and parenchyma cells (see illustration). The sieve tubes lack many of the normal cell structures. They serve as conduits for the passage of sugars and complex photosynthates, such as amino acids, vitamins, and hormones, from the leaves to the stem and roots where they are used to help metabolism. The oldest phloem cells lie on the outside of

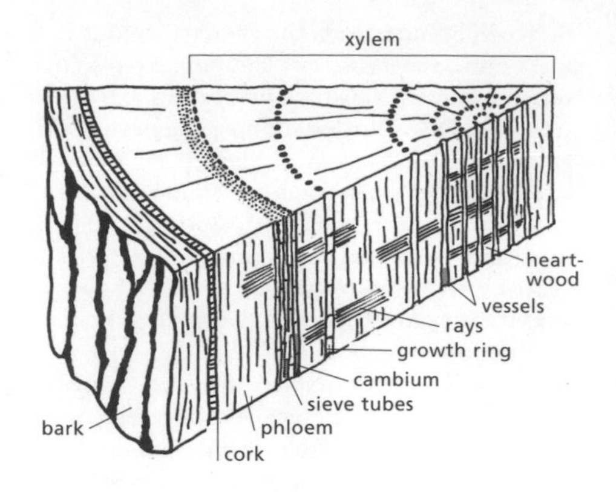

the vascular cambium, the youngest on the inside, next to the cambium. *See also* Bark; Xylem.

PHOTO BASE In photogrammetry, the length of the air base as represented on a photograph. The distance between the principal points of two adjacent prints of a series of vertical aerial photographs.

PHOTOBIONT The photosynthetically active component organism in a lichen. It is the alga of cyanobacterium.

PHOTOGRAMMETRY The art, science, and technology of obtaining reliable information about physical objects and the environment through processes of recording, measuring, and interpreting images and phenomena, such as patterns of electromagnetic radiant energy.

PHOTO INTERPRETATION The detection, identification, description, and assessment of the significance of objects and patterns imaged on a photograph.

PHOTO MAP A single air photo or a mosaic showing grid coordinates and other marginal information. *See also* Orthophoto Map.

PHOTOPERIOD The relative periods of daylight and darkness and the effects that this changing light intensity has on the growth, maturity, and activity of an organism.

PHOTOSYNTHESIS The process by which plants transform carbon dioxide and water into carbohydrates and other compounds, using energy from the sun captured by chlorophyll in the plant. Oxygen is a byproduct of the process. Photosynthesis is expressed chemically as:

$$CO_2 + H_2O \rightarrow C_6H_{12}O_8 + O_2$$

Photosynthesis is the essence of all plant life (autotrophic production) and hence of all animal life (heterotrophic production) on the planet Earth. The rate of photosynthesis depends on climate, intensity and duration of sunlight, available leaf area, soil nutrient availability, temperature, carbon dioxide concentration, and soil moisture regimes. Airborne atmospheric pollution and pollution deposits on the leaves affect the amount of sunlight reaching the photosynthesizing cells in the leaf surfaces. In sufficient concentrations, either form of pollution can seriously restrict photosynthesis.

PHOTOSYNTHETICALLY ACTIVE RADIATION (PAR) The visible part of the light spectrum, generally wavelengths between 0.4 and .75 micrometre wavebands.

PHOTOSYNTHETIC SURFACE The surface of a plant's leaves or needles that are capable of photosynthesizing. The amount of photosynthetic activity is determined by several factors, including the total surface area available, the percentage of this that can actively capture light and undertake photosynthesis, and other environmental factors such as soil and water regimes, and climate.

PHOTOTYPING The delineation and labelling of natural or cultural features on aerial photos. *See also* Forest Type.

PHREATOPHYTE A plant that sends down very long roots in order to utilize groundwater sources of moisture rather than depending upon soil moisture (e.g., willows [*Salix* spp.], cottonwoods [*Populus* spp.]).

PHYCOMYCETE A widely used designation for the so-called 'lower fungi' (Mastigomycotina and Zygomycotina), although no longer considered to be a taxonomically valid grouping. Phycomycetes are characterized by hyphae with few or no cross-walls (septa). They include the damping-off fungae.

PHYLLARY An involucral bract, typical of members of the Compositae family.

PHYLLOCLAD A flattened stem or branch functioning as a leaf (as with the prickly pear cactus [*Opuntia* spp.]).

PHYLLODE An expanded or broadened petiole taking the place of a leaf blade (e.g., *Acacia* spp.).

PHYLLOPODIC In plants, with the lowest leaves well developed instead of reduced to scales.

PHYLLOTAXY The arrangement of leaves or other floral parts on a stem or other axis. It is typically expressed numerically by a fraction, the numerator representing the number of revolutions of a spiral made in passing from one leaf past each successive leaf to reach the next leaf directly above the starting leaf. The denominator represents the number of leaves passed in the progression.

PHYLOGENETIC SPECIES CONCEPT The concept that a species is the smallest discernible cluster of individual organisms within which there is a parental pattern of ancestry and descent. *See also* Biological Species Concept.

PHYLOGENETIC TREE A diagrammatic representation of lines of evolution based on morphology and paleontological evidence.

PHYLOGENY The evolutionary history of an organism. *See also* Ontogeny.

PHYLUM In taxonomic classification a phylum lies beneath the classification kingdom and above the classification class. It is a group of similar classes. *See also* Class; Division; Family; Genus; Kingdom; Order; Species; Taxon.

PHYSICAL BARRIER **1** A human-made or natural feature of the landscape that has three-dimensional and spatial characteristics capable of impeding or preventing organisms moving from place to place. **2** Any obstruction to the spread of fire, it is typically an area or strip devoid of combustible material. *See also* Control Line; Fuelbreak; Psychological Barrier.

PHYSICAL or TECHNICAL ROTATION *See* Rotation.

PHYSIOGNOMY The form and structure of vegetation in natural communities.

PHYSIOGRAPHIC REGION A geographic area having a similar set of biophysical characteristics and processes due to effects of climate and geology, and which result in patterns of soils and broad-scale plant communities. Habitat patterns, wildlife distributions, and historical land-use patterns may differ significantly from those of adjacent provinces.

PHYSIOGRAPHY Pertains to the factors that influence the development of landforms or a landscape, such as relief and topography, bedrock geology and structure, and geomorphological history.

PHYSIOLOGICAL LONGEVITY The maximum life span of an organism under optimum living conditions.

PHYSIOLOGICAL RACE A subgroup of a pathogenic species, characterized by restriction to one or more races, cultivars, or varieties of a single host species.

PHYTOALEXIN A substance that inhibits the development of microorganisms. It is produced in higher plants as a result of chemical, biological, or physical stimuli.

PHYTOCOENOSIS *See* Plant Community.

PHYTOGEOGRAPHY The study of the geographical distribution and relationships of plants.

PHYTOPATHOGEN Any organism that can induce disease in plants.

PHYTOSANITARY CERTIFICATE A certificate of health, attached to plants or plant parts that are to be exported. Typically, the certificate notes the origin of the material and declares the material to be free of potentially damaging diseases.

PHYTOTOXIC Any substance that is toxic to plants.

PICTOGRAPH A number of different techniques used by Native peoples to visually represent ideas, events, or activities (e.g., rock paintings [pictographs] and rock carvings [petroglyphs]).

PIECE RATE A payment schedule where income earned is directly related to output successfully completed.

PIEDMONT **1** As an adjective, lying or formed at the base of a mountain range. **2** As a noun, an area, plain, slope, glacier, or other feature at the base of a mountain.

PIEDMONT SLOPE The dominant gentle slope at the foot of a mountain. Its main components consist of: (1) an erosional surface on bedrock adjacent to the receding mountain front (pediment); (2) a constructional surface comprising individual alluvial fans and interfan valleys, also near the mountain front; and (3) a distal complex of coalescent fans and alluvial slopes without fan form. Piedmont slopes grade to either basin-floor depressions with alluvial and temporary lake plains, or surfaces of through drainage.

PIER The intermediate support between the abutments of a bridge.

PILEUS The cap of a mushroom carrying the spore-bearing tissues (hymenium) on its underside. The pileus can occur in a variety of shapes, some of which are shown in the illustration. *See also* Fungus.

PILING **1** *See* Harvest Functions. **2** Wooden posts, steel tubes, or long sheets of steel that are driven into the ground with a pile-driver. The posts or tubes are typically driven in to provide a foundation for a structure being built on soft ground. Sheet piling is typically driven in such a way as to provide a solid wall of well-anchored steel, which serves to contain or separate two different areas, usually water from solid ground.

PILOSE Hairy; covered with soft, straight hairs.

PILOT BALLOON OBSERVATION (PIBAL) A method of determining winds aloft in the vicinity of an observation station by periodically reading the elevation and azimuth angles of a theodolite, usually at one-minute intervals, while optically tracking the ascent of a small, free-lift balloon. A PIBAL is commonly used for constructing a vertical wind profile. *See also* Minisonde Observation; Rawinsonde Observation.

pileus shapes

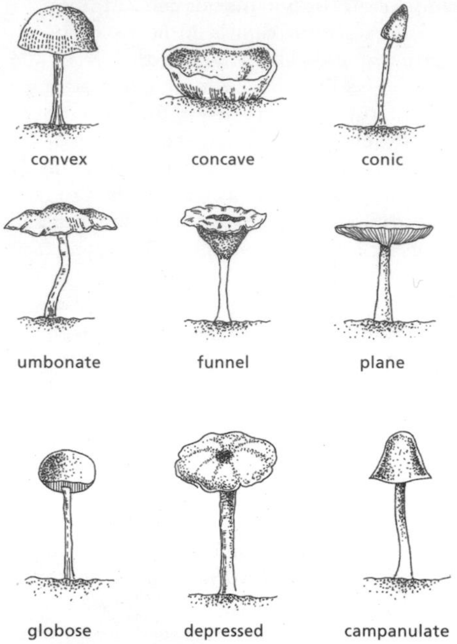

convex
concave
conic
umbonate
funnel
plane
globose
depressed
campanulate

PILOT PROJECT A relatively small-scale field trial designed to evaluate a new material, technique, or strategy in order to determine its effectiveness and feasibility under operational conditions. *See also* Operational Trial.

PINGO A large frost mound; especially, a relatively large conical mound of soil-covered ice (commonly thirty to fifty metres high and up to 400 metres in diameter) raised in part by the hydrostatic pressure of the water within and below the permafrost of Arctic regions, and of more than one year's duration.

PING-PONG BALL SYSTEM A mechanized method of dispensing Delayed Aerial Ignition Devices (DAIDs) at a selected rate. The DAIDs are polystyrene balls, 1.25 inches in diameter, containing potassium permanganate. The balls are fed into a dispenser, generally mounted in a helicopter, where they are injected with a water-glycol solution and then ejected through a chute leading out of the helicopter. The chemicals react thermally and ignite in twenty-five to thirty seconds. The space between ignition points on the ground is primarily a function of helicopter speed, gear ratio of the dispenser, and the number of chutes used (up to four).

See also Ignition Pattern (area grid ignition).

PINHOLES **1** The cross-sections of tunnels made by ambrosia beetle adults, forming small, round holes in timber or timber products. These are often surrounded by a dark brown or black stain produced by the fungus that the beetles introduce into the wood and feed upon. **2** Tiny holes in leaves caused by disease or insect feeding.

PINNA The primary division or primary leaflet of a pinnately compound leaf. If the leaf is decompound, the primary divisions are pinnae and the ultimate leaflets are pinnules. *See also* Fern (for illustration); Sorus.

PINNATE Having the parts, such as veins, lobes, or branches, arranged along both sides of an axis (e.g., a pinnate leaf is compound, with leaflets arranged on both sides of the rachis).

PINNATIFID Cleft or parted in a pinnate manner. *See also* Leaf Margin (for illustration).

PINNATISECT Cut, incised to the midrib in a pinnate manner.

PINNULE A segment of a pinna. A secondary, tertiary, or quarternary leaflet, whichever is the ultimate division of a (usually) pinnately decompound leaf. *See also* Fern (for illustration).

PIONEER **1** A species capable of invading disturbed areas, often in large numbers and over considerable areas, and of persisting until displaced by other species as succession proceeds. **2** Any new arrival in the early stages of succession.

PIONEER BEETLE A bark beetle that searches for and initiates attack on a suitable host tree. *See also* Host Selection.

PIONEERING POPULATION An initial population of animals introduced into previously unoccupied habitat.

PIPING Subsurface erosion of particulate materials by flowing water, resulting in the formation of underground caves and conduits and the development of collapse-depressions at the land surface. *See also* Batholith (for illustration).

PIPING DEPRESSION A small, enclosed depression formed by collapse of the land surface associated with piping.

PISCIVOROUS Fish-eating.

PISTIL The female organ (gynoecium) of a plant, made up of ovary, style, and stigma. It may have one or more carpels; one carpel is a simple pistil, while two or more carpels is a compound pistil.

PISTILLATE A female flower that has pistils but no stamens.

PISTILLODE A rudimentary or vestigial pistil found in certain staminate flowers.

PIT **1** *See* Mine. **2** Botanically, an area in the cell walls of higher plants where the secondary cell wall is absent, creating a gap or cavity. The main parts of a pit are the pit cavity (primary cell wall) and the pit membrane (middle lamella). Typically, one pit membrane serves two pits. Where two cells have pits in adjacent parts of the wall, they may be connected by protoplasmic connections called plasmodesmata. Pits vary in complexity and may include very specific characteristic structures such as apertures, borders, canals, cavities, chambers, margins, membranes, and the torus.

PITCH **1** In air navigation, a rotation of an aircraft about the horizontal axis normal to its longitudinal axis so as to cause a nose-up or nose-down attitude. **2** In photogrammetry, a rotation of the camera or of the photograph coordinate system about either the *y* axis or the exterior *y* axis; a tip or longitudinal tilt. In some photogrammetric instruments and in analytical applications, the symbol phi (Φ) may be used to depict pitch. **3** *See* Resin.

PITCH OUT To repel or drown out an attack of bark beetles by a strong flow of resin or pitch at the point of attack, or at the entrance hole.

PITCH POCKET Also called a resin pocket. A well-defined cavity between or within annual growth layers of coniferous wood, often lens-shaped, containing liquid or solid resinous material (pitch). Some pockets may be empty or contain bark inclusions.

PITCH TUBE A mass of resin and often frass or boring dust at the point of entry of an insect tunnel into the bark, cones, etc., of various conifers. Pitch ducts arise from the severing of resin ducts by the boring activity of the attacking insect.

PITH The soft, spongy tissue that forms a central core in most angiosperm stems, made up primarily of parenchyma tissue. The shape of the pith in cross-section is characteristic to certain species (e.g., star or pentagon shape in oaks and cottonwoods, triangular in alders, or terete in ash and elms). In some species, such as walnut, the pith has distinct chambers.

PITH FLECK A small, localized, isolated patch of wound tissue, darker or lighter than the surrounding wood, appearing on a longitudinal surface as a streak. It is produced by injury to the cambium; in conifers by the feeding of adult weevils, and in hardwoods by the feeding of larvae of flies in the family Agromyzidae.

PIT-RUN GRAVEL Naturally occurring, graded gravel deposited by a retreating glacier. It is used as the subgrade or final surface in road construction.

PITTED A surface having small depressions.

PITTED OUTWASH PLAIN An outwash plain with kettles.

PITTING A feature of some decays in which the wood is honeycombed with small pockets, at first filled with whitish fibre, but later on becoming empty.

PIXEL The smallest, most elementary areal constituent of an image. It is also called a resolution cell, the pixel is comparable to the many dots making up the picture on a television screen. Pixel is derived from Picture × Element.

PLACENTA **1** In plants, the tissue bearing or containing the ovules in an ovary. *See also* Carpel (for illustration). **2** In animals (mammals), the tissue connecting the fetus to the wall of the uterus.

PLACENTATION In plants, the arrangement of the placenta within the ovary. Several distinct types of placentation are recognized (see illustration): (1) **apical placentation**, in which the ovules are reduced to a few or one and are borne at the top of a simple or compound ovary; (2) **axile placentation**, in which the ovules are borne at or near the centre of a compound ovary on the central axis formed by the joined sections (septa) (e.g., most Liliaceae and Scrophulariaceae); (3) **basal placentation**, in which the ovules are reduced to few or one and are borne at the base of a simple or compound ovary; (4) **free central placentation**, in which the ovules are borne on a central column in a compound ovary without septa or with septa confined to the base; (5) **marginal or ventral placentation**, in which the ovules are borne on the wall along the ventral suture in a simple ovary; and (6) **parietal placentation**, in which the ovules are borne on the wall or on slight intrusions within a compound ovary; (7) **lamellate placentation**, in which the ovules are borne on platelike extensions of the placenta into a compound ovary (a modified parietal form).

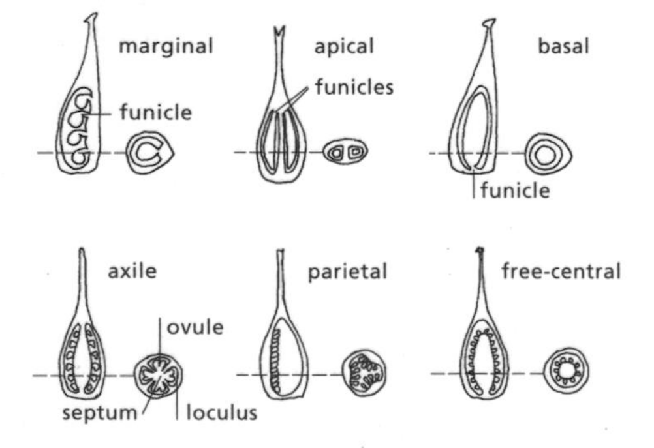

PLAIN **1** A level or very gently sloping planar surface with gradient up to three degrees (5 per cent); local relief is less than one metre. **2** An extensive region of comparatively smooth and level or gently undulating land, having few or no prominent surface irregularities, and usually at a low elevation with reference to surrounding areas.

PLAN A course of action proposed to meet predefined goals, objectives, and policies that lay out management directions; and an ordered set of decisions and actions to be taken to achieve these goals, objectives, and policies. The plan is merely the statement of what is desired. Unless the plan is implemented in the manner intended, the results will not be achieved; thus a plan is a means to an end, but not the end itself.

PLANE A uniformly flat surface at any orientation.

PLANE SURVEY *See* Survey.

PLANETARY BOUNDARY LAYER The atmospheric boundary layer extending from the surface of the planet upwards to a point where frictional forces have no influence.

PLANIMETER An instrument used to mechanically measure an area by tracing its perimeter on a plane surface. Two types are commonly seen. (1) **Polar compensating planimeter** rotates about a fixed point and is limited in the area it can measure. (2) **Linear rolling planimeter** has a small measuring wheel built into the machine and is not constrained by the fixed point.

PLANIMETRIC MAP A map portraying the correct horizontal positions of the features represented, but with no data on relative heights. *See also* Cadastral Map; Topographic Map.

PLANKTON Small (less than two millimetres) plant (phytoplankton) and animal (zooplankton) life-forms that float in saltwater or freshwater and are carried passively by water currents. *See also* Benthos; Nekton; Neuston.

PLANNER One whose profession consists of identifying community or resource management needs, resources, and problems, and assists citizens, bureaucrats, and politicians in making decisions on goals, objectives, policies, priorities, plans, programs, and the methods of implementing plans.

PLANNING The act of deciding in advance what needs to done to achieve predetermined goals and objectives, creating alternative solutions, and selecting one. The planning process is iterative and never complete, since results encountered in the present determine what may or may not be possible or desirable in the future, and these factors constantly change with time.

PLANT ASSOCIATION A plant community represented by areas of vegetation occurring in places where environments are so closely similar that there is a high degree of floristic uniformity in all the layers.

PLANTATION A stand of trees established by human activity to meet predetermined social, environmental, or economic goals.

PLANT COMMUNITY A vegetative complex that is unique in its combination of plants and occurs in particular locations under particular environmental conditions. The plant community is a reflection of the prevailing environmental influences, including soils, temperature, elevation, solar radiation, slope, aspect, and rainfall.

PLANT COMMUNITY TYPE An aggregation of all plant communities with similar structure and floristic composition. A unit of vegetation within a classification with no particular successional status implied.

PLANT CROWN COVER In range management, the proportion or percentage of the ground surface under live, aerial plant parts.

PLANT FORM The shape or form of trees and other woody plants, which is determined genetically and by four main factors during development: (1) the location of leaf and flower buds (terminal or lateral); (2) the pattern of bud break along the trunk and branches; (3) the angle at which branches grow; and (4) the differential elongation of shoots.

Tree forms can be divided into two main categories, excurrent and decurrent. An **excurrent** branching habit is typical of most conifers and a few broad-leaved trees, where the leader and main stem grow faster than the lateral branches, thus forming a tree with a shape that resembles a tall, tapered triangle. A **decurrent** branching habit (sometimes termed deliquescent or diffuse) is more typical of broad-leaved trees, where the leader and lateral branches grow at roughly equal rates, thus forming a more rounded form with no obvious single leader and a series of codominant stems. *See also* Apical Control.

PLANT GROWTH REGULATOR **1** A natural substance that regulates the growth of plants (e.g., by influencing enlargement, elongation, division, or activation of cells). *See also* Hormone. **2** A natural or synthetic chemical which, when applied as a pesticide to plant leaves, stems, or roots, alters the growth and physiology of the plant.

PLANTIGRADE An animal that has the ability to walk on the soles and heels of the foot (e.g., bears [*Ursus* spp.] and humans [*Homo sapiens*]).

PLANTING The establishment of trees by planting seedlings, transplants, or cuttings. *See also* Artificial Regeneration; Natural Regeneration.

PLANT KINGDOM The plant kingdom (the kingdom Plantae) consists of multicellular eukaryotic organisms producing embryos and, typically, able to photosynthesize, but lacking the power of locomotion and having no apparent sensory organs. The primary photosynthetic pigment is chlorophyll a, with chlorophyll b and carotenoids utilized in certain species and conditions. The kingdom excludes fungi and algae.

In contemporary classification schemes there are eleven main phyla. In older schemes this number is reduced by use of the superphylum Spermatophyta, which is then divided into the Angiospermophyta and the Gymnospermophyta. Complete details of the plant kingdom are given in Appendix 1: Classification of Organisms. There remains some disagreement among plant classification authorities about which system is best, or most valid. *See also* Angiosperm; Gymnosperm.

PLASMOLYSIS Occurs when the isostatic contents of plant cells shrink due to water loss by osmosis, resulting in a hypertonic condition. *See also* Hypertonic; Isotonic.

PLASTIC LIMIT The minimum soil water content that permits a soil sample to be deformed without rupture. The lower limit of plasticity.

PLASTIC SOIL In soil texture analysis, any soil capable of being permanently moulded or deformed under moderate pressure. *See also* Consistency.

PLATEAU An extensive upland mass with relatively flat summit area that is considerably elevated (more than 100 metres) above the adjacent lowlands and is separated from them by escarpments. A relatively large part of a plateau surface is near the summit level.

PLATE TECTONICS Plate tectonic theory is used to describe the ongoing evolution and formation of the Earth's crust. Plate tectonics is the study of the movement of Earth's brittle crustal plates above and upon the flexible mantle layer, on continents, and beneath oceans. The illustration shows the major tectonic plates on the planet. Wide arrows indicate the direction of plate movement, thin arrows indicate the direction of plate movement along fault lines. *See also* Pangaea.

PLATFORM In remote sensing, the objects, structure, or base upon which a remote sensor is mounted.

PLATFORM NEST A relatively flat nest constructed on a supporting structure, typically a broken tree top of lateral branches. Well-established platform nests may be decades old and weigh several hundred pounds. They are occupied by birds such as eagles or herons.

PLEATED A surface folded lengthwise several times. It is often seen in the early stages of plant part development, such as a bud.

PLEISTOCENE The first epoch of the Quaternary period after the Tertiary period and Pliocene epoch and before the Holocene epoch. It is characterized by repeated glacial and non-glacial intervals, and also, the corresponding worldwide series of rocks. It began about two million years ago and ended about 10,000 years ago. It corresponds to the Ice Age. It is also termed the Glacial epoch. *See also* Appendix 2: Geological Time Scales.

PLEOMORPHIC *See* Polymorphic.

PLEUROCARPOUS In bryophytes, producing sporophytes laterally from a bud or short branch.

PLICATE Pleated.

PLIOCENE The last epoch of the Tertiary period, following the Miocene epoch and before the Pleistocene epoch, during which humans and most species of modern mammals came into existence, two to seven million years ago. *See also* Appendix 2: Geological Time Scales.

PLOT *See* Sample Plot.

PLOTLESS CRUISING *See* Point Sampling.

PLOTTER A device that can plot computerized graphics images, usually by drawing lines with ink pens. Plotters require that the picture image is coded in vector graphics format (point to point). Flatbed plotters limit the overall size of the drawing to the fixed height and width of the 'bed' onto which the paper is placed for drawing. Flatbed plotters draw by moving the pen in horizontal or vertical axes. Drum plotters limit the size to one dimension only (the width of the drum), but not the other dimension, since the length of the paper is determined by how far the plot needs to travel for completion as it travels over the drum. Drum plotters draw by moving the pen along one axis and the paper along the other. *See also* Stereoscopic Plotter.

PLUMOSE Feathery; with fine, long hairs, these having fine secondary hairs.

PLUNGE POOL A deep hollow scoured in a streambed at the foot of a waterfall.

PLURIVOROUS Describes an organism capable of living on many different hosts.

PLUS STAND A stand having many good phe-

plate tectonics

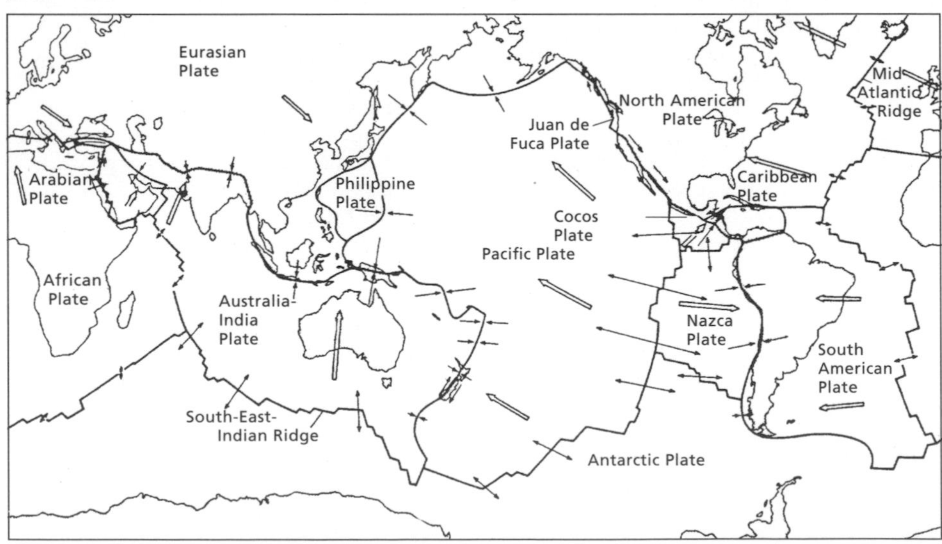

notypic qualities but not necessarily plus trees.
PLUS TREE A phenotype judged (but not proved by test) to be unusually superior in some quality or qualities (e.g., exceptional growth rate relative to site, desirable growth habit, high wood quality, exceptional apparent resistance to disease and insect attack, or to other adverse locality factors).
PLUTONIC ROCKS Coarse-grained rocks, usually of igneous origin, that have formed deep within the Earth, but may also include the associated metamorphic rocks.
PLUVIAL LAKE Generally, a lake formed during a period of heavy rainfall. Specifically, a lake formed in the Pleistocene epoch during a time of glacial advance.
PNEUMATOPHORE Modified roots that may function as a respiratory organ in species subjected to frequent inundation or soil saturation (e.g., Cypress knees).
POCKET ROT Also termed peck. Wood decay localized in small areas, usually forming rounded or lens-shaped cavities, surrounded by apparently sound or only slightly modified wood.
POCKETS OF A FIRE *See* Forest Fire (bays).
POD Technically, a dehiscent, dry fruit, but often used in a very general sense if no other term is available.
PODETIUM A stalklike elevation of a lichen thallus supporting one or more apothecia.
POIKILOHYDRIC The physiological ability to resist drought, reviving and green when moist, dry and brown when water is absent (such as with the lungwort lichen *Lobaria pulmonaria*).
POIKILOTHERM Any animal whose metabolism and body temperatures vary in conformance with the prevailing environmental conditions. It is also called ectotherm. *See also* Homeotherm.
POINT COUNT **1** In avian conservation, a census methodology in which counts are made of the contacts recorded by an observer based at a fixed observation point and over a specified time interval. **Fixed distance (radius) point count** is limited to individuals noted within a single fixed distance. **Variable distance (radius) point count** is limited to individuals within distances according to species-characteristic detection distances (also termed variable circular plot). **Unlimited distance point count** includes all individuals without limits; that is, all detections recorded regardless of distance. It is also termed the station count method. *See also* Strip Transect Method. **2** In timber management, *see* Point Sampling.
POINT OF COMMENCEMENT A fixed landmark, aerial photography tie point, or known survey point, used as a starting point for a walk-through, probe, cruise, or survey of the forest.
POINT SAMPLING A method of selecting trees for measurement and for estimating stand basal area using tree size rather than frequency as the main parameter. Trees are tallied at a sample location or point sample, with the selection probability being proportional to the basal areas of the trees. It is also called plotless cruising, angle count method, and Bitterlich Method. Point sampling is used as an alternative to the fixed-area plot and has no fixed boundary. In point sampling, a 360-degree sweep is made with an angle gauge about a fixed point, and the stems whose breast height diameters appear larger than the fixed angle subtended by the angle gauge are included in the sample. *See also* Basal Area Factor; Sample Plot.
POINT SOURCE A static, identifiable source of air, soil or water pollution. *See also* Non-point Source.
POINT TRANSECT In bird surveys, a transect along which the point count method is used. No recordings are made between stations, as opposed to strip transects with continuous recordings. *See also* Strip Transect Method; Transect.
POINT TRANSFER DEVICE In photogrammetry, a stereoscopic instrument used to mark corresponding image points on overlapping photographs.
POLAR ORDINATION Polar ordination is an indirect ordination technique used by the pioneers of statistical ecology, in which the axes cross in the centre of the ordination. It has been replaced by more robust and representative techniques such as Detrended Correspondence Analysis and Canonical Correspondence Analysis. *See also* Ordination.
POLE STAGE That stage of coniferous tree development between sapling and small sawtimber.
POLICY A set of decisions, methods, or actions designed to fulfil predetermined objectives. *See also* Goal; Objective.
POLICY DIALOGUES Policy dialogues are usually convened and conducted by a mediator and are aimed at developing policy recommendations for consideration by legislative or administrative bodies. Representatives of affected interests are brought together to develop consensus on guidelines for the development of policy or, in some cases, to draft

specific policy directions. Policy dialogues are not usually related to specific disputes and are less constrained by existing administrative practices, rules, or legislation because new directions are being developed.

Policy dialogues may occur at the request of an administrative or elected official or at the independent volition of interested parties. Responsible officials are not pre-committed to adopt policies that emerge from such discussions. However, to the extent that the consensus represents a broad reflection of public and private interests and is based on a carefully reviewed and documented consideration of social concerns and technical realities, such a consensus can be very persuasive and is often translated into formal policy and legislation.

POLLARDING A technique that encourages rapid growth of sprouts from a tree. In a rural setting, the tree is typically cut at a height just beyond the reach of browsing animals, and the resulting sprouts are harvested for use in weaving, willow being a favourite species for this purpose. In amenity trees, the technique is used to shape or form the crown. Once the main scaffold structure has been established, the watersprout growth is pruned back annually to a head or knob of latent buds at the end of each branch. Regrowth is vigorous in species such as London plane, basswood, black locust, and willow.

POLLEN The microspores, spores, or grains contained in the anther of a flowering plant and that contain the male gametes.

POLLEN ANALYSIS *See* Palynology.

POLLEN INFLUX The accumulation of pollen in sediments per unit of volume or time. The absolute pollen influx is the number of pollen grains per square centimetre per year derived from pollen concentration and rate of sedimentation.

POLLEN SAC The pollen-bearing cavity – a microsporangium. In angiosperms, the anther sac.

POLLEN SPECTRA The percentages of pollen and spores in a single pollen grain.

POLLINATION The process in which pollen is transferred from an anther to a receptive stigma.

POLLINIUM The waxy, almost coherent mass of pollen grains, typical of many orchids and milkweeds.

POLLUTION **1** The materials that are considered to be contaminants. **2** The act of contaminating (polluting) the environment. *See also* Contamination.

POLY- A prefix meaning many.

POLYANDROUS **1** *See* Polyandry. **2** Male flowers having many stamens. *See also* Adelphous.

POLYANDRY The mating of a single female with several males in the breeding season. *See also* Polygyny.

POLYAREAL SAMPLE *See* Point Sampling.

POLYCARPIC Seed production in plants that occurs more than once for an indefinite period (e.g., annual fruiting perennials and masting perennials).

POLYESTRUS Having several breeding periods in a year. It is also spelled polyoestrus.

POLYGAMODIOECIOUS A dioecious plant but having some perfect (bisexual) flowers present on some or all plants. *See also* Polygamomonoecious.

POLYGAMOMONOECIOUS A monoecious plant that may have some bisexual flowers present. *See also* Polygamodioecious.

POLYGAMOUS **1** Any species where the male or female of a species breeds with more than one male or female in a breeding season. *See also* Monogamous. **2** A plant having both unisexual and bisexual flowers, either on the same plant or on separate plants of the same species.

POLYGENIC RESISTANCE Resistance to disease, usually quantitative in character, which is controlled by a series of genes. *See also* Horizontal Resistance; Monogenic Resistance; Oligogenic Resistance; Vertical Resistance.

POLYGON In GIS work, a stream of digitized points approximating the delineation (perimeter) of an area (e.g., forest type) on a map. Polygons are often comprised of line segments or arcs that join at nodes to produce a polygon.

POLYGONAL Having many angles, as in a polygon.

POLYGYNY The mating of a single male with more than one female in the breeding season. *See also* Polyandry.

POLYMORPHIC Literally, of many forms. It is also called pleomorphic. In genetics, the occurrence in a population of several alternative alleles at a locus. Polymorphism is the occurrence of more than one distinct form of individuals in a population.

POLYPETALOUS Having a corolla of distinct and separate petals, as opposed to gamopetalous. It is also termed choripetalous.

POLYPHAGOUS An organism that can successfully feed (and reproduce) on a wide variety of foods (i.e., a wide host range). *See also* Host Specificity; Monophagous; Oligophagous; Stenophagous.

POLYPHYLETIC 1 Describes organisms derived from more than one independent ancestral line. 2 A grouping in cladistics that does not include the most recent ancestral form of the organisms in that group. *See also* Cladistics; Monophyletic.

POLYPLOID A cell or organism having three or more complete complements of chromosomes (3n or higher), as opposed to the more normal diploid (2n) or haploid (n) complements.

POLYPORE One of several groups of wood-decaying fungi producing basidiocarps with poroid lower surfaces.

POLYSEPALOUS Having a calyx of distinct and separate sepals, as opposed to gamosepalous.

POMACEOUS Consisting of or pertaining to apples or botanically related fruit.

POME A normally fleshy fruit typical of apples, pears, hawthorns, and some roses (all in the Rosaceae family), where the flesh is derived from the fusion of an inferior ovary and the hypanthium. The seeds are not embedded in pulp. *See also* Fruit (for illustration).

POOL A portion of the stream with reduced current velocity, often with water deeper than the surrounding areas; a smooth, relatively undisturbed surface that is frequently usable by fish for resting and cover. A small body of standing water (e.g., on a floodplain or in a marsh). Pools can be classed as several types, each one having specific characteristics. **Alcove pool** is a backwater along the shoreline where the stream is generally wider than above or below. **Backwater pool** is a pool formed by an eddy along channel margins downstream from obstructions such as bars, rootwads, or boulders, or resulting from back-flooding upstream due to an obstruction. May be separated from the channel by sand or gravel bars. Or, a body of water whose form and duration is controlled by some feature of the channel downstream from the backwater, or in coves, or covering low-lying areas and having access to the main body of water. **Corner pool** is a lateral scour resulting from a shift in the channel direction, causing deeper waters to form on the outside of the streamflow as it changes directions. **Dam pool** is water impounded upstream from a complete or partly complete channel blockage, such as a beaver dam, log jam, rockslide, or habitat improvement activity. **Flat pool** is a wide, shallow pool of low turbulence, also called a glide. **Lateral scour pool** is formed by the scouring action of water flow as it is directed laterally or obliquely to one side of the stream by a partial channel obstruction, such as a fallen log, a gravel bar, or deflection device. **Plunge pool** is a pool created by water passing over or through a complete or nearly complete channel obstruction and dropping vertically, scouring out a basin in which the flow radiates from the point of water entry. It is also called falls pool or plunge basin. **Scour pool** is a series of small pools surrounded by swiftly flowing water, usually caused by eddies behind boulders or logs, or by potholes in the stream bed. It is also called a pocket water pool. **Secondary channel pool** is a relatively small, sometimes isolated pool in a smaller braid of the mainstream and usually associated with gravel bars. **Slack water pool** is a pool-like depression along the stream margin and on the floodplain that contains water only during high flow or after floodwaters recede. More transient in nature than secondary pools, it may contain water for only a few days or weeks. **Trench pool** is a pool characterized by a relatively long, slotlike depression in the stream bed, often found in bedrock-dominated channels. **Under scour pool** is a pool formed by scouring of water under a stream obstruction such as a log. Forms on the upstream side. It is also called an upsurge pool.

POOL/RIFFLE RATIO The ratio of surface area or length of pools to the surface area or length of riffles in a given stream reach. It is frequently expressed as the relative percentage of each category. It is used to describe fish habitat rearing quality. Specific ratios of 1:1, 2:1, 1:2, etc., are considered ideal for different species of fish.

POPULATION 1 In statistics, the entire group or collection of items or individuals under study, from which the sample is taken. Populations can be finite (the total number of sample units can be expressed as a finite number) or infinite (the number of sample units is infinite). A population that is normally distributed has identical mean, median, and mode values. 2 The number of organisms of the same species inhabiting the same area, that potentially interbreed and share a common gene pool. 3 The total number of organisms over a large cluster of areas, such as a physiographic region, or nation. 4 In timber inventories, the population is usually a forested area for which information is required. *See also* Minimum Viable Population; Viable Population.

POPULATION DENSITY The number of individuals of a species per unit area.

POPULATION DYNAMICS The aggregate of

changes that occur during the life of a population. Included are all phases of recruitment and growth, senility, mortality, seasonal fluctuation in biomass, and persistence of each year class and its relative dominance, and the effects that any or all of these factors exert on the population.

POPULATION PERSISTENCE The capacity of the population to maintain sufficient density to persist, well distributed, over time. *See also* Viable Population.

POPULATION VIABILITY The probability x that a population will persist for a specified period y across its range despite normal fluctuations in population and environmental conditions; x and y must be socially determined. Factors affecting viability include habitat change, demographic randomness, environmental randomness, catastrophes, and genetic randomness.

POPULATION VIABILITY ANALYSIS Analysis that estimates minimum viable populations. It is synonymous with population vulnerability analysis.

POPULATION VIABILITY MODELS Mathematical abstraction of a system that is designed to predict the likelihood of persistence of a population under different conditions. Individual models attempt to predict the future state of any one plant or animal population based on its birth and death rates, habitat conditions, and other environmental factors.

PORE A small, typically circular opening in the surface, skin, or epidermis of an organism.

PORE SPACES The spaces between the particles of detrital sediments that are not occupied by mineral matter.

PORE SURFACE The surface of a fruiting body of certain wood-decaying fungi (Polyporaceae) that consists of small openings or pores.

PORICIDAL **1** Opening by pores. **2** A seed capsule dehiscent by pores at the top (e.g., poppy flowers). *See also* Capsule; Fruit (for illustration).

POROID Describes a surface with porelike depressions.

POROSITY **1** The permeability of a substance to fluids, via holes or interstices, and thus a reflection of the volume of air space occupying voids between soil particles, or within rocks. The degree of porosity affects the ability of gases or water to move through the soil or rock. **2** In geology, the percentage volume of air voids within the rock or soil sample.

PORRECT Extending upward and forward.

POSITION The location of a point with respect to a reference system, such as a geodetic datum. The coordinates that define such a location. The plane occupied by a point on the surface of the Earth.

POSITIVE FEEDBACK A loop where one component stimulates a second component and the second then stimulates the first. *See also* Feedback; Negative Feedback.

POSTEMERGENCE TREATMENT Pesticide treatments made after crop plants or weeds emerge through the soil surface. *See also* Pre-emergence Treatment; Preplant Treatment.

POSTERIOR In plants, closest or toward the back, or adaxial surface. In animals, the back or the end farthest from the head. *See also* Anterior.

POSTFLEDGLING MORTALITY The death rate of young after fledging, calculated from the following: the fates of young birds after fledging (or hatching in the case of precocial young), when these fates can be observed directly; and the number of surviving young needed to replace adult losses, when adult mortality rates and the reproduction of fledglings are known.

POSTGLACIAL Pertaining to the time interval since the disappearance of glaciers or an ice sheet from a particular area. It is similar to the Holocene epoch.

POTAMON Fish that live in the lower, warm-water, sluggish zone of stream systems. *See also* Rithron.

POTENTIAL HABITAT A vegetation type not currently suitable for the species under consideration, but with the capability of developing into suitable habitat in the future.

POTENTIAL NATURAL COMMUNITY The community of plants and wild animals that would become established if all successional sequences were completed without interference by people under present environmental conditions. For some forest communities, the potential natural community may be an old-growth stand.

POTENTIAL VEGETATION The vegetation that would develop if all the successional sequences were completed under the present site conditions.

POTHOLE **1** In geomorphology, a pot-shaped pit or hole. **2** In glacial geology, a large kettle formation. **3** In lakes, a shallow depression, typically less than 4 hectares in size, located between dunes on a prairie and often containing an intermittent pond or marsh.

POWER **1** The ability to exert influence over an individual or group in making decisions, establishing norms, or performing an activity. **2** In statistics, the power of a test is defined as 1 – ß where ß is the probability of a type II error. The power of a test is thus inversely related to the risk of failing to reject a false hypothesis.

PRE-ATTACK PLAN A plan detailing predetermined fire suppression strategy and tactics to be deployed following fire occurrence in a given land management unit. A pre-attack plan contains data on fuel types and topographic conditions including fuelbreaks, access routes and travel times, water supply sources, lakes suitable for skimmer aircraft, and existing heliports. It also contains information on existing and/or proposed locations for control lines (including the types and number of fire suppression resources that may be required and probable rates of fire guard construction, and possible constraints), base and line camps, helispots, and the priorities for construction and/or improvement of presuppression facilities. *See also* Fire Management Plan; Fire Suppression Plan.

PRE-ATTACK PLANNING The process of collecting, evaluating, and recording fire intelligence data, in advance of fire occurrence. This information is then used for decisionmaking purposes to increase the chances of successful fire suppression in initial attack and campaign fire situations, consistent with the fire management objectives for a given area.

PRECIPITATION Any or all of the forms of water, whether liquid (i.e., rain or drizzle) or solid (e.g., snow or hail) that fall from the atmosphere and reach the ground. The more common term 'rainfall' is also used in this total sense to include not only amount of rain, but also the water equivalent of frozen precipitation. Precipitation is the preferred general term.

PRECISION **1** In statistics, the variability of a series of sample estimates (i.e., the difference between a sample estimate and the estimate obtained from complete enumeration using the same methods and procedures). The amount of agreement in a series of measurements. Generally, random deviation from the sample mean. The mean square error (MSE), a measure of accuracy, illustrates the relationship with precision and bias, where MSE = $(\text{precision})^2 + (\text{bias})^2$. The precision or sampling error is usually expressed as the standard error of the sample estimate, either absolutely or as a percentage of the estimate. **2** The resolving power of optical instruments. The smallest unit used in taking a measurement; the smaller the unit the more precise the measurement. *See also* Accuracy; Bias; Mean Square Error.

PRECOCIAL Any species of bird that is born with its eyes open and covered in feathers or down (e.g., ducks and chickens). Precocial birds are able to fend for themselves fairly soon after hatching. *See also* Altricial.

PRECOCIOUS Developing or maturing very early. In plants, also refers to when flowers develop before the leaves.

PREDATION An example of interspecific association between species that may be positive or negative. Positive predation occurs when predator populations fluctuate in positive response to variations in prey. Negative predation occurs when high predator population densities produce a local population depression of prey.

PREDATOR Any free-living animal that hunts, kills, and eats other animals that are usually smaller and weaker than itself (i.e., the prey).

PREDATOR CONTROL **1** The relationship between predators and prey in which the predator becomes the limiting factor in the population size of the prey. **2** The harvest of predators to allow higher numbers of prey species to survive. In many cases, the control of predators by humans is a very controversial practice.

PREDICTOR VARIABLE An independent variable.

PREDISPOSITION Susceptibility that is environmentally, rather than genetically conditioned (i.e., the influence of pre-existing living and nonliving stress factors on the susceptibility of an individual host to disease).

PRE-EMERGENCE TREATMENT Pesticide treatments applied after a crop is seeded but before it emerges. The term may also refer to treatment of weeds before they emerge from the ground. *See also* Postemergence Treatment.

PREMORSE Appearing to have been bitten off; coarsely eroded.

PREPLANT TREATMENT A pesticide treatment applied before the crop is planted. *See also* Postemergence Treatment; Pre-emergence Treatment.

PREPUPA In insects, a usually inactive larval stage that occurs after feeding has ceased and before the pupa has formed.

PRESCRIBED FIRE The planned use of carefully controlled fire to accomplish predetermined management goals (e.g., site preparation for planting, reduction of fire hazards or pest problems, improvement of the ease with which the site can be traversed, and creation of better quality browse for wildlife). The burn is set under a combination of weather, fuel moisture, soil moisture, and fuel arrangement (e.g., windrows) conditions that allow the management objectives to be attained, and yet confine the fire to the planned area.

In some cases, a wildfire that may produce beneficial results in terms of the attainment of forest management and other land-use objectives may be allowed to burn under certain burning conditions according to a predefined burning prescription, with limited or no suppression action. In this case, the wildfire may be considered as a form of prescribed fire. *See also* Slash Burn.

PRESCRIPTION A written statement defining the objectives to be attained and the factors involved in aspects such as prescribed fire and silvicultural treatments. The objectives are generally expressed as acceptable ranges of the various indices being used, and the limit of the geographic area affected (e.g., a fire prescription would include coverage of objectives, temperature, humidity, wind direction and wind speed, fuel moisture content, and the soil moisture under which the fire would be allowed to burn).

PRESENT VALUE The value at the present moment of a series of benefits or costs arising at subsequent points in time.

PRESERVATION A land-use designation that signifies little or no human activity or use within the designated area. A somewhat dated term, as it is now generally realized that nothing can be preserved since natural forces are constantly prevailing, and all systems change over time, the main variable being the rate of change.

PRESERVATIVE A chemical substance which, when applied to wood, makes it more resistant to attack by fungi, insects, or marine borers.

PRESSURE ALTITUDE The indicated altitude of an aircraft's pressure altimeter at an altimeter setting of 29.92 inches of mercury. *See also* Density Altitude.

PRESUPPRESSION Those fire management activities undertaken in advance of fire occurrences. These are concerned with the organization, training, and management of a fire-fighting force and the procurement, maintenance, and inspection of improvements, equipment, and supplies to ensure effective fire suppression.

PREVENTION Activities designed to minimize the affect of a pest before an outbreak occurs, including silvicultural activities carried out to increase tree vigour, or otherwise reduce stand susceptibility to pest damage. Prevention requires the incorporation of pest management into the overall forest management strategy in order to create ecological conditions unfavourable to pests.

PRICE DEFLATOR A measure of change in the purchasing power of money used to adjust money incomes, wages, etc., in order to compare their real (corrected for inflation) values over a number of time periods.

PRICE-SIZE CURVE The relationship between price per unit volume (or other measure of quantity) and the volume (or other measure of size) of a tree or log.

PRICKLE A sharp, spinelike outgrowth from the epidermis or bark rather than from the wood itself that is not associated with the conducting tissues. *See also* Thorn.

PRIMARY ASSOCIATION The relationship between a wildlife species and a habitat condition that reflects a dependence on such habitat. The relationship is usually strong and predictable. *See also* Incidental Association.

PRIMARY ATTRACTION The attraction of bark beetles to a host tree as a result of substances released by the tree itself before any beetles have visited it. *See also* Attractant; Secondary Attraction.

PRIMARY CAVITY NESTER Any bird capable of excavating its own nesting space by hammering at the substrate (e.g., woodpeckers). *See also* Secondary Cavity Nester.

PRIMARY CONVERSION The first stage in converting trees to products. The cutting and removal of trees from the forest.

PRIMARY CYCLE The first cycle of a plant disease to begin in any one year.

PRIMARY HOST **1** That host on which the sexual form(s) of an insect or other invertebrate with alternating generations is found. **2** The host on which the first two stages of a rust fungus (pycnial and aecial) exist. *See also* Alternate Host; Principal Host; Secondary Host.

PRIMARY INFECTION The first infection in a sequence of infections, or in any given year. *See also* Secondary Infection.

PRIMARY INOCULUM An overwintering pathogen or its spores that initiate primary infections. *See also* Secondary Inoculum.

PRIMARY INSECT **1** An insect capable of completing development in an apparently healthy, living tree. **2** A bark beetle species capable of killing healthy trees. **3** The first insect species to arrive at or utilize a given host tree. *See also* Secondary Insect.

PRIMARY LOGGING ROAD. *See* Mainline.

PRIMARY LOOKOUT A lookout point that must be staffed to meet planned minimum seen area coverage in a given locality. For that reason, continuous service is necessary during the normal fire season and the lookout (person) is not sent to help on fires. *See also* Secondary Lookout.

PRIMARY PARASITE A parasite of an organism that is not itself parasitic. *See also* Hyperparasite.

PRIMARY PATHOGEN A pathogen that infects the host, producing changes in it before invasion by other, secondary pathogens. By definition, a primary pathogen can induce disease whether or not secondary pathogens become involved. *See also* Primary Insect; Secondary Pathogen.

PRIMARY PRODUCTION The creation of plant biomass and accumulation of energy through photosynthesis or chemosynthesis. Complete photosynthesis, in which all of the sun's energy is assimilated, plus chemosynthesis is gross primary production. Primary producers are plants and are at the base of the trophic level. *See also* Net Primary Production.

PRIMARY PRODUCTIVITY The rate at which energy, produced by photosynthetic or chemosynthetic activity as organic compounds, is stored in an ecosystem or group of communities. *See also* Net Primary Production.

PRIMARY SUCCESSION A successional process starting on bare soil with no biological legacies present from previous ecosystems to influence the successional pathway; no previous seral stages other than bare ground or substrate. *See also* Secondary Succession.

PRIMARY TEPHRA Deposits of volcanic ejecta that remain as deposited by airfall from a volcanic cloud. In cores from lakes or bogs, these deposits represent volcanic ash that fell on the water surface at the time of volcanic eruption. *See also* Lapilli; Redeposited Tephra.

PRIMOCANE In plants, a biennial shoot or cane during its first year of growth and before flowering. Brambles or raspberries (*Rubus* spp.) are examples of plants with primocanes. *See also* Floricane.

PRINCIPAL COMPONENTS ANALYSIS (PCA) An indirect ordination technique that uses multivariate eigenanalysis to extract axes of maximum variation from either an R-mode (species) resemblance matrix or a Q-mode (stand) resemblance matrix, and ultimately produces a stand ordination. R-mode PCA is most typically used in ecological data analysis when the number of stands exceeds the number of species.

In a PCA, a standardized correlation matrix is first created from the raw species data matrix. Standardization of the data occurs when the origin of the original coordinate system is moved to the centre of gravity of the species space. This procedure is known as row centring. Through eigenanalysis, the coordinates of each species relative to the principal axes are calculated by determining the linear combination of weighted species abundances. The multidimensional data is thus transformed onto new axes (principal components), which allow the species to be displayed in fewer (usually two) dimensions by concentrating information on the first components, which usually have the most meaning. These axes can then be rotated using several statistical techniques to expose any underlying ecological patterns. Because PCA is a linear model, non-linear relationships will be poorly represented, and other techniques such as detrended correspondence analysis or canonical correspondence analysis should be used. The term 'classical scaling' is used as a synonym for PCA. *See also* Ordination.

PRINCIPAL COMPONENTS TRANSFORMATION In remote sensing and statistics, the representation of data into a new, uncorrelated (orthogonal) coordinate system or vector space. It produces, in multidimensional space, a data set that has most variance along its first axis, the next largest variance along a second mutually orthogonal axis, and so on. The derived components are linear combinations of the original variables.

PRINCIPAL HOST The host on which a particular parasite most frequently occurs. *See also* Host Susceptibility Rating; Primary Host; Secondary Host.

PRIORITY ANIMAL TAXA In the US, species or subspecies having special significance for management. They include endangered, threatened, and special status taxa.

PRISM An optical instrument used as an angle gauge, consisting of a thin wedge of glass that establishes a fixed (critical) angle of projection in a point sample. *See also* Angle Gauge; Basal Area Factor; Point Sampling; Relascope.

PRISM PLOT *See* Point Sampling.

PRIVATE LAND Land not owned by the Crown or state.

PROBABILITY The relative frequency with which an event might occur over time. The probability of an event (A) occurring is calculated as:

$$P(A) = \frac{x}{n}$$

Probabilities are always positive integers and range from zero to one.

PROBE 1 A ground survey conducted to confirm an aerial survey or derive preliminary information about a pest attack. **2** A ground survey for bark beetle (or other pest) infestations. The term is used freely to describe surveys of various types and intensities, but usually implies a compass line (probe line) through a stand suspected of being diseased, with trees within a set distance on either side of the line being assessed for bark beetle attack. **3** That part of a measuring instrument that is placed in the medium to be measured.

PROBE CRUISE A combination of bark beetle (or other pests) probe and the conventional timber cruise, in which normal prism plots are established to collect the necessary cruise data, and in addition, a strip-cruise is done in between the prism plots of the regular cruise.

PROBING The activity of aphids and other insects that have piercing or sucking mouthparts. Probing is a brief exploratory penetration of host cells by mouthparts or ovipositor to determine suitability of the prospective host.

PROBOSCIS 1 The elongated mouthparts of some arthropods. *See also* Butterfly (for illustration). **2** The elongated snout of some animals (e.g., anteater, elephant).

PROCESS The action of moving forward progressively from one point, task, or observation to another point, task, or observation on the way to completion, or of passing through stages of development from a starting point to an anticipated endpoint.

PROCESSING 1 The operation necessary to produce negatives, diapositives, or prints from exposed film, plates, or papers. **2** The manipulation of data by means of a computer or other device. **3** The physical conversion of one form of material into another (e.g., processing timber into lumber or pulpwood into pulp).

PROCESSOR *See* Harvesting Machine Classification.

PROCTOR DENSITY *See* Soil Compaction.

PROCUMBENT A plant part that is lying flat on the ground, trailing, but not rooting.

PROCUREMENT COSTS The direct and indirect costs involved in the transfer from one stage of manufacture or distribution to another, from the viewpoint of the latter stage.

PRODUCER SURPLUS In economics, the difference between the producer's sale price and the production costs (i.e., the economic rent).

PRODUCTION FOREST A forest specifically under management to provide a harvest of forest products. The biotic and/or abiotic diversity of the forest may be changed over time as a result of management activities such as clearing, burning, planting, brushing, and weeding, and the introduction of faster growing varieties or exotic species. *See also* Forest.

PRODUCTIVITY 1 The rate at which biomass accumulates over a given area in a given period of time. **2** In avian biology, the number of young produced per pair of birds, or the reproductive performance of the population, estimated as the proportion of young in the total population just after the breeding season. *See also* Primary Production.

PROFILE VIEW An illustration in which the features coinciding in space with the plane of sectioning are strongly emphasized (usually by thick linework). Features in the background are usually shown with much thinner linework and without any reduction in size in proportion to their increasing distance from the plane of sectioning (as would occur if they were drawn according to the rules of linear perspective). Underground features are seldom shown in 'profile' type drawings, nor is there ever any exaggeration of the scale of the vertical or horizontal features. *See also* Cross-Section.

PROFUNDAL ZONE That part of a lake where light does not penetrate.

PROGENY The offspring resulting from sexual reproduction, or from one asexually reproducing individual.

PROGENY TEST The evaluation of the genetic constitution of an individual based on the field performance of its progeny.

PROGRAMME EVALUATION AND REVIEW TECHNIQUE (PERT) *See* Critical Path Method.

PROJECT FIRE *See* Campaign Fire.

PROJECTION 1 An extrapolation of a series of past data to make a conditional forecast of future conditions and occurrences. The accuracy of a projection is very dependent on past trends continuing, or else changing in a manner that is already fully understood. A 'projection' differs from a forecast, which is also a prediction of future conditions but is based on an understanding of the system under discussion from current and past data rather than merely continuing and adjusting past trends. The dividing line between the terms is imprecise. *See also* Forecast. **2** Any physical form or shape that projects markedly beyond the general form of the whole body or feature and is therefore more noticeable in its own right.

PROKARYOTE A unicellular microorganism lacking an organized nucleus and distinct organelles; includes bacteria, blue-green algae, and actinomycetes. An organism with these traits is said to be prokaryotic. *See also* Eukaryote.

PROLEGS The fleshy abdominal legs of certain insect larvae.

PROLIFERATION **1** In general, a large and rapid increase in population numbers. **2** In biology, a rapid and repeated production of new cells, tissues, or organs. **3** Producing buds or new shoots in an abnormal manner, such as shoots from flowers, fruits on fruits, plantlets on leaves.

PROPAGATING FLAMING ZONE That portion of the fire front that is largely responsible for preheating fuels ahead of the fire.

PROPAGULE **1** A detachable reproductive structure of plants (cone, seed, fruit, spore, rhizome) or any part capable of growing into a new plant (twig, leaf, root), produced for dispersal and propagation of the species. It is also termed disseminule or diaspore. *See also* Anemochore; Barochore; Hydrochore; Seed; Zoochore. **2** In conservation biology, the smallest number of individuals of a species that can successfully colonize an island with a suitable habitat.

PROPER MARGIN In fungi, the edge of the apothecial exciple containing fungal, but no algal, cells. The proper margin is typically similar in colour to the disc.

PROPHYLL/PROPHYLLUM **1** A bracteole subtending a single flower on a flower stalk, especially one of two subtending the perianth in *Juncus* species. **2** A two-edged first bract on the peduncle, and occasionally on the branches of an inflorescence in palms.

PROP ROOT A rigid aerial root arising from the stem that reaches to the ground and then provides support for the stem.

PROSTRATE General term for lying flat on the ground.

PROTANDROUS/PROTERANDROUS A flower in which the anthers mature and release their pollen prior to the stigma of the same flower being receptive. *See also* Protogynous.

PROTECTANT **1** A pesticide that prevents an attacking organism from establishing itself on the surface of its host. With fungi, it is also termed a fungistatic chemical. *See also* Fungistatic. **2** A chemical applied to a plant surface before it is contacted by a pathogen to prevent infection. *See also* Eradicant.

PROTECTED AREA **1** Generally, an area protected by legislation, regulation, or land-use policy to control human occupancy or activity. Protection can be of many different forms. **2** The World Conservation Union identified eight main categories of protected areas in 1978. In the early 1990s, this system was reviewed and amended to six main categories. The new scheme is outlined below along with its earlier equivalent. **Category I**: Strict Nature Reserve/Wilderness Area is a protected area managed mainly for science or wilderness protection. **Category Ia**: Strict Nature Reserve is a protected area managed mainly for science. (The equivalent category in the 1978 system was Scientific Reserve or Strict Nature Reserve.) **Category Ib**: Wilderness Area is a protected area managed mainly for wilderness protection. (The 1978 system did not have this category, but it was adopted in 1984.) **Category II**: National Park is a protected area managed mainly for ecosystem protection and recreation. (Equivalent to national Park in the 1978 system.) **Category III**: Natural Monument is a protected area managed mainly for conservation of specific natural features. (Equivalent to Natural Monument/Natural Landmark in the 1978 system.) **Category IV**: Habitat/Species Management Area is a protected area managed mainly for conservation through management intervention. (Equivalent to Nature Conservation Reserve/Managed Nature Reserve/Wildlife Sanctuary in the 1978 system.) **Category V**: Protected Landscape/Seascape is a protected area managed mainly for landscape/seascape conservation and recreation. (A Protected Landscape in the 1978 system.) **Category VI**: Managed Resource Protected Area is a protected area managed mainly for the sustainable use of natural ecosystems. (This category did not exist in the 1978 system but may match some aspects of Resource Reserves, Natural Biotic Areas/ Anthropological Reserves, and Multiple Use Management Areas/Managed Resource Areas.)

PROTECTED LANDSCAPE NETWORK Within the concept of wholistic forest use, areas between large, protected reserves that are protected from human use or modification in order to maintain connectivity in the landscape and with it, a full range of biological diversity at all scales. Components of a protected landscape network include riparian ecosystems, representative ecosystems (small nodes of 400 hectares or more, established to protect strategically located, rare, or endangered ecosystem types), sensitive ecosystems, and cross-valley corridors. A protected landscape network forms a framework within which ecologically responsible forest uses may be zoned.

PROTECTION **1** The use of measures for protecting trees or stands, such as chemical sprays, manipulation of biological control agents, or protection of regenerated stands by the removal of residual infected trees. **2** The action of a strain of a pathogen in protecting a host against infection by a second strain of the same pathogen. *See also* Forest Protection.

PROTECTION FOREST All forest land managed primarily to exert beneficial influences on soil, water, landscape, or for any other purpose when production of merchantable timber, if any, is incidental. *See also* Forest.

PROTHALLIUM/PROTHALLUS The gametophyte generation of ferns and some other cryptogams. A small, delicate, flattened, thalluslike structure growing on the ground, bearing the sexual organs of antheridia and archegonium.

PROTOGYNE A reproductive stage of certain eriophyid mites. A malelike female. One of the two forms of the same mite species. *See also* Deutogyne.

PROTOGYNOUS/PROTEROGYNOUS A flower in which the stigma is receptive prior to maturity of the anthers in the same flower. *See also* Protandrous.

PROTONEMA Plural protonemata. A branched, threadlike or platelike growth arising from spores and on which the leafy parts of mosses develop.

PROTONYMPH The second instar of false spider mites, spider mites, and tarsonemid mites. *See also* Instar.

PROVENANCE The region or geographical source where a plant or animal was originally found and is native, and where its genetic constitution has developed through natural selection in between periods of glaciation.

PROVENANCE TEST A replicated experiment that compares trees grown from seed or cuttings from many parts of a species' natural range to determine the most appropriate provenance for use in any one location.

PROXIMAL Describes the location of a feature on an organism that is close to the centre or point of attachment. *See also* Distal.

PROXIMATE FACTOR An event or characteristic that has a direct or relatively direct effect on an organism (e.g., day length). *See also* Ultimate Factor.

PROXIMITY In statistics, a measure of how similar or how different two objects are.

PRUINOSE Having a greyish-white bloom on the surface.

PRUNING **1** Usually, the selective removal of branches to improve timber quality, or to remove dead or diseased wood, or to correct undesirable growth patterns. Natural pruning occurs when the lower branches are shaded by those above, die, and drop off. Bud pruning involves the removal of selected buds to prevent them from developing into branches. **2** The severing of roots to force development of new, more fibrous root structures, or as a means of controlling nutrient supply and forcing flowering and fruiting at a younger age, or as a means of restricting top growth on very vigorous plants.

In wildlife management, branch pruning activities to improve wood quality (timber management) can also severely reduce hiding (security) cover for large animals, although it may provide very minor benefits in terms of better access through the stand, and the temporary creation of improved forage if light levels increase as a result of pruning. *See also* Pruning Cut.

PRUNING CUT The manner in which branches are removed or cut from the main trunk. Two schools of thought are found, one advocating the conventional pruning approach, and the other advocating natural target pruning. The practice of cutting branches flush with the tree surface (conventional pruning) is no longer considered acceptable due to the greatly increased amount of wounded tissue created and the higher risk of disease infection.

Most branches form a distinct bark ridge or collar at the point of attachment. In natural target pruning, the branch is severed just beyond this ridge so as to avoid damaging the integrity of the bark collar. In conventional pruning, the bark ridge is also maintained, but the cut is slightly lower and thus creates a larger wound area. While both approaches preserve the integrity of the bark ridge, the area of wound differs and it is on this point that the disagreement in approach focuses and remains a subject of debate. *See also* Flush Cut.

PSEUD-/PSEUDO- A prefix meaning false, or atypical.

PSEUDANTHIUM A compact inflorescence with

small individual flowers, the whole of which simulates a single flower.

PSEUDOBULB A thickened or bulbiform above-ground stem in certain orchids that, according to the species, varies in shape from globose to long-cylindrical.

PSEUDOCYPHELLUM Plural pseudocyphellae. A white patch, dot, or line on the surface of some lichens, caused by a break in the cortex and the extension of the inner medulla to the surface.

PSEUDOGALL A false gall, appearing to be like a gall but not necessarily an abnormal growth.

PSEUDOPERIDIUM A false peridium.

PSEUDORHIZA A below-ground, rootlike growth at the base of a fungus that may or may not have rhizomorphs. *See also* Fungus (for illustration); Rhizomorphs.

PSEUDOSCLEROTIAL PLATE Describes some wood-colonizing fungi. A hard, dark plate formed within decaying wood, more or less impervious to water, solutes, and organisms, composed of large, thick-walled or encrusted fungal cells, affording protection to the mycelium behind it. Typically seen as a black line (zone line) in transverse view.

PSYCHOLOGICAL BARRIER An obstruction or impediment that is perceived in the mind of an individual or group of individuals, but which is not necessarily a physical barrier. *See also* Attitude; Belief.

PSYCHROMETER The general name for instruments designed for determining the water vapour content of air. A psychrometer consists of dry- and wet-bulb thermometers that, when properly ventilated, indicate the dry- and wet-bulb temperatures used to determine the relative humidity and dew point of the atmosphere, generally with the aid of psychrometric tables or slide rule. A non-ventilated psychrometer relies on the natural movement of air for ventilation, whereas a ventilated psychrometer relies on artificially circulated air (e.g. a sling psychrometer). *See also* Hygrometer; Sling Psychrometer.

PTERIDOPHYTE An obsolete collective term for any plant in the Phylum Pteridophyta, which includes ferns, horsetails, and club mosses. The term has no taxonomic status. *See also* Tracheophyta.

PUBERULENT/PUBERULOUS A surface clothed with minute, soft, erect hairs.

PUBESCENT Covered with short, fine hairs.

PUBLIC INVOLVEMENT The provision of one or more opportunities for the general public to participate, and thereby influence, the process, and the decisions resulting from the process of planning the goals, policies, activities, schedules, and manner of undertaking all of these as they occur on public land over a specified time period. The 'public' is all-inclusive and includes individual citizens, all levels of government, interest groups, or individual companies.

PULPWOOD Trees that will yield logs of suitable size and quality for the production of pulp. It also refers to the logs of such trees. *See also* Fuelwood.

PULVINATE Cushion-shaped, strongly convex, forming a dense, low tuft. *See also* Pulvinus.

PULVINUS A cushion of enlarged tissue typically seen at the base of a petiole where it attaches to the stem.

PUNCTATE A surface dotted with or consisting of small points, spots, depressions, or pits.

PUNGENT **1** Strong-smelling. **2** Ending in a stiff, sharp point or tip.

PUNK KNOT Soft, decayed branch stubs that usually indicate the presence of decay within the tree.

PUNKY A soft, weak, often spongy wood condition caused by decay.

PUPA Plural pupae. Refers to insects with complete metamorphosis. The inactive stage during which the transformation from larva to adult takes place.

PUPAL CHAMBER The chamber excavated in bark, wood, or other material in which pupation takes place. *See also* Gallery.

PUPARIUM The thickened, barrel-like larval cuticle encasing the pupa in certain flies.

PUPATION The transformation of an insect larva into a pupa and the subsequent developmental changes within the pupa.

PURE STAND A stand of coniferous or broad-leaved species where one species occupies more than 80 per cent (may vary by jurisdiction) of the main crown canopy. *See also* Mixed Stand.

PUSTULE In plant pathology, a blisterlike spot on a leaf, stem, or other organ from which erupts a spore-bearing structure of a fungus.

PYCNIDIOSPORE The asexual spore or conidium produced within a pycnidium.

PYCNIDIUM Plural pycnidia. The asexual type of fruiting body, typically flask-shaped, in which asexual spores or conidia are produced.

PYCNIOSPORES *See* Spermatium.

PYCNIUM *See* Spermagonium.

PYRENE The nutlet in a drupe. A seed and surrounding bony endocarp, such as a cherry or peach pit, or the seed of a blackberry drupelet. *See also* Nut.

PYRIFORM Pear-shaped.
PYROCLASTIC Pertaining to fragmental materials produced by usually explosive, aerial ejection of clastic particles from a volcanic vent. The ejected materials can accumulate on land or under water (or glacial ice).
PYXIS A circumscissilely dehiscing capsule, the top coming off as a lid. *See also* Capsule; Fruit (for illustration).

Q

Q-MODE ANALYSIS An ecological data matrix (see diagram) consisting of stands and species that can be studied from two different perspectives: (1) down the columns (the stand) and (2) across the rows (the species). The species (rows) are dependent on each other, while the stands (columns) are independent. Q-mode analysis uses various statistical techniques to measure the similarity or dissimilarity between independent stands in terms of their species composition. Q-mode is the representation of stands in species space. *See also* R-mode Analysis. In the data matrix example below, the presence of each species in each stand has been determined using the Domin-Kragina cover abundance scale.

Q-mode two-way matrix

Species	Stands (columns)				
(rows)	1	2	3	4	5
a	1	2	1	3	2
b	8	8	3	2	4
c	5	2	7	7	6
d	5	6	8	7	8
e	2	4	4	3	2

QUADRAT A small, clearly defined plot or sampling area of known size, used as a part of a sampling or study scheme to ascertain characteristics of a larger ecosystem or vegetation patterns. The shape and size of the quadrats (typically square or rectangular) depend upon the observations that are being made, the total area being sampled, and scale of resolution desired (coarse or fine scale observations). In regeneration studies, frequently one square metre or four square metres in size. *See also* Cruise Line; Transect.
QUADRATIC MEAN DIAMETER *See* Diameter (quadratic mean).
QUALITATIVE The assignment of a value, such as good or bad, to a variable that would normally lack a means of quantification by standard measurement methods (length, width, volume). *See also* Measurement.
QUANTITATIVE The measurement of a value or quantity using standard measurement methods such as volume, duration, length, weight. *See also* Measurement; Qualitative.
QUARANTINE The regulation and restriction of the sale, shipment, or transportation of soil, plants, plant parts, and animals between or within national boundaries, usually to prevent the spread of known pests into new, uninfected areas.
QUATERNARY The second period of the Cenozoic era of geologic time, extending from the end of the Tertiary period (about two million years ago) to the present and comprising two epochs, the Pleistocene (Ice Age) and the Holocene (Recent). The term also describes the corresponding system of earth materials. *See also* Appendix 2: Geological Time Scales.
QUOTIENT *See* Form Quotient.

R

RACE **1** A population or group of populations within a species that is composed of generally similar individuals and is both discontinuous and distinguishable from other populations of that species, though not sufficiently to be considered a separate species. When the distinguishing characteristics of a race are recognizably adaptive, the term is synonymous with ecotype. For example, a population may be described as a **climatic race** if its adaptations are based on climatic factors. A geographically restricted race is termed a **geographic race.** **2** A strain of a pathogen characterized by the limitation of its host range to particular species, cultivars, or varieties. *See also Forma Specialis.*
RACEME An indeterminate inflorescence that has flowers arranged on pedicels along a single stalk. *See also* Inflorescence.
RACEMOSE/RACEMIFORM Like a raceme. Said of flowers borne on a raceme or an inflorescence that is a raceme.
RACE NON-SPECIFIC RESISTANCE Resistance to all races of a particular pathogen. *See also* Field Resistance; Horizontal Resistance.
RACHILLA 'Little Rachis.' The axis of the spikelet in grasses and sedges. *See also* Grass (for illustration).
RACHIS Plural rachises. The main axis of an

inflorescence, compound leaf, or frond. *See also* Fern (for illustration).

RADIAL **1** Generally, a vector extending from a central point to the perimeter of a circle around that point. **2** In photogrammetry, a line or direction from the radial centre to any point on a photograph. The radial centre is assumed to be the principal point (centre of the photograph), unless otherwise designated.

RADIAL LINE PLOTTING A method of triangulation, analytic or graphic, used to locate points on vertical or near-vertical aerial photographs in their correct position relative to each other.

RADIAL STRIP FLANK FIRE *See* Ignition Pattern (maple leaf ignition).

RADIATE **1** Spreading out from a central starting point. **2** To give off waves of energy. **3** A flower structure that has a central area of densely packed flowers surrounded by ray florets as in the typically daisy-like flowers of many Compositae.

RADIATION *See* Heat Transfer.

RADICAL **1** Chemically, a group of atoms or a single atom having an unpaired electron and no charge. Typically, these have a short life span and are very reactive. **2** Botanically, arising directly from the root or root crown. Describes leaves that are basal or rosulate.

RADICAL ENVIRONMENTALISM Refers to that wing of the environmental movement that calls for fundamental and sweeping changes in our philosophies, values, structures, practices, and lifestyles. Some forms of radical environmentalism advocate drastic actions such as ecotage, others are nonviolent and use peaceful tactics to bring about a change in consciousness and thus practices.

RADICLE That portion of an embryo that develops into a root, typically the first structure to emerge from a newly germinated seed.

RADIOCARBON AGE An age determination made on organic substances by measuring the decay of the radioactivity of the Carbon-14 isotope.

RADIO COLLAR Used for tracking wildlife. A collar (or similar fastening device) containing a radio transmitter is fastened onto the animal. Signals from the transmitter are received and used by wildlife biologists to gain information about the animal's position and its movement patterns over time.

RADIOSONDE OBSERVATION An evaluation, in terms of dry-bulb temperature, relative humidity, and pressure aloft, of radio signals received from a balloon-borne radiosonde. The height of each mandatory and significant pressure level of the observation is computed from these data. *See also* Helicopter Sounding; Minisonde Observation; Rawinsonde Observation.

RADIO-TELEMETRY Automatic tracking, measurement, and transmission of data from remote sources via radio to a receiving station for recording and analysis.

RAGHORN A two-year-old bull elk with small, often asymmetrical antlers, frequently having broken tines.

RAIN Precipitation in the form of liquid water drops. *See also* Precipitation.

RAINFOREST A forest biome characterized by high annual rainfall, very infrequent incidences of fire, closed, typically dense vegetation layers, dominated by trees which form a two-or-more layered, dense canopy in which lianas and epiphytes are usually copious, and with a lower, sparse assemblage of smaller trees, shrubs, herbs, and ferns. Globally, two main types are of significance. (1) **Tropical rainforests** have extremely high species diversity, quite disproportionate to the area occupied. Biological complexity is extremely high, and many species and ecosystem relationships are as yet unknown, and possibly not even imagined. Tropical rainforest is widespread around the world at equatorial and subequatorial latitudes. (2) **Temperate rainforests**, located between latitudes 30 degrees and 60 degrees north or south, have much lower species diversity, and cooler year-round climates. As with tropical rainforests, many of the complex ecosystem functions and processes are as yet unknown or poorly understood. Temperate rainforests are not common globally and represent a more endangered ecosystem than tropical rainforests.

RAIN-ON-SNOW EVENT The combination of heavy rainfall with rapid snowmelt, with the ground still largely frozen. It produces exceptionally high volumes of water in a very short period of time.

RAIN SHADOW The area of land lying in the lee of mountains or similar obstructions that receives less rainfall than areas lying further away from the obstructions. The rain received in the shadow is all that remains of the orographic rain. *See also* Orographic.

RAMET Offspring produced from vegetative reproduction.

RAMICORNS **1** Unusually large and persistent branches that project from the main stem at acute angles, often indicating previous attack by weevils. **2** The branched antenna of some insects.

RAMIFYING **1** A process, decision, result, or outcome that has widespread implications and thus ramifies (branches many times) throughout a system. Thus, the results are termed the ramifications. **2** Botanically, having a branching growth habit.

RAMOSE Having, or dividing into many branches.

RAMSAR SITES An international designation for important wetland areas, such as the Everglades in Florida. As with biosphere reserves and world heritage sites, areas on the Ramsar list have no legal standing as a result of such listing, but the international recognition may support their protection.

RANDOM Being or relating to a set or to an element of a set each of whose elements has equal probability of occurrence. It is also characterized by procedures to obtain such sets or elements.

RANDOMIZATION In an experiment, the process of assigning placement of control or experimental treatments, or membership in control or experimental groups, in such a way that the probability of assignment to a particular place, or group, is equal for all treatments or individuals. *See also* Sampling.

RANGE **1** Of a species: the geographical and/or vertical range where a species occurs throughout the day, or seasonally. In mountainous areas, larger animals typically have a summer range area higher up the mountains, while their winter range is lower down or in more sheltered areas, away from the deeper snows and harsher winter weather. *See also* Home Range; Territory. **2** In statistics, a basic measure of the range between the largest and smallest points in a set of random variables. **3** In land classification schemes, land producing forage crops as opposed to other agricultural crops, or forest crops. **4** In radio-telemetry, or other work involving radio signals, the distance over which the signal sent can be clearly received.

RANGE CONDITION In range management, the current status or stage of succession of a plant community, relative to the potential or climax vegetation possible for the site.

RANGE LAND Land not under cultivation that produces (or has the capability to produce) forage suitable for the grazing of livestock. It includes forest land producing forage.

RANGE OF VARIABILITY The spectrum of conditions possible in ecosystem composition, structure, and function considering both temporal and spatial factors.

RANK **1** The position of a taxon in a taxonomic hierarchy. **2** Botanically, a vertical row; typically leaves that are two-ranked (in two vertical rows, alternate or opposite).

RAPATTACK *See* Rappel Crew.

RAPHE **1** A ridge occurring at the point where two structures join or meet (e.g., the junction of the hemispheres in vertebrate brains). **2** The ridge on seeds or most anatropous ovules where the ovule joins the stalk.

RAPHIDE A tiny, needlelike crystal of calcium oxalate found in many vegetative parts of plants.

RAPIDS A relatively deep stream section with considerable surface agitation and swift current. Some waves may be present. Rocks and boulders may be exposed at all but high flows. Drops of up to one metre in elevation are typical.

RAPPEL CREW An initial attack crew trained to descend from a specially equipped, hovering helicopter on a rope fitted with a mechanical device to control the rate of descent. It is synonymous with rapattack. *See also* Rappelling.

RAPPELLING In fire suppression, the act of descending from a hovering helicopter whereby a person slides down a rope to the ground, their rate of descent being controlled by a mechanical device attached to the rope. It is a specialized form of helitack. *See also* Rappel Crew.

RAPTOR Any predatory bird, such as a falcon, hawk, eagle, or owl, that has feet with sharp talons or claws adapted for seizing prey, and a hooked beak for tearing flesh.

RASPING MOUTHPARTS Specialized insect mouthparts that are designed for filing or rasping plant tissue. It is typical of thrips. *See also* Thrips.

RASTER In GIS work **1** the scanned (illuminated) area of a cathode ray tube. **2** A format for data that comprises a set of pixels arranged to represent spatial information in a grid of cells. *See also* Vector Format.

RATE OF AREA GROWTH The speed at which a fire increases its size, expressed in terms of area per unit time. *See also* Rate of Perimeter Growth; Rate of Spread.

RATE OF INCREASE A measurement of the change in numbers of a population. The **finite** or **geometric**, rate of increase λ is the factor by which size of a population changes over a specified period. The **exponential rate** (r) is the power to which e (the base of natural logarithms) is raised such that $e^r = \lambda$. The **intrinsic rate** of increase ρ in the best of all environments, is the rate at which a population with a stable age distribution grows in a given environment when no resource is in short supply. It is also termed the Malthusian parameter. The **observed rate** of increase is the rate at which a population changes over time. The **potential rate** is that rate that would result if the effect of a given agent of mortality were eliminated. The **survival-fecundity rate** of increase is the exponential rate at which a population would increase if it had a stable age distribution appropriate to its current schedules of age-specific survival and fecundity. The **innate capacity for increase** is the intrinsic growth rate of a population under ideal conditions without the restraining effects of competition.

RATE OF PERIMETER GROWTH The speed at which a fire increases its perimeter, expressed in terms of distance per unit time. *See also* Rate of Area Growth; Rate of Spread.

RATE OF SPREAD The speed at which a fire extends its horizontal dimensions, expressed in terms of distance per unit time. It is generally thought of in terms of a fire's forward movement or head fire rate of spread, but is also applicable to backfire and flank fire rate of spread. In Canada, it is measured in metres per minute or kilometres per hour (1.0 metre per minute = 0.06 kilometres per hour). *See also* Rate of Area Growth; Rate of Perimeter Growth.

RATE OF SPREAD FACTOR In fire management, a factor, usually on a scale of 1 to 100, that represents a relative rate of spread for a specific fuel condition and fixed weather conditions (or fuel model). The factors can be used as multipliers, arguments for entering tables, or to provide a ratio of values between two fuels.

RATE OF USE The amount of resource use per unit time, defined in measurable units, such as cubic metres per year.

RATIO MEASUREMENT *See* Measurement.

RAUNKIAER'S LIFE-FORMS *See* Life-Form.

RAVINE A small stream valley, narrow, steep-sided, and typically v-shaped in cross-section. It is larger than a gully.

RAW DATA The values collected for each variable, without any statistical or other manipulation having been done to alter or adjust the data.

RAWINSONDE OBSERVATION A method of determining wind speed and direction, air temperature, relative humidity, and atmospheric pressure at various levels in the atmosphere in the vicinity of an observation station by tracking a transmitting, balloon-borne sensor package with a radio direction-finder or by radar. A Rawinsonde Observation is commonly used in determining atmospheric stability and for constructing vertical temperature and wind profiles. *See also* Helicopter Sounding; Minisonde Observation.

RAY **1** A beam of radiant energy, typically radiating out from a source. **2** Botanically, a branch of an umbel or an umbel-like inflorescence. **3** A component of wood made up of cells and/or structures extending radially and horizontally from the cambium. Softwood rays tend to be uniseriate (one cell wide) but may be many cells high. Hardwood rays tend to be larger and more variable, multiseriate (many cells wide) and of variable height. The arrangement and composition of rays can be used to assist species identification in some cases. *See also* Phloem (for illustration). **4** *See* Ray Flower.

RAY FLOWER A ligulate flower with flattened corolla, typical of the Compositae. The flattening results from incomplete coalescence between two petals of sympetalous flowers. Ray flowers are found on the margin of the flower head, although in some species they occupy the whole flower head. *See also* Disc Flower.

REACH **1** The distance spanned by a skyline in which logs can be extracted from the stump to the landing. **2** *See* Stream Reach.

REACTION WOOD The woody tissues formed as a means of counteracting the affects of gravity (lean) on main stems or branches. In broad-leaved trees, reaction wood forms on the upper surfaces of branches or leaning trunks and is termed **tension wood**. The tension wood acts to pull the branch or trunk back toward the vertical. The wood is typically harder, denser, and sometimes darker than normal wood. The vessels are usually smaller and less frequent. Tension wood is a serious defect in lumber, having higher than usual longitudinal shrinkage (not as high as compression wood) and may collapse due to uneven shrinkage.

In coniferous trees, the reaction develops on the underside of branches or leaning trunks and is termed **compression wood.** Compression wood exerts a pushing force that acts to correct the lean. The phenomenon is easily seen in conifers that have lost their main leader and had it replaced by a lateral branch that changes its growth pattern from roughly horizontal to vertical. Growth rings are wider in compression wood than normal wood, the tracheids are rounder in cross-section and thicker walled, and intercellular spaces are common. Compression wood is a serious defect in lumber, having a lower tensile strength, much higher longitudinal shrinkage rates, and a tendency to fail suddenly under tensile loads. It is also inferior for pulping. *See also* Stress.

REARING HABITAT Areas in rivers or streams where juvenile salmon and trout find food and shelter to live and grow.

REAR OF FIRE *See* Forest Fire (back).

REBURN **1** A repeat burning of an area that has already burned once. **2** The area burned in this manner.

RECEIVING SITE Sites that receive moisture from other, typically higher sites, through subsurface groundwater flows in addition to precipitation.

RECEPTACLE The enlarged or elongated structure supporting the reproductive organs of a plant and some or all of the other flower parts (see illustration). It is also called a thalamus or torus. If the ovary is attached to the receptacle above the attachment of the other floral parts, it is superior. The ovary is inferior when it is below the attachment of the perianth and androecium and embedded in the receptacle. Depending on the position of the ovary, perianth, and androecium, flowers may be hypogynous, epigynous, or perigynous. *See also* Epigynous; Hypogynous; Perigynous.

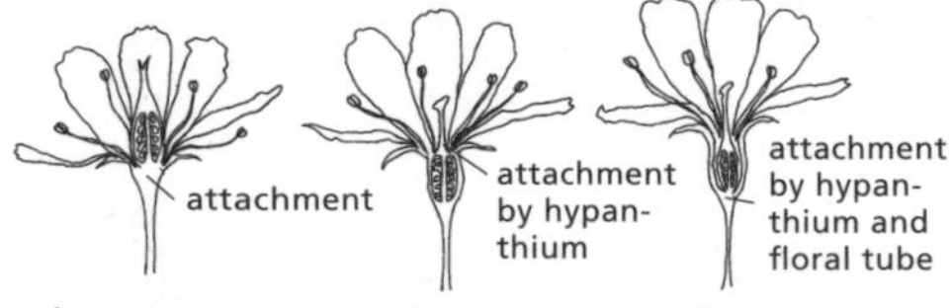

RECESSIVE *See* Dominant.

RECHARGE The addition of water to an aquifer that occurs naturally from infiltration of rainfall and from water flowing over earth materials that allow water to infiltrate below the land surface.

RECLAMATION A planned series of activities designed to recreate the biophysical capacity of an ecosystem in such a way that the resulting ecosystem is different from the ecosystem existing before disturbance. *See also* Restoration.

RECLINATE Bent down, reclining, falling back from the perpendicular.

RECONNAISSANCE **1** Generally, a broad-scale review of an area prior to undertaking a more detailed and systematic inventory or evaluation. **2** In fire suppression, to examine a fire area to obtain information about current and probable fire behaviour and other related fire suppression information.

RECORD In data storage, usually on a computer, one record is a collection of related data treated as a logical unit. In computerized data bases, each record contains one or more fields of data. *See also* Field.

RECOVERABLE WOOD VOLUME The volume of wood in a growing stand that is anticipated to be available for commercial harvest over a specified period.

RECOVERY **1** In fire management, an increase in fuel moisture content as a result of increased relative humidity, usually occurring overnight. **2** The amount of usable wood products generated (recovered) from a round log after manufacture. **3** The ability of a disturbed system to return to its pre-disturbance state. **4** An action that is necessary to reduce or resolve the threats that caused a species to be listed as threatened or endangered.

RECOVERY PLAN A plan that gives details about the actions or conditions necessary to promote a species' recovery. If implemented successfully, the results would improve a species' status, ideally to a point where it would no longer be listed under the US Endangered Species Act or, in Canada, to a point where it is no longer nationally threatened or endangered.

RECOVERY TEAM A technical committee charged with developing a national recovery plan for nationally threatened and endangered species.

RECOVERY TIME The time needed for a disturbed system to replace itself with the components that existed prior to disturbance.

RECREATIONAL OPPORTUNITY SPECTRUM (ROS) A planning approach identifying a range of recreational environments across a spectrum ranging from urban recreation areas, rural countryside, highly developed campgrounds, intensively managed, multiple-use forests, national parks, recreation and scenic areas, roadless wildlands, and wilderness. The ROS defines six classes: primitive, semiprimitive non-motorized, semiprimitive motorized, roaded natural, rural, and urban.

RECRUITMENT **1** Generally, the addition to a population from all causes (reproduction, immigration, stocking). Recruitment may refer more specifically to numbers born or hatched or to numbers at a specified stage of life, such as breeding age or weaning age. **2** In silviculture, *see* Ingrowth. **3** In wildlife tree management, a strategy to retain standing live or dead trees that have the potential to become wildlife trees in the future. **4** In the re-creation of old-growth forest attributes, a measure of potential changes in habitat, such as the recruitment of snags or coarse woody debris in the seral stages developing into old-growth forest.

RECTIFICATION The transformation of an aerial photograph to a horizontal plane to remove displacement caused by tilt and conversion to a desired scale. *See also* Displacement; Orthophotograph; Rubber Sheeting.

RECURRENCE INTERVAL The expected or observed time intervals between hydrological events of a particular magnitude described by stochastic or probabilistic models (log-log plots).

RECURSIVE The process of repeating an operation or group of operations, usually with the result of each repetition being in some way dependent upon the result of the preceding repetition.

RECURVED Curved downwards or backwards. *See also* Declinate; Reflexed.

RED ATTACK Describes a beetle attack code assigned to a tree infested by bark beetles. The crown foliage is in a transition from green to a straw colour and then to a red colour, and finally to a rust colour prior to the needles falling off. At the rust-coloured stage, the bark beetles have usually left the tree to infest a green tree elsewhere. *See also* Green Attack; Grey Attack; Red-Top; Sorrel-Top.

RED-BELT Winter injury to conifers, often a result of unseasonally warm or strong winds, usually confined to altitudinal zones or bands that approximately follow distinct contour lines.

REDD A fish nest made in gravel, consisting of a depression hydraulically dug by a fish for egg deposition (and then filled) and the associated gravel mounds.

REDEPOSITED TEPHRA Deposits of volcanic ejecta that fell out of a volcanic cloud in one setting and were later moved to another setting by natural processes. In cores from lakes or bogs, these deposits represent volcanic ash usually carried into the water by surface runoff sometime after the volcanic eruption. *See also* Primary Tephra.

RED FLAG WATCH/WARNING/CANCELLATION In the US, a set of terms used by fire weather forecasters to alert forecast users to special and/or adverse weather conditions that present a high probability of extreme fire behaviour. **Red Flag Watch** is the first stage. It notifies the using agencies, usually twenty-four to seventy-two hours ahead of the event, that current and developing meteorological conditions may evolve into dangerous fire weather. If the adverse weather pattern continues to develop and adverse conditions are expected within twenty-four hours, the second stage, **Red Flag Warning**, is given. Cancellation of either the watch or the warning is given whenever the special or adverse conditions are no longer expected to develop or have ceased to exist. The watch/warning is carried in all forecasts until specifically cancelled.

RED STAIN A pronounced reddish coloration, often extensive, induced by fungi in the heartwood of conifers and a few hardwoods. The term particularly refers to a firm, incipient decay associated with *Armillaria*, *Fomes*, *Phellinus*, and *Inonotus* species in conifers. It is also termed red heart.

RED-TOP The advanced colour phase of the foliage of a conifer killed by insects or pathogens, usually characteristic of a tree killed during the previous season. Although a red attack tree is a red-top, not all red-tops are red attack trees (e.g., white pine blister rust causes red-tops). The terms are often used interchangeably. *See also* Black-Top; Sorrel-Top.

REDUCTION Any chemical process in which one or more electrons are added to an atom, molecule, or ion. Reduction of one substance always involves the oxidation of another. *See also* Oxidation.

REDUNDANCY ANALYSIS (RA) RA is the canonical form of principal components analysis. *See also* Ordination; Principal Components Analysis.

REEF A ridgelike or moundlike structure, layered or massive, built by sedentary calcareous organisms, especially corals, and consisting mainly of their remains. The structure is wave-resistant and stands above the surrounding contemporaneously deposited sediment. There could also be such a structure that was built in the geologic past and is now enclosed in rock, typically of a different lithology. Reefs are extremely rich in marine life-forms. Often the structure reaches above the surrounding sea or lake bottom to (or nearly to) the surface and may pose a navigational hazard.

RE-EMERGENCE The phase of bark beetle activity during which adults bore back out of the bark after ovipositing, or after abandoning a gallery.

REFERENCE CONDITIONS The conditions characterizing ecosystem composition, structure, and function, and their variability.

REFLECTANCE A measure of the ability of a surface to reflect energy. Specifically, the ratio of the reflected energy to the incident energy. Reflectance is affected not only by the nature of the surface itself, but also by the angle of incidence and the viewing angle.

REFLECTING PROJECTOR An optical image transfer device that is used to project the image of photographs, images, or on occasion, maps, onto a copying table.

REFLEXED Curved abruptly downward. *See also* Declinate; Recurved.

REFORESTATION The natural or artificial restocking of an area with forest trees. Typically, refers to planting.

REFORM ENVIRONMENTALISM A sector of the environmental movement that calls for minor changes and reforms in our practices. Environmental ethics is seen as a necessary extension of our concern for humans and future generations. Reform environmentalism is anthropocentric, whereas radical environmentalism is not. Reform environmentalism continues with business as usual on the basis of the same growth-oriented ideas of progress and technological control of the natural world. Some philosophers regard reform environmentalism as the Shallow Ecology Movement.

REFUGIA **1** Locations and habitats that support populations of organisms that are limited to small fragments of their previous geographic range (i.e., endemic populations). **2** Areas that remain unchanged while surrounding areas change markedly, hence the areas serve as a refuge for those species requiring specific habitats. The changes could be short term, such as wildfires, hurricanes, or volcanoes, and the subsequent revegetation of an area, or much longer term, such as periods of glaciation.

REGENERATION **1** The renewal or restoration of lost or damaged tissues. **2** The renewal of a forest or stand of trees by natural or artificial means, or the stand of young trees under 1.3 metres high that results.

REGENERATION CLASS The area, and the young trees in the area, being managed during the regeneration interval in the shelterwood silvicultural system. In this interval, old and young trees occupy the same area, the young trees being protected by the old ones.

REGENERATION CUT The removal of trees to assist the development of the established regeneration or to make regeneration possible.

REGENERATION LAG The time from harvest until establishment of a regenerated stand. *See also* Green-up Period.

REGENERATION METHOD The cutting method selected that will create a new age class. The major methods fall into three main categories. (1) **Even-aged methods** include the following. (a) **Clearcutting** is a method of regenerating an even-aged stand in which a new age class develops in a fully exposed microclimate after removal, in a single cutting, of all trees in the previous stand. Regeneration is from natural seeding, direct seeding, planted seedlings, and/or advance regeneration. Harvesting may be done in groups or patches (group or patch clearcutting), or in strips (strip clearcutting). In the clearcutting system, the management unit or stand in which regeneration, growth, and yield are regulated consists of the individual clearcut stand. (b) **Clearcutting with reserves (standards)** is a clearcutting method in which varying numbers of reserve trees are not harvested in order to attain goals other than regeneration. (c) **Seed tree** is an even-aged regeneration method in which a new age class develops from seedlings that germinate in fully exposed micro-environments after removal of all the previous stand except for a small number of trees left to provide seed. Seed trees are removed after regeneration is established. (d) **Seed tree with reserves (standards)** is a seed tree method in which some or all of the seed trees are retained after regeneration has become established to attain goals other than regeneration. (e) **Shelterwood** is a method of regenerating an even-aged stand in which a new age class develops beneath partial shade, or in the partially shaded micro-environment provided by the residual trees. The sequence of cutting treatments can include three distinct types of cuttings: (i) an optional preparatory harvest to enhance conditions for seed production; (ii) an establishment harvest to prepare the seed bed and to create a new age class; and (iii) a removal harvest to release established regeneration from competition with the overwood. Harvesting may be done uniformly throughout the stand (uniform shelterwood), or in strips (strip shelterwood). (f) **Shelterwood with reserves (standards)** is a variant of the shelterwood method in which some or all of the shelter trees are retained, well beyond the normal period of retention, to attain goals other than regeneration. The resulting stand may be two-aged or tend toward an uneven-aged condition as a consequence of both an extended period of regeneration establishment and the retention of reserve trees that may represent one or more age classes. (2) **Two-aged methods** are designed to maintain and regenerate a stand with two age classes. *See* Shelterwood with Reserves and Coppice with Reserves. (3) **Uneven-aged (Selection) methods**

are methods of regenerating a forest stand and maintaining an uneven-aged structure by removing some trees in all size classes in the following ways. (a) **Group selection** is a method of regenerating uneven-aged stands in which trees are removed and new age classes are established in small groups. The maximum width of groups is approximately twice the height of the mature trees, with small openings providing micro-environments suitable for shade-tolerant regeneration and the larger openings providing conditions suitable for the more shade-intolerant regeneration. In this system, the management unit or stand in which regeneration, growth, and yield are regulated, consists of a landscape containing an aggregation of groups. (b) **Single-tree selection** is a method of creating new age classes in uneven-aged stands in which individual trees of all size classes are removed more or less uniformly throughout the stand to achieve desired stand structural characteristics. (c) **Coppice method** is a method of regenerating a stand in which all trees in the previous stand are harvested and the majority of regeneration is from sprouts or suckers. (d) **Coppice with reserves (standards)** is a coppice method in which reserve trees are retained to attain goals other than regeneration. The method normally creates a two-aged stand.

REGENERATION PERIOD The time between the removal of the previous forest and the successful re-establishment of a new stand by natural or artificial means.

REGISTERED PESTICIDE A pesticide that has been accepted for registration and specific application, uses, and purposes under the applicable legislation.

REGISTERED USE One of the specific uses (i.e., application to a particular crop and target pest) for which a particular pesticide or other pest control product has been registered.

REGOLITH The unconsolidated and unaltered layer of weathered rock and soil and surficial materials overlying the bedrock.

REGRESSION **1** In statistics, a method of analysis employing least squares to examine data, and to draw meaningful conclusions about dependency relationships (i.e., extent, direction, strength) that may exist with single or multiple independents. **2** A reversion to an earlier stage of succession due to destruction of the vegetation of a site by, for example, fire, grazing, cutting, etc., usually with no subsequent deterioration of the soil by exposure, erosion, and loss of nutrients.

REGRESSION ANALYSIS In statistics, the analysis of the relationship between two variables, one of which is dependent upon another independent variable. It is usually expressed by a mathematical equation representing a straight or curved line.

REGULAR FLOWER A flower in which the members of each circle of parts (at least the sepals and petals) are similar in size, shape, and orientation. It is also termed actinomorphic.

REGULAR UNEVEN-AGED STRUCTURE (BALANCED) A stand in which three or more distinct age classes occupy approximately equal areas and provide a balanced distribution of diameter classes. *See also* Irregular Uneven-Aged Structure.

REGULATION The control of harvest location, quantity, and size of area cut, usually to meet a sustained yield objective. *See also* Annual Allowable Cut.

REGULATORY NEGOTIATIONS (REG-NEG) The use of mediated negotiations to establish regulations. The parties at interest and the responsible agency are brought together to develop standards and procedures that are mutually acceptable. The agency commits to carry forward the agreement as a proposed rule if agreement of all parties (including the agency) is achieved. In the absence of such agreement, the agency will promulgate a proposed rule of its own design, but that rule is likely to be more responsive to the needs of the parties and the public based on information developed and exchanged in the process.

In regulations dealing with technical and scientific matters (chemicals, waste disposal, habitat protection, etc.) there is a prior commitment that any rule developed through the negotiations will be based on an appropriate scientific and technical record.

Regulatory negotiations have been successfully applied in situations ranging from stream protection in timber harvest to protection of eagle-nesting sites to the protection of air quality during off-shore oil exploration and development.

REHABILITATION The restoration of ecosystem functions and processes in a degraded system or habitat. *See also* Restoration.

RE-INVENTORY The remeasurement of an entire survey area to replace (update) an existing inventory in its entirety.

REKINDLE Re-ignition due to latent heat, sparks, or embers or due to the presence of smoke or steam.

RELASCOPE An angle gauge, used in point sampling, in which bands of different widths are viewed through an eyepiece, resulting in different angles of projection. The relascope has other scales and may be used for other purposes, such as the estimation of tree heights. *See also* Point Sampling; Prism; Telerelascope.

RELATIVE ABUNDANCE A rough estimate of population density or relative importance of one species compared to others in the same area. It is calculated from the number of individuals of a certain species sighted over a certain period of time (e.g., number of birds sighted per hour) or in a particular place, divided by the number of all species in a community. Relative abundance is usually expressed as a percentage.

RELATIVE HUMIDITY The ratio, expressed as a percentage, of the amount of water vapour or moisture in the air to the maximum amount of moisture that the air would hold at the same dry-bulb temperature and atmospheric pressure. Relative humidity can vary from 0 to 100 per cent (e.g., 60 per cent relative humidity means that the air contains 60 per cent of the moisture it is capable of holding). *See also* Absolute Humidity.

RELATIVE THINNING INTENSITY The volume of thinnings derived from a stand, expressed as a percentage of its periodic annual increment or as a proportion of the total stand volume.

RELAXATION RATE The rate at which species are lost in any one location after the area has been isolated, and there is no further genetic exchange with any neighbouring areas.

RELEASE TREATMENTS The process of freeing certain tree species or individuals from competition, such that they can dominate the site sooner than would be possible if the site were left untreated.

RELEVÉ A forest sampling stand.

RELICT **1** A regional remnant of a biotic community otherwise extinct. **2** In evolutionary biology, the persistence of an ancient organism. **3** In geomorphology, surface landscape features that have never been buried and are products of past environments no longer in effect in that area.

RELIEF The degree of topographical difference in elevation between high and low points in the landscape. Relief is also used as an index of the potential erosional energy in a watershed. Higher relief equates to steeper slopes, more deeply incised streams, and higher rates of material transport. *See also* Microrelief.

RELIEF DISPLACEMENT *See* Displacement; Relief.

REMNANT PATCH A patch of land in the broader landscape that remains undisturbed but is surrounded by disturbed lands.

REMOTE AUTOMATIC WEATHER STATION (RAWS) A weather station at which the services of an observer are not required. A RAWS unit measures selected weather elements automatically and is equipped with telemetry apparatus for transmitting the electronically recorded data via radio, satellite, or by a land-line communication system at predetermined times or on a user-request basis.

REMOTE SENSING **1** In the broadest sense, the measurement or acquisition of information of some property of an object or phenomenon by a recording device that is not in physical or intimate contact with the object or phenomenon under study. Examples include the utilization at a distance (such as from an airplane, spacecraft, or ship) of any device and its attendant display for gathering information pertinent to the environment (such as the measurements of force fields, electromagnetic radiation, or acoustic energy). The technique employs such devices as the camera, lasers, radio frequency receivers, radar systems, sonar, seismographs, gravimeters, magnetometers, and scintillation counters. **2** The practice of data collection in the wavelengths from ultraviolet to radio regions.

RENEWABLE RESOURCES Any biological resource capable of indefinite renewal (on a human time scale), assuming that the prevailing environmental, social, and political forces permit this.

RENEWABLE RESOURCES ASSESSMENT AND PROGRAM In the US, it is required by the Forest Service (by the Forest and Rangeland Renewable Resources Planning Act [RPA]), as amended by the National Forest Management Act. The RPA calls for (1) the preparation of an assessment of the supply and demand for the nation's forest and rangeland resources; and (2) the development of a management program for national forests that considers alternative management directions and the role of national forests.

RENIFORM Kidney-shaped. *See also* Leaf Shape (for illustration).

REPAIR TIME *See* Machine Time.

REPAND Having an uneven, sinuate margin. *See also* Leaf Margin.

REPELLANT **1** A substance so obnoxious to organisms, especially to birds, insects, and animals, as to deter attack on an object to which the repellant has been applied. **2** A substance that causes an organism to make oriented movements away from the source of the repellant.

REPLACEMENT VALUE The estimated costs at present prices of replacing a tree, stand, or forest (or other capital equipment) with one of equivalent value.

REPLICATION The use of one or more treatments more than one time, in order to increase the precision of comparisons and to provide an assessment of the variability among the experimental units that were treated alike. Unlike repetition, replication involves carrying out the treatments at the same time and place, rather than at different times and places.

REPLUM A persistent, septumlike or framelike placenta that bears ovules on the margins.

REPORT TIME *See* Elapsed Time.

REPRESENTATIVE FRACTION *See* Scale.

REPRESSION *See* Checked.

REPTILE A cold-blooded vertebrate animal in the class Reptilia that has the following characteristics: (1) internal fertilization, with external egg laying; (2) no aquatic larval stage or metamorphosis; (3) the young are born from an egg and resemble the adult form; (4) they possess an internal diaphragm and breathe solely through lungs; (5) the skin is covered with scales or horny plates and is impermeable to water.

There are four orders of living reptiles: (1) Chelonia, including turtles and tortoises; (2) Squamata, including lizards and snakes; (3) Crocodilia, including crocodiles and alligators; (4) Rhynococephalia, represented by a single species, *Sphenodon punctatus,* that inhabits rat-free islands offshore from New Zealand. Other orders represent dinosaurs, pterodactyls, and other extinct reptiles. *See also* Amphibian; Bird; Mammal.

RESCUE EFFECT Immigration (facilitated by humans) of new individuals sufficient to maintain a population that might otherwise decline toward extinction.

RESEARCH NATURAL AREAS In the US, areas set aside to preserve representative ecosystems for scientific study and educational purposes. *See also* Ecological Reserves.

RESERVE In its strictest sense, an area of land designated as being off-limits to any exploitive activities that might change the nature of the area. Not all reserves are so tightly controlled. *See also* Ecological Reserves; Nature Reserve.

RESERVE TREES Trees, pole-sized or larger, retained after the regeneration period under the clearcutting, seed tree, shelterwood, or coppice methods. Reserve trees are also known as standards.

RESIDENCE TIME **1** The amount of time something has been in one place (e.g., the amount of time a log has lain on the forest floor). **2** In fire management, the length of time required for the flaming zone or fire front of a spreading forest fire to pass a given point, most commonly expressed in minutes and/or seconds. Numerically, it is equivalent to the flame depth divided by the rate of spread. *See also* Burn-out Time. **3** In pesticide applications, the time the chemical remains in the ecosystem, or part thereof. **4** In nutrient cycling, the time period an element remains in one pool or compartment.

RESIDENT FISH Also called non-anadromous. Fish that remain in freshwater throughout their life cycle.

RESIDENT POPULATION **1** Generally, organisms inhabiting a given locality throughout the year. *See also* Sedentary. **2** In pest management, a population of insects in a particular locality that persists there for at least one generation, often from year to year. *See also* Immigrant Population.

RESIDENT SPECIES The organisms typically found in an area.

RESIDUAL **1** That part of a substance, or activity left over after the main action has been concluded. **2** In regression analysis, the difference between an observed response and the fitted value is termed a residual.

RESIDUAL SMOKE The smoke produced after the initial fire front has passed through the fuel.

RESIDUAL STAND The trees that remain standing after a natural or human-induced disturbance.

RESIDUAL TREE A tree remaining after logging, generally the same age as or younger than the trees that were logged.

RESIDUAL VALUE The actual or assumed value of a machine after it has been fully depreciated.

RESIDUE A pesticide, or its metabolic derivatives, or degradation products remaining, usually in trace amounts on or in a crop after treatment, or in the soil or water.

RESILIENCE The ability of an ecosystem to recover and maintain the desired condition of diversity, integrity, and ecological processes following disturbances. *See also* Stability.

RESIN Also termed pitch. The secretions of certain trees, insoluble in water but soluble in organic solvents, often exuding from wounds or produced in response to insect attack. *See also* Oleoresin; Resinosis.

RESINOSIS **1** A copious flow of resin or pitch on the bark of a conifer in response to infection, wounding, or insect attack. **2** Impregnation of tissue with resin or pitch.

RESISTANCE **1** The ability of a plant to overcome, retard, suppress, or prevent infection or colonization by a pathogen, parasite, or adverse abiotic factor. **2** The ability of insects, fungi, weeds, or other pests to survive normally lethal doses of an insecticide, fungicide, herbicide, or other pesticide. The opposite of susceptibility.

RESISTANCE TO CONTROL The relative ease of establishing and holding a fireguard and/or securing a control line as determined by the difficulty of control and resistance to fire guard construction. *See also* Difficulty of Control; Resistance to Fire Guard Construction.

RESISTANCE TO FIRE GUARD CONSTRUCTION The relative difficulty of constructing fire guards as determined by fuel type characteristics (e.g., forest floor depth), effects of topography on access (e.g., slope steepness), and mineral soil type. *See also* Difficulty of Control; Resistance to Control.

RESOLUTION **1** A measure of the ability of a remote sensing system to reproduce an isolated object or to separate closely spaced objects or lines. It is usually expressed as the number of lines per millimetre. **2** Solving a problem. *See also* Alternative Dispute Resolution.

RESOURCE **1** Generally, anything that is useful for something, be it animal, vegetable, mineral, a location, a labour force, etc. Resources can be tangible commodities or abstract concepts, such as aesthetics. The concept of 'resource' presupposes an appraisal of the usefulness of an object or environment for some purpose. What constitutes a 'resource' is a relative concept whose definition changes depending on the purpose or point of view. **2** More narrowly, a substance or object required by an organism for normal maintenance, growth, and reproduction.

RESOURCE INDUSTRY An industry based on the primary resources obtained from agriculture, fisheries, forestry, or mining.

RESOURCE PARTITIONING A coexistence strategy evolved by plants and animals to avoid competitive exclusion from a site. It is achieved by taking advantage of the jointly available resources through variations in seasonal growth patterns and resource usage (e.g., understorey plants in deciduous forests compensate for the lack of sunlight throughout most of the year by completing much of their growth in spring before the overstorey leaves block the sunlight. In insects, resource partitioning of plant parts often occurs so that certain species utilize different sizes of branches or different parts of the trunk at the same time.

RESOURCISM A view and approach that espouses the idea that all of the other beings of Earth are here only to serve human needs and desires, that we can use them as experimental subjects and can sacrifice them for our benefit. *See also* Anthropocentric; Deep Ecology; Ecocentric.

RESPONSE TIME *See* Elapsed Time (get-away time).

RESTORATION A process of returning ecosystems or habitats to their original structure and species composition. Restoration requires a detailed knowledge of the (original) species, ecosystem functions, and interacting processes involved. *See also* Reclamation; Rehabilitation.

RESTORATION AND RETENTION BLOCKS Areas of forest reserved and managed to restore or retain old-growth communities and respective plant communities.

RESTRICTIVE LAYER A layer or band in the soil that restricts penetration of moisture or roots. Could be bedrock, cemented soil horizons, extremely compacted materials, or layers having chemical concentrations such as carbonates.

RESUPINATE Describes a fungal body that is reclined or flat on the host or the ground.

RESURGENCE A rapid recovery of numbers of a pest population, which had been significantly reduced by pesticide treatment, due to decreased, intraspecific competition at low densities and/or pesticide-caused mortality of natural enemies.

RETARDANT *See* Fire Retardant.

RETARDANT COVERAGE The area of fuel covered and the degree of coverage on the fuel by a fire retardant, usually expressed in terms of volume per unit area.

RETICULATE A surface or form having a netted or netlike appearance.

RETICULUM A network or netlike arrangement of structures.

RETROGRESSION The retreat or deterioration of a plant community from a later stage of succession to an earlier one, usually brought about by biotic changes or other influences of human activity. *See also* Regression.

RETRORSE Turned backward or downward. *See also* Antrorse; Extrorse; Introrse.

RETUSE Having a shallow, narrow notch in a broad apex. *See also* Leaf Shape (for illustration).
REVERSION SHOOTS **1** Shoots bearing a juvenile form of foliage but appearing on a mature plant. **2** Green shoots appearing on a variegated plant.
REVETMENT *See* Riprap.
REVOLUTE A surface or form that has its margins or apex rolled backwards. *See also* Involute; Leaf Margin.
RHEOLOGIC PROPERTIES The flow characteristics of liquid fire retardants, especially their cohesiveness or ability to hold together while falling through the air.
RHEOLOGY The science of deformation and flow of fire retardants and other liquids, especially of the cohesiveness of liquid bodies and the stress-strain relationship of their particles.
RHEOPHYTE A plant associated with fast-flowing waters.
RHEXISTASY A geological interval when the predominant process was mechanical erosion, which flattens mountains and accumulates heavier deposits at their base. *See also* Biostasy.
RHINARIUM The bare, moist, crinkled, and typically black nosepad of many mammals.
RHIZINE In lichens, the threadlike branched, unbranched, tufted, or brushlike organ of attachment, composed of fungal hyphae.
RHIZOID A filamentous organ, one cell thick, used to assist plants attach to a substrate, and possibly for the absorption of water and nutrients. It is typically found in mosses, ferns, and fungi. *See also* Moss (for illustration).
RHIZOMATOUS In plants, bearing rhizomes.
RHIZOME A rootlike stem, growing horizontally below the ground surface. The rhizome is used for storage of food materials and can produce adventitious roots and shoots. A plant possessing rhizomes is said to be rhizomatous. *See also* Fern (for illustration); Stolon.
RHIZOMORPH A compact, rootlike strand of fungal hyphae that develops by apical growth at the base of a fungus. It transports nutritional materials from one part of the thallus to another and helps to spread the fungi through or over the substratum. *See also* Pseudorhiza.
RHIZOPHORE A leafless stem that produces roots.
RHIZOPLANE The microhabitat on the surface of a root.
RHIZOSPHERE The soil immediately adjacent to plant roots. It is typically very rich in microorganisms.
RHOMBIC/RHOMBOIDAL Diamond-shaped, almost symmetrical, widest at the midpoint, with the sides almost straight to the base or apex. *See also* Leaf Shape (for illustration).
RHYOLITIC Describes rhyolite, a light-coloured, fine-grained volcanic rock.
RIB The prominent vein in a leaf or other plant organ or any prominent vein or nerve.
RIBONUCLEIC ACID A nucleic acid having a single polynucleotide chain that plays a pivotal role in the synthesis of proteins. It occurs in three basic forms: messenger RNA, ribosomal RNA, and transfer RNA. *See also* Deoxyribonucleic Acid.
RIDGES **1** Elongate hillocks with slopes dominantly between 15 and 35 degrees (26 to 70 per cent) on unconsolidated materials and steeper on bedrock; local relief is greater than one metre. **2** A long, narrow elevation of the land surface, usually sharp-crested with steep sides and forming an extended upland between valleys.
RIFFLE A shallow rapids where the water flows swiftly over completely or partially submerged obstructions to produce surface disturbances, but where standing waves are absent.
RIGHT-OF-WAY A cleared area, usually linear, containing a road and its associated features such as shoulders, ditches, cut and fill slopes, or the area cleared for the passage of utility corridors containing power lines or over- or underground pipelines. Typically, the right-of-way is a specially designated area of land having very specific rights of usage attached. Rights-of-way may be owned outright or may be an easement over land owned by someone else.
RILL One of the smallest forms of stream channel, often a surface depression draining runoff water from the soil surface.
RIMOSE A surface marked with numerous cracks.
RING FIRE A fire started by igniting the full perimeter of the intended burn area so that the ensuing fire fronts converge toward the centre of the burn.
RING ROT Any rot localized mainly in the early wood (springwood) of the annual growth rings, giving a concentric pattern of decayed wood in cross-section (e.g., characteristic of rot produced by *Fomes pini*).
RIPARIAN Pertaining to anything connected with or immediately adjacent to the banks of a stream or other body of water.
RIPARIAN ZONE or AREA Those terrestrial areas where the vegetation complex and microclimate conditions are products of the combined presence and influence of perennial and/or intermittent water, associated high water

tables, and soils that exhibit some wetness characteristics. Normally used to refer to the zone within which plants grow rooted in the water table of these rivers, streams, lakes, ponds, reservoirs, springs, marshes, seeps, bogs, and wet meadows. The riparian zone is influenced by, and exerts an influence on, the associated aquatic ecosystem. Some jurisdictions specify a minimum and maximum horizontal distance from top of bank, or the high water mark.

RIPPING The process of breaking up or loosening compacted soil (e.g., skid trails or spur roads) to better assure penetration of the roots of young tree seedlings.

RIPRAP A layer of large rocks placed along stream banks or lake shores to protect them from erosion. It also refers to the rocks themselves. *See also* Bridge (for illustration).

RISK Risk is the probability that an undesirable event will or will not occur. It is the product of the probability of the event taking place, the probability of being exposed to the event, and the probability of certain outcomes occurring if exposure did take place. Risk can be statistically quantified in a risk assessment. *See also* Uncertainty.

RITHRON Fish that live in the upper, cold-water, swift zone of stream systems. Rithron are cold-water stenotherms. *See also* Potamon; Stenothermal.

RIVERINE All wetlands and deepwater habitats contained within a natural or artificial channel that periodically or continuously contains moving water or that forms a link between two bodies of standing water.

RIVER TERRACE A more or less flat surface bounded downslope by a scarp and resulting from fluvial erosion and deposition. It is the same as fluvial terraces and alluvial terraces.

R-MODE ANALYSIS R-mode analysis uses various statistical techniques to determine species affinity by measuring pairwise species resemblances based on data occurring across the rows in an ecological data matrix. R-mode is the representation of species in stand space. *See also* Q-mode Analysis.

RNA *See* Ribonucleic Acid.

ROADLESS AREA An extensive tract of land that contains no developed roads. In the US, it can be an area temporarily withdrawn from management pending the determination of its suitability for possible wilderness classification, or it can be an area designated for active management without the construction of roads (e.g., helicopter logging only).

ROADLESS AREA REVIEW AND EVALUATION I (RARE I) A US Forest Service effort in the early 1970s to systematically inventory, review, and evaluate the relative values for future uses of existing roadless areas. The RARE process identified the extent of roadless lands remaining on the national forests and recommended each area for wilderness consideration, further study, or release for other multiple use.

ROADLESS AREA REVIEW AND EVALUATION II (RARE II) The second Roadless Area Review and Evaluation in 1977-1979 incorporated new roadless area criteria and the requirements of the National Forest Management Act. The final RARE II inventory list included 2,919 roadless areas, including sixty-two million acres in national forests and national grasslands in thirty-eight states and Puerto Rico. Each area's resources were estimated, site-specific information was reviewed, and potential for uses was assessed. RARE II also sought to assess how each area might contribute to qualities of the wilderness system, such as ecological diversity.

ROADSIDE SURVEY A ground survey conducted from a vehicle either with observer and driver or driver alone stopping to observe.

ROCHE MOUTONNÉE A knob of rock with a sheep-back form, the long axis of which is oriented parallel to former ice flow and having a smooth, glacially abraded stoss (up-flow) slope and a much steeper and rougher, glacially plucked lee slope.

ROCK AVALANCHE Rapid downslope movement of a large mass of rock fragments derived from bedrock; the rock fragments in motion, although not saturated, take on the character of a (dry) flow and are highly mobile. It is typically the result of very large rock falls and rock slides.

ROCK CREEP Slow, downslope movement of rock fragments. It is commonly associated with the presence of interstitial ice and/or solifluction.

ROCK FALL The relatively free-falling or precipitous movement of a newly detached fragment of bedrock of any size from a cliff or other very steep slope. It is the fastest form of mass movement.

ROCK GLACIER A tongue-shaped or lobate, ridged accumulation of angular fragments containing interstitial ice that moves slowly downslope. It is morphologically similar to a glacier.

ROCK OUTCROP Any area where the subsurface bedrock (excluding volcanic lava) is exposed.

ROCK SLIDE Rapid or slow downslope movement of a large mass of rock by sliding along one or more well-defined surfaces of rupture.

RODENTICIDE A pesticide used to control or manage rodents.

ROESTELIA Plural roesteliae. In mycology, rusts having a cornute aecium with a pointed apex that typically ruptures along longitudinal slits and is composed of characteristic cells.

ROESTELIOID Resembling a roestelia.

ROGUING The systematic elimination of plants not considered desirable in the population, usually in a seed orchard or a nursery.

ROLL **1** In air navigation, a rotation of an aircraft about its longitudinal axis so as to cause a wing-up or wing-down attitude. **2** In photogrammetry, a rotation of a camera- or a photograph-coordinate system about either the photograph *x* axis or the exterior *x* axis; may be designated by the symbol omega (ω)

ROLLING RESISTANCE The retarding force of the ground against the wheels of a vehicle.

ROOSTING Describes the behaviour of a bird at rest.

ROOST SITE Sites where an animal roosts. It can refer to daytime or nighttime roosting. Roosting sites often provide protection from adverse environmental conditions and predators.

ROOT Plants depend upon roots for anchorage, uptake of water and nutrients, storage of food reserves, and the synthesis of organic compounds. The roots of a tree typically grow in the upper fifty centimetres of the soil and may extend out from the trunk to distances of up to ten times the diameter of the crown foliage. Patterns of root development are less constant than for the branches. Several types of root are recognized. **Tap roots** are made up of one root that may penetrate the soil to depths of several metres by growing vertically downward, but may lack an extensive fibrous root system. Tap roots are associated with conifers and dicotyledonous plants, but usually occur in conjunction with other root forms. **Fibrous roots** are a well-branched system of many small roots all of approximately equal size, typical of grasses. **Heart roots** are roots other than tap roots, which grow downward at an angle away from the tree and usually lend structural support. **Lateral roots** are roots that grow horizontally away from the tree on or just below the soil surface. **Sinker or striker roots** are roots that grow downward from some point along a lateral root, usually near to the trunk, and offer structural support.

Research has shown that the below-ground biomass produced by a tree may exceed the amount of above-ground biomass. Roots transmit disease from one tree to another via root grafts. In some cases, roots have an innate development pattern that is not easily altered. **Plagiotropic** roots will revert to their original growth pattern, so that if the root is turned up it grows back down, or if it is turned down, it grows back up. **Exotropic** roots will revert to their original direction of growth when they encounter an obstacle, even if they have been deflected in a very different direction.

The surface area of roots within the dripline of a tree may often be 2.5 to 4.5 times greater than the surface area of one side of all the leaves on the same tree, and yet the well-being of roots is often ignored. Roots are easily damaged by above-ground activities and are very susceptible to oxygen deprivation caused by flooding or soil compaction. Note that roots absorb nutrients (elements) as inorganic ions regardless of their source (inorganic or organic), with the exception of urea, which can be absorbed as a compound. *See also* Apical Meristem; Mycorrhizae; Root Hairs.

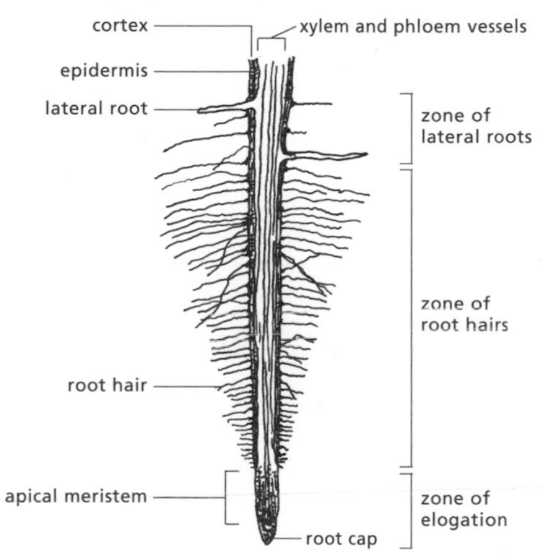

ROOT CAP The cells located at the very outer tip of growing roots, forming ahead of the apical meristem. The root cap serves to protect the root as it forces its way through the soil, and the cap cells slough off to form a simple lubricant for the developing root. The root cap is also termed the calyptra in some texts. *See also* Root (for illustration).

ROOT CLIPPING The cutting or clipping of roots by gophers or other small mammals.

ROOT COLLAR Also termed the root crown. The part of a tree where the main roots join the trunk, usually at or near ground level. It is the transition zone between roots and stem sometimes delineated by a slight swelling.

ROOT CROWN The upper-most portion of the root system where the major roots join together at the base of the stem.

ROOTED VEGETATION Refers to the description of stream banks, where vegetation is drawing its water supply directly from the soils soaked by water from the stream, rather than water draining through the soils into the stream. *See also* Riparian. The two sources of water are used to define a change in bank classification. *See also* Stream Bank.

ROOT GRAFT A naturally occurring vegetative union between roots of different individual trees, through which pathogens or translocated herbicides may pass from tree to tree. Often, sizeable groups of trees may become interconnected. Root grafting may also occur between stumps and living trees, maintaining life in old stumps. Root grafts are most frequent among trees of the same species, but may also occur between different tree species.

ROOT HAIRS The very fine, hairlike, epidermal cells that develop just behind the tip of a root's apical meristem. Root hairs greatly increase the surface area available for water and nutrient uptake, but do not turn into roots, and have a short life, usually only a few weeks. *See also* Root (for illustration).

ROOT KILL The death of trees, shrubs, etc., due to freezing of their roots. It is frequent in regions where precipitation is light and the soil freezes deeply.

ROOT ROT A rot that occurs chiefly in the roots of trees or in the roots of seedlings that have developed woody stem tissues, or any disease with these characteristics.

ROOT SPROUTS Vegetative growth (branches) emerging from a basal root burl or root nodes. They are common in chaparral shrubs.

ROOTSTOCK **1** An underground stem or rhizome. **2** The basic root and stem onto which a scion is united to produce grafted trees or shrubs.

ROOT-TO-SHOOT RATIO The ratio of oven-dry root weight to oven-dry shoot weight in seedlings.

ROOT WAD The mass of roots, soil, and rocks that remains intact when a tree, shrub, or stump is uprooted.

ROOT ZONE The soil volume within which roots grow.

ROSETTE A cluster of leaves or other organs arranged in a circular pattern, often in the basal position.

ROSTELLUM Shaped like a small beak. It is typically the tissue separating the anther from the functional stigma on the column of single-anthered orchids. It is often specialized to assist in pollen transfer by insects or hummingbirds.

ROSTRATE Having a beaklike projection.

ROT **1** A state of decay, usually fairly advanced and obvious, of woody or succulent plant tissue caused by invading plant fungi or bacteria. Many common names, such as brown rot, butt rot, dry rot, heart rot, pocket rot, ring rot, root rot, wet rot, and white rot are based on colour, texture, or location. **2** A disease characterized by the symptoms of rot. *See also* Decay.

ROTATE Of a plant corolla, wheel-shaped; flat and circular in outline.

ROTATION Also called tree age rotation. Broadly, the time needed from regeneration of a crop of trees through to harvestable timber. Rotation can be classified as follows. **Financial rotation**, whereby the time of harvest is determined by an economic determinant that may or may not be related to a physical criterion on site. Ideally, the financial rotation provides the highest net present worth after all costs and benefits have been discounted back to the start of the rotation, using a defined rate of compound interest. Higher interest rates equate to shorter rotations and vice versa. **Physical or technical rotation**, whereby the time of harvest is determined by the point at which the trees reach a certain size or volume to meet manufacturing criteria. It can also mean the point at which the trees reach maximum mean annual increment. **Biological rotation**, whereby harvest takes place as the trees die, but before they have decayed. **Ecological rotation** is the time period for an ecosystem to return to its predisturbance state, especially with respect to the total nutrient capital. *See also* Mean Annual Increment; Stand Age Rotation.

ROT COLUMN The vertical column of rotted wood within the heartwood of a tree invaded by heart rot fungi.

ROTOR DIAMETER The diameter of the main rotor of a helicopter, used to determine the feasibility of landing or taking off in a helicopter and to plan the minimum design configurations necessary to ensure the type of helicopter and landing spot are compatible.

ROTOR DOWNWASH The air turbulence occurring under and around the main rotor system(s) of an operating helicopter.

ROUGH **1** A general term to describe unfinished lumber that has been cut to a nominal set of dimensions but is not yet considered to be finished. **2** In southern pine communities of the US, an accumulation of living and dead ground and understorey vegetation, especially grasses, forest litter, and draped dead needles, sometimes with understorey shrubs.

ROUNDED A shape that has a full, sweeping arc. *See also* Leaf Shape (for illustration).

ROUNDNESS OF CLASTS Pertains to the sharpness or degree of rounding of the edges of clasts. It is commonly described by the terms rounded, subrounded, subangular, and angular.

ROUNDWOOD Sections of tree stems, with or without bark. Includes logs, bolts, posts, pilings, and other products still 'in the round.'

ROYALTY A payment made by the owner or leaseholder of a forest in exchange for predetermined exploitation rights, usually based on a rate per unit of produce removed.

r-SELECTION Describes species living in a patchy and unpredictable environment, with a high risk of mortality for any one individual, and little competition from other organisms. Such species respond to selection pressures by producing large numbers of small offspring and are called r-strategists. Typically, such species colonize early in succession, many are opportunistic species, although some have such narrow environmental tolerances that they cannot be opportunistic. *See also* K-Selection; Selection.

RUBBER SHEETING In GIS work, the fitting of slightly distorted data, such as that found on an air photograph, to its counterpart on a map. One of several computer-based transformations that can produce a mathematical analog of fitting commonly done by projectors. *See also* Orthophotograph; Rectification.

RUBBLE **1** Debris created during demolition of an engineering structure. **2** *See* Substrate Particle Size (Cobble). **3** Angular particles between 2 and 256 millimetres, which may include interstitial sand. **4** Angular rock fragments.

RUDERAL An introduced plant species growing under disturbed conditions, or a native or introduced plant growing in old fields, roadsides, and abandoned sites of human habitation.

RUDIMENTARY Botanically, a plant, plant part, or organ that is imperfectly developed and nonfunctional.

RUGOSE Describes a rough or wrinkled surface.

RUGULOSE Finely wrinkled.

RUMINANT Animals in the suborder *Ruminantia* that have even-toed hooves, chew the cud, and typically have three- or four-chambered stomachs (e.g., deer, sheep, goats, cattle).

RUMINATE Botanically, having the appearance of being chewed.

RUN A swiftly flowing stream reach with little surface agitation and no major flow obstructions.

RUNCINATE Sharply incised or divided with the teeth of each division pointing backward or toward the base of the organ. *See also* Leaf Margin (for illustration).

RUNNER *See* Stolon.

RUNNING CROWN FIRE *See* Forest Fire (independent crown fire).

RUNNING FIRE *See* Fire Behaviour.

RUNNING SKYLINE A system of two or more suspended moving lines, generally referred to as the main lines and haul-back lines. They provide lift and travel (pull) to the load carrier when tension is properly applied.

RUNOFF **1** The part of precipitation and snowmelt that reaches streams by flowing over or through the ground. Surface runoff flows away without penetrating the soils. Groundwater runoff enters streams by seeping through the soils. **2** The shedding of spray from plant surfaces during, or immediately after an application. Droplets may coalesce to form a continuous film and any surplus liquid runs off the surface. Some pesticide directions indicate 'spray to run-off' to ensure complete coverage of the plant surface.

RURAL Any area in which residences and other human developments are scattered and intermingled with forest, range, or farm land and native vegetation or cultivated crops. *See also* Urban.

RURAL-URBAN INTERFACE *See* Urban-Wildland Interface.

RUST **1** A disease induced via parasitization by one of the rust fungi. **2** Masses of orange-coloured spores on leaves, fruits, or stems. **3** A rust fungus.

RUST FUNGUS One of a group of basidiomycete fungi in the order Uredinales, commonly causing blisterlike growth on needles, branches, or stems of host plants. These fungi are characterized by obligate parasitism, restricted host range, and complex life cycles, with as many as five spore types (aecial, pycnial, uredinial, telial, basidial), often involving two or more hosts, and the production of masses of orange spores during one stage.

RUT **1** The periodic sexual excitement of male deer, goats, and sheep that corresponds to estrus in females of the same species. The period during which this activity takes place is referred to as the 'rutting season.' *See also* Estrus (also spelled oestrus). **2** A narrow channel formed in a roadbed by the passage of wheeled or pedestrian traffic.

RUTTING SEASON **1** Loosely synonymous with breeding season. **2** Specifically, the period of maximum testicular activity in male mammals, usually applied to the period of sexual activity in deer.

S

SACCATE Forming a sac or bag-shaped pouch.

SAC FRY *See* Alevin.

SACKUNG On mountainsides, trenches and uphill-facing scarps trending parallel to contours and developed as a result of gravitational movement.

SADDLE A low point on a ridge or crestline, generally a divide or pass between the heads of streams flowing in opposite directions.

SAFETY ISLAND In fire suppression, an area cleared of flammable material and used for escape in the event the control line is outflanked, or in the case of a spot fire causing fuels outside the control line to render the line unsafe. In firing operations, crews progress so as to maintain a safety island nearby, allowing fuels inside the control line to be consumed before proceeding. Safety islands may also be constructed as integral parts of fuelbreaks. They are greatly enlarged areas that can be used with relative safety by firefighters and their equipment in the event of a blow-up in the vicinity.

SAGITTATE Shaped like an arrowhead, with the basal lobes pointing downwards or concavely toward the stalk. *See also* Leaf Shape (for illustration).

SALIENT **1** Projecting outwards or upwards from its surroundings. **2** Prominent, outstanding, striking (e.g., the salient facts).

SALLY *See* Flycatching.

SALMONID Fish of the family Salmonidae, including salmon, trout, chars, whitefish, ciscoes, and grayling. It generally refers to salmon, trout, and chars.

SALTATION The transport of particles through turbulent air or water, whereby the particles skip or jump rather than flow smoothly (saltatory movement).

SALTATORY MOVEMENT Stopping a number of times while moving between two points; jumping.

SALT MARSH A marsh area having high salinities in the ambient water and substrate, typical of estuarine areas, or other areas subject to flooding with ocean water, and characterized by thick mats of halophytic plants.

SALVAGE CUTTING The utilization of standing or down trees that are dead, dying, or deteriorating, for whatever reason, before the timber values are lost.

SALVERFORM Describes a gamopetalous corolla where the slender basal tube abruptly expands into a flat or saucer shaped limb. It is also termed hypocrateriform.

SALVO In fire-bombing operations, the dropping by an airtanker of its entire load of suppressant or retardant at one time. *See also* Incremental Drop; Split Drop.

SAMARA An achene with a single or pair of wings, such as ash, elm, or maple. *See also* Fruit (for illustration).

SAMMOSERE Ecological succession that takes place on sand, away from any wave action. Colonizing plants stabilize the sand and help in dune creation. *See also* Hydrosere; Xerosere.

SAMPLE **1** As a verb, to select sample units and measure or record information contained within these units to obtain estimates of population characteristics. **2** As a noun, a subset of one or more of the sample units into which the population is divided, selected to represent the population and examined to obtain estimates of population characteristics. Samples can be derived in several ways. **Random** is a sample in which every possible sample has an equal probability of being selected and measured. **Stratified** is a sample selected for a population that has been stratified (i.e., divided into parts). The process of stratification is usually undertaken by dividing the survey area into subareas on a map or through interpretation and classification of points from remote sensing imagery. **Systematic** is a sample that is obtained by a systematic method as opposed to random choice. Samples are chosen according to a fixed pattern (e.g., at regular intervals along a line rather than at random intervals). Variation within the sampling area is assumed to be random, so that the resulting set of samples is also considered to be random.

Sequential is a sample based on predetermined abundance classes for the pest, sign, symptom, or other attribute of concern. Basic units (e.g., branches or twigs) are examined until the number found of the pest, sign, symptom, or attribute fits one of the defined classes (e.g., treatment versus no treatment). Considerable research is required to design a sequential sampling scheme, but it can lead to a large reduction in the number of samples required to make a decision and is a useful aid to prediction or decisionmaking. *See also* Randomization.

SAMPLE FRAME The total population of possible sample units or plots within a survey area. A frame may be a listing of all the stands within a forest, all pixels within a Landsat image, all possible 0.1 hectare plots within a big-game winter range, and so on.

SAMPLE PLOT A sample unit or element of known area and shape. *See also* Sample Unit.

SAMPLE SIZE The number of sample units established in a given area.

SAMPLE STRIP *See* Cruise Strip.

SAMPLE UNIT One of the specified parts into which the population has been divided for sampling purposes. Each sample unit consists of only one element, which may be a sample plot, a point sample, or a tree. If the sample unit contains more than one sample element, it is termed a cluster. In probability sampling, the sample units are selected independently of each other while the sample elements within a sample unit (cluster) are not. *See also* Clustering; Sample; Sample Plot.

SAMPLING The selection of a portion (the sample) of a population for measurement in order to make estimates or inferences about the entire population. Several sampling strategies are possible. **Multiphase** is a selection of sample units in which a large sample is taken to estimate a population characteristic for some auxiliary variable, and a small sample is selected to establish the relationship between the auxiliary variable and the primary variable of interest (e.g., double sampling or two-phase sampling). **Multistage** is a method of sampling within sample units or sub-sampling, to estimate characteristics rather than measuring the entire sampling unit. This approach assumes that the sample units are clusters or aggregations of some more basic elements that are of interest (e.g., two-stage sampling). **Nonprobability** is a method of sampling where sample units are not selected with any known probability. **Probability** is a method of sampling where sample units are selected with a known probability and can be used for statistical inference and analysis.

SAMPLING DESIGN The method to determine which sample units will be measured or observed, such as a systematic sample or a stratified sample.

SAMPLING ERROR *See* Precision.

SAMPLING INTENSITY The number of samples taken per unit area.

SAND **1** Soil inorganic particles between 0.062 to 2 millimetres in diameter. **2** A soil textural class in which sand particles are very abundant. *See also* Substrate Particle Size.

SANDSTONE Sedimentary rock made up of predominantly sand-sized clastic materials.

SANITATION **1** The removal and/or destruction of infected plant parts or individual plants. **2** Disinfection and/or disinfestation of tools and machinery to prevent the spread of disease or insects.

SANITATION CUTTING The removal of infected or infested, dead, damaged, or susceptible trees, or parts of them, or of vegetation that serves as an alternative host for pathogens, to prevent or retard the spread of pests or pathogens. *See also* Sanitation Spacing.

SANITATION HARVEST The removal of dead or damaged trees, or trees susceptible to insect and disease attack, such as intermediate and suppressed trees, to prevent the spread of pests or pathogens and to promote forest health.

SANITATION SPACING The cutting of young stands to control density, species composition, or disease level by combining spacing with removal of the residual or young trees that are defective in form or heavily infected with dwarf mistletoe or other diseases. *See also* Sanitation Cutting.

SAP **1** In plants, the fluid contents of the vascular system, carrying dissolved mineral and organic nutrients, or the contents of individual cells. **2** The moisture and dissolved substances in unseasoned wood.

SAPLING The stage of tree development in between the seedling and the pole stage. Saplings are typically one to two metres tall and two to four centimetres in diameter, with vigorous growth, no loose, dead bark, and few (if any) dead branches.

SAPROBE A microorganism, including many fungi and bacteria, living on and deriving nutrition from dead, organic matter. It is also termed, less specifically, saprotrophs or osmotrophs. Saprobic fungi are of economic importance not only to foresters (wood decay) but also to many other human endeavours, since they account for decay in food, leather, paper, and textiles. However, they are also used beneficially in food processing, especially baking and cheese-making, and in the brewing industry. Saprobic bacteria also spoil food and cause food poisoning. Beneficial saprobic bacteria produce many of the important products necessary for the manufacture of antibiotics.

SAPROGEN An organism capable of producing decay in dead, organic material, such as dead wood. Saprogens are able to enter decayed wood and compete with other organisms in the substrate (e.g., Trichoderma).

SAPROLITE A soft, earthy, clay/mineral-rich product of chemical weathering of igneous and metamorphic rocks.

SAPROPHYTE A plant that lives on dead or decaying organic matter and gains its nutrition from this substrate in the form of organic nutrients in solution. Saprophytes are important decomposers of dead, organic matter. *See also* Epiphyte; Saprobe; Saprozote.

SAPROTISM A general term describing the condition of living on dead, organic material. *See also* Saprobe; Saprophyte; Saprozote.

SAPROTROPHS A general term describing any organism capable of deriving its energy and nutrition from dead, organic material (decomposers, detritivores, and detritus-feeders). Saprotrophs depending on dead plant materials or the feces of herbivores (including any organisms living in their alimentary canal) can be considered akin to herbivores, and encompass saprophytes and saprobes. Saprotrophs depending on dead animal materials or the faeces of animals (including any organisms living in their alimentary canal) are akin to carnivores and include the saprobes and saprozotes, as well as the large scavengers such as seagulls, vultures, and hyenas. *See also* Coprophage.

SAPROZOTE An animal or microorganism that lives in decaying, organic material and derives its nourishment from it. *See also* Saprophyte.

SAPSTAIN A stain that predominantly affects the sapwood, particularly those stains resulting from the growth of fungi that do not cause decay. *See also* Bluestain; Brownstain.

SAPWOOD The outer layers of xylem tissue lying immediately interior to the cambium. In the growing tree, sapwood forms the active water-conducting system, containing living cells and food reserve materials, such as starch. Sapwood is typically lighter in colour than heartwood, but may not be clearly differentiated. *See also* Heartwood; Phloem (for illustration); Xylem.

SARMENTOSE Having or producing long flexuous runners or stolons.

SAVANNAH A major global biome consisting of open grasslands containing scattered trees or shrubs.

SAWFLY An insect in the suborder Symphyta of the Hymenoptera. It is characterized by females with a sawlike ovipositor for laying eggs in plant tissue and larvae that are caterpillars.

SAWTIMBER Any tree capable of yielding logs of a size and quality suitable for lumber production. Exact log dimensions and quality attributes vary by jurisdiction.

SAXICOLOUS Plants growing on rocks.

SCAB A dark, crustlike lesion on a leaf or fruit.

SCABERULOUS Minutely scabrous.

SCABROUS Rough to the touch, with short bristly hairs.

SCAFFOLD LIMBS The main or primary branches in a tree, which determine the final shape of the tree and the manner in which the branches are attached to the main trunk. It is usually important in landscape trees where final form determines aesthetic appeal.

SCALE **1** In mensuration work: as a noun, the measured or estimated quantity expressed as the volume, area, length, mass, or number of products obtained from trees and measured or estimated after they are felled. As a verb, the act of measuring or estimating the quantity expressed as the volume, area, length, mass or number of products obtained from trees and measured or estimated after they are felled, but before they are processed. *See also* Map Scale. **2** In considering landscape and biodiversity models, scale is defined on the basis of elements such as size, shape, and distribution of the ecosystem components, using scales at the **coarse** (landscape level); **intermediate** (local ecosystem level); and **fine** (habitat elements such as snags, soil litter, vegetation strata). *See also* Coarse Scale; Fine Scale. **3** Botanically, a small, sharp-pointed, broader at the base, mostly dry, appressed leaf or bract, often only vestigial. It is also, a minute, flattened trichome, of epidermal origin, such as the scales on the lower surface of certain leaves. *See also* Leaf Shape (for illustration).

SCALE INSECT A group of plant-sucking insects, usually immobile, in the order Homoptera. It is characterized by a hard, convex covering over the body with no visible appendages or segmentation. It is usually small, ranging from one to five millimetres in length or diameter.

SCALE-LIKE LEAVES A scale-like structure that is morphologically a leaf, often greatly reduced in size (e.g., bud scale, bracts).

SCALPING The preparation of forest soil for planting, involving removal of ground vegetation and organic mats down to the mineral soil in a small patch at the point where the new tree is to be planted.

SCANDENT Having climbing stems.

SCAN LINE In remote sensing, the strip on the ground that is swept by the instantaneous field of view of a detector in a scanner system. *See also* Instantaneous Field of View.

SCAPE A one- or many-flowered stem bearing no leaves, but which may bear scales or bracts.

SCAPOSE Having a scape or borne on a scape.

SCAR **1** A mark left after regrowth of damaged tissue following an injury (e.g., an oviposition scar or mechanical damage scar). **2** A mark resulting from the natural separation (abscission) of one plant organ from another (e.g., the leaf scar remaining on a stem or twig after leaf fall).

SCARIFICATION **1** The mechanical disturbance of the forest floor (duff, litter, soils) to create better growing conditions for trees that are planted, to create better seedbed conditions for the germination of seeds derived from standing trees or slash, or to promote coppice and suckering from existing stumps. **2** The physical or chemical modification of a hard seed to make it permeable. It is typical of seeds that pass through the gut of birds or animals as a part of their life cycle.

SCARIOUS Not green, but thin, dry and membranous, often almost translucent.

SCARP *See* Escarpment.

SCAT Faecal pellet or dropping; faeces (also spelled feces).

SCENARIO A hypothetical sequence of future events constructed for the purpose of focusing attention on causal processes and decision points.

SCHIZOCARP A dry fruit, developed from a syncarpous ovary, that splits into one-seeded sections.

SCHOOLMARM A tree that originally had a single trunk, but later split into two trunks part way up the tree. The second trunk is usually weakly attached to the first trunk.

SCLEROPHYLLOUS Describes the thick, drought-resistant cuticle that makes leaves hard and tough, and enables plants to withstand the rigours of prolonged periods of dry, hot climate.

SCLEROTIUM A mass of thick-walled, hardened and compact hyphae, or waxy, protoplasmic material formed in some fungi and slime moulds as a resting stage in the life cycle. The sclerotium can survive extended dormancy (an overwinter stage in fungi) or through periods of drought in slime moulds, and then develop an active mycelium when conditions are more favourable. *See also* Microsclerotium.

SCOPE The number of variables to be considered in any problem-solving exercise. In environmental impact assessment work, the scope of the project analysis determines what will or will not be analyzed and is thus an extremely important step because it determines which variables will form the basis for decisionmaking at some future point. A narrow scope might omit important factors that ought to be analyzed in more detail, but a broad scope runs the risk of analyzing almost everything, potentially yielding unusable results in the timeframe needed to make defensible decisions. The activity of deciding the scope is called scoping.

SCORCH Injury to bark, foliage, flowers, or fruit from excessive heat whether from fire or sunlight; from hot, freezing, salt-laden, fume-laden, or unduly strong winds; from unbalanced nutrition; or from poisoning (e.g., due to the misapplication of a pesticide).

SCORPIOID CYME A coiled, determinate inflorescence similar to a helicoid cyme but having the flowers or branches developing alternately to the left and right, as opposed to only one direction. It is also termed a cincinnus.

SCOUR The powerful and concentrated clearing and digging action of flowing air, water, or ice, especially the downward erosion by stream water in sweeping away mud and silt on the outside curve of a bend or during a flood. A place in a stream bed swept (scoured) clean by running water, typically leaving a gravel base. *See also* Fill.

SCOUR POOL *See* Pool.

SCOUT A person in a fire suppression organization assigned duties of gathering and reporting timely information, such as existing location and behaviour of a fire, progress in control, and the physical conditions that affect the planning and execution of the suppression job.

SCREE A slope of loose, rocky debris accumulating beneath a cliff of weathering rock. *See also* Talus.

SCREEFING The removal of herbaceous vegetation and duff to expose a weed-free soil surface for planting. A type of site preparation that may be carried out by mechanical or chemical means.

SCREENING **1** The separation of individuals in a population with respect to a particular pest, pesticide, or adverse environmental factor (e.g., in the initial stages of a breeding program in which resistant individuals are identified). **2** The separation of agents according to their efficacy (e.g., the screening of chemicals for their ability to kill a particular organism).

SCRIBNER RULE Developed around 1846, it is one of the oldest diagram log rules in existence. The rule assumes boards will be one inch thick and uses a one-quarter-inch saw kerf in calculating the likely volume of lumber that can be derived from a log. It makes a generous allowance for slabs, but no allowance for taper (assumes all logs are perfect cylinders). Typically it underestimates the mill output of lumber. For a sixteen-foot log, the basic formula is:

Volume (in board feet) = $0.8\ (D-1)^2 - D/2$

where

D = log diameter in inches.

See also Doyle Rule; International Log Rule.

SCROBICULATE A surface marked with shallow depressions.

SCROBICULATION A pit or shallow depression.

SCROPHULARIACEOUS Belonging to the Figwort family, Scrophulariaceae.

SCRUB *See* Brush.

SCULPIN A small fish.

SCURFY Covered with small, branlike scales.

SCUTATE Shaped like a small shield.

SCUTELLUM In insects, a plate (sclerite) on the dorsum of the thorax that is more or less triangular in shape.

SEASONED Wood that has been dried to a certain moisture content to improve its serviceability. The grading standards of the Western Wood Products Association define seasoned wood as having a moisture content of 19 per cent or less.

SECCI DISC A disc about twenty centimetres in diameter that is marked with alternating black and white quarters. The disc is lowered into the water and the depth at which it can no longer be seen provides a measure of water clarity.

SECONDARY ATTRACTION Attraction of bark beetles to a host tree after initial attack by pioneer beetles in response to release of pheromones by the resident beetles, or increased release of primary attractants (kairomones) due to boring activity of resident beetles, or both. *See also* Primary Attraction.

SECONDARY CAVITY NESTER Any species that occupies a cavity previously excavated by another species. *See also* Primary Cavity Nester.

SECONDARY CYCLE In plant disease, any cycle initiated by inoculum generated during the same season.

SECONDARY FUNGUS A weak parasite or saprophyte that usually invades only predisposed, weakened, or killed host individuals.

SECONDARY HOST **1** A host species attacked less frequently than a main or principal host. It is incorrect to use the term 'secondary host' to mean an economically unimportant host. **2** The host on which the 3rd, 4th, and 5th stages (uredinial, telial, basidial) of a rust fungus develops. **3** For aphids with complex life cycles, the host on which only asexual reproduction occurs. **4** *See* Host Susceptibility Rating (dwarf mistletoe). *See also* Primary Host.

SECONDARY INFECTION **1** An infection resulting from the spread of inoculum produced during a primary or earlier secondary infection, without an intervening inactive season; an infection produced by a secondary inoculum. **2** Infection by dwarf mistletoe of previously infected tissue. *See also* Primary Infection.

SECONDARY INOCULUM Inoculum produced by infections that took place earlier in the same growing season. *See also* Primary Inoculum.

SECONDARY INSECT **1** An insect generally found in unhealthy or dead trees. **2** Any insect that can successfully attack only plants that are already weakened, dying, or dead (e.g., many bark beetles). *See also* Primary Insect.

SECONDARY INVADER A saprophytic microorganism that colonizes dead cells, in association with or after the action of a pathogen. *See also* Secondary Pathogen.

SECONDARY LINE In fire suppression, a fire line constructed at a distance from the perimeter concurrently with or after a primary control line has been constructed on or near to the perimeter. It is generally constructed as an insurance measure in case the fire escapes control by the primary line. *See also* Primary Line.

SECONDARY LOOKOUT **1** A lookout point intermittently used to supplement seen area coverage of the primary lookout system when required by fire danger, restricted visibility, or other factors. **2** The person who occupies this lookout. *See also* Primary Lookout.

SECONDARY PARASITE *See* Hyperparasite.

SECONDARY PATHOGEN A pathogen that

invades the host after establishment of a primary pathogen. Secondary pathogens may or may not be able to induce disease on their own. *See also* Primary Pathogen.

SECONDARY PEST A species that becomes a pest after natural or human interference with processes that normally regulate its density to non-pest levels. It usually occurs after predisposition of a host by another pest species or following the unintended destruction of the natural enemies of the secondary pest species (e.g., as a result of pesticide application intended to control another pest).

SECONDARY SUCCESSION A successional process starting in areas where there are biological legacies present from previous ecosystems to influence the successional pathway. *See also* Primary Succession.

SECOND-GROWTH FOREST Relatively young forests that have developed following a disturbance (e.g., wholesale cutting, extensive fire, insect attack) of the previous stand of old-growth forest. Restricted in application to those parts of the world where clearly discernible, old-growth forests still exist, or did exist not long ago. *See also* Old-Growth Forest.

SECTION **1** A real or imaginary slice through or across a solid to reveal the nature and patterns of the substance underneath the visible surfaces (e.g., a section across a tree trunk, a section through a landform to plot geological strata, or a section across a landform to show the profile). **2** A land survey subdivision equal in area to one square mile (640 acres). The commonly used term quarter section is 160 acres in size.

SECUND Describes an arrangement of plant parts turned to one side, typically by twisting. It is often applied to an inflorescence where the flowers appear to be borne on only one side of the axis.

SEDENTARY Describes the habit of an organism that tends to stay in one place and is generally stationary. *See also* Resident Population; Sessile.

SEDIMENT Fragmented material that originates from the weathering of rocks and decomposition of organic material that is transported in suspension by water, air, or ice, to be subsequently deposited at a new location.

SEDIMENTARY ROCK A rock formed from materials deposited from suspension or precipitated from solution and usually consolidated. The principal sedimentary rocks are sandstones, shales, limestones, and conglomerates. *See also* Igneous Rock; Metamorphic Rock.

SEDIMENTATION The deposition of eroded soil materials suspended in the water of creeks, lakes, or other water bodies. Sedimentation takes place when water velocity falls below a point at which the suspended particles can be carried.

SEDIMENT YIELD The quantity of soil, rock particles, organic matter, or other dissolved or suspended debris transported that is transported through a cross-section of stream in a given period. Measured in dry weight or by volume. Consists of dissolved load, suspended load, and bedload. *See also* Dissolved Load; Suspended Sediment; Bedload.

SEED **1** The propagation unit of plants, consisting of a mature and usually fertilized ovule enclosed by the integuments or testa (seed coat). The embryo is surrounded by stored food in the form of the endosperm, or in the cotyledons. The seed coat protects it from adverse environmental conditions until it is ready to germinate. The endosperm helps the developing seedling survive until it can derive additional nutrition from the soil and sunlight. *See also* Propagule; Spore. **2** In animals, the male gametes or sperm. **3** As a verb, to introduce a different organism or material into an area or substrate where these did not previously exist.

SEED BANK **1** A store of viable seed buried and dormant in the soil or underwater sediments. **2** The place where seeds of rare plants or obsolete varieties are stored in carefully controlled conditions to preserve their genetic material for research and possible future use.

SEEDBED **1** The prepared soil in a nursery, or the soil or forest floor upon which falling seed will germinate and develop.

SEED COLLECTION AREA A forest stand that exhibits good characteristics of growth, form, and vigour, and that is not managed for cone production, but from which seed is collected, usually at the time of harvest.

SEEDING The introduction of seeds into an area to promote natural or artificial regeneration. Several seeding methods are used. **Aerial** is the broadcast application of seeds or seeds in pellets from a plane or helicopter. **Broadcast** is the application of seeds in a uniform pattern over large areas, either by hand or with a mechanical seed spreader mounted on a truck or similar machinery. **Direct** is the sowing of seeds by hand or machinery directly into the ground. **Drill** is the sowing of seeds with a manually or mechanically operated seed drill in shallow furrows in the ground. **Natural** is the natural dispersal of seeds by wind, water, birds, mammals, or gravity from standing trees in or adjacent to the area being regenerated. **Spot** is the sowing of seeds in small, cultivated, or screefed patches throughout the area to be regenerated.

SEEDLING A young tree grown from seed is a seedling from the time of germination through to the sapling stage. Seedlings can be in several forms, including: (1) **bare-root**, in which the seedling is transplanted from the nursery with its roots bare; (2) **container**, in which the seedling is grown in a container and planted with its roots still in the growing medium used in the nursery; and (3) **plug**, in which a seedling is lifted from its container with roots and rooting medium left undisturbed. There is often little difference, except in the shape of the container, between container and plug-grown seedlings.

SEED ORCHARD A plantation of trees, either proven by analysis to be genetically superior, or a plantation of plus trees that are being tested for superior genetic traits. The orchard is isolated to reduce cross-pollination from potentially genetically inferior, outside sources, and is intensively managed to improve the genotype and produce frequent, abundant, and easily harvestable seed crops. A **clonal seed orchard** is established by setting out clones as grafts or cuttings. A **seedling seed orchard** is established from selected seedling progenies.

SEED PRODUCTION AREA A forest stand identified as a good source of seed and in which individual trees are evaluated for desired characteristics. Unwanted trees and competing trees are removed to promote cone production. Seed is collected during the life of the stand.

SEED SOURCE *See* Provenance.

SEED TRAP A device used to trap seeds falling to the ground from trees or shrubs. It is used to determine the amount of seedfall and the time, period, rate, and distance of dissemination.

SEED TREE A tree selected and often reserved for seed collection or provision of seed for natural regeneration.

SEED TREE SYSTEM An even-aged, silvicultural system that retains mature standing trees scattered throughout the cutblock to provide seed sources for natural regeneration.

SEED YEAR The year in which a tree species produces, either as an individual or as a crop, enough seed to ensure regeneration of the species. All tree species have seed years, but some produce seed very infrequently, and then produce vast amounts of seeds in the seed year. The term mast year is also used to mean the same thing, although is more commonly applied to oaks and beeches. The carpet of fallen seed is called mast and is an important food source for wildlife, which then distribute the seed around the landscape.

SEEN AREA In fire detection, the ground seen from a lookout point or flight route is classified as: (1) **visible**, when the ground or the vegetation growing thereon is directly visible from an established or proposed lookout or aerial flight route; (2) **screened**, when the ground or vegetation thereon is not directly visible but over which the lookout's line of sight passes at an elevation not in excess of a given standard; (3) **blind**, in areas not visible to the lookout and more than a given standard elevation below the line of sight. Screened areas at the limit of visibility and not having good background are also classified as blind. All observations are made under specified visibility conditions. It is synonymous with visible area.

SEEN AREA MAP A map showing the different classes of seen area covered by a lookout or lookouts. It may differentiate visible, screened, and blind areas, or only two classes, visible and blind, may be recognized. It is synonymous with visibility or visible area map.

SEEP The point where an aquifer or area of minor groundwater flows out onto the land surface or into a stream channel. Seeps are too small to be a spring and do not produce runoff at a visible rate. *See also* Spring.

SEEPAGE ZONE An area where soil is saturated due to emerging ground water.

SEGMENT **1** In GIS work and computer applications generally, a segment is a division of a record, usually in the form of one or more fields. For polygons, a segment is a line defined by two points. **2** Botanically, a part of a plant organ such as a leaf, petal, calyx, corolla, or perianth that is deeply divided but not truly compound.

SEISMIC Pertaining to earthquakes.

SEISMIC LINES Strips of land that have had the vegetation (and sometimes the surface soils) removed to permit the placement and detonation of underground explosive charges so that the underlying geological structure can be determined by measuring the returning vibrations of deliberately created surface disturbances. 'Shooting' seismic lines is performed extensively in mineral and gas and oil exploration and can have an effect on access to wilderness areas by humans (namely, increased poaching) and on how wildlife uses the affected landscape or habitat.

SEISMIC ZONATION **1** Broad subdivision of a province or country into regions of similar susceptibility to earthquakes. **2** Subdivision of an area according to types of surface materials and their properties with regard to seismic shaking, location of faults, etc., commonly termed micro-zonation.

SELECT GRADE A high-quality lumber. It is the grade recommended for all finishing work where fine appearance is essential, such as interior trim and cabinet work.

SELECTION There are two forms of selection. **Natural selection** is the differential reproduction and survival of individuals, such that poorly adapted offspring do not continue in the population. **Artificial selection** occurs when human manipulations yield specific traits deemed desirable, or when human-induced pressures, such as hunting, prevent or eliminate individuals from reproducing, thus suppressing or eradicating a particular trait. *See also* K-Selection; r-Selection.

SELECTION BIAS A systematic tendency in the sampling procedure to exclude one kind of person or object from the sample. *See also* Bias.

SELECTION CUTTING A silvicultural system used to create or maintain uneven-aged stands, usually by the periodic removal of groups of trees or individual trees. It is undertaken to provide periodic harvests while maintaining full residual stand growth rates. It attempts to develop a balanced, uneven-aged stand structure, including the encouragement of regeneration by providing the cultural measures needed for tree growth and seedling establishment. The selection system refers to the programs used to create or maintain the stand, while the selection method refers to the way in which the stand is regenerated. The cutting usually involves a mixture of regeneration and improvement cuts. Note that selection cutting is not the same thing as selective cutting (logging). *See also* Selective Cutting.

SELECTION DIFFERENTIAL The average phenotypic value of the selected individuals, expressed as a deviation from the population mean.

SELECTION PRESSURE **1** The action of an agent that tends to produce changes in relative frequency of different genotypes in a population by causing differential mortality or fertility of individuals carrying the different genotypes. **2** The degree to which the above occurs (i.e., a quantitative estimate of the differences in mortality or fertility produced).

SELECTIVE CUTTING A system in which groups of trees or individual trees are removed periodically from the forest based on economic criteria aimed at maximizing logging revenues rather than the need to ensure satisfactory regeneration or to maintain stand growth rates and quality of timber production.

The term is often used synonymously with selection cutting, but this is seldom correct, since the management goals of the two systems differ. Selective cutting provides periodic revenues from the forest but is not specifically designed to improve the growing conditions of the trees remaining.

The practice of selective cutting has historically resulted in the selection of all the biggest and best trees for cutting, leaving behind a silvicultural slum of damaged trees and degraded ecosystem functions. *See also* High Grade; Selection Cutting.

SELECTIVE HERBICIDE A herbicide that is more toxic to some plant species than to others. In some cases, a non-selective herbicide can be used selectively if timing of application can take advantage of morphological, biochemical, or physiological differences among plants, thus permitting the target plant to be treated without damage to non-target plants. *See also* Non-selective Herbicide.

SELF-PROPELLED A term used to describe non-motorized recreational activities such as hiking, skiing, canoeing, or kayaking.

SELF-SUSTAINING POPULATION A wildlife population of sufficiently large size to assure its continued existence within the area of concern without introduction of other individuals from outside the area, assuming that the desirable ecosystem conditions are maintained. Note that this term has a time limitation, since all ecosystems change over time.

SEMELPARITY Production of all an organism's offspring in one event, which may occur over a short time. *See also* Iteroparity.

SEMIFOSSORIAL A burrowing animal that is partially adapted to living underground, but also spends time above ground (e.g., marmots [*Marmota* spp.]).

SEMIOCHEMICALS A complex, volatile chemical substance that acts as a message and triggers one or more interactions between organisms (e.g., pheromones). *See also* Allelochemic; Allomone; Kairomone; Pheromone; Synomone.

SEMIPARASITE A green plant having its own

root system, but partly dependent for its nutrition on a functional connection with the roots of other plants.

SENESCENCE 1 Generally, the process of aging in mature individuals, typically toward the end of an organism's life. Organisms at this stage are said to be senescent. **2** In deciduous plants, the process preceding leaf shedding.

SENSITIVE SPECIES 1 In the US, those species that (1) have appeared in the Federal Register as proposed for classification and are under consideration for official listing as endangered or threatened species; (2) are on an official state list; and (3) are recognized by the US Forest Service or other management agency as needing special management to prevent their being placed on federal or state lists. **2** *See* COSEWIC for Canadian designations.

SENSITIVITY The relative likelihood of damage occurring due to an attack by pests, exposure to toxic materials (such as a pesticide), or adverse environmental conditions. The opposite of tolerance. *See also* Immunity; Resistance; Susceptible.

SENSITIVITY ANALYSIS An analytical procedure in which the value of one or more parameters is varied and the changes that this produces are analyzed in a series of iterative evaluations. If a small change in a parameter results in a proportionately larger change in the results, the results are said to be sensitive to the parameter.

SENSOR Any device capable of detecting electromagnetic energy and converting it into a form suitable for gathering and interpreting information about the environment. An **active sensor** records the reflection of the electromagnetic energy it emits (e.g., radar). A **passive sensor** records sources of electromagnetic energy that have been emitted or reflected from other sources.

SENSU LATO Latin, meaning in a broad sense.

SENSU STRICTO Latin, meaning in a strict or limited sense.

SEPAL One of the component parts of the calyx, typically green and foliaceous. Each sepal has the same number of vascular traces as a leaf of the species, and this is sometimes used as a means of confirming identification. *See also* Flower (for illustration).

SEPT A small hollow or depression, such as is seen between the carpels on the outside of an ovary in which the nectaries are developed (e.g., some species of *Allium*).

SEPTICIDAL A seed capsule that is dehiscent lengthwise at the junction of the carpels (e.g., Yucca species). *See also* Capsule; Fruit.

SEPTUM Plural septae. The wall, partition, or wall-like structure between two cells.

SERAL SPECIES Plant species of early, middle, and late successional plant communities of any plant association. The term is often used in a narrower sense in forest management to describe the dominant conifer vegetation that follows major disturbance episodes.

SERAL STAGES Also called successional stages. In a forestry context, the series of plant community conditions that develop during ecological succession from bare ground (or major disturbances) to the climax stage. Five main stages are typically recognized. (1) **Early seral stage** is the period from disturbance to crown closure of conifer stands managed under the current forest management regime. Grass, herbs, or brush are abundant. A period of high diversity, often suitable for a broad group of plants and animals. (2) **Mid-seral stage** is the period in the life of a forest stand from crown closure to first merchantability, usually ages fifteen to forty years. Due to stand density, brush, grass, or herbs rapidly decrease in the stand. Hiding cover may be present. A period of declining diversity, suitable for a narrower group of plants and animals. (3) **Late-seral stage** is the period in the life of a forest stand from first merchantability to culmination of mean annual increment. During this period, stand diversity is minimal, except that conifer mortality rates will be fairly rapid. Hiding and thermal cover may be present. Forage is minimal. (4) **Mature seral stage** is the period in the life of the forest stand from culmination of MAI to an old-growth stage or to 200 years. This is a time of gradually increasing stand diversity. Hiding and thermal cover, and some forage may be present. (5) **Old-growth seral stage** represents the potential plant community capable of existing on a site and is determined by the frequency of natural disturbance events. This final stage continues on until stand replacement occurs and the secondary succession process starts again. In forests where there are long periods between natural disturbance events, the overall forest structure will tend to be more even-aged than forest types undergoing more frequent disturbances. *See also* Old-Growth Forest Succession (for illustration).

SERE The individual stages that follow sequentially in ecological succession.

SERIATE Arranged in series, typically in whorls or rows.

SERICEOUS Silky, covered with soft, fine adpressed hairs.

SERIES **1** In vegetation analysis, an aggregation of taxonomically related associations that takes the name of the climax species that dominates the principal layer. **2** A taxonomic unit in a classification. *See also* Soil Series.

SEROTINOUS **1** Plant species or individuals that flower or fruit late in the season, or plant behaviour that occurs late in the day. **2** It is used specifically to describe cones (typically *Pinaceae* species) that, although containing viable seed, remain on the tree for many years and only open to release their seed when stimulated by the heat of a fire or intense heat from the sun.

SERRATE A margin having a saw-toothed appearance, with the teeth pointing forwards toward the apex of the organ. *See also* Leaf Margin (for illustration).

SERRULATE Minutely serrate. *See also* Leaf Margin (for illustration).

SERVICE TIME *See* Machine Time.

SESSILE **1** It describes insects in stages of their life cycle where they are normally immobile. **2** It describes non-mobile organisms, such as barnacles or corals, or rooted plants that are fixed to a permanent base. **3** It describes stalkless structures directly attached to the main part of an organism, rather than being located at the end of a stem. *See also* Mobile.

SET **1** In fire control: (1) lighting (setting) an individual incendiary fire; (2) the location or point of origin of an incendiary fire; (3) the material left to ignite an incendiary fire at a later time; (4) individual lightning fires or railroad fires, especially when several are started within a short time; (5) burning material at points of origin deliberately ignited for backfiring, slash burning, prescribed burning, or other purposes. **2** In sawmilling, the distance at which individual saw teeth deviate outwards from the plane of the blade. The degree of set determines in part, the width of the kerf.

SETA Plural setae. **1** In insects, a hollow, stiff, hairlike extension of the cuticle. **2** In mosses, the stalk that bears the spore-containing capsule. **3** In plants generally, a bristle. *See also* Moss (for illustration).

SETACEOUS Having a bristlelike texture.

SET-BACKS A general term for buffer zones or more specific zoning requirements where a strip of land is delineated for no or modified activity. The width and configuration depend on the site and purposes intended.

SETIFEROUS/SETIGEROUS Bearing bristles.

SETOSE Covered with bristles.

SETTING The area (cutblock) being logged in any one continuous operation, which may have several landings and extraction points, but is all part of the same logging operation. It is sometimes considered to be the area logged to one landing or set up point for the yarder, thus several settings might make up one cutblock.

SEVERE BURN A degree of burn in which all organic material is removed from the soil surface, and soil surface is discoloured (usually red) by heat. The organic material below the surface is consumed or charred. *See also* Fire Severity; Light Burn; Moderate Burn.

SEX RATIO The number of males in a group divided by the number of females at fertilization (primary sex ratio), at birth (secondary sex ratio), and at sexual maturity (tertiary sex ratio).

SEXUAL DIMORPHISM The differences in size, weight, colour, or other morphological characteristics that are related to the sex of the individual.

SEXUAL STAGE The stage in the life cycle of a fungus in which spores are produced after sexual fusion. It is synonymous with perfect stage.

SEXUPARAE Winged, parthenogenic female adelgids or aphids that fly from the summer host to the overwintering host.

SHADE-INTOLERANT SPECIES Plant species that require open, sunny conditions for optimal growth, and will grow poorly, if at all, in shady conditions, although they may colonize gaps. Typically, easily dispersed plant species that can invade a disturbed site and grow rapidly, to form the first forest community in the next successional sequence (e.g., many pine species, larch, alder, and cottonwood).

SHADE-TOLERANT SPECIES Plant species that have evolved to grow well in shade. Typically, these species grow in the understorey, thus shade-tolerant species often dominate a climax forest type (e.g., hemlock, beech, sugar maple).

SHADOW PRICE The value of goods or services measured by using opportunity cost principles rather than market prices.

SHALE Sedimentary rock formed by induration of a clay or silty clay deposit and having a tendency to split into thin layers.

SHALLOW OPEN WATERS A form of wetland, which includes potholes, sloughs, ponds, and waters along river, coast, and lakeshore areas. Usually small bodies of standing or flowing water less than two metres deep in midsummer, they represent the transitional stage between lakes and marshes. Surface waters are generally free of emergent vegetation. *See also* Bog; Fen; Marsh; Swamp; Wetland.

SHANNON-WEINER INDEX (*H'*) An index of diversity based on the proportional abundance of species in a community. The index should be used when individuals are randomly sampled from a larger population and the assumption is made that all species are represented in the sample. Error therefore, is most likely to occur when all species in the sample community have not been included. The value of the Shannon-Weiner Index usually falls between 1.5 and 3.5 and rarely exceeds 4.5. H' is calculated as:

$$H' = -\Sigma\, p_i \ln p_i$$

where

p_i = proportional abundance of the ith species = $\frac{n_i}{N}$

ln = log normal.

SHAPE OF CLASTS The shape of clasts as defined by the relative lengths of their *a* (long), *b* (intermediate), and *c* (short) axes. Terms, such as spherical ($a = b = c$) and discoid ($a = b > c$), refer to clast shape.

SHEAR-BLADING The use of a bulldozer to cut off trees and brush in frozen ground by pushing the blade along the ground and shearing off the vegetation at ground level. It is often used as a means of clearing seismic lines.

SHEARING **1** Harvesting trees by means of a mechanical shear rather than a saw. **2** The shaping of trees, usually ornamentals or Christmas trees, by clipping and pruning. **3** A method of site preparation in which all standing material is removed at ground line using a shear blade attached to a large tractor. **4** A pattern of wood failure in which the wood fibre breaks cleanly at ninety degrees to the main axis of the stem or branch.

SHEATH A tubular covering, such as the basal part of a grass leaf surrounding the stem.

SHELTERWOOD SYSTEM A silvicultural system used in even-aged stands in which groups of trees are harvested in a design that uses adjacent or overhead large trees for seed or to protect regeneration. Several variations are commonly used. **Irregular shelterwood system** is a harvest pattern that is irregular and gradual, usually in groups of trees, with the final cutting pattern in strips. It relies on natural regeneration using a long regeneration interval, often up to half the rotation length. The resulting stand is uneven-aged and irregular. **Strip shelterwood system** uses regeneration cutting in wide strips, against the prevailing wind and in a short time-frame. Regeneration is natural and occurs in a short time-frame to yield an even-aged and regular stand. **Uniform shelterwood system** is a harvest pattern that is regular and uniform throughout the stand to yield natural regeneration, which may be bolstered by artificial regeneration. A short regeneration period yields a fairly even-aged and regular stand.

SHEPHERD'S CROOK A leader or branch with a downward-curving tip in the shape of a shepherd's crook. It is characteristic of attack by certain insects or pathogens (e.g., terminal weevils on spruce and *Fusarium* root rot in Douglas-fir seedlings). *See also* Crook.

SHIGOMETER An instrument used to detect decay in trees.

SHIPPING DRY Wood having a moisture content (oven-dry basis) of 14 to 20 per cent. This results in reduced shipping weight and less susceptibility to decay, and is a standard widely used in the international lumber trade.

SHOOT **1** The above-ground, generally ascending axis of a plant including, in the seedling and transplant stages, any branches and leaves. *See also* Leader. **2** Any young, slender, above-ground outgrowth from a plant, particularly a sprouting stem or branchlet, often taken to include its leaves.

SHOOT SCAR *See* Basal Cup.

SHORAN An acronym for short-range navigation, SHORAN is an electronic measuring system that computes the distance from an airborne station to each of two ground stations.

SHORELINE The line of intersection between a horizontal plane representing the calm water in a lake, or any tidal height, and the sloping plane that forms the beach or shore.

SHORT-DISTANCE MIGRANTS Bird species that usually migrate just beyond the snow line.

SHORT-TERM FIRE DANGER An assessment of current records and conditions to determine day-to-day fire danger. Factors considered are fuel condition, weather measurements and forecasts, fire risk, fuel types and resulting fire hazards, accessibility, values at risk, and topography. The information is used in day-to-day fire prevention, fire presuppression, and fire suppression planning. *See also* Long-Term Fire Danger.

SHORT-TERM RETARDANT A water-based substance in which water is the fire suppressing agent. Chemicals may be added to the water to alter its viscosity or retard its evaporation, thereby increasing its effectiveness.

SHORT TON In the US, a weight measure of one ton or 2,000 pounds. *See also* Long Ton; Tonne.

SHORTWOOD HARVESTING Extraction of log lengths from the stump to the landing, where the tree has been cut into lengths at the stump, or cut and decked in small piles.

SHOTGUN A two-drum, live skyline yarding system used in uphill logging in which the carriage moves down the skyline by gravity, is lowered to attach logs, and is then raised and pulled to the landing by the mainline.

SHOT-HOLE **1** A type of leaf spot in which the necrotic tissue falls out, leaving a hole in the leaf. *See also* Necrosis. **2** A larger form of pinhole produced in wood by ambrosia beetles, or in bark by emerging bark beetles. **3** A depression in the bark caused by woodpeckers searching for insects at the base of an old fruiting body. An indication of decay. **4** A depression along a seismic line formed when the earth settles due to the underground seismic explosion.

SHRINKAGE The decrease in wood dimensions due to loss of water in the wood cell walls. Shrinkage across the grain of the wood occurs when the moisture content falls below 30 per cent, the fibre saturation point. Below this point, shrinkage is generally proportional to moisture content, down to a moisture content of zero per cent. Shrinkage is expressed as a percentage of the green wood dimensions. Wood can shrink or swell according to moisture content.

SHRUB A woody perennial plant, typically lower than most trees, having multiple stems that branch from the base without a well-defined main stem. It is often used as a descriptive term in a broad sense.

SIALLITIC Soils in which the clay fractions are dominated by siliceous clays, such as illite and montmorillonite. *See also* Allitic; Ferrallitic; Fersiallitic.

SIDELAP *See* Overlap.

SIDE-LOOKING AIRBORNE RADAR (SLAR) A radar system that uses a stabilized antenna oriented at right angles to the flight path of the aircraft.

SIGMOID S-shaped. Having a double curve in opposite directions.

SIGN The visible portion of a pathogen, or pest, or part of it, or its products seen on the host plant and used to associate or identify the cause of a symptom (e.g., a conk or frass). An external manifestation of an internal problem. *See also* Symptom.

SIGNIFICANCE **1** In statistics, the probability of making a Type One error is termed the significance level of the statistical test, and it can be set at any level. **2** A general term often used to describe a threshold beyond which an outcome can be considered of sufficient importance to warrant a different set of actions. The exact definition of where this threshold lies is often difficult. One definition is: Any exercise in judging the significance of an environmental impact should consider (a) the importance of the environmental attribute in question to the decisionmakers, (b) the distribution of change in time and space, (c) the magnitude of change, and (d) the reliability with which change has been predicted or measured. *See also* Scope.

SIGNIFICANT PEST INCIDENCE An occurrence of an indigenous or introduced pest in numbers and circumstances that are judged detrimental to the fulfilment or management objectives.

SILICEOUS Composed of or covered with silica; containing minute particles of silica.

SILICLE A podlike fruit similar to a silique, but shorter, and not more than twice as long as wide. *See also* Fruit (for illustration); Silique.

SILIQUE A podlike, two-carpelled fruit, dehiscing longitudinally leaving a central axis of tissue. It is typical of certain members of the Mustard (Cruciferae) family; much longer than wide. *See also* Fruit (for illustration); Silicle.

SILL Sheets of intrusive, igneous rock that have been forced in between layers of existing rock to depths of a few centimetres to many metres thick. *See also* Batholith (for illustration); Dyke; Laccolith.

SILT **1** Soil inorganic particles between 0.004 and 0.062 millimetres in diameter (i.e., between clay and sand). **2** A soil textural class in which silt particles are very abundant. *See also* Substrate Particle Size.

SILVICS/SYLVICS The study of the life history and general characteristics of forest trees and stands, with particular reference to locality as a basis of silviculture.

SILVICULTURAL CONTROL The suppression or management of a pest population, or the reduction of pest damage by site preparation, growing genetically improved trees, manipulation of species composition/age/stocking, or any other silvicultural manipulations. *See also* Biological Control; Chemical Control; Manual Control; Mechanical Control.

SILVICULTURAL DECISIONMAKING MODEL A computer model or system that permits the simulation and possibly prediction of the interaction of such factors as site class, access, managed-stand volume, and logging costs to assist in decisionmaking with respect to silvicultural practices in individual stands.

SILVICULTURAL PRACTICES The set of field techniques and methods implemented to modify and manage a forest stand over time to meet defined management goals and objectives, which will depend on the silvicultural system being used.

SILVICULTURAL PRESCRIPTION One or more professional recommendations for controlling the establishment, composition, constitution, and growth of forests from seedling through to the desired endpoint of the forest stand.

SILVICULTURAL REGIME A series of stand-tending treatments applied after regeneration to achieve a specific stand management objective.

SILVICULTURAL SYSTEMS One or more planned treatments prescribed for a forest stand that are designed to encourage the generation of a new stand of trees following harvesting and maintain that stand through to the next point of harvest (i.e., one rotation). The term encompasses the type of cutting, the stand treatments, and any intermediate cuttings. *See also* Rotation.

SILVICULTURE The art, science, and practice of controlling the establishment, composition, health, quality, and growth of the vegetation of forest stands. Silviculture involves the manipulation, at the stand and landscape levels, of forest and woodland vegetation, including live vegetation, and the control or production of stand structures, such as snags and down logs, to meet the needs and values of society and landowners on a sustainable basis.

SIMPLE Not compound and not divided into secondary units (e.g., a leaf that is not compounded into leaflets, or an inflorescence that is not branched).

SIMPSON'S INDEX (*D*) This index of diversity is based on the number of samples of random pairs of individuals that must be selected from a community to provide at least a 50 per cent chance of obtaining a pair with both individuals of the same species. It is often referred to as a dominance measure because it is heavily weighted toward the most abundant species in the sample instead of reflecting species richness. A community with only one species would have a D value of 1.0. The value increases as each individual represents an additional species and is calculated as:

$$D = \Sigma \frac{(n_i(n_i - 1))}{(N(N-1))}$$

where

n_i = number of individuals in the ith species

N = total number of individuals.

The reciprocal form of Simpson's Index ($1/D$) is usually used to ensure that the index value increases with increasing diversity.

SIMULATION The use of a computer or mathematical model to predict effects from a management option given different sets of assumptions about population vital rates.

SINGLE-ACTION SHEAR A mechanized cutting tool that uses one hydraulic cylinder to push the cutting blade through the tree while a fixed anvil provides support for the blade on the opposite side of the tree.

SINGLE ENTRY Entering a stand of trees for logging purposes only once within any one rotation period. It is associated with a clearcutting silvicultural system. *See also* Multiple Entry.

SINGLE FRUIT *See* Syncarp.

SINGLE-TREE DISPOSAL The practice of attempting to eradicate small bark beetle infestations by disposing of individual trees, such as by removing and milling, or by cutting and burning them, prior to emergence of the bark beetle brood.

SINGLE TREE SELECTION METHOD A method of regenerating and managing uneven-aged stands in which individual trees are removed fairly uniformly throughout the stand. *See also* Selection Cutting.

SINGLE USE A management regime in which one output is given complete priority over all the other possible outputs. For instance, logging plans that disregard fish and wildlife habitats, aesthetics, water quality, or recreation values would be considered a single use of the land. Conversely, it has also been argued that parks and ecological reserves are also a single use since they do not permit logging. *See also* Multiple Use.

SINK **1** Generally, an area or process that absorbs objects, or ideas, without yielding anything in return. **2** In conservation biology, a population whose average reproductive rate is less than its average rate of mortality. Such a population attracts immigrants that may help to replenish the population. *See also* Sink Habitat; Source. **3** In soils, the capacity of soils to assimilate nutrients, and subsequently provide a source for above- and below-ground vegetative growth.

SINKER **1** The wedgelike structure embedded in the wood of the host plant by the plant parasite mistletoe. **2** In timber management, logs that sink when dumped in the water for transportation. *See also* Floaters.

SINK HABITAT A habitat in which reproduction is insufficient to balance local mortality. The population can persist in the habitat only by being a net importer of individuals.

SINKHOLES A funnel-shaped depression in the land surface that communicates with a subterranean passage developed by solution. It is common in limestone and karst regions. It is also applied to similar features caused by piping.

SINKING FUND A fund accumulated from profits by setting aside regular (typically annual) instalments sufficient at compound interest to replace the capital value of a 'wasting asset' at the end of its useful life (when it is written off). It is a form of amortization.

SINUATE Having a wavy margin. *See also* Leaf Margin; Undulate.

SINUOSITY **1** The ratio of channel length between two points on a channel to the straight line distance between the same two points. **2** The ratio of channel length to down-valley length. Channels with sinuosities of 1.5 or higher are termed meandering.

SINUS **1** Botanically, an indentation or recess in a margin between two lobes or divisions of a leaf or other expanded organ, such as a calyx or corolla. **2** In animals, a cavity within a bone, or a blood-filled cavity in certain arthropods or fish.

SITE **1** Generally, the soil, drainage, slope, climate, and biotic factors that determine the landform and its associated vegetation patterns. **2** In a silvicultural context, an area of land that, because of its various characteristics, is deemed suitable for particular species and silvicultural treatments. **3** The general location where an event (planned or unplanned) has occurred.

SITE CLASS Any interval into which the site index range is divided for the purposes of classification and use. A measure of an area's relative capacity for producing timber or other vegetation.

SITE CLASSIFICATION The assessment of individual forest sites to derive an approximation of long-term growth potential (productivity). Factors affecting the site include climate (regional and local), the current site conditions, historical land uses and vegetation patterns, drainage patterns and water availability, the methods of harvesting employed, and the source and extent of the on- and off-site nutrient pools that will be expected to supply nutrients for future stands. Typically, a site index is derived to produce height/age curves and, in combination with predicted volume/age tables, the site can be assessed to predict the volume of wood likely to grow per hectare. As with all classification schemes, implementation always reveals the needs for improvement and refinements, and there are many variations around the world.

SITE FIDELITY Refers to birds that return to the same nest, territory, or localized area every year.

SITE INDEX A measure of forest site productivity expressed as the average height of the tallest trees in the stand at a defined index age, typically less than the planned rotation ages. Common index ages are 40, 50, 70, 75, and 100 years.

SITE PREPARATION Any action taken in conjunction with a reforestation effort (natural or artificial) to create an environment favourable for survival of suitable trees during the first growing season. This environment can be created by altering the ground cover, soil, or microsite conditions, using biological, mechanical, or manual clearing, prescribed burns, herbicides, or a combination of methods.

SITE PRODUCTIVITY (CAPABILITY) The potential biomass capable of being produced on any one site. Note that productivity may be helped or hindered by various management activities and is a function of site quality. It is measured as the mean annual increment of merchantable volume at or near rotation age, which can be expected from any one site assuming that the stand is fully stocked by one or more species best adapted to the site. Productivity on a high-quality site would normally be greater than that possible on a low-quality site. *See also* Site Quality.

SITE QUALITY The innate ability of a geographic area to produce biomass as determined by the prevailing soil type and condition, the moisture regimes, and the local climatic conditions. Site quality is measured as volume produced per unit area for any one species (M^3/ha) or per year (M^3/year). Site quality can be divided into simple classes such as high, medium and low, and each class has its own range of productivity. *See also* Site Productivity.

SITE REGION In Hill's Ecological Land Classification, a site region is a macroclimatic region that has similar soil and climatic conditions on similar landforms. Vegetation responds to these features and conditions to produce a characteristic forest type.

SITE REHABILITATION **1** The rehabilitation of potentially productive land presently occupied by stands of undesirable tree species, or by brush, to a condition appropriate for the establishment of the more desirable tree species. **2** Stump removal after harvesting to reduce or eliminate root rot infection centres.

SITUATION ANALYSIS An analysis of the factors that influence suppression of an escaped fire from which a plan of attack will be developed. It includes development of alternative strategies of fire suppression and the net effect of each.

SITUATION REPORT (SITREP) An itemized list and/or written account, usually issued on a daily basis, detailing the status of various fire-related activities. A SITREP generally contains information on fire occurrence and area burned to date, fire suppression resources committed to going fires and resources on standby, number of fires in the various stages of control, fire danger class, fire weather forecast, and forest closures (if any).

SIX CLASS SYSTEM An example of an infection rating system for rating the intensity of dwarf mistletoe infection on individual trees. The degrees of infection (the infection ratings) are determined by classifying each third of the crown as either zero (healthy, with no visible infection), one (light infection, up to and including 50 per cent of the branches infected), or two (severe infection, with more than 50 per cent of the branches infected). The three figures are added and a tree is then placed into one of six infection classes.

SKELETAL SOIL A soil having between 35 to 70 per cent by volume of coarse fragments, but also having sufficient fine fractions to fill interstices larger than one millimetre.

SKELETONIZE Describes the results of certain insects or fungi that feed on the soft tissues of leaves, leaving only the basic matrix or veins intact (the leaf skeleton).

SKETCH MAPPING The preparation of additional map information about ground or vegetation features by an aerial observer flying along preplanned flight lines and sketching observed features onto an existing map base.

SKIDDER *See* Harvesting Machine Classification.

SKIDDING *See* Harvest Functions.

SKID TRAIL A path created by dragging logs to a landing. *See also* Landing.

SKIMMER Any aircraft equipped to pick up water while in motion on or over water.

SKYLINE LOGGING A cableway system that uses a main cable tautly stretched between two spar trees or towers. This cable serves as a track for the skyline carriage, which moves to and from the yarder along the cable as logs are hauled into the landing. A **skyline crane** has the added capability of yarding logs laterally into the carriage and then yarding them into the landing, thus providing the system a greater reach from any one set-up point. A **slackline system** is a live skyline system employing a carriage, main line, and haul-back line. Both main and haul-back lines attach directly to the carriage. The skyline is lowered by a slackening of the line to permit the chokers to be attached to the carriage. Lateral yarding is provided by side blocking. *See also* Ground-Lead Logging; High-Lead Logging.

SLABS The outside parts of a log that are removed when the opening faces of a log are cut to produce a cant. Slabs used to be considered waste material but are now more typically chipped and used in pulp mills. *See also* Cant.

SLAR *See* Side-Looking Airborne Radar.

SLASH Debris left as a result of forest and other vegetation being altered by forestry practices and other land-use activities (e.g., timber harvesting, thinning and pruning, road construction, seismic line clearing, etc.). Slash includes material such as logs, splinters or chips, tree branches and tops, uprooted stumps, and broken or uprooted trees and shrubs.

SLASH BURN The deliberate and carefully planned use of prescribed fire to eliminate the accumulated slash lying on the ground. *See also* Prescribed Fire.

SLASH DISPOSAL The treatment or handling of slash to reduce the potential for fire, insect, or disease hazards.

SLASHER-BUNCHER *See* Harvesting Machine Classification.

SLEEPER FIRE *See* Holdover Fire.

SLIDE A type of mass wasting process in which the material moves downslope as a coherent mass along a well-defined surface, such as bedrock. *See also* Creep; Flow; Slump.

SLING PSYCHROMETER A portable, hand-operated psychrometer. The dry- and wet-bulb thermometers are mounted on a frame connected to a handle at one end by means of a bearing or length of chain. Thus it can be whirled by hand to provide the ventilation necessary to obtain a reading. *See also* Psychrometer.

SLOPE The angle at which a planar surface is inclined relative to the horizontal. Slope is a primary determinant in many classification schemes. The typical slope classes are divided as follows:

Slope class		Slope gradient limits (%)	
Simple slopes	Complex slopes	Lower	Upper
Nearly level	Nearly level	0	1-3
Gently sloping	Undulating	1-3	5-8
Strongly sloping	Rolling	5-8	10-16
Moderately steep	Hilly	10-16	20-30
Steep	Steep	20-30	45-65
Very steep	Very steep	45-65	none

The shape of the slopes is also important. The main slope shapes are straight or flat, concave, convex, or S-shaped. The formation of S-shaped slopes is related to hillslope processes, such as water runoff and soil creep. Vegetation is important to the maintenance of these slope shapes. Concave slopes form naturally in areas of rough ground, usually a result of strong erosional forces such as glaciers, or as a result of slumps and associated erosional processes. Removal of vegetation may increase the chances of the slope becoming concave. Convex slopes typically reflect strong underlying rock formations that are resistant to erosion.

SLOPE BREAK The point on a slope where gradient changes rather abruptly.

SLOPE FAILURE Rupture and collapse, or flow of surficial materials, soil, or bedrock due to shear stress exceeding the shear strength of the material.

SLOPE PROCESSES Mass movement processes (such as debris slides) and surface wash whereby fine sediments are transported downslope by overland flow.

SLOPE STABILITY Pertains to the susceptibility of a slope to landslides and the likelihood of slope failure.

SLOPE WASH Fine sediments on or at the foot of hillsides that have been moved downslope by overland flow.

SLOSS (SINGLE LARGE OR SEVERAL SMALL) A subject of considerable, and often controversial, debate that refers to the design of reserves, and whether it is better to have one large reserve or several smaller ones. No consensus exists as to which approach is correct. In the illustration, for each of the six pairs of nature reserve designs, extinction rates may be theoretically

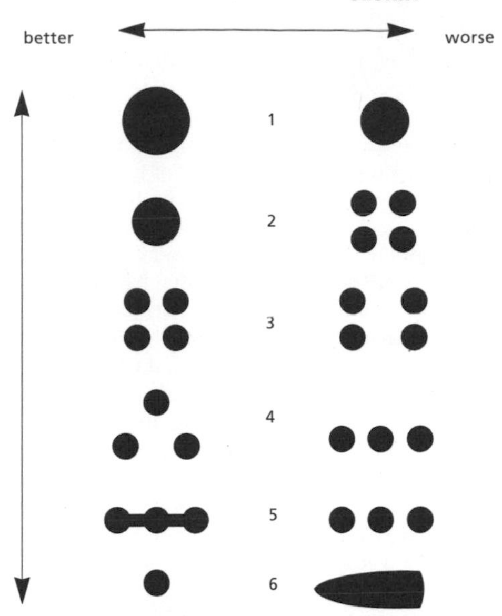

lower for the reserves on the left than on the right. Reserves toward the top of the illustration would theoretically show lower extinction rates than those at the bottom. *See also* Island Biogeography Theory; Species-Area Curve.

SLOUGH **1** Low, swampy ground where water flows sluggishly for long stretches (pronounced 'slew'). **2** Casting off, as in a snake casting off its old skin, or the dead tissue that has become separated from living tissue. **3** Patches of rock separating from the main body of rock (pronounced 'sluff' in definitions 2 and 3).

SLUMP A type of mass wasting process in which a coherent mass of rock or unconsolidated material moves downslope along an upwardly curved surface of short radius. It is also called a rotational slump. *See also* Creep; Flow; Slide.

SLUMP-EARTHFLOW A complex landslide displaying characteristics of a slump in its headward zone and characteristics of an earthflow in its downslope zone.

SLUMP STRUCTURE Warped or faulted bedding or stratification within a deposit resulting from downslope movement due to gravity since deposition.

SLURRY **1** A suspension of insoluble matter in water. **2** In fire suppression, it is a general term applied to any long-term or short-term retardant after the mixing process has been completed. **3** In planting bare-root seedlings, the roots are dipped in a peat slurry to minimize the exposure of fine roots and root hairs to dry air.

SMOKE **1** The visible products of combustion rising above a fire. **2** A term often used when reporting a fire or probable fire in its initial stages. In fire management, the following types of smoke are recognized. **Legitimate smoke** is smoke from any authorized use of fire or other permissible sources, such as permitted debris burning, locomotives, or industrial operations. **False smoke** is any phenomenon mistaken for smoke. **Drift smoke** is smoke that has drifted from its origin and has lost any original billow form. **Intermittent smoke** is smoke that becomes visible occasionally. **Smoke haze** is a haze caused by smoke. **Smoke column** is smoke and other gases that form a column-shaped mass above a fire, characterized by sharply defined billowed edges. It is synonymous with smoke plume. *See also* Convection Column. **Smoke pall** is smoke that forms an extensive, thick blanket spreading more or less horizontally from a fire.

SMOKE CANDLE A pyrotechnical product that emits smoke of a uniform colour, like that of a small fire, and at a standard rate. It is used to check visibility of a simulated small fire and to test the alertness of lookouts.

SMOKE EPISODE A period when smoke is dense enough to be an unmistakable visual nuisance or hazard to driving or flying.

SMOKE JUMPERS Fire fighters trained and equipped to parachute to fires (usually in remote places) for initial attack.

SMOKE MANAGEMENT Scheduling and conducting a prescribed burning program under predetermined burning prescriptions and firing techniques that will minimize the adverse impacts of the resulting smoke production in smoke-sensitive areas. *See also* Mixing Height; Ventilation Index.

SMOKE SENSITIVE AREA An area in which smoke from outside sources is intolerable, owing to heavy population, transportation services, existing air pollution, and/or intensive recreation/tourist use.

SMOLT A juvenile salmonid one or more years old that has undergone physiological changes to cope with a marine environment. It is the seaward migrant stage of an anadromous salmonid.

SMOOTHING **1** In GIS work, the elimination of jagged lines in a polygon by averaging or curve-fitting techniques. **2** In statistics, the grouping of data in order to obtain a smoother-looking distribution.

SMOULDERING *See* Fire Behaviour.

SMOULDERING COMBUSTION *See* Combustion.

SMUDGE *See* Hot Spot.

SNAG Any standing dead, partially dead, or defective tree at least 3 metres tall. A **hard snag** typically has an intact top, a high degree of bark cover, most limbs, and sound wood which might be merchantable. Hard snags are required by a number of wildlife species, including cavity nesters. A **soft snag** is composed primarily of wood in an advanced stage of decay and deterioration, and is generally not merchantable.

The changes in the plant community surrounding the snag (or down log) that take place over time are called **external succession**. The changes taking place inside the snag (or down log) over time, which are a reflection of decay, are termed **internal succession**. *See also* Snag Classification.

SNAG CLASSIFICATION Snags form a vital component in forest ecosystems, providing habitat for a wide range of birds, animals, and insects, as well as a substrate for new plant growth in the later stages of decomposition. Both logs and snags (which essentially are logs still standing) can be classified based on their size (cross-sectional diameter and length) and the stages of decay on the outside and the inside of the snag, which varies considerably between tree species. A nine-stage system is used to describe the decomposition of snags (see illustration). **Stage 1** is a living tree; **Stage 2** is a declining tree; **Stage 3** is a dead tree; **Stage 4** is loose bark on a dead tree; **Stage 5** is a clean snag (no bark); **Stage 6** is a broken snag beginning decomposition; **Stage 7** is a decomposed snag; **Stage 8** is downed material from a col-

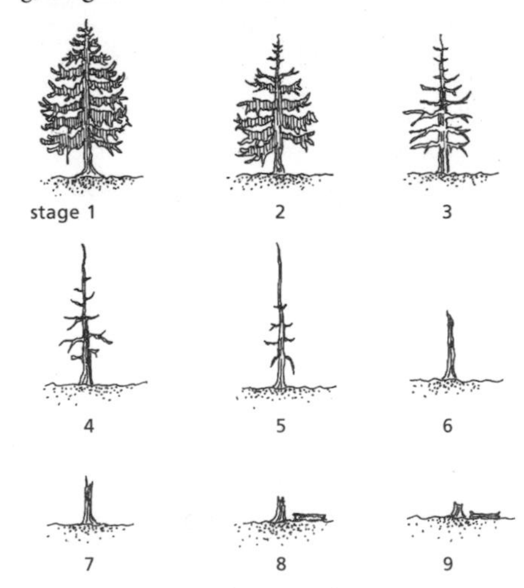

lapsing snag; **Stage 9** is a stump or wood that is incorporated into soil.

This system of snag classification has been utilized as a means of classifying the relative wildlife values of live trees and decaying snags. *See also* Log Classification; Wildlife Tree.

SNAG DENSITY The number of snags per unit area.

SNAG-DEPENDENT SPECIES Birds or animals dependent on snags for nesting, roosting, or foraging habitat.

SNOW-INTERCEPTION COVER A stand of conifers at least ten metres in height and with 60 to 90 per cent canopy closure that provides relatively shallow snow depths and abundant available forage when compared to other stands.

SOBOLIFEROUS Bearing or producing lateral shoots from the ground, forming a clump. It is usually applied to shrubs or small trees.

SOCIAL BENEFIT The non-monetary and not easily calculable returns to society arising from any form of economic activity, such as the creation of recreational areas, parks, etc.

SOCIAL COST The non-monetary and not easily calculable toll on society arising from any form of economic activity (e.g., atmospheric pollution) over and above the costs of the goods and services causing this. *See also* Social Benefit.

SOCIAL DISCOUNT RATE The preference or value expressed by society for the timing of the production of goods, services, and ecosystem states from an ecosystem. A positive discount rate reduces the value of a product produced in the future by a certain per cent annually up to that future time, as compared to the unreduced value of the same product produced in the present. A zero social discount rate presumes that society is indifferent to the time when the product is produced, now or in the future.

SOCIAL ECOLOGY The study of the ecological context of human societies, including the ideological and other dimensions of culture as well as the biological and geological relationships and settings.

SOFT CHAPARRAL Usually non-dense and penetrable stands of limber shrubs such as sage (*Salvia* spp.), buckwheat (*Eriogonum* spp.), and sagebrush (*Artemisia* spp.). *See also* Chaparral; Hard Chaparral.

SOFT PINES The soft or white pines in the subgenus *Strobus* (Haploxylon) usually have needles in clusters of five, with one vascular bundle in cross-section. *See also* Hard Pines.

SOFTWOOD Typically refers to the wood of coniferous trees, although a few hardwood trees have physically soft wood (e.g., balsa or cottonwood). Softwood timbers have a simpler cell structure than hardwoods. *See also* Evergreen; Needle-Leaved.

SOFTWOOD EXCAVATOR Any species of bird capable of excavating its own nesting or roosting cavity in decayed or soft wood.

SOIL The top layer of the Earth's surface consisting of unconsolidated mineral or organic materials derived from geological material and dead, organic matter. These components are modified by biological, chemical, and physical processes. In combination with climatic factors and the actions of organisms acting on the materials, a substrate capable of supporting plant life may be created.

SOIL AMENDMENTS Materials, such as sand, peat, or compost, mixed into soils to improve their physical, chemical, or biological properties. Ammendments are often specified when planting landscape trees to overcome the problem of heavily compacted and nutrient-deficient soils. The amendment needs to be at least 50 per cent of the soil volume to be effective.

SOIL CLASSIFICATION SCHEMES Any scheme used to differentiate the layers, origins, and properties of soils. There is considerable variation between the nomenclature used in Canada, the United States, and other parts of the world. Readers seeking detailed information should consult the accepted scheme in use in their area.

SOIL COMPACTION An increase in bulk density (mass per unit volume) and a decrease in soil porosity resulting from applied loads, vibration, or pressure. More compacted soils (or other materials) can support greater loads (load-bearing capacity). Bulk density can be increased by controlling the moisture content, compaction forces, and treatment procedures, as well as by manipulating the type of material being compacted. The results of the compaction effort are presented in graphical format showing dry density in kilogrammes per cubic metre (pounds per cubic foot) against varying moisture contents (per cent by dry weight). The results produce a series of curves, with the peak of each curve representing the maximum bulk density and optimum moisture content for the compactive effort being employed. Increasing the compactive effort moves the compaction curve upwards and to the left, yielding higher maximum density and lower moisture content. Thus, use of heavy compaction machinery can achieve greater density using less moisture (important in large engineering projects where water has to be added to the surface being compacted). Granular materials have high maximum densities and low optimum moisture contents, while clay soils are the opposite. Note that very silty soils have a very peaked curve and thus moisture content becomes very critical for such soils.

Soil compaction is measured against standardized testing methods. In North America, the Standard Proctor test is common. Compaction densities required are typically specified as a percentage of the maximum density, rather than moisture content or type of equipment needed. For example, a compaction requirement of 95 per cent for a soil having a maximum density of 125 pounds per cubic foot would require compaction in the field that yielded a surface capable of bearing 119 pounds per cubic foot of material tested. Testing involves analysis of the material being used to ensure it complies with the type known to be capable of compaction to the specified density and moisture contents, and then actually loading the material in laboratory conditions to see if the specification can be achieved as written. Loading analysis typically involves a measure of the resistance of the compacted material to penetration by a plate of known size.

SOIL CREEP The slow, downhill movement of soil or overburden on a slope due to the influence of gravity. *See also* Solifluction.

SOIL DISPLACEMENT The removal and horizontal movement of soil from one place to another by mechanical forces, such as a bulldozer blade.

SOIL DRAINAGE The manner in which water-saturated soil behaves under the influence of gravity. Freely draining soils reach field capacity quickly, while those with impeded drainage tend to stay saturated for longer periods. *See also* Percolation.

SOIL HORIZON A layer or zone of soil or soil materials lying approximately parallel to the land surface with physical, chemical, and biological properties or characteristics that are distinct from the adjacent, genetically related layers. *See also* Solum.

SOIL INHABITANT **1** Any organism that lives in the soil during all or part of its life. **2** A microorganism that is usually strongly competitive with other microorganisms normally occurring in the soil, and which can often survive for many years in the complete absence of a suitable host. *See also* Soil Invader.

SOIL INVADER A microorganism that is poorly competitive with microorganisms normally occurring in the soil, and which seldom survives more than one or two years in the soil in the complete absence of suitable hosts. *See also* Soil Inhabitant.

SOIL LIQUEFACTION The change of the strength of a water-saturated, cohesionless soil to that of a liquid, usually from intense ground shaking. Upon liquefaction, a soil loses all of its bearing strength. The process is also known as thixotrophy.

SOIL MANTLE The Earth's surface where geologic and biologic factors have, over time, created a soil mass different from the original materials. The soil mantle serves as a natural medium for plant growth.

SOIL MOISTURE The water content of the soil in its natural state.

SOIL PARTICLE SIZES Soils are classified in several different ways, one of the most common based on the size of the component particles. The scheme used by Agriculture Canada and the US Department of Agriculture is as follows:

Boulders	greater than 25 centimetres
Cobbles	7.5-25.0 centimetres
Gravel	2 millimetres-7.5 centimetres
Sand	0.05-2 millimetres
Silt	0.002-0.05 millimetres
Clay	less than 0.002 millimetres

For engineering usage, the Unified System of Soil Classification recognizes the following divisions:

Gravel	4.75-7.62 centimetres
Sand	0.075-4.75 millimetres
Fines	less than 0.075 millimetres

In this system, clayey and silty soils are distinguished by consistency testing (i.e., according to behaviour) rather than by particle size.

SOIL PIPES *See* Macropores.

SOIL PIT A pit excavated for the purpose of examining the soil. It is most commonly dug by hand using shovels and is usually less than one metre deep.

SOIL PRODUCTIVITY The capacity or suitability of a soil for establishment and growth of a specified crop or plant species, based primarily on nutrient availability.

SOIL PROFILE A vertical sequence of well-defined soil, sediment, or decaying vegetation layers.

SOIL SERIES A group of soils developed from a particular type of parent material having naturally developed horizons that, except for texture of the surface layers, are similar in differentiating characteristics and in arrangement of the profile. The lowest category in the US system of soil taxonomy.

SOIL STRUCTURE Refers to the aggregation of primary soil particles into compound particles that are separated from adjoining aggregates by surfaces of weakness. As shown in the illustration, structure is classified in terms of grade or distinctness (weak, moderate, strong), class or size (fine, medium, coarse, very coarse), and type (granular, platy, prismatic, blocky). Sizes in the illustration are in millimetres.

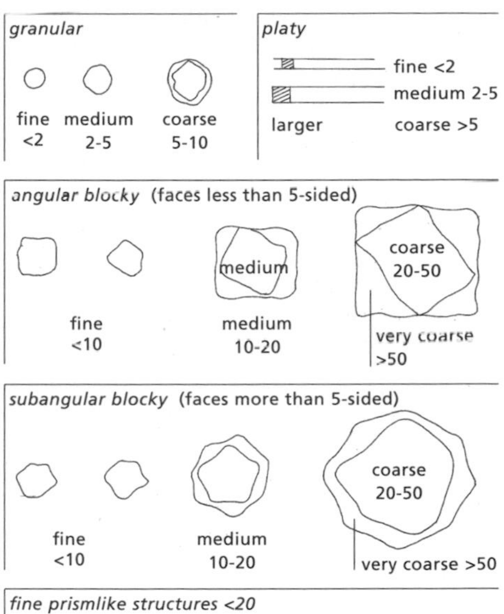

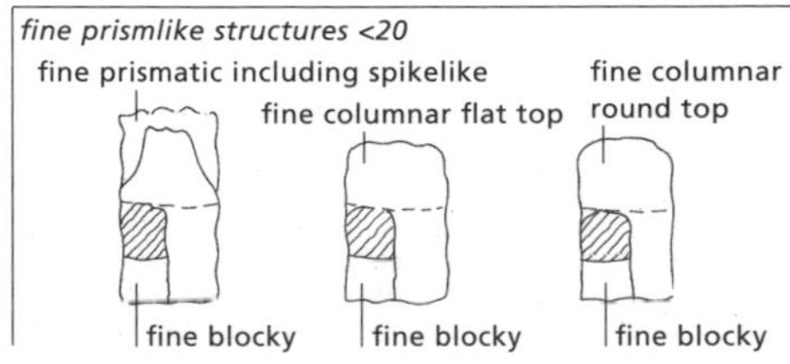

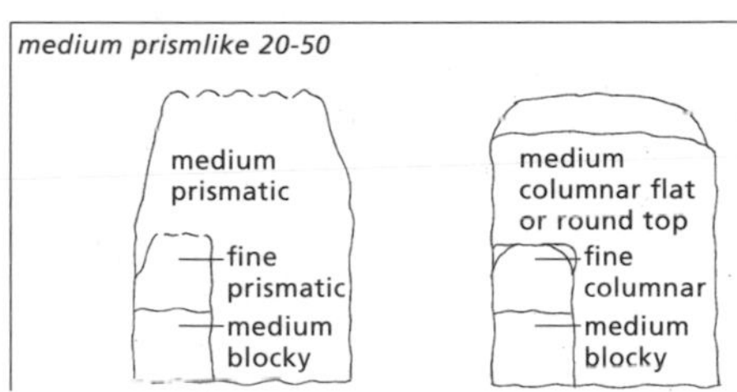

SOIL SURVEYS **1** Mapping the distribution of soil types, which requires air photo interpretation and field work by pedologists. **2** Assessing the engineering properties of surficial materials, such as bearing strength and plasticity, at a site or in an area where construction is proposed. **3** Collecting soil or surficial material samples for geochemical analysis for the purposes of mineral exploration. It is a component of drift prospecting.

SOIL TEXTURE The relative proportions (in per cent) by size of sand, silt, and clay particles in a soil. It is normally assessed in the field by touch or in the laboratory by use of sieves and with reference to the standard soil texture chart. When the proportions of sand, silt, and clay have been determined, the values are projected inward on the chart until the lines intersect. For example, in the illustration, a sample consisting of 75 per cent sand and 10 per cent clay falls in the sandy loam category.

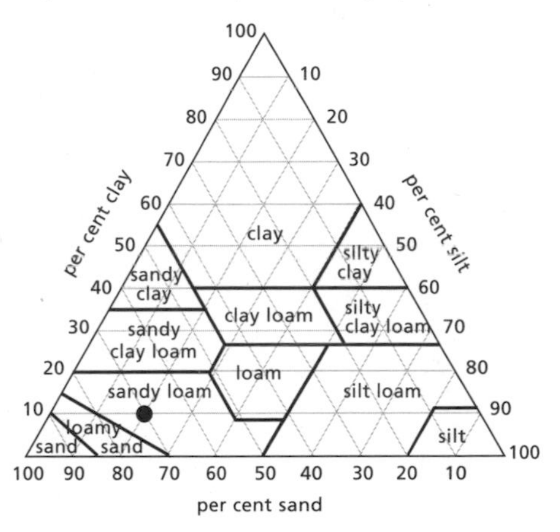

SOIL TREATMENT The application of a water-soluble herbicide to the ground for absorption through the roots of brush species.

SOIL TYPE Pertains to classes of soil defined according to soil horizons present and horizon thickness.

SOIL WATER The water regime of a soil is determined by the physical properties and arrangement of the soil particles. The pores in a soil determine its water-retention characteristics. When all the pores are full of water, the soil is said to be saturated. Large pores allow water to drain from them. Once a soil has freely drained for a few days, the soil's water content is at field capacity. Water is held in smaller pores by capillarity. Other water is adsorbed onto soil particle surfaces. Some capillary water is available to plant roots, but as water is lost, a point is reached where the water tension (the energy required to remove a unit amount of water) is too high and the soil's hydraulic conductivity is too low for significant plant uptake. This point is termed the permanent wilting point, and represents the soil water content below which a plant will not recover overnight without the addition of water to the soil. The soil water present between the field capacity and the permanent wilting point is termed available water.

SOLIFLUCTION The slow, downslope movement of moist or saturated, seasonally frozen, surficial material and soil.

SOLIGENOUS FEN A peatland affected by water originating, at least in part, from areas of mineral soil percolating through it and/or carrying minerals in from the surrounding area.

SOLITARY **1** Species that occur singly or in pairs, but are usually not gregarious. **2** Botanically, occurring singly or borne alone.

SOLUM The *O* (or *L, F, H*), *A*, and *B* horizons in a soil profile. In mature soils, plant and animal activity and soil-forming processes have been confined to this zone.

SOMATIC CHROMOSOME *See* Autosome.

SOREDIUM Plural soredia. A small, powdery propagule of a lichen, containing algal cells and fungal hyphae breaking through the outer layer (cortex) to be released.

SØRENSON INDEX (C_s) An index of community similarity that qualitatively measures beta diversity in pairs of sites. All species are counted equally, and abundances are not taken into account.

$$C_s = \frac{2j}{(a + b)}$$

where

a = species in site A
b = species in site B
j = number of species common to both sites.

In this index, a value of 0 would indicate there is no similarity (no identical species), between the two communities. A value of 1.0 would indicate that the two communities have an identical species composition. *See also* Jaccard Index; Morisita-Horn Index; Sørenson Quantitative Index.

SØRENSON QUANTITATIVE INDEX (C_N) An index of community similarity that quantitatively measures beta diversity in pairs of sites. Abundances of species are taken into account. Results may be influenced by species richness and sample size.

$$C_N = \frac{2_{jN}}{aN + bN}$$

where

aN = number of individuals in site A
bN = number of individuals in site B
jN = sum of the lower of the two abundances of species that occur in the two sites.

See also Jaccard Index; Morisita-Horn Index; Sørenson Index.

SORREL-TOP The initial colour phase (usually chlorotic yellow in spruce or orangeish in firs and pines) of the foliage of a coniferous tree killed by insects, such as bark beetles, or pathogens. It is usually characteristic of a tree killed in the current season. *See also* Black-Top; Red-Top.

SORTIE A single, round trip made by an airtanker from an air base to a fire.

SORTING A geological term pertaining to the variability of particle sizes in a clastic sediment or sedimentary rock. Materials with a wide range of particle sizes are termed **poorly sorted;** materials with a small range of sizes are **well-sorted.** Note that these terms are the reverse of the engineering expressions 'well-graded' and 'poorly graded.'

SORTING COEFFICIENT A measure of the distribution or variability of particle sizes in the substrate. The usual measure, computed as d_{75}/d_{25}, is equivalent to the standard deviation of the log transformed frequency curve, hence a measure of dispersion of particle sizes. A substrate with a large sorting coefficient is termed well-sorted. The terms d_{75} and d_{25} are those diameters for which 75 per cent and 25 per cent of the cumulative size-frequency distributions are larger.

SORUS Plural sori. In rusts, smuts, and false smuts, the fruiting body and the mass of spores produced. In ferns, a collection of stalked sporangia on the lower side of a pinna or pinnule. In seaweeds, the antheridia on the fronds. The illustration shows the sori of *Polypodium glycyrrhiza*, the Licorice fern. *See also* Fern (for illustration); Pinna.

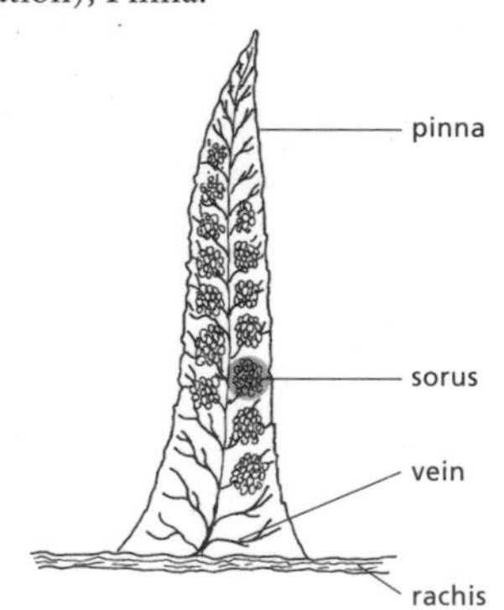

SOUND WARBLER A signalling device mounted on an airtanker that generates a tremulous siren sound to warn firefighters on the ground that a plane is approaching to make a retardant drop.

SOURCE Generally, an area or process that yields objects or ideas. An actively breeding population that has an average birth rate that exceeds its average death rate, and thus produces an excess number of juveniles that may disperse to other areas. *See also* Sink.

SPACING **1** The distance between trees in a plantation, either at the time of planting or after the developing stems have been thinned out at any time in the rotation. **2** The act of altering the distance between adjacent stems by increasing (planting) or decreasing (thinning) the number of stems per unit area.

SPADIX In certain plants (e.g., Araceae), the thick or fleshy flower spike surrounded by a spathe, with the flowers often embedded in the axis. *See also* Inflorescence (for illustration).

SPAN The horizontal distance between skyline supports.

SPAR TREE A tree or mast on which rigging is hung for one of the many cable-hauling systems.

SPATHE A large bract enclosing an inflorescence or spadix. It is often white or highly coloured, but rarely green (e.g., Palmae, Araceae).

SPATHE VALVE One of two or more herbaceous or scarious bracts that subtend an inflorescence or flower and generally envelop the subtended unit when in bud.

SPATHULATE/SPATULATE Shaped like a spatula or spoon, the basal end being narrowed and the apical end rounded. *See also* Leaf Shape (for illustration).

SPATIAL DATABASE A collection of interrelated, geographically referenced data stored without unnecessary redundancy to serve multiple applications as part of a geographic information system. *See also* Geographic Information System; Geographically Referenced.

SPATIALLY EXPLICIT MODEL A model that predicts the future state of an ecosystem or animal population based on mapped locations of organisms and their habitat.

SPECIAL HABITAT A habitat that has a special function not provided by plant communities or successional stages alone. It includes riparian habitat zones, snags, dead and down woody material, and edges. Special habitats are biological in nature but can be created or altered by management. *See also* Unique Habitat.

SPECIALIST A species with narrow food and/or habitat preferences. *See also* Generalist.

SPECIALIZED Evolved characteristics that permit an organism to adapt to a narrow set of environmental conditions.

SPECIATION The process of deriving a new species from its ancestor. The separation of a species into two or more isolated populations, which then evolve separately. *See also* Isolation.

SPECIES A group of individuals that have their major characteristics in common and (usually) can only breed with each other. *See also* Class; Genus; Order; Phylum; Taxon.

SPECIES ABUNDANCE The distribution of the number of species and the number of individuals of each species in a community.

SPECIES-AREA CURVE A graph depicting the relationship between the area of an island, or an analogous patch of forest, and the number of species living there. It is also called area-species curve. The relationship is defined by the following formula:

$$S = cA^z$$

where

S = number of species

A = area

c and z are constants where c provides an estimate of the number of species per unit of area and z indicates how fast new species are added with increasing area.

This model is ecologically simplistic since a small area may have a greater number of species if it has greater habitat diversity. *See also* Island Biogeography Theory; SLOSS.

SPECIES DIVERSITY *See* Diversity.

SPECIES-HABITAT MATRIX A table, book, or database depicting the relative quality of vegetation associations and seral stages for meeting various life needs of wildlife species, typically for reproduction, feeding, and resting or cover.

SPECIES HYPERSPACE Species hyperspace is conceptualized as a single dimension (S-space) or axis for each species in a sample of S species. Stands are placed within the S-space based on the relative abundance of each species in a stand. The distance between stands in S-space represents their similarity or dissimilarity to each other. *See also* Stand Hyperspace.

SPECIES RICHNESS The number of species in a given area regardless of distribution. *See also* Diversity.

SPECTRAL BAND In remote sensing, the spectral band (also called wavelength band) is a distinct range of wavelengths in the electromagnetic spectrum that sensors can detect (e.g., Band 2 in the Landsat MSS is sensitive from 500-600 nanometres).

SPECTRAL REFLECTANCE CURVE In remote sensing, the characteristic spectral wavelengths that are associated with different objects, such as water and vegetation. It is also termed the spectral signature.
SPEED OF ATTACK **1** The elapsed time from fire origin to arrival of the first resources. **2** If the strength of attack is specified, the elapsed time necessary to contain the fire at an acceptable or predetermined limit within a specified fuel type.
SPELEOLOGY The study and exploration of caves and their features.
SPERMAGONIUM Plural spermagonia. A fruit body in certain fungi and lichens containing the spermatia. It is also spelled spermogonium.
SPERMATHECA An internal sac in female salamanders where sperm can be stored.
SPERMATIUM Plural spermatia. The nonmotile male gametes of some lichens and fungi borne in the spermagonium. Spermatia are non-infectious. It is the pycnidiospore in rust fungi; oidium in mushrooms; the small conidium in cup fungi.
SPERMATOPHORE A small packet of jelly containing sperm used as a medium for transporting sperm to the female in some invertebrates, especially molluscs, crustaceans, cephalopods, and some aquatic salamanders.
SPERMATOPHYTE A seed-producing plant. A member of the Spermatophyta, such as a flowering plant or conifer.
SPICATE Spikelike, or borne in a spikelike inflorescence.
SPIKE **1** A male deer or elk with single-point antlers. **2** Botanically, typically an unbranched, elongated, indeterminate inflorescence in which the flowers are sessile. *See also* Inflorescence.
SPIKELET In grasses, the inflorescence may be composed of several spikelets, consisting of one or more florets, which may be surrounded by glumes. *See also* Grass (for illustration).
SPIKE-TOP **1** The pointed, dead tip of a living tree from which most of the needles and branches have fallen. It may be caused by insect attack or severe dwarf mistletoe infection. **2** In general, any tree with such a dead tip.
SPINE A stiff, sharp, and pointed woody outgrowth of a stem. *See also* Prickle; Thorn.
SPINESCENT **1** Having spines. **2** Terminated by a spine or sharp tip.
SPINULE A small spine.
SPINULOSE Covered with small spines.
SPIRACLE The external openings of the respiratory system in insects.
SPIROPLASMA A helical mollicute, resembling mycoplasma-like organisms. The primary cause of Stubborn disease and of economic significance to citrus crops, including grapefruit, sweet orange, and tangelo. Causes suppressed growth, shortened internodes, and the production clusters of shoots in bushlike formations. *See also* Mollicute; Mycoplasma.
SPIT A fingerlike extension of the beach reaching out into the sea, usually comprised of sand or gravel that has been deposited by longshore drifting.
SPLIT DROP In fire-fighting, a retardant drop made from one compartment at a time from an airtanker with a multi-compartment tank. *See also* Incremental Drop; Salvo.
SPORANGIOPHORE A sporangium-bearing hyphae.
SPORANGIUM Plural sporangia. In fungi and mosses, a spore case, capsule, or saclike structure in which spores are produced. *See also* Moss (for illustration).
SPORE The reproductive structure in fungi and lower plants (e.g., ferns, mosses, club mosses, liverworts) consisting of one or several cells and not containing a pre-formed embryo. *See also* Seed. The illustration shows the characteristics of a variety of spore shapes visible under a microscope.

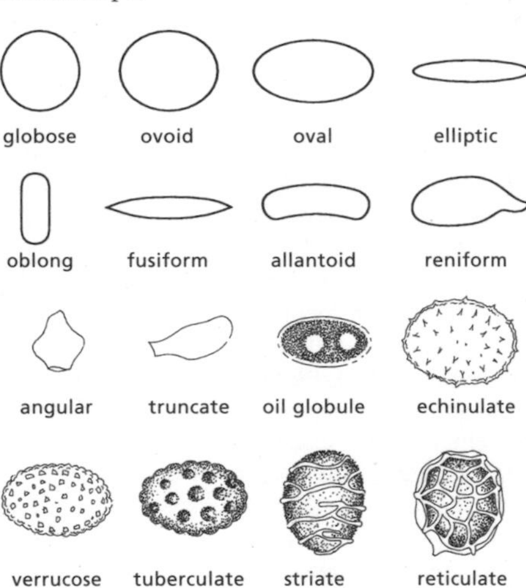

SPOROCARP A large, multicellular structure (fruiting body) that produces spores. *See also* Sporophore.
SPORODOCHIUM A hemispherical mass of hyphae bearing conidiophores protruding above the surface of the substrate. It is similar in origin to an acervulus.
SPOROPHORE A single, fungal strand bearing

spores and located on a complex, multicellular body. *See also* Sporocarp.

SPOROPHYLL A leaf or leaflike organ bearing sporangia. In angiosperms, the comparable organ is a carpel or stamen.

SPOROPHYTE The diploid, spore-producing stage in plants that reproduce by alternation of generations. It is typical of ferns.

SPORULATE The process of producing and releasing spores.

SPOT A discrete lesion, commonly chlorotic or necrotic, differing in colour or tint from the surrounding tissues.

SPOT BURNING A modified form of broadcast burning in which only large accumulations of slash are ignited and fire is confined to these spots.

SPOT FIRE **1** A fire ignited by firebrands that are carried outside the main fire perimeter by air currents, gravity, and/or fire whirls. It is synonymous with jump fire. **2** A very small fire that requires little time or effort to extinguish. *See also* Fire Behaviour.

SPOT IGNITION *See* Ignition Pattern (area grid ignition).

SPOT INFESTATION Pest damage of a local nature confined to small areas of timber. *See also* Infestation.

SPOT-MAPPING METHOD In bird surveys, a census procedure that plots on a map individuals seen or heard in a surveyed area. The survey is usually conducted over a period of days or weeks in a season, and individual territories or home ranges are then demarcated by examining the clusters of observations. It is used in a breeding bird census.

SPOTTER In smoke jumping, rappelling, or paracargo operations, the individual responsible for selecting the drop target and supervising all aspects of dropping smoke jumpers, rappellers, or cargo.

SPOTTING Fire behaviour producing sparks or embers that are carried by wind and which ignite new fires beyond the zone of direct ignition by the main fire.

SPOT TREATMENT **1** A pesticide or fertilizer applied over small, restricted areas of a whole unit, rather than over all of the whole unit (e.g., treatment of patches within a stand). **2** The application of a granular formulation of a herbicide to eliminate individuals or clumps of brush, or directed sprays around planted tree seedlings for herbage control.

SPOT WEATHER FORECAST *See* Fire Weather Forecast.

SPREADING A growth habit that extends outwards horizontally.

SPRING The point where an aquifer intersects with the ground surface and discharges water. *See also* Seep.

SPROUT (WATERSPROUT) *See* Epicormic Shoot.

SPUD *See* Barking Iron.

SPUR **1** Botanically, a tubular or saclike projection from a flower, usually containing a nectar-secreting gland. **2** A short, stiff branchlet bearing whorls of leaves or flowers from tightly spaced nodes. **3** A secondary divide between minor drainage systems.

SPUR ROAD A small branch of a logging road, generally used as a temporary access to a setting.

SQUALL A sudden increase in wind speed to at least seventeen miles per hour (fifteen knots) that is sustained for at least one minute but not more than five minutes.

SQUALL LINE A narrow, organized band of active thunderstorms, often preceding a cold front.

SQUAMA A scale.

SQUAMATE/SQUAMOSE Covered with scales.

SQUAMELLA Small scales.

SQUAMULOSE Covered or furnished with small scales.

SQUARROSE In plants, leaves abruptly spreading or recurved at some point above the base.

STABILITY The ability of an ecosystem to withstand change or, when changed, to develop forces leading back to the original condition. Assessed by examining factors such as population fluctuations, resistance to disturbance, speed of recovery after disturbance, and persistence of community composition. *See also* Resilience.

STABLE AGE DISTRIBUTION The proportions of the population in different age classes when the rate of increase has converged to a constant (which depends on the fixed schedules of survival and fecundity). The ratios between the numbers in the age classes are constants.

STABLE ATMOSPHERE *See* Atmospheric Stability.

STABLE DEBRIS That portion of debris within a stream channel or adjacent to it, which is unlikely to be moved, even at high flows. Stable debris is usually embedded in or attached to the bed or bank and forms a part of the stream's morphological character.

STADIA LINES The set of cross-hairs appearing superimposed on the image being viewed when using a theodolite or surveying level. The stadia lines permit more accurate measurements to be made by ensuring that the same point in the image is always used for readings, either vertically or horizontally.

STADIUM The period between insect moults. *See also* Instar.

STAGE A distinct, sharply different period in the development of a fungus or insect (e.g., the egg or larval stages), which are marked by distinctiveness of form. *See also* Instar.

STAGGERED SETTING One way of arranging cut-blocks across a landscape, such that each area cut is separated from the next area cut by areas of uncut forest of at least equivalent size.

STAG-HEADED A tree dead at the top as a result of injury, disease, or nutrient or moisture deficiencies, with dead branches projecting from the upper crown.

STAGING AREA An area where birds congregate to rest, generally during migration.

STAGNANT **1** Stands or individual trees whose growth and development have been repressed or almost stopped due to poor site conditions or excessive stocking. Growth is said to be stagnant or checked. *See also* Checked; Repression. **2** Water that is stationary and has a low oxygen concentration.

STAGNANT AIR CONDITIONS Atmospheric conditions under which pollutants build up faster than the atmosphere can disperse them.

STAGNANT ICE Part of a glacier or ice sheet within which ice is no longer flowing; stationary ice; usually melting by downwasting.

STAIN A discoloration of wood that does not usually affect its structural properties. It is caused primarily by fungi and chemicals. Names commonly given to different types of stain are blue, chemical, brown, fungous brown, interior sap, iron-tannate, log, mineral, sap, sticker, water, weather, and wound.

STAKEHOLDER Anybody who feels that his/her interests will be affected by the outcome of a decisionmaking process. These interests do not have to be of a financial nature, but may include a whole range of human values, such as the need for natural justice, religious values, ecological principles, and a longing for environmental protection.

STALK The elongate support of a plant organ such as a petiole, peduncle, pedicel, filament or stipe.

STAMEN The male, pollen-bearing organ of a seed plant. It is part of the androecium, typically comprised of an anther and filament, but may be the anther alone. *See also* Androecium; Flower (for illustration); Gynoecium.

STAMINATE A pollen-bearing (male) inflorescence or cone having stamens but no pistils. *See also* Pistillate.

STAMINODE/STAMINODIUM A sterile stamen, or structure resembling a stamen, sometimes resembling a petal.

STAND An aggregation of trees occupying a specific area and sufficiently uniform in composition, age, arrangement, and condition so that it is distinguishable from the forest in adjoining areas. Stands are the basic management unit in silviculture.

STAND AGE ROTATION The sum of tree age rotation plus regeneration lag. It is the time-dependent variable needed by most harvest simulation models to optimize outputs over time. *See also* Regeneration Lag; Rotation.

STANDARD **1** Quantifiable and measurable thresholds that are typically defined in law or regulation, and are mandatory. A statement that outlines how well something should be done, rather than how it should be done. A standard does not necessarily imply fairness or equity, nor an absolute knowledge of cause-and-effect linkages. Standards are typically established using a combination of best available scientific knowledge, tempered by cautious use of an established safety (caution) factor. *See also* Guidelines. **2** A tree selected for retention when the others are harvested, to perform a special function, such as the provision of shelter, a seed source, or the encouragement of special quality or sizes of timber (e.g., coppice with standards). **3** In nursery management, a tall, single-stemmed, young tree. **4** Botanically, the upper, typically broad and erect petal in a papilionaceous corolla of plants in the pea flower. It is also termed a banner or vexillum.

STANDARD ATMOSPHERE A hypothetical vertical distribution of atmospheric temperature, pressure, and density which, by international agreement, is taken to be representative of the atmosphere (e.g., for purposes of pressure altimeter calibrations, aircraft performance calculations, aircraft and missile design, ballistic tables, etc.). Air is assumed to obey the perfect gas law and the hydrostatic equation which, taken together, relate vertical variations in temperature, pressure, and density. It is further assumed that the air contains no water vapour and that the acceleration of gravity does not change with height.

STANDARD DEVIATION In statistics, the square root of the arithmetic mean of the squared deviations from the mean in a data set. In a typical frequency curve, one standard deviation on either side of the average value will encompass 67 per cent of all the deviations. *See also* Variance.

STANDARD ERROR OF ESTIMATE In statistics, an expression about the accuracy of any single observation, often associated with regression analysis. It is also called the root mean square error. *See also* Mean Square Error.

STANDARD ERROR OF THE MEAN In statistics, a measure of the standard deviation about the sample mean. Used to determine confidence limits.

STANDBY A state of readiness to take immediate action upon detection of a fire. *See also* Period of Alert.

STAND CONDITION An assessment of the physical properties of a stand (e.g., crown closure or diameter).

STAND CONVERSION The planned manipulation of species composition within a stand to increase the density of the desirable species. It may involve removal of hardwoods and replacement with conifers. The term may also refer to changing the main stand component from one conifer to another (e.g., by harvesting trees subject to pest attack and replacing them with non-susceptible or less susceptible species).

STAND DENSITY A quantitative measure of the number and size of trees on a forest site. Can be expressed as number of trees per hectare, basal area (M^2/hectare), stand density index, or weight. Unless specified, stand density would include all trees regardless of age. Stand density is not the same as stocking. *See also* Density; Stocking.

STAND DENSITY INDEX Any index used to evaluate the stand density. It is typically based on the number of trees per unit area, and the diameter of the tree of average basal area. For example, Reineke's Index, which is a plot of the logarithm of number of trees per acre (hectare) against the logarithm of average diameter of fully stocked stands, yields a straight line relationship. The slope of the line can in most cases be used to define the limits of maximum stocking. Although stand-density index can be correlated with stand volume and growth, basal area is often as good a measure of density, and since it is simpler to derive, is a preferred measure of stand density.

STAND DENSITY MANAGEMENT DIAGRAM A two-dimensional graph showing the logarithmic relationship between declining mean stand frequency and increasing mean tree size as mean stand diameter and dominant height increase in pure, even-aged stands.

STAND GROWTH When expressed in terms of volume, stand growth can be defined by the following equations:

$$G_g = V_2 + C - I - V_1$$
$$G_g + i = V_2 + M + C - V_1$$
$$G_n = V_2 + C - I - V_1$$
$$G_n + i = V_2 + C - V_1$$
$$G_d = V_2 - V_1$$

where

G_g = gross volume of initial growth
$G_g + i$ = gross growth including ingrowth
G_n = net growth of initial volume
$G_n + i$ = net growth including ingrowth
G_d = net increase
V_1 = stand volume at beginning of growth period
V_2 = stand volume at end of growth period
M = mortality volume
C = cut volume
I = ingrowth.

Stand growth can be considered in terms of the following. **Accretion** is the gross growth of initial volume when calculated using *M* or *C* to represent the volume of *M* or *C* trees at the time of their death and cutting. **Cut** is the volume or number of trees periodically felled or salvaged, whether removed from the forest or not. **Ingrowth** is the volume or number of trees that have grown into a measured category during a specified period (e.g., saplings which have grown into a merchantable diameter class). **Mortality** is the volume or number of trees periodically dying from natural causes. **Survivor growth** is the gross growth of initial volume when calculated using *M* or *C* to represent the volume of *M* and *C* trees at the time of the first measurement (the initial volume of *M* and *C* trees).

STAND HYPERSPACE Stand hyperspace is conceptualized as being *N*-dimensional (*N*-space), in which there is one dimension for each of the *N* stands in the sample. The species are placed within this *N*-space in relation to their stand abundances. The closer species are, the more similar are their respective abundances in the stands. *See also* Species Hyperspace.

STAND INFECTION INDEX An evaluation of the intensity of pathogen infection in a stand based on the average of infection classes for individual trees. The term is applied most frequently to stands infected with dwarf mistletoe.

STAND LEVEL The level of management at which a relatively homogeneous land unit can be managed under a single prescription, or set of treatments, to meet management goals, and objectives. *See also* Stand.

STAND MODEL A computer model that forecasts the development of a forest stand, usually in terms of mean stand attributes (e.g., mean diameter or height).

STAND-REPLACING EVENT A disturbance such as fire, wind, disease, insects, earthquakes, or volcanoes, that are of sufficient severity and extent to eliminate the existing stand and initiate a new stand of some form.

STAND TABLE A summary table showing the number of trees per unit area by species and diameter classes for a stand or type. The data may also be presented in the form of a frequency distribution of diameter classes.

STAND TENDING Activities such as thinning, spacing, removal of mistletoe-infected trees, and weed or brush control, carried out in already established stands.

STATION In avian biology, **1** the area within which observations made from a point are recorded by the observer. It is also termed the point. *See also* Point Count. **2** A monitoring station is an area of usually less than about fifty hectares where intensive censuses, nest searching, and/or mist-netting are conducted.

STATISTICALLY VALID DESIGN A design in which the sample units chosen are representative of the population being examined. It utilizes objective observations and permits the calculation of sampling error.

STEADY STATE A system in equilibrium. A stable level in ecosystem processes over time.

STEFAN-BOLTZMANN CONSTANT A physical constant derived from the Stefan-Boltzmann law, which states that radiancy (the energy emitted per second by a unit surface of a luminous body) is proportional to the fourth power of the absolute temperature:

$$E = \sigma T^4$$

where

E = radiant energy

σ = Stefan-Boltzmann constant, which is equal to 5.67×10^{-8} watts/m^{-2} K^{-4}

T = absolute temperature in degrees Kelvin (K).

The Stefan-Boltzmann constant occurs in formulae used to study plant-atmosphere relationships involving longwave radiation. *See also* Energy Balance.

STELLATE Describes hairs on a plant surface that have branched into a starlike appearance but is also used when only one or two branches occur.

STEM The principal axis of a plant from which buds and shoots develop giving the plant its characteristic form. With woody species, the term applies to all ages and thicknesses, unlike the terms trunk and bole, which refer to tree stems of substantial thickness. *See also* Decurrent; Excurrent.

STEMFLOW The flow of precipitation that is intercepted by canopy vegetation and flows down the stem, as opposed to intercepted precipitation that drips off the canopy. *See also* Throughfall.

STENOBATHIC Any organism restricted to living in certain depths of water. *See also* Stenoplastic; Stenothermal; Stenotopic.

STENOPHAGOUS An organism that is quite restricted in feeding habits, more so than an oligophagous organism and with a limited host range. *See also* Host Range; Host Specificity; Monophagous; Oligophagous.

STENOPLASTIC Organisms having little or very limited variation in the phenotypes of any given genotype.

STENOTHERMAL Any organism restricted to living in a narrow temperature range and unable to survive large variations in temperature. *See also* Stenotopic.

STENOTOPIC Any organism that is restricted to living in one, or a relatively small number of habitats. *See also* Stenobathic; Stenoplastic; Stenothermal.

STEPPE Vegetation dominated by grasses and occurring where the climate is too dry to support tree growth.

STEP TEST A five-minute test used to predict a person's ability to take in, transport, and use oxygen (aerobic capacity), which is the most important factor limiting the ability to perform arduous work. A scoring system rates fitness numerically, based on post-exercise pulse rate, body weight, and age, in terms of millilitres of oxygen consumed per kilogram of body weight per minute. Test scores (aerobic capacity) indicate fitness for various types of field work. Fire suppression jobs have been assigned fitness scores ranging from forty-five for fire line construction and other strenuous work, to thirty-five for jobs involving less effort. Applicants must attain the necessary test score to qualify for these positions.

STEREOCOMPARATOR *See* Stereometer.

STEREOGRAM A set or series of photographs that have been correctly oriented for stereoscopic viewing.

STEREOMETER A stereoscope with special

attachments for measuring parallax.

STEREO PAIR Short for stereoscopic. In aerial photograph interpretation, two photographs taken from adjacent parts of a flight line can provide a stereoscopic image (appears to be three-dimensional to the viewer) when the photographs are correctly aligned.

STEREOSCOPE A binocular instrument used to view overlapping aerial photographs as a three-dimensional model.

STEREOSCOPIC COVERAGE *See* Coverage.

STEREOSCOPIC PLOTTER An optical image transfer device used to transfer stereoscopic images to a base map by radial line plotting, by superimposition of photo and map images, and by floating marks attached to drafting devices.

STEREOSCOPY The science and art of using and interpreting stereo photographs. *See also* Stereo Pair.

STERIGMA Plural sterigmata. In conifers, a short projection on a twig that bears a sessile or petiolate leaf and remains on the twig following leaf fall.

STERILE **1** Nonfunctional, nonproductive organs, such as sterile stamens, or lacking functional sex organs. **2** Plants not bearing flowers. **3** Plants not producing fruit.

STEVENSON SCREEN A boxlike structure designed to protect air temperature and humidity-sensing instruments (e.g., psychrometer) while providing a shaded and ventilated environment. The standard Stevenson screen is made of wood, painted white, and has double-louvred sides and a double roof. When installed at a fire weather station, a Stevenson screen is firmly mounted on a wooden stand with its floor 115 centimetres above the ground and the door facing north.

STEWARDSHIP Caring for the land and associated resources so that healthy ecosystems can be passed on to future generations.

STEWARDSHIP LAND TRUST Land held in trust for the purposes of preservation and human use compatible with the long-term sustainability of the values and qualities of the land under trust. A stewardship trust usually has strict ecological guidelines about what kinds of activities can be practiced on the land. An ecoforestry land trust, for example, would be forest lands held in trust in perpetuity for purposes of practice of ecoforestry. It could be leased to independent, nonprofit societies or small businesses, which would then engage in ecoforestry activity with the oversight and guidance of the trust officers.

STIGMA The apex of the pistil where pollen is received. It is usually covered with a sticky covering to facilitate germination. *See also* Carpel (for illustration).

STIMULANT A chemical substance that elicits such actions as germination, growth, feeding, mating, or oviposition by an organism.

STIPE **1** The stalk of a pistil or other small organ when axile in origin. It is not the same as a pedicel of a flower. **2** The petiole of a fern or palm leaf. *See also* Fern (for illustration). **3** The stem or stalk of a fungus. *See also* Fungus (for illustration).

STIPEL A stipule of a leaflet.

STIPITATE Describes the shape of a sporophore, which has a stem or stalk.

STIPULE A leafy appendage at the base of the petiole. They may be in pairs, one either side, or fused. *See also* Leaf (for illustration).

STOCHASTIC Random, uncertain; involving a random variable. *See also* Deterministic.

STOCHASTIC MODEL A model that includes representation of random events.

STOCK In fish biology, a group of fish that is genetically self-sustaining and isolated geographically or temporally during reproduction.

STOCKING A qualitative measure of the adequacy of tree cover on an area in relation to a predefined norm expressed in the same units of measurement. Unless otherwise specified, stocking includes trees of all ages. The definition of the norm depends upon the purpose of the assessment and might be measured as number of large sawlogs, tree diameters beyond a defined size, stems per hectare, basal area per hectare, crown cover, canopy closure, or volume. While stand density reflects the current condition of the forest, stocking indicates how acceptable this density is when compared to the desired norm (over- or understocked). Stocking assessments include several broad categories or classes, and these may vary locally or regionally. The term stocking assumes a timber management objective as the primary orientation. Land considered understocked by a timber manager may in fact be at an ideal stocking for the wildlife manager. **Fully stocked** defines productive forest land stocked with trees of merchantable species. These trees, by number and distribution or by average dbh, basal area, or volume, are such that at rotation age they will produce a timber stand that fully occupies the potentially productive ground. They will provide a merchantable timber yield according to the potential of the land. The stocking, number of trees, and distribution required to achieve this will be determined from regional or local yield tables or by some other appropriate method. **Non-stocked** defines productive forest land that lacks trees completely or that is so deficient in trees, either young or old, that at the end of one rotation, the residual stand of merchantable tree species, if any, will be insufficient to allow utilization in an economic manner. **Normally stocked** defines productive forest land covered with trees of merchantable species of any age. These trees, by number, distribution, or by average dbh, basal area, or volume, are such that at rotation age they will produce a timber stand of the maximum gross timber yield. This yield must satisfy the site potential of the land as reported by the best available regional or local yield tables. For stands of less than the rotation age, a range of stocking classes both above and below normal may be predicted to approach and produce a normal stocking at rotation age and may, therefore, be included. This is because greater or lesser mortality rates will occur in over- or understocked stands as compared with those in a normal stand. **Not satisfactorily restocked** (NSR) defines an area of forest land that has been either planted or left to natural regeneration, and which has not become sufficiently well established to meet a predetermined stocking level. Factors affecting the lack of establishment might include competing vegetation, animal damage, frost or drought kill, lack of seed, or poor planting stock. **Overstocked** defines productive forest land stocked with more trees of merchantable species than normal or that full stocking would require. Growth is in some respect retarded and the full number of trees will not reach merchantable size by rotation age according to the regional or local yield or stock tables for that particular site and species. **Partially stocked** defines productive forest land stocked with trees of merchantable species insufficient to utilize the complete potential of the land for growth, such that they will not occupy the whole site by rotation age without additional stocking. Explicit definition in stems per hectare, crown closure, relative basal area, etc., is locally or regionally defined and is site specific. **Satisfactorily stocked** defines productive forest land that has been regenerated naturally or artificially to at least a minimum number of well-established, healthy trees of merchantable species that are free to grow and sufficient to produce a merchantable timber stand at rotation age. **Understocked** defines: (1) the condition when a plantation of trees fails to meet the minimum requirements for number of well-spaced trees per hectare; and (2) an area containing fewer individuals of a species, or fewer species of a biota than it is capable of containing under given environmental conditions. *See also* Stand Density.

STOCK TABLE A summary table outlining the basal area or volume of trees per unit area by species and diameter classes, for a stand type.

STOLON A shoot at or just below the ground that roots at nodes or the apex to produce new plants.

STOLONIFEROUS Plants producing stolons.

STOMA Plural stomata. A microscopic pore in the epidermis of a leaf or stem used for gas exchange. *See also* Palisade Layer (for illustration).

STONE Botanically, a large pyrene. *See also* Nut.

STONE LINE A sheetlike concentration of coarse fragments in surficial deposits. In cross-section, the line may be marked only by scattered fragments or it may be a discrete layer of fragments. The fragments are more often pebbles or cobbles than stones. A stone line generally overlies material that was subjected to weathering, soil formation, and erosion before deposition of the overlying material.

STOREY A roughly horizontal layer or stratum in vegetation, which is defined by the canopy in forests. Forests having only one layer are **single-storied**, while those having more than one layer of foliage are termed **multistoried**. The ground vegetation underneath a high overstorey is termed the understorey.

STORM FLOW The rapid, temporary rise in stream discharge caused by heavy rains geographically, or a temporary rise in stream discharge caused by heavy rains or rapid melting of snow or ice. It is also termed a freshet.

STRAIN **1** In pathogens, an infraspecific population defined on an arbitrary basis, such as geographic or host origin. **2** An isolate or group of similar isolates. **3** Any breeding selection of a sexually reproducing cultivar. *See also* Isolate. **4** In mechanics, the extension of a material under tension relative to its original length. *See also* Stress.

STRAMINEOUS Straw-coloured.

STRANDLINE An abandoned shoreline.

STRATEGIC PLANNING A precursor to more detailed planning, strategic planning is essentially a plan for planning and a disciplined effort to produce the basic decisions that shape and guide an organization and determine what it is, what it does, and why. It lays out the organizational goals, examines the internal and external environment and influences that will affect these goals, and then selects the most strategic objectives that will lead to goal achievement. Finally, progress toward the defined goals are continually monitored and adjustments made as needed.

Typically, strategic planning is a senior management-level activity, although lower level involvement would occur, and like comprehensive planning, it has a heavy reliance on analytical procedures. *See also* Comprehensive Planning; Incremental Planning.

STRATIFICATION **1** A horizontal or inclined structure in a sedimentary unit that results from its mode of deposition. The term includes beds, laminae, abrupt and gradual textural changes, and orientation and concentrations of particles. **2** The classification and mapping of terrestrial or aquatic habitats/communities into well-defined layers or zones, based on light, temperature, moisture, and physical structure regimes. **3** A technique used for conditioning seed embryos and breaking dormancy in those seeds requiring cold, moist temperatures prior to germination.

STRATIFIED In geology, materials arranged in strata or layers. In soils, layers accumulating from soil-forming processes are termed horizons, while those inherited from the parent material are termed strata.

STRATIGRAPHIC POSITION Refers to the dating of a particular layer in a sequence of sedimentary deposits according to the relative order in which all the layers making up the sequence were deposited. Generally, this means that any given layer is considered older than the layers above it and younger than the layers below it.

STRATIGRAPHIC UNIT A bed or series of beds with characteristics that differ from those of overlying and underlying materials. It is a subdivision of a larger sequence of sediments or sedimentary rock.

STRATUM **1** A subdivision of the forest area or population to be inventoried. Sample populations are usually stratified (divided into strata) to obtain separate estimates for each stratum. **2** In geology, a distinct band or layer of rock representing one activity or geological period.

STREAM A natural watercourse containing flowing water, at least part of the year, supporting a community of plants and animals within the stream channel and the riparian vegetation zone. Streams in natural channels may be classified according to their relation to season, space, or groundwater.

In relation to season, streams can be categorized as follows. **Ephemeral** is a stream that flows briefly only in direct response to precipitation in the immediate locality and whose channel is at all times above the water table. **Intermittent** or **seasonal** is a stream in contact with the groundwater table that flows only at certain times of the year, such as when the groundwater table is high and/or when it receives water from springs or from some surface source such as melting snow in mountainous areas. It ceases to flow above the stream bed when losses from evaporation or seepage exceed the available streamflow. **Perennial** is a stream that flows continuously throughout the year. It is also called a permanent stream.

In relation to space, streams can be: (1) **continuous** in which there are no physical interruptions in stream continuity; (2) **interrupted** in which some sections of the stream are perennial, intermittent, or ephemeral; or (3) **beaded** in which a stream consisting of a series of small pools or lakes is connected by short stream segments (e.g., a stream commonly found in a region of paternoster lakes or an area underlain by permafrost).

Streams can be related to the groundwater in the following ways. **Insulated** defines a stream or stream reach that neither contributes to nor receives water from the zone of saturation. It is separated from the zones of saturation by an impermeable bed. **Gaining** defines a stream or stream reach that receives water from the zone of saturation. **Losing** defines a stream or stream reach that contributes water to the zone of saturation. **Perched** defines either a losing stream or an insulated stream that is separated from the underlying groundwater by a zone of aeration. *See also* Paternoster Lakes.

STREAM BANK The rising ground bordering a stream channel, below the level of rooted terrestrial vegetation and above the normal streambed, which restricts lateral movement of water at normal water levels. The left and right banks are defined looking downstream. The lower bank is considered to be the portion of the channel cross-section periodically submerged from the high water line to the water's edge during the summer low-flow period. The upper bank is that portion of the topographic cross-section extending from the break in the general slope of the surrounding land down to the normal high water line. *See also* Riparian; Rooted Vegetation; Top of Bank.

STREAM CORRIDOR A stream flowing through a channel created by geomorphic features, with the corridor occupying the continuous low profile of the valley. The corridor may contain a perennial, intermittent, or ephemeral stream and its associated vegetative fringes.

STREAM DENSITY The relative density of natural drainage channels in a given area, expressed as kilometres of stream per square kilometres of drainage area.

STREAM IMPACTS The results of changing the terrestrial or vegetative conditions in areas surrounding or uphill from a stream system (e.g., the removal of forest cover reduces evapotranspiration rates and increases stream flows, alters water temperatures and light regimes in the stream, and eliminates certain sources of nutrient inputs to the stream, such as leaf litter and insects). In addition, the lack of forest cover eliminates interception of precipitation, and thus increases runoff volumes.

Road and other construction activities cause compaction and altered surface and subsurface drainage patterns, leading to either increases (channelization) or decreases (higher infiltration due to blocked seepage) in water flows, especially peak flows and low summer flows. Road construction and logging lead to extensive soil disturbance, and unless adequate protection measures are taken, high rates of soil erosion and downstream siltation will occur, leading to loss or severe modification of stream habitats. Other examples include fertilizer and pesticide runoff from agricultural activities.

STREAM ORDER A system of stream classification based on a number from one to six or higher, ranked from headwaters to river terminus, that designates the relative position of a stream or stream segment in a drainage basin. The smallest, unbranched, perennial tributaries, terminating at an outer point, are first-order streams. Two first-order streams join to make a second-order stream. A third-order stream has only first- and second-order tributaries, and so on. The illustration shows a hypothetical stream with four orders.

STREAM REACH A relatively homogeneous section of a stream having a repetitious sequence of physical processes, characteristics, and habitat types. Any specified length of a stream. A regime of hydraulic units whose overall profile is different from another reach.

stream order

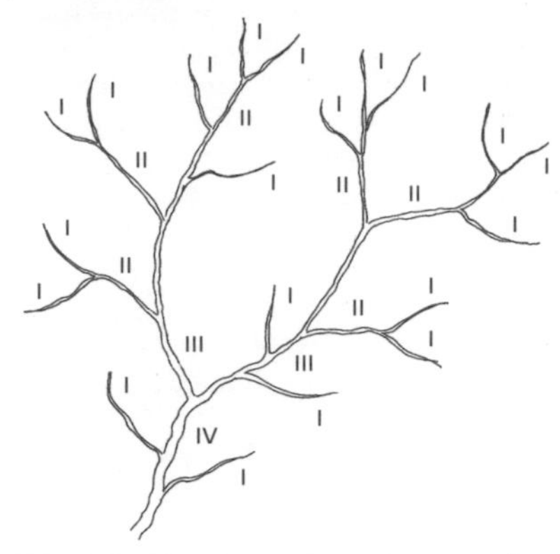

STREAM REACH CLASSES and LAKES A method used to classify the fisheries habitat values and integrate these with planned forest management activities within the entire watershed. Three classes are recognized (based on the British Columbia scheme), and are typically mapped at a scale of 1:20,000 for initial planning, and at a scale of 1:5,000 for operational planning. Classification schemes will vary by jurisdiction. **Class A** includes streams or portions of streams that are frequented by anadromous salmonids and/or resident sport fish or regionally significant fish species; or streams that have been identified for fishery enhancement in an approved fishery management plan. Stream gradient is usually less than 12 per cent. The objective is to maintain the productive capacity of fish habitats, including water quality and stream channel characteristics. **Class B** includes streams or portions of streams that are populated by resident fish not currently designated as sport fish or regionally significant fish. Stream gradient is usually 8 to 20 per cent. The objective is to maintain the genetic stock of indigenous species and maintain stream-channel integrity necessary to protect downstream Class A waters and marine-sensitive zones that may be affected by accelerated transport of sediment or debris or increased stream temperatures. **Class C** includes streams or portions of streams that are not frequented by fish. Stream gradient is usually greater than 20 per cent. The objective is to maintain stream-channel integrity necessary to protect downstream Class A and B portions of streams and marine-sensitive zones that may be affected by accelerated transport of sediment or debris or increased stream temperatures. **Lakes** include lakes that are frequented by anadromous salmonids and/or resident sport fish species, or regionally significant fish species are Class A. Lakes that contain only resident, non-sport fish species or fish species not designated as regionally significant fish are Class B. Lakes not frequented by fish are Class C.

STREAMSIDE MANAGEMENT ZONES The land and the vegetation it supports immediately in contact with the stream or sufficiently close to have a major influence on the total ecological character and functional processes of the stream. The zone is measured from stream margins, generally considered to be the point at which frequent wetting takes place in the high water season, and where a vegetation change is clearly seen. The size and configuration of a streamside management zone depends on the site, the fisheries value classification (Stream Reach Class I to IV), and the purposes intended. *See also* Buffer Zone; Stream Reach Classes and Lakes.

STRESS **1** Any environmental factor that restricts growth and/or reproduction of an organism or a population (e.g., significant shortage of soil moisture may place a plant under stress). **2** Any stimulus or other factor acting to disturb the steady state of an organism or other system. **3** In mechanics, a force distributed over an area, arising from the action of one body on another, or one part of a body on another part. In wood, stress refers to forces developed in resistance to loading. This resistance may be lessened by pest damage, especially fungal action. *See also* Reaction Wood; Strain.

STREAM TERRACE One of a series of platforms in a stream valley, flanking and more or less parallel to the stream channel, originally formed near the level of the stream and representing the dissected remnants of an abandoned floodplain, stream bed, or valley floor produced during a former stage of erosion or deposition. Erosional surfaces cut on bedrock and thinly mantled with stream deposits (alluvium) are designated 'strath terraces.' Remnants of constructional valley floors are termed 'alluvial terraces.'

STREAM TRANSPORT CAPABILITY The capability of a stream to move organic debris or sediment down the stream channel during seasonal water flows. It may not occur every year and is determined by many complex factors, including volume, intensity, and timing of water flows; condition, age, and stability of the debris; and channel shape.

STRESS **1** Any environmental factor that restricts growth and/or reproduction of an organism or a population (e.g., significant shortage of soil moisture may place a plant under stress). **2** Any stimulus or other factor acting to disturb the steady state of an organism or other system. **3** In mechanics, a force distributed over an area, arising from the action of one body on another, or one part of a body on another part. In wood, stress refers to forces developed in resistance to loading. This resistance may be lessened by pest damage, especially fungal action. *See also* Reaction Wood; Strain.

STRESSOR Any chemical, physical, or biological entity that can induce adverse effects on individuals, populations, communities, or ecosystems.

STRIAE, STRIATIONS Finely cut lines (scratches) on the surface of bedrock or clasts formed by glacial abrasion. They are oriented parallel to former ice-flow direction. More than one ice-flow direction may be represented by criss-crossing striae.

STRIATE Marked with lines, channels, or ridges.

STRICT Botanically, standing upright, and straight.

STRIGOSE Covered with flattened, fine, bristle-like hairs.

STRIKE The compass bearing of the line of intersection formed by a structural rock feature (bed or fault) with the horizontal surface of an imaginary plane. Strike is at ninety degrees to the dip. *See also* Dip.

STRING DROP *See* Incremental Drop.

STRIP CRUISE A cruise in which the plots measured are in the shape of long, narrow strips.

STRIP CUTTING The removal of trees in one or more passes in a system of strips of various widths. It is designed to encourage regeneration on difficult and/or fragile sites.

STRIPPING **1** Completely peeling the bark off a tree or log. It is often done to expose bark beetle broods to adverse environmental conditions or to physically remove and destroy them. **2** A technique used by First Nations cultures for gathering bark for material to make clothing, baskets and other containers (especially red or yellow cedar bark), the preparation of medicinal concoctions, and other uses.

STRIP TRANSECT METHOD In avian conservation, a procedure using a strip of land or water of fixed direction that is sampled visually and/or aurally by an observer. Counts may be one of the following: fixed distance (width) counts, limited to a strip of set width for all or specially chosen species; variable distance (width) counts, with different, species-specific widths that are determined to reflect detection attenuation; or unlimited distance counts, in which all detections are recorded regardless of distance. It is also termed belt-transect. *See also* Point Count.

STROBILE/STROBILUS A conelike reproductive structure having a central axis or branch bearing sporophylls. It is sometimes used incorrectly as an equivalent to the more restrictive term cone. *See also* Cone.

STROMA Plural stromata. **1** In fungi, a mass of hyphae with or without plant tissue or other substrate, in or on which spores or fruiting bodies are produced. They can be micro- or macroscopic, colourless to bright or dark in colour, and can form on or in the substrate. **2** In plants, the colourless regions in chloroplasts in between grana, containing enzymes associated with the fixation of carbon dioxide. **3** In animals, the supporting tissue around organs, including the nerves and blood vessels. It also refers to the transparent, spongy framework around red blood cells.

STRUCTURAL BACKSLOPE *See* Dipslope.

STRUCTURAL BENCH A platform-type, nearly level to gently inclined erosional surface developed on resistant strata in areas where valleys are cut in alternating strong and weak layers that have an almost horizontal attitude. In contrast to stream terraces, structural benches have no geomorphic implication of former, partial erosion cycles and base-level controls, nor do they represent a stage of floodplain development after an episode of valley trenching.

STRUCTURAL DEFECT In hazard-tree assessments, any internal or external points of weakness that might reduce the stability of the tree or its component parts.

STRUCTURAL DIVERSITY The diversity of forest structure, both vertical and horizontal, that provides for a variety of forest habitats for plants and animals. The variety results from layering or tiering of the canopy and die-back, death, and ultimate decay of trees. In aquatic habitats, structural diversity results from the presence of a variety of structural features, such as logs and boulders, that create a variety of habitats. *See also* Horizontal Diversity; Vertical Diversity.

STRUCTURAL RETENTION Harvest practices that leave physical elements (e.g., green trees, snags, down logs, coarse, woody debris) of the late successional or old-growth forest on site after harvest.

STRUCTURE **1** In forestry generally, the various horizontal and vertical physical elements of the forest. **2** In landscape ecology, the spatial interrelationships between ecosystems, including energy fluxes, distribution of materials and species relative to the sizes, shapes, numbers, kinds, and configurations of the ecosystems. **3** The distribution of trees in a stand or group by age, size, or crown classes (e.g., all-aged, even-aged, uneven-aged, regular, and irregular structures). *See also* Horizontal Diversity; Vertical Structure.

STUB **1** In wildlife tree retention, an artificially created wildlife tree at least three metres in height or a standing, dead tree broken off at about six metres, with few if any remaining branches. **2** In pruning, a short piece of branchwood not pruned off. Stubs are considered to be a major site of disease infection and are a sign of poor pruning technique.

STUBBLING A method of killing brush and small-diameter trees. The competing vegetation is slashed or felled and the remaining stubble is sprayed with a herbicide. *See also* Hack-and-Squirt.

STUMP The woody base of a tree that remains upright after the rest of the tree has fallen as a result of decay or rotting or having been cut down. *See also* Root Wad.

STUMPAGE The price charged for the right to harvest timber from publicly or privately owned forest land.

STUMP TREATMENT The application of herbicide to or near stumps to prevent the growth of sprouts and suckers, or treatment with a chemical substance that prevents or inhibits the spread of disease.

STUNTED A plant that is smaller and less vigorous than would be typical, due to unfavourable environmental conditions or disease.

STUNTING The natural, or genetically or environmentally induced dwarfing of the whole plant.

STYLE The middle portion of the pistil, often elongated, between the ovary and the stigma. *See also* Carpel (for illustration).

STYLET The needlelike part of the piercing-sucking mouthparts of certain insects.

STYLOPODIUM An enlargement or disc-like expansion at the base of the style, as exemplified in some Umbelliferae.

STYPTIC A substance that when applied to an

open wound in animals, causes contraction of the nearby tissues, especially the blood vessels, and thus acts to slow or stop the bleeding.

SUB- A prefix meaning: (1) nearly, somewhat, slightly; or (2) below, under.

SUBCLIMAX COMMUNITY A successional stage along a sere that has been prevented from progressing to the climax or steady-state community by fire, grazing, or similar disturbances.

SUBCOMPARTMENT A division within a compartment that permits a more detailed level of treatment.

SUBCUTICULAR Beneath the cuticle of a plant, on the epidermis.

SUB-DRAINAGE A land area (basin) bounded by ridges or similar topographic features, encompassing only part of a watershed. *See also* Drainage; Watershed.

SUBEROSE Corky in texture and appearance.

SUBGLACIAL Pertaining to the area underneath a glacier or the base of a glacier.

SUBGLACIAL TILL Material that accumulates directly from melting ice at the base of a glacier. It includes basal till and lodgement till.

SUBHERBACEOUS Herbaceous, but becoming woody later in the growing season.

SUBJECTIVE The use of one's own worldview, attitudes, or opinions as a basis for decision-making, rather than using the merits or facts of the matter in a more objective way. Most objective decisions include a degree of subjectivity. *See also* Balanced Objectivism; Objective.

SUBLETHAL A stimulus or substance that impairs functions but does not cause death.

SUBMERGENT VEGETATION Plants that are rooted in and grow in the sediments at the bottom of a freshwater or saltwater body. *See also* Emergent Vegetation.

SUBPETIOLAR Located under the petiole and often enveloped by it.

SUBPOPULATION A well-defined set of interacting individuals that compose a proportion of a larger, interbreeding meta-population.

SUBSHRUB A suffrutescent perennial plant having basally woody stems, or a very low shrub that might more often be considered a perennial herb.

SUBSIDENCE **1** In meteorology, a term referring to the descending motion of air in the atmosphere, usually extending over a rather broad area and accompanied by warming and drying. *See also* Convection. **2** In a geological sense, the collapse or sinking of the ground's surface due to subsurface changes in structure.

SUBSIDY Economic assistance granted directly or indirectly by governments or other agencies or entities to facilitate actions or activities that are deemed to be socially desirable and in the broad public interest. Typically, it is a means of reducing or defraying the true costs of a project.

SUBSOIL The B horizon of a soil profile.

SUBSPECIES A taxon of a rank situated between species and variety. The term has various implications depending on the user and can mean a distinct geographical distribution, a group of varieties, or a distinct variety if only one infra-specific variety is in use.

SUBSTRATE **1** The abiotic material forming the bed of a stream, lake, or ocean. **2** The nutrient medium or physical structure on which an organism feeds and develops. In fishery management, the substrate is of great importance in ensuring successful fish spawning. The gravel substrate of spawning rivers needs to be between one and fifteen centimetres in diameter. This permits water to flow between the gravel and provide adequate oxygen supply to fish embryos and alevin while at the same time removing organic wastes. Larger substrate sizes provide habitat for benthic invertebrates and hiding cover for young fish. *See also* Substratum. **3** The material upon which plants grow.

SUBSTRATE PARTICLE SIZE The abiotic materials of a stream bed are classified by size as shown:

Particle name	Size (millimetres)	Size (inches)
Large boulder	> 1,024	40-160
Small boulder	256-1,024	10-40
Large cobble (rubble)	128-256	5-10
Small cobble (rubble)	64-128	2.5-5
Gravel	2-64	0.08-2.5
Sand	0.062-2	
Silt	0.004-0.062	
Clay	< 0.004	

SUBSTRATUM **1** The material underlying something, such as the soil below plants and animals. **2** A lower layer of soil or rock.

SUBSURFACE FIRE *See* Forest Fire (ground fire).

SUBTEND Standing below and close to another part (e.g., a bract immediately below a flower).

SUBULATE Awl-shaped, linear, and very narrow, tapering from the base to a sharp apex. *See also* Awl-Shaped; Leaf Shape.

SUCCESSION A series of dynamic changes in ecosystem structure, function, and species composition over time as a result of which one group of organisms succeeds another through stages leading to a potential natural community or climax stage. For example, the series of plant communities (seral stages) following a major disturbance. Primary succession occurs when organisms colonize a previously sterile area (i.e., it has no biological legacy to pass on). Secondary succession occurs on sites that have previously been colonized and subsequently disturbed in some manner. The illustration shows a typical series of successional changes in a southern Ontario Carolinian forest stand. *See also* Seral Stages.

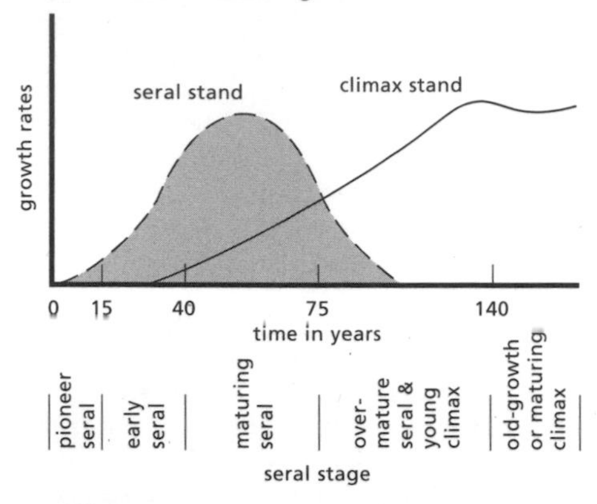

SUCCESSIONAL PATHWAY The probable course of plant community development within a defined framework of seral stages for a particular disturbance regime.

SUCCULENT Juicy, fleshy, soft in texture, and usually thickened. A characteristic of plants capable of storing water within the cells of stems and/or in leaves, which are often considerably modified in form to minimize water losses.

SUCKER *See* Epicormic Shoot.

SUCTORIAL Any insect adapted for sucking out fluids from a host through specialized mouthparts that can pierce cells.

SUDDEN LIMB DROP The sudden failure of branches within a tree, often seen in warm weather with no winds. It is characteristic of some species, such as elms, although it is often difficult to predict which limbs might fail.

SUFFRUCTICOSE A degree above suffrutescent, where the woody stems are permanent and persistent but still close to the ground.

SUFFRUTESCENT A plant having the lower part of the stem only just above ground level, woody at the base, and perennial.

SUGAR BUSH Colloquial for a stand of sugar maples from which maple sap is harvested.

SULCATE Grooved or furrowed along the main axis.

SUMMER PLUMAGE The plumage of a bird that replaces the worn winter feathers during the breeding season. Summer plumage is often more brightly coloured than winter plumage and serves to advertize the individual's sex and/or sexual maturity. Summer plumage plays an important role in the quest for a mate. It is synonymous with breeding plumage. *See also* Winter Plumage.

SUMMER RESIDENT A species of organism that moves into an area for feeding and/or reproductive reasons during the summer period.

SUNSCALD Localized injury to bark and cambium often resulting in wounds or a blanching of leaves. It is caused by a sudden increase in exposure of the plant to intense sunshine and high temperatures. *See also* Leaf Scorch; Winter Sunscald.

SUPER-/SUPRA- A prefix meaning above, beyond, greater than, superior to.

SUPERFICIAL On the surface only; shallow, lacking depth.

SUPERIOR Describes the relative position of a part of an organ; above, higher, on top. *See also* Inferior.

SUPERPARASITISM **1** The simultaneous infestation of an individual host by two or more individuals of the same parasite species. **2** In entomology, the infestation of an individual host by a greater number of individuals of one parasite species than can be supported for complete development by that host. *See also* Hyperparasite; Multiple Parasitism; Parasite; Parasitoid.

SUPERSPECIES Two closely related species that are believed to have diverged relatively recently.

SUPINE Prostrate, lying down, reclined.

SUPPLY **1** The functional relationship between the price of a given commodity or service and the quantity that sellers would be willing and able to sell in a given market during a specified time period. It is typically expressed as a mathematical equation (showing quantity supplied as a function of price) or as a curve showing price per unit plotted over quantity. **2** The actual quantity of a commodity or service offered by sellers in the market over a period of time. *See also* Demand.

SUPPRESSANT An agent used to extinguish the flaming and smouldering or glowing stages of combustion by direct application to burning fuels. *See also* Short-term Retardant.

SUPPRESSION **1** The reduction of a pest population to socially, politically, and economically acceptable levels by the application of silvicultural, mechanical, manual, biological, and/or chemical control measures. *See also* Direct

Suppression; Indirect Suppression. **2** In fire management, the immediate containment of all fires and the use of active measures to control and extinguish the fires.

SUPPRESSION CREW A unit of fire fighters assembled and organized for conducting fire suppression, either for initial attack and/or continuing work on fires. Crew size, specialization, and configuration are determined by agency procedures. It is synonymous with fire crew.

SUPRAFOLIAR Borne above a leaf or leaves.

SUPRAGLACIAL Pertaining to the upper surface of a glacier.

SURFACE EROSION The detachment and transport of soil particles by wind, water, or gravity. Surface erosion can occur as the loss of soil in a uniform layer (sheet erosion), in dry rills, or by dry ravel. A group of processes whereby soil materials are removed by running water, waves and currents, moving ice, or wind.

SURFACE EXPRESSION Refers to small topographic features and landforms that are not usually shown adequately on a topographic map, and to the relation of a surficial material to the underlying surface; terminology, such as 'terrace,' 'cone,' is defined in a non-genetic sense.

SURFACE FIRE *See* Forest Fire.

SURFACE FUELS All combustible materials lying above the duff layer between the ground and ladder fuels that are responsible for propagating surface fires (e.g., litter, herbaceous vegetation, low and medium shrubs, tree seedlings, stumps, downed, dead roundwood). *See also* Aerial Fuels.

SURFACE WIND Wind measured at a surface observation station, customarily at some distance (usually six meters or twenty feet) above ground to minimize the distorting effects of local obstacles and terrain.

SURFACTANT Short for surface-active agent. Surfactants are chemicals that modify the relationship between the surfaces of two liquids or a liquid and a solid, thus facilitating and enhancing the emulsifying, dispersing, wetting, spreading, sticking, and penetrating properties of the liquids. They are used to increase the retention and penetration of herbicides on and into plants.

SURFICIAL GEOLOGY The geology of surficial materials.

SURFICIAL GEOLOGY MAP A map that shows the types and distribution of surficial materials in a chronostratigraphic framework.

SURFICIAL MATERIALS Relatively young, nonlithified sediments, usually of Quaternary age; usually classified as to their genesis, hence fluvial sediments, colluvium, glaciolacustrine sediments, etc.

SURVEILLANCE In pest management, pest detection carried out by field personnel in conjunction with other routine activities, such as inventory, trail maintenance, fire reconnaissance, or stand tending. Surveillance consists of recognizing and reporting unusual pest activity and abnormal tree or stand conditions. It is sometimes used synonymously with the term monitoring. *See also* Monitoring.

SURVEY As a verb, the systematic measuring and/or observation of attributes to determine their relative position on, above, or below the Earth's surface (e.g., in a forest area to detect pest outbreaks, estimate pest abundance and/or evaluate damage). As a noun, the results of survey activities, or the organization responsible for undertaking a survey. Surveys are undertaken by means of: (1) **aerial surveys**, which utilize aerial photographs as part of the surveying operation, or the process of taking aerial photographs for surveying purposes; (2) **ground surveys**, which utilize measurements made from the ground that may or may not include the use of aerial photographs; and (3) **photogrammetric surveys**, which utilize either ground or aerial photographs.

Surveys that make no allowance for the curvature of the Earth are termed **plane surveys.** Surveys that include an allowance for the curvature of the Earth's surface are termed **geodetic surveys.**

SURVEY AREA The land base about which information is needed. It is the total land base from which a sample is drawn.

SURVEY INTENSITY (LEVEL) Expresses the relation between map scale and the amount of field checking carried out during preparation of a terrain map.

SURVIVAL The proportion of newborn individuals alive at a given age.

SURVIVAL RATE The average proportion of individuals in a sample or a proportion that survive for a given period.

SURVIVORSHIP The rate of survival or the proportion of individuals of a species or population surviving over a specified period, such as a development stage, generation or age class.

SURVIVORSHIP CURVE Data regarding the number of survivors at the start of each age interval in a life table can be graphically represented by a survivorship curve. Cohort life tables are constructed by monitoring the survival of a group of individuals (cohort), until they are all dead. Static life tables are constructed by examining the age-class structure of a population at a particular moment in time. While there are four major types of survivorship curves to which a population may conform (see illustration), other populations may be characterized by curves intermediate to the main types. **Type I** is a survivorship curve in which population mortality occurs near the end of the life span of the organisms. **Type II** is a survivorship curve in which population mortality is evenly distributed across all age classes, resulting in a constant number of deaths over time, and a fairly uniform percentage decrease in the number of survivors. **Type III** survivorship curves occur when there is a constant percentage of mortality amongst the remaining members of each age class. **Type IV** is a survivorship curve in which population mortality is heavy in the juvenile age classes, followed by a low and constant mortality for the rest of the age classes. *See* illustration.

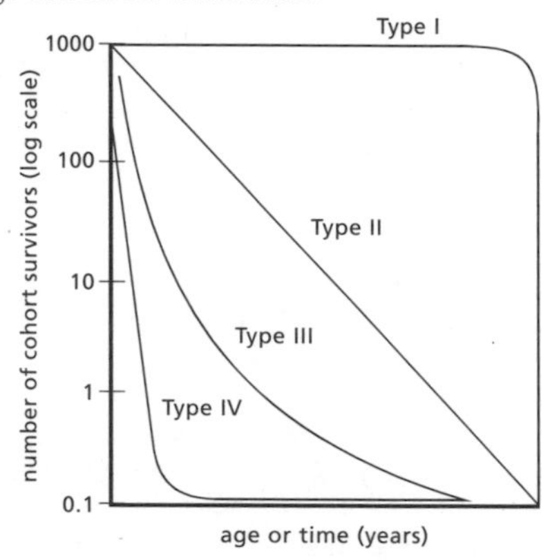

SUSCEPTIBLE Lacking the ability to withstand attack by an organism or abiotic agent without incurring serious damage and/or injury. The degree to which an organism is subject to infection or infestation by another organism. It is the opposite of resistance. *See also* Sensitivity.

SUSPECT TREE Any tree that upon detailed inspection appears to have some internal problems that are being manifested by external indicators. Indicators of decay include signs on or immediately adjacent to the trunk of the tree, such as conks, blind conks, scars, fork or crook, frost crack, trunk infections of mistletoe, rotten branches, cavities, dead or broken tops. External indications of insect problems include discoloured foliage, frass or boring dust, entry or exit holes. External indicators of root damage include otherwise inexplicable dieback on one side of the tree (typically above the damaged roots), fruiting bodies at the base of the tree, changed soil grades or soil compaction.

SUSPENDED SEDIMENT Sediment suspended in a fluid by the upward components of turbulent currents or by colloidal suspension. *See also* Bedload; Dissolved Load; Sediment Yield.

SUSTAINABILITY The ability of an ecosystem to maintain ecological processes and functions, biological diversity, and productivity over time.

SUSTAINABLE DEVELOPMENT A conceptual ideal where development (in whatever form that might be) meets the needs of the present generations without compromising the ability of future generations to meet their own needs. It implies meeting the basic needs of all and extending to all the opportunity to fulfil their aspirations for a better life. It is not a fixed state of harmony, but rather a process of change in which the exploitation of resources, their renewability, the direction of investments, the orientation of technological development, and institutional needs are made consistent with future as well as present needs.

The concept has conceptual merit, but practical difficulties, including political and economic realities, as well as technological limitations, may act to temper the ideal. Projected over a long enough time span, the concept may be unrealistic, since the burgeoning global population daily places ever-increasing rates of stress on finite resources in a non-sustainable manner. However, as a concept, it has made some profound changes in the attitudes as to how these finite resources are being developed.

SUSTAINABLE FOREST DEVELOPMENT Maintaining, without unacceptable impairment, the productive and renewal capacities, as well as the genetic, species, and ecological diversity of forest ecosystems.

SUSTAINABLE FOREST MANAGEMENT Forest management regimes that maintain the productive and renewal capacities, as well as the genetic, species and ecological diversity of forest ecosystems. Sustainable forest management is required to obtain sustainable forest development.

SUSTAINABLE GROWTH An oxymoron. No biotic or abiotic features on the planet have the capacity for indefinite growth.

SUSTAINABLE HARVEST SURPLUS *See* Harvestable Surplus.

SUSTAINABLE MANAGEMENT Managing the use, development, and protection of natural and physical resources in a manner or at a rate that enables people and communities to provide for their social, economic, and cultural well-being, and for their health and safety while (1) sustaining the potential of natural and physical resources (excluding minerals) to meet reasonably foreseeable needs of future generations; (2) safeguarding the life-supporting capacity of air, water, soil, and ecosystems; and (3) avoiding, remedying, or mitigating any adverse effects of activities on the environment.

SUSTAINABLE USE Use of an organism, ecosystem, or other renewable resource at a rate that does not exceed its capacity for renewal.

SUSTAINED DEVELOPMENT Development that has been, is now, or is planned at a rate that has little or no regard for social and ecological constraints, and is thus, in the longer term, unsustainable.

SUSTAINED YIELD **1** The quantity of a resource that can be produced continuously under a given management regime (i.e., the rate of harvest equals the rate of production). **2** In timber management, a theoretical calculation of the yields of wood fibre possible on a continuing basis from a forest under a specified management regime. The calculations are based on data about the age-class composition; species; site productivity; the extent of the land base available now and in the future; the past, present, and predicted management and growth rates; and the likely extent of losses due to fire, pests, and diseases. By iteratively modelling a range of optimistic or pessimistic scenarios, a long-run, sustained-yield figure can be chosen that satisfies predetermined management and societal goals. This long-term, sustained-yield figure can then be used to organize and schedule all other management activities in the shorter and longer terms, including the establishment of an allowable annual cut figure. However, if any of the factors subsequently prove to have been incorrect, the scenario must be recalculated to better reflect the changing circumstances. The phrase sustained yield is not necessarily synonymous with sustainable development, since maximizing one output from the forest land base (e.g., sustained timber yields) may minimize other outputs of potentially equal or greater value to society. *See also* Annual Allowable Cut; Sustainable Development.

SUTURE A line, groove, or seam where two or more surfaces or margins join or split apart.

SWALE A slight depression in generally level ground that may be slightly swampy.

SWAMP A type of wetland where trees or tall shrubs dominate a landscape characterized by periodic flooding. Swamps have a nearly permanent, subsurface, nutrient-rich water flow through the substrate of mineral sediments and organic materials; peat accumulations are seldom present, unless in the form of well-decomposed wood. *See also* Bog; Fen; Marsh; Wetland.

SWARM The simultaneous emergence or assembly of large numbers of one species of insect in one place or locality.

SWATH CUTTER *See* Harvesting Machine Classification.

SWEEPER LOG **1** A long log overhanging the back end of a logging truck, thus posing a danger to other traffic on the haul road as the log tends to 'sweep' the road width on curves and corners. **2** Logs jammed or otherwise hung-up in rivers that pose a hazard to navigation on the river. *See also* Large Organic Debris.

SWING The rotation of a photograph in its own plane around the photograph perpendicular from some reference direction (e.g., the direction of flight). Swing may be designated by the symbol kappa (K). Swing is also the angle at the principal point of a photograph that is measured clockwise from the positive *y* axis to the principal line at the nadir point. *See also* Nadir Point; Yaw.

SWITCHING A change in the focus of a bark beetle aggregation and attack from one host tree with a relatively large number of beetles on it, to another as yet uncolonized tree.

SYLVICULTURE *See* Silviculture.

SYMBIONT One of the organisms involved in a symbiotic relationship. It is also a form of mutually beneficial parasitism. *See also* Parasite.

SYMBIOSIS **1** Generally, a long-term association between two different species living together. **2** May be restricted to organisms that have mutually beneficial relationships (mutualism), but can also include commensalism and parasitism that would be harmful to one of the organisms.

SYMMETRICAL **1** A body capable of division into approximately equal halves. **2** Less correctly, the term is used in more restrictive ways, such as radial symmetry (equal radial parts around a centre point), trilateral symmetry (division into three equal parts). **3** It describes flowers having similar numbers of parts in the calyx, corolla, and androecium. *See also* Actinomorphic.

SYMPATRIC Living in the same place. Typically, refers to areas where species populations overlap. *See also* Allopatric; Parapatric.

SYMPETALOUS A flower in which all the petals are coalescent at the base and possibly further up; gamopetalous.

SYMPHYSIS The junction boundary between two bones that have grown together.

SYMPODIAL A growth habit in which the growth of the stem or rhizome is periodically stopped by the death of the terminal bud or development of an inflorescence, with subsequent growth continued by a lateral branch. *See also* Monopodial.

SYMPTOM **1** The visual evidence of a host plant reacting to infection, disease, or other forms of pest attack (e.g., chlorosis, necrosis, galls, brooms, or stunting). **2** The external and internal reactions or alterations of an organism as a result of a disease or pest. *See also* Sign.

SYNANDRIUM An androecium where the anthers are fused or connate.

SYNANGIUM An aggregation of connate sporangia.

SYNCARP A structure having the appearance of a compound fruit, but is actually composed of several fruits almost coalesced. Fruits from a single flower, such as magnolia, are termed aggregate fruits, while those arising from several flowers, such as pineapple, are termed multiple fruits. *See also* Fruit (for illustration).

SYNCARPOUS Having carpels united. It describes an ovary of two or more carpels, but sometimes used when the separate pistils within one flower are partially united. *See also* Apocarpous.

SYNCLINE A linear, downward fold in sedimentary strata. *See also* Anticline; Fold; Monocline.

SYNDROME **1** The pattern of symptoms and signs in a disease. **2** The totality of effects produced in a host by a particular disease, whether simultaneously or successively and whether detectable to the unaided eye or not.

SYNECOLOGY The study of the ecology of groups of organisms (i.e., communities in relation to environmental conditions). *See also* Autecology.

SYNERGISM The phenomenon where two or more biotic or abiotic substances or processes interact at one time, or in sequence, with the net effect being greater than the sum of the independent effects of each substance or process. In pesticide formulation, the effect sometimes leads to a toxicity higher than would be expected from the individual active ingredients.

SYNGAMEON The most inclusive group of species capable of limited interbreeding.

SYNGENIOUS Having the anthers connate in a ring around the style (e.g., the stamens in Compositae).

SYNNEMA Plural synnemata. **1** In fungi, an aggregation of conidiophores bound together into an elongate, spore-bearing structure, sometimes large enough to be seen with the naked eye. It is also termed coremium, plural coremia. **2** In plants, the united stamen filaments borne on a monadelphous flower.

SYNOECIOUS Plants having perfect flowers.

SYNOMONE A semiochemical emitted by an individual of one species that, when contacted by an individual of another species, induces a behavioural or physiological response favourable to both. *See also* Allelochemical; Allomone; Kairomone; Pheromone; Semiochemicals.

SYNONYM In plant nomenclature, a name no longer in use due to re-arrangement of the classification because another plant was already named earlier with the same name, or because the name does not comply with internationally accepted codes.

SYNOPTIC CHART Any map on which weather data and analysis are presented depicting the state of meteorological conditions over a large area at the Earth's surface and at various levels in the upper atmosphere at a particular time. It is synonymous with weather map.

SYNSEPALOUS Having connate sepals; gamosepalous.

SYNTHETIC APERTURE RADAR (SAR) A side-looking airborne or space-borne imaging system that uses the Doppler principle to sharpen the effective beam width of the antenna. The result is improved resolution in the azimuth direction (direction of vehicle travel) and constant resolution in the range direction (direction of radar to target). The radar backscatter is recorded on tape or on film and must be digitally or optically processed to form radar images.

SYNTOPIC Describes populations or species that occupy the same macrohabitat.

SYNTYPE *See* Type.

SYNZOOCHORE *See* Zoochore.

SYSTEMATICS The determination of the groups to be used in taxonomic classifications based on evolutionary, genetic, and phenotypic differences or affinities. *See also* Binomial Nomenclature; Taxonomy; Appendix 1: Classification of Organisms.

SYSTEMIC Any substance or influence capable of affecting or spreading throughout the whole plant.

SYSTEMIC INFECTION **1** An infection affecting or spreading internally throughout the host's body and not localized. **2** A dwarf mistletoe infection in which the absorptive system of the parasite is in the terminal bud of the host twig and keeps pace with the twig's growth.

SYSTEMIC PESTICIDE A chemical that is transported through the vascular system of a plant. In the case of an insecticide or acaricide, the purpose is to reach the sucking insects or mites. In the case of a translocated herbicide, the chemical can pass through the plant and even to other plants, via root grafts, producing its effects throughout the plant, rather than merely at or near the points of contact. In the case of a fungicide, the target fungus is affected at points beyond the point of contact.

T

TAGLINE An extra length of line at the end of a main line. It is used as an extension for carrying additional choker hooks, or to dampen the swing of a bucket or grapple on a boom-type loader.

TAIL BLOCK A block fixed to a stump at the outer edge of a setting in ground-lead or high-lead cable logging, or to the tail spar in skyline cable logging. The haul-back line passes through the tail block for returning the main line and butt rigging to the loading point.

TAILED Botanically, anthers having spurlike appendages on the back (e.g., some of the Ericaceae), or at their base (e.g., some of the Compositae).

TAILHOLD In cable logging, the anchorage at the outer end of the skyline away from the landing. It is also the line securing a machine to a stump.

TALLY In inventory work, as a noun meaning a record of the number of units counted or measured, by one or more classes. As a verb, the recording of the number of units counted or measured by one or more classes.

TALUS Angular rock fragments accumulated at the foot of a steep rock slope and being the product of successive rock falls; a type of colluvium.

TALUS SLOPE A slope of about thirty-five degrees, the natural angle of rest of non-cohesive rock fragments, and underlain by talus. It is usually located at the foot of a rock slope that is steeper than thirty-five degrees. The illustration shows how a talus slope develops from broken rock fragments at the base of a cliff. *See also* Angle of Repose.

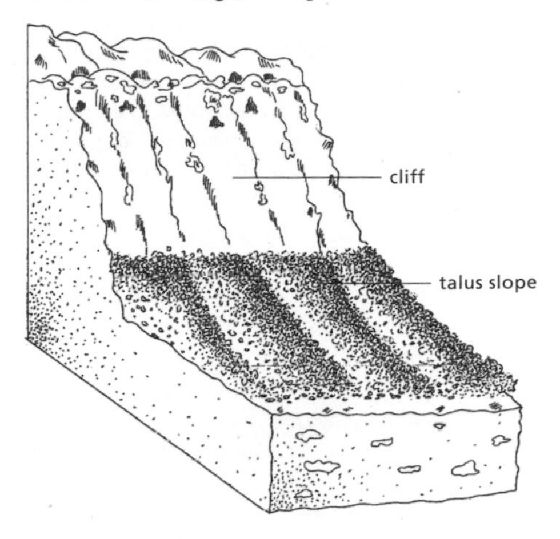

TAPER The decline in diameter of a tree stem or log moving from the base (larger) to the top (smaller). The taper factor is an indication of how large the taper is and is used in the calculation of tree volumes.

TARGET **1** In photogrammetry, one or more distinctive marks placed on the ground or a clearly identifiable ground feature that can be used in identifying locations on an aerial photograph. It is also the location of the actual ground target on an image. **2** The organism at which a particular chemical or other control or management treatment is directed. *See also* Non-target Organism. **3** A fire location for fire-bombing controllers. **4** In hazard-tree assessment, people or property that are within the striking range of a tree, or part of a tree, were it to fall.

TARGET AREA **1** The area to which a pesticide or other treatment is to be applied. **2** The surface area of potential hosts exposed to fungal spores or dwarf mistletoe seeds. **3** The area that would be affected if a hazard tree were to fail.

TARIFF An official schedule of taxes (customs duties) imposed on imported (less commonly on exported) goods, either as a percentage of their value (ad valorem tariffs) or as an amount per unit of measure, generally weight or volume (specific tariffs).

TARSPOTS **1** Large black blotches on the foliage of hardwoods due to the presence of fungi. **2** The common name for the leaf spot diseases of maples due to the fungus *Rhytisma.*

TARSUS **1** Ankle bones in humans and terrestrial vertebrates. **2** The foot of an insect, consisting of one to five segments.

TAXON Plural taxa. A category in classification systems, such as class, family, or phylum.

TAXONOMIC DIVERSITY A measurement of species diversity that takes into account the relatedness of species. For example, the land has many more species that the sea, but the species on land are more closely related to each other that the species in the ocean. Thus, the diversity of marine ecosystems is higher than a strict count of species would imply.

TAXONOMY A means of classifying living or extinct organisms based on their anatomy, morphology, and biochemical and genetic characteristics. It is often used synonymously with systematics. *See also* Binomial Nomenclature; Systematics; Appendix 1: Classification of Organisms.

TECHNICAL EFFICIENCY The degree to which a business as a whole, or a machine or process used in that business, employs technically valid knowledge in an efficient manner to facilitate the production of outputs (goods and/or services).

TELERELASCOPE A relascope coupled with enlarging optics designed for use as a dendrometer. *See also* Dendrometer; Relascope.

TELIOSPORE The spore of the rust fungi from which the perfect stage of the basidium and basidiospore arise.

TELIUM Plural telia. In rust fungi, a fruiting body composed of teliospores, produced after the uredinial stage in the life cycle of a rust.

TELOCENTRIC A chromosome having a terminal centromere. *See also* Acrocentric; Metacentric.

TEMPERATE NORTH AMERICA That area of land and water that lies between the Tropic of Cancer and the Arctic Circle.

TEMPLATE In photogrammetry, a template is a graphical representation of a photograph. It records the directions or radials taken from the photograph. A **hand template** is made by tracing the radials from a photograph onto a transparent medium, such as a sheet of plastic. Hand templates are laid out and adjusted manually to form the radial triangulation. A **slotted template** is where the radials are represented as slots cut into a sheet of card or metal. *See also* Radial.

TENDING Any activity designed to improve the overall characteristics of individual trees, entire stands, or entire forests. Tending takes place throughout the life of a forest and includes the activities taking place after tree establishment, such as removal of competing vegetation (weeding, cleaning, girdling), thinning, spacing, pruning, and fertilization.

TENDRIL A twining, threadlike process or extension by which a plant grasps or clings by adhesion as a means of gaining support. It can be a part of a branch or a leaf. Initially soft and pliable, tendrils usually harden once support has been obtained.

TENERAL ADULT *See* Callow Adult.

TENSION CRACKS Open fissures in bedrock or surficial materials resulting from tensile stress. It is typically located at or near the crest of a steep slope and is indicative of potential slope failure.

TENSION WOOD *See* Reaction Wood.

TENSION ZONE The zone of constant change along the boundary of an inherent edge. *See also* Edge.

TENT CATERPILLAR A larva of the moth family Lasiocampidae which, in its earlier stages, lives gregariously in a large silken nest or matting that is woven onto and sometimes envelops the host plant. The term is also applied to some insects that do not construct true tents (e.g., the forest tent caterpillar).

TENURE **1** The relationships established among humans regarding their various rights to own, use, and control land, or the resources on that land. **2** The holding of an official post or office for a predefined length of time.

TEPAL A unit of undifferentiated perianth where the petals and sepals are similar in appearance and not readily distinguishable from each other. It is lacking a clearly differentiated corolla and calyx.

TEPHRA A collective term for all pyroclastic sediments; volcanic ejecta.

TEPHROCHRONOLOGY The dating of layers of volcanic ash in order to establish a sequence of geologic or archaeological events. This is possible because the tephra produced during any given eruption often have unique physical and chemical properties that allow the correlation between an ash deposit and the eruption that formed it.

TERATOLOGICAL Abnormal growth form or structure. The study of these forms is called teratology.

TEREDO Also known as the shipworm. A

wood-boring marine mollusc, living in saltwater conditions, belonging to the genus *Bankia* or the genus *Teredo*, that damages pilings and logs stored in water. *See also* Gribble.

TERETE Slender, cylindrical, of approximately circular cross-section, varying in diameter.

TERMINAL **1** Located at the apex or tip of a stem or summit of an axis. **2** A condition known to have a definite endpoint.

TERMINAL BUD The bud at the apex of a stem or branch.

TERMINAL MORAINE The moraine formed at the farthest point of glacial advance, usually seen as a massive arcuate ridge or complex of ridges underlain by till and other drift types. *See also* Drumlin (for illustration).

TERNARY PLOTS A triangular diagram that graphically depicts the composition of a three-part mixture.

TERNATE Divided into three (e.g., the leaves of the Trillium plant). **Biternate** means the primary leaves are divided into three and again divided into three secondary leaves. **Triternate** means the primary and secondary leaves are divided into three more sections.

TERNATE-PINNATE A compound leaf where the three primary divisions are then pinnate.

TERRACE **1** Any relatively level or gently inclined surface, generally less broad than a plain, and bounded along one side by a steeper descending slope or scarp and along the other by a steeper ascending slope or scarp. **2** A relatively flat area that has been naturally eroded into the side slope of a valley wall, or has been artificially created by humans, usually for agricultural use.

TERRAIN **1** A comprehensive term to describe a tract of landscape being studied with respect to its natural features. **2** Pertains to maps showing surficial materials, material texture, surface expression, present-day geomorphological (geological) processes, and related features.

TERRAIN ANALYSIS The process of terrain mapping and interpretation or assessment of terrain conditions for a specific purpose, such as construction of logging roads or urban expansion.

TERRAIN CLASSIFICATION A scheme used to analyze the land base to assist the planning of engineering, logging, and silviculture activities. The terrain classification can be used to determine site suitability for different types of machinery, logging methods, and where to best locate access roads. Typically, terrain classification examines the following characteristics. **Ground strength** is the compactibility or trafficability of the soils, where rocky soils are hard and will accept heavy machinery, as opposed to deep, wet soils that are soft and will bog down machinery. It is normally measured in summer, unless the ground is deeply frozen in which case the measurement is of less importance. It is usually measured in kilopascals (pounds per square inch in Imperial measurement). **Ground roughness** is the permanent topography of the site, independent of slope (e.g., continuous hummocks, rock outcrops, depressions, or flat areas). It is usually assessed using a count of the number of obstacles per hectare and the height of the obstacles. **Slope** or **grade** is the gradient of slopes, usually in per cent.

Combinations of these factors yield terrain classes, each one having an associated limit of acceptability for the purposes of planning and operational activity.

TERRAIN STABILITY MAP A map indicating the susceptibility of the land to mass wasting. On the basis of the features mapped, managers attempt to predict the likely response of the land to disturbances such as fires, road construction, logging, and pest outbreaks. Stability is classified subjectively, usually in five classes ranging from stable (Class 1) to unstable (Class 5).

TERRANE Area of the lithosphere distinguished by a certain assemblage of rock types.

TERRESTRIAL Of or concerning the land. An organism whose primary habitat for growth, reproduction, and survival is on or in the land. *See also* Aquatic.

TERRICOLOUS A plant growing on soil. *See also* Saxicolous.

TERRIGENOUS Refers to sediments or other materials derived from the land. *See also* Biogenous.

TERRITORY The area that an animal defends, usually during breeding season, against intruders of its own species. *See also* Home Range.

TERTIARY The first period of the Cenozoic era, following the Mesozoic era preceding the Quaternary (approximately sixty-five to two million years ago). The Tertiary period is divided into epochs, which in order of increasing age are Pliocene, Miocene, Oligocene, Eocene, and Paleocene. *See also* Appendix 2: Geological Time Scales.

TESSELLATE A surface marked with a mosaic or checkered design.

TESSERA The smallest homogeneous unit visible at the spatial scale of a landscape.

TEST The external shell or covering of many

invertebrate animals. Applies mainly to armoured scale insects.

TESTA The seed coat; the hardened outer integument.

TETRADYNAMOUS Having four long and two short stamens (e.g., members of the Cruciferae).

TETRAHEDRAL Having the form of a solid body that has four planes; a pyramid with a base and three sides.

TETRAMEROUS Any shape or form occurring in multiples of four.

TETRANDROUS Having four stamens.

TETRAPLOID Having four basic sets of chromosomes (4n) per cell rather than the more normal two.

TEXTURE (OF AN ECOSYSTEM) The relative surface smoothness of an ecosystem determined by remote sensing technology, or the distinctiveness of the transition between two distinct ecosystems.

TEXTURE (OF SEDIMENTS) Pertains to the grain sizes, shape, and arrangement of particles in a sedimentary unit.

THALAMUS *See* Receptacle.

THALLOPHYTE **1** An obsolete term used to designate the algae and fungi among the so-called nonvascular plants. Modern classification schemes do not consider algae or fungi to be true plants. **2** A cryptogam where the plant body is a thallus (e.g., bacteria, algae, fungi).

THALLOSPORE An asexual spore that has no conidiophore or is not separate from the hypha or conidiophore that produced it.

THALLUS A plant body not divided into leaves, stems, or roots, and lacking a true vascular system, such as lichens. Can be single-celled or a colony of cells (e.g., algae), or a mycelium or collection of packed mycelia (e.g., mushrooms), or a complex and multicellular structure. It is less commonly termed the thallome.

THALWEG A line connecting the lowest or deepest points along a stream bed or valley bottom.

THECA A small case or pouch. **1** In flowering plants, a pollen sac on an anther. **2** In mosses and related plants, a capsule.

THEMATIC MAP A map that portrays selected information in themes, such as fish habitat, stream quality, forest cover.

THEMATIC MAPPER A scanner used in producing satellite imagery that has more spectral, radiometric, and geometric sensitivity than its predecessors and is part of the capabilities of Landsat satellites.

THEME In mapping, sets of data are called a theme (e.g., all the areas mapped that contain sensitive fisheries habitat might be one theme). Other themes are then mapped and can later be related among each other. *See also* Thematic Map.

THERMAL BELT An area of mountainous slope (usually the middle third) that typically experiences the least variation in diurnal temperatures and has the highest average temperatures and, therefore, the lowest relative humidity. Its presence is most evident during clear weather with light wind.

THERMAL COVER Cover used by animals to lessen the effects of weather on body temperature.

THERMOGRAPH A self-recording thermometer or an instrument that records air temperature automatically and continuously on a chart.

THERMOHYGROMETER *See* Hygrothermograph.

THERMOKARST A topographic feature, similar in form to karst, produced in a permafrost region by the local melting of ground ice, followed by settling of the ground.

THERMONEUTRAL ZONE An area where the ambient conditions do not trigger a metabolic response on the part of the animal occupying the area.

THERMOREGULATION The physiological and biological process whereby an animal regulates its body temperature.

THICKET A dense patch of bushes, small trees, and shrubs.

THIN CLOUD LAYER A layer of clouds whose ratio of dense sky cover to total sky cover is one-half or less. *See also* Ceiling; Cloudy; Dense Cloud Layer.

THINNING The removal of selected stems from a developing stand in order to salvage potential mortality, and promote silvicultural or other objectives (enhanced growth in the remaining trees, increased water yields, improved wildlife habitat, etc.). In a managed stand, thinning will affect stand density, and diameter classes can be controlled, but variation in height classes will be less apparent. Several types of thinning are recognized. **Commercial thinning** is a partial cut in older, immature stands, where trees have reached merchantable size and value, to provide an interim harvest while maintaining a high rate of growth on well-spaced, final crop trees. **Precommercial thinning** is a silvicultural treatment to reduce the number of trees in young stands (improve spacing), carried out before the stems are large enough to be used or sold as a forest product. The intent is to concentrate growth per unit area on fewer stems, thus increasing mean stand diameter, retaining more live crown, creating opportunities for commercial thinning, accelerating stand operability, and improving wildlife habitat. **Crown thinning** is (1) in the silvicultural sense, the removal of trees from the dominant and codominant crown classes to favour the best trees of those same classes. It is also termed thinning from above or high thinning; and (2) in the arboricultural sense, the careful removal of a percentage of the crown foliage in order to lighten the crown, or as a means of reducing branch weight, or to let more light through the crown, or to allow more wind to pass through the foliage and thus reduce the chances of windthrow. **Free thinning** is the removal of trees to control stand spacing and favour desired trees using a combination of thinning criteria without regard to crown position. **Low thinning** is the removal of trees from the lower crown classes to favour those in the upper crown classes. It is also termed thinning from below. **Row thinning** is the removal of trees by cutting out narrow strips or lines of trees at fixed intervals throughout a stand. **Selection thinning** is the removal of trees in the dominant crown class in order to favour trees in the lower crown classes. It is also termed dominant thinning. **Mechanical thinning** is row thinning performed by machinery, either by cutting down and extracting the tree, or by knocking it down to the ground and chipping/slashing it. It is also termed geometric thinning. **Spacing** is the retention of trees at fixed intervals with all the other trees being cut down.

THINNING CYCLE The time period between thinning operations in any one stand.

THINNING GRADE The severity of low thinning based on the crown classes removed, ranging from very light (Grade A) to very heavy (Grade E).

THINNING INTENSITY The characteristics of a thinning prescription determined by the severity and frequency of thinnings.

THINNING SERIES Two or more adjacent forest plots that are thinned differently so that a comparison can be made between the subsequent annual increments within each plot.

THIN SKY COVER A sky cover through which higher clouds or the sky can be detected. *See also* Ceiling; Cloudy; Dense Sky Cover.

THIXOTROPHY *See* Soil Liquefaction.

THORAX **1** In vertebrate animals, the body cavity containing the lungs and heart, separated from the abdomen by the diaphragm. **2** In arthropods, that part of the body lying between the head and the abdomen, which in insects is also the point of attachment for the legs and wings. *See also* Abdomen; Butterfly (for illustration).

THORN A sharp, woody, spinelike outgrowth from a stem, and a form of modified, greatly reduced branch. *See also* Prickle; Spine.

THOUSAND BOARD FEET A unit of measurement for sawn lumber equivalent to one thousand lineal feet of wood one foot wide and one inch thick. *See also* Board Foot.

THREATENED SPECIES In the US, those plant or animal species likely to become endangered species throughout all or a significant portion of their range within the foreseeable future. A plant or animal identified and defined in accordance with the 1973 Endangered Species Act and published in the federal register. **2** *See also* COSEWIC.

3/2 POWER LAW OF SELF-THINNING Dense populations of trees in even-aged stands that have reached a size at which mortality occurs (self-thinning due to competition) demonstrate a relationship between the logarithm of mean plant weight and the logarithm of stand density. The relationship typically has a slope of −3/2 but varies by species.

THRESHOLD PHENOMENON Pattern or trend in population growth that exhibits relatively long periods of slow change followed by precipitous increase or decrease in response to an environmental gradient.

THRIFTY Describes plants, especially young seedlings or trees that are growing vigorously.

THRIPS Small insects, one to two millimetres long, having narrow, nearly veinless wings, fringed with relatively long hairs. Weak fliers, but aerially dispersed often for many kilometres. Several species are associated with North American ornamentals and cause economic damage by injuring flowers, stippling or bleaching the foliage, or by causing structural abnormalities in the callus tissue, galls, malformed leaves, and leaf blisters.

THROAT Botanically, the opening of a sympetalous corolla, calyx, or perianth. The location at which the tube joins or expands into the spreading limb.

THROUGHFALL The total amount of precipitation that reaches the forest floor, minus the stemflow volume (i.e., water dripping from the canopy plus direct precipitation).

THUNDERHEAD A popular term for a cumulonimbus cloud formation associated with a thunderstorm. It is characterized by a large, vertical column topped by a mushroom- or anvil-shaped head.

THUNDERSTORM A localized storm, invariably produced by a cumulonimbus cloud accompanied by lightning and thunder. It is synonymous with electrical storm.

THYRSE/THYRSUS A densely crowded panicle-like inflorescence where the main axis is indeterminate, while the lateral axes are determinate and cymose.

TIDAL FLAT An extensive, nearly horizontal, marshy or barren tract of land that is alternately covered and uncovered by the tide, and consisting of unconsolidated sediment (mostly mud and sand). It may form the top surface of a deltaic deposit.

TIDE The naturally occurring periodic rise and fall of the oceanic water levels. It is caused by the rotation of the Earth and the combined gravitational influences of the Earth, moon, and sun and varies directly with their associated masses and inversely as the square of their distances apart. The type of tide varies according to the relative juxtaposition of the planets. **Apogean tide** occurs when the moon is at its furthest distance from the earth, thus gravitational forces are lessened, yielding lower than normal high tides and higher than normal low tides, consequently the tidal range between low and high is also less than the normal. **Neap tide** occurs when the sun and moon are at right angles to the Earth (the first and last quarter phases of the moon), yielding tidal forces that are in opposition. Tidal range is reduced with high low tides and low high tides. **Perigean tide** occurs when the moon is at its closest position to the Earth, its gravitational force is high, and consequently, high tides are higher than normal and low tides are lower than normal. **Spring tide**, which is a bimonthly tide of higher than normal range, is associated with the alignment of the Earth, sun, and moon so that the gravitational forces are in conjunction (new moon) or in opposition (full moon). High tides are higher than normal and low tides are lower than normal.

TILL **1** Material deposited by glaciers and ice sheets without modification by any other agent of transportation. *See also* Ablation Till; Basal Till; Drumlin (for illustration); Flow Till; Lodgement Till; Meltout Till. **2** To prepare the soil for planting using hand tools or machinery.

TILLER A sprout or branch that grows from the base of a plant, especially those of the grass family.

TILL PLAIN A level or gently undulating surface underlain by till.

TILT In remote sensing, tilt refers to vertical aerial photography, and is the deviation of the camera axis from the vertical.

TIMBERLINE The upper elevational limit of timber that has commercial value, normally in a closed forest system. *See also* Tree Line.

TIMBER MANAGEMENT The activity involving the allocation of forested lands for harvesting of the timber on that land. Timber management may involve planning, road-building, logging extraction of merchantable timber for processing off-site, and varying intensities of silvicultural activity to encourage another stand of trees to grow back. Timber management is an important subset of forest management, but it is not an equivalent activity. *See also* Forest Management.

TIMBER STAND IMPROVEMENT Refers to all the intermediate treatments made to improve the composition, structure, condition, and increment of either an even- or uneven-aged stand.

TIMELAG The drying time under stated conditions of dry-bulb temperature, relative humidity, wind speed, and time of the year, required for dead fuels to lose about two-thirds of the difference between their initial moisture content and their equilibrium moisture content. The timelag represents the rate of moisture change in a fuel. Dead forest fuels can have timelag values from minutes to months. The fuels represented by the Fine Fuel Moisture Code, Duff Moisture Code, and Drought Code in the Canadian Forest Fire Weather Index System have timelag values of two-thirds (or sixteen hours), twelve, and fifty-two days in average weather.

TIMING OF APPLICATION The most efficacious time to apply a pesticide in order to maximize its potential effects on the target pest. This requires a detailed knowledge of the pesticide and the time when the target pest is most vulnerable. With herbicides, the time of emergence and dormancy are important factors, hence herbicides can be classified as post-emergent, or pre-emergent.

TISSUE CULTURE The cultivation (sometimes commercial) of plant or animal tissues, cells, or organs in an artificial nutrient medium.

TOESLOPE In geomorphology, the outermost, gently inclined surface at the base of a hillslope with a linear form. In terms of gradational processes, they are constructional surfaces forming the distal part of a hillslope continuum that grades down to the valley floor.

TOLERANCE **1** The relative ability of an organism to endure injurious effects of an adverse environmental condition. The opposite of sensitivity. **2** A host-pest interaction in which the host exhibits signs and symptoms characteristic of a susceptible interaction but is damaged less by the interaction, or can recover more readily than can a susceptible host. **3** The range of chemical, biological, and physical conditions that permit an organism, or a population, or a biological process to continue to subsist. The outer ranges of any of these environmental conditions define the limits of tolerance, which is termed the ecological amplitude for any species, population, or process. *See also* Immunity; Resistance; Susceptible.

TOLERANCE LEVEL The amount of a pesticide that may safely and legally remain as a residue in a food plant, or in meat or fat.

TOMENTOSE Having a tomentum.

TOMENTUM A covering of densely matted, short, woolly hairs.

TON *See* Long Ton; Tonne; Short Ton.

TONNE A measure of weight equal to 1,000 kilograms or approximately 2,205 pounds. It is sometimes termed a metric tonne. *See also* Long Ton; Short Ton.

TOOTHED SURFACE The tooth-like texture of the spore-bearing surface of certain wood decay fungi (e.g., Indian paint fungus).

TOP-KILL **1** Relatively rapid death or dieback of the leader and more or less of the upper crown portion of the crown. **2** A tree with a portion of the crown and stem killed, from the top down, by insects or some other cause, with the remainder of the stem and lower crown remaining green. *See also* Spike-Top.

TOP OF BANK The point at which the topography of bank slopes shows a significant and continuous change to a less steep slope. In flat landscapes it could be the normal high water mark, but more typically, it is the top of the slope leading down to the water. It is an important criterion since many other management activities, such as leave strips, buffer zones, and set-backs are measured from the top of bank. *See also* Bank.

TOPOGRAPHIC MAP A map portraying the correct horizontal and vertical position of the features represented. It is typically used to display the landforms of any one area by use of contour lines. *See also* Cadastral Map; Contour Lines; Planimetric Map.

TOPOGRAPHY The relative position and elevations of the natural or human-made features of a landscape, used to describe the surface configurations.

TOPOLOGY The study of topography; the description or features of an area. Topology is a branch of geometry dealing with the properties of a figure or form that remain unchanged if the figure or form is stretched, twisted or bent. In landform analysis, topology deals with the way in which geographic elements are linked together.

TOPOSEQUENCE A group of related soils or parent material sequences that differ from one another in some properties, mainly due to the differences in topography as it affects soil formation. *See also* Chronosequence; Lithosequence.

TOPOTYPE *See* Type.

TOPPING **1** *See* Harvest Functions. **2** A pruning technique to reduce the height of trees. When applied to the entire top of a tree, it is considered to be very poor arboricultural practice, since it creates major points of entry for disease at the top of the tree and any new growth will be structurally weak with a higher than usual potential for failure.

TOR A small, castellated hill of bedrock with open joint planes rising abruptly from a relatively smooth hilltop or slope. It is commonly surrounded by fallen blocks.

TORCH or TORCHING *See* Fire Behaviour.

TORRENT A temporary flow condition in streams created by heavy rainfall or rapid snowmelt, characterized by near flood conditions, large increases in flow velocity, standing waves, and loss of the typical stepped profile and hydraulic diversity of habitat.

TORULOID In botany and mycology, describes a shape that is almost cylindrical, but with pronounced swellings or beads at intervals. It is generally used to describe a fruit that is coarsely and irregularly moniliform. It is also termed torulose.

TORULOSE *See* Toruloid.

TORUS The receptacle of a flower or of a head.

TOTAL DIVERSITY INDEX A number that indicates the relative degrees of total diversity (induced diversity and inherent diversity) in habitat per unit area produced by all edges within or on the periphery of the area. Expressed mathematically as:

$$\text{Total DI} = \frac{TE_c +_s}{2\sqrt{A\pi}}$$

where

$TE_c +_s$ = total length of all inherent and induced edges

A = area

π = 3.1416.

Total diversity index is the sum of inherent diversity index and induced diversity index. Total DI expressed as a percentage is calculated by multiplying total DI by 100.

TOWER CUPOLA *See* Lookout Cupola.

TOWERMAN *See* Lookout.

TOXIC Any substance capable of acting as a poison.

TOXICANT A poisonous substance, regardless of origin, usually one used to kill rather than repel.

TRACHEOPHYTA In some plant classification schemes, a collective term indicating all vascular plants, including the pteridophytes and spermatophytes, which are placed in the phylum tracheophyta (plants with tracheids) to distinguish them from the nonvascular plants.

TRADE OFF The exchange of one thing or value in return for another, usually the loss of one benefit and the gain of a different benefit. Trade offs involve weighing many different factors in the decisionmaking process, and include issues of how equity will be distributed among those that might gain and those that might lose (now and for future generations, and including nonhuman life-forms), costs of the trade off, the time required to realize benefits and losses, and a sense of whether or not the trade off proposed will meet or assist management goals.

TRADITIONAL FOREST A natural forest under a traditional pattern of management utilizing harvesting and cultivation methods based on long-established customs or practices, usually to serve limited local needs. *See also* Forest.

TRAILING In plants, prostrate, but not rooted.

TRAMPLING The action of walking on vegetation by humans and padstock which may cause abrasion of vegetation, abrasion of surface soil organic layers, and compaction of soils.

TRANSECT A straight line across a landscape along which plot surveys are undertaken to provide a cross-section of the area under study. The transect may be a series of plots, a belt or strip, or merely a line, depending on the purpose of the survey and the statistical design being used. Transects are typically used to determine vegetation changes along a gradient. *See also* Cruise Line; Quadrat.

TRANSFORMATION The process in which one photograph is projected by mathematical, graphic, or photographic means, from its own plane onto another plane by translation, rotation, and/or scale change.

TRANSITION PERIOD A period of environmental change during which a population increases or decreases to a new stable equilibrium level.

TRANSLATIONAL LIFT Lift that is gained when a helicopter translates from a hover into forward flight. The additional lift increases with increasing airspeed and is derived by the main rotor system moving into undisturbed air. *See also* Ground Effect.

TRANSLOCATION **1** The active movement of dissolved substances from one part of a plant to another, often using the phloem as the main conduit of movement. **2** The transfer of a part of one chromosome from one locus to another locus in the same, or in another chromosome.

TRANSMISSION The transfer of an infectious agent from one host individual to another. *See also* Vector.

TRANSPIRATION **1** The loss of water vapour through the stomatal openings in plants, or by evaporation from cell tissues. **2** The movement of vaporized liquids or gases across a membrane or similar surface (e.g., perspiration through animal skin).

TRANSPLANT A seedling that has been replanted one or more times in a nursery to improve its size and growth potential characteristics, or a tree that has been moved from one site to another (transplanted).

TRANSPORTATION ZONE In hillslope erosion processes, the transportation zone carries soil and rock materials collected from the erosion zone to the deposition zone via saltation, surface creep, or suspension in air or water. *See also* Erosion; Hillslope (for illustration).

TRAP TREE A tree treated in some manner to make it an acceptable host for bark beetles or other pests (e.g., felled in the shade for spruce beetle, or standing and baited with semiochemicals for mountain pine beetles). Lethal traps are treated so as to kill the insects arriving at or infesting them (e.g., with surface or systemic insecticides or herbicides). Otherwise, infested trap trees are harvested and the insects killed in timber processing and manufacturing activities. Trap trees that have been felled, limbed, and bucked are sometimes termed trap logs.

TRAVEL CORRIDOR A route used by animals along a belt or band of suitable cover or habitat.

TRAVEL TIME *See* Elapsed Time.

TRAVERSE A survey line applied to various kinds of surveys, including topographic, geological, soil, and biological surveys.

TREE A woody plant characterized by one main trunk, bearing a more or less distinct and elevated crown of branches. Typically, trees are larger than shrubs.

TREE LENGTH HARVESTING Extraction of the complete tree length, minus top and branches, from the stump to the landing. The tree is then cut up into smaller logs in preparation for loading and hauling, but may also be hauled away in one piece.

TREE LINE The limits of tree growth in the subalpine zone, which lies beyond the upper elevational edges of the timberline. Trees in this zone seldom reach commercial size or form, and those that do occur in scattered islands that do not justify the costs of exploitation. In some cases, tree line and timberline coincide, but more typically the tree line extends several hundred metres beyond the timberline. *See also* Krummholz.

TREE-RING CORRECTED The method of radiocarbon dating that assumes a constant rate of atmospheric carbon isotope production and decay. This assumption is not true, so radiocarbon ages cannot be directly converted into calendar years. To overcome this, values for radiocarbon-dated tree rings of known age are applied to correct the radiocarbon date to actual calendar ages. Differences between a radiocarbon and a tree ring age can be significant. For example, the radiocarbon age for the eruption of Mount Mazama in the United States is about 7000 BP, but the tree-ring corrected age is closer to 8000 BP.

TREE RINGS *See* Dendrochronology.

TRI- A prefix meaning three.

TRIANGULAR DIAGRAM A diagram constructed by plotting three related variables that graphically displays the relationships between them. Typical variables would be site, place, population, soil texture, etc. In the illustration, eight sites are located on the triangle according to their July mean precipitation, air temperature, and potential evaporation values. *See also* Soil Texture.

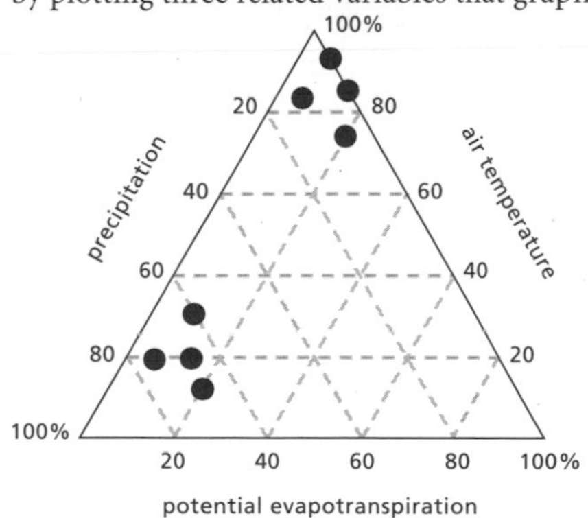

TRIBUTARY A stream feeding, joining, or flowing into a larger stream.

TRICHOME A tiny projection from a plant epidermis; may be hairlike, spiny, or glandular.

TRICHOTOMOUS Forking regularly and repeatedly into three further divisions or branches.

TRICOLPATE Pollen grains having three grooves on the outer surface.

TRIFID Cleft or split into three lobular divisions.

TRIFOLIATE Having three leaves.

TRIFOLIOLATE A leaf having three separate leaflets. *See also* Compound Leaf.

TRIGONAL/TRIGONOUS Having three angles.

TRIMEROUS Having parts in multiples of three.

TRIMORPHIC Occurring in three different forms.

TRIPINNATE Thrice pinnate; where the secondary leaflets are further divided into tertiary leaflets. *See also* Compound Leaf.

TRIPLOID Having three basic sets of chromosomes (3n) per cell rather than the more normal two.

TRIQUETROUS Three-angled in cross-section.

TROPHIC LEVEL The level in the food chain at which an organism sustains itself. The feeding level that energy passes through during its passage through an ecosystem. *See also* Autotrophic; Carnivore; Frugivore; Herbivore; Heterotrophic; Omnivore.

TROPHIC STRUCTURE The organization of the community based on feeding relationships of populations.

TROPICS An area of the planet that lies between the Tropic of Cancer (Latitude 23°27' north) and the Tropic of Capricorn (latitude 23°27' south).

TROPOSPHERE The gaseous medium surrounding the Earth. The troposphere is the lower layer of the Earth's atmosphere stretching from the ground up to seven to seventeen kilometres, where it blends into the upper atmosphere (stratosphere). In the lower layer temperature decreases with altitude at a regular rate, and it is in this layer that most of the planetary weather systems occur. *See also* Bisophere; Hydrosphere; Lithosphere.

TROUGH In geomorphology, **1** any long, narrow

depression in the surface of the Earth, typically a long, broad, elongate, U-shaped valley having no surface outlet for drainage. **2** The channel in which a stream flows.

TRUNCATE Ending abruptly, having the appearance of the end being cut off sharply. *See also* Leaf Shape.

TUBER A thickened, short, usually but not always underground stem, branch, or root often bearing buds or eyes, that serves as a storage organ containing reserve food (e.g., a potato).

TUBERCLE A small, rounded nodule or projection from the surface of an organ.

TUFF A compacted deposit consisting of at least 50 per cent volcanic ash or dust.

TUMID Swollen, inflated.

TUNIC Botanically, a loose, membranous outer skin that is not the epidermis. It applies especially to the membranes wrapped around a corm or bulb.

TUNICATED **1** Having a tunic. **2** Having concentric layers of membranous coat (e.g., an onion).

TURBIDITY A measure of water clarity, or the degree to which water is opaque due to suspended silt or other sediments. High turbidity over prolonged periods of time will alter the aquatic habitat by reducing light penetration levels (reduced photosynthetic activity reduces autotrophic, and hence heterotrophic activity). Turbidity also modifies the substrate, since the sediment that settles out leads to accretion in gravel beds and reduction of suitable habitat for benthic invertebrates, as well as reduced spawning habitat for fish.

TURBINATE Inversely conical, shaped like a top.

TURBULENCE The motion of a fluid characterized by constant, random fluctuations and changes in the local velocity and direction of the flow. Surface waters are disturbed and surface levels are uneven. *See also* Laminar Flow.

TURGID A cell that has its maximum amount of water, thus causing full distension of the protoplast. Normally applied to plant cells, the condition is termed turgor.

TURION **1** A young shoot or sucker, such as the emerging stem of asparagus. **2** A swollen winter bud in many aquatic plants, containing stored food.

TURN A general term describing the logs yarded out in any one cycle, or trip. The number of logs in the turn is dependent on the size of each individual log and the hauling capacity of the yarding machinery.

TURNOVER **1** Extinction of some species and replacement by others. The turnover rate is the number of species eliminated and replaced per unit time. **2** In hydrology, the period of time taken for large bodies of water to circulate. **3** In nutrient cycling, the time period between use and replacement of one or more nutrients in the nutrient pool.

TUSSOCK A thick tuft or clump of vegetation forming scattered hummocks of more solid terrain within a wetland.

TUSSOCKOSIS An allergic reaction of humans in response to contact with the irritating body hairs of Douglas-fir tussock moth larvae, often shed by the larvae and carried on the wind, or left embedded in the egg masses of this insect. *See also* Urticating Hair.

TWIG The current season's growth, or the latest growth (last year's) of a branch. Twigs have important features for different species and are important in identification keys (e.g., buds, leaf scars, surface characteristics, and pith type). The branchwood below the twig often loses some or all of these features.

TWINSPAN Two-way Indicator Species Analysis (TWINSPAN) is a hierarchical, polythetic, divisive classification technique that is based on the statistical ordination technique of reciprocal averaging.

Given a data set consisting of stand and species information, the TWINSPAN program classifies both the stands and species into groups, and constructs a two-way table from a stand-by-species matrix. First, through ordination, the stands are divided and subdivided into groups based on the preference of each species for one group or another. Species are then classified based on their presence in particular groups of stands. The species most responsible for the division of each group are identified as 'indicators.' Lastly, a two-way table is constructed from both the stand and species classifications so that groups of stands are arranged across the table according to their affinities for species listed down the table. A dendrogram can then be hand-constructed from the information in the table. *See also* Classification; Dendrogram.

TYPE The element of a taxon to which the name of that taxon is permanently attached. The type of the name of a species or of any taxon of lower rank (i.e., subspecies, variety, or forma) is ordinarily a preserved specimen, which serves as the standard or criterion for application of the name. The type of genus or of any taxon between genus and species is a species; that of a family or of any taxon between family and genus is a genus. In the systems of plant nomenclature, the source of the material is important, leading to the following additional terms. **Cotype** is an additional specimen from the same plant as the holotype. **Holotype** is the original specimen used by the author of a name, or designated by the author, as the nomenclatural type. **Isotype** is a duplicate specimen of the holotype. **Lectotype** is a specimen from the original material that can serve as the nomenclatural type, either because the holotype was not designated at the time of publication, or when the holotype is missing. **Neotype** is a specimen selected to serve as the nomenclatural type of a taxon where all of the original material, upon which the taxon is originally based, is now missing. **Paratype** is a specimen other than the holotype that is cited with the original description. **Syntype** is one of two or more specimens used by an author when no original holotype was designated, or as a substitute for the holotype, or when one of two or more specimens were designated at the same time as the type. **Topotype** is a specimen collected at the type locality where the holotype was originally collected.

TYPE MAP Any map depicting the distribution of attributes (e.g., forest cover types, soil types, etc.).

TYPICAL Botanically, it means the inclusion of the nomenclature type of a taxon of higher rank. In a variable species with more than one variety, the typical variety is that which includes the original type of the species itself (i.e., has the same type), and therefore has the varietally distinguishing characteristics of the species as it was originally typified. Hence, use of the descriptor 'typical' does not necessarily mean the 'commonest' or the 'most representative.'

U

ULTIMATE FACTOR An event or characteristic (e.g., in evolution or geologic history) that causes or controls a proximate factor. Environmental factors of direct importance to the well-being of an organism. *See also* Proximate Factor.

UMBEL A flat-topped or convex inflorescence in which the pedicels of the flowers arise from a common point. In a compound umbel all peduncles supporting each secondary umbel arise from a common point on the primary ray. *See also* Inflorescence (for illustration).

UMBELLATE Flowers borne in an umbel, or resembling an umbel.

UMBELLET A secondary umbel within a compound umbel.

UMBILICATE Having a navel-like, typically central, depression.

UMBO A conical projection, often centrally located, as in the raised portion of the scale in a pine cone.

UMBRELLA SPECIES A large-bodied, popular species having a large home range and broad requirements for habitats and resources, that can be managed to also provide habitats and resources for other species. It is similar to flagship species.

UNARMED Botanically, a surface having no spines, prickles, or other sharp projections.

UNAVOIDABLE Any adverse effect that cannot be avoided, even with the best possible planning, implementation, on-site supervision, and education of all levels of workers. It does not include adverse effects that arise due to measures, or lack of measures, dictated by cost considerations (i.e., lack of funds).

UNCERTAINTY The process of making decisions where there is no objective basis for assigning numerical probability weights to the possible different outcomes, or there is no way to describe the outcomes. In practice, a probability distribution is often assigned to uncertain factors using a combination of experience, intuition, knowledge, and lack of knowledge. Risk is based on an objective assessment of likely outcomes, while uncertainty is always more subjectively based, less easily quantified, and less predictable (i.e., random). *See also* Risk.

UNCINATE Hooked, or bearing a hook.

UNCONFORMITY A substantial break or gap in the geologic record where a rock unit is overlain by another that is not next in stratigraphic succession, such as an interruption in the continuity of a depositional sequence of sedimentary rocks or a break between eroded igneous rocks and younger sedimentary rocks.

UNCONSOLIDATED MATERIALS *See* Surficial Materials.

UNCONTROLLED FIRE Any fire that threatens to destroy life, property, or natural resources, and (1) is not burning within the confines of firebreaks, or (2) is burning with such intensity that it could not be readily extinguished with ordinary tools commonly available.

UNCONTROLLED MOSAICS *See* Aerial Photograph Mosaic.

UNDERBURNING Prescribed burning of the forest floor or understorey vegetation for botanical or wildlife habitat objectives, fire hazard reduction, or to meet silvicultural objectives.
UNDERCUT A wedge-shaped notch cut in the base of a tree to govern the direction of its fall. It is sometimes termed a box or a notch. *See also* Backcut.
UNDERCUTTING The root pruning of seedlings in a nursery bed.
UNDERPLANTING The planting of young trees of the same or different species under the canopy of an existing forest.
UNDERSTOCKED *See* Stocking.
UNDERSTOREY The trees and other woody species growing under the canopies of larger adjacent trees and other woody growth. *See also* Storey.
UNDULATE **1** A surface that is wavy; widely sinuous across the breadth. **2** Having a wavy margin. As applied to leaves, it describes the up-and-down undulations, rather than any in-and-out changes, which would be sinuate. *See also* Leaf Margin.
UNDULATING Gently sloping hillocks and hollows with multidirectional slopes generally up to fifteen degrees (26 per cent); local relief is greater than one metre.
UNECONOMIC Any action or process that does not add to the total stock of useful goods and services, or else produces a good or service less effectively or at higher cost than an alternative method.
UNEVEN-AGED MANAGEMENT A combination of practices for a whole forest under sustained yield management that simultaneously maintains continuous tall forest cover, recurring regeneration of desirable species, and the orderly growth and development of trees through a range of diameter classes, or age classes with at least ten to twenty years between them. Cutting methods that develop and maintain uneven-aged stands are single-tree selection and group selection. *See also* Even-Aged Management.
UNGUICULATE Having the base contracted into a claw or petiole-like base.
UNGULATE **1** Any animal in the group *Ungulata*: hoofed, grazing mammals, many of which have horns (e.g., deer). **2** Hoof-shaped.
UNIFIED SOIL CLASSIFICATION SYSTEM Soil classification used by engineers. It is based on particle size of coarse materials and consistency of fines (silt/clay mixtures).
UNIFORM FUELS Fuels that are distributed continuously and therefore have the potential to provide a continuous path for fire to spread.
UNIGENERIC Monogeneric.
UNIJUGATE A compound leaf having one pair of leaflets.
UNILOCULAR Having a single locule, chamber, or cell.
UNIQUE ECOSYSTEMS Ecosystems embracing special habitat features such as beaches and dunes, talus slopes, meadows, and wetlands. *See also* Special Habitat; Unique Habitat.
UNIQUE HABITAT A wildlife habit that has special functions and that is geomorphic in nature (abiotic origins) (e.g., cliffs, caves, and talus). *See also* Special Habitat; Unique Ecosystems.
UNIRAMIA The largest subphylum of Arthropoda. The uniramia have unbranched (uniramic) limbs and stout mandibles. The subphylum is very diverse and there is some disagreement among authorities on classification as to details. In general, there are five or six classes recognized including centipedes (Chilopda), millipedes (Diplopoda), and insects (Insecta).
UNISEXUAL Of one sex. Botanically, with staminate only, or pistillate only flowers.
UNISTRATOSE Having cells in one layer. *See also* Bistratose; Multistratose.
UNITYPE SPECIES A wildlife species that uses and requires only one kind of habitat or successional stage, typically interior conditions. *See also* Multitype Species.
UNIVERSAL SOIL LOSS EQUATION (USLE) An equation for predicting *A*, the average annual soil loss in mass per unit area per year, and is defined as $A = RKLSPC$, where *R* is the rainfall factor, *K* is the soil erodibility factor, *L* is the length of slope, *S* is the per cent slope, *P* is the conservation practice factor, and *C* is the cropping and management factor. *See also* Erosion; Wind Erosion Equation.
UNIVOLTINE The condition of an animal (e.g., an insect or nematode) in which only one generation is produced per year or season. *See also* Bivoltine; Multivoltine.
UNMERCHANTABLE Any tree or stem that by dint of size, shape, fibre quality, decay or structural factors, or volume, is not sufficient to attract a financial return for harvesting and extraction.
UNSTABLE **1** In engineering, a determination that the ground or built structures are not stable and require additional work to reduce the chances of failure. For example, slopes of loose or poorly consolidated materials that are

beyond their angle of repose, geological features that have a high probability of failure, or soils that will not support loads. **2** In fisheries management, unstable streambanks are those that are actively deteriorating.

UNSTABLE ATMOSPHERE *See* Atmospheric Stability.

UNTRAMMELLED Any process, substance, or area that is not subject to human controls and manipulations that hamper the free play of natural forces. It is often considered to be an essential aspect of wilderness areas.

UPDATE In inventory work, to consider the changes that have taken place since the last inventory, and bring databases and/or computer models up to date so they better reflect actual conditions on the ground.

UPLAND Land that generally has a higher elevation than the adjacent alluvial plain or low stream terrace, or land above the footslope zone on a hillslope continuum.

UPLIFT In plate tectonics, a structurally high area in the crust resulting from positive movements underground that raise or upthrust the rocks into domes or arches.

UPPER RIDGE A meteorological term referring to an elongated area of relatively high atmospheric pressure in the upper atmosphere. It is usually associated with warm and dry weather conditions at the Earth's surface. It is the opposite of an upper trough.

UPPER RIDGE BREAKDOWN A weakening or collapse of an upper ridge. It is generally associated with an increase in fire weather severity at the Earth's surface.

UPPER TROUGH A meteorological term referring to an elongated area of relatively low atmospheric pressure in the upper atmosphere. It is often associated with cool and showery weather conditions at the Earth's surface. It is the opposite of an upper ridge.

UPSET PRICE Describes a predetermined, minimum acceptable price necessary for a sale to go through at an auction.

UPTHRUST **1** A violent upheaval of rock. **2** A high-angle gravity or thrust fault where the relatively upthrown side was the active element.

URBAN An area in which residences and other human developments form an almost solid covering of the landscape, including most areas within cities and towns, subdivisions, commercial and industrial parks, and similar developments whether inside city limits or not. *See also* Rural.

URBAN FORESTRY A specialized form of forest management concerned with the cultivation and management of trees in the entire area influenced and/or utilized by the urban population. It includes trees on streets, in parks, on private property, as well as watersheds. Urban forests provide many benefits, including climate amelioration, engineering, architectural, and aesthetic uses. *See also* Forest.

URBAN-WILDLAND INTERFACE A line, area, or zone where structures and other human development meets or intermingles with undeveloped wildland or vegetative fuels. The interface is often a zone of conflicting resource management values signalling changing attitudes toward what once was, and what might be in the future.

URCEOLATE Describes the shape of a flower corolla that is urn- or pitcher-shaped.

UREDINIOSPORE One of the many spore stages produced by the rust fungi in their complicated life cycle. These spores are produced in a fruiting body called a uredium.

UREDINOLOGIST A botanist specializing in the study of rusts.

UREDIUM Plural uredinia. One of the many types of fruiting bodies formed by the rusts in their complex life cycle. Urediniospores are formed in this fruiting body.

URTICATING HAIR Small bristles or hairs on the bodies of certain insects that release rash-causing chemicals when touched. *See also* Tussockosis.

USUFRUCT The right of using, enjoying the benefits of, and profiting from property, short of destroying or damaging the property and its benefits.

UTILITY CORRIDOR A linear strip of land identified for the present or future location of utility lines within its boundaries.

UTM Universal Transverse Mercator grid system. A system established to fix a position anywhere on the planet between latitudes 84 degrees north and 80 degrees south, by exact measurement of longitude (east to west around the globe) and latitude (north to south around the globe). The planet is divided into 60 grid zones, each one representing 6 degrees of longitude and 8 degrees of latitude – an area of 1 million hectares. Starting at 180 degrees the first line of longitude is line 1. The next, at 174 degrees, is line 2, and so on. Lines of latitude are designated by letters, starting at latitude 80 degrees south, letter C, and running northwards from letter C to letter X, omitting letters L and O to avoid confusion. Thus Grid Zone

10U represents that part of the planet situated between 120 degrees to 126 degrees west and 48 degrees to 56 degrees north.

Each grid zone is then further subdivided into a finer grid of 100,000 square metres. Labelling these smaller grids is accomplished as follows. Starting at 180 degrees and reading east at 100,000-metre intervals the squares are labelled A to Z, omitting I and O. Every 18 degrees, the lettering starts again. Starting at 80 degrees south and reading north at 100,000-metre intervals, the squares are lettered A to V, omitting I and O. This sequence repeats every 2,000,000 metres along the lines of latitude. Thus, the next nearest similar grid reference is 101 kilometres away (63 miles).

Using this system, detailed grid coordinates can be derived to within 10 metres. A full UTM grid reference has the grid zone, the 100,000-metre-square identification, and the 1,000-metre grid coordinates. For example, the grid reference for the offices of UBC Press are 10UDK4981354568, broken down as 10U (grid zone), DK (100,000-metre quadrangle), 49813 (eastings), and 54568 (northings). The illustration shows how North and Central America are divided into longitudinal grid zones. *See also* National Topographic Service.

UTRICLE A bladder-like, one-seeded fruit, usually indehiscent. *See also* Fruit (for illustration).

UTM grid system

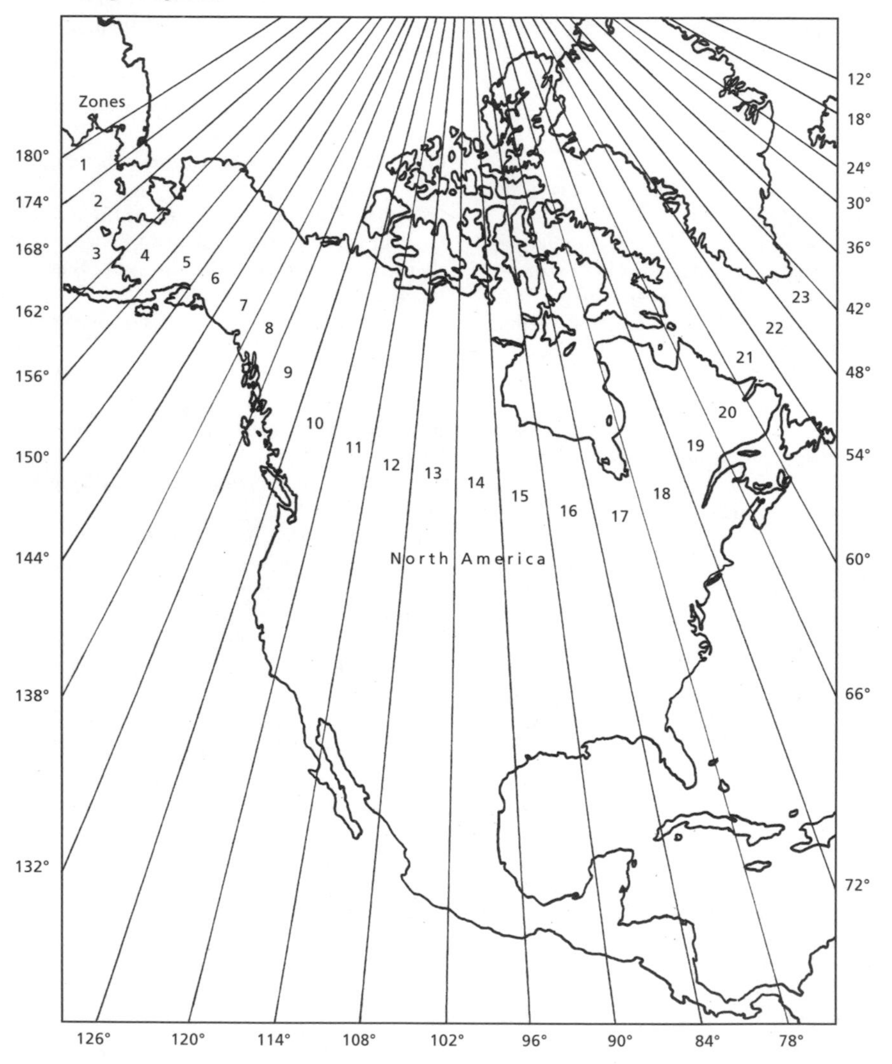

V

VADOSE ZONE A zone of soil lying between the land surface and the water table. It is subdivided into the belt of soil water, the intermediate belt, and the capillary fringe. It is also called the zone of aeration. *See also* Water Table.

VAGILE Capacity of any organism to become widely dispersed. *See also* Labile; Mobile; Volant.

VAGINATE Having or being enclosed by a sheath.

VALLECULA Describes the grooves occurring in the intervals between the ridges on a plant stem. A surface having such grooves is said to be vallecular.

VALLEY An elongate, relatively large, externally drained depression of the Earth's surface that is primarily developed by stream erosion.

VALLEY FILL Surficial materials that fill or partly fill a valley.

VALLEY GLACIER A glacier confined by valley sides. It is usually much longer than broad.

VALVATE **1** Opening by a series of valves, usually by splitting along regular vertical lines, leaving valves in between. **2** Meeting at the margins without overlapping. Both senses apply to leaves and sepals that do not overlap in the bud.

VALVE Botanically, **1** One of the segments of an open capsular fruit; the area between two lines of dehiscence. **2** A flap over a pore in a poricidal anther or capsule.

VARIABLE Something that is measured or counted. *See also* Dependent Variable; Dummy Variable; Independent Variable; Nominal Variable.

VARIABLE CEILING A cloud ceiling of less than 915 metres (3,000 feet) that rapidly increases or decreases in height by one or more reportable values during the period of observation.

VARIABLE COSTS The costs that result from running a machine, calculated on a periodic basis. They include the cost of labour and items such as fuel, oil, wire rope, and replacement parts. It is also termed operating costs. *See also* Fixed Costs.

VARIABLE SKY CONDITION A sky condition that varies between reportable values of sky cover amounts during the period of observation.

VARIABLE VISIBILITY A condition in which the prevailing visibility is less than 4.8 kilometres (3 miles) and rapidly increases or decreases by one or more reportable values during the period of observation.

VARIABLE WIND DIRECTION Wind direction that varies by sixty degrees or more during the period of time that the wind direction is being determined.

VARIANCE In statistics, variance is a measure of the dispersion of individual values about their mean. The square root of variance is the standard deviation. *See also* Standard Deviation.

VARIETY **1** A category of taxa intermediate between subspecies and forma. **2** A division of a free-living species which, on the basis of characteristics of form and physiology, can be differentiated from another group of individuals of the same species. **3** One or more races of a pathogen or parasite that are characterized by the limitation of their host range to organisms in certain taxa. *See Forma Specialis.* **4** An assemblage of cultivated plants that are distinguished by any characteristics (morphology, physiology, etc.) significant for the purposes of horticulture, agriculture, or forestry, and that, when reproduced sexually or asexually, retain their distinguishing features. The term cultivar (cultivated variety) is considered by some to be preferable to the term variety when applied to a deliberately selected variant of a cultivated plant. The term variety is then reserved for a variant found in nature. *See also* Cultivar.

VARVE A distinct repeating band representing the annual deposit in sedimentary materials regardless of origin and usually consisting of two layers, one a thick, light-coloured layer of silt and fine sand and the other, a thin, dark-coloured layer of sand. It is characteristic of glaciolacustrine and lacustrine sediments.

VASCULAR A term applied to the conducting tissues of a plant, which typically consist of phloem and xylem.

VASCULAR PLANTS Plants having well-developed vascular components (xylem and phloem) capable of transporting water, sugars, nutrients, and minerals between the absorbing tissue in the roots and the photosynthesizing tissue in the leaves.

VECTOR **1** Any organism, or abiotic force (wind, water) capable of transferring a pathogen from one organism to another (not necessarily of the same species). **2** An organism that contains or carries a pathogen in an infectious stage, and is normally a necessary link between one or several hosts. A mechanical vector carries the pathogen externally. A vector carrying the pathogen internally, where it may multiply and or maintain itself, may be considered as a host in its own right. *See also* Carrier. **3** A straight line in space characterized mathematically by its direction and magnitude. It is used in GIS work to create a file of points such that vectors can be drawn from point to point to portray line segments. **4** As a noun, the flight path of an aeroplane. As a verb, to direct the flight path of the aeroplane, typically from, or in relation to, the ground.

VECTOR FORMAT In GIS work, a computer file representing spatial information in such a manner that the lines and areas are coded to express size, direction, and degree of connection between the various data points (i.e., along vectors). *See also* Raster.

VEGETATION MANAGEMENT The act of manipulating vegetation and microenvironments to direct site resources into producing the vegetation complex desired to meet management objectives, while at the same time, meeting the concerns for improving wildlife habitat, grazing, scenic value, recreation, and watershed concerns. Some of the objectives may be diametrically opposed and mutually exclusive.

VEGETATIVE Describes plant or fungal organs or parts which usually have absorption, growth and development functions rather than reproductive ones.

VEGETATIVE INFECTION **1** Generally, the presence of a parasitic plant growing on another plant. **2** A dwarf mistletoe infection that does not produce aerial shoots. It usually occurs on heavily shaded branches or on incompatible hosts.

VEGETATIVE PHASE Describes the growth stage of a microorganism, fungus, or plant in contrast to the reproduction stage. It involves the absorption and buildup of nutrients into complex constituents of the organism.

VEGETATIVE REPRODUCTION Asexual reproduction in plants that includes layering, and sending out stolons, or the deliberate propagation of plant materials by root cuttings.

VEIN **1** In plants, a vascular bundle. *See also* Palisade Layer. **2** In animals, a component of the blood circulatory system, carrying the deoxygenated blood back to the heart from the body tissues.

VELAMEN The thick, corky covering of aerial roots in epiphytic orchids. It serves to absorb moisture from the air.

VELOCITY The distance travelled divided by the time required to travel that distance (e.g., kilometres per hour).

VELUTINOUS Clothed with a velvet-like covering of erect, straight, moderately firm hairs.

VENATION In plant leaves, the mode of veining.

VENEER **1** A thin mantle of surficial material that does not mask the topographic irregularities of the surface upon which it rests. It ranges in thickness from ten centimetres to about one metre. **2** A thin peeling of wood used to create plywood, or to be applied on top of a base as a decorative finish.

VENTILATION INDEX A numerical value relating the potential of the atmosphere to disperse airborne pollutants from a stationary source, such as smoke from a prescribed fire. It is calculated by multiplying the mixing height by the average wind speed in the mixed layer. It is also called ventilation factor.

VENTRAL Describes the location of a feature that is on the underside of a plant, animal, or organ, or on the side facing the ground (the front in humans). *See also* Dorsal.

VENTRICOSE Swollen more on one side than the other. It is a more pronounced swelling than gibbous.

VERNAL Appearing in the spring.

VERNAL OVERTURN *See* Lentic.

VERNATION The arrangement of leaves in a bud, or the manner in which a single young leaf develops.

VERRUCOSE Describes a surface covered with small, rounded or truncated, wartlike protrusions.

VERSATILE **1** Botanically, an anther attached at the middle on the apex of a filament and capable of free movement such as rotation. **2** Any species having the capability of, or already being, adapted for survival in several plant communities or successional stages or both.

VERSATILITY INDEX A figure indicating relative degrees of versatility between species in terms of the number of plant communities and successional stages used by individual species for feeding and reproduction. The greater the number of communities and successional stages used, the more versatile the species. *See also* Vulnerability.

VERTICAL DIVERSITY The diversity in a stand that results from the complexity of the aboveground structure of the vegetation. The tiers of vegetation or the more diverse the species makeup (or both), the higher the degree of vertical diversity. *See also* Biological Diversity; Horizontal Diversity; Structural Diversity.

VERTICAL EXAGGERATION In photogrammetry, the size of the vertical scale or dimension seen in a stereo model, in comparison to the hori-

zontal scale or dimension ratio of the actual object being viewed. *See also* Base-Height Ratio.
VERTICAL FUEL ARRANGEMENT The relative heights of fuels above ground and their vertical continuity that influences fire reaching various levels or strata of the forest.
VERTICAL INTENSIFICATION The spread upward of dwarf mistletoe within a tree. It is also termed upward spread.
VERTICAL RESISTANCE Also termed race specific resistance, or specific resistance. Resistance to some but not all races of a particular pathogen. The ranking of host varieties by degree of resistance may thus vary depending on the genotypes of the pathogens to which they are exposed. Conversely, ranking of the pathogen genotypes by degree of virulence may vary depending on the genotypes of the hosts to which they are exposed. Vertical resistance is usually monogenic or oligogenic. *See also* Horizontal Resistance.
VERTICAL STRUCTURE Also referred to as vertical stratification, in which plants are arranged into several layers in the canopy.
VERTICAL TEMPERATURE PROFILE A plot of actual air temperature against height above the Earth's surface. It is most commonly determined by a Rawinsonde observation. *See also* Helicopter Sounding; Minisonde Observation.
VERTICAL WIND PROFILE A plot of winds aloft against height above the Earth's surface. It is most commonly determined by a pilot balloon observation. *See also* Minisonde Observation; Rawinsonde Observation.
VERTICIL A whorl, a ring of three or more parts at one node.
VERTICILLASTER A much condensed cyme which appears to be a whorl, but really arises in the axils of opposite leaves.
VERTICILLATE Arranged in, or appearing to be arranged in whorls or rings.
VESICLE An air- or fluid-filled cavity, like a bladder.
VESPID WASP A social wasp that constructs nests made of bark, transformed into 'paper' by the mastication of woody materials.
VESSEL *See* Xylem.
VESTIGIAL Imperfectly developed, atrophied, and no longer functional, but was known to be fully developed and functional in ancestral forms. It is typically a smaller, degenerate form, of less complexity that its prototype.
VESTITURE/VESTURE Pubescence; any surface covering of hairs that makes it other than glabrous. *See also* Indument.
VETERAN Refers to mature trees that are considerably older than the rest of the stand. Usually, veterans are trees remaining from a previous forest that have survived while a new forest has been growing up around them. Different jurisdictions have set different age thresholds for the age at which a tree becomes a veteran.
VEXILLUM *See* Standard.
VIABILITY **1** The ability of a wildlife or plant population to maintain sufficient size so that it persists over time in spite of normal fluctuations in numbers. It is usually expressed as a probability of maintaining a specific population for a specified period. **2** In seed testing, the percentage of seed tested that contains sufficient live endoplasm for the seed to germinate. **3** The capacity of a seed, pollen grain, or spore to germinate and develop under given conditions.
VIABLE POPULATION A wildlife or plant population that contains a number and distribution of reproductive individuals in an area sufficient to provide *x* likelihood of persistence to *y* date. *x* and *y* must be specified. *See also* Minimum Viable Population.
VICARIAD One of two or more related organisms occurring in similar habitats and environmental conditions, but in distinct, and often widely separated areas.
VIEWSHED The landscape that can be directly seen from a viewpoint or along a transportation corridor.
VILLOUS Bearing long, straight, soft hairs.
VIRGA Wisps or streaks of water or ice particles falling out of a cloud but evaporating before reaching the Earth's surface as precipitation.
VIRGATE Wand-shaped; long, slender, straight, and erect.
VIRGIN FOREST Any forest that has had no visible evidence of human influence in its development history. There is considerable debate about whether any such forests could now exist anywhere in the world, since human influences are globally pervasive. *See also* Forest; Old-Growth Forest; Second-Growth Forest.
VIRULENCE The degree of pathenogenicity attributable to an isolate, pathotype, or strain of an organism.
VIRULENT Having the capacity to cause disease; strongly pathogenic.
VISCID Having a sticky feel when touched.
VISCOSITY The relative ability of a fluid to resist flow.
VISCOUS WATER Water that contains a thicken-

ing agent to reduce surface runoff. It tends to cling to burning fuels and spread in layers that are several times thicker than plain water, thereby having an increased capacity to absorb heat, cool fuel, and exclude oxygen. *See also* Wetting Agent.

VISIBILITY The greatest distance at which selected objects can be seen and identified, or its equivalent derived from instrumental measurements.

VISIBLE AREA *See* Seen Area.

VISIBLE AREA MAP *See* Seen Area Map.

VISUAL ACUITY A measure of the human eye's ability to separate details in viewing an object.

VISUAL FLIGHT RULES (VFR) Basic weather conditions prescribed for flight under visual flight rules. These are a cloud ceiling above one thousand feet and flight visibility in excess of three miles. *See also* Instrument Flight Rules.

VISUAL IMPACT ASSESSMENT An assessment of the landscape and its scenery components before development, such as the installation of new facilities or timber harvesting, takes place. The assessment reviews the component parts of the scenery and outlines ways in which the visual impact of the proposed development can be lessened or eliminated over a stated period of time.

VISUAL RESOURCE The visible physical features of a landscape.

VISUAL RESOURCE MANAGEMENT The inventory and planning actions taken to identify values and establish objectives for managing those values, and the management actions necessary to achieve those objectives.

VISUAL RESOURCE MANAGEMENT CLASSES Categories assigned to lands based on scenic quality, sensitivity level, and distance zones. Four classes are defined in the US, each one having an objective that prescribes the amount of modification allowed in the landscape.

VITAL RATES Rates of key demographic functions within a population, such as birth rate and survival rates.

VIVIPAROUS **1** Botanically, seeds that germinate in the fruit or while still otherwise attached to the plant. **2** Shoots that form plantlets while still on the parent plant (i.e., develop into vegetatively reproductive structures rather than flowers). **3** In animals, the young developing inside the body of placental mammals.

VIVITOXIN A toxic material produced within the infected host, or by the pathogen within the host.

VOLANT Any organism capable of flying. *See also* Mobile; Vagile.

VOLATILES In fire management, readily vaporized organic materials which, when mixed with oxygen, are easily ignited.

VOLATILITY The tendency of a substance to evaporate or be vaporized (i.e., change from a solid or liquid to a gas, at ordinary temperatures and atmospheric pressures). Use of highly volatile pesticides increases the likelihood of contamination beyond the target area.

VOLCANIC The deep-seated, igneous processes causing magma and its associated gases to rise up through the Earth's crust and be extruded onto the surface and into the atmosphere, sometimes with great force and violence. It is also the landforms, structures, and rocks that this produces.

VOLCANISTIC The entire spectrum of fragmental materials having a preponderance of clasts of volcanic origin. The term not only refers to pyroclastic materials but also to epiclastic deposits derived from volcanic source areas by normal processes of mass wasting and stream erosion (e.g., welded tuff, volcanic breccia).

VOLUBILE/VOLUBLE A twining growth habit.

VOLUME The amount of wood or fibre contained in a tree, stand, or forest, or parts of these measured in cubic units (e.g. square metres or cubic metres per hectare) inside the bark. **Gross merchantable volume** is the volume of the main stem, excluding stump and top, but including defective and decayed wood. **Gross total volume** is the volume of the main stem, including stump and top as well as defective and decayed wood. **Net merchantable** volume is the volume of the main stem, excluding stump, top, and defective and decayed wood.

VOLUME EQUATION A statistically derived expression of the relationship between volume and other tree or stand variables like age or site quality. It is used to estimate volume from more easily measured variables such as diameter at breast height, tree or stand height, taper factors, and crown closure. *See also* Volume Table.

VOLUME TABLE A table showing the estimated average tree or stand volume corresponding to selected values of other, more easily measured, tree or stand variables. Volume tables are used in the same manner as volume equations, from which they are usually constructed. Occasionally, volume tables may be constructed from a graphically derived relationship between volume and other tree or stand variables like age or site quality. Volume tables are constructed for individual species or species groups.

For a stand, volume tables are given in cubic metres per hectare. **Aerial volume table** is one where the independent variables must be measurable on aerial photographs, and often include stand height and crown closure. For an individual tree, volume tables for individual trees are given in cubic metres and can be in the following form: (1) **aerial volume tables**, as for stand volume tables; (2) **form class volume tables**, where the standard tree volume equations are constructed for different form classes; (3) **local volume tables**, where the diameter at breast height is the only independent variable. Data is collected from a small, local area. Local volume tables may sometimes be constructed from a standard tree volume equation by applying it to a local height/diameter relationship; (4) **standard volume tables**, where the independent variables are diameter at breast height and tree height. The data are collected from a large area (extensive) such as a province, state or region. *See also* Volume Equation.

VOLVA The fleshy remains of the partial veil found at the basal end of the stipe of a basidiomycete fungus. It may be above or below ground. *See also* Annulus; Fungus (for illustration).

VUGHS Relatively large soil voids, irregular in shape, and not normally interconnected to other voids.

VULNERABILITY The relative probability of timber management activities having an adverse effect on the numbers of a wildlife species. It is measured as the inverse of the versatility index. *See also* Versatility Index.

W

WAKES Boat-generated waves. *See also* Fetch.

WALK-THROUGH The least intensive type of ground survey to determine insect or disease damage, or to gain a preliminary sense of the biotic and abiotic attributes and features present. It is usually used to gain a qualitative estimation.

WARM FRONT *See* Front.

WART A raised gland on the skin of a toad or other amphibian that contains a poison.

WASHBOARD MORAINE *See* Corrugated Moraine.

WASHING Removal of fines from a surficial material due to the action of waves or running water; winnowing. It results in the formation of lag deposits.

WATER BARS Transverse ditches dug into the surface of an abandoned road to divert surface runoff water into the lateral ditches.

WATER BOMBER *See* Airtanker.

WATER QUALITY The chemical, physical, and biological characteristics of water.

WATERSHED An area of land, which may or may not be under forest cover, draining water, organic matter, dissolved nutrients, and sediments into a lake or stream. The topographic boundary, usually a height of land, that marks the dividing line from which surface streams flow in two different directions. In the US, a Key Watershed is defined by the National Forest Service and Bureau of Land Management District fish biologists as one containing: (1) habitat for potentially threatened species or stocks of anadromous salmonids or other potentially threatened fish; or (2) greater than six square miles with high quality water and fish habitat. *See also* Drainage; Sub-drainage.

WATERSHED ANALYSIS A systematic procedure for characterizing watershed and ecological processes to meet specific management and social objectives. In the US, watershed analysis is a stratum of ecosystem management planning applied to watersheds of approximately 20 to 200 square miles. Other jurisdictions apply differing size limits to the basin area.

WATERSHED RESTORATION Improving current conditions of watersheds to restore degraded fish habitat and provide long-term protection to aquatic and riparian resources.

WATERSPROUT *See* Epicormic Shoot.

WATER TABLE The upper limit or level in the ground of groundwater. It forms the boundary between the zone of saturation and the zone of aeration. In some cases, a surface water body or an upper water table (unconfined aquifer), may be separated from an underlying layer of groundwater by an impermeable layer of soil – this is called a perched water table. The illustration shows the movement of water from the atmosphere through the zone of aeration and into the saturated groundwater zone. Where

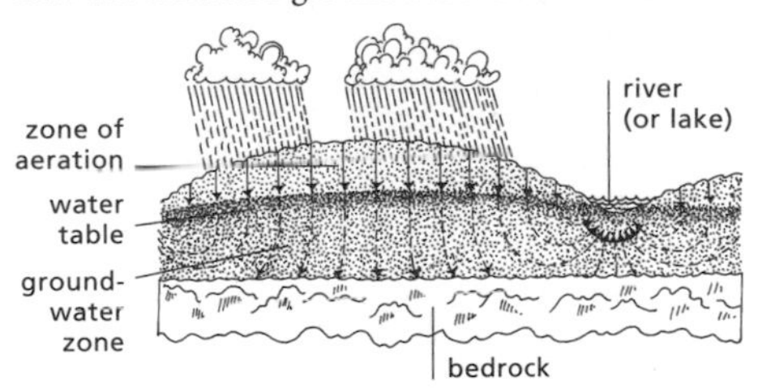

erosional processes have cut down into (possibly through) the water table and created depressions, such as valleys, bodies of water, such as rivers and lakes, may form. *See also* Perched Water Table; Vadose Zone

WATER YIELD The quantity of water derived from a unit area of watershed.

WEAK EXCAVATORS Species of birds capable of excavating a nest cavity, but require the wood to be softened by fungus or other agencies (e.g., chickadees, nuthatches).

WEATHERED BEDROCK Bedrock that has decomposed or disintegrated in place due to mechanical and/or chemical weathering.

WEATHERING The physical or chemical disintegration and decomposition of rock at or close to the surface of the Earth.

WEATHER MAP *See* Synoptic Chart.

WEATHER RADAR A radar device designed to operate on certain radio frequency bands to detect the presence (i.e., direction and distance) of precipitation, clouds, or both. Some types of weather radar are used to determine the amount of precipitation and wind speed and direction.

WEATHER STATION *See* Fire Weather Station; Stevenson Screen.

WEDGE SYSTEM A modification of the strip shelterwood system in which cutting begins as narrow, interior, wedge-shaped strips with the apex pointing into the prevailing winds. The strips are progressively enlarged and advanced. The system yields natural regeneration within a short period and leads to establishment of a fairly even-aged stand.

WEED A plant growing where it is not desired (i.e., a plant interfering with human activity or welfare) and is therefore considered to be a pest. The term includes herbs, shrubs, and trees and may include specimens of desirable species (e.g., when stands are overstocked and the superfluous trees are considered to be weeds).

WEEDING The removal or suppression of weeds from stands at the seedling stage, by cultural, physical, or chemical means.

WEED TREE Any tree considered to have little or no economic or other value. As utilization standards and technology change, many trees formerly considered to be weeds are now of significant economic value.

WEEVIL A beetle of the extensive family Curculionidae, characterized by the adult head being more or less elongated into a beak or snout, bearing clubbed, elbowed antennae, and by curved, legless larvae (grubs). Many species of weevil, in their adult or larval form, are serious forest pests, particularly as root and terminal shoot borers in conifers, and as root pests in nurseries.

WEIGHTED MEAN A value derived by multiplying each of a series of values by its assigned weight and dividing the sum of those products by the sum of the weights.

WEIR **1** A notch or depression in a levee, dam, embankment, or other barrier across or bordering a stream, through which the flow of water is measured or regulated. **2** A barrier placed across a stream to divert fish into a trap. **3** A small dam in a stream used to raise the water level or divert its flow.

WELL DISTRIBUTED A geographic distribution of habitats that maintains a population throughout a planning area and allows for interaction of individuals through periodic interbreeding and colonization of unoccupied habitats.

WENTWORTH PARTICLE SIZE SCALE A logarithmic scale for size classification of sediment particles; defines terms such as silt, pebbles, and boulders.

WET-BULB TEMPERATURE Technically, the temperature registered by the wet-bulb thermometer of a psychrometer. It is the lowest temperature to which the air can be cooled by evaporating water into it at a constant atmospheric pressure.

WET-BULB THERMOMETER In a psychrometer, the thermometer whose bulb is covered with a clean jacket of muslin saturated with distilled water before an observation is made. It measures the wet-bulb temperature once it is properly ventilated.

WETLAND A general term used to describe areas of land that are inundated by surface water or groundwater. This inundation has a frequency sufficient to support, and under normal circumstances does support, a prevalence of vegetative or aquatic life that require saturated or seasonally saturated soil conditions for growth and reproduction. These inundation patterns promote ecosystem processes that produce specific soil and vegetation patterns. In the Canadian Wetland Classification, a three-tiered approach is used to produce five wetland classes, seventy wetland forms, and numerous wetland types based on vegetation physiognomy. The five wetland classes are Bogs, Fens, Marshes, Swamps, and Shallow Open Waters. *See also* Bogs; Fens; Marshes; Shallow Open Waters; Swamps.

WET MEADOWS Areas where grasses predominate; normally waterlogged within a few inches of the ground surface.

WET ROT **1** A rot that is accompanied by release of water from the disintegrating cells. **2** A decay of wood characterized in its active state by a high water content, and the rotting mass of wood readily yielding water under moderate pressure, as in some white rots.

WET STORAGE **1** An area where powders or granular substances have been mixed with water or other liquids and can be stored without deterioration or drying out. **2** In fire-fighting, the storage of liquid chemical retardants stored at air bases and available for immediate use. *See also* Dry Storage.

WETTING AGENT A chemical that reduces the surface tension of water causing it to spread and penetrate more effectively. *See* Surfactant.

WET WATER Water with added chemicals that reduce the surface tension of water, causing it to spread and penetrate more effectively.

WETWOOD Wood, especially heartwood, with an abnormally high water content and a translucent, glassy appearance. The condition develops in the living stem and not by soaking in water. It is found in both softwoods and hardwoods and is of uncertain origin (e.g., in elms, may be associated with bacteria).

WHITE ROT In wood, any decay or rot attacking both the cellulose and the lignin, to produce a generally whiteish cellulose residue that may be spongy or stringy in texture, or may occur as pocket rot (e.g., *Heterobasidion annosum*). *See also* Brown Rot.

WHOLE TREE HARVESTING *See* Full Tree Harvesting.

WHOLISTIC FOREST USE A practical, ecosystem-based system for planning forest use, that protects all aspects of the forest ecosystem both during and after human use, accommodating at the same time the principles of landscape ecology, ecologically responsible forest use, and balanced forest use. Under wholistic forest-use planning, the ecological characteristics of the landscape are first protected by establishing large, protected reserves and a protected landscape network. Various ecologically responsible forest uses are then zoned on a watershed-by-watershed basis, accommodating the most sensitive and easily damaged human uses first before allocating zones for more aggressive uses. Timber extraction is considered as only one of the many possible forest uses and is recognized as having potentially large, negative impacts on other forest uses and on future forest functioning.

WHOLISTIC FOREST-USE ZONE Within the wholistic forest-use concept, an area designated for one or more ecologically responsible forest uses. Major zones include culture (areas that are culturally or historically important to local people), ecologically sensitive (small, sensitive areas not identified in the protected landscape network), fish and wildlife habitat, recreation-tourism-wilderness, ranching and trapping, and wholistic timber management.

WHOLISTIC TIMBER MANAGEMENT Within the wholistic forest-use concept, a zone where timber extraction is determined to be an acceptable human use of the forest. By applying partial cutting methods and rotation periods of 150 to 250+ years, fewer trees are cut under wholistic timber management than under conventional timber-cutting systems, while community economic needs are met through labour-intensive practices and value-added manufacturing. Consistent with wholistic forest-use principles, any practices that might degrade ecosystem functioning (such as conventional clearcutting, slashburning, highgrading, and pesticide applications) are avoided. The primary standard for wholistic timber management (also known as ecologically responsible timber management) is that all plans and activities must protect, maintain, and restore (where necessary) a fully functioning forest ecosystem at all temporal and spatial scales.

whorl

Chimaphila umbellata (Pipsissewa)

WHORL A circle of three or more leaves (see illustration), flowers, or other organs at one node. *See also* Alternate; Opposite.

WIDOW-MAKER A loose limb or tree top, or piece of bark lodged in a tree, which may fall on anyone working underneath it, causing serious injury or death.

WILD AND SCENIC RIVER SYSTEM In the US, those rivers or sections of rivers designated by Congressional action under the Wild and Scenic River Act (Public Law 90-542, 1968), as supplemented and amended, or those sections of rivers designated as wild, scenic, or recreational by an act of the legislature of the state or states through which they flow. Each designated river may be classified and administered under one or more of the following categories. **Wild river areas** are those rivers or sections of rivers that are free of impoundments and generally inaccessible except by trail, with watersheds or shorelines essentially primitive and waters unpolluted. These represent vestiges of primitive America. **Scenic river areas** are those rivers or sections of rivers that are free of impoundments with watersheds still largely primitive and shorelines largely undeveloped, but accessible in places by roads. **Recreation river areas** are those rivers or sections of rivers that are readily accessible by road or railroad, that may have some development along their shorelines, and that may have undergone some impoundment or diversion in the past. *See also* Canadian Heritage Rivers System.

WILDERNESS **1** In the US, areas formally protected by congressional action under the 1964 Wilderness Preservation Act and its extension to eastern lands by the so-called Eastern Wilderness Act, to public lands by the Federal Land Policy and Management Act of 1976, and to Alaska by the Alaska National Interest Lands Conservation Act of 1980. In the US, the legal definition of wilderness, under the Wilderness Act of 1964, is: 'A wilderness, in contrast with those areas where man and his works dominate the landscape, is hereby recognized as an area where the earth and its community of life are untrammelled by man, where man himself is a visitor who does not remain.' **2** More generally, wilderness is an area established to conserve its primeval character and influence for public enjoyment, under primitive conditions, in perpetuity, without permanent improvements or human habitation. Wilderness areas are protected and managed to preserve their natural conditions, which generally appear to have been affected primarily by the forces of nature, with the imprint of human activity substantially unnoticeable. Such areas have outstanding opportunities for solitude or for a primitive and confined type of recreation. Wilderness areas in the US include at least 5,000 acres or are of sufficient size to make practical their preservation, enjoyment, and use in an unimpaired condition. They may contain features of scientific, educational, scenic, or historic value as well as ecological and geological interest.

Note that there is a significant attitudinal aspect to the connotation of what is or is not a wilderness. Although they are defined by US legislation to be quite large areas, many people consider much smaller areas to be wilderness worth retaining in an undeveloped state, hence the emerging concept of 'pocket wilderness areas' as small, often quite isolated remnants of the formerly undisturbed landscape.

De facto wilderness is public or private land considered to be wilderness because it is undeveloped and unroaded, but it is not designated by legislation as being a wilderness area, national park, or other formal land protection category.

WILDERNESS-DEPENDENT WILDLIFE Species that are dependent on conditions of naturalness and solitude and thus have their continued existence dependent on and/or reflective of wilderness conditions.

WILDERNESS OPPORTUNITY SPECTRUM (WOS) A spectrum of wilderness conditions including finer gradations of naturalness and solitude (i.e., primitive conditions). The WOS includes, for example, pristine, primitive, and portal designations, indicating decreasing degrees of naturalness and solitude. Like the Recreation Opportunity Spectrum, WOS is a kind of zoning, which delineates particular areas where different management prescriptions or restrictions on visitor behaviour apply.

WILDFIRE An unplanned or unwanted natural or man-caused fire, as contrasted with a prescribed fire. *See also* Prescribed Fire.

WILDLANDS Land that is now, and has been in recent history, uncultivated and relatively uninfluenced by human activities (e.g., tundra, barrens, alpine areas). There are legal definitions of what constitutes wildlands in some jurisdictions.

WILDLIFE Any species of amphibian, bird, fish, mammal, and reptile found in the wild, living unrestrained or free-roaming and not domesticated. Some definitions include plants, fungi, algae, and bacteria.

WILDLIFE MANAGEMENT The art and science of manipulating wildlife populations and their habitats to meet specific objectives, which can be scientific or recreational.

WILDLIFE TREE A classification scheme derived from the concepts outlined in snag classification. A wildlife tree is any tree that provides present or future habitat critical (but may not be in the US legal sense of 'critical') for the maintenance or enhancement of wildlife. The assessment of a wildlife tree as critical habitat may be determined by one or more physical attributes, such as structure, age, condition, abundance, species, geographic location, or surrounding habitat features. A high-quality wildlife tree has the following attributes: (1) a standing, dead tree greater than fifteen metres in height; (2) at least thirty centimetres in diameter at breast height; (3) preferably with a broken top; (4) some of the bark is intact; (5) the tree is windfirm; and (6) lean is minimal.

However, all snags and stumps, whether standing or lying on the ground have wildlife value for a range of species. In British Columbia, snags are classified for their utility as wildlife trees into one of nine classes based on their ability to provide perching, roosting, nesting, or feeding opportunities for a range of wildlife. *See also* Snag Classification.

WILDLING A naturally grown seedling that is suitable for replanting into a stand.

WILT **1** The loss of rigidity and subsequent drooping of plants. It is caused by a loss of turgor pressure within the cells due to lack of water. **2** A disease characterized by this symptom, due to a vascular infection that interferes with normal water uptake or conduction. *See also* Blight.

WILTING POINT *See* Soil Water.

WIND BREAK A barrier that provides shelter from the wind on the downward side.

WIND DIRECTION The direction from which the wind is blowing. Wind direction is most commonly referred to by cardinal direction (e.g., north, east, south, west) but may also be expressed in degrees (1 degree to 360 degrees).

WIND EROSION EQUATION An equation for predicting E, the average annual soil loss due to wind in mass per unit area per year, and is defined as $E = IKCLV$, where I is the soil erodibility factor, K is the soil ridge roughness factor, C is the local climatic factor, L is the field width, and V is the vegetative factor.

This is now being replaced by a simpler Revised Universal Soil Loss Equation (RUSLE). This is conceptually similar and uses the same equation. However, the rainfall erosivity factor R is based on more data and more sophisticated predictive relationships. The soil erodibility factor K is improved and now takes into account some geographic variation of soil characteristics, including special features of volcanic soils, and seasonal variation associated with climatic variables. The L and S factors (slope angle and slope length effects) have been modified, and may be combined into a single factor. The C and P factors are now based on more extensive data (e.g., the C factor now takes into account prior land use, plant canopy, soil surface cover, and surface roughness. *See also* Erosion; Universal Soil Loss Equation.

WINDFALL Trees or parts of trees felled by high winds. *See also* Windthrow.

WINDROW The machine piling of slash and logging debris into lines with cleared ground in between. Windrows may be burned or just left to decay.

WINDROW BURNING The burning of woody debris that has been piled into long, continuous rows.

WINDS ALOFT A meteorological term referring to the wind speeds and wind directions at various levels in the atmosphere above the domain of surface weather observations. The most common method of determining the speed and direction of winds in the upper air is by visually tracking a small, free-lift balloon. *See also* Minisonde Observation; Rawinsonde Observation.

WINDTHROW A tree uprooted by the wind. Windthrow may indicate the presence of a pest problem, such as root rot. It is synonymous with blowdown.

WING **1** A movable organ, often the forelimb, designed to allow or assist flight in birds, insects, and bats. *See also* Butterfly. **2** A thin, membranous structure on a seed or fruit that aids in wind dispersal. **3** A membranous outgrowth on a plant, typically, a flange on a stem. **4** One of two lateral petals of a papilionaceous flower.

WINGWALL An extension of a bridge abutment, constructed to retain the fill material of a road bed and prevent it from spilling or slumping into a watercourse. *See also* Bridge (for illustration).

WINTER BIRD POPULATION STUDY In the US, a program of the National Audubon Society involving census of wintering birds by counting and mapping, but not depending on persisting occupation of territories or home ranges.

WINTER DRYING The desiccation of foliage or twigs by dry winds at times when water conduction is restricted by cold soil, or the freezing of plant tissues, or the soil.

WINTER PLUMAGE The plumage that a bird moults into after the reproductive phase of the year is over (often after migration). It is often less brightly coloured than summer plumage.

WINTER RANGE The geographical and/or vertical range where a species occurs after both the reproductive and migratory phases of the year are completed. *See also* Summer Range.

WINTER SUNSCALD Localized injury to bark and cambium, often resulting in wounds or cankers, caused by freezing following the unseasonable heating of the bark by the sun in winter. It is usually localized on the side of the stem that is exposed to the midday and afternoon sun.

WIN-WIN A situation in which neither side in a dispute loses out to the other. Both sides win a little, as compared to a fifty-fifty split. Neither side wins everything.

WITCHES' BROOM A characteristic plant form of woody plants. It is caused by an abnormal shortening of internodes and proliferation of weak shoots, to create a dense, brushlike mass of twigs. It is typically induced by dwarf mistletoe, rust fungi, or other organisms, but can also be a response to abiotic environmental stresses. Mistletoe brooms are evergreen, while the needles of brooms induced by rusts usually only last for one year.

WITHDRAWAL Forested land removed from the operation base used to calculate available timber or mineral supplies. Typically, lands are withdrawn for other purposes that are mutually exclusive to logging and mining (e.g., parks, ecological reserves, impoundments).

WITHE/WITHY A slender, flexible branch or twig.

WOLF TREE A tree of good vigour but poor form that occupies space, and nutrient and water potential that might better be utilized by another tree of similar vigour but better form.

WOODLAND In the US, forest land producing trees not normally used for saw timber products, and not included in timber volume calculations for the purpose of allocating timber sales. In more general terms, an ecosystem that has trees as the tallest stratum, but where their canopy cover does not exceed about 30 per cent.

WOOLLY APHID An aphid covered by waxy scales or threads (e.g., the balsam woolly aphid *Adelges piceae*).

WORD In computer science, a storage unit equivalent to a character of information, consisting of a group of bytes. A word is usually four bytes, but may range from two to eight or more. *See also* Bit; Byte.

WORKING GROUP An aggregate of forest stands, or forest stand and forest sites, which are grouped for the purposes of applying a common set of silvicultural treatments (also called operational group).

WORLD CONSERVATION STRATEGY A set of national and subnational strategies designed to achieve a more balanced integration of conservation and development around the world. The *World Conservation Strategy*, published by the International Union for the Conservation of Nature in Switzerland (IUCN) in 1981, was predicated on three main objectives: (1) essential ecological processes and life-support systems must be maintained; (2) genetic diversity must be preserved; and (3) any use of species or ecosystems must be sustainable.

Since its release, many countries have written and implemented national conservation strategies. The World Conservation Strategy was further elaborated in 1991 with the release of *Caring for the Earth: A Strategy for Sustainable Living*, also published by the IUCN.

WORLD HERITAGE SITES An international classification system to recognize and designate areas which represent a major stage of the Earth's evolutionary history; significant ongoing geological processes, biological evolution, and man's interaction with his natural environment; superlative natural phenomena, formation, or features; and has natural habitats where threatened or endangered species of animals or plants of outstanding universal value can survive.

WOUND GUM A dark, amorphous gummy substance produced in the wound of hardwoods and some conifers in response to injury, infection, or other irritation.

WOUND PARASITE A parasite that can enter a host and establish itself only through wounds or injured tissue.

WOUND STAIN A discoloration of wood originating in or developed as a result of a wound in a tree.

WRENCHING The disturbance of seedling roots in a nursery bed (e.g., with a tractor-drawn blade) with the objective of stimulating the development of a fibrous root system.

X

XENOGAMY Cross-fertilization between flowers on different plants. Outcrossing. *See also* Geitonogamy.

XERIC Environmental conditions and associated habitats lacking water due to low rainfall. *See also* Hydric; Mesic.

XEROPHYTE Plants growing where soil moisture conditions are very dry most of the time. *See also* Halophyte; Hydrophyte; Mesophyte.

XEROSERE Ecological succession that takes place on bare rock, away from any wave action. Colonizing plants are lichens and some mosses that can withstand prolonged drought, temperature extremes, and a lack of nutrients. *See also* Hydrosere; Sammosere.

X-MOTION In a stereoplotting instrument, the x-motion is a linear correction that lies approximately parallel to a line between two projector stations. *See also* Y-Motion.

XYLEM The conducting tissues of vascular plants, characterized by the presence of vascular bundles containing elongated, tubelike cells (tracheids and vessel elements), parenchyma, and xylem fibres.

The tracheids have thick walls; the vessels have thinner walls. Both cell types are seen in angiosperms, but only tracheids are seen in gymnosperms. Tracheids and vessels are linked at their ends by perforated walls, and form the pathway by which water and dissolved nutrients can pass upwards from the roots to the leaves. They have no living contents.

The axial and radial parenchyma cells, located in the sapwood, are used for food storage in the trunk and branches, and lateral movement of materials across the stem. The fibres provide tensile strength to the tree. The central part of the trunk or branch contains the oldest xylem, which is typically physiologically inactive and known as the heartwood.

The initial or primary xylem supports vertical growth. Secondary xylem is responsible for radial growth. Xylem formed early in the season has lighter coloured cells with thinner walls, in contrast to later formed xylem cells which are fewer in number and have thicker walls. This difference in wall thickness and colour makes up the width of one annual ring and provides a means of differentiating annual or seasonal growth. The main bulk of wood is made up of secondary xylem. *See also* Bark; Heartwood; Phloem (for illustration); Sapwood.

XYLEM STIMULATION Hypertrophy or hyperplasia of xylem cells of the host, usually due to infection by organisms such as dwarf mistletoe, which produces grossly distorted annual rings.

XYLOMETER The apparatus used to determine the volume of wood pieces, by measuring the amount of water displaced when the pieces are immersed in the xylometer.

Y

YARDING The moving of logs from the point where they were felled to a central collection and pickup point, known as the landing. *See also* Harvest Functions.

YAW **1** In air navigation, the rotation of an aircraft about its vertical axis so as to cause the aircraft's longitudinal axis to deviate from the flight path. It is also called crab. **2** In photogrammetry, the rotation of a camera or photograph coordinate system about either the photograph *Z* axis or the exterior *Z* axis. In some photogrammetric instruments and in some analytical applications, the symbol kappa (K) may be used. *See also* Crab; Swing.

YEARLING A one-year-old individual in its second year of life.

YELLOWS A disease in which yellowing or chlorosis of plant tissue is the principal symptom (e.g., elm yellows). *See also* Mycoplasma.

YIELD **1** The accumulated volume or biomass remaining from gross production after accounting for losses due to respiration during production, herbivory, litterfall, and other factors that decrease the remaining available biomass. **2** In timber management, the volume of wood available for harvest at the end of a rotation period, usually measured as unit volume per unit area (e.g., cubic metres per hectare) or the amount of output actually harvested and usable (e.g., volume of timber extracted, volume of lumber produced from the timber extracted). *See also* Biomass Production.

YIELD TABLE In its simplest form, a plot of expected fibre yield in terms of volume per unit area, against the stand age. The basic plot produces a **normal yield table** that assumes the site is fully stocked or has a normal stand density. A derivative form is the **empirical yield table** in which the stocking is assumed to be average rather than full or normal. This eliminates the problems of assuming full stocking, but only applies to the average stand densities found at the sample plots. A third derivative is the **variable-density yield table**, which uses multiple regressions to account for various stand density levels.

Y-MOTION In a stereoplotting instrument, the y-motion is a linear correction that lies approximately perpendicular to a line between two projector stations. *See also* X-Motion.

Z

ZOEAMEGALOPS The final larval stage of crabs and shrimps. It is typically the point in the life cycle at which the organisms settle to the ocean bottom.

ZONE **1** In planning, a geographically defined area, or a temporal space on the planet in which activities, events, or features occur by design or otherwise. **2** In vegetation analysis, the geographic area of uniform macroclimate where the climatic climax associations share the same characteristic species of the principal layer.

ZONE LINE A black line visible in decaying wood when a cut or fracture crosses a pseudosclerotial plate.

ZONE OF INITIATION The point on the landscape at which mass wastage movements originate. *See also* Mass Wasting.

ZONE OF SATURATION In soils, the zone found below the permanent water table. *See also* Illuviation.

ZOOCHORE A propagule dispersed by animals. Characteristics of zoochory include fleshy fruit, nut-like fruit, or adhesivity (barbs). If the dispersion involves passage of the propagule through the digestive tract of an animal it is **endozoochory**. If dispersion is achieved by being carried on the outside of an animal, it is **exozoochory**. Where a cache of propagules, such as seeds or nuts are buried or piled by an animal, it is termed **synzoochory.** *See also* Anemochore; Barochore; Hydrochore; Myrmecochore; Propagule.

ZOOGEOGRAPHY The study of the evolutionary history and prehistoric and current distributions of animals.

ZOOSPORE A spore produced by algae or fungi, that is motile by means of flagellae.

ZYGOMATIC ARCH In mammals, the cheek bones in the skull running below the eye to form an arch.

ZYGOMATIC WIDTH In mammals, the width of the skull measured at and including the zygomatic arches.

ZYGOMORPHIC Bilaterally symmetrical, having the capability to be divided into two equal halves in one plane only (see illustration). *See also* Actinomorphic; Symmetrical.

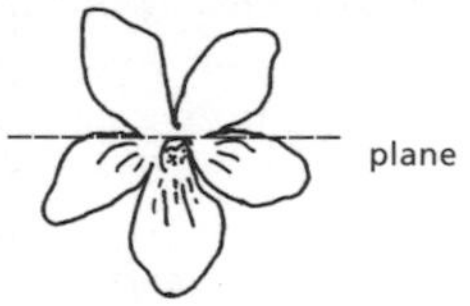

plane

ZYGOSPORE A thick-walled resting spore in certain fungi that is formed by the fusion of two gametes and borne on somatic hyphae. It is characteristic of zygomycetes.

Appendix 1
Classification of Organisms

The classification of organisms has long been a source of controversy. Organisms are classified on the basis of characteristics such as size, structure, colour, and number of similar features (e.g., number of teeth and appendages). In very early classification schemes only two kingdoms were recognized and all organisms were considered to be either plants or animals. More recently it was realized that certain organisms needed their own kingdom due to basic differences that separate them from either the plants or the animals. As a result a third kingdom, the Protoctista, was added to differentiate the single-celled organisms. As more research work elucidated the intricacies of life, it became apparent that even the three-kingdom system did not provide enough separation for all organisms. A four-kingdom scheme arose where the single-celled creatures were divided into the kingdom Monera and the kingdom Protista. Most recently, a fifth kingdom has been accepted, the kingdom Fungi. It should be noted however, that there remains considerable variation in the schemes adopted. For example, some authorities have a six-kingdom scheme using Protista, Plantae, Animalia, Fungi, and the Monera divided into two kingdoms, the Archaebacteria, and the Eubacteria. The distinguishing characteristics of the five-kingdom scheme are outlined below.

Kingdom Monera
Unicellular organisms, which may be seen in colonies. They have prokaryotic cells, lack plastids and mitochondria, and do not have membranes around the cell organelles.
Reproduction is asexual by fission, nutrition is absorptive or photosynthetic, and motion is by means of flagella.

Kingdom Protista
Unicellular organisms, which may be seen in colonies. They have eukaryotic cells and a complete set of cell organelles. Reproduction is asexual and sexual, nutrition can be absorptive, ingestive, or photosynthetic, and motion is by means of cilia or flagella.

Kingdom Fungi
Eukaryotic cells lacking plastids and photosynthetic materials. Reproduction is asexual and sexual, they are immobile, and the cells typically lack definite boundaries between each other.

Kingdom Plantae
Eukaryotic cells with distinct cell walls, but a simpler set of organelles than the protists. Reproduction is sexual and asexual, and they are immobile, multicellular structures that use photosynthesis as the main source of nutrition.

Kingdom Animalia
Eukaryotic cells without walls, and that lack plastids and photosynthetic pigments. Reproduction is typically sexual and nutrition is ingestive. They are mobile, multicellular structures.

To further confuse the classification scheme, some authorities place the same names in different parts of the classification. For example, one scheme may discuss the kingdom Protista, the phylum Sarcomastigophora, and the subphylum Mastigophora, while another will show the Sarcomastigophora as a subphylum of the Phylum Protozoa, with Mastigophora shown as a class. While this is confusing, it is more important to be able to agree on the classification of the organisms within each particular section. In the following detailed classification, we have noted the classification scheme adopted within each kingdom, representing the most commonly accepted version available at the time of publication. We have not included extinct organisms, nor have we broken all of the classifications down beyond the level of class. Suggestions for improvement are welcome. Because of the ever-changing nature of classification schemes, it is likely that future schemes will introduce other changes, once better evidence about origins and commonalities is more widely accepted.

Plant Kingdom: Kingdom Plantae (Metaphyta)

The classification of plants has long been a source of debate among botanists, and several classification systems are still in use. While most elements of these classification schemes are agreed upon, the exact placement of certain plants within these schemes remains variable. All of them utilize the evolutionary origins and current phylogenetic appearances as the basis for placement, but some botanists tend to lump groups together under one category, while others prefer to split out subtle differences into several categories. In the following classification scheme, the angiosperms are classified according to Cronquist's classification scheme. A complicating factor in plant classification schemes is that different names are given to the same categories. For example, some authors refer to the Anthophyta, while others refer to the Angiospermophyta – both meaning the angiosperms, or flowering plants. The two main groups of plants are the Bryophyta (the non-vascular plants), which include mosses, liverworts, and hornworts, and the Tracheophyta (the vascular plants), which encompass all the other plants. Throughout the following scheme, alternative names are placed in parentheses after the currently accepted name.

Phylum	Class	Subclass	Order	Family
Bryophyta				
	Bryopsida (Musci)(mosses)			
			Sphagnidae (peat mosses)	
			Andreaeidae (granite mosses)	
			Bryidae (true mosses)	
Hepatophyta (liverworts)				
		Takakiales		
		Haplomitriales		
		Marchantiales		
		Metzgeriales		
		Jungermanniales		
Antherocerophyta (hornworts)				
Psilotophyta (psilopsids)				
Lycopodophyta (club mosses)				
Sphenophyta (horsetails)				
Pterophyta (ferns)				
Cycadophyta (cycads)				
Ginkgophyta (ginkgo)				
Gnetophyta (gnetophytes)				
Coniferophyta (conifers)				
				Araucariaceae (Chile pine)
				Cephalotaxaceae (Cow's tail pine)
				Cupressaceae (cypress, false cedars, junipers)
				Pinaceae (fir, true cedar, larch, spruce, pine, hemlock)
				Sciadopitaceae (umbrella-pine)
				Podocarpaceae (yellow wood)
				Taxaceae (yew)
				Taxodiaceae (swamp cypress)

Plant Kingdom, *continued*

Phylum	Class	Subclass	Order	Family	Family, *continued*
Anthophyta (Angiospermae) (flowering plants)					
	Magnoliopsida (Dicotyledonae)				
		Magnoliidae			
			Magnoliales		
				Winteraceae	Magnoliaceae
				Degeneriaceae	Lactoridaceae
				Himantandraceae	Annonaceae
				Eupomatiaceac	Myristacaceae
				Austrobaileyaceae	Canellacea
			Laurales		
				Amborellaceae	Calycanthaceae
				Trimeniaceae	Idiospermaceae
				Monimiaceae	Lauraceae
				Gomortegaceae	Hernandiaceae
			Piperales		
				Chloranthaceae	
				Sauraceae	
				Piperaceae	
			Aristolochiales		
				Aristolochiaceae	
			Illicialies		
				Illiciaceae	
				Schisandraceae	
			Nymphaeales		
				Nelumbonaceae	
				Nymphaeaceae	
				Cabombaceae	
				Ceratophyllaceae	
			Ranunculales		
				Ranunculaceae	Lardizabalaceae
				Circaeasteraceae	Menispermaceae
				Berberidaceae	Coriariaceae
				Sargentodoxaceae	Sabiaceae
			Papaverales		
				Papaveraceae	
				Fumariaceae	
		Hamamelidae			
			Trochodendrales		
				Tetracentraceae	
				Trochodendraceae	
			Hamamelidales		
				Cercidiphyllaceae	Myrothamnaceae
				Eupteleaceae	
				Platanaceae	
				Hamamelidaceae	
			Daphniphyllales		
				Daphniphyllaceae	
			Didymelales		
				Didymelaceae	
			Eucommiales		
				Eucommiaceae	

Plant Kingdom, *continued*

Phylum	Class	Subclass	Order	Family	Family, *continued*
Anthophyta (Angiospermae) (flowering plants)					
	Magnoliopsida (Dicotyledonae)				
		Hamamelidae, continued			
			Urticales		
				Barbeyaceae	Cecropiaceae
				Ulmaceae	Urticaceae
				Cannabidaceae	
				Moraceae	
			Leitneriales		
				Leitneriaceae	
			Juglandales		
				Rhoipteleaceae	
				Juglandaceae	
			Myricales		
				Myricaceae	
			Fagales		
				Balanopaceae	
				Fagaceae	
				Betulaceae	
			Casuarinales		
				Casuarinaceae	
		Caryophyllidae			
			Caryophyllales		
				Phytolaccaceae	Chenopodiaceae
				Achatocarpaceae	Amaranthaceae
				Nyctaginaceae	Portulacaceae
				Aizoaceae	Basellaceae
				Didiereaceae	Molluginaceae
				Cactaceae	Caryophyllaceae
			Polygonales		
				Polygonaceae	
			Plumbaginales		
				Plumbaginaceae	
		Dilleniidae			
			Dilleniales		
				Dilleniaceae	
				Paeoniaceae	
			Theales		
				Ochnaceae	Tetrameristaceae
				Sphaerosepalaceae	Pellicieraceae
				Sarcolaenaceae	Oncothecaceae
				Dipterocarpaceae	Marcgraviaceae
				Caryocaraceae	Quiinaceae
				Theaceae	Elatinaceae
				Actinidiaceae	Paracryphiaceae
				Scytopetalaceae	Medusagynaceae
				Pentaphylacaceae	Guttiferae
			Malvales		
				Elaeocarpaceae	Malvaceae
				Tiliaceae	
				Sterculiaceae	
				Bombacaceae	

Plant Kingdom, *continued*

Phylum	Class	Subclass	Order	Family	Family, *continued*
Anthophyta (Angiospermae) (flowering plants)					
	Magnoliopsida (Dicotyledonae)				
		Dilleniidae, continued			
			Lecythiadales		
				Lecythidaceae	
			Nepenthales		
				Sarraceniaceae	
				Nepenthaceae	
				Droseraceae	
			Violales		
				Flacourtiaceae	Ancistrocladaceae
				Peridiscaceae	Turneraceae
				Bixaceae	Malesherbiaceae
				Cistaceae	Passifloraceae
				Huaceae	Achariaceae
				Lacistemataceae	Caricaceae
				Scyphostegiaceae	Fouquieriaceae
				Stachyuraceae	Hoplestigmataceae
				Violaceae	Cucurbitaceae
				Tamaricaceae	Datiscaceae
				Frankeniaceae	Begoniaceae
				Dioncophyllaceae	Loasaceae
			Salicales		
				Salicaceae	
			Capparidales		
				Tovariaceae	Resedaceae
				Capparidaceae	
				Cruciferae	
				Moringaceae	
			Batales		
				Gyrostemonaceae	
				Bataceae	
			Ericales		
				Cyrillaceae	Epacridaceae
				Clethraceae	Ericaceae
				Grubbiaceae	Pyrolaceae
				Empetraceae	Monotropaceae
			Diapensiales		
				Diapensiaceae	
			Ebenales		
				Sapotaceae	Symplocaceae
				Ebenaceae	
				Styracaceae	
				Lissocarpaceae	
			Primulales		
				Theophrastaceae	
				Myrsinaceae	
				Primulaceae	

Plant Kingdom, *continued*

Phylum	Class	Subclass	Order	Family	Family, *continued*
Anthophyta (Angiospermae) (flowering plants)					
	Magnoliopsida (Dicotyledonae), continued				
		Rosidae			
			Rosales		
				Brunelliaceae	Connaraceae
				Eucryphiaceae	Anisophylleaceae
				Cunoniaceae	Alseuosmiaceae
				Davidsoniaceae	Crassulaceae
				Dialypetalanthaceae	Cephalotaceae
				Pittosporaceae	Saxifragaceae
				Byblidaceae	Rosaceae
				Hydrangeaceae	Neuradaceae
				Columelliaceae	Crossosomataceae
				Grossulariaceae	Chrysobalanaceae
				Greyiaceae	Surianaceae
				Bruniaceae	Rhabdodendraceae
			Fabales		
				Leguminosae	
			Proteales		
				Eleagnaceae	
				Proteaceae	
			Podostemales		
				Podostemaceae	
			Haloragidales		
				Haloragidaceae	
				Gunneraceae	
			Myrtales		
				Sonneratiaceae	Myrtaceae
				Lythraceae	Punicaceae
				Penaeaceae	Onagraceae
				Crypteroniaceae	Oliniaceae
				Thymelaeceae	Melastomataceae
				Trapaceae	Combretaceae
			Rhizophorales		
				Rhizophoraceae	
			Cornales		
				Alangiaceae	
				Nyssaceae	
				Vornaceae	
				Garryaceae	
			Santales		
				Medusandraceae	Misodendraceae
				Dipentodontaceae	Loranthaceae
				Olacaceae	Viscaceae
				Opiliaceae	Eremolepidaceae
				Santalaceae	Balanophoraceae
			Rafflesiales		
				Hydnoraceae	
				Mitrastemmataceae	
				Rafflesiaceae	

Plant Kingdom, *continued*

Phylum	Class	Subclass	Order	Family	Family, *continued*
Anthophyta (Angiospermae) (flowering plants)					
	Magnoliopsida (Dicotyledonae)				
		Rosidae, continued			
			Celastrales		
				Geissolomataceae	Icacinaceae
				Celastraceae	Aextoxicaceae
				Stackhousiaceae	Cardiopteridaceae
				Salvadoraceae	Corynocarpaceae
				Aquifoliaceae	Dichapetalaceae
			Euphorbiales		
				Buxaceae	
				Simmondsiaceae	
				Pandaceae	
				Euphorbiaceae	
			Rhamnales		
				Rhamnaceae	
				Leeaceae	
				Vitaceae	
			Linales		
				Erythroxylaceae	
				Humiriaceae	
				Ixonanthaceae	
				Linaceae	
			Polygales		
				Malpighiaceae	Polygalaceae
				Vochysiaceae	Xanthophyllaceae
				Trigoniaceae	Krameriaceae
				Tremandraceae	
			Sapindales		
				Staphyleaceae	Julianiaceae
				Melianthaceae	Simaroubaceae
				Bretschneideraceae	Tepuianthaceae
				Akaniaceae	Cneoraceae
				Sapindaceae	Meliaceae
				Hippocastanaceae	Ptaeroxylaceae
				Aceraceae	Rutaceae
				Burseraceae	Zygophyllaceae
				Anacardiaceae	
			Geraniales		
				Oxalidaceae	Balsaminaceae
				Geraniaceae	
				Limnanthaceae	
				Tropaeolaceae	
			Apiales		
				Araliaceae	
				Umbelliferae	
		Asteridae			
			Gentiales		
				Loganiaceae	Asclepiadaceae
				Gentianaceae	
				Saccifoliaceae	
				Apocynaceae	

Plant Kingdom, *continued*

Phylum	Class	Subclass	Order	Family	Family, *continued*
Anthophyta (Angiospermae) (flowering plants)					
	Magnoliopsida (Dicotyledonae)				
		Asteridae, continued			
			Solanales		
				Duckeodenraceae	Menyanthaceae
				Nolanaceae	Polemoniaceae
				Solanaceae	Hydrophyllaceae
				Convolvulaceae	
			Lamiales		
				Lennoaceae	
				Boraginaceae	
				Verbenaceae	
				Labiatae	
			Callitrichales		
				Hippuridaceae	
				Callitrichaceae	
				Hydrostachyaceae	
			Plantaginales		
				Plantaginaceae	
			Scrophulariales		
				Oleaceae	Acanthaceae
				Scrophulariaceae	Pedaliaceae
				Globulariaceae	Bignoniaceae
				Myoporaceae	Mendonciaceae
				Orobanchaceae	Lentibulariaceae
				Gesneriaceae	
			Campanulales		
				Pentaphragmataceae	Donatiaceae
				Sphenocleaceae	Brunoniaceae
				Campanulaceae	Goodeniaceae
				Stylidiaceae	
			Rubiales		
				Rubiaceae	
				Theligonaceae	
			Dipsacales		
				Caprifoliaceae	Morinaceae
				Adoxaceae	
				Valerianaceae	
				Dipsacaceae	
			Calycerales		
				Calyceraceae	
			Asterales		
				Compositae	
	Liliopsida (Monocotyledonae)				
		Alismatidae			
			Alismatales		
				Butomaceae	
				Limnocharitaceae	
				Alismataceae	
			Hydrocharitales		
				Hydrocharitaceae	

Plant Kingdom, *continued*

Phylum	Class	Subclass	Order	Family	Family, *continued*
Anthophyta (Angiospermae) (flowering plants)					
	Liliopsida (Monocotyledonae)				
		Alismatidae, continued			
			Najadales		
				Aponogetonaceae	Najadaceae
				Scheuchzeriaceae	Zannichelliaceae
				Juncaginaceae	Posidoniaceae
				Potamogetonaceae	Cymodoceaceae
				Ruppiaceae	Zosteraceae
			Triuridales		
				Petrosaviaceae	
				Triuridaceae	
		Arecidae			
			Arecales		
				Palmae	
			Cyclanthales		
				Cyclanthaceae	
			Pandanales		
				Pandanaceae	
			Arales		
				Araceae	
				Lemnaceae	
		Commelinidae			
			Commelinales		
				Rapateaceae	
				Xyridaceae	
				Mayacaceae	
				Commelinaceae	
			Eriocaules		
				Eriocaulaceae	
			Restionales		
				Flagellariaceae	
				Joinvilleaceae	
				Restionaceae	
				Centrolepidaceae	
			Juncales		
				Juncaceae	
				Thurniaceae	
			Cyperales		
				Cyperaceae	
				Gramineae	
			Hydatellales		
				Hydatellaceae	
			Typhales		
				Sparganiaceae	
				Typhaceae	

Plant Kingdom, *continued*

Phylum	Class	Subclass	Order	Family	Family, *continued*
Anthophyta (Angiospermae) (flowering plants)					
	Liliopsida (Monocotyledonae), continued				
		Zingiberidae			
			Bromeliales		
				Bromeliaceae	
			Zingiberales		
				Strelitziaceae	Zingiberaceae
				Heliconiaceae	Cannaceae
				Musaceae	Marantaceae
				Lowiaceae	
		Liliidae			
			Liliales		
				Philydraceae	Agavaceae
				Pontederiaceae	Xanthorrhoeaceae
				Haemodoraceae	Hanguanaceae
				Cyanastraceae	Taccaceae
				Liliaceae	Stemonaceae
				Iridaceae	Smilacaceae
				Velloziaceae	Dioscoreaceae
				Aloeaceae	
			Orchidales		
				Geosiridaceae	
				Burmanniaceae	
				Corsiaceae	
				Orchidaceae	

Animal Kingdom: Kingdom Animalia (Metazoa)

The classification of invertebrates within the animal kingdom remains in a state of flux, with several schemes in use. In some classifications the protozoans are included in the animal kingdom. In the following scheme they are excluded and placed in a separate kingdom, the Protista.

Phylum	Subphylum	Class	Subclass	Order (Suborder *and* Family *not shown*)
Subkingdom PARAZOA				
Porifera				
	Symplasma (glass sponges)			
	Cellularia (other sponges)			
Subkingdom METAZOA				
Cnidaria (Coelenterata)				
		Anthozoa (Actinozoa) (sea anemones)		
			Alcyonaria (soft corals, sea fans)	
			Zoantharia (stony corals, sea anemones)	
		Hydrozoa (hydroids)		
		Scyphozoa (jellyfish)		
Ctenophora (comb jellies)				
		Tentaculata (with tentacles)		
		Nuda (without tentacles)		
Platyhelminthes (flatworms)				
		Turbellaria (free-living flatworms)		
		Mononenea (ectoparasitic flukes)		
		Digenea (endoparasitic flukes)		
		Cestoda (tapeworms)		
Nemertea (Rhyncholoela) (bootlace worms)				
		Anopia		
				Paleonermertea
				Heteronemertea
		Enopia		
				Hoplonemertea
				Bdellonemertea
Gnathostomulida (acoelomate worms)				
Entoprocta				
Rotifera				
Nematoda (Nemathelminthes) (roundworms)				
		Adenophorea		
		Aphasmida		

Animal Kingdom, *continued*

Phylum	Subphylum	Class	Subclass	Order	(Suborder *and* Family *not shown*)
Gastrotricha					
		Macrodasyida			
		Chaetonotida			
Kinorhyncha (Echinoderes)					
		Cyclorhagida			
		Homalorhagida			
Nematophora (hair snakes, horse hair worms)					
		Nectonematoida (marine)			
		Gordioida (freshwater/semiterrestrial)			
Acanthocephala (spiny–headed worms)					
		Archiacanthocephala			
		Eocanthocephala			
		Palaeacanthocephala			
Tardigrada (water bears)					
		Heterotardigrada			
		Eutardigrada			
Bryozoa (Ectoprocta)					
Brachiopoda					
		Inarticulata			
		Articulata			
Phoronida					
Mollusca					
		Monoplacophora			
		Aplacophora			
		Polyplacaphora (Amphineura – Chitons)			
		Scaphopoda			
		Gastropoda			
		Bivalvia (Pelecypoda)			
		Cephalopoda			
				Nautiloidea	
				Ammonoidea	
				Coleoidea	
Annelida					
		Polychaeta (ragworms, lungworms)			
		Myzostomaria			
		Oligochaeta (earthworms)			
		Hirudinea (leeches)			
Sipuncula (peanut worms)					
Pogonophora (beard worms)					
Echiura					
Priapulida					

Animal Kingdom, *continued*

Phylum	Subphylum	Class	Subclass	Order	(Suborder *and* Family *not shown*)
Arthropoda					
	Trilobita (extinct forms)				
	Chelicerata				
		Merostomata (horseshoe crabs)			
		Arachnida (mites, spiders, scorpions)			
		Pycnogonida (sea spiders)			
	Crustacea (lobsters, crabs, water fleas, barnacles)				
	Uniramia				
		Onychophora			
		Myriapoda (centipedes, millipedes)			
		Hexapoda (Insecta)			
			Apterygota (silverfish)		
			Pterygota		
				Ephemeroptera (mayflies)	
				Odonata (dragonflies)	
				Dictyoptera (cockroaches)	
				Isoptera (termites)	
				Orthoptera (grasshoppers)	
				Hemiptera (bugs)	
				Diptera (flies)	
				Siphonaptera (fleas)	
				Lepidoptera (butterflies, moths)	
				Coleoptera (beetles)	
				Hymenoptera (ants, wasps, bees)	
Echinodermata					
		Crinoidea (sea lilies, feather stars)			
		Asteroidea (starfish)			
		Ophiuroidea (brittle stars)			
		Echinoidea (sea urchins)			
		Holothuroidea (sea cucumbers)			
Chordata					
	Urochordata (sea squirts)				
	Cephalochordata (amphioxus)				
	Vertebrata (vertebrates)*				
		Agnatha (Cyclostomata)			
				Petromyzoniformes (lampreys)	
				Myxiniformes (hagfish)	
		Selachi (Chondrichthyes) (sharks, rays)			
		Osteichthyes (bony fish)			
			Actinopterygii (ray-finned fish): includes the infraclasses Chondrostei, Cladistia, Neopterygii. The Neopterygii includes the division Teleostei and contains the superorders of: Protacanthopterygii (salmon), Ostariophysi (carp), Paracanthopterygii (cod), Acanthopterygii (perch)		
			Crossopterygii		
				Coelacanthini	
			Dipnoi (lungfish)		

Animal Kingdom, *continued*

Phylum	Subphylum	Class	Subclass	Order	(Suborder *and* Family *not shown*)
Chordata, continued					
		Amphibia (amphibians)			
			Lissamphibia		
				Salientia (frogs, toads)	
				Urodela (newts, salamanders)	
		Reptilia (reptiles)			
			Anapsida (primitive reptiles)		
				Apoda	
			Chelonomorpha (tortoises, turtles)		
			Lepidosaura		
				Squamata (lizards, snakes)	
			Archosauria		
				Saurischia and Ornithischia (dinosaurs)	
				Crocodilia (crocodiles)	
		Aves(birds)			
			Neornithes		
		Mammalia (mammals)			
			Prototheria (egg-laying mammals)		
				Monotremata (duck-billed platypuses, spiny anteaters)	
			Theria (mammals giving birth to live young)		
			Infraclass Metatheria		
				Polyprotodonta (opossums)	
				Diprotodonta (kangaroos)	
			Infraclass Eutheria		
				Insectivora (shrews, moles, hedgehogs)	
				Scadentia (tree shrews)	
				Chiroptera (bats)	
				Primates (monkeys, apes)	
				Carnivora (dogs, cats, bears, skunks, etc.)	
				Pinnipedia (seals)	
				Cetacea (whales, dolphins, porpoises)	
				Proboscidea (elephants)	
				Perissodactyla (horses, rhinoceroses, tapirs)	
				Artiodactyla (cows, pigs, hippopotamuses, camels, deer, elk, bison, sheep, antelope)	
				Rodentia (squirrels, rats, mice, beavers, porcupine, gophers)	
				Lagomorpha (rabbits, hares)	
				Sirenia (sea cows, manatee, dugong)	

* Some authorities add in two superclasses within the phylum Chordata; the superclass of Pisces (all fish) and the superclass Tetrapoda, the four-legged land vertebrates.

Kingdom Protista

The algae and certain unicellular organisms were formerly placed in either the plant (algae) or animal (protozoans) kingdoms, but in modern classification schemes they now have a separate kingdom. The kingdom Protista contains eukaryotic unicellular and multicellular aquatic or terrestrial organisms, having nutritional modes that include ingestion, photosynthesis, and absorption. Many of the organisms reproduce sexually and move by means of 9-plus-2 flagella, although some are non-motile. The divisions include heterotrophs (water moulds, slime moulds, and chytrids) and autotrophs (algae).

Phylum	Subphylum	Class	Subclass	Order (Suborder *and* Family *not shown*)
Sarcomastigophora				
	Mastigophora			
	Opalinata (Protociliata)			
	Sarcodina (Rhizopda) (amoebas, foraminiferans)			
	Telosporea			
	Piroplasmea			
Cnidospora				
	Myxospora			
	Microsporea			
Ciliophora				
	Ciliata (Infusoria)			
Dinophyta (Pyrrhophyta) (Dinoflagellates)				
Parabasalia				
Metamonada				
Axostylea				
Kinetoplastida				
Euglenophyta				
Cryptophyta				
Opalinata				
Heterokonta				
Chloropyhta				
Haptophyta				
Choanoflagellida				
Rhizopida				
Actinopoda				
Sporozoa (Apicomplexa)				
Microspora				
Oomycota (water moulds)				
Chytridiomycota (chytrids)				

Kingdom Protista, *continued*

Phylum	Subphylum	Class	Subclass	Order	(Suborder *and* Family *not shown*)
Acrasiomycota (cellular slime moulds)					
Myxomycota (slime moulds)					
Chrysophyta					
		Chrysophyceae (golden algae)			
Rhodophyta (red algae)					
		Xanthophyceae (yellow-green algae)			
Phaeophyta (brown algae)					
		Bacillariophyceae (diatoms)			
Chlorophyta (green algae)					

Kingdom Monera

It is generally accepted that bacteria and similar prokaryotic cells belong in a distinct kingdom, although much debate continues about the exact placement of certain organisms. Classification of the organisms in this kingdom is far from complete or agreed upon but includes:

- anaerobes that photosynthesize or form endospores
- Archaebacteria
- chemoautotrophic bacteria
- cyanobacteria
- aerobic, nitrogen-fixing bacteria
- omnibacteria
- spirochaetes.

Kingdom Fungi

Once considered part of the plant kingdom, fungi are now considered as separate organisms based on their unique life cycles, modes of nutrition, and patterns of development. Fungi are eukaryotic, multicellular structures (occasionally unicellular) in which the nucleus is found in a continuous mycelium, which can be always septate or septate only at certain stages of the life cycle. Fungi are heterotrophs and obtain their nutrition by absorption. They can reproduce both sexually and asexually, and many life cycles include both forms. The kingdom Fungi includes extremely diverse morphological forms, and at least 100,000 species are known to science. They play an extremely important role in ecosystem functions, which has only recently been fully appreciated. Phyla in the kingdom are listed below.

Phylum Ascomycota
Terrestrial and aquatic fungi characterized by the formation of an ascus in sexual reproduction. All members of the Ascomycota can also reproduce asexually. The division includes cellulose, decomposing fungi, mycorrhizal fungi, yeasts, morels, and truffles. At least 30,000 species are known to science.

Phylum Basidiomycota
Terrestrial fungi characterized by the formation of a basidium containing basidiospores in sexual reproduction. Important components of many ectomycorrhizae, there are at least 25,000 species known to science. Important classes include: Hymenomycetes (mushrooms, coral, and bracket fungi); Gasteromycetes (puffballs, earthstars, and stinkhorns); and Teliomycetes (rusts and smuts).

Phylum Deuteromycota
Also termed the Fungi Imperfecti. This division is considered to be rather artificial by some mycologists but is still widely used by others. Fungi in this division have no known sexual (perfect) stages and apparently reproduce asexually by budding, production of conidia, or oedia. These fungi contain certain stages more typical of Ascomycetes and Basidiomycetes. They are of economic importance in the manufacture of cheese, antibiotics (e.g., penicillin), and as plant pathogens.

Phylum Mycophycophyta
The lichens. A symbiotic association between Ascomycetes and certain green algae or cyanobacteria. They are very widespread and occur in many different forms around the world. They are very sensitive to air pollution and are classified on the basis of their growth habit (crustose, foliose, or fruticose). About 20,000 species have been described.

Phylum Zygomycota
Terrestrial fungi lacking septate walls, except during the formation of reproductive bodies (conidia) or the conjugation of cells of different types to form zygospores. Many species form an important component of the endomycorrhizae seen in approximately 80 per cent of all vascular plants. Almost 800 species have been identified and include fungi that parasitize insects (Entomophthorales) and certain protists (Zoopagales), as well as the moulds (Mucorales).

Appendix 2
Geological Time Scales

PHANEROZOIC EON

Cenozoic Era

Quaternary Period		
Holocene Epoch	10,000 years ago to present	Modern times. Glaciers retreat and the last ice age ends. The age of human beings begins.
Pleistocene Epoch	1.64 million to 10,000 years ago	The ice age. Wide climatic fluctuations, many glacial advances and retreats, and the final uplift of mountain ranges occurs. Early humans appear toward the end of the epoch. Many large mammals and birds become extinct.
Tertiary Period		
Pliocene Epoch	5.2-1.64 million years ago	Dry, cooler climates. Deserts form. Mountains are uplifted and built. Widespread glaciation occurs in the Northern Hemisphere. The uplift of the Panama region joins North and South America. Early human-like apes appear.
Miocene Epoch	23.5-5.2 million years ago	Moderate climates. Forests dwindle, grasslands expand. Mountain ranges form. Widespread glaciation starts again in the Southern Hemisphere. Grazing animals and apes evolve.
Oligocene Epoch	35.5-23.5 million years ago	Cool climate. Uplifting and formation of the European Alps and the Himalayas. South America separates from Antarctica. Mammals start to resemble modern forms.
Eocene Epoch	56.5-35.5 million years ago	Climate mild to very tropical. Australia separates from Antarctica. India collides with Asia. Widespread forests and mammals.
Paleocene Epoch	65-56.5 million years ago	Climate mild to cool. Extensive forests. Shallow, continental seas disappear. Many new mammal forms evolve, including the early insectivores and primates.

Mesozoic Era

Cretaceous Period	146-65 million years ago	Tropical to subtropical climates prevail. Africa and South America separate. Insects and many angiosperms develop and gain dominance. The age of reptiles. At the end of the period, the dinosaurs become extinct.

Jurassic Period	208-146 million years ago	Mild climates. Large, shallow, continental seas. Gymnosperms, and especially cycads, are dominant. Birds evolve.
Triassic Period	245-208 million years ago	Dry land, many deserts. Continents are mountainous and joined into one supercontinent. The first dinosaurs and mammals appear. The forests are dominated by gymnosperms and ferns.
Paleozoic Era		
Permian Period	290-245 million years ago	Extensive glaciation in the Southern Hemisphere, world-wide aridity. Early forest types dwindle. Reptiles evolve and diversify.
Carboniferous Period	363-290 million years ago	Climate is warm, with little seasonal variation. Extensive seas, swamps, and glaciation. Widespread formation of coal deposits. The first amphibians move onto land. Forests start to appear and gain dominance in the landscape. Insects and reptiles evolve. The age of amphibians.
Devonian Period	409-363 million years ago	The age of fishes. Land plants start to evolve, primitive vascular plants become extinct. The first amphibians start to appear.
Silurian Period	439-409 million years ago	Continents flat, mild climate. Extensive ice coverage of land and seas. The period sees a major extinction event. The oldest fossil plants are seen in this period. The first fish with jaws evolve.
Ordovician Period	510-439 million years ago	Extensive land masses later becoming covered with shallow seas. Period starts with a major extinction event. The oldest fossil crustaceans are seen in this period. Molluscs evolve and diversify. Land plants and the first fungi evolve.
Cambrian Period	570-510 million years ago	Widespread seas. The first shelled animals appear, and external skeletons in animals evolve. Many new plants and animals appear. Chordates evolve.
PRECAMBRIAN TIME		
Proterozoic Era	2,500-570 million years ago	The formation of the earth's crust. Shallow seas, very simple life forms. The origin of eukaryotes (at least 1.5 billion years ago) and multicellular animals (700 million years ago). The earliest fossil record of life is seen about 3,800 million years ago.
Archean Era	3,800-2,500 million years ago	
Pre-Archean Era	4,600-3,800 million years ago	

Appendix 3
Conversion Tables and Other Measurements

CONVERTING MAP SCALES

Map scales are typically shown as an Imperial ratio, such as 1 inch = 50 feet, or as a simple ratio, such as 1:1,000, which is called a representative fraction. To convert an Imperial ratio to a simple ratio (sometimes incorrectly called a metric scale), multiply the 50 feet by 12 (representing 12 inches in a foot). The resulting new scale is 1:600. In this new scale the 1 is simply the expression of a unit of measurement on the map; it is not necessarily a centimetre or a metre, but rather one unit of measurement on the map representing 600 units of the same measurement on the ground.

If 1:600 is not the desired working scale, it could be enlarged to get a larger scale. e.g., 2× to get 1:300, or reduced to get a smaller scale, e.g., 1:1,200. Scales such as 1:600, 1:300, or 1:1,200 are not common, so maps or plans are usually adjusted to a more common scale, such as 1:500, 1:250, or 1:1,500.

Useful Representative Fraction Conversions

The following conversions represent the equivalents of some common scales. For example, a scale of 1:1,000,000 means that 1 kilometre on the ground is equivalent to 10 centimetres on a map. At the same scale, a mile on the ground is represented by 15.782 inches on a map. Conversely, a tenth of a centimetre (one millimetre) on the map represents one kilometre, and one inch would represent 0.0634 miles on the ground.

Scale (representative fraction)	1 kilometre on the ground is represented by *x* centimetres on the map	1 centimetre on the map represents *x* kilometres on the ground	1 mile on the ground is represented by *x* inches on the map	1 inch on the map represents *x* miles on the ground
1:100,000	10.0	0.1	15.782	0.0634
1:500,000	5.0	0.2	7.891	0.127
1:100,000	1.0	1.0	1.578	0.6336
1:50,000	0.5	2.0	0.789	1.267
1:25,000	0.25	4.0	0.395	2.534
1:10,000	0.1	10.0	0.1578	6.366
1:2,500	0.025	40.0	0.0395	25.34
1:633,600	6,336.0	0.1578	10.0	0.1
1:63,360	0.6336	1.578	1.0	1.0

Converting Imperial Scales to Representative Fractions

To convert the following Imperial scales, often used by architects and engineers, use the following chart:

Imperial (inch = feet)	*Representative fraction*
1/32 = 1	1:384
1/16 = 1	1:192
1/8 = 1	1:96
3/16 = 1	1:64
1/4 = 1	1:48
5/16 = 1	1:38
3/8 = 1	1:32
1/2 = 1	1:24
3/4 = 1	1:16
1 = 1	1:12
1.5 = 1	1:8
3 = 1	1:4
Half size	1:2
Full size	1:1
Double size	2:1

It can be seen from the above that the representative fractions from the conversions are not readily usable numbers and therefore are difficult to work with. To overcome this, the so-called 'metric' scales have been developed, e.g.,1:50, 1:100, and 1:200, which are the closest rounded representative fractions to 1/4 inch = 1 foot, 1/8 inch = 1 foot, and 1/16 inch = 1 foot.

DETERMINING THE PER CENT REDUCTIONS NECESSARY FOR IMAGE MANIPULATIONS

In order to make graphic images fit within reports or to bring a photographic image to a common scale, it is often necessary to enlarge or reduce the original image. Simply divide the width of the reproduction size desired by the width of the original image and multiply this by 100. To check the reproduction height, just multiply this percentage number by the height of the original and divide by 100.

step 1 $$\frac{\text{Reproduction width} \times 100}{\text{original width}} = \%\ \text{reduction} \qquad \text{e.g.,}\ \frac{3.5'' \times 100}{8.5} = 41.2\%\ \text{reduction}$$

step 2 $$\frac{\%\ \text{reduction} \times \text{original height}}{100} = \text{reproduction height} \qquad \text{e.g.,}\ \frac{41.2 \times 11}{100} = 4.5''$$

If the image being manipulated is to be used in any measurements, it is extremely important to have an accurate scale for the original image being used. If working from a photocopy, be sure the scale bar is accurate, otherwise measurements may be wrong, leading to incorrect calculations later on. Many drawings will state right on the paper DO NOT SCALE FROM THIS PLAN. This is to ensure that an original copy, known to be accurate, is used. Photocopied plans should only be used as a rough indication of distances and elevations, which may be suitable for preliminary field or office work.

CALCULATING CIRCULAR AND SQUARE PLOT DIMENSIONS

Using Imperial Units

Area		Radius of circular plot		Side of square plot		Diagonal of square plot	
Acres	Square feet	Feet	Chains	Feet	Chains	Feet	Chains
1.00	43,560.0	117.75	1.784	208.71	3.162	295.16	4.472
0.50	21,780.0	83.26	1.262	147.58	2.236	208.71	3.162
0.25	10,890.0	58.88	0.892	104.36	1.581	147.58	2.236
0.20	8,712.0	52.66	0.798	93.34	1.414	132.00	2.000
0.10	4,356.0	37.24	0.564	66.00	1.000	93.34	1.414
0.05	2,178.0	26.33	0.399	46.67	0.707	66.00	1.000
0.01	435.6	11.78	0.178	20.87	0.316	29.52	0.447
0.001	43.56	3.72	0.056	6.60	0.100	9.33	0.141

Using Metric Units

Area		Radius of circular plot	Side of square plot	Diagonal of square plot
Hectares	Square metres	Metres	Metres	Metres
1.00	10,000	56.41	100.00	141.42
0.50	5,000	39.89	70.71	100.00
0.25	2,500	28.21	50.00	70.71
0.20	2,000	25.23	44.72	63.24
0.10	1,000	17.84	31.62	44.72
0.08	800	15.96	28.28	39.99
0.06	600	13.82	24.49	34.63
0.05	500	12.62	22.36	31.62
0.04	400	11.28	20.00	28.28
0.03	300	9.77	17.32	24.49
0.025	250	8.92	15.81	22.36
0.02	200	7.98	14.14	20.00
0.01	100	5.64	10.00	14.14
0.0016	16	2.26	4.00	5.66
0.001	10	1.78	3.16	4.47
0.0004	4	1.13	2.00	2.83

CONVERSION FACTORS FOR UNITS OF LENGTH

	millimetre	centimetre	metre	kilometre	inch	foot	yard	chain	mile
1 millimetre =	1.0	0.1	0.001	–	0.0394	0.0033	–	–	–
1 centimetre =	10.0	1.0	0.01	10^{-5}	0.3937	0.0328	0.0109	–	–
1 metre =	1,000.0	100.0	1.0	10^{-3}	39.3701	3.2808	1.0936	0.04971	0.00062
1 kilometre =	10^{6}	10^{5}	1,000.0	1.0	39,370.1	3,280.83	1,093.61	49.7096	0.62137
1 inch =	25.4	2.54	0.0254	–	1.0	0.0833	0.02778	–	–
1 foot =	304.8	30.48	0.3048	0.3048×10^{-3}	12.0	1.0	0.3333	0.01515	0.00018
1 yard =	–	91.44	0.9144	0.9144×10^{-3}	36.0	3.0	1.0	0.04545	0.00056
1 chain =	–	2,011.68	20.1168	0.0201	792.0	66.0	22.0	1.0	0.0125
1 mile =	–	–	1,609.347	1.6909	69,360.0	5,280.0	1,760.0	80.0	1.0

Additional measurements:
100 links = 1 chain; 1 link = 0.66 feet or 7.92 inches; 1 furlong = 10 chains
1 English nautical mile = 6,080 feet = 1,853.18 metres
1 international nautical mile = 1,852 metres = 6,076.12 feet
1 fathom = 6 feet = 1.829 metres

CONVERSION FACTORS FOR UNITS OF AREA

	Cm^2	M^2	Hectare	Km^2	$Inch^2$	$Feet^2$	$Yards^2$	$Chains^2$	Acre	$Mile^2$
1 $centimetre^2$ =	1.0	0.0001	10^{-8}	–	0.15500	0.001076	1.196×10^{-4}	–	–	–
1 $metre^2$ =	10,000.0	1.0	0.0001	10^{-6}	1,549.997	10.76387	1.19599	0.00247	0.000247	3.861×10^{-7}
1 hectare =	10^8	10,000.0	1.0	0.01	15.50×10^6	107,638.7	11,959.9	24.7104	2.471044	0.003861
1 $kilometre^2$ =	10^{10}	10^6	100	1.0	–	10,763,867.0	1,195,985.0	2,471.04	247.104	0.3861
1 $inch^2$ =	6.4516	6.4516×10^{-4}	–	–	1.0	0.006944	0.7716×10^{-5}	–	–	–
1 $foot^2$ =	929.034	0.092903	–	–	144.0	1.0	0.11111	0.00023	0.000023	–
1 $yard^2$ =	8,361.31	0.836131	–	–	1,296.0	9.0	1.0	0.002066	0.000207	–
1 $chain^2$ =	–	404.687	0.040469	0.00004	627,264.0	4,356.0	484.0	1.0	0.1	0.000156
1 acre =	–	4,046.87	0.404687	0.004047	6,272 640.0	43,560.0	4,840.0	10.0	1.0	0.001562
1 $mile^2$ =	–	258,999.7	258.9997	2.59	–	27,878,400.0	3,097,600.0	6,400.0	640.0	1.0

Additional measurements:
1 hectare = 100 are
1 are = 100 square metres = 0.01 hectare
1 mil-acre = 4.84 square yards = 1,000 square links = 4.046856 square metres
1 square metre = 0.247105 mil-acres
1 inch = 1,000 mils
1 chain = 4 rods = 22 yards = 100 links
640 acres = 1 section; 36 sections = 1 township = 6 x 6 miles = 36 square miles or 23,040 acres
1 square foot per acre = 0.2296 square metres per hectare
1 square metre per hectare = 0.4356 square feet per acre

CONVERSION FACTORS FOR UNITS OF VOLUME

	cubic centimetre	litre	cubic metre	cubic inch	cubic foot	cubic yard	US gallon	UK gallon
1 cubic centimetre =	1.0	0.001	0.000001	0.061023	–	–	–	–
1 litre =	1,000.00	1.0	0.001	61.0237	0.035315	0.0013	0.264179	0.219975
1 cubic metre =	106.0	1000.00	1.0	61,023.7	35.3145	1.308	254.2	220.0
1 cubic inch =	16.3872	0.016387	16.38×10^{-6}	1.0	0.000579	21.43 × 106	4.329×10^{-3}	3.605×10^{-3}
1 cubic foot =	28,317.0	18.316	0.028317	1,728	1.0	0.03704	7.480	6.229
1 cubic yard =	764,555.0	764.56	0.76456	46,656.0	27.0	1.0	201.96	168.18
1 US gallon =	3,785.412	3.785	3.785×10^{-3}	231.0	0.1337	3.60	1.0	0.8327
1 UK gallon =	4,546.092	4.546	4.546×10^{-3}	277.4	0.1605	4.33	1.201	1.0

Additional measurements:
1 bushel = 32 quarts in US dry measure
1 acre foot x 1,233.482 = cubic metres
1 gallon = 4 quarts = 8 pints

OTHER CONVERSION FACTORS

Timber Measures

1 cunit = 100 cubic feet of wood = 2.83168 cubic metres of wood
1 cord of stacked wood = 128 cubic feet = 3.625 cubic metres*
1 cubic metre of stacked wood = 0.2759 of a cord*
1 cord of wood per acre = 8.956 cubic metre per hectare*
1 cubic metre per hectare = 0.11165 cords per acre*
1 Hoppus cubic foot = 1.273 cubic feet
1 Hoppus cubic foot per acre = 0.089 cubic metres per hectare
1 cubic metre per hectare = 11.224 Hoppus cubic feet per acre
1 cunit per acre = 6.997 solid cubic metres per hectare
1 solid cubic metre per hectare = 0.1429 cunits per acre

* the volume occupied by the stacked wood, but not the actual volume of wood

Temperature

y° Celsius = (1.8 × y°) + 32 Fahrenheit
y° Fahrenheit = 0.55 × (y° Fahrenheit – 32)

Solutions

1 part per million = 1 cc per litre = 1 cc per kilogram = 0.0001 per cent
1 per cent = 10,000 parts per million = 10 grams per litre = 10 grams per kilogram = 1.33 ounces per gallon of water

Rates of Application

1 square foot per acre = 0.2296 square metres per hectare
1 square metre per hectare = 4.35597 square feet per acre
1 cubic foot per acre = 0.0699 cubic metres per hectare
1 cubic yard per acre = 1.889 cubic metres per hectare
1 cubic metre per hectare = 14.29 cubic feet per acre
1 cubic metre per hectare = 0.529 cubic yards per acre

The International System (SI) of Units and Their Prefixes

Factor	Prefix	Symbol
10^{18}	exa	E
10^{15}	peta	P
10^{12}	tera	T
10^{9}	giga	G
10^{6}	mega	M
10^{3}	kilo	k
10^{2}	hecto	h
10^{1}	deka	da
10^{-1}	deci	d
10^{-2}	centi	c
10^{-3}	milli	m
10^{-6}	micro	μ
10^{-9}	nano	n
10^{-12}	pico	p
10^{-15}	femto	f
10^{-18}	atto	a

Planting Spacing Figures

Distance apart in feet	Number of trees per acre	Number of trees per hectare
3 × 3	4,840	11,960
4 × 4	2,722	6,726
5 × 5	1,742	4,305
6 × 6	1,210	2,990
7 × 7	889	2,197
8 × 8	680	1,680
9 × 9	537	1,327
10 × 10	435	1,075
12 × 12	302	746
15 × 15	193	477
20 × 20	109	269

To calculate the number of trees per acre or per hectare when planting in a square pattern, divide the area to be planted in square feet or square metres by the square of the planting distance. The resultant figure is the number of trees per acre/hectare. For example:

planting distance = 5 feet, 1 acre = 43,560 square feet

$$\text{thus } \frac{43{,}560}{5 \times 5} = 1{,}742 \text{ trees per acre}$$

If a planting system is used involving lines of trees on a rectangular (but not square) pattern, the calculation is similar, except that the area to be planted is divided by the product of the distance between the lines and the distance between trees along the lines.